The Golden Tradition

The Golden Tradition

Jewish Life and Thought in Eastern Europe

Lucy S. Dawidowicz

SCHOCKEN BOOKS · NEW YORK

All rights reserved under International and
Pan-American Copyright Conventions. Published
in the United States by Schocken Books Inc.,
New York. Distributed by Pantheon Books, a
division of Random House, Inc., New York.

Published by agreement with Holt, Rinehart &
Winston, Inc., New York.

Library of Congress Cataloging in Publication Date
Main entry under title:
The golden tradition.
Reprint. Originally published: New York: Holt,
Rinehart, and Winston [1967].
Bibliography: p.
Includes index.
1. Jews—Europe, Eastern—Addresses, essays,
lectures. 2. Europe, Eastern—Ethnic relations—
Addresses, essays, lectures. I. Dawidowicz, Lucy S.
DS135.E8G65   1984   305.8'924'047   84-5560
ISBN 0-8052-0768-6

Manufactured in the United States of America

9   8   7   6   5   4   3   2

IN REMEMBRANCE OF

Zelig and Riva Kalmanovich

d. Estonia, 1943

TWO OF SIX MILLION

Many friends and colleagues have helped and encouraged me in the course of this work. I am especially indebted to Dr. John Slawson, executive vice-president of the American Jewish Committee, for a liberal gift of time; to Milton Himmelfarb, director of the Committee's Information Service, from whom I have learned more than I could possibly acknowledge; to the National Foundation for Jewish Culture for a grant to defray some of the expenses I incurred, and to Arthur A. Cohen, Holt, Rinehart & Winston's editor-in-chief, for his interest.

I owe thanks also to Isaiah Trunk, of the Yivo Institute for Jewish Research, for having saved me from errors of historical fact; to Miss Dina Abramowicz, librarian, and Berl Kagan, of Yivo, for their unfailing helpfulness; to Dr. Marvin Herzog, associate director of the Language and Culture Atlas of Ashkenazic Jewry at Columbia University, for assistance in locating many place names; to Vincent Kotschar for his skill in giving my memoirists a geographic form and place; to Miss Rose Grundstein for her assistance and encouragement, and to Mrs. Estelle Weinstein for her indefatigable typing.

My husband Szymon has had a great share in this book. Without him it would not have been possible.

L. S. D.
June 1966

Contents

I   Early Hasidism

II   The Haskala

III The Quest for Education

IV The World of Tradition

V Scholars and Philosophers

VI Literary Men

VII   The Arts

VIII   Marginals

IX   In the Zionist Movement

X   In the Revolutionary Movements

XI   In Political Life

Introduction:

The World of East European Jewry

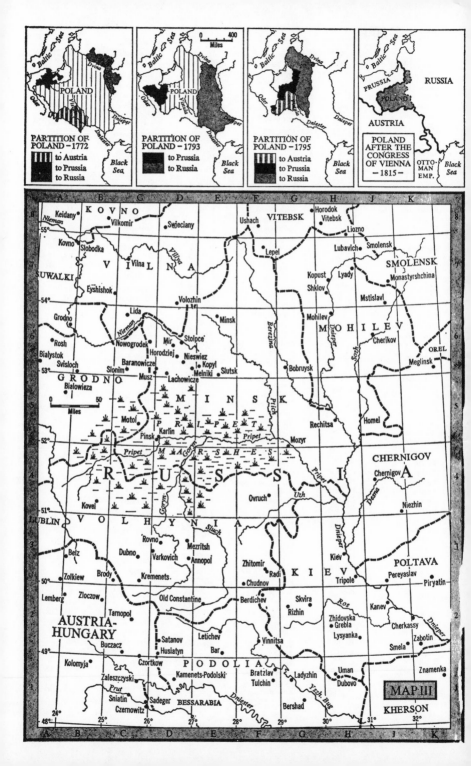

PARTITION OF POLAND – 1772
to Austria
to Prussia
to Russia

PARTITION OF POLAND – 1793
to Prussia
to Russia

PARTITION OF POLAND – 1795
to Austria
to Prussia
to Russia

POLAND AFTER THE CONGRESS OF VIENNA – 1815 –

MAP III

KEY TO MAPS

Introduction

THIS is a book about East European Jews in crisis, challenge, and creativity from the end of the eighteenth century until their cataclysmic destruction in the Second World War.

In the sixteenth century, the center of world Jewry moved to Eastern Europe, which until 1939 remained the region of greatest Jewish population and density. Eastern Europe was the cradle of almost every important Jewish cultural, religious, and national movement and the area where Jewish faith, thought, and culture flourished unsurpassed. Thence came the impetus and vitality that preserved the Jewish people intact in prosperity and adversity. East European Jewry became a reservoir of manpower and from the nineteenth century on provided the overwhelming bulk of migrants to the United States, to Israel, and many far-flung communities.

Enlightenment came to the relatively small communities of Western Jews before it went east, and emancipation followed shortly thereafter with the French Revolution. The enlightenment shook the foundations of traditional Judaism, unprepared for its assault; emancipation toppled that traditional Jewish society. Western Jews could not resist the lures of enlightenment, emancipation, and the opportunity to enter the larger society. They rushed to embrace it, though emancipation often turned out to be a mirage and enlightenment a dead end. In a brief span, West European Jewish communities were decimated, having paid heavily for emancipation with conversion.

Eastern Europe was different, and East European Jews responded differently to enlightenment and emancipation. They searched for ways to harmonize tradition and modernity, to preserve their Jewish identity and retain their community. This book is an attempt to show what they did and what the outcome was.

I have here assembled autobiographies, memoirs, reminiscences, and letters of some sixty persons whose lives document these East European Jewish responses to modernity. "Autobiography," Wilhelm Dilthey wrote, "is the highest and most instructive form in which the understanding of

5

life confronts us." The most direct form of history, autobiography is history's most intimate disclosure, a man's assessment of his life, his acts and ideas, successes and failures; an analysis of his origins, his milieu, the flow of events around him.

The autobiographies I sought were those of men, in William James's words, "whose genius was so adapted to the receptivities of the moment, or whose accidental position of authority was so critical that they became ferments, initiators of movement, setters of precedent or fashion." But because the material was not always available, I have tried to repair the gaps with memoirs about them.

I was guided also by the desire to show the diversity of Jews and their culture, the centripetal and centrifugal forces that moved them, and the variety they brought to Jewish thought and life. East European Jewry was not, as the sentimentalists see it, forever frozen in utter piety and utter poverty.

The historical review that follows is an attempt to put these memoirs in the perspective of their time and place and to describe some relevant social, political, and economic currents that affected our memoirists. I have tried to show the tension betwen assimilatory tendencies and survivalist values among East European Jews, and I have cited the autobiographies as illustrative documents.

East European Jewry was cruelly cut down. But vital elements of its culture survive. Perhaps we, heirs of that culture, can continue its tradition of conserving Jewish identity by fusing the old and the new.

1   Preamble:
Contours of East European Jewry

In 1764 about a million Jews lived in the commonwealth of Poland. From Courland in the north on the Baltic Sea, Poland extended as far south as the Dniester, across which lay Moldavia in the Turkish Empire. Poland's northern tier stretched from the North German plains east of the Oder toward the Warta River, across the Central Polish flatlands beribboned with lakes and rivers — the Bug, the Vistula, the Nieman. Thence it ex-

tended across ten thousands of square miles of the Pripet Marshes north-
ward to the Russian lowlands, eastward through great coniferous forests
all the way to the Dnieper, which marked the Russian border. The central
Polish belt swept from Upper Silesia over the loess plains of Galicia across
the *ukraine* (frontier) where the Zaporogian Cossacks lived. Its southern
tier rose and fell in the peaks and foothills of the Beskids and the High
Tatras, extending southward toward the Carpathians, eastward toward the
Black Earth of Russia, and westward toward the Sudeten Mountains.

The lay of the land and the course of its rivers channeled immigration
into Poland from the Baltic and Russian lands to the northeast, across the
ukraine from the southeast, from Moravia and Bohemia in the southwest,
from Silesia and Prussia to the East. The earliest settlers, the Polanie,
"dwellers in the plains," gave the lands its name of Polska. Then came
Mazovians, Pomeranians, Litts, Prussians, Bielorussians, and Ruthenians.
The migrations followed the pattern of the land, and various ethnic and
cultural groups distributed themselves in its separate pockets.

The Jews had migrated as early as the eleventh century from the
German lands. From the fifteenth century onward their population grew
and prospered during the golden age of the Polish-Lithuanian commonwealth under the Jagiellonian dynasty, from about 25,000 at the end of the
fifteenth century to several hundred thousand, perhaps even a half million,
150 years later. They lived mostly in towns, controlled the kingdom's ex-
port trade (mostly agricultural produce), the import trade, and the domestic
trade through the fairs. The Jews sometimes leased the royal lands and sometimes lands of the nobility, tax farming their meadows, woodlands, and fish
ponds. The Jews planted crops, bred livestock, fished, lumbered, and manufactured flour and spirits. They leased inns and taverns where the peasants
came to drink and carouse. The Jews handled money, extended credit, and
held mortgages. They developed their own crafts in competition with the
Christian craft guilds, pioneering in that most characteristic form of early
capitalism — the ready-made clothing industry.

Though mainly gentry, the Jews lived as a separate estate. Their affairs
were regulated by their own autonomous organization, the Vaad Arba
Arazot, Council of the Four Lands, a self-governing body that represented
the Jews in their relations with the state and with the formal institutions
of the other estates. The Council came into being as an authoritative body
in the second half of the sixteenth century. Its basic unit was the local
kehilla, or *kahal,* the word for both the Jewish community and its autonomous government. Kahal conducted its own administrative, legislative,
judicial, fiscal, religious, educational, and charitable institutions. Elected

laymen, the community elders, conducted administrative affairs. The rabbis supervised religious and judicial affairs and exercised unparalleled authority in regulating the moral, religious, and cultural life of the Jews. Problems beyond the competence or purview of local councils were submitted to provincial bodies consisting of representatives of local councils. These provincial councils usually held their meetings or congresses during the great fairs; the most important one was convened at Lublin's winter fair and later, alternately, at the summer fair at Yaroslav in Galicia. The four provinces, or lands, represented at these congresses were Great Poland (capital, Posen), Little Poland (Cracow), Polish or Red Russia, consisting of Podolia and Galicia (Lemberg), and Volhynia (Ostrog, Kremenets). Until 1623 the Lithuanian Jews had had representatives in the Council of the Four Lands, but later organized their own council which, while authoritative in local matters, worked with the Council of the Four Lands.

The very fact that the autonomous Council represented in one organization the Jews of all the provinces in the Polish-Lithuanian commonwealth strengthened Jewish solidarity and stressed the communality of Jewish interests. Simon Dubnow saw the institutions of Jewish autonomy as the means of Jewish national and cultural survival:

> . . . kahal as the nucleus of self-government and the associations of local kehillot with their central organs had enormous significance for the communal life of Polish Jewry. This whole organization of autonomous communities provided law and order among the Jewish population. It disciplined the masses beyond the state's jurisdiction. It gave a people without a state a surrogate for national political activity, thereby sustained its awareness of its autonomy, safeguarded and developed its own individual culture.[1]

That culture — rabbinic Judaism — reached its height in this era of Jewish autonomy. At a time when literacy in Eastern Europe was an accomplishment only of the nobility and higher clergy, Jewish learning was transmitted in an extensive school system based on the *heder* (elementary school) and the *yeshiva* (secondary school). "In no other country," wrote Nathan-Note Hannover, the chronicler of the mid-seventeenth century, "is the study of the Holy Torah as widespread among our brethren as in the Kingdom of Poland."

In this period the most authoritative code of Jewish law came into existence, the *Shulhan Arukh* (literally, "the set table"). Originally the product of Joseph Karo (1488–1575), the Shulhan Arukh was a codification of law and custom derived primarily from Sephardic and Oriental Jewish traditions. Glosses added by the great Polish rabbi Moses Isserles (ca. 1520–1572), founder of the Cracow yeshiva, incorporated German-Polish traditions and practices. The Shulhan Arukh at first acted as a powerful and conserving element in Jewish life; later it became a timid and conservative one.

Karo, the Jewish legist, lived in Safed in Upper Galilee, where many exiles from Spain and Portugal had settled. There lived also Isaac Luria (1534–1572), the mystic philosopher who constructed a theosophic system based on the Kabbala. The Lurianic Kabbala invaded Poland in the seventeenth century; Polish rabbis and Kabbalists became its chief disseminators and interpreters. The Lurianic doctrines were to have a profound influence on a subsequent movement of Jewish mysticism: hasidism. Thus Polish Jewry accepted, validated, and preserved both a code of law and a philosophy of mysticism that were legacies of the Spanish Jewish exile.

Polish Jews became also the chief consumers, and then the most prolific producers, of a rising religious and secular Yiddish literature. *Bovo-bukh,* a Yiddish version of contemporary Italian romances, by Elijah Bahur (ca. 1468–1549), a Hebrew grammarian living in Italy, became one of the most popular books in Poland. To counteract its secular influence, the anonymous *Maase-bukh* appeared at the end of the sixteenth century, combining Talmudic legends and medieval folktales. Yiddish morality books and prayer books, directed primarily to women, were published with increasing frequency. The crown of these works was the *Tsena-Urena* by Jacob Ashkenazi (1550–1628). A translation of the Pentateuch, embellished with legends and moral precepts, the *Tsena-Urena* was published in about thirty-five editions from 1622–1725. *Yosifon,* a Yiddish adaptation of a Hebrew version of Josephus's *Antiquities,* was one of the many histories in Yiddish; it remained in the traditional Jew's library until modern times.

In the middle of the seventeenth century, this Jewish traditional society was shaken by a series of cataclysmic events. During the next century the social, economic, and cultural institutions of Polish Jewish life began to deteriorate and disintegrate. That disintegration paralleled and was largely a consequence of the disintegration of the Polish commonwealth and its continuous wars with Russia and Sweden. The breakup began violently in 1648 under John Casimir II, whose reign came to be known in Polish history as The Deluge. That deluge, beginning with the uprising of the Zaporogian Cossacks, inundated also the Jews.

The Ukraine had come under Polish rule in 1569 and had been subjected to a harsh policy of Polonization and Catholicization: the Eastern
Orthodox Church was suppressed and the Ukrainian peasants enserfed to
the Polish nobility. The rise of towns on the steppe where Cossack horse-
men once rode wild horses and the increasingly powerful economic role of
urban Jews mediating between the Polish nobility and the Ukrainian peasants compounded the political and religiocultural tensions. Bogdan Chmielnitsky (1593–1657), hetman of the Zaporogian Cossacks, led a Cossack
uprising to liberate the Ukraine from Poland. Chmielnitsky agitated against
Poles and Jews: "You know the wrongs done us by the Poles and Yids,
their leaseholders and beloved factors, the oppressions, the evil deeds, and the
impoverishment, you know and you remember."

Chmielnitsky did not succeed in liberating the Ukraine, but in the subsequent decade of war and violence, interrupted only by brief intervals of
negotiations among the Poles, Russians, Swedes, and Turks, the Cossacks
with their murderous bands of peasants, called Haidamaks, slaughtered
hundreds of thousands of Jews, sacking and destroying hundreds of Jewish
communities. That was the beginning of a series of blood-drenched encounters between Jews and Ukrainians that were to endure in Jewish historic
memory. About one-tenth of the Jewish population remained in the Polish
Ukraine, Volhynia, and Podolia. The other survivors emigrated into Lithuania, Poland proper, and to the Western European countries. In 1654,
Chmielnitsky accepted Moscow's protection, and finally in 1667, the
Truce of Andrusovo split the Ukraine, with Kiev, its cultural center, and
the left bank of the Dnieper going to Russia, and the right bank remaining
with Poland.

With the entry of Russia and Sweden into the wars, the Jewish communities in the northern provinces, previously little affected by the Cossack
uprisings, now also came under the sword. Nathan-Note Hannover closed
his chronicle of those dreadful events with the prayerful hope: "May God
hear our lament and gather us together from all corners of the world, and
send us the sainted Messiah soon in our lifetime."

This longing for the Messiah had obsessed the Kabbalists even before
the calamitous days. But with the Third Destruction, as a contemporaneous
rabbi characterized the massacres in the wake of the Cossack rising, a fever
of Messianic expectation seized the Jewish people. The community leaders
were not unaware of the political, religiocultural, and economic factors
whose hapless conjunction led to the wars and massacres. But between
despair and mystic expectancy, the Polish Jews believed that God had
inflicted these sufferings, whose severity presaged the coming of the Mes-

siah. Only Messianic hopes, it seemed, could redeem the Jews from death and disaster. With the coming of Sabbatai Zevi, who publicly proclaimed himself the Messiah in 1665, God's prophecy appeared to have been fulfilled. Rapidly the movement spread from Palestine, where Sabbatai Zevi disclosed his mission, through the Turkish provinces of Eastern Europe into Podolia and Volhynia. Nor did it decline with Sabbatai Zevi's public apostasy to Islam in 1666, for his adherents continued to believe in Sabbatai Zevi's expected return as the true Messiah. But the years passed and nothing happened. Meanwhile, rabbinic Judaism kept persecuting the Sabbatians for their heresy, with the result that what had once been a movement became a heretical sect; the ecstatic expectations for the Messianic coming expired in shame, confusion, disillusion, and despair. Believers in the heresy remained, practicing their nihilistic doctrines in secret, encouraging radical and heretical opposition to traditional rabbinic Judaism, in the very name of that Judaism.

From the end of the seventeenth and into the eighteenth century, war, disorder and anarchy gave Poland no respite. Russia, Prussia, and Austria began to exploit their interest in the Polish lands with political and military adventures, while successive Polish rulers engaged in futile and wasteful wars against the Swedes to the North and the Turks to the South. To satisfy their rising financial obligations, the Polish rulers began to press the Jewish autonomous organizations for ever larger tax contributions to the state, but the Vaad and its constituent bodies had become financially crippled in the decades following the Chmielnitsky uprisings. The financial needs of the Jewish community during The Deluge had been enormous; the ravaged and dispersed Jewish communities did not have the resources to meet the exorbitant fiscal demands of the Polish rulers. The Western Jewish communities, still reeling from the impact of the Thirty Years' War and, additionally, absorbing thousands upon thousands of refugees from Poland, were unable to assist.

The Vaad, then, and local communal bodies began to borrow heavily not only from Jews and Jewish institutions, but from the landed nobles and the Catholic orders. To meet their debts the communal councils began to levy heavy excise taxes on the Jews, which particularly burdened the poor, aroused widespread dissatisfaction and opposition, and eventually undermined kahal's authority. In 1764 the Polish Diet moved to dissolve the Vaad, abolishing its tax-collecting function; thenceforth Jews would be required to pay head taxes directly to the state. The demise of the Council of the Four Lands and of the Lithuanian Council preceded by a few brief years the demise of Poland itself.

In the prevailing anarchy of early eighteenth century Poland, brigand bands of Cossacks and runaway Ukrainian serfs roamed the country, murdering and robbing, incited by the Great Russians to harass the Poles and Jews. In 1768, when Poland stood at the brink of dissolution, Cossack hordes under their Zaporogian leader Maxim Zheleznyak descended. A runaway Ukrainian serf spread a rumor that Catherine II, Tsarina of Russia (1762-1796), had ordered the Greek Orthodox populace to join the Cossacks in a crusade to murder the Jews and Poles in the Polish Ukraine. At Uman, Zheleznyak's Haidamak bands joined forces with insurrectionist Ivan Gonta, commander of a detachment of Cossack militia. They slaughtered about 20,000 Jews and Poles, under the slogan: "A Pole, a Jew, and a dog above them — their faith is all the same." To the Jews, the Cossack massacres were a dread repetition of the Chmielnitsky massacres of 1648 and revived the despair and Messianic hope that had stirred Jewish communities a century before.

From out of a secret Sabbatian sect came Jacob Frank (1726-1791), declaring himself Sabbatai Zevi's successor and preaching a doctrine even more heretical and antinomian. In 1759 Frank came to Podolia, his birthplace, claiming that the divine revelations vouchsafed to him demanded his conversion and that of his followers to Christianity as a step toward the future Messianic religion. Later that year Frank was baptized in Warsaw; about 500 of his followers were converted to Catholicism. Soon the Catholic ecclesiastical authorities realized that Frank and his followers were not truly Catholics; a Church tribunal convicted Frank for spreading a pernicious heresy. He was imprisoned in the fortress at Czestochowa, where he remained until after the first partition of Poland. In 1773, after his release, Frank and his followers left Poland for Moravia, later travelling into Germany. Many Frankists remained in Warsaw, for several generations a marginal group between Jews and Catholics.

The Ukrainian uprisings of 1768 brought Russian troops once again to Poland. Fearful that Russia would devour all of Poland on the pretext of defending the Orthodox minority, Frederick II of Prussia proposed a threeway partition of Poland in which also he and Habsburg Empress Maria Theresa would share. In 1772 the first step in the dismemberment of Poland was taken. Poland lost nearly 4 million inhabitants, 35 percent of her population. Austria emerged the largest gainer, with about a third of the partitioned land and about half the population. Russia received the most land — Polish Livonia and White Russia — and about 1.3 million inhabitants, many Greek Orthodox. Prussia received the smallest share in people and land — West Prussia.

Twenty years later, Catherine the Great moved against Poland again, behind the strategy of Field Marshal Alexander Vasilevich Suvorov, whose triumphs in the Russian-Turkish war had extended Russian hegemony over the Black Sea steppes and the Crimea. Despite resistence, Poland in 1793 had to submit to another partition, in which Prussia shared with Russia about half of remaining Poland. To all intents, Poland had already become merely a Russian protectorate, yet in a revolutionary outburst of nationalism, Thaddeus Kosciuszko in 1794 led a desperate insurrection for Polish freedom that ended in disaster opposite Warsaw, at Praga, on the Vistula's right bank. There Suvorov and his soldiers slaughtered not only Praga's defenders, but its defenseless population. In 1795 Poland, a country with more history than geography, ceased to exist, divided once again among Russia, Prussia, and Austria.

Of the nearly one million Jews that had lived in Poland before the partitions, Prussia inherited about 150,000, Austria about 250,000, and Russia well over half a million. Prussia expelled thousands of its Polish Jews who then migrated into Russia's newly acquired Polish lands. When Napoleon emerged victorious over Prussia at Jena in 1806, he created the semi-independent Duchy of Warsaw out of Prussia's share of Poland. After the Congress of Vienna in 1815, most of the Duchy of Warsaw was converted into a semiautonomous Kingdom of Poland attached to Russia, known thenceforth as Congress Poland. After an unsuccessful Polish uprising in 1831, it became incorporated as a province of Russia. Russia, then, came to control about three-fourths of the former Polish commonwealth.

Thus the Jews of Poland, for centuries governed by their autonomous institutions in a near-feudal society, were catapulted into a modern political world. They became subjects of three states ruled by absolutist monarchs, shortly to be joined in a Holy Alliance against the threatening storm of liberty and equality which the French Revolution had set in motion. Internally, too, Jewish traditional society was being severely shaken. Traditional rabbinic authority, whose omnipotence had lessened with the decline of the councils, was being undermined by mystical and Messianic movements originating in the East. New currents of social and political thought were sweeping eastward in the wake of the French Revolution.

2 Hasidism and Haskala

Rabbinic judaism, which had for centuries exercised a powerful hegemony over East European Jewry, was in the eighteenth century assaulted from east and west. *Hasidism,* a revolutionary movement of religious renewal, arose in the Ukrainian provinces of Podolia and Volhynia. *Haskala,* or Enlightenment, began in Berlin, the Prussian capital and center of emergent German nationalism. The originators of both movements were contemporaries: Israel Baal Shem Tov (ca. 1700–1760) and Moses Mendelssohn (1729–1786). In their time rabbinic Judaism still claimed one figure of uncontested, universal authority and matchless scholarship: the towering Elijah ben Solomon, the Vilna Gaon (1720–1797).

The apparent compatibility of haskala and hasidism in a joint attack on rabbinic traditionalism paralleled the temporary union in the Christian world between rationalism and pietism, opposing rigid Protestant formalism and scholasticism. But these alliances were brief. Within a quarter of a century, hasidism and rabbinic Judaism reconciled their differences and consolidated their forces against the haskala.

Likenesses between hasidism and haskala were as striking as their differences. Hasidism and haskala each in its own way dignified the individual and enhanced his personal status in relations with God and fellowmen. The haskala made Judaism a private matter between man and God, to be transacted in private. Haskala denationalized Judaism and decommunalized its teachings, observances, and symbols. Hasidism, for its part, demanded individual spontaneity and genuineness in place of mechanical performance and formalistic ritual; communion with God was conditional on inwardness and authentic religiosity. To help its followers attain that communion, hasidism provided them with the *zaddik* (saint, pious man), the charismatic religious leader through whose extraordinary mystical powers ordinary men could be brought closer to God. Investing the zaddik with divine grace and insisting on naturality, sincerity, and spontaneity, hasidism downgraded rabbinic study and traditional rabbinic authority, both long honored in Jewish communal life.

Haskala, too, struck at traditional communal leadership, opposing its inflexible control over Jewish educational and religious affairs and its unwillingness to adapt to changing times. The haskala strove toward complete emancipation, when Jews as free citizens would serve the state directly, without the kehilla as intermediary.

Hasidism directed itself toward improving the inner man; haskala, the outer man. Hasidism wanted to perfect man for communion with God; haskala wanted to refine and cultivate him for communication with non-Jews. The hasid, striving for inwardness, disregarded appearance, manners and costume; to achieve humility, he assumed a boorish mien, concealing the subtle spirituality and intellectuality of hasidic teachings. The *maskil*, the enlightener, stressed outwardness — elegant speech, modern clothing, good manners, wit, and erudition to dazzle non-Jewish society. Hasidism warned its followers to eschew pride, self-love, and ostentation. Haskala valued achievement and accomplishment.

Both haskala and hasidism spoke of equality, but meant different things. Hasidism preached an egalitarian doctrine of spiritual liberation, proselytizing rich and poor alike, skeptic and believer, German Jew and Polish Jew. Hasidism tried to strengthen the Jew's inner resources and increase his self-esteem, combatting those feelings of Jewish inferiority which characterized the early maskilim. The maskilim, for their part, dedicated though they were to civic equality, never hesitated to set themselves apart and above the mass of Jews. In the dozens of petitions they submitted to European monarchs they contrasted their own readiness for citizenship with the educational disqualifications of their unenlightened brethren.

Voltaire's crusade against religion and intellectual backwardness ("Écrasez l'infâme"), his contempt for Christianity (suitable, he thought, for chambermaids and tailors but not for an educated elite), and his ardent espousal of science, scholarship, and literature endeared him to Western Jews. They even internalized his savage hostility toward Jews, for in their eyes Western culture and humanism were rational, enlightened, progressive, *ergo* good; whereas Judaism was irrational, superstitious, backward, separatist, *ergo* bad. The dazzling proof of the equation was Moses Mendelssohn, then the most famous Jew in Europe, and Count Mirabeau's most persuasive argument on behalf of Jewish emancipation:

> May it not be said that his example, especially the outcome of his exertions for the elevation of his brethren, silences those who, with ignoble bitterness, insist that the Jews are so contemptible that they cannot be transformed into a respectable people?

That notion became legend. (It still persists.) It was told again and again; the Jews were sunk in ignorance and superstition, unfit for citizenship or the intercourse of noble men, until Moses Mendelssohn, the hunchbacked Berlin Socrates, physically ugly but intellectually radiant, led them from darkness toward enlightenment, liberating them from the bondage of the Jewish past, and setting them on the path to political emancipation. Mirabeau and Gotthold Lessing were not the only ones who saw the Jewish situation that way. The same picture was drawn by German Jews and East European Jews. Upon Mendelssohn's death, his followers published an extravagant eulogy: "Truth and the authentic interpretation of the Torah were obscured in darkness for generations, until God commanded: 'Let Moses appear,' and at once there was light!"

The portrait now seems a caricature. Mendelssohn was not the first Jew educated in Western culture, but he dramatized Jewish acceptance, and its dizzying perspectives at the pinnacles of intellectual society. His friendship with Lessing and his intercourse with the most eminent philosophers, thinkers, and nobility of Western Europe became legend. Young Jews, East and West, dedicated themselves to emulating him, matching his education and intellectual attainments, and, as a seemingly natural accompaniment, achieving a great place in Gentile society. The Mendelssohnians thought that place could be attained by adapting Judaism to the time. Little did they realize how brief would be the duration of that particular time. The Berlin haskala began to discard and disown the national elements in Judaism and pare down its beliefs and observances. First of all, the Berliners disowned the East European Jew, whose very dress and coiffure called attention to Jewish differences. Then they eliminated Yiddish, in their eyes a vulgar distortion of German, the articulated symbol of the disparity between Jew and German. Mendelssohn's German translation of the Bible, printed in Hebrew letters with modern Hebrew commentaries (*biurim*), was intended to discourage the use of Yiddish in expounding and interpreting the Bible, to replace the traditional commentary with a more rationalist and critical interpretation, and, finally, to encourage and stimulate the use of German among Jews.

The rapid abandonment of Yiddish and then Hebrew, of belief in the Messiah's coming and in the unity of the Jewish people, did not guarantee entry into Christian society, for not enlightenment but apostasy was the right price of admission to Gentile society. Heine, who paid it, remarked that "the baptismal certificate is the admission ticket into European civilization." Many enlightened Berlin Jews had little difficulty paying that price. The Mendelssohnian haskala set off an epidemic of voluntary conversions unparalleled in Jewish history. "They were like moths, fluttering around the flame, till they were consumed," writes Graetz. So pervasive was this headlong flight to Christianity, that even those who remained Jews justified the apostates. Lazarus Bendavid, a Mendelssohnian and a Kantian, empathized: "One cannot reproach these converts because they prefer the living, joyous church to the forlorn, dreary synagogue and rush to save themselves and their children."

Some Mendelssohnians, like David Friedlaender (1750–1834), hesitated to plunge into the baptismal waters. In an anonymous letter in 1799 to *Oberconsistorialrat* Teller on behalf of a group of Jewish patresfamilias, Friedlaender proposed in the name of Enlightenment, Reason, and Moral Feeling, their wholesale baptism and conversion on condition that they be excused from believing in Jesus' divinity. The Protestants were not interested. Friedlaender died a Jew, but all his children converted unconditionally; a century later their descendants no doubt qualified as pure Aryans when German nationalism triumphed over Enlightenment, Reason, and Moral Feeling.

No wonder, then, that "Berlin," "Berlinchik," and "biur" became anathema among pious Jews and defenders of tradition. In 1799, Israel Leibel, formerly a preacher in Mohilev, White Russia, a combatant in rabbinic Judaism's war on hasidism, came to Frankfort to publish an antihasidic tract. Friedlaender's *Sendschreiben* so shocked him that he trained his polemical talents against "the new heretics" instead of the hasidim.

The notion that civic emancipation was conditional on religious enlightenment was imported from the Berlin Mendelssohnians into Eastern Europe. Mendel Lefin, who played a seminal role in connecting the Berlin haskala with Galicia, Russia, and the Ukraine, urged the Polish diet in 1791 to reform Judaism and Jewish traditional education. Lefin praised Judaism's rationalist qualities as exemplified by Maimonides in the past and by Mendelssohn in the present, while denouncing the spread of hasidism in Eastern Europe. Jewish political emancipation and cultural enlightenment, he argued, could be achieved only by drastic reforms in Judaism and Jewish education, whose enforcement required the state's authority. But he did not impress the Poles. The short-lived Constitution of May 3, 1791, did not grant Jews any rights.

In Galicia, Joseph II, an admirer of Rousseau and Voltaire, brought modernity and efficiency into an empire where despotism had been tempered only by Viennese *schlamperei*. His *Toleranzpatent* gave religious freedom to the Protestants and Greek Orthodox who had languished under Maria Theresa's policy of Catholicization. "Nobody should suffer any more tribulations in consequence of his faith," he wrote. He even extended the privilege of religious tolerance to the Jews — on condition that they abandon what he understood to be the false and harmful religious teachings in

the Talmud and in Jewish prayer books. Demonstrating his religious tolerance, he promulgated a harsh germanizing policy, establishing a secular
school system for Jewish children with German the language of instruction.
The Jewish enlighteners, like their opposite numbers among the Czechs
and Hungarians, regarded German as the vehicle for Western culture and
hailed Joseph's policies. Thus, the haskala first came to Galicia under the
inauspicious sign of forced assimilation and anti-Judaism.

In Russia, too, the handful of early Mendelssohnian maskilim regarded
the haskala as the means of admission to Gentile society. Case histories are
instructive, Judah Leib Nevakhovich (1776–1831), a student of philosophy, and Abraham Peretz, son-in-law of Joshua Zeitlin, the Maecenas of
early Russian maskilim, with other merchants and government contractors
from Shklov formed the nucleus of a Jewish community in St. Petersburg, where they resided despite Catherine's prohibition, because of close
business associations with high government officials. In 1803, when a governmental committee was convened to consider the legal status of Jews in
Russia, Nevakhovich wrote a Russian pamphlet, *Outcry of the Daughter of
Judah* (issued a year later in Hebrew), which hailed eighteenth-century
humanism extravagantly, rhapsodized Russia and its people, and pleaded for
the emancipation of the worthy Jews. Nevakhovich, Peretz, and their circle
petitioned the Tsarist government also to introduce reform in Jewish education and religion, thus enabling the less worthy Jews to qualify for emancipation. But the Statute of 1804, while liberal in some regards, did not fulfill
their hopes. Nevakhovich consoled himself shortly thereafter by converting
to Greek Orthodoxy. His friend Peretz followed suit. Peretz's son Hirsch
(Grigory) also apostatized. (Later, arrested as a Decembrist, he was said to
have used the Hebrew *herut* [freedom] as a password.)

Western-educated Hirsh Ber Hurwitz (1795–1857), son of Hayim
Heikel, merchant-maskil of Uman, also adhered to the Berlin pattern. The
younger Hurwitz believed that "reforms" in Jewish society could be enforced only by an enlightened absolutism, which would liberate Jews from
the Talmud and from their "superstitions." He held New Testament morality to be the pinnacle of ethical thought, with which Jews should be familiar. Above all, the younger Hurwitz wanted the Tsarist government to forbid traditional Jewish garb which, to him, was a badge of shame. In 1822
Hirsh Ber founded a secular school in Uman but abandoned it under the
pressure of the hasidim. Shortly thereafter, Hurwitz left Uman and, via
Berlin, came to England, where he converted to Christianity. As Hermann
Bernard, he was appointed *praeceptor linguae sacrae* at Cambridge in 1837.

The suicidal consequences of the Berlin haskala and of its disciples in Poland, Galicia, and Russia solidified traditionalist resistance to what was modern and secular. That siege mentality had not been characteristic of Judaism in the past, when secular education had been considered compatible with Judaism. Among Jews, the study of mathematics, astronomy, and medicine had a venerable tradition and the abundance of Hebrew publications in those fields during centuries when most Europeans did not know their own alphabets testifies to the harmony between normative Judaism and secular knowledge. That tradition the Vilna Gaon continued. He pursued and advocated the pursuit of the secular learning as a basis for understanding Judaism better: "Every lack of knowledge in secular subjects causes a hundredfold lack in the study of the Torah, for Torah and knowledge are joined together." He himself wrote treatises on Hebrew grammar, trigonometry, geometry, algebra, and astronomy. Baruch Shick of Shklov (1740–1812), an East European precursor of the haskala, wrote: "The Vilna Gaon advised me to translate as many scientific books as possible into our sacred tongue to disseminate learning among our people of Israel lest the Gentiles ridicule us for our ignorance and in their pride ask: 'Where is your wisdom?' "

Whereas dozens of documents describe the bitter war between the Vilna Gaon and the hasidim, no historical evidence has been adduced that the Gaon ever criticized Mendelssohn's Bible translation and biur. In fact, most orders from Poland for Mendelssohn's Bible came from Vilna. Contrary evidence may be gleaned from the history of Solomon Dubno (1738–1813), the Volhynian poet, grammarian, Biblical exegete, and Mendelssohn's original collaborator. After some orthodox rabbis condemned Mendelssohn's translation of Genesis, with Dubno's commentary (1778), Dubno broke with Mendelssohn. But Dubno completed his own Biblical commentary and received testimonials for its publication from scholars close to the Vilna Gaon, including Rabbi Hayim Volozhiner, the Gaon's most eminent disciple.

In the second half of the eighteenth century in Poland, general education was much prized by the emergent Jewish middle class. Literate in Hebrew or at least Yiddish, many Jews knew, although not always well, the local language: Polish, Ukrainian, German, Lithuanian, or Lettish. Even Mendelssohn owed part of his secular education to an East European Jew, Israel Zamosc (ca. 1700–1772), who came to Berlin in 1742 after having taught at the yeshiva of Zamosc. Hired to instruct Mendelssohn in mathematics, Zamosc, obviously a man of uncommon abilities and ambition, was nevertheless not unique among pre-Emancipation East European Jews in his acquisition of general knowledge. Education was a necessity for merchants engaged in foreign trade, according to the memoirs of Ber Bolechower (1723–1805).[2] The son of a wine merchant in Eastern Galicia, Ber was proficient in Polish, Latin, and other subjects, long before Mendelssohn and Solomon Maimon were heard from. Some years later, in a small town near Stanislawow where he lived with his in-laws, Ber Bolechower joined a circle of young people who devoted themselves to reading literary Hebrew. A successful merchant, he continued studying rabbinic literature, foreign languages, and the humanities.

Ber Bolechower was typical for that upper stratum of Jewish merchants whose commercial activities took them beyond the confines of their own towns. Jews travelled extensively, responsible for much of Poland's foreign trade. Statistics of the Leipzig fairs show an attendance in 1756 of twenty Gentiles and eight Jews from Poland, but a decade later three times as many Jews as Christians came from Poland, and that Jewish proportion kept increasing.

Many Jewish communities were commercial centers, situated at the crossroads of European trade routes: Brody, Berdichev, Lemberg, Lublin, Yaroslav, Poltava, Brest-Litovsk, Warsaw, Odessa, Shklov. Towns and cities in Eastern Europe were then centers mainly of commerce and finance, neither industrial nor manufacturing centers. The population was mostly rural, but the Jews were ensconced in the very center of trade, commerce, and finance — an urban population when urbanization was in its infancy.

In the early nineteenth century, hasidism became Judaism's dominant mode in Eastern Europe. Only the Lithuanian stronghold of the Vilna Gaon's descendants remained untouched. Pockets of German culture remained here and there, as in Courland, and embattled haskalic islands survived in larger communities. The history is yet to be written of how the hasidim captured the masses, won loyal disciples also among the social elite, and emerged triumphant over their opponents, called *mitnagdim*. Since hasidism had never questioned the authority of Jewish law and had always identified with the whole Jewish community, hasidim and mitnagdim soon learned to live in peace, if not always in mutual respect. But hasidim waged war against the haskala.

Hasidism had originated as a kind of anti-intellectual movement, dignifying the common and uneducated Jew over the Talmudic scholar. Since traditionalist Jewish scholarship by itself could not guarantee any man the world to come, of what value then was general scholarship? The early maskilim had little to recommend them to hasidim, who considered love of one's people a virtue. The common people distrusted first the educated and then, from their example, education. Educated upper-class Jews increasingly began to appear as agents of officialdom, ungenerous to their people and lax in their religion. The masses, more than the *rebbes,* exerted pressure against modernists and advocates of secular education. Not all rebbes approved these anti-intellectualist moods, but few could resist conformist pressures. Some rebbes were themselves men of the world, Talmudic scholars, some with secular education, who had traveled throughout Eastern and Central Europe. Many came to hasidism from traditional rabbinism, having undergone a profound religious experience.

Hasidism took three courses as it expanded. In the Ukraine, where it originated, and thence into Galicia, the rebbe, the zaddik ruled supreme. In the smaller towns in the Russian and Austrian backwaters, the hasidic thrust was toward simplicity, sincerity, spontaneity, gladness, and purposefulness in devotion to God. The rebbe's eminence reached kingly stature with Israel of Rizhin (1813–1850), who, having fled the Tsarist police in the Ukraine, came to Sadagora (Yiddish name: Sadeger), where his court enjoyed extraordinary prosperity and his influence spread far, even into Bukovina and Rumania.

In White Russia and Lithuania, hasidism took a distinctive course with Habad hasidism, founded by Rabbi Schneur Zalman of Lyady (1745–1813). Its name "HaBaD," an acronym for *hokhma* (wisdom), *bina* (understanding), *da'at* (knowledge), epitomized the singularities in its founder's doctrine. Schneur Zalman combined an original philosophical system with rabbinic learning and an individualistic strain of mysticism.

In Poland, where the somewhat more urbanized Jews looked derisively upon wonder-working rebbes, hasidism under Simha Bunam of Pshiskha and Menahem Mendel of Kotsk took a sophisticated and highly individualized direction, demanding of each hasid greater self-reliance and less dependence on the rebbe, insisting on each man's own perfectability through his own efforts. Polish hasidism never depreciated Talmudic study; indeed, Rabbi Isaac Meir Alter, the rebbe of Ger (Góra Kalwarja), foremost disciple of Kotsk, restored Talmudic study to its original prehasidic eminence. (In Galicia, too, the great dynasty of Belz restored a more traditional rabbinic mode to hasidism.)

Indirectly, but unmistakably, the hasidic movement spurred rabbinic learning. Hayim of Volozhin (1749–1821) having accepted the post of rabbi at Volozhin in 1773, founded a yeshiva there in 1802 to counteract hasidic influences and revive Talmudic study. Drawing its student body from all Eastern Europe, the yeshiva at Volozhin eventually became the most distinguished center of Torah scholarship in the nineteenth century. Its establishment, in turn, stimulated the founding of other yeshivot at Mir, Slonim, Vilna, Telshe, and eventually the *musar* yeshivot.

The hasidim also stimulated greater literacy and the spread of books when they began publishing their rebbes' biographies and apothegms. The last quarter of the eighteenth century witnessed an extraordinary growth and expansion of Hebrew and Yiddish printing in Poland, in part a result of the government's efforts, between the first two partitions, to encourage domestic book production. Printing presses became common in the dense hasidic centers in the Ukraine, while in White Russia and Lithuania, where hasidism was less vigorous, book production was more traditionalist. By the end of the eighteenth century, Hebrew presses in Podolia, Volhynia, White Russia, and Galicia were producing standard Talmudic and rabbinic works, prayer books, and Yiddish books, besides polemical hasidic and antihasidic tracts.

Despite their other-worldliness, the rebbes were concerned with this world too. Many hasidic rebbes undertook, as their mission, to convert the "enlightened" and return them to God and Judaism. Zusya of Annopol and Simha Bunam proselytized Jews to return to Judaism. Levi Yitzhak of Berdichev (ca. 1740–1809), known for his exaltation of the common man, his preference for faith over scholarship, engaged in public disputes with mitnagdim and maskilim to defend hasidic teachings and win Jews for Judaism.

Even Nahman of Bratzlav (1772–1810), the mystic who elevated faith and simplicity, who aggrandized the role of the zaddik in mediating between the pious and God, even he, who was said to have composed a prayer against the haskala ("O Lord, grant us the good fortune to avoid occupying ourselves with Gentile writings and languages"), distinguished between two kinds of secular knowledge: the scientific, which he thought contained sparks of holiness, and the rationalist, which led to disbelief. He is said to have spoken contemptuously of those rationalist maskilim who claimed that the highest degree of knowing was not knowing. But he did not lose hope in recovering them for Judaism. In poor health the last year of his life, he moved to Uman, wanting to be buried with the martyrs of Gonta's Cossack massacres of 1768. Uman then had a small colony of maskilim, including Hayim Heikel Hurwitz (ca. 1750–1822), an admirer of Mendelssohn, and his son Hirsh Ber. Hasidic and maskilic sources document the encounters between Nahman and the Hurwitz circle. A maskilic memoir reports: "[Hirsh Ber] Hurwitz read and explained the German classics to him, and Nahman listened with great eagerness. When he was pleased by an idea

that was read to him, he immediately transposed it into his work and attributed it to a zaddik." Nahman's hasidim, it is told, complained he spent
too much time with nonbelievers; he justified himself by explaining that
that way he hoped to turn them to righteousness.[3]

Schneur Zalman of Lyady, too, mingled with maskilim, and tales are
told of his exchanges with Joshua Zeitlin of Shklov, another central figure
of the early haskala. Each rebbe had his maskil with whom he wrestled for
the victory of faith over skepticism. The hasidic versions of these encounters, however apocryphal, indicate that ideas were perhaps more freely ex-
changed than we have been given to believe.

The Berlin haskala encountered only one opponent, traditional Judaism, which it attacked with a totality that foreclosed compromise. But the
haskala in Galicia, Russia, and Congress Poland encountered, besides rabbinic Judaism, also hasidism, which became a buffering third force in the
conflict between traditionalism and modernity and a source of life-giving
energy to both a desiccated rabbinism and an arid rationalism. In Galicia,
the haskala combined with rabbinic orthodoxy against hasidism to produce
a modernized style of Judaism and a high level of Hebrew culture. In Russia, hasidim and mitnagdim collaborated against the maskilim, amassing
enormous religious and cultural resources that enriched and endowed later
radical movements with Jewish content. In Congress Poland, Polish nationalism became a third party to the tensions between Orthodoxy and haskala.

These internal Jewish conflicts, reconciliations, and accommodations occurred in a political climate totally dissimilar from that of the Berlin haskala. The brief flirtation of Europe's absolutist rulers with enlightenment
had ended with the Napoleonic wars. In the midst of an accelerating and
polarizing struggle between reaction and revolution in the Austrian and
Russian empires, in which they were both subjects and objects, Jews tried to
create for their own community a synthesis between tradition and modernity.

Unlike its Berlin predecessor, the haskala in Eastern Europe was not
monolithic, the maskilim not cast from one mold. Witness Nahum Sokolow's description of the Hebraist maskilim:

. . . How great the distance between the maskil, the dreamer and striver
    who lived in the environs of knightly castles, had something of young
    Werther's sorrow, reared on Goethe and Schiller, who wrote preten-
    tiously about spring in colorless, naïve Biblical Hebrew, sans life, sans
    thought; and between the maskil, the refiner of Hebrew, the methodi-

cian of the ancient language who fondled it like an idol or a beloved; and that maskil, the scholar of Judaism, who strove to enclose ideas of faith, tradition, and Jewish life in a frame of philosophic method; and between that maskil who burst forth from the exact-scientific section of the Talmud.[4]

In Galicia, the haskala's generator, or regenerator, was Nahman Krochmal (1785–1840), one year old when Moses Mendelssohn died. Krochmal was born in Brody, at Galicia's Russian border— the second largest city after Lemberg, the Jewish capital of Galicia, and one of the great trading centers linking Europe and Asia. The nucleus of a group of lesser commercial towns, including Tarnopol and Zolkiew, and coupled with Lemberg, Brody became the center of the Galician haskala. There Mendel Lefin came in 1800 and stayed many years, the living link between Mendelssohn and East European Jews, who innovated the use of Yiddish for enlightenment, thus creating new possibilities for synthesizing tradition and modernity.

Krochmal became the master and standard-bearer of an extensive and highly differentiated circle of maskilim — some close to traditional Judaism, and some radical reformers. The first outstanding maskil to combine modern scholarship and faith, he enlarged the Jewish intellectual environment. He used Jewish history as a revivifying element in the modern man's search for Jewish identity.

Hebrew scholarship and Hebrew publishing, which had withered in Berlin, revived in Galicia and flourished for many decades. Even after 1848, with the politicalization and germanization of the Galician haskala, the Hebrew press continued to retain its readership, drawing upon the inexhaustible reservoir of hasidim who, having tasted modernity, became addicted to it.

The commercial and rationalist outlook of the Galician merchants-scholars, unreceptive to mysticism and hostile to zaddikism, turned the Galician haskala violently antihasidic. Joseph Perl (1774–1839), the innovator of educational and religious reform in Tarnopol, bitterest and most vituperative antihasid, even invoked the state police to break up hasidic prayer meetings. Repelled by this excessive antipathy toward hasidism and its resort to the repressive arm of the imperial government, lifelong maskil Jacob Samuel Bick (ca. 1770–1831) demonstratively sold his copy of Maimonides' *Guide to the Perplexed* (the maskil's symbol of Jewish rationalism). Bick's maskilic friends could not fathom how anyone who had enjoyed rationalism and enlightenment could choose to return to utter darkness. Bick tried to explain to his friend Rapoport: "Why have you, who loves Schiller so deeply and has translated his poems into Hebrew, not taken to heart for yourself his cosmopolitan verse 'Diesen Kuss der ganzen Welt!' You do not fulfill this verse toward the people of Israel. Embrace and kiss all our Jewish brothers with a whole heart and an undivided soul, even if one must pay with both reason and soul." [5]

The Russian haskala in its early years lacked a commanding intellect like Krochmal and lived off the reflected brilliance of its charismatic father, Mendelssohn. Russian maskilim regarded Berlin as their Athens and Mendelssohn their Socrates. In Russia, not only Jews, but also educated Russians looked westward for intellectual stimulation and educational models. (Baltic Germans then were the highest elite in Russia, dominating the top ranks of the army, the diplomatic service, and the state bureaucracy.)

Some early Russian maskilim went abroad; a few found refuge in Mitau and Hasenpot in Courland, where Prussian culture paired well with the Berlin haskala. Others formed small pockets of modernism. These included Menasseh of Ilye (1767–1831), an autochthonous Russian maskil who, in the tradition of the Vilna Gaon, studied mathematics, astronomy, and philosophy, then intended to set out for Berlin. The story has it that the traditionalists induced the Prussian authorities at Koenigsberg to refuse him a passport, lest he be lost to Judaism in Berlin. Baruch Shick, the Vilna Gaon's admirer encountered earlier, returned from England, where he had studied medicine, to his native Shklov, translating into Hebrew Euclid and works on algebra and trigonometry. There he was befriended by Joshua Zeitlin (1742–1822), merchant and contractor for the Russian army, who had established a nearby academic retreat for scholars and writers. For Shick he set up a chemical laboratory. Mendel Lefin, too, was a resident scholar at Zeitlin's estate.

Young Jews, stirred by the new world, eager for novelty and freedom, found Mendelssohn's Bible translation and biur the key to secular culture. Lev Mandelstamm, the first Jewish university student in Russia, started his secular education with Mendelssohn and continued with *Ha-Me'assef*.

The Russian maskilim began to publish when hasidism and rabbinic Judaism were beginning to accommodate each other. Attacking both, the maskilim isolated themselves from the poor Jewish masses, from the Talmudic scholars, and even from the thin stratum of upper-class Russian-speaking merchants and doctors who wanted assimilation, not enlightenment. Unlike their Berlin models, early Russian maskilim like Isaac Ber Levinsohn (1788–1860) and Abraham Ber Gottlober (1811–1899) were cut off also from Russian society, without knowledge or appreciation of contemporary politics. At a time when Alexander I had conceived of a Holy Alliance as a bulwark against the political and religious liberalism released by the French Revolution and when Metternich's shadow darkened Europe, Levinsohn, Gottlober, and their company were still thinking in Mendelssohnian terms of the enlightened absolutism of Frederick II, Joseph II, and Catherine the Great. These Russian maskilim mistook the aggressively Christian antisemitism of Alexander I and Nicholas I for a rationalist contempt of supernatural religion. Yet despite their shortcomings and their recurrent cravenness before authority, these maskilim were imbued with *ahavat yisrael*, love of the people of Israel, even when they mocked and ridiculed Jewish ways and customs. They wanted European culture combined with Jewish tradition, Jewish political equality to be accompanied by patriotism, and the Jewish economic position improved. They thought the haskala would bring this to pass.

The Russian maskilim turned to Yiddish, the language of common and uneducated folk, though for that same reason they despised it. Mendel Lefin's first Yiddish translation of the Bible (Proverbs) infuriated maskil Tobias Feder (1760–1817) into writing a choleric Hebrew pamphlet that frightened Lefin away from Yiddish forever after. But life's logic dictated the use of Yiddish and by cultivating the folk language, the maskilim eventually came into closer, if not intimate, rapport with the masses. Similarly, maskilic experiments in modernizing Hebrew helped bring the haskala to those Palestine-oriented nationalists who were to reconstruct modern Hebrew culture.

Vilna and Zamosc became the citadels of haskala, new centers for Hebrew and Yiddish literature. The Odessa Jewish community, largely seeded by migrants from Brody, in a city new to Russia and new to the Jews, without rabbinic, hasidic, or any Jewish tradition, became a Russian maskilic Mecca. In Jewish folklore, Odessa became synonymous with disbelief, sinfulness, and frivolity.

The Gaon's rationalist traditions had made Vilna hospitable to a Hebraist and conservative haskala. Modern Hebrew fiction emerged in the naïve and primitive romances of Abraham Mapu (1808–1867) and in the romantic fiction of Kalman Shulman (1819–1899). Mordecai Aaron Gunzburg (1795–1846), called the father of Hebrew prose, Abraham Ber Lebensohn (1789–1878), poet and scholar, and his far more poetically gifted son, Micah Joseph (1828–1852), formed the nucleus of Vilna's budding modernist Hebrew literature.

Yiddish haskala literature was, to begin with, didactic and antihasidic. Its first true literary talent was Solomon Ettinger (1800–1855), who had studied medicine in Lemberg. He settled in Zamosc, writing Yiddish poems and a play *Serkele,* considered the first modern Yiddish drama. Israel Aksenfeld (1787–1868), a practicing notary public in Odessa, was a prolific producer of prolix Yiddish fiction, once characterized as "naïve-primitive realism."

The outstanding figure of this early Russian-Polish haskala, Hayim Selig Slonimski (1810–1904), known as the Jewish Humboldt, all his life an observant Jew, combined traditionalism in perfect harmony with scientific study. A gifted popularizer of science and invention, who fashioned a Hebrew modern scientific vocabulary from biblical and Talmudic sources, Slonimski was exceptional in that he had the approval and admiration of both traditionalist and modernist Jews.

But Slonimski, traditionalist and scientist, was unique. The literary haskala ended in despair and futility, for, cut off from living realities and contemporary problems, it led nowhere. Peretz put it this way: "It is already long past the haskala era. We have renounced it. We regard it as a hoopskirt when slim skirts are in style. We accuse it: it did not convey water and minerals to the roots, nor air and light to the branches, but merely broke off twigs and grafted them on foreign trunks. No one knows exactly how to have done otherwise. But that was not the way." [6]

Had the time produced men of greater intellectual and moral stature, the introduction of science and secularism into traditional society, inevitable as it was, might have been accomplished with less injury to the religious culture. Eventually the East European haskala became the instrumentality of change and accommodation, the change itself becoming incorporated into the tradition.

3 Education, Reform, and Assimilation

TRADITIONAL JEWISH society began to show marked signs of change and disintegration in the first third of the nineteenth century. The Jewish family, for centuries the underpinning of Jewish tradition and continuity, became strained by the tensions between hasidism and haskala. The rebbe had preempted the hasid's devotion. On solemn and festive holy days hasidim repaired to their rebbes, leaving their families unmanned. Maskilim, for their part, having discovered romantic love in the German fiction they admired, rebelled against traditionally arranged marriages. Quarrels between traditionalists and modernists frequently divided families as well as communities: marriages were dissolved, wives abandoned. Husbands who turned maskilim were often forced by traditionalist in-laws to divorce their wives even when the couple lived in harmony, while other maskilim fled inflexible in-laws and tearful wives, seeking "progress" and "light."

Economic life, too, was changing Jewish society. Governmental decrees in Galicia, Congress Poland, and Russia restricted Jews in their place of residence and choice of occupation. Their economic insecurity spurred them to explore and enter the new occupations and businesses developing in a newly urbanizing and industrializing society which required an expanded middle class.

In Russia and Poland, Jews had long fulfilled a life-giving role as merchants, traders, and financiers, buying and selling, exporting and importing, and providing capital. They were among the Russian pioneers of the domestic textile industry, sugar production, railroad building. Under Nicholas I, a new Russian occupation was managing the liquor industry, whose production and sale had become a government monopoly. The government leased all its operations to private entrepreneurs, most of whom turned out to be Jews. Operating liquor leases required a large staff, extensive organization, much paper work, and connections and talent to negotiate with the Tsarist bureaucracy. About eight thousand Jews were said to have been employed at various functions in the operation of liquor leases.

These people, knowing the utilitarian value of general education, regarded it as a necessity, not a heresy. To this expanding Jewish middle class, traditional Judaism often appeared an embarrassment and a liability as they sought financial success and social acceptance in the non-Jewish world. They thus reinforced the maskilim and gave a practical purpose to what had appeared a futilitarian ideology. The combination of the rising business elite with the emergent Jewish intelligentsia turned the haskala into a practical reform movement to modernize school and synagogue. It no longer sufficed to apostrophize that heavenly daughter enlightenment in extravagantly ornate Hebrew verse. Deeds were required.

In early nineteenth-century Galicia and Russia, state schools were open to Jews, but they clung to *heder* and yeshiva. Even those attracted to secular education found the state schools inhospitable, for in the Austrian and Russian empires state and school were both wedded to church — Roman Catholic and Greek Orthodox, then the two most bigoted and intolerant religions in Europe. The school curriculum, saturated with Christian content and Christian prejudice, infected its Christian pupils and humiliated its Jewish ones. Jews complained in 1817 to the authorities in Lublin that Jewish children in the state schools were abused by teachers and fellow pupils, ridiculed for their traditional dress, shamed and insulted for being Jews. In 1830, after more than a quarter of a century of the privilege of attending state schools, only 408 Jewish pupils were enrolled in the Galician state schools; in Russia in 1841, out of a population of over a million, only 230 children attended state schools; in Congress Poland, the Jewish proportion was higher: 2,000 out of half a million. To remedy this situation, maskilim in larger communities tried to establish private schools for Jews, combining Jewish studies with a general curriculum.

The earliest and most successful school was inaugurated in Tarnopol in 1813 by Joseph Perl, that rabid antihasid. A man of considerable means, a highly successful wine merchant, Perl at first financed the school himself. It opened with thirteen pupils; six years later it had over a hundred. In 1820, Austrian authorities gave the school formal recognition and financial support. Based partly on German models, the school combined Jewish and secular studies: Hebrew, prayers, Talmud, and Bible, with German, arithmetic, history, geography, and morals.[7] Similar schools were successfully established in Warsaw and Odessa; unsuccessful attempts at secular schools were made in the 1820's in Vilna, Uman, Siedlce, Kalisz, and Lublin. A decade later, a modern school was finally established in Vilna.

In 1839, Riga Jews imported from Munich Dr. Max Lilienthal to be their rabbi and principal for their new school. His arrival inaugurated a fateful chapter in Russian Jewish history. His Riga reputation as a modernist brought him to the attention of the Nicolaitan authorities, who had concluded that general education, forcibly administered, would eventually assimilate (read: convert) the Jews. Precisely when the Russian and Austrian despots had come to regard general education and enlightenment as dangerous and radical, they were seized with an itch to educate the Jews.

Nicholas I, who ascended the Russian throne in 1825 following the Decembrist uprising, was consumed by a hatred for Jews and Judaism (the Talmud was his greatest bugaboo) and obsessed with the wish to convert the Jews. Most of his anti-Jewish legislation — six hundred decrees in his thirty-year reign — was designed "to diminish the Jews in the empire," that is, to convert them. Yet when he did not have his Christian mission in mind, he persecuted Jews, making their life as bitter as in ancient Egypt. He decreed their arbitrary expulsion from the villages where they had resided; he taxed them exorbitantly; he abolished the kehillot except as government fiscal agents; he tried forcibly to modernize Jewish traditional dress. In 1836, out of paranoia and to the premature satisfaction of the maskilim, the Nicolaitan government closed down all but two of the numerous Hebrew presses (at this time printing many hasidic works) and installed a foolishly meddlesome and strict censorship over all Hebrew and Yiddish publications. (Censorship of Russian books was just as foolish and strict.)

The conscription law of 1827 was the cruellest — demanding that Jews furnish the state with a higher proportion of recruits than non-Jews, do so more frequently, and for longer periods of time. Conscription lasted twenty-five years, but Jewish children conscripted or kidnapped, as many actually were, between the ages of twelve to eighteen, or even younger, were first assigned to "preparatory establishments," and their twenty-five-year service period began at eighteen. Nicholas's conversionist pressures on the Jewish conscripts, especially children, gave rise to a folkloristic, memoiristic, and fictional literature depicting the pitiable sufferings of children torn from parents and community, thrust into a brutish military life, condemned to loneliness, humiliation, and cruelty. The Nicolaitan regime offered enticing inducements to convert: money, privileges, acceptance. In some military companies all the Jewish recruits were baptized; in others "only" half. In 1842–1843 alone, over twenty-two hundred Jewish minors were converted, without their parents' permission or knowledge, of course. In the nine-year period 1846–1854, out of fourteen thousand cantonists, nearly seven thousand were baptized.[8]

In civilian life, too, the regime penalized Judaism and lured converts with many pleasing prospects: apostates were given equal civic rights with Christians; they were exempted from taxes for three years; criminal offenders were given leniency. All through Russia, domestic and foreign missionary societies operated with governmental blessing.

In 1844 the Nicolaitan government issued an edict announcing the establishment of crown schools for Jewish children and of two rabbinical seminaries in Vilna and Zhitomir, equivalent in curriculum to the gymnasium, whose graduates could become crown rabbis (recognized by the authorities as responsible heads of the Jewish community). To prepare the Jews to accept these schools, Lilienthal had toured the major Jewish cities in Russia, but wherever he went, he met tremendous opposition. The Jews understood that the schools were intended to convert rather than educate, that the state's educational policies were dictated not out of love for education, but out of hate for Jews. A secret decree did not equivocate:

"The purpose in educating the Jews is to bring about their gradual merging with the Christian nationalities and to uproot those superstitions and harmful prejudices which are instilled by the teachings of the Talmud."

Uvarov too was explicit: "The training in the newly established schools is calculated gradually to destroy in the Jews their fanatical separatism and incorporate them into the common body of citizenry. In this the Jews are not mistaken, for is not the religion of Christ the purest symbol of universal citizenship?"

Lilienthal's name became a household epithet for atheist and misleader, the subject of mocking and contemptuous Yiddish folksongs among the traditionalist Jewish masses. But Uvarov was determined to push his "educational" reforms.

In operation, the schools confirmed Jewish fears. The Christian principals and administrators meddled in the Jewish religious curriculum. They forced the Ashkenazic prayer book, with a German translation, upon a hasidic population that followed the Sephardic ritual. In 1853, they discontinued teaching Talmud. They introduced Russian textbooks that were antisemitic and wildly superstitious about Jews and their Talmud.

Pupils in these schools were sometimes enrolled by conscription, the community recruiting the poor or orphaned, as hostages for the more favored. In 1854, about three thousand Jewish children attended some seventy crown schools and in 1863 about four thousand were in ninety-eight schools. (The number of children attending *hedarim* grew far more rapidly — from seventy thousand in 1844 to nearly seventy-six thousand in 1847.)

Lilienthal's precipitous departure for the United States confirmed the worst fears Jews had had about the crown schools. Some years later he admitted, in the *Allgemeine Zeitung des Judentums* (1848): "The Tsar will be satisfied only when the Jew will bow to the Greek cross."

With more irony than logic, the officious and meddling intrusion of the Nicolaitan bureaucracy in internal Jewish affairs fashioned a new class, a Jewish intelligentsia supported somewhat precariously by the government out of the onerous taxes exacted from Jews. Maskilim, educated and half-educated, who could find no place in Russian society, taught Jewish subjects in the crown schools and rabbinic seminaries, censored Jewish books on behalf of the government, wrote government-financed textbooks for the crown schools, and produced instructive manuals for the general Jewish public. A new profession, too, came into being in 1844: *uchony yevrey* ("learned Jew"), the expert on Jewish affairs, attached to the governor-general's offices in the Pale, or in the educational ministry and in other ministries where Jewish expertise was wanted.

Many of the thousand or more graduates of the crown rabbinical seminaries entered the universities. To some, the seminary was an avenue to general secular culture and an escape hatch from the traditional commu-

nity. Other seminary graduates returned to the Jewish community as in-
novators: Abraham Goldfaden, the first modern Yiddish playwright; Aaron
Lieberman, the first Jewish socialist; Lev Levanda, Russian journalist and
novelist who advocated russification as the solution for Jewish problems;
Solomon Mandelkern, who single-handedly compiled a biblical concord-
ance; Abraham Harkavy, who became an outstanding Orientalist and a historian of Russian Jewry.

The movement for educational reform was accompanied by stirrings of
religious reform. Mendelssohn's biur continued to have its impact in Eastern Europe as each rising generation of yeshiva students discovered it anew.
Two new editions were published for Russian and Polish Jews, one in
Warsaw in 1836 and another a decade later in Vilna.

The German Reform movement stimulated some small changes in the
synagogue service of some East European congregations. But reform and
changes in the liturgy and the service were not innovations in themselves.
Long before German Reform, the Vilna Gaon himself had abolished the
recitation of much of the *piyyut* ("hymns") and had introduced congrega-
tional singing. Also, Menahem Mendel of Kotsk had recommended abridg-
ing the piyyut.

In the forties, in Riga, Odessa, Lemberg, Cracow, Warsaw, and Vilna,
a few modest reforms began to be made in synagogues attended by well-to-
do merchants, financiers, and industrialists. A musically trained cantor and
a male or mixed choir were introduced, though an organ was rarely used.
Most widespread was the rabbi's delivery of the sermon in German, Polish,
or Russian — whatever language the upper class favored at that particular
time or place. The Tsarist government conceived the notion of having the
prayer book translated into Russian, an innovation that even radical assimilationists did not conceive of for another two decades, but Hebrew remained the liturgical language. These synagogues, sometimes called "German" or "choir" synagogues, were the religious sanctuary of the more privileged Jews. They had practically no impact on traditionalist prayer houses
or hasidic *shtiblekh*.

The modest reforms in services were accompanied by loud publicistic
and literary demands for reforms in traditional observances. Moses Leib
Lilienblum and Judah Leib Gordon launched attacks against the rigid and
mechanistic application of the Shulhan Arukh, demanding reforms to meet
modern needs. Their intemperate onslaught so savagely mocking traditionalism, their intent so iconoclastic, they succeeded only in reinforcing the
traditionalists in their unalterable conformity.

At that time, when the modernists kept leaping over the fences the Orthodox tried to build around a Judaism encrusted with tradition, a new religious movement arose in Lithuania, in the heartland of intransigent rabbinism. Known as *musar*, an untranslatable word generally meaning chastisement, but here meaning religious ethics, the new movement renewed and refreshed rabbinism, preaching a doctrine of ethics and morality based on traditional Judaism. To be sure, musar encountered antagonism and opposition among the Orthodox. Israel Salanter, its founder, sensitive to the currents of the times, aware that custom had displaced meaningfulness in the mechanical fulfillment of the Shulhan Arukh, was a reformer and a radical in the sense that he downgraded the routine performance of religious duties. He demanded instead service to God through self-discipline and self-knowledge: "Know whence thou art come, whither thou art going, and before whom thou art destined to give an account and reckoning." Man was created in the image of God; as God is merciful, so must man be. Salanter believed that man's highest service to God was rendered through service to one's fellow man. (Felix Adler, founder of the Ethical Culture Society in New York, was said to have once heard Israel Salanter preach in Berlin and to have been impressed by his doctrine of religious ethics.) Salanter's influence was most widely felt in Kovno and throughout Lithuania, where he kindled sparks in dry and rationalist rabbinism. Kovno had been under the influence of the German haskala, but Israel Salanter's musar movement eventually turned Lithuania into a fortress of Judaism whose Talmudism was moderated by inwardness and whose love of God was accompanied by love of man. In time musar's emphasis shifted to asceticism and withdrawal from society. Self-discipline became self-denial; the spirit's strength was used to mortify the body; joy became sin and lust; pain, pleasure. From Israel Salanter down to the radiant Old Man of Slobodka, until our own times, musar sought to rescue man from his evil impulses and from the illusions of society.

The revolutions of 1848 in the Habsburg Empire and Nicholas I's death in 1855 launched an era of political reform which to Jews heralded a time when all men, Jews and Gentiles, would be as brothers. Everywhere the Jews were beneficiaries of the reforms, and they responded with fervent patriotism and an ecstatic embrace of the prevailing culture. Political emancipation, or the promise of it, began to differentiate East European Jewry in class and status, in new political allegiances. The once unitary and integral Ashkenazic Jewish culture took on multiple forms. Germanization, Polonization, Russification became the watchwords of middle-class Jews eager to prove their patriotism and become Germans or Austrians, Poles or Russians of Jewish faith.

The revolution in Austria gave Jews equal civic rights, though, to be sure, these were not given ungrudgingly. (Two Jews had been among five students killed in the first clash between the military and the students in Vienna in 1848, and all five were buried in a common grave. The rabbi, participating in the services with the Christian clergy, appealed: "You have wished that these dead Jews should rest with you in your earth, in the same earth. Do not begrudge it that those who have fought the same battle with you, a hard battle, should live with you upon the same earth, free and untroubled, as yourselves.")

The oppressive taxes on Jews were removed, restrictions on their rights of residence lifted. (The reaction reinstated nearly all of these, but beginning in the late fifties lifted them one by one until the 1867 Constitution gave Jews civic equality and political representation.) The Jewish population increased, by continuous migrations from Russia and Congress Poland, from about 350,000 in 1850 to nearly 600,000 in 1869. The explicitly Catholic and Catholicizing policies of the state school were moderated, with the consequence that whereas only thirty-two Jewish students had been enrolled in Galician gymnasia in 1848, Jews were 9 percent of the pupils in 1869. Jews thronged to the Austrian universities, overwhelmingly in the faculties of law and medicine. In 1848, only three Jews were jurists; by 1887, they were 35 percent of the profession.

The revolution lifted Austria's rigid censorship and the Jewish press, too, began to flourish. A decade after the revolution, Lemberg and Vienna became centers of Hebrew publishing from which emanated a wide variety of journals dedicated to political and business news, Western culture, Jewish scholarship and literature.

In Cracow, the ancient capital of Jagiellonian Poland, as in all Western Galicia, the Jews were infected with Polish nationalism, but in Lemberg, as in all Eastern Galicia, the Jews, surrounded by a Greek Catholic peasant population, looked toward Vienna and the imperial government as the citadel of their political Jewish enlightenment. Amid a sea of illiterate, superstitious, and brutalized peasants, Jews more successfully resisted the assimilationist attractions that political reform encouraged. The great hasidic dynasties entrenched in Eastern Galicia wielded enormous influence over their followers. Belz was first among the Orthodox to turn civil emancipation to account for Orthodoxy and to elect an ultra-Orthodox rabbi to the Reichsrat. To counteract the reformist and assimilationist trends among Jews in Lemberg, the Belz dynasty formed a society called Mahzike Ha-Dat ("Upholders of the Faith") and, in one of the most radical steps taken by traditionalist Jewry, published a Hebrew paper to propagandize its point of view and oppose the modernists. It was the first step in the politicalization of hasidism.

In Congress Poland, Alexander Wielopolski, on behalf of Alexander II, gave the nearly 600,000 Jews full civic and political rights and unprecedented freedom to express their Polish loyalties and demonstrate on behalf of Polish independence. In proclaiming Polish patriotism the Jews found fraternity with Poles. Jewish blood shed for Polonia Restituta on the thirtieth anniversary of the 1830 Polish uprising opened hitherto closed doors. A Polish leader deplored exclusionary policies against Jews in the guilds: "Poland demands that all its natives feel like brothers. Let us then set aside the prejudices which erect a wall between us and let us not permit religions to divide us." [9] The Tsar crushed the uprising in 1863 and his vengeful policy of forced russification stifled everything Polish in official society. By limiting the rights which Wielopolski had given the Jews, the Tsar intensified Jewish loyalty to Poland, its language and culture. That Polonism persisted with a unique passion among Jews until finally Poland was reconstituted as an independent state.

Those brief years of liberalization dichotomized Polish Jews in two camps more estranged from each other than from Jews in Galicia or Russia. The polonized, reform-minded Jews, the "progressists," had little in common with the rapidly growing hasidic population, unlearned, mostly poor, and pious. The uppermost stratum among the very assimilated converted and passed into Christian society. Some who converted for career retained an abiding sense of identity with Jews and whenever and wherever possible exercised their influence on behalf of Jews. Yet these extremes managed to produce a synthesis in the characteristically Warsavian Jewish communal leaders, lukewarm in religion, but generous in philanthropy (was it *noblesse oblige?*), who built and operated hospitals, old-age homes, vocational schools, orphanages, and libraries for the Jewish community, who managed Jewish communal affairs with competence and dignity, and preserved the record of Jewish antiquity in Poland. These men were the distinctive product of Polish patriotism, Hebrew enlightenment, and a diluted modernist Judaism.

When Nicholas I died in 1855, Peter Kropotkin described how ". . . at St. Petersburg . . . men of the educated classes, as they communicated to one another the news, embraced in the streets." The 2.5 million Russian Jews rejoiced no less. The Haman of Russian-Polish Jewry had passed away.

At his coronation of unprecedented splendor on August 26, 1856, Alexander II issued a manifesto which included more than thirty clauses of amnesties and remissions of taxes and fines. The Decembrist exiles were pardoned; the peasants would be liberated from bondage. The Tsar bestowed his grace on the Jews, too, in that coronation manifesto, and in his first official act with regard to the Jews, he abolished the conscription of Jewish children, equalizing Jewish military obligations with those of the entire population.

Finally, on February 19, 1861, perhaps too late and providing too little, the Emperor signed the liberation manifesto and freed about thirty million serfs. Just as exciting was the liberation of the printed word from Nicholas's morbid fears of subversion and perversion.

Nekrasov celebrated the new freedom in a poem:

> My favorite idea
> That the Petersburg climate is terrible
> I can now insert
> In every article without fear. . . .
> At length in old age I have attained happiness:
> I have smoked cigars on the street
> And written without censorship.[10]

The Jews, too, took advantage of freedom, though their press permits were slower in coming. (Ha-Maggid, the first modern Hebrew weekly newspaper, began to come out in 1856 in Lyck, East Prussia, but was directed toward Russian Jews, bringing them news of political developments in Europe. With four hundred subscribers at the start, it had two thousand in 1864.) Three Jewish journals began to appear in Russia in 1860, two in Hebrew and one in Russian. Ha-Karmel, published and edited in Vilna by Samuel Joseph Fuenn (1819–1891), scholar, maskil, and former instructor in the Vilna crown rabbinical seminary, concentrated on literary and scientific subjects. It represented a compromise between a conservative Lithuanian haskala and an equally conservative Talmudism. Ha-Melits, founded and edited in Odessa by Alexander Zederbaum (1816–1893), was an aggressive organ of haskala and perhaps the most influential spokesman for the Russian Jews. Its avowed purpose was to mediate between the government and the Jews, between enlightenment and Judaism. It appeared, except for a few brief intervals, for forty-three years and published nearly every important Hebrew writer of that time. Razsvet ("Dawn"), published in Odessa, undertook to combat "bigotry and stagnation" within the Jewish community and the denial of human and religious rights from the outside. After publishing some fifty issues, the paper ceased publication, for it had worked itself into an intolerable situation: without a mass base, disapproved of by traditionalist Jews, its outspoken editorial policies had kept it too embroiled with a suspicious Tsarist bureaucracy.

In 1862, Zederbaum began publishing a Yiddish weekly, *Kol Mevasser*, first as a supplement to *Ha-Melits* and later as an independent organ. The pioneer of modern Yiddish journalism, it was radically maskilic, assailing the old traditionalist order. There Mendele Mokher Sforim, the grandfather of Yiddish literature, made his debut in Yiddish literature with his first novel *Dos kleyne mentchele* ("The Little Man").

Educational policies, too, were liberalized and education for all classes encouraged. The Jews, too, benefited. The carrot replaced the stick: conversionist measures were abrogated and incentives were offered instead: Jews with higher education could live outside the Pale of Settlement, enjoy the right to hold office, and engage in certain professions. The enrollment of Jewish children in the elementary state schools rose slowly but steadily and soared in the secondary schools. Whereas only twelve Jews had attended the gymnasia in the Western Russian provinces in 1833, in 1865 Jews in the Pale were 7.5 percent of pupils in the gymnasia, nearly 10 percent in 1870, and 15 percent in 1872.

The most radical reform (if short-lived) was the restoration of autonomy to the universities. A new humanism and progressive spirit infused them, with the result that the number of students increased very rapidly, with young men enrolling from all levels of society. (In 1853, nearly three-quarters of the students at Petersburg University had been of the nobility.) The new middle class, the Jews among them, basking in the pale spring sun of Russian liberalism, seized their chance. The numbers of Jews enrolled in the universities rose, mostly in the faculties of law and medicine. To the Jews breaking out of traditionalist society, Alexander II's regime appeared to offer everything. That was when Jews thought they stood at the threshold of a new society, a neutral society of rational men, neither Jews nor Christians. Vladimir O. Harkavy (1846–1911), a Moscow jurist, described how he and a Jewish friend felt on being enrolled in the Moscow University in 1864: "When we came out of the old university building, we crossed to the other side of the street and, respectfully doffing our hats, bowed before the sanctuary that had opened its doors to us and we embraced each other. Proudly we walked home, eager to shout to everyone we met: Have you heard? We are students. All at once it was as though the alienation from the Christians around us had gone. We felt like members of a new society in which there were neither Jews nor Greeks." [11]

Russification for economic improvement and emancipation was the purpose of the Society for the Promotion of Culture among Jews, founded in St. Petersburg, December 18, 1863. Its prime mover was Baron Joseph Yozl (Ossip) Günzburg, the head of Russia's most prestigious Jewish family of financiers, philanthropists, and communal leaders. The first officially sanctioned voluntary Jewish organization in Tsarist Russia, the society existed sixty-six years until the Soviet Union's Communist Party dissolved it in 1929. The society undertook to encourage and promote knowledge of Russian among Jews, to provide financial aid to needy university students, and to publish educationally useful works.

Assimilationist as the Petersburg group was, it seemed moderate in comparison with its Odessa section of extremist russifiers, who wanted to substitute Russian for Hebrew in the prayer book and service. Here, amidst Russia's most highly educated and russified Jews, a three-day pogrom erupted Easter, 1871. Jews were beaten, their property looted and destroyed, while the police stood by idly. "The anti-Jewish excesses of Easter," E. M. Soloveitchik, a former editor of *Razsvet*, wrote to the society in Petersburg, "have completely destroyed the faith of the Odessa leaders of the society in the efficacy of their purpose. They have concluded that their striving to bring Jews closer to the Russian people will be fruitless so long as the Russian masses are submerged in ignorance and civic immaturity." [12] And indeed, the Odessa branch did not renew its work until 1878, and then limited itself to subsidizing needy students.

The disappointment with the Russians for failing to create a neutral society in which educated, russified Jews would be welcome foreshadowed the disappointment that was to recur on a grander scale after 1881.

4   New Religions:
Science, Progress, Humanity

As the second half of the nineteenth century unfolded, the political, social, and industrial changes that had transformed Western Europe moved east. Nationalism became the prevailing revolutionary ideology everywhere in the Habsburg Empire: Hungarians (even in their own Kingdom), Poles, Czechs, Croats, Ruthenians, Slovaks, Rumanians dreamed of national liberation, when their language, culture, historic and religious traditions could flourish in a country of their own. "Nationality," Mazzini had written, "is a holy thing." The nationalist and separatist aspirations of the Hungarians and the Poles spurred the nations without history, as Frederick Engels first characterized them — the Slovaks, the Ruthenians, the Czechs — to their own national awakening, cultivating their hitherto despised folk languages and searching for their cultural roots in ancient folklore and history. In Russia nationalism took the form of Slavophilism with its sense of Russian mission to unite all the Slav peoples, and though at first a conservative philosophy, it eventually pervaded much of radical thought. In Congress Poland, meanwhile, Polish nationalism smoldered dangerously under forcible russification.

The industrial revolution and the great technological changes that England and Western Europe had undergone decades earlier came eastward more slowly. Congress Poland took a great leap forward industrially after the suppression of the 1863 uprising. The textile mills of Lodz and Warsaw were mechanized; the wool, tanning, and alcohol industries expanded; new mining and metallurgy industries were established. Railroads opened new economic and developmental possibilities in Russia. In 1857, Russia had only 663 miles of railroad lines; in 1871, 6,762. The liberation of the serfs had created a landless peasantry that in time became an oppressed industrial proletariat.

The second half of the nineteenth century became an age of accelerated scientific productivity and scientific synthesis. Ideas about the influence of environment and about evolution as progress through conflict flourished. August Comte, Herbert Spencer, Henry Thomas Buckle, Karl Marx, Thomas Malthus applied these concepts in their sociological, historical, and economic studies of human society. Darwin's *Origin of the Species* (1859) was most provocative, for it challenged not only past knowledge, but the belief in divine cosmogony. Natural and social sciences alike formulated materialistic theories which explicitly denied the existence of a Creator.

Comte's religion of humanity, the English Ethical Culture movement threatened traditional religion. (Nationalism, too, fusing race, culture, and politics, became a substitute for religion.) Positivism, Progress, Culture, History became new dogmas. In Russia, under Nicholas I, the Orthodox Church had suppressed works that conflicted with its teachings. Charles Lyell's *Principles of Geology* (1830–33) was kept out of Russia for thirty years because the official censors thought it contravened the biblical story of creation.

These ascendant scientific theories and philosophical currents had an explosive effect on the emerging educated classes in Eastern Europe. They had a convulsive effect on Jewish traditional society.

In Poland, after the uprising of 1863 was suppressed, young Polish patriots turned to positivism to replace that visionary nationalist romanticism they felt had destroyed Poland. They extolled work and physical fitness, technical education and vocational training, determined to make the Poles fit for survival in the struggle with Russia by developing Poland's economic possibilities. Polish positivism condemned national chauvinism; its leading writers uncompromisingly fought antisemitism and bigotry, with the not entirely unanticipated consequence that positivism was later attacked in Poland as a Jewish invention.

In Russia proper, under Alexander II's short-lived liberalization of censorship, the new science and the philosophy of progress inundated Russia. Spencer, Mill, Darwin, Buckle, Comte, Buechner, Moleschott, and Vogt were read avidly in English, German, and in Russian translations by university and gymnasium students, by intelligentsia and pseudo-intelligentsia. Even usually frivolous upper-class young women took to such books, according to a contemporary journalist who reported this conversation:

"I am reading Buckle," she told me, although I had reason to suspect that she had never read anything before in her life.

"But you don't know any history," I observed. "What are you going to get out of him? And anyway, why read him?"

"Goodness! Everybody nowadays reads Buckle," she objected. "There is no God, you see."

"What has become of him?" I asked.

"There never was any. People have invented all this. There is nature, and nothing else." [13]

The Russian apostles of positivism and utilitarianism were Nikolai Chernyshevsky (1828–1889), Nikolai Dobroliubov (1830–1861), and Dimitri Pisarev (1840–1868). Chernyshevsky and Dobroliubov, sons of priests, had been educated in Orthodox seminaries (Turgenev called them "our unwashed seminarians"). Both had lost their faith on reading Ludwig Feuerbach's *Das Wesen des Christentums*. They were the angry young men of Russia in the sixties and seventies, whose disappointment in Alexander II's miserly reforms set them on a revolutionary anticonstitutional course and whose despair at the human waste in Russian society made them sneer at esthetics and subtle sensibilities. In their articles in the radical periodicals, popularizing science and criticizing esthetics and literature, they propounded the utilitarian notion that morality was merely enlightened self-interest and the materialistic philosophy that matter determined mind and spirit (Feuerbach's *Man ist was man isst*). They popularized Buechner, Moleschott, Darwin, and Buckle.

Chernyshevsky's unbelievably bad didactic novel *What Is To Be Done?* (1864), probably the most widely read book during the sixties and seventies, became Holy Scripture among the radical intelligentsia.[14] (Lenin was so impressed, he was to use Chernyshevsky's title for a major political tract.) Replete with Aesopianisms, the novel advocated establishing relations between the sexes of the basis of equality, freedom, and self-interest, liberating women from the tyranny of common morality, and creating workers' cooperatives and study circles in a Fourierist vision of a socialist society.

What Is To Be Done? was one of the three most influential books that deeply affected East European Jewish youth (the others were Mendelssohn's biur, of course, and Moses Leib Lilienblum's *Hattot Ne'urim*.) The few hundred Jews in the universities and the thousands in the gymnasia were deeply attracted to the new science, the faith in humanity and in progress, and the philistine optimism about life and society that Russian positivism generated. The works of the German idealistic philosophers, the English Utilitarians, the French Positivists, the progressists, evolutionists, and historicists had an unparalleled influence on the Jewish student youth for the next two and three decades and influenced the direction that modern Jewish scholarship was to take.

Young Russians, liberals, radicals, even Slavophils, thought Western intellectual life superior to Russia's. That xenotropia, the attraction to the different, was even stronger among those Jews whose Jewishness often consisted of little more than a sense of inferiority. The very notion of progress defeated their sense of worth, for they were the reluctant scions of a culture so old it must surely be backward, and a religious one to boot. On first reading Buckle, Dubnow wrote: "This great freethinker subverts the feeling of love for one's people."

Uri Kovner and Moses Leib Lilienblum introduced positivism into Hebrew literature. Kovner, an erratic, unstable and neurotic personality whose self-destructive impulses eventually led him to apostasy, began his career as a Hebrew journalist by attacking the haskala for its concern with dead and useless subjects. Instead of flowery Hebrew rhetoric and obscure philological studies, he asserted, the Jews needed science and practical knowledge.

To a friend he wrote: "Like Pisarev I too am ready to exchange a thousand poems of your Pushkin, Lermontov, or Micah Joseph Lebensohn for a simple but utilitarian article on how to fertilize the soil." [15] Having mocked Hebrew literature, he then abandoned it and turned to Russian journalism, a field in which he acquired some small success.

Lilienblum, more Jewishly oriented, discovered positivism when his faith in haskala was running out. Disappointed by its inutility and impracticality, its absorption in trivialities like poetry and archeology, Lilienblum felt then that only science and a practical vocational education mattered. At thirty, having gone through several cycles of belief and despair, he wrote his "Confessions" that others might learn from his experiences and mistakes. Addressing himself to the young men in the yeshivot whose aspirations to know more of the outside world were being stifled by the rigidity of traditional society and to their parents as well, Lilienblum warned that unless the youth were to be educated for a useful life in a practical world, the flight from Jewish society and traditional Judaism would accelerate. He was a kind of Jewish Chernyshevsky with a positivist and timidly socialist message to the Jews.

Secular knowledge and socialism (usually in tandem) had begun to infiltrate traditional Jewish society. Even at that most traditionalist yeshiva at Volozhin many of the hundreds of students surreptitiously read forbidden books in Hebrew and Russian and dreamed of another world. In the late seventies, the Education Ministry had proposed that the yeshiva introduce secular subjects in its curriculum, but its ultraconservative leaders refused. Nevertheless, the yeshiva students and other young Jews like them began to study Russian from Lev Mandelstamm's Hebrew-Russian and Russian-Hebrew dictionaries (1859) and from the later ones by Joshua Steinberg (1878). Clandestine reading circles and circulating libraries had begun to spring up in the cities under the aegis of radical groups who, true disciples of Chernyshevsky, coupled self-study with socialist propaganda. The doctrines of positivism became the agitational material for the populists.

Populism, Russia's indigenous socialist movement, agrarian and Bakuninist, largely innocent of Marx and West European industrial socialist movements, insisted on the centrality of the peasant commune in the new society. In the "mad summer" of 1874, about 2,000 student-populists set out for villages in deep Russia in a spontaneous movement to agitate the peasants to revolt against the Tsar and seize the land. They were "going to the people." But instead the shrewd and stubborn peasants, with their deep religious faith and steadfastness to their traditional way of life, subverted the student radicals. These positivist-utilitarians, already anti-intellectual, began to perceive the peasants in religiomystical terms, in whom innate and transcendant wisdom resided, from whom they, intellectuals, alienated from the soil, could learn. Rousseauian anticivilization notions and Slavophilism permeated Populist socialism with Russian nationalism and religious Orthodoxy.

The Populists were mostly students in universities and technical schools, even in gymnasia, from the upper classes and the clergy, a proportionately large number of Jews among them. (The records of one police department for 1873–1877 classified radical propagandists who were arrested, tried, and sentenced to prison, banishment, or exile in these categories: 279 nobles, 197 sons of priests, 117 sons of high officers, and 68 Jews.)

Many Jews among the early Populists came of well-to-do families, assimilated or tolerant of assimilation. They were the first sizable generation of Russian Jews brought up without substantial Jewish education and with little knowledge of the Jewish tradition. Many were students in the Petersburg Military-Medical Academy, which in 1869 had been the scene of revolutionary activities.

A few early Populists emerged from the Vilna crown rabbinical seminary, which nurtured a spirit of hostility to traditional society. The prevailing attitude among the non-Jewish faculty there undoubtedly magnified the sense of inferiority among many students. One was Aaron Lieberman (1842–1880), the only Jewish Populist of that time who propagandized socialism in Hebrew among Jews. His first agitational leaflet was distributed among the students at the Volozhin yeshiva, with no perceptible effect. In 1875, when the police uncovered the Populist circle to which he belonged, Lieberman fled Vilna for Berlin and then Vienna, where he published *Ha-Emet,* a Hebrew socialist paper with a short life and a singular lack of success. He was aggressively hostile to everything Jewish. The prospectus for his paper attacked the Hebrew press for treating "only religious and national questions and other nonsense." Fundamentally a yeshiva-*bokher* too suddenly catapulted into a revolutionary society, unable to find a place in the Populist movement, he tried to create one for himself among Jews, despite his self-hate. He expatiated on how he felt about Jews in a letter in 1876 to Valerian N. Smirnov, an editor of *Vperiod* ("Forward"), a biweekly which Peter Lavrov published in London for distribution in Russia. Smirnov, a non-Jew, had criticized Lieberman's Hebrew paper as a symptom of nationalist separatism. Lieberman replied: "You know well that I abhor Jewry just as I abhor all other national isms. . . . You know just as well that I am an internationalist, but I am not ashamed of my Jewish origin and, like all oppressed people, I love that segment of humanity which current national and religious principles designate as Jews. And indeed I do not love them all, but only the suffering masses and those fit to join us. Otherwise I would not be worthy of the name socialist." [16]

Lieberman had no lasting influence among Jews and remains only a historical curiosity, a precursor without any direct followers. He emigrated to America in 1880 and shortly thereafter committed suicide.

An extremist of another sort was Populist Joseph Aptekman, born in Pavelgrad, province of Ekaterinoslav, in 1850. His father combined traditionalism with modernity, and enrolled his son in a gymnasium. "I grew up under the same influences as all Russian youth," Aptekman wrote. "In addition, there was the oppression of my own people and all together that made a revolutionary of me." He mentioned the great impact Buckle's *History of Civilization in England* had on him. While studying medicine in St. Petersburg, he became active in revolutionary circles. He found that his Jewishness alienated him from the Russian people and created an obstacle to his "going to the people." He had no feeling of debt to the Russian people, no sense of repentance or renunciation. "Where should I get it from? As a member of an oppressed people, I should rather have presented a bill for payment than myself pay some imaginary debt." He went on: "I did not know the Russian people, for born in town I practically never saw the village. Besides, I was alien to this people by blood. I knew Russian history very poorly and I must admit I did not care for it. I was a Jew. How would the Russian people receive my propaganda? Would they take it from me?"

The religious currents of the period infected him, and he was seized with an apocalyptic vision of the future: "I was then in a state of exaltation, and religious exaltation at that. It was a complex and rather confused spiritual state when the practical socialist world view within me merged with a Christian evangelical one . . . and I decided that before I went to the people I would take the Greek Orthodox faith. . . . I was baptized and I tell you: I felt like newborn. I am going to the people, I thought, not a Jew any more, but a Christian, I became fused with the people." [17]

Aptekman's evangelical approach to the Russian peasant in which the eschatalogy of the socialist revolution was fused with that of the New Testament was not typical of all Jewish revolutionaries. More rationalist, they were inclined to invest their revolutionary passion in organization, in technical and tactical matters like smuggling literature into Russia and men out, distributing propaganda, establishing clandestine printing plants, and maintaining vigilance against informers and the secret police. They lived hunted lives, in prison or in exile. Some were shot and some were hanged and some died natural deaths, young and unfulfilled. Yet, however practical and rationalist, they were all imbued with a fervent messianic belief in the coming of socialism and held a vision of the ultimate transformation of society.

This revolutionary messianism was perhaps their only remaining distinctively Jewish trait, one that Saint-Simon had brilliantly described a half century earlier in *The New Christianity*:

> The people of God, that people which received revelations before the coming of Christ, that people which is the most universally spread over the surface of the earth, has always perceived that the Christian doctrine founded by the Fathers of the Church was incomplete. It has always proclaimed that a grand epoch will come, to which it has given the name of Messiah's Kingdom; an epoch in which religious doctrine shall be presented in all the generality of which it is susceptible; that it will regulate alike the action of the temporal and that of the spiritual power; and that then all the human race will have but one religion and one organization. . . .[18]

This religious messianism permeated a seemingly materialist ideology, and when not expressed in secular terms, took on an explicitly Christian character. Solomon Wittenberg, a Jewish terrorist whose father had hoped he would become a rabbi, wrote a farewell letter to his comrades in 1879, after he was sentenced to death for involvement in a plot to assassinate the Tsar: "Certainly I do not want to die and it would be untrue on my part if I said I would die willingly. But let no one cast doubt on my faith and on the firmness of my convictions. Remember that the highest example of love for man and of self-sacrifice was surely that of the Savior. Yet He too prayed: 'Let this cup pass from me.' How then can I do otherwise? And like Him I tell myself: 'If it could not be different, if it is necessary for the victory of socialism that my blood be shed, if the transition from the present order to a better one is not possible except by stepping over our bodies, then let our blood be shed as a sacrifice for humanity. That our blood will enrich the soil from which the seeds of socialism will sprout, that socialism will triumph, and soon indeed — in that I believe." [19]

These early Jewish Populists had in common, besides the messianic complex, an obsessive urge to escape from the Jewish group and to obliterate their Jewish identity. The vision of the new revolutionary society offered them the promise of a world without Jews. Their sense of Jewish inferiority was nourished by Russian literature on which they had been bred and from which they absorbed the seemingly ineradicable anti-Jewish attitudes of Russian writers and thinkers. One Jewish Populist wrote: "Russian literature imbued us with love of the Russian peasants while it transmitted to us a picture of the Jews as a class of parasites." No Russian novelist or poet, neither Gogol nor Pushkin, Turgenev nor Lermontov, depicted Jews as other than repulsive caricatures. The press was not more favorable. While Jews may have been without interest to the liberal press, they emerged as monsters in the reactionary press. The outstanding socialist theoreticians of the time, Marx and Bakunin, could not be counted among the friends of Jews, poor or rich. Their opinions, too, had a crippling effect on the youthful naïve Jewish revolutionaries who uncritically accepted anti-Jewish prejudices as "scientific" social and economic doctrine.

In 1876, Zemlya i Volya ("Land and Liberty"), an agrarian, Bakuninist revolutionary organization, was formed. Its program was vague: land to the peasants, liberty to the people. Its relentless terrorist policy and continuing attempts to assassinate the Tsar and his entourage split the organization in 1879. The smaller fraction, Chorny Peredel, was beginning to orient itself toward the emerging working class. From it the Marxist Social-Democratic organization was to emerge. The larger group, Narodnaya Volya ("The People's Will"), authentic heir of the Populist tradition, was composed of revolutionaries turned conspirators and assassins. Regicide became their program. Undaunted by police surveillance, arrests, imprisonment, sentences to hard labor, banishment to Siberia, and hanging of its members, Narodnaya Volya's carefully elaborated plans came to fruition on March 1, 1881. Alexander II was assassinated on his way home from a review of the Imperial Guards.

His son Alexander III (1845–1894) succeeded him. The revolutionary uprising the terrorists hoped for after the assassination did not materialize. Narodnaya Volya's Executive Committee sent the new Tsar a respectful ultimatum: Russia was at the crossroads. The Tsar could choose to turn toward the people, offering political amnesty and a constituent assembly with free elections. Or there would be revolution. Alexander III replied by publicly hanging the conspirators. His chief advisor became Constantine P. Pobedonostsev, Over-Procurator of the Holy Synod, who was to restore Nicholas I's principles of nationality, Orthodoxy, and autocracy, and who held that "the sovereignty of the people" was "among the falsest of political principles."

Novoe Vremya, Petersburg daily and chief organ of Russian reaction, and other papers close to officialdom began hinting the Jews were to blame for the assassination and for the revolutionary movement as well. According to Dubnow, mysterious emissaries from Petersburg appeared in South Russia, with secret talk that the "people's wrath would be vented on the Jews." On April 15, just six weeks after the Tsar's assassination, a pogrom broke out in Yelisavetgrad, a South Russian city of about 30,000. That started a wave of pogroms that continued well into 1882, affecting some 225 communities. About 20,000 Jews were made homeless, 100,000 ruined, Jewish property valued over 80 million dollars was destroyed. Men, women, and children were attacked, raped, killed.

Both liberal Russia and radical Russia remained silent. There was no public outcry, no protest, no challenge to brutality. The voices of the great Russian writers and liberals, humanitarians and moralists, were hushed. Tolstoy spoke not a word. M. E. Saltykov-Shchedrin, the satirist and fablist, was the one exception. After the wave of pogroms in 1881 he wrote: "History has never recorded in its pages a question more difficult, more inhuman, more painful than the Jewish question. . . . No history is more heartrending than this history of unending torture by one man of another."

The default of liberal Russia staggered the Jews who had believed they could eventually assimilate into Russian life and society. The default of radical Russia was even more shattering to radical Jewish youth. Narodnaya Volya's executive committee had issued a leaflet applauding the revolutionary energy the peasants used in turning on the Jews. That was the most shocking betrayal of all. The radical youth turned in anguish away from the revolutionary movement and back to the Jews.

The pogrom wave reached Congress Poland, despite assurances by the Polish press that a pogram "could not and would not happen in Warsaw," for it contradicted "traditional Polish tolerance." But on Christmas Day, 1881, a pogrom broke out in Warsaw. Alexander Kraushar (1843–1931), assimilated Jewish historian and jurist, wrote a poem, "Polish-Jewish Idyll," which went like this: "On March 2 [1861] a holiday was celebrated and I was greeted with fraternal words and as a symbol of eternal peace I received the title of Jewish Pole. But those exalted days did not last long. God knows if I can understand for what sins years later in December days [1881] my bedding was torn to bits." [20]

The year 1881 radically affected the course of Jewish history. It marked the first major rupture among modernist Jews with the philosophy of enlightenment and emancipation. Like a prism, 1881 refracted the Jewish experiences of the past and bent them in another direction. Not since 1648 had the consciousness of being Jewish in an alien and hostile world been so vivid. First the paralyzing shock, then the visceral reaction: flight.

There were two kinds of flight, internal and abroad. The internal flight was by way of the baptismal font. (A little antisemitism, the cynics say, helps Jewish survival, but not necessarily and not predictably.) With each new penalty that the Tsarist government bestowed on Jews for being Jewish, the flight from Jews and Judaism accelerated among the careerists and self-seekers, the anxious and the unstable, the self-haters and xenotropists. The pogroms were just the start of what was to become Pobedonostsev's long-range "legal" solution to the Jewish problem: one-third to emigrate, one-third to convert, and one-third to die of hunger. The regulations restricting Jews to the Pale of Settlement began to be stringently enforced; the admission of Jews to secondary schools and universities was restricted and a quota introduced; Jews were prohibited from acquiring rural property and deported from villages; thousands were expelled from Moscow, excluded from the legal profession, hounded, harassed, and pauperized.

Conversions increased. Synod statistics on the annual average number of conversions show the correlation between persecution and apostasy. Under Nicholas I's policy of forcibly baptizing juvenile conscripts, the annual average had been about fifteen hundred. It dropped to about four hundred during Alexander II's reign and then rose steadily until it reached nearly one thousand in the nineties. The catastrophic expulsions from Moscow were said to have produced about 3,000 conversions. In 1891, an observer remarked on the frequent items in the Russian press that "sixty young Jews wishing to be admitted to the university renounced the law of Moses," that forty others were converted because their business affairs demanded their presence outside the Pale of Settlement, and that many others "for equally good reasons" were each month admitted to the flock of the faithful. In Minsk, Jewish secondary-school graduates formally debated the question of baptism from the ethical point of view, with the majority favoring baptism. There was even briefly a flurry of conversions to Islam to obtain admission to universities, but the government soon halted that.

For the Jewish future, the more important Jewish flight was abroad. Emigration began spontaneously. Despite the Jewish notables in Petersburg, the financiers and railroad contractors, who feared emigration would brand the Jews (and them) as unpatriotic, the Jewish exodus accelerated under the continued persecution. In the last two decades of the century about a million Jews emigrated from Russia.

A few weeks after the first pogrom in Yelisavetgrad, two maskilim conceived the plan to emigrate to America where they would found cooperative colonies in the spirit of Robert Owen, Fourier, and Tolstoy. Thus began the movement known as Am Olam ("Eternal People"), dedicated to redemption by working the soil. The ideal of Jewish agricultural pursuits was a heritage of the haskala, reinforced by Populist notions about Jewish unproductivity. (That concept was a staple of antisemitic propaganda, deriving from an agrarian, anti-industrial, and anti-urban mentality.) The movement attracted only a small proportion of the swelling tide of Jewish emigration to America. They founded a few agricultural colonies in far-flung places (for example, Crémieux and Bethlehem Judea in South Dakota, New Odessa in Oregon), but none endured. At the time of America's unparalleled industrial development and capitalist expansion they came with eighteenth-century notions that had failed a half-century earlier. Nor did their Jewish mission have any relevance to America, where economic productivity was then being demonstrated, not on the farm, but in mine and factory.

The first emigrants to Palestine shared the social and political outlook of Am Olam. Russified and radical students, they organized in 1882 to form the Bilu society (Bilu: an acronym for the Hebrew "House of Jacob, come, let us go!"), to colonize Palestine. The movement attracted only a few hundred members, not all of whom went to Palestine. Of those who did go, few endured the physical hardship. Antisemitism had returned them to the Jewish milieu, but their inner Jewish resources were still inadequate to sustain them in the primitive conditions of Palestinian colonization in those days. In a few years the Bilu movement disappeared. Yet unlike Am Olam, which remained only a curiosity in Jewish history and the end of a chapter in Russian Jewish history, Bilu signalled the beginning of a new Jewish nationalism.

5 National Renewal

THE RUSSIAN pogroms after Alexander II's assassination coincided with the accelerating progression of political antisemitism in Europe. In Russia, severe political repression accompanied the anti-Jewish persecutions, and the government continued its seemingly inevitable, predestined journey to disaster.

In the decades after 1881 the contours of East European Jewry began to change. Massive emigration provided the manpower that was to build in the United States the largest, the most prosperous, and most secure Jewish settlement at any time in Jewish history in the dispersion. East European Jewry furnished also the manpower and the intellectual undergirding that created a Jewish state and a new Jewish-Hebraic culture in Palestine. But the overwhelming majority of Jews remained in Russia, Congress Poland, Galicia, and Rumania. Their communities became laboratories for testing new theories designed to preserve national Jewish existence and to strengthen Jewish identity in the modern world and for experimenting with new styles of Jewish communal life.

The great transformation occurred among those who disengaged themselves from the traditionalist community, the educated and half-educated, with faith or without, who could no longer tolerate Orthodoxy's refusal to make peace with the modern world. Yet masses of Jews remained in that world of traditional piety, accepting pogroms, economic hardships, and deprivations as God's will. They had spared themselves at least that traumatic disillusion in Gentile society. Among believing Jews, those calamitous events evoked no mystical responses, no messianic stirrings, as in past catastrophes. Perhaps that was because the secular Jewish movements had usurped the messianic impulses in the Jewish tradition and transformed them into modern ideologies.

The new ideologies of national renewal were products of modernity — fashioned mostly by men estranged from Judaism's traditional way of life. These new movements — Zionism, autonomism, Bundism, Hebraism, Yiddishism — all tapped authentic sources in the Jewish past and the very traditions against which they rebelled. The past and the future became syncretized in movements that comforted Jews in adversity and introduced Jewish content into modernity.

"Zionism," Theodor Herzl once said, "is a return to the Jewish people even before it is a return to the Jewish homeland." That was true for himself and for his ideological precursors. In Odessa, Leo Pinsker returned to the Jewish people in 1881 to become the first East European ideologue of Zionism.

Pinsker (1821–1891), an Odessa physician, had been an active member of the assimilationist Odessa branch of the Society to Promote Culture among Jews. The Odessa pogrom of 1871 had temporarily shocked Pinsker into inaction and apathy, as it had the Society's other members. But 1881 transformed him. In 1882, under the anonymity of "A Russian Jew," he published a German pamphlet called *Auto-Emancipation,* in which he set down his ideas about the homelessness and alienness of Jews, dispersed and unwanted among the nations of the world. He appealed to the Jews to reclaim their self-respect and dignity and to the non-Jews to recognize that Jews were indeed a nation: ". . . grant us only what you granted the Serbians and Rumanians." Pinsker apparently did not know that, twenty years earlier, Moses Hess, a German Jew and leading European socialist, had traversed the same path from assimilation to nationalism. Hess's extraordinary little book *Rome and Jerusalem,* in which he developed his ideas of a Jewish national state as part of a world comity of socialist nations, had evoked mostly hostile criticism from assimilationists and socialists alike and was, it seems, shortly thereafter forgotten. (In 1896, when Herzl wrote *Der Judenstaat* under the impact of the Dreyfus case, he too approached the question *de novo,* unaware of either Hess or Pinsker.)

Auto-Emancipation was not to the liking of German Jews on whose support Pinsker had counted. But in Russia it galvanized the struggling Bilu groups and the handful of Hoveve Zion ("Lovers of Zion") societies dedicated to colonizing Palestine.

That infant Zionist movement whose first major thrust came from antisemitism and whose models were European liberal nationalists like Mazzini was invigorated and authenticated by two specifically Jewish elements: the binding power of the Hebrew language, and the holiness of Palestine in rabbinic and Kabbalistic thought. In traditional Judaism, the people of Israel and the land of Israel were subordinated to the God of Israel. Though hubristic nationalism reversed those positions, the idea of returning the people of Israel to its land drew upon the oldest and most potent of Jewish traditions.

For believing Jews, Palestine's transcendent meaning was immanent in Judaism: the messianic hope of the return to Zion — Return, Redemption, and the end of the Exile. The holiness of Eretz Israel attracted pious Jews in all ages: "The merit of living in Palestine equals the merit of observing all the commandments." (Great merit was attached also in dying there.) Some devout Jews believed a special reward accrued from performing the commandments relating to Palestine. Kabbalists performed mystic rites dramatizing the catastrophe of the Exile and the promise of Redemption, which was to begin in Palestine.

The pious Jews who came to Palestine to await the Messiah were usually indigent, and to support them, European Jews organized a charitable fund known as *halukka.* At the end of the seventeenth century the idea of collection boxes to raise these funds was put forward by one Rabbi Meir Ba'al ha-Nes (Meir the miracle-worker) for whom they were named. The boxes had a place in every God-fearing home, even until our own times, and came to symbolize the attachment of Orthodox Jews for Palestine. In the second half of the eighteenth century hasidim from every important dynasty established their foothold in the Holy Land in readiness for the Messiah's coming.

Kabbalistic mysticism and practical colonization in Palestine had long been paired. Rabbi Zvi Hirsch Kalischer (1795–1874), a Talmudist and mystic, was instrumental in getting the Alliance Israélite Universelle to buy land for an agricultural colony in Palestine. Kalischer, immersed and confined in the old Talmudic world, was convinced by his study of the Talmud that the Redemption required preparation, not just by observing the commandments in exile, but also by doing practical work in Palestine. Kalischer's son-in-law once told Nahum Sokolow how the Rabbi used to describe those who sit and wait: "To whom can they be compared? To a sick man who comes to a doctor and is advised: Here is a tried and true remedy, but you must take it a thousand years. The sick man may possibly be cured in a thousand years, but who lives that long?" [21]

The Hoveve Zion touched deep Jewish sensibilities and helped to restore trust between the once-alienated intellectuals and the traditionalist masses. A fund-raising campaign which the Hoveve Zion undertook in 1884 showed how extensive that Jewish sentiment was. To celebrate Sir Moses Montefiore's one-hundredth birthday (he lived to 101), the Hoveve Zion sold his photograph throughout the Pale. Montefiore's worldwide intercessions on behalf of Jews had won him their love and esteem; besides, he was associated especially with Palestine, which he had visited seven times and where he had endowed innumerable educational, religious, and economic institutions and enterprises. That photograph raised the then colossal sum of thirty thousand rubles and, like Meir Ba'al ha-Nes's collection box, became a staple of every Jewish household. (Eventually, Theodor Herzl's portrait displaced Montefiore's.)

The Hoveve Zion movement was sentimental and philanthropic, though Pinsker in *Auto-Emancipation* had been national and political. The absence of national content and national purpose, the national flaccidity in the movement spurred Ahad Ha'am to write his first and now classic essay "That Is Not the Way" (*Ha-Melits*, 1889) in which he argued that the strong sense of national unity lacking among the Hoveve Zion could be cultivated only by selfless devoted men committed to an intensive program of cultural and educational renewal. That very year, a semisecret society, B'nai Moshe ("Sons of Moses"), was formed, dedicated to the ethical and cultural purposes set forth in that article. Ahad Ha'am headed the group for a time. The B'nai Moshe set up a publishing house, Ahiasaf, which Ahad Ha'am directed, and later a journal, *Ha-Shiloah*, which he edited (1896–

1903), striving to make it the Hebrew equivalent of high-culture European journalism, like *The Nineteenth Century*. B'nai Moshe in Warsaw also pioneered in modern Hebrew education.

While Ahad Ha'am was trying to evolve a philosophy of modern Jewish existence and Jewish nationalism and when Chaim Weizmann was raising money in Pinsk for the Hoveve Zion, Theodor Herzl announced his plan to restore the Jewish state and thus to solve the plight of the Jews. *Der Judenstaat* was Herzl's ringing solution to antisemitism and in it he called on the unity and will of the Jews: "We are a people — *one* people," he wrote. "The Jews who will it shall achieve their State." What the pogroms had worked on the Jewish intellectuals in Russia, the Dreyfus Affair had effected on this assimilated, Western-educated Jew who had only a rudimentary Jewish education. Herzl's charisma turned the Hoveve Zion into the Zionist Organization; a Jewish Colonial Trust and a Jewish National Fund were established; members were recruited, propaganda distributed, funds laboriously raised.

The East European Jews were the mainstay of the Zionist movement, the foot soldiers in Herzl's battalions. The Russian Jews were the heart and guts of this army, the volunteers; the Galician Jews fell into line slowly, while Polish Jews remained reluctant. The Russian Jews then had the overwhelming numbers in any case — nearly 4 million Jews in the Pale to 1.3 million in Congress Poland. (Galicia and Bukovina had about 900,000.) On August 16, 1903, on his way home from secret negotiations with Plehve, Herzl stopped in Vilna to see the Russian Jewish masses he had heard so much about. He noted in his diary the "tumultuous Jewish streets" through which he rode, the "packed throngs" and the crowds that the police dispersed. A young man even proposed "a toast to the day when *ha-melekh Herzl* [King Herzl] would reign."

Yet despite the busyness, the Congresses, the sales of shekalim, the pathos for a national home, Jewish settlement in Palestine was a future vision, as remote from the reality of life in the Pale as the messianic redemption. While agitating for Zionism and Palestine the Promised Land, the Jews migrated in masses to America the Golden Land.

By the end of the century, only some five thousand colonists had settled in some twenty-five agricultural colonies in Palestine. But the new Labor Zionism that matured during the 1905 revolution and Weizmann's "synthetic" Zionism, combining practical colonization with diplomacy, changed the character of the Zionist movement qualitatively and even quantitatively. More Jews became prepared to translate Zionist ideology into reality. By the outbreak of the first World War, the number of colonists in Palestine had more than doubled: about twelve thousand in forty-three colonies. They were to provide the future leadership of the Jewish state.

A paradox: though Zionism appropriated the symbols of Judaism and tapped barely submerged messianic longings, it was a revolt against the old Jewish way of life. The Zionist movement drew into its active ranks both modern-minded Jews who all their lives had scorned traditionalist Jewish ways and rebels fresh from yeshivot and prayer houses. Zionists chose to revolutionize their own Jewish society, to "normalize" the Jewish people, make it like all other peoples, and, above all, to repudiate Israel's chosenness. They blamed the oppression and prejudice Jews endured in the Diaspora on Jewish uniqueness and the way Jews lived; they came to loathe the Jewish Diaspora, the good and bad without distinction: the inflexibility of religious tradition, the Yiddish language and its folk culture, the Jewish gift of accommodation and nonviolent resistance, even Jewish intellectuality and scholarship, which they were willing to relinquish for a "normal" distribution of tillers of the soil. The philosophic concept of the negation of the *galut* became, among many Zionists, a negation of Jewish creativity in the Diaspora. Zionists attacked traditional society sometimes even more savagely than the haskala had, for while the haskala had striven to reform the old society, Zionism wanted to destroy the old and build anew.

Ahad Ha'am was different. He believed that Zionism must be concerned not, as Herzl put it, with the plight of the Jews, but with the plight of Judaism. By Judaism he meant the sum total of Jewish experience and the accumulation of Jewish learning. Without Jewish national culture, a Jewish state could not preserve Judaism: his evidence was Palestine in Herodian days. Ahad Ha'am conceived Palestine as a spiritual center of the Jewish people, where an intellectual and culturally creative elite would develop and enrich Jewish national culture. Emanating from this center to the majority of Jews remaining in the Diaspora, that national culture would sustain and invigorate them. The restoration of Jewish national culture in Palestine must proceed simultaneously with colonization. He believed that "the foundation of a single great school of learning or art in Palestine, the establishment of a single university for the study of language and literature, would be . . . a national work of the highest importance, and would do more to bring us near to our aims than a hundred agricultural colonies." [22]

Ahad Ha'am rejected Herzlian political messianism and the notion that the new state would gather in all the Jews. Jews would, he felt, always continue to live in the dispersion, and Jewish survival was not contingent on the Zionist ingathering. He seemed to have accepted the permanence of the galut as a realistic fact of life. Yet he wrote: "Dispersion is a thoroughly evil and unpleasant thing, but we can and must live in dispersion, for all its evils and all its unpleasantness. Exodus from the dispersion will always be, as it always has been, an inspiring hope for the distant future; but the date of that consummation is the secret of a higher power, and our survival as a people is not dependent upon it." Even allowing for irony, can we conclude that Ahad Ha'am was too traditionalist to be seduced by pseudomessianic hopes?

An agnostic, with an ineradicable distaste for hasidism (a visit as a child to the Sadegora rebbe soured him on hasidism for the rest of his life), Ahad Ha'am tried to come to terms with Judaism. In a letter to Judah Magnes in 1910, Ahad Ha'am wrote: " 'National religion' — by all means: Judaism is fundamentally national, and all the efforts of the 'Reformers' to separate the Jewish religion from its national element have had no result except to ruin both the nationalism and the religion. Clearly, then, if you want to build and not to destroy, you must teach religion on the basis of nationalism, with which it is inseparably intertwined." But Ahad Ha'am warned Magnes against "excluding from the ranks of the nationalists all those who do not believe in the principles of religion." In his view, "our religion is national — that is to say, it is a product of our national spirit — but the reverse is not true. If it is impossible to be a Jew in the religious sense without acknowledging our nationality, it is possible to be a Jew in the national sense without accepting many things in which religion requires belief. . . ."

Simon Dubnow was Ahad Ha'am's contemporary and friend, and for many years they discussed and debated how to ensure the survival of Jewish culture. Both men agreed that Jewish national culture was the vital element in Jewish life. While Ahad Ha'am believed that Palestine as a spiritual center would ensure that culture, Dubnow believed in national-cultural autonomy, evolving his theory from that period in Jewish history most beloved to him — Jewish autonomy in the Polish commonwealth, when, under the Council of the Four Lands, Jews and their culture flourished.

His essay "The Survival of the Jewish People" most succinctly expressed his idea of national cultural autonomy. "The principles of the national commandments are known: perennial struggle for communal autonomy — autonomy of the cells that make up the body of the nation — in a form that is appropriate to the conditions of the time; a struggle for national education at home and in schools established for this purpose — education in the ancient national language and the vernacular languages developed in the Diaspora which unite the entire people or large sections of it; a struggle for the cultivation of all basic national possessions and their adaptation to universal culture without damaging their own individuality." [23]

Dubnow and Ahad Ha'am differed in emphasis and in some particulars

(Yiddish, for instance, which Ahad Ha'am rejected totally), but they were otherwise remarkably alike. An agnostic like Ahad Ha'am, a product of positivism and historicism, Dubnow was, nevertheless, too much a Jew to exclude Judaism from his concept of Jewish nationality. In "The Doctrine of Jewish Nationalism," the first in the series "Letters on Old and New Judaism," which he wrote between 1897 and 1907, Dubnow evolved a position on Judaism somewhat more affirmative than Ahad Ha'am's:

> If we wish to preserve Judaism as a cultural-historical type of nation, we must realize that the religion of Judaism is one of the integral foundations of national culture and that anyone who seeks to destroy it undermines the very basis of national existence. Between us and the orthodox Jews there is only this difference: they recognize a traditional Judaism the forms of which were set from the beginning for all eternity, while we believe in an evolutionary Judaism in which new and old forms are always being assumed or discarded and which adjusts itself unceasingly to new cultural conditions.

Like Ahad Ha'am again, Dubnow rationalized the galut and accepted it as part of the Jewish condition. In "The Emancipation Movement and the Emigration Movement," another letter on the old and new Judaism, he characterized Jewish migration as "the wanderer's staff" on which the Jews had relied for thousands of years. He cited a Talmudic passage, "The Lord has done kindness to Israel in scattering it among the nations" (Pesahim, 87b), and a medieval sage's comment thereon: "A king in one country issues decrees against our money and our lives, while in another country another king has mercy and saves those who escape." Dubnow remarked that from a religious point of view that interpretation was astonishing, for the Lord could have saved the chosen people from ruin. "But," he went on, "the saying contains a sound historical observation: without migration, not even a small remnant would have been left of the Jewish people after all the misfortunes, crusades, expulsions, persecutions, inquisitions, and pogroms. And what would have been our fate in Russia during the last twenty years had we not been able to drill a hole in the boiling cauldron in which we were being roasted and let the steam escape?"

Perhaps similar temperaments made Dubnow and Ahad Ha'am amiable adversaries and dear friends. Both were pessimistic, rationalist, humanist, influenced by positivism, searching the Jewish historical past for lessons on the Jewish future, and distrustful of the Gentile world. They were Girondists among Jacobins, traditionalists among messianists. With equanimity both accepted the uniqueness of Jewish existence, in contrast to the secularly messianic Zionists and the secularly messianic revolutionaries, who hoped to liberate the Jews from uniqueness or chosenness. Both men analyzed the galut and its problems rationalistically, yet both harbored a mystical concept of a Jewish will to live and survive until the real End of Days would come. Both struggled with the problem of Judaism, the faith of their fathers which they had lost, and both found a place for it within their scheme of things, though its place within their own hearts was ambiguous. Thus, they stood apart from the run of Zionists and nationalists of their time.

To that extraordinary duo, a third must be added: Nathan Birnbaum. His course in search of his Jewish identity was lonely and anguished. Associated with Herzl for a year or so in the Zionist Organization, Birnbaum soon concluded that the way to Jewish national renewal lay elsewhere. A more intimate knowledge of East European Jews led him to that conclusion: "I found in them a nation with all the characteristics of a living distinctive people, and it became clearer to me that we do not have to create anew a nation that already exists but it is essential that we nurture it. So I conceived galut-nationalism. In Western Europe I championed East European Jewry, stressing their vibrant peoplehood; of East European Jews I demanded that they preserve what they had, and not dissipate it for futuristic visions." [24]

Birnbaum espoused Jewish national-cultural autonomy as the means to preserve the Jewish people and enrich authentic Jewish culture. Like Dubnow and Ahad Ha'am, he rejected secular messianism ("the futuristic visions"), choosing instead the continuity of Jewish culture and traditions.

Between 1905 and 1910, national-cultural autonomy became a cardinal principle of all modern Jewish movements, in their innumerable sects, schisms, and splinters. (Nahman Syrkin characterized that era as "the period of theoretical chaos.") The Zionists, too, incorporated the principle of national-cultural autonomy in their domestic program. That was no time to live in a messianic future, for in that period of convulsive social and political upheaval in Russia, Palestine assumed an aspect of unreality. The Jewish situation in Russia demanded immediate attention and relief. Nor could any Jewish movement remain indifferent to the general political situation. In 1906, the Russian Zionists adopted a program dealing with the here and now (*Gegenwarts-program*, as it was called in the Zionist patois).

Radical ideologies penetrated the Zionist movement. The fusion of socialism and Zionism produced several groups. The idea of territorialism (a Jewish state, but not in Palestine) merged with socialism, and that with national cultural autonomy. The radical groups — Zionist, territorialist, socialist — found their rationale for national-cultural autonomy not in the Jewish past, like Dubnow, or in the Jewish present, like Birnbaum, but in a socialist analysis of nationalism derived from the experiences of the Habsburg Empire. Karl Renner and Otto Bauer, gifted Austrian socialist theoreticians, conceived a systematic theory of harmonizing rival national interests within an economically and politically unified state. They advocated a scheme of local governments which would recognize legitimate national aspirations (an educational system, cultural associations, and official recognition of the mother tongue in institutions of local government). The Austrian Social-Democratic party itself had originally been organized along national lines: separate nationality parties, according to language, in a federated system. In 1907, that was changed to a loose association, and in 1909, differences between the German and Czech parties disrupted the unity of whole movement. Ideology notwithstanding, loyalty to nation transcended loyalty to class, a difficult lesson for class-conscious Jews to learn.

Among Jews, too, a new proletariat had begun to emerge. Artisans long before the factory system, skilled and sophisticated in the rational production of goods, they were nevertheless excluded from most government-operated factories and other large industrial establishments, sometimes because of Sabbath observance and sometimes because of prejudice. Engaged in home industries or in small factories, Jewish artisans outnumbered the employment opportunities in the congested Pale of Settlement: in 1898 there were over 500,000 Jewish artisans, 100,000 Jewish day-laborers, and at least 50,000 Jewish factory workers. Despite the enormous emigration to America, Jewish artisans had increased about 20 percent since 1887. Concentrated in light industry, they vastly outnumbered non-Jewish artisans in the same cities. (In Grodno, a typical example, Jews, 17 percent of the population in 1897, were 61 percent of the artisans. In Galicia in 1890, 26 percent of Jews were industrial workers, compared to 9 percent of Poles and 1 percent of Ukrainians.)

This newly fledged proletariat became the focus of the new revolutionary movement of the nineties. Jewish radical intellectuals in Vilna and Minsk then organized a few socialist circles to which they attracted Jewish stocking-makers and tailors employed in small shops. These workers were natural Jews, an organic part of Jewish society, though they had broken radically from Jewish tradition. They lived totally within a Jewish milieu, spoke Yiddish, and could not conceive of themselves as other than Jews. In 1892, about one hundred Jewish workers attended an illegal May Day meeting in the woods outside Vilna. While one worker rushed to embrace the future religionless society ("We Jews, Jewish subjects, repudiate our own holidays and fantasies which are valueless for human society: we join the ranks of the socialists and adopt their holiday. . . ."), another's speech was permeated with Jewish pathos and a Jewish messianism straight out of Jewish tradition: "We Jews must not feel humiliated or ashamed that we belong to the 'pernicious' Jewish race. Jewish history justifies us; it too has its pages of splendor. Never in the world was there a people like the Jews that could die with resolution for the Sanctification of the Name. Let us, then, the younger generation, follow the example of our fathers and demonstrate our resolution in the struggle for the liberation of humanity." [25]

These worker-pioneers of the Jewish labor movement regarded their revolutionary circles as vehicles for a sort of socialist haskala that would lead them to enlightenment and emancipation, an outlook with which professional revolutionaries had little sympathy. Julius Martov, later a leader in the Russian Social-Democratic movement and a close associate of Lenin, who began his career organizing Jewish workers in Vilna, wrote of them:

> . . . their whole manner of social thinking was idealistic . . . their socialism was still thoroughly abstract and utopian, and . . . the idea of employing the class struggle to transform the uncultured environment itself, in protest against which their own social awakening had occurred, was still alien to them. . . . They considered self-education, in the noblest sense of the word, the alpha and omega of the socialist movement. . . .[26]

The organization of strikes and strike funds, as the new method of socialist organization, was introduced in Russia by Martov and his colleague Arkady Kremer. Kremer (1865–1935), the son of a poor Lithuanian maskil, had come to Vilna, where he began to agitate among Jewish workers. The new tactics of organizing strike funds and strikes (several occurred in Vilna in 1892 and 1893) and agitating on purely economic issues did not sit well with the Utopian-minded Jewish workers Martov described. To convince them, Kremer wrote a pamphlet *Ob agitatsii* ("On agitation"), which Martov edited, that eventually became a guidebook on revolutionary tactics. Martov left for St. Petersburg and the Russian movement. Kremer remained in Vilna, where he continued his work which led in 1897 to the founding of the Jewish Labor Bund. From its small illegal beginnings, the Jewish Labor Bund later evolved into a major force in Jewish life, the only modern movement that in the lifetime of East European

Jewry successfully competed with Zionism, offering both masses and classes another mode of Jewish identification. The Bund became a channel through which many alienated and assimilated Jews returned to their own people and their own culture.

Most early Bundist leaders were *intelligentn,* many with university education. They had sympathy for the Jewish workers they encountered and a sense of their responsibility toward the proletariat of their own people, a socialist *noblesse oblige.* By contrast, the Jews active in the Russian Social-Democratic movement — Axelrod and Trotsky, for example — wanted to escape from their unwanted Jewishness by agitating for a new society of universal brotherhood. Early Bundist leaders did not ponder much on the Jewish component of their program, for they were interested only in propagandizing a proletariat whose language happened to be Yiddish. They were, at best, indifferent to any expansion of specifically Jewish activities.

Slavic nationalism had been one of Marx's bugaboos. The Russian socialists, too, regarded nationalism as bourgeois and reactionary, though they failed to recognize their own Great Russian chauvinism for what it was. They were critical of Polish separatist nationalism for defying the laws of scientific socialism and shattering working-class unity. For Jewish national-cultural autonomy (a far cry indeed from national chauvinism), the Russian Social-Democrats had only contempt. The Bund, at its 1900 convention, under cross-pressures of the Russian movement's antinationalism and the natural Jewish impulses of its members, curbed those impulses: "Considering demands for Jewish national autonomy to be premature, this convention holds it sufficient for the present to fight for the abolition of all anti-Jewish discriminatory legislation, to publicize and protest against the oppression of the Jewish nation, avoiding any amplificaton of national feeling, which can only reduce the class consciousness of the Jewish proletariat and lead to chauvinism." [27]

But thereafter, at first slowly and tentatively but ever more surely, the Bund began to acknowledge its specifically Jewish character and to champion its own brand of Jewish national culture. In 1903 the Bund withdrew from the Russian Social-Democratic Labor Party (RSDLP), to which it had belonged since 1898, after the RSDLP convention refused to recognize the Jews as a nationality and give the Bund the exclusive franchise to organize Jews. Lenin, in *Iskra,* had characterized the idea of Jews as a nationality "reactionary" and "medieval." In Galicia, too, the Polish and Austrian Social-Democratic parties, supported by assimilationist Jews who out-Polonized the Poles, for years obstructed the efforts of Jewish workers' organizations in Lemberg and Cracow to form a Jewish party, with Yiddish as its language. In 1905, finally, such a Jewish party was organized, despite Polish opposition. Also in Congress Poland, Polish socialists had a double standard: Polish nationalism was good but Jewish national identity was bad. Founded in 1892, the Polish Socialist Party (PPS) combined Marxism and Polish separatist nationalism in a policy of "permanent insurrection." Its Jewish members were as assimilationist and Polonist as those in the Galician Polish party.

The Jewish workers whom the Bund recruited came from the depths of the Jewish Pale, wretched and miserable, with the bare rudiments of a traditional education, ignorant of the world beyond their cheerless milieu. They were disdained by Jewish society, which the aristocracies of rabbinic learning and wealth dominated, intermarrying to maintain that dominance. The worker was the *am ha-arets* ("ignoramus"). Was it mere coincidence that the Jewish labor movement arose in Lithuania, that for years its stronghold was Vilna, that the Bund grew more rapidly in places where hasidism never flourished? Hasidism had been the only Jewish movement that championed the common man and gave him and the more advantaged equal standing before God. Rabbinic Judaism was aristocratic and patrician; haskala, upper class and snobbish; Zionism, bourgeois and philanthropic. The Bund was the first Jewish movement after hasidism to comfort the common people and give them a sense of their individual worth and dignity. To speak to these workers as members of an exploited class, the Bund had to address them as Jews, in a tongue familiar not only linguistically but also culturally, the Yiddish of the folk culture. At the outset, the Bund's national-cultural aspirations were limited by the cultural backwardness of its members (Dubnow was justified then when he criticized the Bundist concept of Jewishness as "only an ethnic or folk quality, not national-cultural"). But eventually the Bund opted for more and devoted itself not only to the economic and political problems Jews faced but also to enlarging and enriching their cultural horizons. By World War I, the Jewish Labor Bund had begun to organize a Jewish school system with Yiddish as the language of instruction and to support national-cultural autonomy. The Jewish culture which the Bund fostered, exclusively Yiddishist and explicitly secular, nonetheless embodied traditional Jewish values (social justice originated in Jewish Law, did it not?).

Several socialist-Zionist groups soon emerged, spin-offs from the Zionist movement or the Russian socialist movement, and competed with the Bund for the allegiance of the Jewish proletariat. Nahman Syrkin (1867–1924), founder of socialist Zionism, had formulated the idea of a Jewish socialist state in 1898. Socialism, Syrkin thought, would solve the Jewish problem and would liberate Jews from antisemitism and assimilation. Since Jews of all classes suffered in capitalist society, all Jews, proletariat and bourgeoisie, ought to support socialism. Syrkin's propaganda led to the formation of a small group of socialist Zionists in Berlin in 1901. A more class-conscious Zionism, synthesizing Marxism and Zionism, was formulated by Ber Borochov (1881–1917), who had been expelled from the RSDLP for Zionist nationalism, with groups in Yekaterinoslav, Minsk, Poltava, Vitebsk. The Uganda debacle in 1903 (when Herzl was prepared to accept East Africa for a Jewish homeland in lieu of Palestine) split the Zionist movement into pro-Palestinians and territorialists. The embryonic socialist-Zionist organizations also divided into bewildering multiplicity of groups: socialists who were Zionists, socialists who were territorialists, and national autonomists who were all three.

Despite their ideological antagonism, Bundists and Zionists, especially socialist Zionists, resembled each other in their goal to remake Jewish traditional society and in their scorn for those traditional Jewish attitudes of accommodation and nonviolent resistance that had served Jews in adversity in the Diaspora. Zionists and Bundists alike extolled physical resistance and Jewish preparedness to fight. They leaped back over nineteen hundred years of Jewish life in the dispersion to find a Jewish tradition by which to legitimate themselves. A Bundist leader rhapsodized: "The old heroic spirit was reborn among the Jews. It has come to life in the hearts of the Jewish proletariat. For centuries the Jew had lived like a slave. He considered suffering and silence his highest virtues. When his blood was shed, he fell like a dumb animal under the hand of the slaughterer, without struggle, without resistance. . . . The soul of the ancient Jewish heroes, wandering in the world of chaos, has finally found its place. The Jewish worker-heroes acquired it." [28]

After the outbreak of the Kishenev pogrom Easter Sunday, 1903, the Bund began to organize its young men in armed resistance groups, called *zelbshuts* (self-defense), prepared to fight pogromists. The Labor Zionists followed suit. Exploiting a Maccabean tradition, the zelbshuts was nonetheless a product of Jewish modernity, a revolt against Jewish traditionalist acceptance of Jewish suffering as the disorder of the world which would be set right with the coming of the Messiah.

On July 14, 1904, a Socialist Revolutionary assassinated Interior Minister Plehve, hoping, as revolutionaries had hoped in 1881, the deed would stir the people to a revolutionary upsurge. And indeed: unrest spread among practically every group in the Russian population. Russia's involvement in the bloody war with Japan increased discontent. In 1905 the revolution came, a brief and fragile revolution, followed by a far longer period of black reaction. The revolution had tragic consequences for Jews, for it unleashed a new wave of pogroms. The only difference between 1905 and 1881 was the presence of the Jewish self-defense, which in some places helped to ward off calamity. But the Jews were no match for the Black Hundreds, a counterrevolutionary force of obscure origin, consisting of peasants and workers, devoted to monarchy and church.

The Bund denounced the pogroms as the arm of counterrevolution. A few RSDLP local groups publicly condemned them, too, but the party itself remained silent. At the RSDLP's convention in 1906, the Bund, having rejoined, proposed a resolution on the party's responsibility in counteracting the Black Hundreds, antisemitic agitation, and pogroms, but the RSDLP shelved it for lack of time. (In 1903, the RSDLP had declined to hear a report on the Kishenev pogrom.) Russian socialists, it appeared, suffered from a somewhat milder strain of the same disease that infected most Russian society. The impotence of the Bund in the RSDLP and the indifference of the Russian socialists to the pogroms foreshadowed the later powerlessness of Jewish politics in Russia and Poland.

The proletarianization of the Jewish masses and their accelerated urbanization began to disrupt segments of traditionalist society where earlier modernist movements had not penetrated. The rigorous demands of industrial labor changed the Jewish flow of time that had been regulated by prayers and religious observances. Jewish workers turned to the Bund, as rabbis and rebbes took sides in the class war within the Jewish community, supporting Jewish employers against their workers or preaching caution out of timidity. (The strike of the prayer-shawl weavers in Kolomea, Galicia, was different. Pious Jewish workers took an oath on the Torah, administered by a rabbi, to strike until they won an improvement in their working conditions. All through the strike the rabbi supported them.)

Within a decade or two these Jewish masses — proletarian, plebian, common — emerged as actors in Jewish history. Heretofore, these hewers of wood and drawers of water, *am ha'aratsim,* had had no say in the community. History had been made by rabbis and scholars, rebbes and zaddikim, the wealthy, well-born, and well-connected, the court Jews, the philanthropists, and, finally, writers and intellectuals. But after 1881 the masses — raw, ignorant, and unprepared — began to act and to determine their own fate. They emigrated to America, they raised money for Palestine, they organized labor unions and struck shops, they took up arms in self-defense.

These emergent masses wanted education and culture. Hebrew literature and some of the earlier nineteenth-century Yiddish literature, didactic and reformist, were more suited to the classes, maskilim, communal leaders, educated men. The masses required a culture to cheer and entertain, while lightly instructing. Since the middle of the nineteenth century, the few Yiddish books of this quality had enjoyed phenomenal success. Tales and novels by Isaac Meir Dik (1814–1893) were best sellers even by our standards (his stories sold about 100,000 copies). Vilna housewives, marketing for the Sabbath, bought Dik's paper-pamphlet novelettes to increase their Sabbath joys. Dik, though critical of the traditional society he depicted, differed from other haskala writers in that he exploited the literary resources of the people: folklore, folktales, customs, and, most important of all, folk humor. His social criticism was humorously good natured, neither bitter nor satirical.

Isaac Joel Linetsky (1839–1916), Dik's successor, became an overnight sensation in 1868 with the publication of his novel *Dos poylishe yingl*, a satirically humorous yet sentimental novel about a hasidic youth. In 1875, Linetsky and Abraham Goldfaden jointly published *Yisrolik*, a humorous Yiddish weekly, a first attempt at popular journalism. Goldfaden was already known for his collection of Yiddish songs *Dos yidl*, first published in 1866, the most reprinted and beloved work of Yiddish verse. In the late seventies, Goldfaden found that a public brought up on this popular literature was ready for the theater. For them he composed Yiddish musical comedies and dramas, whose subject matter was Jewish history or humorous social criticism of Jewish life.

Early modern Yiddish literature was, as a perceptive literary critic once remarked, a literature of readers rather than of writers, "inspired and dictated by those for whom it was created, not by those who created it. That tradition persisted . . . till nearly the end of the nineteenth century." [29] Unlike Hebrew, Yiddish possessed a mass culture before it attained high culture. The increasing vulgarity of that mass culture and its subliterary productions elicited contempt for Yiddish among people with more refined literary tastes. Nahum Meir Shaikevich (1850–1905), known by his pen name Shomer wherever Yiddish was read, was in the eighties the most prolific producer of that mass literature and the most popular. In his lifetime he wrote approximately two hundred novels and stories, many of enormous length, and some thirty or forty plays. His novels, improbable stories of love and adventure (yeshiva student meets princess), used to appear in weekly installments.

Sholem Aleichem (1859–1916), pen name of Sholem Rabinovich, started his literary career with the explicit purpose of weaning the mass reader from Shomer. Prepared to compete for the common reader, Sholem Aleichem offered high-culture literature in popular form. Dubnow was among the first critics to notice. In 1887 Dubnow reviewed Sholem Aleichem's story *Dos meserl* ("The Penknife"), calling it a "pearl" among the literary refuse to which he had long consigned Shomer. Sholem Aleichem was the only one of the three modern Yiddish classicists who directly took the path of popular literature. Mendele Mokher Sforim, the grandfather of Yiddish literature, had started with Hebrew and haskala. In his youth, Isaac Leib Peretz began to write poems in Polish, turned to Hebrew, and then came to Yiddish literature, and as a Yiddish writer passed through several periods of experimentation before he found his way to authentic Jewish sources. Yet these were literary sources rather than human ones. Sholem Aleichem was unique in that his literary genius drew its resources from the living people, their way of life, their manner of speech, their idiom, and ironic humor. Mendele's literary endowments had enabled him to transcend his didactic purposes. "Mendele," wrote Bialik, "created style in our literature." But Mendele never became the literary interpreter of the masses that Sholem Aleichem was nor their literary ambassador abroad.

Among the Hebraists, Chaim Nahman Bialik was Sholem Aleichem's counterpart to the extent that he, too, became a spokesman for the common folk and their aspirations. Bialik wrote both Hebrew and Yiddish and, modernist as he was, relied almost exclusively on the Jewish traditional culture and its prophetic flavor for his diction, symbols, style, and allusions.

At the end of the eighties, the new literature began to take shape. An innovation of the haskala, it had been mellowed by national feeling and refined by estheticism. Classics of European literature were being translated into Yiddish and Hebrew, dispelling Jewish literary provincialism. The new literature in Hebrew and Yiddish (Charney-Niger's formula: "two languages and one literature") was modernist, its writers rebels against traditionalist society. Yet they created a new literature that was permeated with Jewish traditional values, with Jewish culture both traditional and modern, and with love for the Jewish people. Warm, often sentimental, the new literature rejected the corrosive self-hate that had characterized haskala literature. Bialik could write with affection of the yeshiva and the prayer house which he had left. Even Mendele, who earlier had written savage satires on traditionalist society, became more tender. In 1899, in the introduction to his autobiographical novel *Shloyme Reb Khayims* he wrote: ". . . the life of the congregation of Israel, though it appears outwardly ugly, is nevertheless inwardly beautiful. A powerful spirit dwells in Jewish life, a divine spirit which like a gusting wind raises waves to cleanse them of filth and decay. Beneath the refuse in the heder, the yeshivot and the prayer houses, the flame of the Torah glows, casting light and warmth among the whole people. All our children, poor and rich, small and great, have mastered the Hebrew letters and are immersed in study. Such a life we say is right, and it is fitting to record it for generations to come."

In this vein Sholem Asch began his career with his stories about the *shtetl*, romanticized idylls of the Jewish town in Poland, suffused in nostalgia for traditional Jewish life. Later, Asch began to write about Jewish big-city life, but the shtetl remained a basic motif in Yiddish literature, not as satire (Mendele) nor idealized (Asch), but often in the raw, as depicted by the later Yiddish naturalists and realists. The shtetl, too, became a creative element in Marc Chagall's art.

The new culture began to stir the new proletariat. Self-study groups, calling themselves "jargonist committees," arose in the early nineties in workers' circles. Its organizers wanted to improve their members and liberate them from Shomer's fantasies. They organized libraries of Yiddish belles lettres and popular science. David Pinsky, the short-story writer and dramatist, then a Bundist, first invited Peretz to read his poems and stories to working-class audiences. Their intelligence and literary appreciation induced Peretz to publish *Yomtov-bletlekh* (1894–96), journals which became the literary treasure of the jargonist committees.[30]

The political movements rushed headlong into the literary and cultural world. Most writers were committed to one ideology or another, few stood apart from ideological conflicts. Indeed, their contributions to national and political polemics raised the level of Jewish journalism. The Bund, heir to the jargonist committees, became the champion of Yiddish literature, printing poetry and stories in its underground publications. (The Russian censors were ever present.) In the words of a Yiddish literary critic, "under the influence of socialism which penetrated Jewish life, Yiddish literature blossomed into a beautiful flower." Hebrew had been preempted by the Zionists who shared the assimilationists' contempt for Yiddish, which to them symbolized everything hateful and ugly in the Diaspora. To Yiddishists and Hebraists, the cultivation of their language and the enrichment of their literature became matters of transcendent national importance. Language and literature became surrogates for land and state, and even an alternate for religion.

Chaim Zhitlowsky formulated a theory of Yiddishism upon which he predicated the existence and survival of the Jewish people: ". . . everyone must admit that the Yiddish language is the breath of life whose very inhalation renews the existence of the Jewish people. As long as Yiddish lives, there can be no doubt that the Jewish people will live." His theory had considerable vogue among anti-Zionists and anti-traditionalists.

Another sort of Yiddishist was Nathan Birnbaum, who in 1908 convened a conference in Czernowitz on the Yiddish language. Participants included writers, scholars, communal and political Jewish leaders. He wanted Yiddish proclaimed *the* national Jewish tongue. Peretz, whose presence lent enormous prestige to the conference, held that Jews had no national language: Hebrew had lost that status, while Yiddish had not yet attained it. Finally, the conference adopted the formula that Yiddish was *a* national language. (Birnbaum was then on the eve of a momentous revelation: that language by itself was insufficient to keep a culture alive, that national survival needed the motivating energy of transcendent values.) The excess of ideological debate prevented the conference from acting on Birnbaum's concrete proposals to standardize Yiddish spelling and punctuation and to compile a Yiddish dictionary.

In the same period, Dubnow and a corps of young university-trained Jews, mostly jurists, were compiling sources for the history of Jews in Russia. They had undertaken work in this field out of a desire, sometimes inarticulated, to find a place for themselves in the Jewish community, to satisfy Jewish needs that otherwise might have remained unfulfilled. Amateur historians, they laid the groundwork for studies in Russian Jewish history, thus strengthening their own sense of Jewish identity.

To ideology, linguistics, and history as sources of Jewish identity were added the cult of hasidism and the study of Jewish folklore. The exploration of these Jewish traditions and customs animated Jewish literature and scholarship, art and music, with authentically Jewish moral and spiritual values. The cult of hasidism and the literary pursuit of traditional sources manifested the craving to return home among intellectuals and radicals whom modernist currents had swept from their old Jewish moorings.

That Yiddish writers should turn to hasidism for renewed vigor was most fitting, for hasidism had created its own Yiddish literature, one that had remained untouched by modernism. That literature recorded hasidism's oral tradition. In epigrams, apothegms, and aphorisms; in wonder tales and allegories; parables and myths, hasidim recounted the wisdom of their rebbes, the mysteries of the Torah, and the mysticism of the Kabbala. "When all is said and done it is this myth which represents the greatest creative expression of hasidism," Gershom Scholem writes. "Triviality and profundity, traditional or borrowed ideas and true originality are indissolubly mixed in this overwhelming wealth of tales. . . ." [31] In contrast to the literalist and rationalist productions of the haskala, dry unto aridity, hasidic tales contained a wealth of poetic imagery and lyricism, symbolism and subtlety.

Peretz and Berdichevsky came to the hasidic literary treasury by different routes and sparked a neohasidic literary vogue. They became not hasidim, but hasidim of hasidism, devotees of its life-giving literary attributes and its love of the Jewish people. (Other writers — Judah Steinberg and S. J. Agnon, for instance — took more from hasidism.) Bialik, and later also Berdichevsky, explored older traditional literary sources: Bible, Talmud in its dual legal and moral aspects, rabbinic literature, and the secular Jewish poetry of Arabic Spain.

Jewish folklore and customs, as a source of literary enrichment, had long been neglected, except as a subject of study among antiquarians. Herder's romanticism of the *Volk* had prepared the ground for German nationalist exploitation of folk literature as the expression of the folk ethos. Later in the nineteenth century, folk culture was exploited to justify aspirations for political independence among the nationalities in the Habsburg Empire. Perhaps because Jewish intellectuals had long been estranged from their people, Jewish folklore had been bypassed in the movements of Jewish national renewal. But in the closing years of the nineteenth century, Jewish folklore began to elicit their interest. Peretz, once more, was among the first to collect Jewish folksongs. He was to build his most solid literary reputation on his *Folkstimlekhe geshikhten* ("Stories in the Folk Spirit"). The first major collection of some 375 Yiddish folksongs was published in 1901 in St. Petersburg and kindled further interest among writers and scholars. In 1912, under the auspices of the newly organized Jewish Historic-Ethnographic Society in St. Petersburg, S. Ansky launched an extraordinary expedition into the Ukraine to collect Jewish, particularly hasidic, folklore. Ansky once remarked that Jewish folklore lacked hedonist and heroic elements: ". . . Jewish folklore is permeated with the conviction that spiritual (intellectual and moral) perfection is loftier, more substantial and mightier than corporeal, physical power, no matter how heroic."

The folklore expedition lasted three years, right into World War I. A member of that expedition recalled: ". . . the expedition, under Ansky's direction, roamed into the remotest corners of the Ukraine, everywhere collecting the remaining treasures of our past; notated stories, legends, historical events, spells, charms, remedies; tales about *dibbukim*, demons, and evil spirits; songs, proverbs, maxims, sayings; recorded on phonograph discs: old melodies, prayers, and folksongs; photographed old synagogues, historic places, gravestones, prayer houses of zaddikim, various ritual scenes; picked up and purchased: Jewish antiques, documents, communal record books, ceremonial objects, jewelry, clothing, and all sorts of Jewish antiquities for a Jewish museum." [32]

Joel Engel, one of the first Jewish composers to incorporate Jewish folk themes in his work, was a member of that expedition. From the hasidic folk legends Ansky derived the material for his play *Der Dybbuk*, probably the most renowned Yiddish drama of all time.

Jewish folklore, steeped in ancient Jewish religious traditions in which rabbinic, hasidic, and secular motifs were intermingled, helped to enrich secular Yiddish and Hebrew literature and culture. By way of folklore, some modernist writers and scholars were able to bridge the old world and the new, to embellish their Jewish cultural equipment, and to authenticate their credentials as Jewish survivalists.

6   Jewish Politics:
Under Despotism and Dictatorship

From their experience of centuries of autocratic rule, subjected to arbitrary despotism and mob violence, Jews looked to a constitutional order, a society governed by law, for civic equality and protection. They were encouraged to believe that the extension of democracy through parliamentary representation was the ultimate political consummation. Universal suffrage would render Jews equal, and the exercise of political liberty would enable citizens of the polity to rule themselves wisely and justly.

But ironically, in most European parliamentary democracies where the franchise was universal, or nearly so, antisemitism became a matter of politics. All over Europe, decisions about the civic and economic status of Jews were being made by prejudiced masses and dishonorable politicians. In Eastern Europe particularly, politics became the means, not of regulating society for the common good, but of coercing it into submission. In the Russian empire, and most markedly in Congress Poland, in the first floundering steps toward parliamentary representation, antisemitism became a vehicle for political power. The liberating nationalism of the mid-nineteenth century became the relentless totalitarianism of the twentieth. The old notions about the rights of man gave way before the rights of nations.

Eastern Europe was multicultural, multilingual, multinational. Jews lived amid people divided by language, religion, and culture, all striving for independence and political power. Situated among antagonistic contending ethnic groups, Jews often became party to their conflicts, without wishing to. Jews, aspiring to high culture, usually chose to identify themselves with the more Western culture in their milieu. They came in conflict, then, with the nationalist ambitions of the other ethnic cultures. Between 1848 and the last decades of the nineteenth century, assimilated Jews in western Galicia, for instance, were culturally Germanist amid a Polish population. Eastern Galician Jews, amid Ruthenian peasants, were more likely Polonist. Russian Jews chose the literary culture of Great Russia rather than the folk culture of the Ukrainians, White Russians, Litts, or Letts. (In Courland, Jews often chose German culture in preference to Russian.) In Congress Poland, many assimilated Jews were Polonist, though the Jewish migrants to Poland from Russia preferred Russian. In the western reaches of Congress Poland, Jews espoused German culture rather than Polish. These cultural choices that Jews made assumed political significance when the ethnic groups under Austrian and Russian imperial rule began to seek political power. Jewish support for rival national cultures reinforced an already full-blown antisemitism fostered by the Christian churches.

The first East European Jews to have the right to vote, Galician Jews in 1873 elected four Jewish deputies to the Reichsrat. Members of the Liberal Party, Austrian centralists, these Jewish deputies had been elected with Ruthenian support. Thenceforth, the separatist Poles turned to the Jews to defeat their Ruthenian rivals. In exchange, Poles helped elect some Jewish deputies, all of whom joined the Reichsrat's Polish Club. (That recalled a more freely rendered Jewish political choice of an earlier era: In 1848 Dov Berish Meisels, an Orthodox rabbi and fervent Polish nationalist, elected to the Austrian Constituent Assembly, demonstratively joined Franz Smolka's nationalist Polish bloc.) These Jewish deputies in the Polish Club represented no articulate point of view in the Jewish community and themselves had no Jewish policies or politics. Though the government had enacted legislation restricting Jewish economic opportunities, they never asked questions in the Reichsrat about the treatment of Jews. Rabbi Simon Sofer, a Reichsrat deputy from 1879 to 1885, elected with the support of the rebbe of Belz, became a member of the Polish Club; he never uttered a public word during his term of office.

Universal suffrage was enacted in Galicia in 1907, with a system of national representation. But the Jews were not recognized as a nationality, nor was Yiddish granted status as their national language. Some 250 petitions on behalf of Jewish national status were rejected. The Jewish claim had been supported only by the Ruthenians, who hoped to weaken Polish hegemony in Galicia. The Poles, for their part, categorically declared they would prevent recognition of a third nationality politically equal to them and the Ruthenians. In that 1907 election, four Zionists campaigning on a Jewish ticket were elected with Ruthenian support. They formed the first (and only) Jewish club in the Reichsrat.

These four Jewish deputies restored Jewish dignity and self-esteem, but what role could they play in a parliament of 516, torn by violent and seeming irreconcilable national conflict? The Poles moreover continued to enjoy the support of an unlikely pair of Jewish political bedfellows — the assimilationists and the hasidim. In 1911, the last election under Habsburg auspices, Polish nationalist chicanery, with the connivance of Jewish assimilationists, prevented the election of several Zionists. In a tussle over invalid ballots in Drohobycz, twenty Jews were massacred and many wounded. The subsequent public outrage stilled the rhetoric of Polish antisemitism in the Reichsrat, but it did not prevent the Poles, politically and economically dominant in Galicia, from exercising the more deadly weapon of economic antisemitism: boycotts and legalized stratagems to drive Jews out of the professions, light industry, commerce, and services. That was an omen of things to come. A minority amid minorities, novices in politics, Jews had much to learn about the exercise of the franchise and the uses of political power.

Russia until 1905 was a country of power without politics, an autocracy operated by a venal bureaucracy. The establishment of constitutional government and the diffusion of political power absorbed the attention of the middle-class and professional men in Russia, but their quiet and reasoned voices remained unheard in the struggle between autocratic power and revolutionary terror.

Jews were the most defenseless group in Russia, deprived of the limited franchise, restricted in residence, occupation, and educational opportunity, utterly dependent upon a friend at the Court, if there was one, to speak on their behalf. To present their case to the Tsar, the Jews could depend only on *shtadlanim,* men whose prestige, wealth, or Court connections qualified them as intercessors. The first eminent shtadlanim were the Günzburgs, a family of financiers, philanthropists, and communal leaders, on whose founder, Joseph Yozl (Ossip), a hereditary baronetcy had been bestowed in exchange for financial services. The Günzburgs were conscientious shtadlanim who spoke with dignity on behalf of Jews and were sensitive to their hardships. Yet even the Günzburgs failed to put the Jewish case in a political perspective, whether for reasons of temperament or conservatism. Shortly after he became Prime Minister in October 1905, Count Witte received a Jewish deputation, which included, among others, Baron Horace Günzburg, Petersburg attorney Henry Sliosberg, and Maxim Vinaver. They came to plead for full rights for Jews. Before he could bring their case to the Tsar, Witte told them, the Jews would have to promise publicly to abstain from revolutionary activities. "Of late years," Witte said, "the Jews have come to the fore as leaders of various political parties and advocates of the most extreme political ideas. Now, it is not your business to teach us. Leave that to Russians by birth and civil status, and mind your own affairs." Witte reported that Baron Günzburg expressed agreement with his opinion. Vinaver, then already an influential figure in the newly organized Constitutional Democratic Party (Cadets), and to become an outstanding Jewish political leader, took exception. He declared, in Witte's account, "that the moment had now come when the Russian people were going to obtain political freedom and full rights for all the citizens irrespective of race or faith, and that it was the duty of the Jews to offer every possible support to those Russians who were fighting for the political emancipation of the country." [33]

The difference between shtadlan and political leader was unmistakable.

Though the Revolution of 1905 was snuffed out before the year's end in pogroms and brutal punitiveness against all insurgents, and though the autocratic character of the regime remained unchanged, the Tsar kept his promise made in the October Manifesto of 1905 to convene a Duma, an elective legislative assembly. On that basis, Russian Jews began to work energetically to secure equal rights and, first of all, the right to vote for deputies in the forthcoming Duma. The Jewish national movements and groups formulated political positions and strategies, in sharp contrast to the Jewish deputies in the Austrian Reichsrat. Jewish political activists rallied constituencies, debated policies, sought qualified candidates, considered alternative tactics, and made political alliances on the basic issue of rights for Jews. (The Bund and the Social Democrats boycotted that election, on the ground that suffrage was not universal and the Duma had been stripped of real authority.)

Twelve Jewish deputies, 6 of them Zionists, were elected to the first Duma, convened on May 10, 1906. Of 497 deputies, the Cadets, representing the liberalism of the urban professionals, led the largest bloc. The natural leaders in the Duma, but without a majority, they had to maneuver between contending views, maintaining opposition to the Tsarist regime sufficiently forceful to win political concessions, yet not so rebellious as to invite suppression.

During a debate on the government's role in fomenting the pogroms of 1905, news came about a new pogrom in Bialystok from June 14 through 16, 1906, in which eighty Jews were killed and hundreds wounded by a sadistic and savage slaughter. A parliamentary committee was dispatched to Bialystok and a fresh interpellation put to the government. The parliamentary investigation disclosed that the pogrom had been planned by the police "on the ground that the Jews were participants in the Liberal movement." The committee unhesitatingly condemned the government: "The official reports on the reasons, the pretexts, and the course of events are contrary to the truth." The Duma demanded the resignation of the responsible ministry. Two days later, on July 21, when the deputies arrived at the Duma, they found the doors locked and posted with an Imperial manifesto declaring the Duma dissolved for "having gone into an area outside its jurisdiction" (land reform) and for having "occupied itself with investigating acts of the government" (pogroms). That night, about half the deputies assembled just across the border in Viborg, Finland, and adopted an impassioned manifesto to the Russian people, calling on them to refuse cooperation with the government until the Duma was restored. But no one heeded them. That was Russia's first and last liberal parliamentary assembly. The signatories of the Viborg manifesto were forbidden to participate in the Second Duma; many were arrested and exiled.

The Second Duma (March-June, 1907) had only four Jewish members, three Cadets and one Social-Democrat, none active in Jewish communal affairs. Dubnow characterized that Duma as the "black and the red," for it was composed of rightists and leftists, with a weak center. In its short life, the Second Duma briefly discussed the situation of Jews, with no result; it was dissolved summarily by Prime Minister Stolypin. The electoral law was drastically changed, giving disproportionate representation to the landowners and the propertied urban class. As a result, the Third and Fourth Dumas (October, 1907-1912; 1913-1915) became predominantly rightist and the political arm of the Black Hundreds, giving parliamentary sanction to the government's enactment of further draconic restrictions on the Jews.

In Congress Poland, elections to the Duma intensified Polish nationalism. The National Democrats emerged as the most powerful political Polish party, supported by the landed gentry and the rising Polish middle class; the *Lumpenintelligenz*, the educated class that could not be absorbed in the too-slowly developing economy; Polish artisans, merchants, and traders who found the economic positions they wanted already preempted by Jews. Polish economic antisemitism started with slogans to "nationalize" — Polonize — the economy, and in 1909 and 1910 an anti-Jewish economic boycott was initiated. The Jewish striving for cultural autonomy added more fuel to Polish chauvinism: the National Democrats charged that Jews wanted to create a new Judea on the banks of the Vistula. In that period of intense antisemitism, the ideal of assimilation among Jewish Polonists became impossible to uphold. One of its former advocates announced assimilation's bankruptcy in 1910: "One is either a Jew or a Pole. Polish culture is not merely Polish; it is first of all a Catholic culture." [34]

In this climate elections to the Fourth Duma were held in 1912. In a complicated curial system, different categories of eligible voters (by property) chose electors who then elected a deputy. The Polish propertied bloc in Warsaw split its vote disastrously between two nationalist candidates, with the result that the Jewish national bloc elected forty-six electors while the Poles succeeded in electing only thirty-four. (The Bund supported the Polish Socialist party candidates in the working-class curia.) Sensitive to Polish nationalism and to the symbolic and political significance the Poles attached to having one of them represent Warsaw in the Duma, the Jewish national electors expressed their willingness to vote for the Polish nationalist candidate if he would support equal rights for Jews. But he evaded a clear answer, contradicted himself, and finally refused. The Jewish national electors decided to support Eugeniusz Jagiello, the Polish Socialist candidate, whose position on Jewish rights was unequivocal. The nationalist Poles then threatened economic reprisals, violence and pogroms, total boycott. Their economic survival at stake, the Jewish national bloc nevertheless remained unintimidated. Maxim Vinaver came from Petersburg to support them in their courageous decision. Nahum Sokolow wrote of that historic Jagiello election: "We will vote for the man who favors full civic equality. Even we, the Jewish bourgeoisie, will vote against our economic interests for a Polish socialist because of something higher: Jewish honor . . . I am proud to say that that was an example of Zionism." [35]

That honorable Jewish decision, carried out in full awareness of its consequences, was, as a Polish historian wrote, "the spark that fell on powder long since prepared." Jewish support of Jagiello became the pretext for the expanded economic war the Poles waged against the Jews, boycotting Jewish stores and businesses, refusing to buy Jewish goods or to hire Jewish workers. The Jagiello election became a portent of the new Poland.

(Russia had only one more election, decreed by the provisional government after the bloodless revolution of March, 1917, but held after the Bolshevik seizure of power on November 7. Having failed to manipulate a Bolshevik victory at the polls — the Socialist Revolutionaries won 60 percent of the seats to the Constituent Assembly — Lenin ordered the assembly dissolved on the first day it convened, as imperiously as Nicholas II had dissolved the First Duma.)

World War I brought enormous suffering, losses in lives and livelihood throughout Europe. The Jewish population in the Russian Pale, Congress Poland, Galicia, and Bucovina found itself on the main battlefields of the eastern war zone. As Imperial Russia's army advanced, it arrested, tortured, deported, and massacred the Jews; retreating, the Russians repeated the process. Six times the Russians advanced into Galicia and Bucovina, and six times they retreated. Many Poles assisted the Russians in tormenting the Jews, as many were later to assist the Nazi Germans.

During 1915, the Germans occupied Congress Poland and most of the Pale and inaugurated a systematic and orderly economic exploitation of resources and labor which, on top of the war ravages, pauperized the Jewish population. Hunger, disease, and destitution were the common Jewish condition then, and without the private philanthropy of American Jews and the communal funds sent by the American Jewish Joint Distribution Committee Jews could not have survived.

Inspired by the hope of a new political order in Eastern Europe, Jews began to draft proposals to submit to the coming peace conference. Without dissent, East European Jews endorsed demands for individual civic rights and for legally guaranteed minority (group) cultural rights, with the claim to government support for schools conducted in the minority language. The unanimity among East European Jews for national-cultural autonomy and the emotional force with which they advocated it induced the delegation of American Jews at the Paris Peace Conference to support that demand. Eventually, Poland, Rumania, Austria, Hungary, Czechoslovakia, Bulgaria, and Yugoslavia agreed, reluctantly in many cases, to the incorporation in their peace treaties of guarantees of civic and cultural rights to their national minorities. The new states of Lithuania, Latvia, Estonia, and Finland pledged themselves to respect minority rights.

In the Ukraine, Jewish cultural autonomy had a most promising start soon after the March, 1917 revolution. The Central Ukrainian Council (Rada) recognized the rights of its national minorities, including the Jews, and provided for them in a Statute of National-Personal Autonomy, adopted January 9, 1918. A Ministry for Jewish Affairs, with a staff of about one hundred, was established. The two million Jews in the Ukraine elected a Jewish National Council to shape their cultural policies. But in rapid succession came the Bolshevik coup, the German occupation, the Ukrainian uprising, and the creation of the Ukrainian Directory, under Semyon Petlura's leadership. The Directory renewed the promise of cultural autonomy, but whatever hope Jews had had for a life in the Ukraine was drowned in a tidal wave of bloody pogroms accompanying the civil war. The Whites and the Ukrainians (and even sometimes the Reds) pogromized Jews, but the Ukrainian national army under Petlura's political leadership particularly distinguished itself. From 1919 to 1921, nearly two thousand pogroms in about seven hundred places took the lives of at least twenty thousand Jews.

In newly independent Lithuania (Lithuanian nationality, Paris peace conferees quipped, was invented in Germany in 1916), Jewish cultural autonomy had an auspicious start. The government pledged itself to respect minority rights, and it established a ministry of Jewish affairs. The 150,000 Jews in Lithuania formed a Jewish National Council to represent them in formulating educational and cultural policies. In its first optimistic report, the council declared: "We are now experiencing, perhaps for the first time in our long history, an era when we are not, as we used to be, merely silent witnesses to the restoration of other nations, but we are participants in our own renascence, which will give our life a new quality, liberate it, enrich it, beautify it." [36] That hope, too, expired, not in blood as in the Ukraine, but in political reaction. In 1923, the government dissolved the Jewish National Council and the ministry of Jewish affairs. In 1926, Voldemaras's virtual dictatorship obstructed the activities of voluntary Jewish communal bodies and pared state subventions to Jewish schools. The Lithuanian parliament ceased to function. There was no one of whom to demand an accounting.

The ninety thousand Jews in Latvia enjoyed individual civil rights and state support for Jewish schools, as long as such rights existed — until 1934, when Karlis Ulmanis, in a fascist coup, dissolved the Latvian parliament and introduced dictatorship.

The German occupation of Congress Poland and the Western Russian provinces from 1915 through 1918 had an enormous impact on the organization of Jewish religious and cultural life, its influence enduring in later reconstituted Poland. Early in 1916, Pinhas Kohn and Emanuel Carlebach, two German Orthodox rabbis attached to the German civil administration of the Generalgouvernement of Poland, came to Warsaw to counsel the German administration on Jewish policies and help the Jewish community organize itself along Western lines. They advised in the organization of the Agudat Israel, which became the political voice of Orthodox Jewry, and guided them in modernizing their educational system. Antagonistic to the secular nationalists, Zionists, and Bundists, and their demands for Jewish cultural autonomy, Kohn and Carlebach believed the Jewish community could have only a religious character. (Besides, they feared that Jewish insistence on national-cultural autonomy would exacerbate Jewish-Polish relations.) Yet except for die-hard assimilationists, Polish Jews, the Orthodox included, regarded themselves as a national community, or a national-religious community. So pervasive was this concept among Polish Jews that little Jewish boys in Warsaw used to run after Rabbis Kohn and Carlebach with derisive taunts "*Nor a religye, nor a religye!*" ("Just a religion, just a religion").[37]

The Jewish community was organized as a religious kehilla, but under German protection from Polish antisemitism the Jews assiduously cultivated also a Jewish national culture. In those years, Bundists and Left Labor Zionists took the first steps in building a Yiddish school system; Zionist groups began to organize modern Hebrew schools. Unfettered by Tsarist censorship, the Yiddish press flourished. Libraries sprang up, choral societies and cultural clubs were formed. A high-culture Yiddish theater came into existence.

The new Poland agreed, most reluctantly, to provide minority rights. Its Constituent Sejm (parliament) of 1919 promised cultural autonomy to minority groups and approved the provision for minority rights in the peace treaty. Poland's constitution later reaffirmed those rights. But from the outset, these guarantees were a dead letter, a silent testimony to Polish national honor.

All through Eastern Europe, cultural autonomy fell the first victim of rightist reaction and fascist dictatorship.

Reconstituted independent Poland became the war zone of Jewish politics and the laboratory of Jewish cultural creativity. The 2.1 million Jews in 1921 were the second largest minority after the Ukrainians-Ruthenians.[38] (Other substantial minorities were White Russians and Germans.) The new Polish state carried over, with some changes for the worse, the wartime heritage of Rabbis Kohn and Carlebach, recognizing Jews as a "religious union," and giving the religious kehillot civic-legal status, under the supervision of the Ministry of Religion and Education. Kehilla officials were publicly elected and membership was obligatory. The kehillot were given authority over all religious affairs: the rabbinate, synagogues and prayer houses, ritual baths and cemeteries, religious education, supply of kosher meat, establishment and operation of philanthropic institutions for the Jewish needy, and the administration of kehilla property. Responsible for the support of these institutions, the kehillot were authorized to tax adult Jews to raise the necessary funds. The statute also provided for a central religious council, but the government failed to implement it.

Though the Polish government defaulted on its promises for cultural autonomy and in fact ruthlessly promoted Polonization, the Jews continued to cultivate their national-cultural institutions, maintaining them out of their own financial and moral resources and in defiance of Poland's antisemitism and chauvinism. Polish Jews maintained three private school systems: the Agudist Yesode ha-Torah school for boys (about 50,000) and the Beth Jacob schools for girls (35,000); the Zionists organized Tarbut, a modern Hebrew school system, with about 37,000 pupils; the Bundists and Left Labor Zionists operated the Central Jewish School Organization, a Yiddish school system with 20,000 pupils. All three systems included high schools and teacher-training institutions.

Poland's electoral law provided for proportional representation, a system which all ideological strains in Polish politics and all ethnic minorities regarded as a guarantee of the fullest measure of political democracy and a protection against inundation by the majority. With proportional representation, parties proliferated, class interests and national loyalties intersecting each other. In the twenties, the deputies in Poland's Sejm and Senate represented some thirty parties, with over thirty other parties competing for those seats. The Ukrainians alone had ten different parties, all nationalist, ranging from Left to Right, but mostly Right.

The Jews, too, contributed to this plethora of parties, with eight, representing a variety of class interests and Jewish philosophies. On the Jewish political Right, the largest party was the Agudat Israel, ultra-Orthodox and anti-Zionist, in which the hasidic dynasty of Ger played a leading role. Its deputies sat in each of Poland's six Sejms (1919, 1922, 1928, 1930, 1935, 1938) and supported the government bloc, even in its most reactionary period. Also on the right were the Zionists-Revisionists, who had split from the Zionist Organization. Antilabor, the Revisionist party advocated the philosophy of a corporative state and the planned mass evacuation of Jews to Palestine. Its chief source of support appeared to be among Jewish war veterans and assimilationists.

The Jewish political center was occupied by the General Zionists and the Mizrachi (Orthodox Zionists), who formed the backbone of the Sejm's Jewish Club, and the small Folkist party, a survival of Dubnovian autonomism, whose declining strength came from non-Zionist middle-class Jews and Jewish artisans' associations. The Hitachdut (Palestine Labor League, an association of Labor Zionists), whose socialism was subordinated to its Zionism, gradually withdrew from general political activity and concentrated on emigration to Palestine.

The strength of the Jewish Left was overwhelmingly in the Bund, whose support was derived from the working class and the lower middle class, and whose chief political ally was the Polish Socialist Party. The small Left Labor Zionist party was closer to the Communists. (The Communist party, functioning illegally under political pseudonyms, attracted a substantial Jewish following, especially when the government's antisemitic and fascist policies compelled the Jews to positions of radical opposition.)

Each party's political course was shaped by its view of the Jew in society and by its attitude toward power politics. The Agudat Israel held the traditionalist Jewish view that Jews, a minority amid a Gentile majority, had no alternative but accommodation to the wishes of that majority. Consequently, the Aguda supported the government bloc, though its deputies publicly criticized anti-Jewish government policies.

Conservative Zionists believed in the efficacy of political negotiation, in the possibility of a political give-and-take with Polish conservatives and from time to time negotiated such political compromises. The centrist Zionists, in contrast, too modernist to be accommodationist, sought political allies among non-Jewish parties and entered into election coalitions with them. That strategy put them in direct and defiant opposition to the Polish majority, simultaneously strengthening Ukrainian nationalists who were usually as antisemitic as they were anti-Polonist.

The Bund and the Left Labor Zionists, too radical to compromise, more often than not refused to be party to the illegalities perpetrated in national Polish politics and abstained from the elections, preferring to remain uncorrupted tribunes, demanding legality, justice, and equality for Jews and for all citizens.

No Jewish strategy succeeded in Poland; none could have in that accelerating dictatorship. Now it appears that Jewish politics in Poland was a wearisome and tragic exercise in futility. But then Polish Jews thought otherwise. They wanted a voice to speak for them in Sejm and Senate. The overwhelming majority of Jews elected men to Sejm and Senate who would represent them as Jews and defend with dignity their Jewish interests. Centrist Zionists received by far the largest Jewish vote. Agudist candidates ran a distant second.

As Poland's government grew more dictatorial and the Sejm ceased to be even a forum, the Jews lost interest in national politics. After Pilsudski's death in May, 1935, the Sejm became a tool of Rydz-Smigly's dictatorial clique. Most opposition parties and Jewish parties, too (Agudat Israel and Galician Zionists excepted), boycotted the September, 1935 elections. The government bloc received 86 percent of the votes cast, but less than half the eligible voters went to the polls. That was a "plebiscite of silence." By 1938 few Jews bothered to vote. Poland had become a semifascist dictatorship.

Jews concentrated their political energies on municipal elections: in 1935, the Bund received a plurality of Jewish votes and in 1938, in eighty-nine cities and towns, it received 55 percent of the total vote cast for Jewish parties. Strongest in industrial urban centers like Lodz and Warsaw (in Warsaw, seventeen of twenty Jewish councilmen elected were Bundists), the Bund enjoyed wide-ranging support for its councilmanic candidates, from hasidim on the right to proletarians on the left. In the municipalities, economic issues affecting Jewish employment and business were debated — sometimes decided — and municipal subsidies for health and educational institutions were allocated. Thus, Bundists became Jewish communal spokesmen and aggressive advocates of financial aid to all Jewish institutions, including yeshivot and religious institutions.

Politics, then, became an instrumentality for strengthening Jewish identity and increasing Jewish self-reliance. Parliamentary government, even at its most undemocratic and dictatorial, provided a public forum in which the Jewish case and the Jewish view of society could be expressed with dignity. When that political forum was abolished, Jewish parties took their case to public opinion. They rallied multitudes to strikes, protests, and demonstrations against the violence of pogroms and the denial of Jewish rights. After a pogrom in Przytyk in which four Jews were killed and several score wounded, the Bund called a general strike on March 16, 1936. "Three and a half million Jews went out on strike. At noon all Jewish workers left their work; all Jewish stores shut down; Jewish pupils walked out of school. The streets of Poland were filled with fiery people, proud, battle-ready." [39]

The scene was repeated in October, 1937, when all Jewish parties joined in issuing a general strike call to protest the infamous introduction of ghetto-benches for Jewish students at the universities.

Did the multiplicity of Jewish parties not splinter Jewish solidarity? Perhaps, but also it provided Polish Jews with a diversity of political styles and the possibility of choice. Out of the interaction between masses and political leaders, between voters and their representatives, emerged an authentic Jewish leadership, responsive to its people's needs and articulating what the people wanted articulated. For the first time in modern society, masses of Jews were themselves able to fashion their own political points of view.

A minority in the Gentile world, Jews lacked political power to transform their ideas into political reality. Their political powerlessness, however, gave them moral authority, a unique Jewish quality that no other politically powerless minority in Poland exercised. Jews introduced a moral vocabulary into the language of Polish politics. In the chambers of the Sejm and in the streets of Polish cities, Jews reminded the political masters of Poland of an ancient law: "And if a stranger sojourn with thee in your land, ye shall not do him wrong. The stranger that sojourneth with you shall be unto you as the home-born among you, and thou shalt love him as thyself."

7 Opening the Gates

TRADITIONAL JUDAISM and its traditionalist society in the nineteenth century appeared immutable and immovable amid the political, social, and economic transformations of Eastern Europe. Nevertheless, slowly and tardily, it underwent change. No tradition, if it was to survive, could remain impervious to the altered quality of society. Accommodations to new ways of living and new modes of thought gradually became incorporated into the old tradition, and soon it seemed that the new had always been part of the old. As traditional Judaism became more self-reliant in the modern world, it grew more willing to accept what was socially necessary and Jewishly healthy and, doing so, put on them its own stamp of tradition.

After Israel Salanter's doctrine of musar, no significant theological, ethical, or philosophical innovation was introduced in East European Judaism. In the late nineteenth century, hasidism's revolutionary élan had waned. A few rebbes could still generate spontaneity and freshness, but most had become satisfied with the mechanical fulfillment of the Shulhan Arukh and the punctilious observance of every custom sanctioned by long usage. The relentless spread of modernity had compelled Orthodoxy into a posture of obstinate resistance to all change and innovation. Before haskala and hasidism, rabbinic Judaism had been more worldly, more tolerant, and more responsive to social change. After the haskala, rabbinic Judaism became conservative, inflexible, and repressive; hasidism, too, followed suit. The haskala's extreme demands for religious reform caused rabbinic Judaism to lean more heavily than ever on past authority and rendered the rabbis more fearful of exercising independence in interpreting the Law. The smallest deviations from the prescribed way of life became magnified into enormous heresies. Sins of immorality and venality were outranked by sins of modernity, which became identified with atheism and even apostasy. Cutting one's earlocks, wearing a coat shorter than the traditional style, reading "modern" books — these were the most pernicious sins of all.

The hasidic dynasties of Belz in Galicia and Ger in Poland were the first to apply modern tactics against modernity. ("Nothing," says Voltaire, "is so common as to imitate the practice of enemies and to use their weapons.") In the seventies, the rebbe of Belz founded Mahzike ha-Dat, a society to counteract the propaganda of the maskilim, and later also a newspaper with the same name. In 1907 the hasidim of Ger first published a Hebrew-Yiddish newspaper. These periodicals succeeded in circulating new currents of thought among the hasidim and in stimulating hasidic initiative to cope with modern problems instead of remaining unalterably committed to past custom.

Uvarov's schools had confirmed the traditionalists in their view that secular education was an instrumentality for apostasy and had made the issue of secular education in the last decades of the nineteenth century a central point of conflict between traditionalists and modernists. The heder remained the predominant form of Jewish education until World War I. (Poor children attended a communal Talmud Torah for about three years before being apprenticed to learn a trade.) In 1911, only about 10 percent of the Jewish children in the Pale of Settlement attended private or state schools. Jewish literature is rich in lachrymose descriptions of the heder, its harsh discipline, its obscurantist *melamdim,* its inadequate facilities, and antiquated educational methods. (Instruction in Russian and arithmetic was required by the state and usually, but not always, taught by non-Jewish teachers.)

Despite rabbinic opposition, small modifications gradually entered the Jewish educational system. By the end of the nineteenth century, secular subjects had been introduced into the curriculum of communal Talmud Torahs in larger cities. A new type of heder, *heder mesukan,* was created, too, combining general and Jewish studies with modern pedagogical methods in congenial physical surroundings. (Shmarya Levin tried, unsuccessfully, to establish one in Warsaw in 1894.) The heder mesukan remained experimental; where it existed, it attracted children of somewhat secularized, well-to-do parents.

Under the sensitive guidance of Rabbis Kohn and Carlebach, ultra-Orthodoxy in wartime Poland modernized its schools, realizing eventually that Orthodoxy was not imperiled by teaching secular subjects. An educational innovation among the Orthodox in Poland was the establishment in 1917 of the Beth Jacob schools by Sarah Schenirer. The formal education of girls had no importance in the Orthodox scheme of things, for girls required training only in the principles of Judaism and in responsibilities, upon marriage, to keep a Jewish home in accordance with those principles. But since there was no rabbinic injunction against secular education for girls, it became fashionable for well-to-do Orthodox Jews to send their daughters to public or private schools. The simple-minded understanding of Judaism that many of these girls had derived from parental indoctrination and unquestioning obedience rarely withstood the onslaughts of the secular world, and these girls became the carriers of secularism into ultra-Orthodox society. The Beth Jacob schools, then, provided a new religious bulwark but incorporated elements of modernity.

Accommodation to secular education at the secondary level of the yeshiva was more urgent, and by failing to make this accommodation until the twentieth century, Orthodox rabbinic leadership in effect became party to the flight from the yeshivot and the rise of secularism. The yeshivot turned out rabbis whose lack of secular education and whose inadequate knowledge of the official language restricted their role as communal leaders and limited their effectiveness as authoritative spokesmen for the traditional community. In contrast, students at the crown rabbinical seminaries at Vilna and Zhitomir, with a passable secular education, were deficient in Jewish learning. Most graduates of these seminaries who became crown rabbis, responsible for keeping vital statistics about the Jewish community and for supervising the collection of the special Jewish taxes, were incompetent in matters of Jewish law. The rabbinical profession became dichotomized: crown rabbis performed official duties, while true rabbinic authority resided in men who usually held no official communal post.

The ultra-Orthodox in Russia and in Galicia, hasidim and mitnagdim alike, opposed all efforts to establish rabbinical seminaries combining general education with a high standard of rabbinic training. In the late seventies in Galicia, Rabbi Simon Sofer, a true son of the Hatam Sofer (who believed that whatever was new was forbidden by the Torah), branded the proposals put forward by liberal Jews for a modern rabbinical seminary as "harsher persecutions against Jews than the expulsion from Spain and Portugal." In Russia in 1882, Rabbi Isaac Jacob Reines proposed a curriculum of rabbinic and secular studies that would prepare rabbis according to the highest rabbinic standards and also meet the requirements set by the government, but his Orthodox colleagues opposed him and he was forced to close his own experimental yeshiva after a brief period. In 1905, he founded a new yeshiva in Lida, which offered secular subjects in addition to the traditional ones, and it enjoyed considerable success.

The yeshiva at Volozhin, which had become the outstanding center of Talmudic and rabbinic study, attracting the best Jewish brains in Eastern Europe (who of our great men did not attend Volozhin at one time?), ought logically to have taken the leadership in coupling rabbinic and secular studies. But repeatedly, in the course of decades, its administration refused to make any concessions to general education, either in response to the demands of the Tsarist authorities (who closed it for that reason in 1892) or the yeshiva students, who even staged several brief insurrections on behalf of secular instruction. The students consequently resorted to surreptitious study of secular subjects within the yeshiva and outside it. At Volozhin, Bialik learned Russian, even though the yeshiva, in defiance of the government, did not offer Russian as a course of study.

The supervisors, who monitored the students to prevent their reading forbidden books, did not pursue them outside the yeshiva. On their own, the students caught up with positivist and progressist thought still popular in Jewish circles:

Look only at that undergraduate, how, after a heavy day's work he is stand-
    ing there in the street reading Buckle's *History of Civilization* in the
    moonlight! Poor man, he is not so romantic as to prefer the moonlight to
    a cheerful, warm room, with the more prosaic light of a candle, but he
    has got tired of knocking at the door, for his landlady, to whom he has
    neglected to pay rent for the last three terms, made up her mind to let
    him freeze to-night. But still more cruel to him is his fellow-sufferer,
    who is also wandering in the streets with an overloaded brain and
    empty stomach; he roughly shakes him out of his dreams by telling him
    that Buckle is long ago antiquated, and that he had better study the
    works of Herbert Spencer, who has spoken the last word on every vital
    subject in the world.[40]

Volozhin's failure left a void in higher Jewish education which by a stroke of irony was filled in Odessa, the hotbed of modernity. Mendele Mokher Sforim had long been interested in a modern rabbinical seminary. That plan became practicable when Chaim Tchernowitz (1871–1949) arrived in Odessa in 1896. Known later under his pen name Rav Tsair ("The Young Rabbi"), Tchernowitz had just been ordained by Rabbi Isaac Elhanon of Kovno. He was Mendele's ideal candidate for dean of the seminary, and under Mendele's tutelage, Rav Tsair was initiated into Odessa's Jewish intellectual climate and gained a modern insight into the Talmud: ". . . one must perforce differentiate between essential and unessential portions of any tractate." [41] It took nearly a decade before the modern yeshiva began to function. Its staff included Bialik and Joseph Klausner, later professor of Hebrew literature and Jewish history at the Hebrew University of Jerusalem. The new yeshiva attracted students of high caliber and achieved some renown during its brief existence.

From time to time Tsarist authorities convened rabbinic conferences on matters affecting the Jewish community, but the government desired only the rabbis' cooperation, not their opinions. Communal representation had fallen first to the shtadlanim and later to the modernist movements. The organized kehillot in Cracow, Lemberg, and Warsaw were controlled usually by assimilationists and reformers. From these kehillot, Orthodox rabbis and laymen kept aloof, but eventually as the assimilationists became more responsive to Jewish communal needs, Orthodoxy began a slow conciliatory process.

Outstanding among rabbis who accepted communal responsibilities was Rabbi Isaac Elhanan Spektor of Kovno. One of the great rabbinic scholars of his day, he used his enormous prestige on behalf of the Jewish community — its poor and persecuted Jews and its beleaguered institutions — and he encouraged other rabbis to follow suit.

Zionism put the traditionalists in a perplexing dilemma. To devout hasidim and Kabbalists Zionism appeared to be an insolent intervention in the divine process. Mitnagdim were more prosaic. Seeing that most Zionist leaders and activists were lax in their observance of the commandments and some were even freethinkers, rabbinic authorities set a seal of disapproval on the movement. These objections were brushed aside by only a scattering of rabbis, whose standard-bearer was Rabbi Samuel Mohilever (1824–1898). Devoted all his life to the Hoveve Zion movement and to colonization in Palestine, Mohilever persuaded Baron Edmond de Rothschild to interest himself in the agricultural colonies in Palestine, whose benefactor he remained the rest of his life. (Legends about Mohilever's charismatic impact on the Baron coursed among pious Jews and resembled the hasidic tales of wonder-working rebbes.) Too feeble to attend the first Zionist Congress in 1897, Mohilever sent greetings with his grandson. In that message, he justified his participation in a movement which included nonobservant Jews:

Our attitude toward those among us who do not observe the religious precepts must be, as it were, as if fire had taken hold of our homes, imperiling our persons and property. Under such circumstances would we not receive anyone gladly and with love who, though irreligious in our eyes, came to rescue us? [42]

Also Rabbi Isaac Jacob Reines, innovative in education, was not to be coerced on Zionism. He continued where Mohilever left off, active in the general Zionist movement despite the abuse and the threats from anti-Zionist Orthodoxy.

At the turn of the century, questions of social and economic justice came to the forefront in the Jewish community, but few rabbis addressed themselves to these questions. Often rabbis and rebbes feared to support a cause associated with dangerous revolutionaries; sometimes the rabbis found themselves in natural alliances (through marriage, philanthropy, and general conservatism) with the well-to-do in the Jewish community, employers, administrators, manufacturers. Few rabbis preached on social conditions, as Levi Yitzhok of Berdichev once did about working conditions in the matza bakeries: "The Gentiles accuse us of using Christian blood in preparing our matzot. That is not true: we use Jewish blood."

Rabbis whose independence and courage made them respected by workers and employers alike intervened to improve labor conditions, as in Brest-Litovsk, for instance, where Chaim Soloveitchik (1853–1918) was rabbi. An outstanding rabbinic authority who had taught at Volozhin until its closing in 1892, he played an important role during the strikes and labor disturbances in 1905. With the workers' approval, he interceded with the Jewish manufacturers, inducing them to meet the workers' demands.

In reconstituted Poland, the Agudat Israel transformed Orthodox Jewry into a militant force by applying modernist tactics to enforce traditionalism. But traditional society, even among the hasidim of Ger, the Aguda's stronghold, had changed. "Pious young Jews read practically everything and were knowledgeable about the programmatic concepts of the Jewish parties in new Poland. They knew Polish and it even became permissible to read Yiddish books and other once forbidden books. Hasidic young men flaunted their fearlessness of free-thinking Yiddish literature. They, the pious, knew how to adapt themselves and how to fight fanatically for the old Judaism in new times." [43]

One of the Aguda's best known political talents was Rabbi Aaron Lewin (1879–1941), for many years deputy in the Sejm. Though politically conservative, he spoke passionately on all questions affecting Polish Jews: the catastrophic economic boycott, the anti-Jewish demonstrations at the universities, the threatened ban on *shehita,* the rights of religious institutions. He took part also in debates on social issues which were morally relevant to Judaism. On one occasion, he addressed the Sejm on capital punishment. Calling for its abolition, he quoted the Mishna: "A Sanhedrin which executes one person in seven years is called destructive; Rabbi Eliezer ben Azariah says, 'One in seventy years'; Rabbi Tarfon and Rabbi Akiva say, 'Were we in the Sanhedrin, nobody would ever have been killed.' " [44]

In Western Europe the end of the nineteenth century witnessed a reaction against positivism and determinism, against the optimism that promised Progress and the rationalism which claimed knowledge of everything knowable. Religion suddenly attracted the scholars, who examined its sociology, its history, its philosophy, its psychology. Mystics and saints fascinated the intellectuals who envied the believers their vision and illumination.

Western Jews, including Henri Bergson and Freud, were among the leaders of the revolt against materialism and determinism. Bergson and others equally ignorant of Judaism and its diversity turned toward Christianity. Others inclined in that direction, like Franz Rosenzweig, discovered the living Judaism of Eastern Europe and turned back. From the elements of hasidism, Martin Buber constructed his philosophy of Judaism. Ahron Marcus (1843–1916), born and educated in Hamburg, having lost his faith, rediscovered it among Galician hasidim amid whom he settled. Unwilling to exploit his enormous Jewish learning for a livelihood, he became a wine merchant. In his leisure, he wrote on philosophy, psychology, and Judaism (*Hartmann's Inductive Philosophie im Chassidismus,* Lemberg, 1889: *Der Chassidismus,* Pleschen, 1901; *Barsilai oder Sprache als Schrift der Psyche,* Berlin, 1905). Jiri Langer (1894–1943) grew up in Prague in a modern Jewish home, where Jewish education ended with bar-mitzva. He and a friend, similarly brought up, became engrossed in mysticism: Langer's friend became a Catholic, but Langer became a hasid and for years was a disciple with the rebbe of Belz.[45] (Franz Kafka, a friend of Jiri Langer, visited the rebbe of Belz, but remained suspended between attraction and repulsion.)

On Shabbat Shuva, the Sabbath of Return, the Prophetical Portion (Hosea 14: 2–10) begins: "Return, O Israel, unto the Lord thy God." Rabbinic literature, too, is rich on the subject of repentence and return, and the hasidic rebbes always summoned backsliders to return. Rabbi Joseph Isaac (1880–1950), the sixth rebbe of the Lubavich dynasty, used to say: "A Jew should not despair, nor should one despair of a Jew. There is always the hope that he will repent."

East European Jews, too, turned and returned. Though they had not abandoned Judaism or Jews, they had fought against the obscurantism of traditional Judaism and become freethinkers. Some had advocated assimilation, others had devoted themselves to the radical movement. Their return was toward a more intense form of Jewish identity and a passionate reaffirmation of their ties with the Jewish community and its fate. Every Jewish movement, no matter how secular, offered the possibility of such return. Thus, Moses Leib Lilienblum, who lost his faith in the Jewish God and in the Jewish community, returned to the community by way of Zionism. Chaim Zhitlowsky turned, at least partially, via Yiddish. Vladimir Medem, baptized as a child, returned to the Jewish people and its culture upon his encounter with the Bund and simple Jewish workers. Joel Engel turned with Jewish music, and Ansky began his way back with folklore.

Berdichevsky in his last years, shaken by the catastrophes that had befallen the Jews and the death of his father in the Ukrainian pogroms of 1919, turned from his iconoclasm toward a restoration of Jewish tradition as he saw it. Ansky eventually turned full circle. In their youth, when they were most russified, Zhitlowsky talked to Ansky about the Yiddish language as a means of bringing alienated Jewish intellectuals back to the Jewish people. Ansky commented: "If I decided to return to the Jewish people, I would not be satisfied with that. I would return wholly." [46]

"The Jews had always known piety and Sabbath holiness," Abraham Joshua Heschel writes. "The new thing in Eastern Europe was that somewhat of the Sabbath was infused into every day. One could relish the taste of life eternal in the fleeting moment." [47] Perhaps this life eternal in the fleeting moment was what Nathan Birnbaum tasted in his encounter with East European Judaism. One of the most remarkable men of his era, Birnbaum was a Western-educated Jew who returned first to his people when he became a Zionist, then to its culture when he convened the Conference on the Yiddish Language in Czernowitz, and finally, irrevocably, to its faith. Birnbaum turned from modernity to traditional Judasim as it was practiced in Eastern Europe and found therein the power to sustain him and the illumination to guide him.

East European Jewry stood at the threshold of a new era in which traditional Judaism, at last ready to encounter the modern world, faced two opponents: an aggressive secularism that was aggressively Jewish and a self-destroying assimilationism. The drama in that encounter had resonances of an encounter at the beginning of the modern era, when rabbinic Judaism faced hasidism and haskala. But the new drama was not acted out; its dramatis personae were cut down forever.

Notes to the Introduction

1 Simon Dubnow, *Di velt-geshikhte fun yidishn folk*, VI, New York-Buenos Aires, 1952, pp. 349–50.

2 Ber Bolechower, *Zikhroynes* (ed. M. Wischnitzer), Berlin, 1922.

3 Israel Zinberg, *Di geshikhte fun der literatur bay yidn*, Vilna, 1936, Vol. VII, Part II: *Khesides un oyfklerung*, pp. 178–82; Chaim Liberman, "Reb Nakhmen Bratslaver un di umaner maskilim," *Yivo-bleter*, XXIX (1947), 201–19.

4 From his portrait of Hayim Selig Slonimski, in *Perzenlekhkeytn*, Buenos Aires, 1948, p. 91.

5 Zinberg, *op. cit.*, pp. 71–74; S. Verses, "Yakov-Shmuel Bik, der blondzhendiker maskil," *Yivo-bleter*, XIII (1938), 505–36.

6 Y. L. Peretz, *Mayne zikhroynes*, Vilna, n.d., p. 92.

7 Philip Friedman, "Yosef Perl vi a bildungs-tuer un zayn shul in tarnopol," *Yivo-bleter*, XXXI–XXXII (1948), 131–92.

8 Saul M. Ginzberg, *Historishe verk*, III, New York, 1937, pp. 62–63.

9 Quoted in Jacob Shatsky, *Geshikhte fun yidn in varshe*, II, New York, 1948, p. 216.

10 Quoted from Stuart Ramsay Tompkins, *The Russian Intelligentsia: Makers of the Revolutionary State*, Norman, Okla., 1957, p. 26.

11 "Otrivki Vospominanii," *Perezhitoe*, IV (1913), St. Petersburg, 281. The literary allusion is to Galatians 3:28: "There is neither Greek nor Jew, there is neither bond nor free, there is neither male nor female, for ye are all one in Christ Jesus." The reference reveals more about the state of mind among assimilated Jews than they were willing to acknowledge.

12 Quoted from E. Tcherikower, *Istoriia Obshchestva dlia rasprostranenia prosveshchenia mezhdu evreyami v Rossii*, St. Petersburg, 1913, I, pp. 249–50.

13 Quoted from E. Lampert, *Sons against Fathers: Studies in Russian Radicalism and Revolution*, London, 1965, p. 107.

14 An abridged English translation has been published in the Vintage Russian Library series, New York, 1961.

15 Quoted from E. Tcherikower, "Yidn-revolutsyonern in rusland in di 60er un 70er yorn," *Historishe shriftn fun yivo*, III, Vilna-Paris, 1939, p. 120.

16 Kalmen Marmor, ed., *Aron Libermans briv*, New York, 1951, p. 82.

17 Tcherikower, "Yidn-revolutsyonern," *op. cit.*, p. 132; Lev Deutsch, "Di yidn in der rusisher revolutsye," *Zukunft*, 1913–1914.

18 Quoted from J. L. Talmon, *Political Messianism: The Romantic Phase*, New York, 1960, p. 70.

19 Tcherikower, "Yidn-revolutsyonern," *op. cit.*, pp. 138–40.

20 Shatzky, *op. cit.*, III, pp. 98–107. Kraushar's disappointment in Polish behavior did not prevent his later apostasy.

21 In Sokolow, *Perzenlekhkeytn*, *op. cit.*, pp. 201–11.

22 Ahad Ha'am, *Selected Essays*, Philadelphia, 1936, p. 290.

23 Simon Dubnow, *Nationalism and*

History: Essays on Old and New Judaism, ed. Koppel S. Pinson, Philadelphia, 1958, p. 333.

24 Nathan Birnbaum, "An iberblik iber mayn lebn," in Yubileyum-bukh tsum zekhtsikstn geburtstog fun Dr. Nosn Birnboym, Warsaw, 1925, p. 13.

25 "Fir redes fun yidishe arbeter oyf der may-fayerung 1892 in vilne," in Historishe shriftn, III, op. cit., pp. 615, 625.

26 Quoted from Richard Pipes, Social Democracy and the St. Petersburg Labor Movement, 1885–1897, Cambridge, Mass., 1963, p. 61.

27 Quoted in J. S. Hertz, Di geshikhte fun Bund, I, New York, 1960, pp. 180–81.

28 A. Litvak quoted in Shloyme Mendelson: Zayn lebn un shafn, New York, 1949, p. 419.

29 Samuel Charney-Niger, "Di yidishe literatur — un der yidisher lezer," Lezer, dikhter, kritiker, I, New York, 1928, pp. 100–101.

30 Cf. A. Litvak, Vos geven, Vilna, 1925, pp. 69–85, 94–115.

31 Major Trends in Jewish Mysticism, New York, 1961, p. 349.

32 Abraham Rechtman, Yidishe etnografye un folklor, Buenos Aires, 1958, p. 15.

33 Sergei Witte, Memoirs, New York, 1922, pp. 381–82.

34 Quoted from Jacob Shatzky, "Di yidn in poyln fun 1772 biz 1914," in Di yidn in poyln, New York, 1946, p. 724.

35 Nahum Sokolow, "Avrom Podlishevsky: a kharakter-bild," in Avrom Pod-

lishevsky: Memuarn, Warsaw, 1931, pp. 45–48.

36 Der yidisher natsyonal-rat in lite: barikht vegn zayn tetikeyt 1920–1922, Kovno, 1922, p. 1.

37 Alexander Carlebach, "A German Rabbi Goes East: Emanuel Carlebach's Letters from Warsaw, 1916–1918," in Leo Baeck Institute, Year Book, VI, New York, 1961, 60–121.

38 Ukrainians and Ruthenians are ethnically and linguistically the same. The Ruthenians, to the west, were Greek Catholics, while the Ukrainians, in the east, were Greek Orthodox.

39 Shloyme Mendelson, "Tsvey veltanshoyungen," in Shlyome Mendelson: zayn lebn un shafn, New York, 1949, p. 302.

40 A description of Volozhin by Solomon Schechter, "Rabbi Elijah Wilna, Gaon," in Studies in Judaism, New York, 1958, pp. 318–19.

41 Chaim Tchernowitz, "Grandfather Mendele As I Remember Him," Commentary, VI (1948), 436–43.

42 Quoted from Arthur Hertzberg, The Zionist Idea, New York, 1960, p. 402.

43 J. I. Trunk, Poyln, VI, New York, 1951, p. 78.

44 Quoted from Isaac Lewin, Late Summer Fruit: Essays, New York, 1960, p. 32.

45 See Frantisek Langer, "My Brother Jiri," in Jiri Langer, Nine Gates to the Chassidic Mysteries, New York, 1961.

46 Chaim Zhitlowsky, Zikhroynes, I, New York, 1935, p. 87.

47 The Earth is the Lord's: The Inner World of the Jew in East Europe, New York, 1950, p. 97.

I
Early Hasidism

1 The Proselytizer: Zusya of Annopol

RABBI ZUSYA OF ANNOPOL* was one of seven sons born to well-to-do villagers near Tiktin in the early eighteenth century. He and his older brother Elimelekh (Rabbi Elimelekh of Lizhensk [Lezajsk], born 1717) devoted themselves to the Torah and its secret mystical teachings, studying the writings of Isaac Luria, founder of the modern Kabbala (1534–1572). At Zusya's initiative, both brothers made a pilgrimage to Dov Ber, the Great Maggid of Mezritsh (Miedzyrzec), and under his influence became hasidim.

Elimelekh became an important leader in the hasidic movement, but Zusya continued to lead a life of wandering, poverty, and inwardness long past his youth.

According to tradition, the Shekhina, the Divine Presence, has gone into weeping exile with Israel. By sharing the fate of the Shekhina in suffering exile and poverty, many Jewish mystics, Zusya among them, sought union with God. The story is told that he once came to a crossroads and did not know which road to take. Then he raised his eyes and saw the Divine Presence leading the way. He lived among the common people and, loving them, sought to bring them closer to God by his own example. Before his death, he said: "In the next world I will not be asked 'Why were you not Moses?' but 'Why were you not Zusya?' "

Zusya died in 1800 after a long illness. On his tombstone, it is said, these words were written: "One who served God with love, who rejoiced in suffering, who wrested many from their sins." His teachings have been preserved in the writings of his followers and collected in *Menorat Zahav* (Warsaw, 1902). The following tale has been selected from the hasidic lore about Zusya.

WHEN Rabbi Zusya went to suffer the exile in Germany, he came to a city of Reform Jews. When they saw his ways, they mocked him and thought he was crazy. When he came into the synagogue, some of them poked fun at him, and when the children saw their parents ridiculing him,

---

* "Rabbi" has been generally used to translate both *rav* and *rebbe*. *Rav* designates the appointed spiritual head of the community, its authority on the Law, its interpreter and arbiter. *Rebbe* designates the leader of a hasidic sect, often a charismatic figure. (Sometimes one person combined both functions.) *Rebbe* (plural: *rebbes*) has been occasionally used to avoid ambiguity or to stress saintly mystic qualities.

they thought he was crazy and began to pull at him, and tug at his belt. Then he beckoned to the children and said: "My dear children, gather round and I will tell you something." The children thought he would show them a trick. They all stood around him and he in the middle. And he said to them, "My dear children, look well at me, do not take your eyes off me." The children, because they thought he was going to show them something, looked steadily at him, and he also looked steadily at each child separately. After that he told them to go home.

When the children came home and were given their food, they refused to eat. One said that the meat had not been salted, and it must not be eaten. Another asked how one could eat unclean meat. And so all the children refused to eat. They said the dishes were unclean and the food was unclean.

Then, as women do, one went to another and told her that all of a sudden her son came home from the prayer house and refused to eat; whatever was given him, he said it was unclean. Then her neighbor said that her son too refused to eat and shouted that everything was unclean and that one could not pray in her house because her hair was uncovered. Then another neighbor came in and also told such things about her son — the whole town was amazed! Then they each learned that their sons were not the only ones who suddenly became pious. They said that the visitor whom they had ridiculed and thought crazy was none other than a saint. By looking at the children, he had instilled in them the idea of Judaism. The parents became afraid that they had shamed him and went to beg his forgiveness. And Zusya forgave them all.

2   A Hasid Prays for Napoleon: Menahem Mendel of Rymanow

MENAHEM MENDEL, son of Joseph Harif, was born in 1745 in Neustadt-Schirwindt (Wladyslawow). He studied in the Berlin prayer house founded by the German Jewish court banker, Daniel Itzig; later, in Moravia, in the company of his friends, the Maggid of Kozhenits (Kozienice) and the Seer of Lublin, he was a student of Rabbi Shmuel (Shmelke) of Nikolsburg. Steeped in Talmudic literature, Menahen Mendel concentrated especially on the works of Isaac Alfasi (1013–1103), famous for his abridgment of *halakha*.

While studying with Rabbi Shmelke, Menahem Mendel became a hasid and eventually a disciple of Elimelekh of Lizhensk. After Elimelekh died, many of his followers became disciples of Menahem Mendel, who moved to Prystyk and then to Rymanow, where he settled and won great renown as a hasidic leader. He sought renewal and spontaneity in faith and worship. A story is told that on Shavuot he released his congregation from the compulsion of having accepted the Torah. "You are once again free to choose," he told them. And it is said they all responded "We too accept the Torah."

Menahem Mendel died in 1815. One of his former disciples, Rabbi Eze-

kiel Panet of Karlsburg, Transylvania, wrote down Menahem Mendel's teachings and published them.

The upheavals of the Napoleonic wars and the sufferings they brought aroused Messianic expectations among the hasidim. Menahem Mendel was one of those who believed that Napoleon heralded the coming of the Messiah. Other rabbis, particularly Schneur Zalman, founder of Habad, disagreed. (Martin Buber's *For the Sake of Heaven* is a fictional account of these disputations about the Messiah's coming.) The following story, from a collection of tales about Menahem Mendel, shows how this-worldly social and political considerations about Jews and Judaism were intertwined with the mystical belief in the imminence of the Messiah's coming.

I N 1812 when Napoleon waged war on Tsar Alexander I of Russia, Rabbi Menahem Mendel, the Seer of Lublin, and the sainted Maggid of Kozhenits saw the time had come for the Jews to be delivered, and they prayed for Napoleon to triumph in the war against the Tsar of Russia. They hoped Napoleon was Gog and Magog. But the sainted Rabbi Schneur Zalman of Lyady, the Ba'al Tanya, prayed that Tsar Alexander should triumph. He said that if Napoleon won the war, disbelief would spread among Jews. Schneur Zalman wrote a letter to a disciple of his in these very words: "On the first day of Rosh ha-Shana, before *musaf* (additional service), I realized that if France will win the war, riches will increase among Jews and they will prosper. But they will become estranged from God, blessed be He. But if Alexander, the Tsar of Russia, will win the war, the Jews will become impoverished but their hearts will be joined with God, blessed be He."

But Menahem Mendel of Rymanow, while baking matzohs for Passover, prayed hard for Napoleon to win the war, and that very day Napoleon won. At that time, the sainted rebbe of Ropshits (Ropczyce) happened to be present. He wept and said to the rebbe of Rymanow, "I foresee, if it will be so, that many Jews will be killed and blood rise to the feet. The time of redemption will arrive and the Messiah will come."

The next year, in 1813, on Yom Kippur, before musaf, Menahem Mendel of Rymanow asked the rebbe of Ropshits, who was praying before the lectern, to pray for Napoleon's victory in the war. But the rebbe of Ropshits did not agree. Immediately after Yom Kippur, he went to see the Seer of Lublin to convince him not to pray for Napoleon. But he was quite unsuccessful.

From Lublin, the rebbe of Ropshitz travelled to Kozhenits. It was on the eve of the holy Sabbath and the Maggid was in the ritual bath. Then the rebbe of Ropshits lay down on the Maggid's bed. When the Maggid returned from the bath and wanted to lie down in his bed, the rebbe of Ropshits refused to arise until the Maggid promised he would not pray for Napoleon. On Friday night, when the Maggid was at the point of singing the Sabbath Psalm, he said, "People claim that Napoleon is already in Moscow. At the end of this psalm we sing 'Only to be destroyed forever, but Thou, O Lord, shalt be exalted forever.' And the meaning is that God will destroy Napoleon." In the morning came the news that Napoleon had fallen.

But Menahem Mendel of Rymanow refused to yield and prayed for Napoleon to win the war and for the redemption to begin. He said of himself that he hoped to live to see 1815, when Messiah Ben David would surely come and the true deliverance would be here. Passover at the *seder*, he said if only one righteous man of our time would support him, he would be assured that the Messiah would come.

It is told in Napoleon's history that Napoleon said that in all his victorious battles he saw a redheaded Jew praying for him, just as Alexander the Great had seen the figure of the High Priest Simeon the Just. But in the last battle near Waterloo, where Napoleon lost the war, he had not seen the redheaded Jew. He was referring to Menahem Mendel of Rymanow, who was redheaded.

3   Hasid of Inwardness: Simha Bunam

SIMHA BUNAM was born about 1762 in Wodzislaw, where his father, Zvi Hirsh, was one of the outstanding preachers of the period. Simha Bunam studied in yeshivot at Mattersdorf and at Nikolsburg, where he was particularly influenced by his rabbi and teacher, later chief rabbi of Moravia, the outstanding Talmudist Mordecai Benet.

Returning from Nikolsburg, Simha Bunam married Rebecca of Bedzin. During his stay with his in-laws, he became attracted to hasidism. At the advice of the Maggid of Kozhenits, he worked as a manager in the Bergson logging and lumber business. He chose to be a man of the world, in the world; he studied European languages, wore European clothes, and eventually became a licensed pharmacist. A disciple of the Seer of Lublin and then of Yaakov Yitshak, the Holy Jew (*yid ha-kodesh*) of Pshiskha (Przysucha),

Simha Bunam was reluctant to become a rebbe, but after the Holy Jew's death, many hasidim insisted in becoming his disciples.

Simha Bunam initiated a new direction in hasidism — inwardness, individualism, and disciplined study. His many followers later headed the most important Polish hasidic dynasties. He was highly respected also among maskilim. His teachings have been collected in the writings of several of his disciples. He is the subject of a vast treasury of tales, from which the following four have been selected. He died in 1827.

How to Serve God: Four Tales

REPETITION

R ABBI BUNAM once said to Rabbi Mendel, his disciple: "What do I need so many hasidim like these for? A few who really are hasidim would be enough for me."

"Why did the former zaddikim not do the same?" answered Rabbi Mendel. Long afterward, when his master had been dead for many years and he himself was the rebbe of Kotsk (Kock), Rabbi Mendel once said to his disciple, Rabbi Hirsh of Tomaszow: "What do I need so many hasidim like these for? A few who really are hasidim would be enough for me."

"Why did the former zaddikim not do the same?" answered Rabbi Hirsh.

BY NIGHT

Two hours every night, as he lay in bed, Rabbi Bunam would listen to his disciple Mendel, later the rabbi of Kotsk, while he read to him out of the Book of Splendor. Sometimes, Rabbi Bunam fell asleep for a little while, and the reading was interrupted. When he awoke, he himself resumed it.

But once when he woke, he said to his disciple: "Mendel, I have been thinking it over: Why should I go on living as I do? People keep coming to me and prevent me from serving God. I want to give up my service as a rabbi; I want to devote myself to the service of God." He repeated this again and again. His disciple listened and said nothing.

Finally, Rabbi Bunam dozed again. After a few breaths, he sat up and said: "Mendel, no rabbi has been permitted to do so, I am not permitted to do it either."

THE ORDER THAT WAS RESCINDED

The Russian government gave orders that the hasidim were no longer to be allowed to visit the zaddikim. Temerl, a noble lady who had provided for Rabbi Bunam in his youth and in whose service he used to sail down the Vistula to take lumber to Danzig, spoke to the governor of Warsaw and succeeded in having the order rescinded.

When Rabbi Bunam was told about it, he said: "Her intentions were good. But it would have been better had she induced the government to build a wall about every zaddik's house, and surround it with Cossacks to allow no one to enter. Then they would let us live on bread and water and do our job."

IN A BROTHEL

A lumber merchant once asked Rabbi Bunam to take his son, who was to attend to some business for him, to Danzig, and begged him to keep an eye on the youth.

One evening, Rabbi Bunam could not find him at the inn. He left immediately and walked along the street until he came to a house where he heard someone playing the piano and singing. He went in. When he entered, the song had just come to an end, and he saw the lumber merchant's son leave the room. "Sing your best selection," he said to the girl who had been singing, and gave her a gulden. She sang, the door of the room opened, and the youth returned.

Rabbi Bunam went up to him and said in a casual tone, "Oh, so there you are. They have been asking for you. How about coming right back with me?" When they reached the inn, Rabbi Bunam played cards with the youth for a while and then they went to bed. The next evening, he went to the theater with him. But when they returned, Rabbi Bunam began to recite psalms and spoke with great force until he had extricated the youth completely from the power of materiality, and brought him to the point of perfect turning.

Years later, the zaddik once told his friends: "That time in the brothel I learned that the Divine Presence can descend anywhere and if, in a certain place, there is only a single being who receives it, that being receives all of its blessings."

He Walked Humbly
by Pinhas Zelig Gliksman

Pinhas Zelig Gliksman (1869–1942) wrote articles and books about Jewish traditional life in Poland and historical studies, particularly about Lodz, where he lived. The following selection about Simha Bunam has been taken from a study of Bunam's leading disciple, Menahem Mendel of Kotsk.

RABBI BUNAM used to say that one ought to have for himself two rabbis, an earthly one and a heavenly one, that is, one who had passed on but whose religious works merited study. As his heavenly rabbi, he chose Judah Loewe ben Bezalel, Maharal of Prague.

Simha Bunam introduced a new trend in hasidism. He set rationality over ecstasy and feeling and designated the study of the Talmud and the Maharal's works as the foundation of hasidism. Study of Kabbala and the secrets of the Torah he set aside, on the ground that no one of his time was proficient in the wisdom of the Kabbala. His homilies were based on passages of the Talmud and Midrash, not on the Zohar's "Secrets of the Torah."

A fundamental precept of his hasidic approach was "to walk humbly," to cover up one's devoutness and conceal one's virtues from outsiders, putting on the appearance in public that one did not observe all the commandments. He was not strict about praying at the appointed times. This provoked much opposition from both mitnagdim and disciples of other hasidic rebbes.

Rabbi Bunam was the only one of his generation who thought of buying Palestine from Turkey. In fact, he expressed his surprise that Moses Montefiore had not formed a corporation with other Jewish magnates to buy Palestine. When someone asked him, "What is the use of this, if it is not in God's plans for us to settle there?," he answered: "Do not speak that way. When the land will pass out of their possession, our deliverance will be close."

Bunam was teacher, master, and rabbi for thirteen years and died in his sixties, on the 12th day of Elul, 1827.

4 Rebbe of Mystery: Menahem Mendel of Kotsk

MENAHEM MENDEL was born in Goray, near Lublin, in 1787. His father, Leibush Morgenstern, was a mitnagid, a strong opponent of hasidism. Menahem Mendel had a strict Talmudic upbringing. During the brief period that Lublin was under Austrian rule (1795–1809), Menahem Mendel learned German and, in compliance with Austrian law, a trade — pharmacy, though he never practiced it. In 1807, he married Glikel Nei of Tomaszow. While at his in-laws he became a hasid and a follower of the Seer of Lublin. Then he became attached to the Holy Jew and thereafter to Simha Bunam.

Menahem Mendel continued and intensified Simha Bunam's inward and individualistic approach in hasidism, even to the extreme of withdrawing from his own followers. When a hasid asked him about man's way to God, he cited Numbers 31:53: "For the men of war had taken booty, every man for himself." He had many disciples among the rising leaders of Polish hasidic dynasties, the most outstanding of whom was Isaac Meir Rothenberg of Ger (Gora Kalwarja), brother-in-law of Menahem Mendel's second wife. Menahem Mendel spent the last years of his life as a recluse, refusing to see his followers; mystery shrouds his person and beliefs.

Menahem Mendel's teachings are to be found scattered in many works, but two notable collections of his words are *Ohel Torah* and *Emet ve-Emuna*. He died in 1859. The following tale has been selected from the extensive legendry that developed about him.

I Am Not a God: A Hasidic Tale

I t was a bitter frosty winter. One night, Menahem Mendel, the old rebbe of Kotsk, sat all alone by his stove, deep in study of the Gemara. The windows were covered with frost. He was reciting aloud at the top of his voice. He did not see or hear a sleigh pulling up before his house and a man asking to see him.

In the vestibule, the rebbe's attendant dozed by the stove. When the man, dressed in a fur coat and covered with frost, entered, the attendant awoke and asked what he wanted.

The man put down the driver's whip near the door, shook off some of the ice, rubbed his hands. "I must see the rebbe, I have come from a village many miles away, on behalf of my only daughter who has been three days in labor. It is a matter of life and death. Let me see the rebbe."

So absorbed was the rebbe in his study, reciting so loudly, the attendant was afraid to enter. The man pleaded with him, even promising him vodka. But the attendant stood tiptoe at the door, listening. The man became impatient, as if he were on hot coals. He cajoled and he threatened, but it was no use. It was no small matter interrupting the rebbe at his studies! The man, seeing the attendant was afraid to enter, said: "I will go in myself." The attendant tried to stop him, they struggled; the man pushed the attendant aside, and threw open the door. He began to weep: "Sainted rebbe, a daughter of Israel is in danger. She has been three days in labor. There is no doctor in the village and the weather is too frosty to bring her into town. Rebbe, have pity, pray for her!"

The rebbe looked at him, then he went to the door and shouted: "I am not a god. What do you want of me? Why are you pleading with me? Plead with God!"

He told the man to leave and returned to his studies. The man was so upset that the attendant tried to comfort him: "God will help. With God's help, your daughter will be all right. Don't worry, the rebbe knows what he's doing."

But the man would not be comforted. With renewed courage, once again he burst open the door to the rebbe's study and fell at the rebbe's feet, imploring him. The rebbe's wife and children came running to see what was the matter. The women, too, began weeping, and the rebbe's wife entreated: "Mendel, say something to him. It is a matter of life and death."

The rebbe did not reply, his head still bent over the Gemara. The man still lay on the floor, bleating like a calf. The neighbors, too, had come running. Then, pacing up and down his study, the rebbe shouted, "What do these village Jews think? Do they think I am a priest that they kiss my shoes? I am not a god. Go home, pray to God, and your daughter will be well."

But the man kept wailing. "Rebbe, help me; only you, sainted rebbe; I will stay here until you promise me that the birth will go well."

The study was full now. The neighbors were crying, some women even said the man was right to insist on the rebbe's blessing. The rebbe himself stood at a window, his head pressed against a frozen pane. The room was heavy with anguish. Then the rebbe cried out: "Fools, dolts, why have you come here? Do you think I am a god? That I can bring the dead back to life? You think that I, Mendel Kotsker, have influence in Heaven? That if I choose I can turn the frost into a heat wave? Fools, asses. Out! Out! Out!"

The attendant drove all the people out of the study, but the man would not leave. He remained on the floor, like a madman. The rebbe returned to the Gemara, his voice rising ever higher as if he wanted to blot out the incident. The man lay on the floor, perhaps an hour, sighing from time to time. When the rebbe finished, he put his kerchief on the Gemara, and turned to the man. They looked at each other. Then the rebbe said, "Your horse must be frozen. Why are you waiting?" The man began to weep anew: "I cannot go home, rebbe, unless you help me!"

"How can I help you?" asked the rebbe calmly. "I am not a doctor and certainly not a god. Go home. God will probably help you."

His words took effect. The man arose and said goodbye. He took his whip, got into his sleigh, and quickly drove away.

The next day the man returned, cheerful. The attendant asked, "Are congratulations in order?"

"Double congratulations. My daughter had two boys."

The rebbe received him with a smile; "Did you need my blessing?"

"Rebbe," replied the man, "Your last words yesterday helped. At the very moment you were telling me to go home my daughter gave birth."

Menahem Mendel's Hasidic Mode

by *Pinhas Zelig Gliksman*

The following selection has been translated from
Gliksman's two-volume work about Menahem
Mendel of Kotsk.

AFTER Bunam's death, his followers parted company. Some became disciples of Rabbi Menahem Mendel of Tomaszow; others remained with Bunam's only son, Abraham Moses. It was said that Menahem Mendel's followers were more religiously learned and more committed than the others. In Tomaszow, Mendel exercised his rabbinic leadership with great spiritual vigor and inspiration. He deepened and broadened Bunam's approach to hasidism, walking humbly, studying Gemara and Tosefot, and concentrating on the Maharal's works.

In 1829, a little more than a year after Bunam's death, Mendel settled in Kotsk, a small town in the province of Lublin, on the highway to Warsaw. According to an 1853 census, Kotsk had 1,652 Jews and 1,270 Gentiles. After Mendel settled there, Kotsk's reputation spread among Jews, and many hasidim made pilgrimages there. In many cities and towns, congregations of disciples of the Kotsker rebbe were organized. Great scholars and magnates attended Kotsk-oriented prayer houses. In Kotsk itself, the rebbe's congregation was enormous; it became a great center which attracted rabbis, scholars, learned men, promising young people, and the aristocratic among the rich. The influence, too, of the rebbe of Ger, the Hiddushe ha-Rim, was significant, for he seized every opportunity to spread the teachings of Kotsk. He brought his influence to bear on the sons of wealthy Warsaw Jews who studied with him, urging them to visit the rebbe of Kotsk, to strive toward purity and sincerity in their thoughts, and to try to approach the true will of the Creator.

The late Wolf Landau of Strykow, one of the most distinguished of Kotsker hasidim, at the Sabbath table once told us:

"I will tell you the first discourse I heard from the rebbe of Kotsk. I had already heard many of his sayings on the Torah, but with this discourse he inflamed my heart. When he sat down Friday night, after blessing the wine, his face became transfigured, disembodied. He stretched out his hands, washed them, and after blessing the bread, said, 'All that the Lord has spoken we will do and obey. In this world there are wise men, scholars, philosophers who study and search for the recognition of God. But what can they comprehend? Only as much as the level of their intelligence permits. But the Jews have instruments, that is, observance of the commandments, which makes them comprehend more than the level of their intelligence would permit, in fact upward to the level of the ministering angels. That is the meaning of "We will do and obey." If we have the instrument for doing — the performance of the commandments, then we may heed, comprehending everything that is on high.' "

A hasid, always absorbed in his business affairs, once told the rebbe of Kotsk he regretted his business allowed him no time for the Torah and hasidism as he had when he lived with his in-laws. To this, the rebbe replied:

"The Mishna says: 'Rabbi Hananya ben Akashya said: "The Holy One — blessed be He! — desired to enlarge Israel's merits. Therefore he multiplied for them Torah and commandments." ' At first, this is hard to understand. For if He had given the Jews fewer commandments, it would be easier to fulfill them, whereas the many commandments cannot be fulfilled because of the press of business. But the explanation is different. The Lord interposed commandments in everything that man does and creates. For example, when he builds a house, he is commanded to make for it a parapet on the roof, a mezuza and a *sukka*. When he plows and sows his field or his vineyard, he must observe the negative commandments not to mix seeds, not to reap to the edges of the field, not to gather the gleanings but to leave them for the poor and the stranger, and the positive commandments of offerings and tithes, and, in the seventh year, of observing a Sabbath year of rest. The Torah gave you commandments affecting your business, buying and selling, to give true weights and measures, to abjure falsehood and deceit, to be honest in yea's and nay's, and to avoid looking at women. This is what Rabbi Hananya ben Akashya meant when he said that the Lord multiplied the Torah and commandments for the Jews and gave them every opportunity, in all human activity, always to be able to observe the commandments, at leisure and in the press of business."

The Holy Zohar commented on the biblical verse that in the six hundredth year of Noah's life all the fountains of the great deep were broken up. He said this meant the year 5600 (1840) and that the floodgates and fountains of wisdom would then open. The rebbe of Kotsk said that the fountains of wisdom did indeed open at that time — accounting for the important scientific discoveries and inventions of the time. Because of our sins we were not worthy enough to receive these new sources of wisdom, and so the unbelievers seized and used them for worldly purposes.

When a bridegroom on the eve of his marriage came to ask the rebbe of Kotsk for his blessing, the rebbe asked, "Do you know why our holy sages selected the words 'Be thou sanctified unto me' to say at the marriage ceremony, when according to the Gemara it is sufficient to say 'Be thou betrothed to me,' 'Be thou my spouse'? The reason is that this saying suggests that a man ought to enter upon marriage in holiness and purity. Otherwise, the depths of hell will not suffice."

The rebbe of Kotsk said: "Whoever rejects knowledge, saying 'If only I did not know that,' of him it is said: 'Because thou has rejected knowledge, I will also reject thee.' " He also said on this subject, as it is told: "Koheleth said: 'He that increaseth knowledge, increaseth sorrow.' But I say, 'Suffer, if you must, but increase your knowledge.' " This was the teaching of his heavenly rabbi, the Maharal of Prague.

It was the Kotsker rebbe's custom to speak short and sharp that his words might reach the heart. Once a Habad hasid visited him. The rebbe asked what he aimed at, as he recited the shema and the Eighteen Benedictions. When the hasid told him, the rebbe snapped, "But what about the guts?" For his approach was, so to speak, to reach a man's core. A hasid of Kotsk once said to another rebbe's hasid "Your rebbe preaches his wisdom to the heavens, but our rebbe speaks to our guts."

The hasidim of Kotsk were deeply concerned that every religious service, a prayer or a physical act, even a groan, be done without ulterior motive, but only sincerely to do God's will. Otherwise, they described it as "service to oneself," a sort of idolatry. For what difference if one worships an idol or oneself? The Kotsker hasidim vigorously combated egoism, which poisons and seduces the soul, intoxicating with its selfishness, preventing the attainment of truth and fulfillment. The rebbe of Kotsk taught that the "I" is a thief in disguise, insinuating itself in man and corrupting him, without his own realization. The one affected does not know that he has been affected.

To resist, one must delve deep into oneself to search out the hidden thief, the "I," using different remedies to pluck it from his heart. This process the Kotsker hasidim called "departure from the domain of self," to be cleansed of every self-interest, even the slightest. Traits of conceit and pride were associated with "non-departure from the domain of self."

The Kotsker hasidim repudiated services too exalted for the person expected to perform them. It is a fraud for a person to do something he is not fit for, a sort of self-delusion based on lies and hypocrisy. The Kotsker hasidim strove therefore after self-perception, each man to know himself and his place in the world. When a man made a promise he did not keep, or gestured or sighed in a way not his own, not authentic and openhearted, the rebbe of Kotsk called that stealing.

The Kotsker rebbe was enormously sensitive in recognizing frivolous words or an insincere gesture. At first glance, he penetrated a person's thoughts and he could tell how much that man's "I" had hurt him, though the man himself was quite unaware of the disease in his soul. But the rebbe's sharp barbs cured that man. A man whose sense of smell is most acute can smell a very faint unpleasant odor to which others are insensitive.

The Kotsker rebbe's hasidim explained their rebbe's recognition of truth in the same way. He had come so close to the truth that he was immediately sensitive to even the slightest inauthentic gesture, so fastidious was his own sense of the truth.

To attain the truth, to eradicate selfishness and ulterior motives, the hasidim of Kotsk strove to walk humbly, to serve God secretly while in public appearing not to. They delved deeper to remove vanity and pride, so that their walking humbly was a walking humbly even for themselves, lest they themselves think they were doing good or were good.

A wise rabbi once joked that hasidim of Kotsk do good in private and act bad in public, while others act bad privately and do good publicly. Yet, he quipped, it was easier to catch one of these others in a bad deed than a Kotsker hasid in a good one.

The former rabbi of Staszow, Judah Leib Grąubart, in his study "Justifying the Righteous" wrote that the hasidism of the Kotsk school embraced five essential points:

1. Its rock-bottom foundation was the study of Torah, the Prophets and the Writings, the Talmud and its commentators. All Kotsk hasidim used to study day and night or, to be exact, night and day, because they studied mainly at night when most people, sleeping, could not see them.
2. Intention and thought: Every wise man acts thoughtfully. Everyone ought to act with reason, afterthought, and meaningfulness. And with purposefulness. It is right to disregard what is outward and strive for the heart of the matter, for inwardness, to know what is essential and what is secondary, to repudiate the evil spirit, the empty shell, and to separate the chaff from the wheat.
3. Curtailing some recitations during services — supplicatory prayers and liturgical hymns.
4. Be critical. One must consider what one is doing, not merely thoughtlessly imitate others, just out of habit. One must not accept everything that is taken for granted, out of a foolish belief, held by a foolish hasid.

5. Keep a distance from the vulgar crowd. Hasidim of Kotsk did not care to please others, though others disparaged them. They even acted so that others should think they were changing Jewish customs, and so speak ill of them and keep distance. They strove to be separate in their own limited society, without close relations to others.

5   The Rebbe of Lubavich Bests Count Uvarov
by Chaim Meir Hellman

MENAHEM MENDEL SCHNEERSOHN was the third generation of Habad rabbis, the grandson of Schneur Zalman of Lyady, founder of Habad hasidism.

When Menahem Mendel was two years old, his mother, daughter of Schneur Zalman, died, and the boy was brought up by his grandfather. When he was thirteen, he was said to be so learned in Torah and Talmud that his grandfather advised him also to study Kabbala. After his grandfather's death, he remained close to his uncle and father-in-law, Dov Ber, the middle rabbi of Habad, who had settled in Lubavich after the Napoleonic wars. Menahem Mendel continued to study and became renowned for his great learning, even assisting his uncle in the formulation of responsa. After Dov Ber's death in 1827, Menahem Mendel became head of the Habad dynasty and ruled it for nearly forty years.

His most famous work is *Tsemah Tsedek*, commentaries and responsa on the Mishna and the Shulhan Arukh. Another work, *Or ha-Torah*, deals with Kabbala.

Menahem Mendel consolidated the Habad movement, reuniting dissident elements that had split away after his grandfather's death. Under his leadership, the movement spread far beyond White Russia and Lithuania. Because of his rabbinic learning, he was widely respected by the great Talmudists and rabbis of the day, who held most hasidic rebbes in contempt.

He devoted much time to communal affairs. He bought a large tract of land in the province of Minsk, where he founded a Jewish agricultural colony, hoping to improve the economic conditions of Jews. To lighten the impact of the Cantonist decree of 1827, which forced minor children into military service, he established a clandestine organization to rescue children "snatched" for service and, where that could not be done, he instituted an underground program to encourage the young recruits to remain faithful Jews and resist conversionist pressures.

During his time, the Russian government undertook to change the Jewish educational system. The following story (apocryphal, to be sure) deals with his role in the educational commission which Count Uvarov had convened. (It is said that at that meeting Menahem Mendel reluctantly consented to the publication in Russia of Mendelssohn's *biur*.) Again, in 1848, Menahem Mendel corresponded with Lev Mandelstamm on questions of religious education. In response to Mandelstamm's proposal to translate the prayer book into German rather than Yiddish, Menahem Mendel wrote: "It is not right to force upon the Jewish people a language which they do not understand at all and thus abolish their own language, Yiddish, which they have been speaking for some hundreds of years."

In 1856, opponents informed against him to the government, as in earlier conflicts between hasidim and mitnagdim, when opponents had informed against his grandfather and later against his uncle. Menahem Mendel and his family remained under police surveillance for some time.

In 1860, he became ill and remained so for the next six years. He died in 1866, leaving seven sons and two daughters, who in their lifetime spread Habad hasidism to the towns of Kopust, Ovrutch, Niezhin, Bobruysk, and Rechitsa.

Chaim Meir Hellman, born in Lepel, White Russia, in 1856, was a Habad hasid. He is known for his book *Bet Rabbi*, a three-part biography of the first three generations in the Habad dynasty, published in Hebrew in 1900 and in Yiddish in 1904, from which the following selection is taken.

I N 1843 an order came from St. Petersburg that our brethren, the sons of Israel, were to select several of their great men to go to St. Petersburg. A commission, in which Minister Uvarov himself would take part, was to consider the Jewish religion, to decide which group is right — mitnagdim, hasidim from White Russia, hasidim from Poland, or maskilim. Each group selected a representative — the mitnagdim, the learned scholar Rabbi Isaac of Volozhin; the hasidim of White Russia, Rabbi Menahem Mendel Schneersohn of Lubavich; the Polish hasidim, the wealthy hasid Israel Halperin of Berdichev; the maskilim, Bezalel Stern, director of the Jewish school in Odessa. The Minister also invited from abroad the sainted dignitaries Moses Montefiore, Adolph Crémieux, and Rothschild, but they did not come. However, Dr. Max Lilienthal and other maskilim came. The commission itself consisted of only five people, the four that have been listed and the Minister of Education, who was the chairman. Every member was permitted to have advisors with whom he could consult. Menahem Mendel took along his son, Judah Leib, and Shmarya Feitelson as translator.

Count Uvarov immediately informed the commission that the Tsar definitely did not want to convert the Jews, that the writings of Jewish sages remained holy, that none of their laws would be touched. He wanted only to explain everything and establish order among the different Jewish customs. Many questions were put, and the commission replied to all.

Menaham Mendel towered above all the great men in the commission. The Minister was gracious to him, noting his great wisdom and learning. Menahem Mendel could substantiate everything by citing the great Jewish sages. He stood firm lest any Jewish law or custom be touched. He had to deal mostly with the study of Kabbala and hasidism because of the opposition to it. But he remained firm and God, blessed is He, gave him success and all ended well.

In conclusion, the commission turned to questions of Kabbala and hasidism. The question was put: What is the purpose of studying Kabbala and hasidism? What use is it?

Stern said that it was unnecessary, of no use at all. Rabbi Isaac of Volozhin kept silent, saying neither yes nor no. Only Menahem Mendel and Israel Halperin said studying Kabbala and hasidism was indispensable and that everyone could benefit from it.

Once, on Friday afternoon before the Sabbath, the Minister said: "In the matter of Kabbala and hasidism, we will do as it is written in the Torah: incline to the majority. Schneersohn and Halperin say it is essential, Stern and I say it is not. Isaac is silent, and that means he also is against it. Then we are the majority, and we must abolish the study of Kabbala and hasidism."

Menahem Mendel stood aghast. With a bitter cry, he said, "Whatever may be, the study of Kabbala and hasidism cannot be abolished."

The Minister became enraged and ordered his attendants to arrest the rabbi at once. In a moment they escorted him into another room, where he sat in seclusion. The Minister paced up and down the room, his face aflame with wrath. The members of the commission were petrified.

Menahem Mendel began to recite the afternoon prayers. In great ecstasy he chanted *hodu* (Give thanks) and *patah Eliyahu* (Elijah began) to the melody created by Schneur Zalman. The words rose from the depths of his heart with great passion. His voice was heard everywhere. It was so sweet that the Minister was transported. He asked the commission what the rabbi was saying. They told him: "He is reciting the afternoon prayers and chanting patah Eliyahu. This is a most profound portion of the Kabbala, of which we were talking." The Minister sat down and listened in fascination to the whole service. Then he opened the door and said, "Schneersohn, come out. You are freed."

Rabbi Menahem Mendel joined the rest of the commission. The Minister said, "Perhaps we can figure another way. Since Isaac is silent, that means he favors the study of Kabbala and hasidism. Then you have the majority."

Meanwhile, the Sabbath eve came on. The commission decided to hold its final meeting after the Sabbath. On the appointed day, all except Menahem Mendel had assembled. While waiting, Stern went for a walk in the park.

Menahem Mendel said to his son Judah Leib, on the way to the meeting, "Let us walk through the park." There they met Stern. The rabbi took him by the hand and implored, "In the holy Gemara it is written: 'Rabbi Judah ha-Nasi wept and said there are those who can attain the world to come in an hour.' Now this providential chance has been given you to attain the world to come in an hour, if you will tell the commission that the study of Kabbala and hasidism is indispensable." His words penetrated so deeply into Stern's heart that he spoke on behalf of Kabbala and hasidism at the meeting. And Rabbi Isaac did not remain silent; he, too, agreed. So the commission decided in favor of Kabbala and hasidism. With that, its work was over.

Rabbi Menahem Mendel departed from St. Petersburg with honor, glory, and great joy. Some years later, the Tsar bestowed upon him and his children in perpetuity hereditary honorary citizenship.

II

The Haskala

6 I Served Haskala in Russia

by Abraham Ber Gottlober

ABRAHAM BER GOTTLOBER, maskil, teacher, and writer, was born in Old Constantine (Starokonstantinov), Volhynia, in 1811 and died in Bialystok in 1899. Contemporaneous with nearly the whole nineteenth century, his life was a microcosmic reflection of the trends in Jewish life during that epoch.

In addition to a traditional Jewish education, he received instruction also in modern Hebrew. At fourteen, he was married to the daughter of a wealthy Habad hasid in Chernigov and settled there, taking up the study of Kabbala. In 1827, to avoid the newly enacted repressive Tsarist decree forcing minors into military service, he fled to Tarnopol, Galicia, where he came under the influence of Joseph Perl, leading Galician maskil, man of Hebrew letters, and proponent of modern Jewish education. When he returned a maskil to his wife and hasidic father-in-law, the hasidim forced his wife to divorce him and drove him out of town. For this he never forgave them: his later writings lampooned and ridiculed hasidim, their beliefs, and their behavior.

Gottlober's family married him off again, but he found this second wife unbearable and divorced her shortly afterward. In 1832, he married for a third time.

He moved about from town to town, tutoring and teaching, studying, meeting maskilim, and trying his hand at writing. In 1851, he passed the qualifying examination to teach in the newly established government schools for Jewish children. He taught in such schools until 1865, when he became a teacher in the government-sponsored rabbinical seminary in Zhitomir, remaining there until it was closed in 1873. These were the happiest years of his life, coinciding with the high point and blossoming of the haskala.

He was a prolific Hebrew writer of poetry, history, novels, articles, and translations from German. He wrote also in Yiddish, using it essentially as an educational medium to bring enlightenment to the masses. From 1876 intermittently until 1886, he published a Hebrew journal, *Ha-Boker Or*, to which many important contemporary writers contributed. The following selection is taken from his memoirs.

IN 1830, I left my second wife and returned home to my mother in Old Constantine, where I stayed all winter diligently studying German. My friend Joseph Weisner helped me. I read many German books and made much headway. I also studied the Bible with Moses Mendelssohn's commentary and knew it practically by heart.

While I had briefly been in Bar (Podolia) during my second marriage, I became acquainted with Meir Reich, a student of Mendel Lefin. At Reich's house I saw Mendel Lefin's Hebrew works and his Yiddish translation of Proverbs, which he had published in Tarnopol in 1812. Besides the published works, Reich also had manuscripts of Yiddish translation of Psalms, the Song of Songs, and Ecclesiastes.

The great scholar Mendel Lefin was born in Satanov about 1749 and died about 1827, at seventy-seven or seventy-eight. (Despite great effort, I could not obtain the exact dates of his birth and death; even the scholars who had been personally acquainted with him did not know.) Mendel Lefin had been raised in traditional Judaism and as a youth knew the whole Talmud and its commentaries. He was reputed to be a prodigy. In the prayer house, he came upon Joseph Solomon Delmedigo's *Elim*. Interested in speculative exercises, he became absorbed in the book and made important comments on it. He mastered this field, even as he was later proficient in other scholarly areas. Day and night studying many books with diligence, his eyes went bad, and he had to go to a hospital in Berlin to seek a cure. Moses Mendelssohn befriended Lefin. Two years Lefin lived in Berlin and Mendelssohn came to regard him as rabbi and teacher.

It was then the haskala movement among Jews matured. The people who had been kept in darkness about all worldly knowledge saw a great light in the person of Moses Mendelssohn. Torah, wisdom, and reverence for God were combined in this man. His friendship with Lessing won him great renown in Germany, and he was ranked among the German scholars. Young Jews envied his eminence and began to model themselves after him, studying foreign languages and history, and forming study groups to educate themselves.

When Mendelssohn translated the Pentateuch in German, many people had already wanted to do the same for the whole Bible (they finally did). The entire system of study was radically changed and a new spirit governed the young people. Whoever wants to have some notion of the spirit that then prevailed in Germany, particularly in Prussia, need only examine our present situation in our blessed Russia.

In that chaotic time of transition from one way of life to another, two brilliant men lived in Berlin who differed in their purposes. Isaac Satanov did not neglect any field of study. He dipped into all, though he never knew one thoroughly. He wrote many books, yet none (except perhaps his *Sefer ha-Midot*) was useful. He was a keen-witted man of learning whose heart was open to all scholarship and tightly sealed against any good deed, a man who understood Kant perhaps better than his contemporaries but did not understand himself or his purpose in the world.

At that time, Mendel Lefin too lived in Berlin, listening to the wisdom and learning of Moses Mendelssohn. The great tempest that toppled mountains and stood the world on its head did not touch him. He emerged from Berlin, his faith and his Torah intact, as when he had arrived. Then, it appears, the rare thought occurred to him to do in his country what Moses Mendelssohn had done in Prussia — to translate the Bible in the language which the Jews speak in the lands called Poland. This idea pursued him until he fulfilled a part of it.

Girding his loins, he translated into Yiddish — the language of the people and the only one they knew — Ecclesiastes, Proverbs, the Song of Songs, Lamentations, and Psalms. He also accomplished something important in that he found a way to reach the students in the prayer houses; to inspire them to self-education, he wrote in popular Talmudic style *Iggerot ha-Hokhma* ("Letters on Wisdom") and *Heshbon ha-Nefesh* ("Moral Stocktaking"), which influenced many young people in the small towns to form ethical societies. He also translated Tissot's manual of popular medicine from French into Hebrew.

Mendel Lefin's works were most beneficial, for he opened the eyes of many and made knowledge increase. In my youth, I myself knew many people whose incentive to seek education came from Mendel Lefin's Hebrew translations, which they had read in manuscript. Thus, they were prompted to educate their children and teach them languages. If the reader can imagine the obscurantism of that time in the region of Podolia, then he will understand how much Lefin accomplished.

Mendel Lefin's Yiddish translations encouraged me to speak to our people in their own language. From that time, I began to try out my talents in Yiddish. The readers of my Yiddish poems will admit, I am sure, that I was popular and helped to enlighten the people. Only a few of my Yiddish books have been published, but I hope, God willing, to publish those still in manuscript at my own expense. (The Petersburg maskilim wanted to publish them in honor of my seventieth birthday in 1881, but had to abandon the idea because of the bitter times that visited us, when the Jews were plundered and pogromized.)

In 1830, when I was in Odessa, I came upon *Te'uda be-Yisrael*, a book by Isaac Ber Levinsohn, of Krzemieniec (Kremenets), published in 1828 in Vilna. I read it with great eagerness because its subject was Jewish life in Russia, which was my native land and to which I was loyally attached. The author, I saw, was aiming toward the same ideas with which I had been preoccupied. I devoured the book, each word was like balsam. From then on, I loved that writer and I yearned to know him personally, to talk with him, tell him everything hidden in my heart and prove to myself whether I was on the right path or going astray. But it took a long time until I was able to be where I longed heart and soul to be.

All the while the maskilim in Odessa exerted themselves, in storm and stress, to strengthen education and knowledge in our land and illuminate the darkness among our people in Russia, great tumult reigned in Jewish ranks, like the roar of ocean waves on a stormy day, and a bitter struggle reigned between the right and the left. At this time, a new stream from a small source quietly issued forth from an isolated small town, like the waters of the Shiloah which flow softly, whose ripples disturb no one's peace, and which bring restoration to those who drink of them.

Amid the cliffs of Krzemieniec, near the Russian-Austrian frontier, stands a small, poor, and isolated cottage. Who would have imagined that from this humble house would go forth a new light for the Jews in Russia that would open blind eyes, not with brute force or strong arm, but with its powerful spirit, a spirit of knowledge and reverence for God, with the pen of a talented writer speaking to his people from the depths of his heart with understanding and conviction, and that the words of his wise books, emanating from a pure heart and a reverential spirit, would be heeded by listeners whose eyes would light up?

The intelligent reader will know I am speaking of the famous scholar, the only one of his time valued by his people, Isaac Ber Levinsohn, born in Krzemieniec on Rosh ha-Shana in 1788 and died the 24th day of Shevat, 1860. This extraordinary man had been chosen by God to bring new light to his brothers in his native land. From the day the radiance of his light began to spread over the country, the wrath of stupidity quieted and its sword was sheathed. The fanatics ceased to persecute those who sought learning, as they had done in earlier days, for they feared the truth, which spoke out of Levinsohn's books. Many of those who had been lulled to sleep by foolishness came to life, and the spirit of enlightenment seized and transformed them.

True, in the early days he was a target for the wrath of the fanatics and obscurantists, but after he had published *Te'uda be-Yisrael* and had won renown from notables, even from the Tsar himself, Levinsohn's enemies became silent, seeing that God was with him and had given him favor in the eyes of the Tsar and his officials. Nor could they find fault with his work.

When Levinsohn was still a young man he had settled in Brody, then and later a city of maskilim and writers. There he met the greatest scholars of that time — Solomon Judah Rapoport, Nahman Krochmal, Joseph Perl. He knew personally Mendel Lefin, then an old man, Berish Blumenfeld, who translated Job into German, Jacob Samuel Bick, Jacob Bodek, Dr. Isaac Erter, Judah Leib Mieses, and many more. In their society, he was stimulated to do more for his brothers in Russia, to raise them from their lowliness and liberate them from their enslavement to ignorance and superstition. Returning home to Krzemieniec, after several years of tutoring in wealthy homes, he began to carry out his plan. He decided to remain alone, having divorced his wife (their only child had died as a baby), and to devote himself entirely to his people and to improving their lot. Thereafter he remained within the abode of Torah and learning. His pen did not leave his hand until his dying day.

Te'uda be-Yisrael appeared in 1828, shortly after the Russian government had begun to conscript Jews. No doubt the government meant no harm for the Jews, but wanted to make them equal with the other inhabitants of the country. Had the Jewish leaders had the sense to accept this decree in good grace and thank the government for accepting the Jews for military service along with the other nationalities under its protection, the government would have then watched over the Jews. But the Jews could not understand that the government meant well; they considered the decree a calamity and marked it as a fast day, weeping and wailing at their misfortune. The hasidic rebbes found a loophole for themselves, registering as merchants of the first class, and abandoned the people to the mercy of God. Then, Solomon Isaiah Landsberg of Krzemieniec a maskil, in a broadside attacked the hasidic rebbes, calling them rogues and swindlers. As far as I know this was the first time a Russian Jew dared to speak out publicly against these misleaders. *Te'uda be-Yisrael* had just been published. Its purpose was to explain how important education was, that besides learning Hebrew systematically, one should learn other languages, especially the language of the country, without which one cannot get along and is like a stranger in his own fatherland. The book appeared at a propitious time and became very popular, its readership increasing from day to day. Countless young people began to study Hebrew systematically, and also Russian. They were courageous and unafraid of the fanatics who tried to hinder them.

Levinsohn accomplished something still more important. Not content with stimulating the young people to seek knowledge, he also petitioned the government to establish Russian-language schools for Jews and teach them skills necessary to till the soil. Alone, dejected, living in great penury, he appealed to the esteemed government, submitting letters and petitions to high officials in Petersburg, but no one knew of his efforts on behalf of his brothers in need.

The government soon became more attentive to the Jewish situation and decided to finish what it had begun. As far back as 1804, a government issued a decree, which was strengthened in 1835, providing that Jews who wanted an education were not to be refused entrance to government schools but were to be received courteously and admitted just as non-Jewish pupils were. But very few parents dared to sent their children to the Russian schools, for it seemed to them then, as it still does to many, that these schools were a misfortune, leading their children astray from Judaism and toward conversion; for in those schools they had to write on the Sabbath and on holy days. Those people did not understand that their children could remain loyal Jews, even if, God forbid, they had to write a few characters on the Sabbath. Even if, in an emergency, a Jew violated one of the 613 commandments, that did not turn him into a disbeliever or make him cease to be a Jew. At any rate, this was the reason the Jews did not care to enjoy the benefits the government wanted to bestow upon them, also along with the other citizens of the country. Experience later showed that they were wrong to cut themselves off from the rest of the population and to refuse to make it possible for their children to earn their bread in dignity. As a result, many were later forced to engage in illegal occupations and were intricated in a chain of lawbreaking which shamed and degraded them in the eyes of the Russian people.

In 1832, when I was twenty-one, I left Old Constantine for Krzemieniec, where I first met the great Isaac Ber Levinsohn. I was attracted to him by his appearance and his agreeable conversation. My heart clung to him and I cherished him for the rest of my life.

In 1839, Max Lilienthal came to Mohilev. The whole town was in a hubbub. The most distinguished Jews, who already then dressed in European style and whose children spoke half-German, half-Yiddish, received Lilienthal in awe, standing like vassals before him. The humbler people feared Lilienthal at first, but he won their confidence with his sweet and pleasant talk. In the three days he spent in Mohilev, I wrote many letters for him to the Jewish communities, and for two nights in a row I hardly got to sleep. After his departure, I wrote my friend Isaac Ber Levinsohn about everything that I had witnessed myself. This is what he answered:

"You wrote in your letter how you were privileged to serve this great man, the chief rabbi and befriender of his people and great scholar, Lilienthal, and that you wrote many letters for him. I declare you were indeed privileged to do a great and important thing, for this man is one of the truly rare sages whom God chose to help us and be our leader because it suited him and he was fit for it."

7   Rebel and Penitent: Moses Leib Lilienblum

MOSES LEIB LILIENBLUM was born in Keidany, Lithuania, in 1843 and died in 1910 in Odessa. A Hebrew writer, first a maskil and later a Zionist, he was one of the most influential Jewish writers of his time, the champion and hero of the rising secular Jewish generation.

He had a traditional Jewish education and, according to Jewish custom, was married at fourteen. He moved to Vilkomir, continuing his studies while living with his in-laws. In 1865, he established a yeshiva to support himself and his family. He also managed a small library in town for young people, and though he excluded explicitly anti-religious books, he was interested in the new Hebrew literature of the haskala. The townspeople came to believe that he was a maskil and hence, in their eyes, an atheist. They denounced and persecuted him. He then began to publish articles advocating reforms in Judaism. Their publication served only to intensify the denunciations and the persecutions he suffered from his Orthodox tormentors.

His autobiography, *Hattot Ne'urim* ("The Sins of Youth"), was published in 1876 and became the perhaps most widely read book of the time because of its openhearted and dramatic depiction of the conflict between rigid Orthodoxy and rationalism which young Jews all over Eastern Europe were experiencing for themselves. But Lilienblum soon learned that the haskala was a barren tree that would yield no fruit. In the time of his despair at the emptiness of life, he encountered the Russian positivists Chernyshevsky and Pisarev. Then he began to advocate education for a practical course in life and also socialism; some of these ideas remained with him long after he had rejected a positivistic outlook.

After the pogroms of 1881, Lilienblum turned nationalist. Active in the Hibbat Zion movement, he became the secretary of an early society to colonize Palestine, which was headed by Leon Pinsker, author of *Autoemanzipation*. Lilienblum later wrote *Derekh Teshuva* ("The Way of Repentance") as a supplement to his autobiography, which described his reaffirmation of Jewish life and acknowledged the failure of the haskala to solve the problems of modern Jewish existence by its futile and naïve hopes for assimilation. Selections from both parts of Lilienblum's autobiography follow.

The Sins of My Youth

by Moses Leib Lilienblum

SAMUEL DAVID LUZZATTO once wrote that biography is superior to fiction. A novel is the product of the writer's imagination, whereas biography describes events that actually happened. Though I do not completely agree with Luzzatto, having read many biographies — including his — and gained nothing from them, while I learned much from the many novels I read, Luzzatto is right on the whole. A biography recording a person's actions and behavior, his opinions and mode of thinking, his sufferings, and an analysis of his experiences and their effect can be more enlightening than the best novel.

There are two sorts of biography: the biography a famous person writes for his admirers, because the public likes to know everything about celebrities, and autobiography, usually written because the events are worth recording for themselves, not because of the person to whom they happened.

Biographies of famous people written in Hebrew we have many, but I know of only two autobiographies — Luzzatto's, and M. A. Gunzburg's *Aviezer*. Luzzatto's autobiography is as hollow as the parched ears of corn in Pharaoh's dream, whereas *Aviezer* was written to tell about events — the system of Jewish education in our country. But *Aviezer* is limited to the author's childhood and boyhood, and tells nothing of his later life, which might have been instructive for the young people of my native land. This defect I wish to repair: I want here to set down events of my life, from my childhood until I became a mature man.

I am an ordinary man. Hebrew is the only language I have written — some articles in periodicals and a few books. I have no particular distinction, yet my experiences can be instructive, even though they are not spiced with tall tales and extraordinary accomplishments. My life is a sort of Jewish drama. I came on stage and played it for my readers. They ridiculed me, shook their heads in disapproval, and held me up as a horrible example.

My troubles did not arise from passion or evil, as in a French drama, but out of foolishness, for that is the basis of Jewish drama. A maskil once wrote, "The life of the Jew begins in triviality and foolishness and ends in sorrow and woe; the beginning a comedy and the end a tragedy." My life was a tapestry woven of small and large errors my parents made and I myself made, of idle dreams I dreamed about myself and which others dreamed about me. The threads became warped and tangled around my neck, sapping my strength.

Now I am twenty-nine, and old age has already overtaken me. I have given up the idea of living a vital life. My eyes have become heavy with weeping and the source of my tears has dried. But my self-esteem does not let me rest. Perhaps my tears and despair can serve as a lesson to others. That is why I am writing the story of my life.

Who am I? What is my name?

A living person am I, not a nonexistent Job, nor Ezekiel's dry bones. I belonged to that dead Talmudic world that brought Hebrew literature back to life. Yet it was a dead literature, whose life juices were too weak to restore life, sufficient only to keep it hovering between life and death. I am a Talmudist who sinned and went into seclusion, a believer who repudiated the lovely visions and joyful hopes, handed down by my ancestors. I am a failure and an unfortunate man who has abandoned hope of anything good. And my name? I have said before that in autobiography not the name but the events are the point.

I passed through four periods: the days of chaos, in my native town, when I was still unformed clay waiting to be shaped; the days of darkness and the beginning of the transition, when I lived in Marshalov with my in-laws. There I stuffed my head with harmful nonsense. The world became dark and its monstrous darkness began to oppress me. Then came the time of disbelief, when I thought I had discovered the truth and fought for it, as Don Quixote fought the windmills. I was satisfied with myself, though I had nothing to be satisfied with. Finally came the time of crisis and despair, when I travelled and discovered a new world that I had never known in dream or reality.

Once, in the summer of 1861, a friend and I happened to talk about the disagreement between Rashi and Rabbenu Tam about the order in which to insert into the phylacteries the parchment slips with the Biblical inscriptions. There was a legend that Moses came down from heaven and sided with Rashi this dispute. I had read this story long ago, but only now did I disbelive it. I said to my friend, "The Tannaim in the Talmud disagreed about many things. Because of a dissent, the Tanna Eliezer the Great was excommunicated by the Sanhedrin, yet Moses was never brought down to give his opinion. The Talmud itself says: 'The Torah is not in heaven.'" We talked a lot more until I said the whole story was a lie and even convinced my friend of that. For a whole day I rejoiced that I had the high privilege of finding the truth, not as it is in books or accepted by the common people. Eight years later, when I rejected Maimonides' articles of faith, I did not rejoice.

The fact is that I did not want to become an unbeliever. Whenever I doubted something in the Talmud, I used to look for a great authority on whom to lean. When I could not find one I forced my mind to believe. True, one cannot force the independent mind to believe, but mine was then ruled by a frightful confusion of foolish disputations and philosophies. Besides, I was cowardly submissive toward the great rabbinic scholars.

On Rosh ha-Shana in 1861, I was filled with religious ecstasy. Wherever I was, wherever I went, I concentrated on the Tetragammaton. The two days of Rosh ha-Shana and the Sabbath of Return I was in this frenzy. On the fourth day, a frightening idea suddenly floated into my consciousness: "Who can prove there is a God?" Had this thought arisen out of rational doubts, my question might have been put this way: "We assume nothing happens without cause and all causes derive from the laws of nature. What, then, do we gain from the belief in Providence? We assume that nature has always gone on its accustomed way, and we know neither its beginning nor its end. From what ground, then, do we deduce a Creator and a Maker? It is hard to understand how nature first originated, but the question can be put about the Creator Himself. It is easy to say God created nature and His Word created the heavens, but it is hard to comprehend how the Creator created something from nothing with a word. Left without reasonable answer, we ask who can prove there is a God." Had I found rational answers to rational questions, I might have eliminated the doubt in my heart. But my doubts had their source in my total concentration on the Tetragrammaton. This cruel thought "Who can prove there is a God?" must have come to me only because I concentrated on God's existence. My heart was tormented by this inner voice: "Who can say there is a God?" I tried to still this cry by immersing myself in religious books, but everyone knows that no matter how hard one tries to banish a hateful idea, it keeps returning. Then came the Day of Atonement.

After Kol Nidre service, I recited the Great Confession and the first four Psalms, as was my custom to prevent nocturnal emission, and I went to bed. In the middle of the night I awoke suddenly and my heart died within me at what I saw. . . . I would be in anguish for a whole year.

Do not mock me, dear reader, nor shame me.

That Day of Atonement I was, as if, struck by thunder. Obviously God had punished me for my evil thoughts, for doubting His existence. Yet that thought persisted, and my heart quivered at that remorseless voice: "Who can say there is a God?" The cantor chanted the prayer, "Here am I, poor in good deeds." The congregation trembled at his voice. I saw everyone lifting hands and heart to God, while I — where was my God? I covered my face with the prayer shawl and dissolved in tears. The day after, I began to recite certain Yom Kippur liturgical poems which were supposed to be a sure remedy for someone who had had an emission. These prayers were to be repeated for thirty consecutive days. I vowed that if that cruel doubt would return to plague me, I would reject it and immerse myself in the Talmud.

I was weary and exhausted from studying the Talmud, its disputations and various absurdities. When I heard of something new that was rational, I was drawn to it, just like an escaped prisoner coming upon a field of flowers. Every haskala book I came upon, I devoured like the fruits of summer. It was not that I loved the haskala, for at that time I did not rightly know what it was, but so weary was I of the casuistic books and their sophistries that I looked for spiritual sustenance in other sorts of books.

I had no teacher or guide in studying the literature of the haskala. In my town, I was the first to show public interest in the haskala and I did not care what the fanatics said. There was no one to advise me wisely "Stop sleepwalking and chasing shadows. Live, for you are a living person." Undiscriminating, I read everything that came into my hands, oblivious of how the days were slipping away.

DAYS OF MY DISBELIEF

Here is a letter, with all its foolishness and high-flown rhetoric, which, in my naïveté, I wrote to a friend, and which shows what I was going through that summer.

I want to tell you what I believe and I want you to uphold me or condemn me, as you see fit. I am not the hypocrite the rabbi accuses me of being.
I believe in the Holy Torah which was given by Moses, which he wrote down from God's words, and in the songs which he sang with His Holy Spirit, like the Song of the Sea, Hazinu, and his blessings before his death, for in all these the Spirit of God spoke.
I believe in the words of the prophets in whom God's spirit spoke. I am loyal to the tradition and disapprove of the reformers. I do not believe in the new critics who say that the words of comfort in Isaiah are not his, that Chapter 40 and after were added later.
I believe that God will shed His spirit upon a man of the House of David

who will rule over us in our land. But I do not believe in the Messianic legends of our Talmudic sages, nor do I believe in the other Talmudic legends. I believe that our dead will be resurrected, that the good and the pious among the Gentiles will partake of the world to come. I hold sacred all the laws based on the Talmud. But I have no regard for customs not based on the Talmud.

I have told you, dear brother, everything I believe. Hide this letter, do not show it to anyone. There are enough fanatics in your town to say even you have been ensnared by the words of the impious.

The whole town was in an uproar over me. It hurt me to see my wife's suffering because of my conduct and I was very worried about my little boy's health. But neither the uproar of the townspeople, nor my wife's weeping, not even the pleadings of my Torah-true friends who tried to convince me to yield to the rabbi, swayed me one bit. They decided, once and for all, that I was an unbeliever and they kept clear of me. I was satisfied that an iron wall had arisen between me and my Torah-true friends. I ceased to be under their watchful eye and became free, free to write whatever I wanted. In clear Hebrew, I began to describe the barbarities of my townsmen and their foolish deeds. To all these articles I signed my name. The townspeople made even more of an uproar, threatened me, but I ignored them.

Then my heart was seized with new sorrow. For Judaism was dying, and with it the Jewish people would perish. One must seek a cure for this curse. I concluded that the only remedy was to make it easier to observe Judaism, so Jews could always fulfill the commandments as written in the Torah — not as interpreted in the Talmud. Though some fences around the Torah were needed, encumbrances and customs that make Judaism difficult to practice and unattractive to people who cannot tolerate absurdity ought to be removed.

If I regarded each nation not as a world in itself, but as a part of humankind which people, rather than nature, separated into groups, I would make peace with the idea that the end of the Jews would be like the end of all other peoples, that eventually all groups would revert to a common substance. They would cease being peoples and become just people. If I did not love Judaism in which I believed with my whole heart, I would not care if it disappeared. But now, wanting to preserve forever the Jewish people and Judaism, I was convinced the cure for the disease was lifting some of the Talmudic restraints and fences. I had a tested cure for the mortal illness, but there was no one to administer it to the patient.

Since my eyes were opened and I perceived the darkness, I have been persecuted. The foolish rabbi of Marshalov aroused the whole town against me because I had secular books in my possession. They regarded me as a *Berlinchik.* In one moment I, the head of a yeshiva, was turned into an unbeliever. The desire for revenge, a natural and human thing, made me expose them in the newspapers. At this, too, my townsmen were enraged. Yet I always observed the commandments and never intentionally violated the slightest prohibition of the later Talmudists. Even now, I never eat cheese less than six hours after eating meat. I imbued the young people of my town, over whom I have had influence, with love for the Jewish people, respect for Judaism, and the aversion of evil. Yet I was considered the town atheist and endured affliction and sorrow, poverty and hunger. When I wrote about reforming Judaism, bringing the practice of religion closer to reality, my mind was full of ideas but my stomach was empty. My reward for this article was disgrace and dishonor, shame and sorrow. The town elders tried, on false charges, to have me banished to Siberia. The kinder ones were ready to contribute fifty rubles for my children's welfare if I would disappear. They incited street urchins against me; wherever I went, young rascals trailed me, shouting "Freethinker, unbeliever." Scurrilities about me were scribbled on the walls of the prayer houses, the kiosks, the outhouses. Every Saturday, preachers agitated the people against me. Some people informed government officials against me. Some said I issued false receipts, while others said I was teaching deceit to the young. Some hasidim even tried to poison me. They called my children offspring of unclean parents, and the other children bullied them. Everyone fled from me and even my friends were afraid to speak with me on the street. That was how I passed that summer, until I could no longer earn enough for bread. Then the community of Odessa invited me.

All my life I was never beholden to anyone nor had I taken gifts, until last summer, when the committee helped me settle in Odessa. Nor did they instruct me to write one way or another. They saw the troubles I suffered at the hands of the fanatics, and they found a place of refuge for me, where the reach of the fanatics would not extend. Had these not tried to drive me out of town because of my articles, the Odessa committee would never have heard of me. My only lament is that my upbringing had stunted my abilities and hung a millstone on my neck before I was sixteen. Now, with a wife and three children, I am a miserable creature unsuited to any kind of work.

For many years I was tormented by an inner struggle that progressed step by step. After denying the power of amulets and charms, I then questioned the existence of demons. Having finished off demons and magic, I turned to the Zohar. After Zohar and Kabbala, the existence of angels; then the legends in which I had believed. After that, the commentaries on the Talmud about the religious laws, and then, the traditional law. Then I had radical thoughts about Providence, about natural change, about reward and punishment, and about man's soul.

All my days passed in emptiness, without pleasure, for the air around me was poisoned by the inhabitants of the prayer houses. Yet, except for the events of 1869 when I was denounced and forced to leave my home, I found deep satisfaction in prayer. I was raised as a mitnagid, and our services were not marked by fervency as among the hasidim. Yet often ecstasy seized me, especially during the Rosh ha-Shana and Yom Kippur services. When I recited the prayer *U-ve-khen ten pahdekha,* proclaiming man's recognition of God's sovereignty, the song of unity which most deeply touches the heart of everyone who loves God, I was immensely affected. To those who do not know what this is like, I can tell them that it is like embracing one's beloved.

Now what am I? My heart is cold and dried like wood. It is all the same to me whether it is the Sabbath or Yom Kippur, Passover, the Fast of Esther, or a weekday. The poetry, too, has been torn out of my heart. My heart is frozen with hoarfrost. How bitter for one who once was passionate! If I had filled my head with pure science, or if I were rich and enjoyed worldly pleasures, perhaps I would not feel the lack of that illusion. That was the end of the intoxication and of the illusions I had which stemmed from the chaotic haskala — to which I had been so susceptible only because of the bad education I had received.

Once I lived with illusion instead of truth, but I did not know that it was illusion; I thought it was the truth. That is why I was happier then than now.

I have written this book for myself and for others: to lighten my own lot with this funeral oration on my wasted life; and to show others the mistakes and the sins of my youth which they should avoid. I hope that copies of my book will not be eaten by the moths in the bookstores but sold and read by parents and children. Some parents, I suppose, will draw an a fortiori conclusion: See what has become of this writer who had studied all sixty books of the Talmud at eighteen, was steeped in the responsa literature at nineteen, and at twenty, subject to judgment of the Heavenly Court, he fasted and studied all day in prayer shawl and phylacteries so that he might enter the fifty gates of holiness. Though he lived among Talmudic sages and God-fearing men, where no one doubted God, yet even his Torah study and piety could not resist the Devil, and he became an unbeliever. How much easier, then — these parents think — for their children to be corrupted.

If parents understand me, they will not prevent their children from becoming educated out of fear they will be ruined nor marry them off prematurely. If parents want to protect their children from atheism, they should keep them from speculative thought, bar them from studying even a page of Talmud, and teach them a trade instead. Otherwise, their children will come to the same end as I.

I would like to hope that my book will influence the young people who have become absorbed in the futile chaos our writers call haskala. They must learn from my fate and turn to more practical things: learn living languages (I do not mean Hebrew — those reading this book know it already), mathematics, penmanship, natural sciences, and a trade by which they can live.

Boys ought to be prepared for the world while they are still young. Those who escape from the Talmud run toward the chaos of the new literature. This flight has been going on for about a hundred years. All the younger generation is fleeing, but they do not know where to. It is high time for us to stop a moment and ponder where are we running and why. Are we not fleeing into a bottomless pit? Have we no other way except flight?

I am not the first victim of the haskala; many writers and maskilim secretly bewail the sins of their youth for it is too late to correct them. But they continue to lead new enthusiasts on the same futile path along which they went, calling on young people to build and repair the Hebrew language, to raise the walls of Zion, to serve in the temple of the haskala, and other such rhetorical phrases. But I hide only my face, not my ruination, neither the sins of my youth nor the afflictions and sorrows that destroyed my life.

THE WAY OF REPENTANCE

Dear Friend, J. L. Gordon!

I see from your letter that you did not care for my Russian article in which I advocated creating a Jewish literature in Russian, not for our non-Jewish neighbors but for our own children who are becoming estranged from us. I suppose you disliked most of all my saying that the foolish notion, now in fashion, about the speedy assimilation of the Jews did not bring good but, like all foolish notions, only harm. If my guess is right, I will tell you, the banner bearer of assimilation, once again without mincing words, that this notion was foolish and harmful.

I said that back in 1874. Why should we Jews relinquish our nationality and assimilate with the people we live among? We will not be merging with all humankind, but only with one people. The name of Israel will be erased, but the division of nations will remain and humanity will gain nothing from this. There is a story about Francis Deák, the Hungarian patriot, and Emperor Francis Joseph. The Emperor declared that the Hungarians would sooner or later have to assimilate with the Germans and it would be better if they did so sooner. Deák then asked: "Your Majesty, are you a Christian?" "Certainly," the Emperor replied.

"Yet," said Deák, "Your Majesty prefers to enter the Kingdom of Heaven later rather than sooner."

Obviously, assimilation is the death of the nation — and who wants to die? I do not know if these words will influence you at all, but I do not want my people to die.

12th of Tishri [1881], at night on my couch. They write: "One should collect and assemble the data about those Jewish activities which harm the natives." We, then, are not native. During the pogroms, a native woman, ragged and drunk, danced in the streets, joyously shouting: "This is our country, this is our country." Can we say the same, even without dancing in the streets, without being drunk? Yes, we are aliens, not only here but in all of Europe, for it is not our fatherland. Now I understand the word "anti-semitism." This is the secret of our affliction in exile. Even in Alexandria, in the time of the Second Temple, and in all the lands of our dispersion, we were aliens, unwanted guests. We were aliens in Europe, when religion flourished because of our religion; now when nationalism reigns, we are aliens because of our origin. We are Semites among Aryans, the sons of Shem among the Sons of Japheth, a Palestinian tribe from Asia in the European lands.

Yet we dream we will become children of the European nations, children with equal rights. What can be more fatuous? For we are aliens and will remain aliens. Our future is fearful, without a spark of hope or a ray of light — slaves, aliens, strangers forever. Yet why should we be aliens in alien countries if the land of our fathers has not yet been forgotten and remains vacant? It can absorb our people! We must cease to be aliens, and return to our fatherland. We must buy land there, little by little, becoming rooted there, like other people who live in the land of their fathers. We are being uprooted from the land of our residence, the gates are open for us to leave. We are, in fact, fleeing. Why, then, flee to America and be alien there, too, instead of to the land of our fathers?

I was exalted by this lofty thought of return. It is the salvation for the Jewish people, and the assurance of their eternal existence, which hitherto only our declining religion had secured.

The oppressive weight rolled from my heart. It was a revelation. I became exalted and transfigured. The dew of renascence fell upon me and melted the fearful ice which for so many years had congealed my heart.

In September, I stopped attending classes at the gymnasium.

The pogroms taught me their lesson, and I was in despair about our future. My studies seemed a sin against my unfortunate people. Our sons were robbed and derided, our daughters shamed, and all our hopes for equality came to naught. Our people were fleeing the sword, misfortune all around, the present bitter, the future fearful — and I was thinking of entering the university! For years I had striven toward this. But now I am convinced that our misfortune is not the lack of general education but that we are aliens. We will still remain aliens when we will be stuffed with education as a pomegranate is with seeds. I terminated my studies and, with great dedication, I began to prepare myself for my new ideal, though I did not know how.

After the *Sins of Youth* came the *Way of Repentance*. If the repentance has not been commensurate with the sin, no matter, for the sins were against myself, not others. In such cases, even the strictest interpreters of the Law rule that repentance need not be commensurate with the sin. With those who say "Fortunate is old age that atones for childhood," I can in good conscience say, "Fortunate is the childhood that does not disgrace its old age." If I had erred in my judgment of the Torah, I returned to the truth later and showed that the people of Israel and the Torah are one. Nor do I continue to condemn the education my father gave me. I have rectified some of its shortcomings in the last four years. Had my father given me another upbringing, I would not be today what I am. Thus the sins of youth are finished and so, too, the way of repentance.

He Was Called Lilienblum

by David Frischman

David Frischman was born in Zgierz, near Lodz, in 1860 and died in Berlin in 1922. He was a Hebrew and Yiddish writer, poet, editor, and translator, whose first Hebrew short stories were published by Peretz Smolenskin in *Ha-Shahar* in 1878. Frischman also translated many great works of European literature into Hebrew in an effort to raise literary tastes and standards. His own essays of literary criticism are considered his most enduring contribution to Hebrew and Yiddish letters. The following essay was written shortly after Lilienblum's death.

HE was called Lilienblum and also Zelophehad, the son of Hushim, the One Who Strayed. And, I think, some other names — in short, in my eyes, practically a legendary figure. No wonder, for they told deeds about him that stirred the imagination of a twelve-year-old. Every day a new deed, every day a heroic action. Above all, the persecutions inflicted upon him. He stood in the vanguard of the great war against the rabbis and rabbinism. Because he wanted to reform Judaism, they persecuted him. He was a hero. Once I even dreamed about him. Somehow he became confused in my mind with Martin Luther, burning the papal bull at Wittenberg. Then, suddenly he was not Luther but Judah, of the extraordinary physical exploits in *Sefer ha-Yashar,* lifting a hundred-pound rock and crushing it. But as soon as I looked closely, he turned out to be an African-Indian chief.

I had not yet read a single word he had written. *Ha-Boker Or* ("The Morning Light") was publishing, in installments, Reuben Asher Braudes' novel *Ha-Dat ve-ha-Hayim* ("Religion and Life"). It was said Moses Leib Lilienblum was the model for Samuel, the novel's hero, in his war against the Shulhan Arukh.

About that time I came across a copy of *Hattot Ne'urim.* I read it and could not fall asleep. It was perhaps the most extraordinary confession of a human being I had read in all my life. No one had ever been so sincere and openhearted. The fundamental trait of the book was its honesty, practically to fanaticism. Not yet thirty, he had written this book out of despair. All his ships had sunk, all his suns had set. There was no youth, there was no beauty, no haskala, and no fight. There was nothing to fight for. Again I recognized the same trait: also in his despair he came near fanaticism. The book attracted and repelled. Attractive were its wonderful structure and particularly its honesty; repellent, the extremism of his despair. For the world was beautiful and I loved it; youth was beautiful, the cause for which I fought and the combat itself were beautiful, and I loved them. I felt, obscurely, that I was of another world, that one must take life somewhat lightly. He took this hurly-burly so seriously, so narrowly and so naïvely.

Then somewhere I came across several volumes of *Ha-Melits* and eagerly pounced upon his *Orhot ha-Talmud* and other of his writings. What a warrior, what a combative nature! He was a revolutionary to the core, every word a bomb, every sentence a revolt. And what sacrificial honesty! If he would ever come to believe he had assaulted windmills, he might kill himself. Once again I observed this extraordinary trait: he was in fact a fanatic. It does not much matter whether he was a fanatic when he headed the yeshiva in Vilkomir or when he was embattled for youth and freedom. The main thing was that basically he was not a free spirit, nor had he ever been one. His mind was always subject to the despotism of an idea which tyrannized him. I did not know then that I would, in time to come, have the chance of observing him as a fanatic, dedicated to a cause until mania.

I read *Kehal Refa'im,* which Smolenskin had compared to Dante's *Divine Comedy.* I read his poems and his essays — everything he wrote. No, his was not a creative mind, but he was a fighter for his causes, and a fanatic.

I was drawn back to *Hattot Ne'urim.* I read it twice and then a third time. Inwardly antagonistic, yet I read page after page and suffered with the unfortunate author as with no other author. Just as one of his worlds collapses, another arises. His faith dies within him, and he consigns it to the grave. An ideal of his utters its death rattle, and he lays it to rest in the cold ground. He had a beloved and then she was gone; he finds poetry, and then there is no poetry. There was a Day of Atonement, and he wanted to believe and to pray, yet he could not. Only Nahman Krochmal remains, with his *Guide to the Perplexed of Our Time.* Yet even this tree begins to lose its leaves, to bow and fall. Silence is everywhere. Only a melancholy breeze stirs and a yellow leaf falls to the ground. Everything becomes empty, bare.

Fear for the end of this unfortunate overtakes the reader. For he was no Solomon Maimon, whose cynicism helped him survive his hardships. He was basically honest and sound. But he could not live without something affirmative. Would he go tomorrow to the nearest body of water and drown himself? Would he, like that one, knock at some Lutheran pastor's door?

Suddenly, practically overnight, the incredible happened. Practically overnight, I said. It took one day, not two. He became the main pillar of that society. Hundreds of people heard about it and clucked in amazement. But the incredible was not at all incredible. It was actually the natural consequence and only solution. He was looking for something positive, something to clutch lest he drown. One quiet evening he read Dr. Pinsker's famous pamphlet. From everywhere came the terrifying reports of the pogroms. The heart ached to hear them. Dr. Pinsker had a marvelous plan for self-emancipation. Lilienblum clutched at it like a drowning man. This was positive, something to live for.

This, the only positive cause he had, he defended until his last breath with a fanatic's zeal. He ceased to exist as a person, existing merely as defender and guardian of the only positive cause he ever had. He was a kind of Persian dervish. His love of Zion had something of a religion about it.

I used to clash with him. Now I bow my head in respect for his limitless honesty. Few were as sincere as he.

8   Lion of Poets, Pilot of Reform:
Judah Leib Gordon

JUDAH LEIB GORDON was born in Vilna in 1831 and died in St. Petersburg in 1892. The leading Hebrew poet of his time, he helped to renew the Hebrew language. A graduate of the government-sponsored rabbinical seminary in Vilna, he taught many years in government schools for Jewish children. In 1872, he became the secretary of the Society for the Promotion of Culture among the Jews of Russia in St. Petersburg.

He was a leading advocate of reform in Judaism and of secular education, contributing articles to the Hebrew and Russian press on these subjects and satirizing his Orthodox opponents. In 1879, because of his advocacy of reform in Judaism and of modernism in Jewish communal affairs, some hasidim denounced him to the Tsarist police as a traitor. He and his family were imprisoned for about six weeks and then exiled to northern Russia for some months until their innocence was proven.

Upon his return to St. Petersburg in 1880 he joined Alexander Zederbaum as co-editor of *Ha-Melits,* where he remained until 1888.

As a token of appreciation for his services in support of the Russian government's educational policy toward Jews, Gordon received the title of "Honorary Citizen." The following selection is an extract from his diary.

An Entry in My Diary
by *Judah Leib Gordon*

To record daily events is no idle matter or easy task, for as soon as the daily entries become perfunctory, behold, it is a burden on one's neck and an oppressive weight. At times, out of sheer laziness and negligence, the diarist will not notice the beam of an olive press in his eyes; at other times, out of boredom and idleness, his attention will be diverted by tiny splinters and straws or he may strive after wind and follow the east wind, involving himself in abstract matters which have no root or branch in his daily life.

People ask: "If all children are wise, where do the fools forever come from?" The answer is clear: The fools are the wise children, people who have grown physically but not mentally — physically matured, but with childish minds. All children are wise and good in the eyes of their parents, but the teachers and tutors are to blame for not knowing how to develop the child's intellectual potentialities step by step with his physical growth. Nature endowed the child with a fair share of endowments, but bad education spoiled them.

Many ask: The biblical verse says that all the nations shall say, "surely this great nation is a wise and understanding people," yet we hear the name of Israel reviled by all the peoples around them, who say the Jews are foolish. What, then, became of Moses' blessing? Here also the teachers who were supposed to help are to blame. The Torah — whose original substance and natural character was in the image of our people — gave us statutes and ordinances which truly embodied its wisdom and understanding "in the sight of the people." But wisdom and understanding were sufficient only as long as our nation was as a child among nations themseves children. These did not have the intellectual aptitudes nor the attractive ethical inclinations that our child had. But when they became men, their mental development progressed with their physical growth. They made up for their lack of talent by perseverance and diligence, perfecting themselves partly by their own efforts and partly by emulating our child. But our child remained a child even in growing up, because his teachers and mentors did not attempt to harmonize his mental abilities with his physical ones in order to develop him. They boasted of his natural abilities, engaged him in trivialities and childish activities. For this reason, until today the nations of the world speak of Israel as the "youth."

What is this great fear and trembling among the educators for any reform of religion? The major principle, "He shall not change his God, nor shall he change his religion," and "this Torah shall not be changed, nor shall there be another Torah," would not be invalidated by reform or by changing it for the better, in order to attune to the requirements of modern times, for reform does not mean change or substitution. The verbs *to change* and *to substitute* mean to put one thing in place of another but not to change the nature of the thing itself. The Scripture says about sacrificial animals "He shall not change it, nor substitute a good one for a bad, nor a bad one for a good." Is it conceivable that it is forbidden to fatten up the animal in order to improve it? Our sages also maintained that under no circumstances should the cattle be changed or substituted, but they do not imply that the cattle must not be improved.

Yet the pious in our midst, who flee from the slightest reform in religion as from a lion, are not quite as concerned about the Torah as they are about the Talmud and its regulations. The Talmud itself says that "the Talmudic sages were stricter about their own teachings than about those of the Torah," for they themselves changed or completely abolished many laws of the Torah. But no decision even by one of the later sages has been nullified by our contemporary rabbis. They cite the Mishna that no court of law may upset the ruling of another court, unless it surpasses the latter in wisdom and in the number of judges.

What actually is the essence of the Talmud that we guard and cherish its contents far more than the teachings of Moses? For what have we sacrificed ourselves and endured sufferings and harsh persecutions for generations? What is it that, if touched, is as if the pupil of our eye were touched? Those who walk in darkness say the Talmud is above life itself. It is the tree of life to all who grasp it, and each one who partakes of its fruit will live forever, whereas life itself is but a withered tree that does not bear fruit, whose leaves have shrivelled and whose every endeavor fails. But to the clear-sighted, the Talmud was as preserving salt which helped safeguard the existence of Jewry, much as salt is used to preserve fatty meat for the winter. But when mealtime comes, who would be so foolish as to serve the meat without rinsing the salt off, leaving only a trace to make it palatable?

Can we really continue the same way of life by the waters of Europe and other countries that we led by the waters of Babylon? Are the philosophies and teachings of ancient times appropriate for the times we live in and are they adapted to the present status of knowledge? The Talmud is dear to us as an ancient book, a precious chronicle of historic events, a source for enriching our language (of course, purifying and sifting it with thirteen sieves). It is as important and valuable as the poultice on a wound. But if the Talmud with its pedantry, with its overlapping additions and rabbinic commentaries, becomes a guide for our people, then we will be like those who follow the pillar of clouds in the night and we will wander bewildered in the world. We shall be sealed forever in the desert without hope of ever returning to the world around us, to a life of bodily vigor.

Do you know who are the most vocal opponents of religious reform? Those who have liberated themselves from the burden of the Torah and its law. One of my colleagues, who shared an office with me, expounded on the merits of the laws regarding permitted and forbidden foods while eating a breakfast of non-kosher food. He argued that there was no need for change and reform — just leave the Jews alone and they will correct themselves. The theory of these people follows the well-known theory that "let the drunkard alone, he will fall of himself." I do not deny that some orthodox rabbis take the same position when they see how free the present generation is, everyone doing as he pleases. The rabbis make no attempt to introduce useful reforms to lighten the burden, that our religion should not be a millstone.

Are they right who speak this way? Woe to the tenant of a house where the ceiling is cracked, and the builder does not repair it, because it will eventually collapse, and thereby cease to be a danger!

I Meet the Mountain Lion
by Gershom Bader

Gershom Bader was born in Cracow in 1868 and died in New York in 1953. Though he came of a family with great rabbinic prestige, he rejected traditional Judaism, becoming first a Hebrew teacher and later a Hebrew and Yiddish journal-

ist. From 1894 until 1912, when he lived and
worked in Lemberg, he played a considerable role
in the social and literary life of Galician Jews as
writer, lecturer, and editor. In 1904, in Lemberg,
he founded the *Togblat,* the first Yiddish daily
newspaper in Austria. In 1912, he came to New
York, where he continued his career as a journalist. His encounter with Gordon is described in his
memoirs.

AFTER I began to teach Hebrew in the Cracow seminary I used to be
seized with travel fever in the summers. So it happened that in August
1891 I was in Berlin, where *Ha-Maggid,* the oldest Hebrew weekly, was
published. Visiting the editorial office, I learned that the great Judah Leib
Gordon had come from St. Petersburg for an operation and was now recu-
perating in a Berlin hotel.

In those days everyone thought Gordon was the mountain lion of Hebrew poetry. To me, he was the modern Judah ha-Levi, as Heine had described him: whose soul God had kissed when He created it, a kiss which
resounded in all his poems. Gordon's poems used to inspire us, and we
recited them as if they were pious hymns. Once, when I and some other
young maskilim spent the Ninth of Ab together, so that the more radical
maskilim would not know we kept the fast and ridicule us for that, we
recited Gordon's "In the Depths of the Sea," about the banishment of the
Jews from Spain, and "In the Lion's Jaw," about the Jewish war with the
Romans. I shed more tears over these than do pious Jews chanting the
lament of the Ten Slain Martyrs.

I decided to visit Gordon. He had been the first to accept a piece of
mine for publication in *Ha-Melits,* and he had written me a friendly letter
commending my Hebrew style.

We talked about many things. He dazzled with flashes of wit and *bon
mots.* About Baron Horace Günzburg, he said: "A Petersburg philanthropist; when you come close, the chill can freeze you in the middle of the
summer." About the Orientalist, Professor Abraham Harkavy: "The
difference between me and Harkavy is that he is interested in how Jews
once lived, and I want to know how they live today. He exhumes the dead
of the past to find out if they were buried in a large shawl (*tallit*) or a small
one (*arba kanfot*); I want to know if they are hungry or well fed."

I asked his opinion about the Hibbat Zion movement, for it was
thought Gordon opposed it. But he denied this. It was just that he feared

the rabbis would exploit the idea of Hibbat Zion to usurp authority in Palestine. All his life he had fought against rabbinic domination of Jewish life. He was uneasy that the Jews, coming to Palestine, instead of finding refuge, would be trapped in observing new commandments which the Bible made dependent on living in the land of Israel.

Then I asked him about political conditions in Russia. He cautiously weighed his words. He told me about his troubles in 1879 when, because his enemies spread lies about him, he had been interned 120 days in a distant Siberian village. Then he said: "Historical births are like natural births: they cannot occur painlessly. The arrival of a new historical period means the destruction of the present one, for without strife and conflict, historical progress is inconceivable."

A few days later I visited Gordon again. That day the news of the death of the great Jewish historian Professor Heinrich Graetz in Munich had just arrived. I brought Gordon this news. It stunned and depressed him. He lay in bed in stricken silence. Then he asked me to hand him pencil and paper. On his back, he wrote a poem on Graetz's death, which he called "Words from a Sickbed."

9   A Pilgrimage to Peretz Smolenskin
by Samuel Leib Citron

PERETZ SMOLENSKIN, Hebrew novelist and editor, was born in Monastyrshchina, province of Mohilev, in 1842 and died at Meran, Austria, in 1885. Brought up in poverty, he received a traditional Jewish education and studied at a yeshiva. Then he stayed at the Habad hasidic court of Menahem Mendel of Lubavich, but after some months turned his back on the movement. He went to Mohilev, then to Odessa, earning his way as synagogue singer, preacher, and Hebrew teacher, all the while learning modern European languages and gleaning some general secular education.

Determined to publish a Hebrew journal, but unable to secure a permit in Russia, he made his way, via Germany and Prague, to Vienna. In 1869, his monthly journal, Ha-Shahar, began to appear, continuing until 1884, shortly before his untimely death from tuberculosis at forty-three. Besides editing Ha-Shahar, Smolenskin wrote several Hebrew novels, the most noteworthy a lengthy fictional autobiography, Ha-To'eh be-Darke ha-Hayim ("Astray on the Paths of Life").

Smolenskin represented a new generation of Russian maskilim, rejecting the influence of the Berlin haskala, repudiating the Mendelssohnian concept of Jews only as a religious group, decrying the assimilation that the Berlin Enlighteners and their Russian imitators had advocated or encouraged. (Gottlober, one of his targets, founded *Ha-Boker Or* largely to combat Smolenskin's views and defend his own.) From his knowledge of Jewish history, Smolenskin advanced a theory of Jewish national identity transcending religion, which logically led to his espousal of a revived Hebrew language and literature and of the Hibbat Zion movement. Thus he helped to restore a Jewish dimension in the secularizing process by introducing Jewish national, albeit non-religious, elements in the outlook of the modern Jew.

Samuel Leib Citron, prolific Hebrew and Yiddish essayist, novelist, and popularizer, was born in Minsk in 1860 and died in Vilna in 1930. The following selection has been taken from his memoirs of Yiddish and Hebrew writers.

WHILE I was studying at the yeshiva at Volozhin — I was about thirteen —I began corresponding with Peretz Smolenskin, editor of the Hebrew monthly, *Ha-Shahar*. I had just begun reading, surreptitiously of course, the books of the haskala. One of the earliest to come into my hands was Smolenskin's novel *Kevurat Hamor* ("The Donkey's Burial"), depicting the social life of Russian Jews. It enchanted me. From then on, Smolenskin became my hero. The yeshiva ceased to interest me, and I began thinking about a general education. About this I corresponded with Smolenskin. A little later, I visited him in Vienna.

My first visit fell on the first day of Shavuot, the Feast of Weeks. It was so memorable that I recall it until today.

As I came close to Smolenskin's house, I grew excited and my heart thumped wildly. My emotional state was like that of a person approaching the threshold of his holy of holies. The moment the maid at the door said "Mr. Smolenskin is not at home," I felt relieved, as if a heavy stone rolled off my heart. But Mrs. Smolenskin heard me and invited me into her husband's study. She said he ought to be arriving shortly. There I found two youngish men and one older one. The younger men were the Socialists Aaron Samuel Lieberman and Eliezer Zukerman. The older man was the apostate Isaac Salkinson, an outstanding Hebrew stylist famous for his translations of Shakespeare.

Salkinson and Lieberman were playing chess; Zukerman was following the game. Salkinson kept creasing his brow, racking his brain, pondering every move. Lieberman moved with ease and speed, routing the enemy from one position after another. He conquered Salkinson's knights one by one, captured his bishop, was poised to take his queen, all the while humming an aria, but ending with the strains of Kol Nidre.

Salkinson made a bad move from which he could not extricate himself. He became rattled and wanted to replay his last move.

The doorbell rang. I became tense. Smolenskin came in and, behind him, an old man, his coat cut long, his face waxen. The old man had been the head of the yeshiva in Shklov where Smolenskin had studied as a boy and which he immortalized in his autobiographical novel *Ha-To'eh be-Darke ha-Hayim*. He had come to Vienna for medical consultation — he had stomach cancer. Smolenskin had taken him to see a renowned specialist.

Screwing up my courage, I haltingly introduced myself to Smolenskin, but I could not utter another word. Thinking I was shy before strangers, he took me into another room. There I told him the purpose of my trip to Vienna to seek general education. Then we returned to his study and he introduced me. "This young man has come from the famous yeshiva at Volozhin. You ought to know he is one of our heroes, persecuted by the fanatics for seeking the light."

Lieberman murmured, as if reciting Lamentations, "The hallowed stones are poured out at the head of every street." Then, impassionately, he inveighed: "The yeshivas of Volozhin, Mir, and the others consume the best we have. The young people are buried alive in these deserts without dew or sunlight. We established institutions to study the Torah, but the Torah congests the heart and mind and withers every blossom. We need institutions to educate proud people with uplifted heads who will have the spirit and the courage to oppose the despotic government and the feudal order. I once tried to liberate these unfortunate souls from these dark institutions. When I published my Hebrew proclamation *To the Young Men of Israel,* I had copies distributed among the students at the Volozhin yeshiva. I had hoped that the sharpness of the pamphlet would stir them, touch their hearts, and point them in the direction they ought to take. But weeks passed and months: I had no response from Volozhin. That is the Torah for you!"

"Quite right, quite right," Smolenskin replied somewhat excitably. "Our Torah stands like an iron wall against every destructive theory. As if bearing axes, you come to wreck the existing order, but you encounter our Torah, which obstructs your passage and prevents you from putting your thoughts in action. Our Torah is, in biblical epithet, a tree of life, that is, a

Torah of creation, not of demolition. Wherever students of the Torah will be found, you will not gain influence."

Smolenskin then expounded on the meaning of the Torah in the history of the Jewish people. Lieberman tried to interrupt, to argue, but Smolenskin ignored him and continued to develop his subject. His enthusiasm grew and new ideas kept tumbling out of his mouth. He leaped from one era to another, from one problem to another. His large black eyes gleamed like torches. More than an hour passed and still Smolenskin talked. The historian had become an advocate, a prophet.

Salkinson had turned from the chessboard to listen attentively. Zukerman made a sour grimace, biting his upper lip, and looked as if he were sitting on hot coals. Lieberman smiled all the time: he obviously disagreed with everything Smolenskin was saying. The light of pure pleasure was evident only in the parchment face of the old yeshiva principal.

When Smolenskin finished, Lieberman said very calmly, "This is not the time for discussions, especially when these discussions lead nowhere. We have discussed these matters so many times and each one sticks to his opinion. But I must say one thing briefly: We do not demolish, we build. We are building the kingdom of the future." Lieberman did not speak briefly, and I have long forgotten the details of what he said. I remember only that he cited the Bible and the Talmud to prove that the fundamental principles of Marxism had their origins in the Torah of Moses.

"I worried," said the old yeshiva principal, "that I would have to spend Shavuot away from home, without words of Torah. But here I found what I did not expect: learned Jews in a dispute about the Torah, citing Talmud and the commentaries."

Ha-Shahar, the monthly which Smolenskin began to publish in the late sixties, was an extraordinary happening in the life of that Jewish intelligentsia which resisted the assimilatory currents and heeded the Hebrew word. For the Orthodox youth educated in the yeshivas and prayer houses, *Ha-Shahar* was practically a revolutionary upheaval. Every copy in the hands of these young people was like a match put to a powder keg. *Ha-Shahar* revolutionized their minds, undermined old ideas infested with traditional moldiness, sti:.ulated them to new ideas. It brought light into the most dismal Jewish byways, rescuing thousands of talented young people who otherwise would have exhausted their talents in sterile pastimes.

This was why the fanatical guardians of traditional Jewry vented their wrath on *Ha-Shahar* more than on other forbidden books. Woe to the yeshiva student caught with *Ha-Shahar*! He took a drubbing, he suffered various indignities (his "eating days" were withdrawn). Sometimes he was even expelled from the yeshiva. Yet despite their vigorous efforts, the officials of the yeshiva failed to bar *Ha-Shahar*. When they chased it from one door, it came in through seven others. There was not one yeshiva in all the Russian Pale to which Smolenskin's *Ha-Shahar* had not found its way. The young people devised cunning ways to deceive their guardians. They read *Ha-Shahar* on the Gemara and under the Gemara and sat up nights with it. Today this seems incredible. Yet the Orthodoxy considered *Ha-Shahar* as unclean, feeding on poison emanating from the anti-divine, while the young people looked upon it with piety and love, as something sacred.

This piety and love they conferred also on *Ha-Shahar*'s founder. They idealized and idolized Smolenskin. He became their symbol of beauty and ennoblement. They deluged him with letters about the problems that tormented them. Some dreamed of going to Vienna to meet Smolenskin personally. Some young people, intoxicated by *Ha-Shahar*, set out on foot for Vienna. More than once, Smolenskin would find on his doorstep unknown young people who had come from the distant Russian Pale to meet him and hear from his own mouth advice about the future course of their lives.

When I was in Vienna, I met several such talented young people. Smolenskin showed them great cordiality, enrolled them in various schools, prevailed upon welfare institutions and well-to-do persons to give them grants. With his help, some of these young people made brilliant careers for themselves.

Some of the young people he helped brought him anguish. Life in the bustling Austrian capital, with all its attractions, had a demoralizing effect: they stopped going to classes or study and went instead in pursuit of frivolous amusements and cheap pleasures.

To guarantee *Ha-Shahar*'s continued publication, Smolenskin used to serve as a guide for wealthy Russian Jews visiting Vienna. He used to show them the sights of the city, escort them to museums and theaters, to the large stores, and even to renowned medical specialists. The rich tourists also asked his advice about private matters and especially about how to educate their children. I remember one incident involving a well-to-do father and daughter. They came from Mohilev, where the flight from Jewishness to the radical movement was epidemic. The father had brought his daughter to Vienna to hear Smolenskin's advice. But in Vienna, by prearrangement, she met one of her Populist friends and they fled to Switzerland. The father complained bitterly that Smolenskin, who taught everyone else wisdom, could not prevent his daughter's flight.

Smolenskin's answer was calm: "If as you say, I teach, I teach the fathers rather than the children. But not all fathers have heeded me. You, for example, who read *Ha-Shahar*, certainly ought to know my views on Jewish education. But how did you bring up your daughter? You had governesses and tutors, teaching her foreign languages. You sent her to high school, where she learned about other peoples. Did you teach her about our own people? Did you teach her our own language? Did you interest her in our own history? Did you want her to know about our own people and our own national aspirations? To whom, then, should you bring your complaints, if not to yourself?"

III

The Quest for Education

10 My Near-Conversion

by Solomon Maimon

SOLOMON MAIMON, philosopher and skeptic, was born at Nieswiez, White Russia, in 1754 and died at Siegersdorf, Lower Silesia, in 1800.

His extraordinary autobiography depicts his life's wanderings in quest of education and learning. After mastering much of rabbinic literature, he immersed himself in the study of the Kabbala and mysticism, and then, having learned some German, he turned to science. His pursuit of knowledge offended his orthodox in-laws (he had, as was the custom, been married at twelve) and the Jewish community that took him for an unbeliever.

After wandering for two years, sometimes in the company of a professional beggar, he came to Berlin, where Moses Mendelssohn, recognizing his extraordinary talents, received him well. In Berlin, Maimon studied philosophy and wrote critical philosophic studies, making his reputation with an analysis of Kant. But after a while, Maimon's scandalous profligate conduct alienated his friends and supporters. He left Berlin and resumed his wanderings. He returned to Berlin in 1790, after Mendelssohn's death. Some

time thereafter, a wealthy Silesian nobleman, Count Adolph Kalkreuth, who admired Maimon's writings, offered him the refuge of his estate at Siegersdorf. There, Maimon spent the last years of his life in productive philosophic work.

Despite his flight from Jewish tradition and a near conversion, described in the following selection from his autobiography, Maimon remained a Jew, who, though himself unbelieving, regarded Judaism as a more ethical religion than Christianity. But his marginal Jewish status was acknowledged and perpetuated when the Jewish community of Glogau buried him at the edge of the cemetery. He was the first modern East European Jew who, emerging from the confining world of traditional and obscurantist Judaism into the brilliant glare of the world of high scholarship, philosophy, and rationalism, made a name for himself in that world. Yet few philosophers today recall his contribution. Solomon Maimon is remembered rather as that brilliant and erratic wandering Jew who found no secure place in whatever society he lived.

I TRAVELED back to Hamburg, but there I fell into the deepest distress. I lodged in a miserable house, had nothing to eat, and did not know what to do. I had received too much education to return to Poland, to spend my life in misery without rational occupation or society, and to sink back into the darkness of superstition and ignorance, from which I had delivered myself with so much labor. On the other hand, I could not reckon to succeed in Germany, owing to my ignorance of the language, as well as of the manners and customs of the people to which I had never been able to adapt myself properly. I had learned no particular profession, I had not distinguished myself in any special science, I was not even master of any language in which I could make myself perfectly intelligible. It occurred to me, therefore, that there was no alternative left but to embrace the Christian religion and get myself baptized in Hamburg. Accordingly, I resolved to go to the first clergyman I should come across and inform him of my resolution, as well as of my motives for it, without any hypocrisy — in a truthful and honest fashion. But as I could not express myself well orally, I put my thoughts into writing in German with Hebrew characters, went to a schoolmaster, and got him to copy it in German characters. The purport of my letter was in brief as follows:

I am a native of Poland, belonging to the Jewish nation, destined by my education and studies to be a rabbi; but in the thickest darkness I have perceived some light. This has induced me to search further after light and truth and to free myself completely from the darkness of superstition and ignorance. As this could not be attained in my native place, I went to Berlin, where through the support of some enlightened men of our nation I studied for some years — not indeed with any plan, but merely to satisfy my thirst for knowledge. But as our nation is unable to use not only such planless studies but even those based on the most perfect plan, it cannot be blamed for becoming tired of them, and pronouncing their encouragement to be useless. I have therefore resolved, in order to secure temporal as well as eternal happiness, which depends on the attainment of perfection, and in order to become useful to myself as well as others, to embrace the Christian religion. The Jewish religion, it is true, comes, in its articles of faith, nearer to reason than Christianity. But in practical use, the latter has an advantage over the former; and since morality, which consists not in opinions but in actions, is the aim of all religion, clearly the latter comes nearer than the former to this aim. Moreover, I esteem the mysteries of the Christian religion for that which they are, that is, allegorical representations of the truths that are most important for man. Thus I make my faith in them harmonize with reason, but I cannot believe them literally. I beg therefore most respectfully an answer to the question, whether after this confession I am worthy of the Christian religion or not. If I am, I am prepared to carry my proposal into effect; but if not, I must give up all claim to a religion which enjoins me to lie, that is, to deliver a confession of faith which contradicts my reason.

The schoolmaster to whom I dictated this was astonished at my audacity; never before had he listened to such a confession of faith. He shook his head with concern, interrupted the writing several times, and became doubtful whether the mere copying was not itself a sin. With great reluctance he copied it, merely to get rid of it. I went then to a prominent clergyman, delivered my letter, and asked for a reply. He read it with great attention, was equally astonished, and on finishing began to converse with me.

"So," he said, "your intention is to embrace the Christian religion merely in order to improve your temporal circumstances."

"Excuse me, Herr Pastor," I replied, "I think I have made it clear enough in my letter that my object is the attainment of perfection. For this, it is true, the removal of all hindrances and the improvement of my external circumstances are an indispensable condition. But this condition is not the chief end."

"But," said the pastor, "do you not feel any inclination to the Christian religion without reference to any external motives?"

"I should be telling a lie if I were to give you an affirmative answer."

"You are too much of a philosopher," replied the pastor, "to be able to become a Christian. Reason has taken the upper hand with you, and faith must accommodate itself to reason. You hold the mysteries of the Christian religion to be mere fables, and its commands to be mere laws of reason. For the present, I cannot be satisfied with your confession of faith. You should therefore pray to God, that He may enlighten you with His grace and endow you with the spirit of true Christianity; and then come to me again."

"If that is the case," I said, "then I must confess, Herr Pastor, that I am not qualified for Christianity. Whatever light I may receive, I shall always make it luminous with the light of reason. I shall never believe that I have fallen upon new truths, if it is impossible to see their connection with the truths already known to me. I must therefore remain what I am — a stiff-necked Jew. My religion enjoins me to *believe* nothing, but to *think* the truth and to practice goodness. If I find any hindrance in this from external circumstances, it is not my fault. I do all that lies in my power."

With this I bade the pastor goodbye.

11   My Educational Mission in Russia
by Max Lilienthal

MAX LILIENTHAL, rabbi and educator, was born in Munich in 1814 and died in Cincinnati in 1882. He was invited to Riga to become principal of a newly established Jewish school which opened in January, 1840 and also to be preacher of a congregation there. A German Jew guiding German, Russian, and Polish Jews, Lilienthal introduced Reform practices in his congregation and conducted a modern, Western school. His reputation had become known among Tsarist officials and in December, 1841, Lilienthal was invited to undertake an official mission on behalf of Count Uvarov, Minister of Education, to lay the groundwork for government-sponsored Jewish secular schools. That mission is described in the following excerpts from his memoirs.

Aware finally that the despotic Tsarist government was using him to further its program of forced assimilation without giving the Jews elementary civic rights, Lilienthal left Russia suddenly and went to the United States where he was active as rabbi, author, and communal leader.

TOWARD the end of the year 1841, I received a communication, addressed to me by Prince Shirinski-Shikhmatov, the Director of the Department of Public Instruction, informing me that Nisan Rosenthal of Vilna having represented to the minister the possibility of establishing another flourishing Jewish school in that city, His Excellency ordered me to accompany him thither as soon as Rosenthal would call on me, and then to report to him on the progress I had attained. A week afterward, Rosenthal, a modernized Polish Jew, a very handsome man indeed, entered my room. He had just been decorated by the emperor with the golden medal for some services rendered to the crown, and tried, like the politicians in this country, to gain some distinction and to make a living by all kinds of schemes and plans. He stood not in the best graces of his coreligionists, being considered as one of the new lights or Berliners, as the reformers, adjudged to be the followers of Mendelssohn in Berlin, are called in Vilna.

Vilna, even in Poland, is called *ir ve-em be-yisrael*, the metropolis of Israel! And when Napoleon I, on a Friday afternoon in 1812, having entered the gates of this city rode through its streets, he exclaimed to his marshals: "Gentlemen, I think we are in Jerusalem." Coming from Germany, where in all the cities the Jews are in the minority, entirely disappearing amongst the larger majority of their Christian fellow citizens, I did not know what to make out of this swarming beehive of Jews. I, too, believed myself to be in Palestine instead of in Russia, so entirely and thoroughly Jewish appeared to me the city of Vilna.

On a Thursday night an assembly of the representatives of the congregation was convened in order to hear the propositions I had to make to them by order of the government. A committee led me into the vestry, where I found some hundred men assembled, all dressed in their *zhubetses* and their fur caps. I felt so lonesome in the midst of these strange faces — the only *daytshl* in the crowd of Polish Jews. The president of the congregation, a wealthy man, but of a very insignificant appearance, a great Talmudist, but without any other education, who, on account of his riches and his fanatically orthodox ideas exercised a great influence, welcomed me in the name of the illustrious congregation, gave me his chair, and requested me to state the purpose of my visit with which I had honored them.

I stated to the meeting that my visit was of no official character. They were well aware that the emperor had appointed a special committee of ministers to take into consideration the affairs of the Jews from a religious as well as from a political and educational point of view, that the imperial government was determined upon introducing a wholesome change and that its intentions could not be eluded this time. Minister Uvarov, a friend of the Jews, had ordered me to tell my coreligionists that they should not let the opportunity presented to them escape as they had done in the time of the late Emperor Alexander, when the delegates called to the capital were dismissed with the greatest disgrace to themselves as well as to their constituents; that His Excellency wished the Jews to establish schools in accordance with the spirit of the time and the demands of the age before the government would order and compel them to do so. By such a procedure, they would dispose the government in their favor, and being aware what an immense influence the Jewish metropolis of Vilna exercised upon the Russian Jews in general, he hoped that by setting a glorious example they would take the whole matter into their hands, thereby becoming the benefactors and regenerators of their race.

I had been listened to silently. The younger generation in Vilna, imbued with the progressive spirit of our age and well versed in the Hebrew, Russian, Polish, German, and partly French languages, were enthused by my short address; they hoped to see their favorite dreams and hopes fulfilled at last.

But the elders sat there absorbed in deep contemplation. Some of them, leaning on their silver-adorned staffs or smoothing their long beards, seemed as if agitated by earnest thoughts and justifiable suspicions; others were engaging in a lively but quiet discussion on the principles involved; such put to me the ominous question: "Doctor, are you fully acquainted with the leading principles of our government? You are a stranger; do you know what you are undertaking? The course pursued against all denominations but the Greek proves clearly that the government intends to have but one church in the whole empire; that it has in view only its own future strength and greatness and not our own future prosperity. We are sorry to state that we put no confidence in the new measures proposed by the ministerial council, and that we look with gloomy foreboding into the future."

"I am well aware of your apprehensions," I answered the respectable old man who had been the interpreter of the feelings of the gray-headed and silver-bearded assembly, "and was well informed of all that is going on during my sojourn in Riga. The question we have to consider is this: Can we avoid the threatening danger by the useless answer that we do not want to have anything to do with it? I am convinced that the Jewish affairs are now in such hands that they surely will be acted upon. What will we gain by a willful resistance? We will draw the dissatisfaction of the government upon ourselves, will provoke justifiable ill feeling and merely expose ourselves to dangers still more discouraging. I have pondered upon this subject carefully; but after mature and serious consideration, I have found it best to take this matter at once in our hands, and having established schools according to our plans, our means and under our own superintendency, we will anticipate the measures of the government. By thus presenting our intentions and views in a favorable light, I entertain not the least doubt that our schools will be sanctioned and our plans ratified by the department of public instruction."

"But what guarantee," asked another gentleman, "can you offer us that our religion will not be encroached upon?"

"Gentlemen," I replied, "born in Russia, you know a great deal better than I that I am unable to offer you any guarantee on the part of the department. The emperor's will reigns supreme and autocratic; he can recall today what he has promised yesterday; he changes his officers and their systems whenever he pleases. How should I, an humble stranger, be able to offer you a guarantee? I am not empowered to do it. All that I can promise you as your coreligionist is that I shall not go a step further in promoting the plans of the government before having obtained the assurance that nothing will be undertaken against our holy religion, that I shall lay down my office as soon as I shall become convinced of the contrary, and that no offense on the part of my brethren shall excuse me for breaking this promise I am giving you in this solemn hour."

This assurance was received with general satisfaction. Some of the members present hurried up to me and shook my hands heartily; others welcomed me in the most friendly manner, and the confidence and good understanding seemed to be restored.

After having passed the whole day examining the schools, I received in the evening an invitation from the *shtot-magid* (chief preacher) of the city to visit him at ten o'clock the same evening. The late hour of the appointment indicated to me that the rabbi wished to know the result of the examination in order to prevent me from making to the government a one-sided or too hasty report. I repaired to his humble rooms at the fixed time. He received me very kindly, and after having entertained me for about half an hour with some Torah, brandy, and cakes, he left the room, inquiring whether all his housemates were already asleep. Being assured that he was safe from all listeners, he took his seat at the oak table opposite my chair and in a low voice began to ask me:

"Well, doctor, you are firmly resolved upon introducing a change in our school system?"

"It is the will of the emperor and the order of the government, rabbi."

"Are you also aware of all the consequences that this change will effect in our religious views?"

"You see specters, rabbi, where there are none. I come from Germany where no one dreams anymore of such an opposition as the Russian Jews make to the establishment of better schools; and having quenched our thirst at the fountain of universal science and knowledge, we feel ourselves as good Jews as you do who are still frightened at the aspect of a *trefa pasul.*"

"You must not suppose, doctor, that I am entirely opposed to the introduction of your sciences. I have studied too frequently the immortal works of Maimonides, Ibn Ezra, and their successors not to be impressed with the importance, usefulness, and necessity of acquiring the knowledge of profane literature; yea, the Talmud itself recommends it highly unto us, and you know that the members of the Sanhedrin must be well versed even in seventy languages. But we are informed by our merchants visiting the large fair at Leipzig that your brethren in Germany deal very slightly with religion, and that the religious commands are not as strictly observed as in this country."

"Rabbi, for all that we have not as many converted Jews as there are in this country. Besides, I have already heard that if a Polish Jew puts off his *zhubetse,* he treats religion with more disdain and disregard than is customary in Germany. But both our arguments lack a solid foundation; there are good and bad men amongst every nation, in every climate and under all circumstances. But granted even that the reform begun in Germany by the great Mendelssohn has led to some lamentable extremes, the false steps taken in the beginning have been remedied long ago, and you may profit by our experience to avoid all injurious extravagances."

"Doctor, I will tell you; we are ashes, all ashes; and as soon as anyone touches us, the whole edifice will crumble to pieces!"

He looked uneasily about after having uttered that gloomy sentence, whilst I stared in his face at this bold and thoughtful expression.

"You are wrong, rabbi, entirely wrong," I continued, interrupting the uncomfortable silence. "Our religion is not ashes; you confound the eternal truth contained in our doctrines with outworn and antiquated ceremonies. They, indeed, are ashes, and whether we touch them or not, time will destroy them, as in Western Europe it has already destroyed a great deal of them. Put those ashes away, and the jewel of our creed shall shine forth in all its brilliancy. We and all mankind will be benefited by the removal of these your ashes."

"But the whole mass of the people will not know how to discern between the ashes and the jewel, dear doctor. If you remove the ashes they will throw away the jewel, and then what will become of our creed for which our ancestors have suffered so much, for which we ourselves undergo such endless tortures, such awful agonies? It will be surrendered in course of time, and will you be the instrument for such a calamitous and sinful destruction?"

"My dear rabbi, I have too high an idea of the eternal truth of our creed to be in the least afraid of such gloomy consequences. Our creed and our people have outlived and outlasted quite other periods than that of a desirable reconciliation with the advancement and enlightenment of our age. I, on my part, consider it a sin to believe and to assert that our creed is not compatible with science and knowledge itself; its principles are light and nothing but undimmed light; its doctrines are true and eternal as God is; how can you suppose for a moment that by the reconciliation with the irrefutable demands of our age the existence of our sacred creed will be endangered? Your Polish rabbis excommunicated the immortal Mendelssohn, when first he published his German translation of the Pentateuch; you cried 'Murder!' when the pious reformer began the immense task of introducing his isolated brethren into the active arena of life; could you stop the onward march of the bold reformer? Could you bring back our brethren in Western Europe to the spirit of bigotry darkness, and isolation which you considered the only safeguard of our creed? His name stands in bold relief before posterity, and the names of all these Jewish inquisitors are forgotten. Are you resolved upon repeating the same fruitless transaction?"

The rabbi sighed and kept silent for some time, absorbed in deep meditation. "But his pupils," he continued, "have become apostates to our creed. Some members of his own family, I have been told, have become converts to Christianity. If apostasy should be the consequence of your proposed reform I, in the name of all my Jewish brethren, protest against it, and prefer our isolated position to all the allurements of civilization."

"Rabbi, you again confound the levity and frivolity of a few with the good and importance of the cause. The mischief, committed at the first outburst of inexperienced and unbridled wantonness and presumptuousness, has been remedied in Germany long ago. A sincere attachment to the creed of our ancestors, a profound knowledge of science and the arts; a readiness to support every good institution, unbounded and unexampled charity, the dear heirloom of Israel, are the principal virtues marking our brethren at present, and there is not the least apprehension that the old blunders will be committed again and again! And the schools we are proposing are the medium by which our brethren in Russia will avoid the reproaches you are making to Mendelssohn's school. Draw up a perfect plan for the proposed schools we intend to establish; appoint such teachers in whose religious views you can put implicit confidence; impress upon the susceptible mind of the young the doctrines of our faith, and you may instruct them afterward in any science you please — there will be no danger to the religion. And if men of your stamp would take the subject of reform into your own hands, men whose orthodoxy no one dares to doubt, men whose profound Talmudical learning fits them for this responsible and enormous task, the people, fully confiding in your integrity, will gladly abide by your decisions. You will lay the cornerstone for the glorious edifice that the future generations will erect. While your present system is unable to stop the wheels of human progress, the course I propose to you will enable you to direct its motions and become the benefactors of your people."

The clock struck midnight. The rabbi rose from his seat. "He sleeps not and slumbers not, the Guardian of Israel," he said. "Into His hands I confide the future of my brethren. He knows best how to accomplish His end." And shaking my hand heartily, he bade me good-night.

12   From Shtetl to the Capital
by Lev Ossipovich Mandelstamm

LEV OSSIPOVICH MANDELSTAMM, educator and scholar, was born in Zhagory, in Lithuania, in 1809 and died in St. Petersburg in 1889. He was the first Russian Jew to complete a Russian university.

His early marriage having been terminated by divorce because his pursuit of education made him appear free-thinking to his wife's family, Mandelstamm then entered the University of Moscow, later transferred to St. Petersburg, and in 1844 received the bachelor's degree in philology. In 1845, he succeeded Lilienthal as advisor to Count Uvarov on Jewish education, holding this position until 1857, while he also wrote and edited texts for use in Jewish schools.

His translation of the Bible into Russian (twenty-four volumes), with notes, and four volumes of extracts from Maimonides' *Yad ha-Hazaka* in a German translation which he supervised, were published by the Russian government. He also wrote poetry and articles. After many unsuccessful business ventures, he died poor and forgotten. His library was sold to the New York Public Library and became the nucleus of its Jewish division.

Mandelstamm became an educated man and tried to serve the Russian Jews as he understood their needs. His autobiography, from which the following selection is taken, depicts his attempt to reconcile the apparent irreconcilables: his loyalty to the Jews and pity for their social and economic backwardness with his loyalty to the greater Russia, its culture and society. He remained marginal in both worlds and is now remembered only as the first Jew to complete a Russian university.

I WAS born July 11, 1809, in the little town of Novoye Zhagory located on the border between the provinces of Courland and Vilna. Although the town was in the Vilna province, its culture was distinctly that of Courland; hence, I have been in the habit of considering myself a Courlander. My mother was a simple, good-natured Jewish woman; my father, a strong-minded individual with a passion for work. Having had occasion, frequently, to be in Germany on business, he had observed how beautifully Judaism could be combined with education — that education which the Jews of western Russia continue to harass.

My older brothers profited by my father's enlightenment; had circumstances permitted, they might have been able to give me an education that would have been consistent with my personal inclinations and gifts. But the struggle for a livelihood — Scylla and Charybdis for Jewish talents — deprived me of both my father's supervision and my brothers' instruction for they were forced to earn their living far from home and family.

Thus, despite my parents' goodwill in the matter, I had no choice but to follow the example of all my friends: besides having each day to study the Bible in the German translation by Mendelssohn (which, however, I did only casually and superficially), I had to study Talmud, literally night and day, as is the custom among Jews in western Russia. So it was that by the age of twelve, I simultaneously acquired my reputation as a genius and the symptoms of tuberculosis.

But what I lacked by way of formal education, I acquired partly by chance. From childhood, I used to converse with the army officers and, in general, with all the upper-class Christians who frequented our billiard room, the only one in town. They knew about me because of my skill in chess, a game I handled rather well for a small fellow. Their acquaintance was valuable to me mostly because it put me in touch with something new, unconstrained and yet refined.

As I said, my health had deteriorated. Upon the doctors' recommendations, I was released from the burden of school, of Talmud. It is to their recommendations that I owe my thorough grounding in Hebrew literature, a subject thought to be extraneous for a student of Gemara and not worth wasting much time on. But having discovered a new tree of knowledge in the magazine *Ha-Me'assef*, known to us because of the renewed interest in Hebrew literature, I, like our Biblical ancestor Adam, obeyed the charmed half of my self — my sensitivity; tasted the wine of heavenly fruit — enlightenment; and began to know good and evil. It goes without saying, there were people then who believed the Satan-serpent had transformed himself into *Ha-Me'assef* and corrupted my soul.

My ideas about literature then were both wild and shallow. I read the works of our writers like a young girl without critical judgment but with a feeling of conviction to guide me, and I was convinced that I could, and indeed should write something. I wrote countless graceless verses and prose pieces in Hebrew, injecting into them my own childish logic and rabbinic-style casuistic reasoning.

When I regained my health, I took an entirely different view of the sacred Talmud. No longer satisfied with its conclusions and inferences, I searched in Talmud for unity and order. And I gave my teachers no rest until they had sought help from Moses Maimonides. But the study of Maimonides entailed Talmudic laws and pure theology — theosophy, to be more exact — while I, understanding only the practical aspects and not the system of *A Guide to the Perplexed*, withdrew more and more in my thinking from the blind piety of my teachers. Soon I moved on from theology to philosophy, a field of study that has so frequently been ill used by half-educated people. After long and difficult interpretations of the mathematical and astronomical points in Talmud and in Maimonides, I began to study algebra and geometry with a Jewish friend of my older brothers. But scarcely had six months gone by, when my teacher was obliged to put his algebraic formulas to practice — that is, to keep his father's accounts. Since I had just come across a Russian grammar in Hebrew in Vilna, I gave up mathematics, plunged into this erroneous grammar, learned it by heart, and forgot it.

I was fourteen years old at the time and reputed to be quite the philologist, since I could read the alphabets of three languages, besides Hebrew. My family's circumstances were such then that my father was forced to put my fame to use and arrange what looked like a good match for me. Some merchant arrived from Keidany, friends gathered, spent a pleasant evening together, and the next morning, as happens among us Jews, not having seen or spoken to my fiancée, I found myself betrothed. But however devastating these early betrothals, mine had fine consequences since it left me free to pursue my studies independent of the teacher of Talmud. And so I set to work immediately reading the literature we termed "Gentile."

The first books I came across were not texts of grammar, rhetoric, or logic but the writings of Mendelssohn and Spinoza. My older brothers had often read these writers, and I wanted to be like them. Thus, having no knowledge of what a system was, I exhausted myself with haphazard attempts to explain philosophical systems to myself. I can still remember the formula I evolved comparing Spinoza's position that "All is one and the one all" with Maimonides' doctrine that all the planets are living beings like ourselves. Having neither guidance nor texts, I wasted my time in profound but wild speculations. Then circumstances left one of my brothers free to give me some supervision and, of course, he saw to it immediately that I gave up philosophy for grammar. Although I felt somewhat offended at first by this loss of scholarly rank, I soon grew sensible, added Tappe's Russian grammar to Gesenius' German, and studied the two languages simultaneously.

But fate had apparently arranged things so that I was always to learn practice before theory. I had not yet finished my work in grammar, when once again I lost my brother's guidance and instruction. The struggle for a livelihood had taken everyone away again. As earlier, the rash thinker charging among philosophies, I now became the reckless linguist assaulting languages. Everyone knows how a self-willed philosopher can blunder, particularly if he has no knowledge of life or method to guide him; similarly, I wasted time in a frenzy of composition instead of putting it to use to get a solid mastery of language. Which is like forcing an unripened flower to open before its time and so to fade.

Later, when writing began to bore me, I took up the New Testament, studied it only so far, lost myself trying to resolve the questions it posed, and once again dropped everything. Such methods of study might have ruined me forever and left me unfit for any sound scholarship, except that I had then reached the age of seventeen and was forced to give up the innocent, pensive life of childhood for the misfortunes of married life, which, nonetheless, had important consequences in deciding my contest with fate.

Until this time I had devoted only three or four hours a day to languages and spent the rest of my time in religious study, which, among us, was considered the only fit occupation for the mind. But in Keidany, where my wife's parents lived, superstition and prejudice were so severe that I was forced to give up these "extraneous" activities and devote myself body and soul to Talmud again. This accomplished the reverse of its purpose. It was as though I had been wound up too tight; I recoiled from everything that seemed to me inimical to study, and there, in Keidany, I first had a sense of my originality and my destiny in life.

But I was alone there; I had no one with whom I could share impressions or exchange experiences, no one I could confide in. My pensiveness expressed itself first in bitter tears, then in melancholy, and, finally, in a serious nervous ailment. Recovering, I felt as though I had awakened from a deep sleep: I saw myself in a new and more attractive light. Through Captain Melyantev of the Artillery, I learned something of literary theory, while Lieutenant Colonel Engelbach encouraged my studies, lent me the latest works in Russian literature, and, what was even more important, supervised my study of French. When my in-laws became indignant with me because of my studies, I left Keidany and returned home to my father and brothers.

Freer now to study languages, I read the classics in Russian, German, and French; I also did work in history, geography, and other basic fields of study. Again the creative urge began to torment me and I wrote articles, dialogues, critical essays, and many short prose pieces of varied quality in the different genres. I became acquainted with the new school of Romanticism, and, together with my brothers, worked on some pieces of Hebrew literature.

Finally, I divorced my wife.

At present I know myself to be a wild, strong, free child of nature. I love my country and the language of my land but, at the same time, I am unfortunate because of the misfortune of all my fellow Jews. Their rigidity has enraged me, because I can see it is destroying their gifts; but I am bound to their affliction by the closest ties of kinship and feeling. My purpose in life is to defend them before the world and to help them to be worthy of that defense. They are neither bad nor beyond improvement, but they are like someone who, desperately ill, clenches his teeth and refuses the medicine with which his physician wishes to cure him. Perhaps one of their own, a son who shares their spirit and has suffered together with them, can make them yield.

Although I have not yet reached Moscow, I cannot refrain from telling you my first impressions of this new and splendid pursuit of mine. My journey has been delayed too long, like a lengthy intermission in the theater before the curtain rises. Hence, without waiting for fate to lift the curtain on my role in Moscow, I will describe some of the circumstances that may explain both my actions and my distress about the future. And let this account be a kind of prologue to the drama of my life.

Three ideals have guided my heart and spirit up to now: enlightenment, my family, and my people. You can, I think, judge the power of the first by my year and one-half struggle with fate during which I, so to speak, stormed the fortress of the university. In part, it was the bold hopes I entertained that made me rush off all alone, with no help or guidance, to a distant, strange, labyrinthian city — as though I were Don Quixote in search of his beloved.

The love I feel for my parents and my brothers is most pure and powerful; without them, my desires would have lost their reverent quality, my joys would have had no charm, and all my hopes would have been empty. Past, present, and future seem to me but the frames for a spiritual picture — my family. They are what fills the emptiness of my space and time; for them I struggle; with them I can find rest. Whatever I may come to have, whatever I become — is theirs. I do not believe that love for a woman will ever seem as powerful to me as this childlike devotion to my people. And do not think, my reader, that this is simply the intoxication of early youth, from which I have not yet awoken. No, this is genuine love — the kind of love which, though we experience it for just a moment, we retain forever; it is a love that graces our periods of misfortune with fond memories and hopes. Thus, while it makes us suffer here on earth, it is a love that exalts, because it is based on full trust in God.

Finally, the devotion, the compassion — or pity — I feel for my poor people has been a great influence upon my work. The Jews themselves do not sense their misery as keenly as I; their nervous temperaments throw them into a fever, their religion isolates them from the peoples of the world and promises them heavenly paradise. It is the reasonable guardian and physician who alone realizes the danger of their position. Christians cannot know our suffering as fully as I; they know of it through hearsay or reading, as they would a story or a formal document. But I see it and feel it; the story of my people's misery has been inscribed in my heart and soul. If Fate, which has deprived me of the happiness of a home until now, will allow me to help the government educate and improve our Russian Jews, I will not complain that I was born a son of this people.

> Mein Herz, mein Herz,
> Du machst mir Schmerz;
> Du jagst mich 'naus
> Von Vaters Haus;
> Dein Stolz vertrieb
> Von mir die Lieb'
> Ich, armer Mann,
> Was bleibt mir dann
> Zum Gluckesstand?
> Das Vaterland!

I have been in Moscow for more than a month and the month's result is that I was not yet expelled nor have I fled. In the language of the calendar, I survived another thirty days of my bitter life.

An extraordinary result! Truly everything I did this month was concentrated on removing the obstacles in the way of my residence here. I had to struggle with myself, reluctant to degrade myself and beg, as a beggar for alms, for permission to remain here, and finally, as with poor people to try to survive another month.

I have tried to improve myself, to raise myself. This was naïve, childish, natural yet not thought through, for I never considered what would come of raising myself. I came to Moscow with this childish notion. I wanted to reject my experience and solidity as an adult and, childlike, listen to talk about science and poetry. But no one perceived me in my childlike feelings. They accepted me as a thirty-year-old withered ancient (though it was still to take me ten years more to understand Pushkin's poetry). A Jew, and a young one at that, they thought, cannot want to study for the sake of study alone, without any practical purpose. So they asked me why I wanted to study. At first, I could not understand the question, but stared foolishly at the inquirers. Then I thought to tell them that I wanted to become a poet, but that would have appeared even more foolish. Then they asked if I wanted to become a teacher, and that served as my answer. But I could never understand that people studied in order to teach others, and those others study to teach still others and so without end.

Besides all this, my Russian accent was so bad that people were doubly prejudiced toward me — as a Jew boy and an ignoramus.

It would seem then that I had been ill received. But, no, I was received politely. But this politeness which I had to beg for like alms ate away at my heart and wounded my pride. Am I one who needs charity — I, who hope to be the spokesman for my people? They are perhaps a deviant people, but still one of the earliest, ancient peoples of the world.

But I am not one of those patients who ease their pain with groans and sighs. I swallow the pills of circumstance and do not grimace. Fate may oppress me but it will not make a simpleton of me. It may destroy me, but it will not bow me.

At the start, I had reason enough to be dissatisfied with my life here. Instead of poetic tranquility which I had dreamed of, I was burdened with prosaic worries — about a residential passport, a place to live, clothing. Even the university did not at first satisfy me. I looked upon the discipline and formality as compulsion, as a limitation of freedom. The lecture was just the opposite of my simple system of self-education. Besides, it seemed to me that everyone was so busy with important matters of scholarship that I simply did not have the heart to bother them by introducing myself.

All that was at the beginning. Later, everything changed. I came to know several distinguished and friendly professors. My writings, poetry and prose, were praised and I even decided to publish some of my poems.

13　Memoirs of a Grandmother

by Pauline Wengeroff

PAULINE WENGEROFF was born in Bobruysk, White Russia, in 1833 and died in Minsk in 1916. In her life all the major currents affecting Russian Jews were played out: from rabbinic orthodoxy to hasidism, to haskala, to general education, Europeanization and complete secularization, until, finally, the great tragedy of her life — the apostasy of her children.

Herself without influence on her times, or even on her own children, her own life faithfully reflected the centrifugal forces of modernity that whirled around her. That life she described in detail in her memoirs, from which an extract follows. These currents of political and religious liberalism and that pursuit of education and career on the part of middle- and upper-class Jews in this period brought about the collapse, among them, of the traditional Jewish society into which she had been born and the disintegration of the values that that society had cherished.

Born at the beginning of the 1830's in Bobruysk and brought up by strictly observant parents, I was in a position to see the transformation which European education wrought on Jewish family life. I can see how easy it was for our parents to educate us and how hard it was for us, the second generation, to bring up our children. Though we became acquainted with German and Polish literature, we eagerly studied Pentateuch and Prophets, for they gave us pride in our religion and its traditions and bound us to our people. Biblical poetry stamped itself on the untouched childish mind and provided for the days to come chastity and purity, buoyancy and inspiration.

But how hard for us was that great transition period in the sixties and seventies. We had achieved a degree of European education, but we knew of the wide gaps in our knowledge. We did our utmost so that our children would not lack what we had missed. But we overlooked the wisdom of observing moderation. So we have only ourselves to blame for the abyss between us and our children.

We must now obey our children and submit completely to their will, just as once obedience to our parents was inviolable. As once with our parents, so now with our children, we must hold our tongues, and it is harder now than then. When our parents talked, we listened respectfully, as now we listen, in pride and joy, as our children talk about themselves and their ideals. Our submissiveness and admiration make them tyrannize us. This is the reverse side of the coin, the negative impact of European culture on the Jews of Russia. No group but the Jews so swiftly and irrevocably abandoned everything for West European culture, discarded its religion, and divested itself of its historical past and its traditions.

My parents were God-fearing, deeply pious, and respectable people. This was the prevalent type among the Jews then, whose aim in life was above all the love of God and of family. Most of the day was spent in the study of Talmud, and only appointed hours were set aside for business. Nevertheless, my father's business affairs often involved hundreds of thousands of rubles. Like my grandfather, my father was a contractor, an occupation which in the first half of the nineteenth century played a great economic role, enabling the Russian government to erect fortifications, build roads and canals, and thus supply the army.

A marriage was arranged between me and Hanan Wengeroff, and at eighteen I became the bride of a man I loved deeply but knew not at all. Konotop, where my husband's parents lived, was to be my new home. A small town of ten thousand inhabitants, it yet looked like a village. The inhabitants were mostly Christians; the few Jews were grain merchants and tavern keepers. My father-in-law, the richest man in town, held the government's wine and liquor concession. I remember the way the house was furnished — the large rooms, expensive furniture, beautiful silver, carriages and horses, servants, frequent guests.

Most Konotop Jews, including the Wengeroffs, were hasidim. A daughter of mitnagdim, I saw and heard much that was new.

I read a lot in Konotop, especially Russian. First I read the German books I had brought from home — Schiller, Zschokke, Kotzebue, Bulwer. Then I started on the Russian books which stood on the shelves of the Wengeroff library. I read *Moskauer Nachrichten* and taught my husband, eager to learn, German. But his chief study was Talmud. Every Monday and Thursday he spent the night with his rabbi, hunched over great tomes.

Since our betrothal, my husband experienced mystical religious moods and devoted himself to the sacred mysteries of the Kabbala. Then, this fervent young man yearned to make a pilgrimage to Lubavich, the seat of the head of the Lithuanian hasidim. The rabbi would surely have the complete answers to all disturbing questions and enigmas. Yet barely two years before, my husband had advocated modern ideas which led to conflicts with his parents.

One morning while I was busy at household tasks, my husband came into the kitchen and told me, elatedly, excitedly, that his father had permitted him and his elder brother to go to Lubavich in the company of their rabbi.

What happened there I do not know, for my husband never spoke of this tragic experience. All I know was that this young man, hopeful and inspired, made a pilgrimage to the rabbi, hoping he would unveil the great mystery, but returned sobered. He continued his religious observances and studied with the rabbi, but the magic and ecstasy had gone. Thereafter, little by little, he began to neglect his religious observances. Then he decided to cut his beard. We had our first quarrel. I begged him not to yield to vanity and let his beard grow. He would not hear of it. He reminded me that he was the man of the house and demanded my obedience and submission.

Four years later we left Konotop and the patriarchal way of life we had led. My husband had obtained the liquor concession in Lubny, where we were to start our own independent life. Now, without having to worry about his parents, my husband organized his life as he desired. Daily prayers, in prayer shawl and phylacteries, ceased, though he continued to study the Talmud. He used to discuss it at length with the town rabbi, who was our frequent guest, but his interest was just scholarly.

In 1859, my husband's father, grandfather, and another partner obtained the leasehold on liquor for the province of Kovno. My husband was put at the head of the office. We liquidated our business in Lubny, packed our possessions, and moved.

But before I go on about myself, I want to say something about 1855, which marked a new era in Russia, especially for Jews. It was the year Alexander II ascended the throne. He liberated sixty million peasants from bondage and the Jews from their chains. He opened the gates of his main cities into which swarms of Jewish youth thronged to quench their thirst for European education in the universities.

In this brilliant period of intellectual flowering, the Jews took part in the ferment in the whole country, the rise of the fine arts, the development of the sciences. The effects of the reforms in the forties were apparent now: a succession of Jewish professors, doctors, engineers, writers, musicians, and sculptors had won recognition abroad and brought fame to their country.

This made it possible also for the Jews to attain an unexpected influence in commerce and industry. Never before or after did the Jews in St. Petersburg live in such wealth and distinction as then, when a good part of the financial affairs of the capital city were in their hands. Jewish banking houses were founded. Corporations headed by Jews were organized. The stock exchange and the banks grew to immense proportions.

My wise mother once said: "Two things I know for certain. I and my generation will surely live and die as Jews. Our grandchildren will surely live and die not as Jews. But what our children will be I cannot foresee." The first two parts of this prophecy came true. The third is now coming true, for our generation is some kind of hybrid. Other peoples and other nations have drawn from modern, alien currents and ideas only what is congenial to their own character and thus have preserved their own individuality and uniqueness. But the course that befell the Jews was that they could not acquire the new, the alien, without renouncing the old and repudiating their unique individuality, and their most precious possessions. How chaotically these modern ideas whirled through minds of young Russian Jews! Traditional family ideals disappeared, but new ones did not arise in their stead. These young Jewish men had no sense of moderation nor did they want it. In this transitional period, the woman, the mother, was cru-

elly brushed aside, for clinging to tradition; she wanted to impart to her
children the ethics of Judaism, the traditions of its faith, the sanctity of the
Sabbath and the Holy Days, Hebrew, Bible study. She wanted to transmit
this great treasure along with the enlightenment, with the new currents of
West European culture. But the husbands had the same answer to all
pleas: "The children need no religion." In their inexperience, they wanted
to take the dangerous leap from the lowest level of education to the highest,
without any intermediate step. They demanded not only assent from their
wives, but also submission. They preached freedom, equality, fraternity in
public, but at home they were despots.

Kovno was a pretty, provincial town when we settled there. Near the
Prussian border, it was natural that a German style of life influenced the
whole town. Though the Jewish tradition remained intact in the small
Lithuanian towns, in Kovno the enlightenment was in full swing. In progressive Jewish homes, mostly among wealthy families whose fathers and
sons were engaged in commerce with Germany and who frequently travelled across the border, the deviation from Jewish tradition was great.
About the only thing that remained unchanged was the kosher kitchen.

The Sabbath was no longer kept holy, nor did it disturb the passion for
business. The wife, clinging tenaciously to the traditions, used to light the
Sabbath candles, but her enlightened husband lit his cigarette. He invited
his friends for cards. The *kiddush* cup filled with wine stood on the table,
but no one touched it; it had become a symbol. Only the peppered stuffed
fish remained. Apostasy did not go so far as to banish that from the Friday
evening meal. Instead of Sabbath songs, there were jokes and anecdotes.

A few years later we moved to St. Petersburg. I was going toward a
future which would, in transforming the past, surpass all my expectations.
The society we became part of consisted of distinguished and cultivated
people, most of whom lived a carefree existence in wealth and luxury.

The St. Petersburg Jewish community had a magnificent synagogue
and even two rabbis —one modern and seminary-trained, the other Orthodox. But the Jewish community had abandoned many Jewish customs and
traditions. The more fashionable even celebrated Christmas. Only Yom Kippur and Passover were observed, but in an up-to-date way. Some Jews
drove to the synagogue in their carriages and ate in the intervals between
the Yom Kippur service. Passover was kept, even among the most progressive. It remained a festival of remembrance, joyful because it recalled not
the Exodus from Egypt, but one's own childhood in the *shtetl*. The *seder*

was observed, in a highly abbreviated form. Even baptized Jews kept the *seder*. Though they did not themselves make the holiday feast, they welcomed invitations from their not-yet baptized friends.

These were the customs of the upper stratum of Jewish Petersburg. To live in this milieu and remain impervious to it required a strong character and religious fidelity which my husband lacked. Yet here in Petersburg, I often witnessed the strong feeling of solidarity among these Jews who had given up traditional Judaism. Jews in trouble with the authorities anywhere in Russia used to turn to the Petersburg Jewish community for help. Petersburg Jews spared neither money nor time. They appealed to the highest authorities on behalf of the oppressed Jews. Their concern was natural and understandable. This Jewish solidarity became proverbial all over the world. Even the baptized Jews were not immune to it.

In our family, the struggle to keep the Jewish tradition went on in much the same way as in so many other families. First my husband requested, and then demanded, that his wishes be fulfilled. It was not enough for him to have complete freedom over all matters outside our home: I had to "reform" myself and my home. It began with small things, intimate things, dear to me.

As soon as we settled in Petersburg I had to discard the peruke which pious Jewish women wore. It was here in Petersburg, after a violent struggle, that I ceased to keep a kosher kitchen. Little by little, I had to drive each cherished custom from our home. "Drive" is not the right word, for I accompanied each to the door with tears and sobs. I loved my husband intensely and as faithfully as in the first days of our marriage, yet I could not submit without resistance. I wanted to preserve this cherished tradition for myself and my children, and I fought a battle of life and death.

In Petersburg, a thousand different experiences always seemed to converge on the one problem of Judaism. What a time of heartbreak when my son attended the *gymnasium!* Simon was a fourth-year student. The students were taken to the chapel for religious services. All but Simon kneeled before the icons. When the teacher ordered him to kneel, he refused: "I am a Jew. My religion forbids me to kneel to an image." After the service, the enraged teacher told Simon he was expelled. I went to the school superintendent, imploring and weeping. I wanted to tell him my son had not willfully been disobedient; he wanted only to remain loyal to his own upbringing and religion. I could not speak; my throat was tight and the tears flowed. I foresaw that my son's whole life would be destroyed. The school superintendent reflected. The boy was dismissed from this gymnasium, but he would arrange to have Simon admitted to another. I was relieved and also proud. Simon was the flesh of my flesh. But ought I to expect that my children, growing up under alien influences, would follow the ways of their mother? They understood, in their way, what was happening and often took their father's side. I felt alone and abandoned by my husband and society. I submitted. But no one suspected the tragedy I experienced that day. Only a few yellowed pages to which thirty-eight years ago in an hour of despair I confided my unhappiness are the silent witness of my suffering. These words, which I first wrote April 15, 1871, I have set down again for they seem to express the woe and despair which so many wives and mothers suffered in that transitional era in Jewish life.

It was a piece of good luck for us when my husband was offered the position of vice-director of the Commerce Bank in Minsk. We did not ponder long, but packed our things and moved. That was at the end of 1871 and the end of our financial worries. In a short time, my husband became director of the bank and we once again led a comfortable and prosperous life.

The third generation came, fearing neither God nor the devil. They paid highest homage to their own will, raised altars to it, and shamelessly offered the most sacred sacrifices to it. This was the generation that grew up without tradition, without the memories of Judaism. The laments of the Ninth of Ab were foreign to them; foreign, too, the thrice-daily-repeated longing for Zion in the prayers; alien the cycle of the Jewish festivals, in which a solemn one was succeeded by a gay one. This generation were atheists.

In time, the fathers who had reared their children in a manner of modern enlightened Europeans came to see their fateful mistake. Though they themselves had cast off Judaism and its traditions, they still remained Jews in their hearts, good Jews in a national sense, proud of their past. But their children no longer had memories of a Jewish past.

One partial remedy would have been the study of religion in the government schools. Able teachers might easily have interested their pupils in the Jewish past, introduced them to ancient Hebrew poetry, guided them through Jewish history, and so awakened their pride in belonging to a people whose culture and history were ancient, meaningful and impressive. These young Jews might, then, perhaps not have felt the humiliation at every reminder of their Jewish origin, nor would they have turned from their own people in rage, putting their abilities in the service of others.

In the sixties the government had begun its policy of russifying the Jews. After the Polish uprising of 1863, Russian was made compulsory in the Jewish schools in Poland and Lithuania. Then, the subject matter began to be regulated. Gradually, Jewish studies were shortened to make more time for the general curriculum. But the government's policy articulated the unspoken wish among the young generation, and especially their Jewish teachers, that general education be given priority. No wonder, then, that in the cold, dark and stormy eighties and nineties, our children in their frail boats, tossed on the raging waves of life, wanted to bring their little boats to safety. A safe harbor to them was baptism.

So this terrible word comes like a plague. The word has rarely crossed my lips for it was too close, piercing a mother's bleeding heart. After the terrible events, I never spoke of them, and confided only to my diary, damp with tears, and preserved them deep, deep in my memory — until today.

In those transitional seventies, all sorts of high-flown words become current: nihilism, materialism, assimilation, antisemitism, decadence. "Nihilism" made its appearance in Turgenev's *Fathers and Sons*. Our young people responded enthusiastically to the book and its hero, with whom they identified. Conflict between parents and their children became more embittered, and the young people became more alienated from their parents, often ashamed of them. They viewed in their parents only a purse which enabled them to satisfy their desires. But there was no respect. After all, one could only respect a person of high culture. If the relations between parents and children in the forties and fifties were tragicomic, these relations in the eighties and nineties were pure tragedy.

Jewish youth abandoned itself to total assimilation. Then came March 1, 1881, and the sun which had risen on Jewish life in the fifties suddenly set. Alexander II was killed by a bomb on the bank of the Catherine Canal in St. Petersburg. The hand that had freed sixty million serfs was stilled. The lips which had pronounced the great word of liberation were forever silenced.

The City Council of Minsk sent two delegates to St. Petersburg to place a wreath on his fresh grave. The mayor of Minsk and my husband were chosen. It was the first time in Russian history that Jews had participated in a demonstration of mourning.

But different times came. The reptiles that had shunned the light emerged. Antisemitism erupted; the Jews were forced back into the ghetto. Without ceremony, the gateways to education were closed. The jubilation of the fifties and sixties turned into lamentation.

The few rights Jews had enjoyed were withdrawn. Disabilities began to pile up. Rights of residence for Jews in the cities became ever more restricted. An academic education became more and more difficult for Jews to attain, for only a very small Jewish quota was admitted to the gymnasium and even fewer were admitted to the universities.

Pogrom was a new word, coined in the eighties. The Jews of Kiev, Romny, Konotop were among the first to experience the savage assault of the local mobs.

That was the beginning.

In the eighties, with antisemitism raging all over Russia, a Jew had two choices. He could, in the name of Judaism, renounce everything that had become indispensable to him, or he could choose freedom with its offers of education and career — through baptism. Hundreds of enlightened Jews chose the latter. These apostates were not converts out of conviction, nor were they like the Marranos of an earlier age. These apostates disbelieved in all religions: they were nihilists.

My children went the way of so many others. The first to leave us was Simon. Upon learning this, my husband wrote him: "It is not becoming to abandon the camp of the besieged."

Volodya, my favorite child, no longer among the living, followed Simon's example. After completing the gymnasium in Minsk with a brilliant record, he applied to the university at St. Petersburg. He submitted his papers. The admissions clerk rejected them. "These are not your papers. You must have stolen them. You are a Jew, but these papers refer to someone with a Russian name — Vladimir." Several times more he applied to the university, with the same results. Then he took the fateful step, and was immediately accepted.

The baptism of my children was the hardest blow of my life. But the loving heart of a mother can bear a great deal. I forgave them; the blame was on us parents. My sorrow gradually lost its personal meaning, but evermore took on the character of a national misfortune. I mourn it not only as a mother, but as a Jewess mourning for the Jewish people that has lost so many of its noblest sons.

IV

The World of
Tradition

14 Truth and Legend About Israel Salanter

by Jacob Mark

ISRAEL SALANTER, rabbi and preacher, was born in Zhagory in 1810 and died in Koenigsberg in 1883. His family name was Lipkin, but he took the name of Salanter after settling in the town of Salanty. Much of his life story is told in the following memoir.

Israel Salanter was one of the first among East European rabbis to try to conciliate Jewish orthodoxy with modernity, to bring to the modern urban Jew a Judaism relevant to his times and condition, and to halt the flight of young Jews from Judaism. He preached inwardness, self-awareness, ethical behavior and personal morality — known under the general term of *musar*. He established study centers, had moralistic works published, and went from city to city to bring his message to Jews in great urban centers.

In his emphasis on individual morality, Israel Salanter differed from his traditionalist contemporaries. He argued it was as important to abstain from dishonesty in business dealings as to abstain from prohibited food, and equally important to abhor both out of knowledge and self-knowledge. His teachings appear to have had much in common with those of Simha Bunam of Pshiskha in an earlier generation. In a sense, it may be said, Israel Salanter tried to synthesize the best of both Talmudic Judaism and hasidism, by combining learning and *mitsvot* with self-knowledge and saintliness.

Jacob Mark was born in Polangen in 1860 and died in New York about 1929. He was an observant Jew and a maskil. The following essay was taken from his memoirs of great men he knew.

WHEN I was young I often met Rabbi Israel Salanter. I heard his sermons and his private discourses and had the opportunity to observe him at close quarters. I once had the great privilege of being examined by him on my knowledge of Gemara.

Rabbi Israel was born in 1810 in Zhagory, Kovno province, where his father, Rabbi Wolf Lipkin, taught Talmud. After studying at home, Israel was sent to Salanty to study with Rabbi Hirsh Braude, who was renowned as an explicator of Talmud and a man of rare sensibleness. Under his influence, Israel put an end to casuistry and devoted himself to learnedness. But Israel's next teacher, Rabbi Joseph Zundel, an extraordinary man, had a far greater influence over him. All his life, Rabbi Joseph lived like an ordinary, simple man, earning a livelihood as part-time teacher, part-time merchant, notwithstanding his wide repute as a scholar and a saintly man, a disciple of Rabbi Hayim Volozhiner and Rabbi Akiva Eger. When he earned enough to sustain him for a few weeks, he would retire to a nearby town and live for a while in seclusion, in study and prayer. His whole bearing was saintly in every respect. This extraordinary man became the exemplar whom Israel sought to emulate. As a youngster, Israel used to follow Rabbi Zundel when he would withdraw into seclusion to meditate and study musar. Once, Rabbi Zundel saw him. "Israel," he said, "study musar and be a God-fearing man." Thereafter, Rabbi Israel stayed at his side in the twenty years he lived in Salanty. He used to say even later that in musar and good deeds he could not hold a candle to his peerless Rabbi Joseph Zundel.

Rabbi Israel was the first of his time to heed the danger to Jewry from the oncoming haskala. Paradoxically, Judaism and the study of the Torah were then in full flower. The great yeshivas of Volozhin, Vilna, Slutsk, Minsk, Karlin, and Lublin were crowded with students. Practically every little town in Lithuania boasted a yeshiva.

Not only yeshiva students but ordinary householders filled the prayer houses, studying Torah. The singsong Gemara intonation of "the Rabbis teach" was heard from one end of the Pale of Settlement to the other. Since Jews were Jews never had Isaiah's prophecy been so well fulfilled: "And all thy children shall be taught of the Law." The Shulhan Arukh reigned supreme in the Jewish world, while the Pentateuch in Yiddish and morality books ruled the Jewish home.

Small wonder, then, that the rabbis could not understand what Rabbi Israel had in mind when he appealed to them to find ways to safeguard Judaism. Some were incensed at him and responded only with the formula that "innovations are prohibited according to the Torah." But Rabbi Israel's vision was clearer. He foresaw that for all its Judaism and Torah Lithuania would be less resistant to the haskala than Poland, White Russia, the Ukraine, and Galicia, where hasidism had become entrenched; where the authority of the rebbe and zaddik prevailed, where the tradition of the Jewish sages governed the community.

Pondering along these lines, Rabbi Israel concluded that the only way to safeguard Torah and Judaism from the onslaughts of the time was to teach ethics, morality, and the fear of God not only to the young but to adults, married folk, and parents. He used to say educating parents was more urgent and useful than educating children. If parents were more God-fearing, they would not surrender their children to alien influences.

In a small town like Salanty, Rabbi Israel had little opportunity to put his ideas to practice, but his arrival in Vilna marked a new period in his life. Not yet thirty, he became renowned in and around Vilna as a great scholar and pious Jew. He organized societies to study ethical works like Bhaya Ibn Pakuda's *Duties of the Heart* and Moses Hayim Luzzato's *The Path of the Upright,* and he himself studied with them. He also preached sermons in the synagogues.

Vilna provided Rabbi Israel with numerous opportunities to do good deeds and, indeed, many stories were told of his charity and kindness in helping the needy and oppressed. I want to dwell particularly on one story which has frequently been told about him. During a cholera epidemic, to discourage people from fasting on Yom Kippur, he was supposed to have pronounced a benediction on wine in the Great Synagogue of Vilna, despite the objection of the authoritative rabbis in matters affecting Jewish law. This story entered our literature (Steinschneider's "The City of Vilna" and Frischman's "The Three Who Ate") as a true incident, but it is only a myth. I once talked with Rabbi Simeon Strashun of Vilna, who had been in the synagogue on that occasion. This is what happened. The day before Yom Kippur, with the concurrence of the authoritative rabbis, Rabbi Israel had announcements posted in the synagogues that because of the epidemic, the liturgical poems could be omitted, the prayers were to be shortened as much as possible, and the people were to stay in the fresh air as long as possible. Tiny portions of sponge cake were to be on hand in an antechamber of the synagogue, to be used if necessary. After the morning services, Rabbi Israel mounted the pulpit and announced that anyone feeling weak could partake of food in the antechamber, without asking a doctor's opinion. Then, the head of the authoritative rabbinical body followed Rabbi Israel to the pulpit, protesting the announcement. But Rabbi Israel himself did not, in fact, taste any food.

But another story often told about Rabbi Israel is true, not a legend. As a child I heard it from my mother, who was born in Salanty and grew up with Rabbi Israel's children. This incident took place in Salanty.

People had congregated in the synagogue for Kol Nidre. They waited for Rabbi Israel but he did not appear. Since it was getting late, they recited Kol Nidre without him. Then they sent out to look for him, but no one could find him. The crowd was growing panicky; soon the service would be over. Then, abruptly he entered, took his accustomed place, drew the prayer shawl over his head and began to pray. Everyone was astonished at his appearance: his coat was rumpled; his hair and beard full of down. After he finished his prayers, he recounted what had happened to him.

On his way to the synagogue for Kol Nidre, he heard a child crying. He went in the house, saw an infant crying in its cradle, a bottle of milk just out of its reach. The mother had prepared the bottle and gone off to the synagogue, expecting her six-year-old daughter to give the baby its bottle. But the little girl had fallen fast asleep and did not hear the baby crying. Rabbi Israel fed the baby and put it to sleep. When he was ready to leave, the little girl awoke and begged him not to go for she was afraid to be alone. Reluctant to leave small children alone with low-burning candles, he stayed until the mother returned from the synagogue. He rejoiced he had been given the opportunity to do a good deed at a time as sacred as Yom Kippur. His listeners were amazed: How could one miss the Yom Kippur services because of a child's crying? Rabbi Israel scolded them: "Do you not know that, even in the case of a double doubt about saving a life in jeopardy, Jews are permitted not only to omit the prayers but even to profane the Sabbath?"

This simple story characterized Rabbi Israel. It embodied his love of all living creatures in its full radiance. For a saintly Jew like him, the sanctity of Yom Kippur, when the temporal in man ceases to exist and he becomes as an angel, is most solemn. Yet he was willing to forego prayer and confession with the congregation on that Yom Kippur because he did not want a child to cry nor to bring grief to its mother by having her called out of the synagogue.

Or consider this true story. Once, in Salanty, he could not be present to supervise the baking of his *matza shemura* (observance matza). His disciples who undertook the supervision asked him what they were to guard against. He replied that he asked of them only one thing: that in their zealousness they were not to scold the woman kneading the dough for being slow: "Bear in mind," he said, "she is a widow and one ought not to grieve a widow."

Rabbi Israel's compassion for humankind seemed limitless. He wanted every Jew to have a great share in the world to come and to escape the pangs of hell, worse even than the sufferings of this world. To this end, he strove always to be among the people, to live in different cities and countries, though by nature he preferred seclusion. Wherever he went, he summoned to repentance and good deeds. Once Rabbi Israel was told about a recluse in Vilna, an ordinary carpenter who wore his phylacteries all day, his lips moving as if in constant prayer. People asked Rabbi Israel to see him and penetrate his extraordinary qualities. But Rabbi Israel was skeptical of this man's wisdom or reverence for God. Otherwise, he said, the man would not seclude himself from the world, especially nowadays, but he would want to help the Jews of today.

When Rabbi Israel delivered a sermon, looking at his audience with his gentle kind eyes, it seemed to me that his first thought probably was: How I pity these poor dear Jews who will someday endure great sufferings for their sins. From his heart the words cried out: "Turn Thou us unto Thee, O Lord, and we shall be returned." Observing that the congregation wept, too, he thought they were surely repenting, and then his face became radiant with joy.

Rabbi Israel taught musar by trying to improve human nature and the relations between people. His watchword was "Know thyself." Each man was to analyze himself, improve himself, learn his weaknesses in order to conquer them. If pride was one's weakness, a man should try to wean himself from it. Or if one was given to anger, stubbornness, obduracy, he ought to learn little by little to master his rage, his obstinacy, his inflexibility. Rabbi Israel used to say that every man could improve himself until love of mankind came naturally to him. He used to teach that a man should not desire another's property not because the Torah commanded "Thou shalt not covet," but because one would scorn an ugly distasteful act, much as one would spurn rotten fish. Only by self-discipline can man reach this state.

The first five years Rabbi Israel lived in Vilna, he was an enigma to the rabbis because he wanted to safeguard Judaism from the dangers they could not yet perceive. Some rabbis even protested that Rabbi Israel's teaching of ethics and morality brought on neglect of the Torah. But came 1844, and they realized how shortsighted they had been. That was the year the Russian government opened a rabbinical seminary in Vilna; its purpose was to educate rabbis also in the general culture so they could spread general education among all Jews. (Nowadays we think an institution is ideal when it combines Torah and secular learning, but in the view of our good parents — and perhaps they were right — that was the beginning of the end of Torah and Judaism.)

As soon as the rabbinical seminary opened, many students began to abandon the traditional yeshivas, and their Judaism, and flocked to the seminary. Rabbi Israel's prophecy came true sooner than even he had foretold. This sudden innovation brought such an enormous degree of laxity among the young people that even the Vilna maskilim began to fear that this long-coveted seminary would graduate skeptics instead of educated men and unbelievers instead of rabbis.

The Vilna maskilim even tried to induce Rabbi Israel to head the seminary, to lend it his high prestige so it would become more popular with traditional Jewry and simultaneously strengthen respect for Judaism among its students. But he declined, despite the concessions which were made to attract him and the offer of an immense salary for that time, said to have been about a thousand rubles a year. But the maskilim refused to take his "no" for an answer. They asked Count Uvarov, Education Minister, to order Rabbi Israel to accept the post, hoping he would not wish to transgress the precept of the Talmud that "the law of the government is the law." Just at that time, Uvarov happened to be in Vilna. Accompanied by Hayim Leib Katzenellenbogen, instructor in Bible and Talmud at the seminary, Uvarov sought out Rabbi Israel at his yeshiva and offered him the post. But Rabbi Israel declined on the ground that authoritative rabbis could not be trained in an institution where general subjects were essential and Jewish ones secondary.

In 1848, when the first rabbinical conference was convened in Petersburg, it is said Uvarov asked Rabbi Isaac Volozhiner to urge Rabbi Israel to attend. Rabbi Isaac tried to convince Rabbi Israel that his obstinacy contravened the ruling of "a law of the government is a law." To this, Rabbi Israel is said to have replied — so I have it from someone who was there — "Rabbi Isaac, you are in error, not I. This is not a governmental law, but a governmental persecution. Nor is it the kind of persecution we are accustomed to, rather it is intended to convert us. The government of Nicholas I does not seek our welfare, but simply wants to convert our children. The applicable ruling in this case is 'to be killed but not to transgress.'" After this, Rabbi Israel felt he could no longer remain in Vilna. He moved to Kovno.

There he continued his lifework, teaching ethics and morals to the young men studying for the rabbinate.

In 1857, in his best years and at the height of his career, Rabbi Israel left Russia for Germany. He went originally for medical treatment to Halberstadt. Then, seeing the sorry situation of Judaism among the German Jews, he thought he could accomplish more in Germany than in Russia. He remained abroad until the end of his life.

The contributors to *Ha-Shahar*, being greatly interested in Rabbi Israel's life and work, once criticized him for leaving Russia, his native land, where he had a vast arena in which to work, and dedicating himself to foreign Jews — only about one-tenth the number of Russian Jews. I think I understand why. Rabbi Elijah Levinson of Kroettingen, Rabbi Israel's close friend and advisor, once told me how Rabbi Israel himself had explained it. "When horses panic and start galloping downhill, anyone who tries to stop them midway risks his life. The horses will trample him. But after the horses have rushed down the hill, it is possible to halt and bridle them. So, too, with the Jewish communities. In the large Russian cities, they are still in headlong downward flight and nothing can be done for them. But the communities abroad have long ago levelled off and now something can be done for them."

In 1858, Rabbi Israel lived in Koenigsberg, trying to strengthen Judaism especially among the student youth. Then he moved to Memel, which he liked most and where he stayed the longest. Memel was then a bustling commercial city whose trade always brought thousands of Jews from the dozens of surrounding provincial towns. In Memel he applied to the Prussian government for citizenship and studied to perfect his German so that he could deal with the public officials in matters concerning the Jewish community.

Neither his age nor his ill health kept him from seeking to reinforce traditional Judaism so it might better resist modern trends. Seeing how great was the ignorance of Judaism even among the Orthodox, he concluded that preaching on ethics and morals was inadequate when the study of Torah was being neglected. He tried to introduce modern methods to study the Talmud, for young people could no longer devote to it eight to ten hours a day for many years. He first sought Orientalists to prepare a dictionary of the Aramaic words in the Talmud. He went to Berlin on this mission, but nothing came of it. It then occurred to him to have the Talmud translated into Hebrew and published with a brief and simple commentary. It was his plan to assign about one hundred rabbis to this task, each to translate about thirty leaves. But nothing came of this either. Perhaps the rabbis opposed the idea as "reform" or perhaps few knew Hebrew well enough. Then, seeing that young people were giving up the Talmud altogether, Rabbi Israel thought of translating it into a modern European language — a notion that aroused considerable protest at that time among the Orthodox. Rabbi Israel believed the Gentile world ought to be acquainted with the enormous cultural riches in the Talmud. Gentile students, he thought, would more likely sharpen their wits on the Talmud's logic and reasoning than on Greek and Latin classics. It was his conviction that the younger Jewish generation would have more respect for the Talmud if the Gentiles recognized it as a great cultural monument. They would remain closer to the Jewish tradition, then, and take pride in their people and their religion. But unable to accomplish anything in Germany on this project, Rabbi Israel, then over seventy, went to Paris hoping to find greater understanding there. But there also, after two years, he was unsuccessful; I heard from his close friends that he deeply regretted this trip.

In his day Rabbi Israel was about the only notable mitnagid who had won the respect of the hasidic world. He was a disciple of the Vilna Gaon and disliked many hasidic customs because he thought they led to frivolity, yet many hasidim thought highly of him, and he was quite influential among the hasidim of Lubavich. One hasidic rabbi expressed it this way: "After many generations God had pity on the unfortunate mitnagdim and sent them the soul of a rebbe — Rabbi Israel Salanter. But those bunglers deadened his spirit too."

Rabbi Israel used to say that both the hasid and mitnagid ought to be reproved: the hasid for saying "Why do I need a book for religious study, when I have a rebbe?" The mitnagid for saying, "If I have a book for religious study, why do I need a rebbe?"

Rabbi Israel first met the Lubavicher rebbe at a German spa, where they used to take the waters. A story is told about their encounter. The Lubavicher rebbe used to ride in a handsome coach accompanied by servants and disciples. Rabbi Israel used to walk. It was said Rabbi Israel did not approve of the Lubavicher's riding in a carriage — it was not clear why, but hasidim thought it was because Rabbi Israel suspected *sha'atnez*, that the upholstery was made of a mixture of wool and linen, impermissible according to Jewish law. The Lubavicher was not impressed with this argument, because Rabbi Jacob Reischer's *Shevut Ya'akov* was lenient on this subject. One day, the Lubavicher in his carriage passed Rabbi Israel on foot. The Lubavicher invited Rabbi Israel to join him, "Rather than walk, it is better to lean on *Shevut Ya'akov*." The hasidic version of the story tells that Rabbi Israel then stepped into the carriage and both rode together every day thereafter. The mitnagdim tell it differently. Rabbi Israel is said to have replied, "As for the charge of sha'atnez, I would surely lean on *Shevut Ya'akov*, but what about the charge of pride?"

To this, the hasidim retort with a remark the Lubavicher is said to have made: "On the contrary. This is the only way to achieve humility — to ride in a handsome carriage, surrounded by servants, be honored, and yet remain humble."

But this was not Rabbi Israel's concept of humility. He did not think he was better than anyone else; he did not want to be honored by others. Nor could he understand how one could simultaneously practice both pride and humility. His humility was natural, without deviousness. He refused to accept money beyond his immediate needs. He dressed simply, avoided ostentation. He attributed his great learning to a heavenly gift, not to his merit. For he held that even more important than respect for the Torah was respect for each living man.

15   The Old Man of Slobodka
by M. Gerz

NATHAN (NOTA) ZEVI HIRSH FINKEL, the "Old Man" of Slobodka, was born in 1849 and died in 1928. For about fifty years he headed the musar yeshiva at Slobodka. His biography is that of the yeshiva and the development of his ideas and teachings of musar, recounted in the following memoir. He was one of the last in the great tradition of musar, combining Talmudic scholarship with the highest level of personal ethical conduct.

M. Gerz, pen name of Gershon Movshovich, was born in Pikeln, province of Kovno, in 1892. He studied at the yeshiva of Slobodka and later became a Yiddish journalist. He survived World War II in Russia, returning to Riga in 1945, but nothing has been known of him since 1947. The following essay is taken from his memoirs of the yeshiva of Slobodka.

ATOP the Alexot hill you look down upon two worlds poised against each other as in a duel. On one side is Kovno with its ancient woods, tall mountains, dreamy hills, and blossoming valleys. At its foot flows the mighty Niemen, linked eternally with the placid Viliya. Roundabout nature calls to joy and life. And on the other side stretches a long sickly quagmire on whose surface twist vermicular narrow streets with their wretched hunched hovels. It is quiet here in the slime of Slobodka.

The men are logrollers, river lumbermen, logging long months in far places to earn their meager daily bread. The women help eke out their bitter livelihood, wearing away their days and years at the needle and spindle. Children grow sparsely here. From their earliest days, the sickly slime devours them.

From time to time, the dismal stillness of the narrow streets is disturbed. At the start of summer and winter, furtive shadows sidle by; emaciated young bodies, torn from their mothers' arms, are sent here to study Torah. They hasten, these Jewish youngsters, from the other side of the bridge to the Slobodka yeshiva. They will remain here always. For the Old Man of Slobodka said, "The bridge between Kovno and Slobodka was built to go from Kovno to Slobodka, but not back."

No one in Slobodka knew the Old Man. Even the students at the yeshiva scarcely knew him. He lived in seclusion from his family, in a separate room.

He never attracted anyone's notice. A simple man, dressed plainly in a black rep hat and a long topcoat, like a small-town shopkeeper. His suit was what a common man would wear, the jacket often unbuttoned; he kept his hands in his trouser pockets, like a low-class villager. Only an acute eye could tell that what looked like an ordinary beard was only a twig of the long beard tucked deep beneath the collar of his shirt. Three times a day he could be seen at prayer in the anteroom of the yeshiva. Having prayed, he turned about, sometimes had a brief chat with someone — and he was gone. He used to disappear, quickly, sidling furtively down the street.

He kept apart from everyone in the yeshiva. Only a few students used to visit him and presumably were close to him. He was known in the yeshiva as "the Old Man" (his real name was Nota Hirsh Finkel), though his youthful face showed no sign of age. He was hale and fresh as if he were still growing, his eyes clear and limpid. A smile usually clung to his moist lips. He was the real head of the Slobodka yeshiva and of the other yeshivot in the province. He was the father of the musar movement.

He used to say, "Walk humbly. Carry the whole world in your heart, but let not the world know of it. Do only good, for that is why you were created. But who need know about it?"

This is what he preached: Man was created in the image of God. The sages say that when man was created the angels took him to be a god and wanted to sing his praises. The source of man is God. God was Lord of the world before even the world was created, yet God created the world. For what purpose did God do this? He did it out of great love, to bestow upon man a wide and beautiful world. Is love a human trait? As God is filled with mercy, so man is filled with good. If man does a good deed, he does so for himself, for that is his nature. He cannot do otherwise. He is weighed down with goodness and before he can spend it, he does good for his own sake because he is filled with love and wants to find an outlet for it, for his own pleasure. Then why need someone else know about it?

For half a century, the Old Man directed the yeshiva, yet he never signed a letter, a document, any paper connected with a yeshiva. His one book, *Ets Peri* ("A Fruit Tree"), was published anonymously in 1881. He never authored any other book, for he discovered that one should devote himself to people, not books. "My life is my book," he used to say.

He taught the majesty of man. Man is great, man is good, but man must never cease striving ever higher, toward the better, the more beautiful. Life is a ladder on which one ascends or descends, but one never stands in one place. If one does not ascend, one descends; better then to go up.

He used to preach: If man is by nature noble, then why did the Torah instruct us to do good? It would be so obvious. Doing good is itself a natural human thing. Even unbelievers do good deeds and charity. This signifies, then, that we are speaking about a love for man that we would not comprehend without the Torah. For example, a wealthy man gives generously to a poor man. The poor man is pleased, yet the donor has not discharged his obligation. For by the standard of the poor man, benighted and unfortunate, the gift was charitable. Yet it was inadequate by a higher standard. The poor man, however benighted, is God's creature. Whatever he may seem to be, you know he is a man created in God's image. Then know it!

Proof from the Gemara: Rabbi Johannon said to his children: "Hire workmen for me." The children contracted with the workmen that they would pay for their work with food. But Rabbi Johannon told them again to stipulate exactly what he would pay, for promising merely food, even the repasts of Solomon, would not discharge his obligation. To be sure, hungry and exhausted workers will be happy with a chunk of meat, but man must be guided by a nobler concept and a higher standard than the base psychology of the recipient. The Old Man used to cite Abraham, our father, who slaughtered three calves for his three guests (who appeared to be lowly Arabs) that he might set before each of them a "tongue with mustard."

Or he would preach: A man, for instance, gives to the poor as much as he can afford. He does not stint money or time to help the poor, the sick, the unfortunate. Common sense says he is a good man, that is the world's understanding. But the Torah understands love differently. If a man supports the poor and unfortunate, that itself is not proof of love for man, nor proof that he heeds the commandment "thou shalt love thy fellowman like thyself." For were the needy whom he helps rich and enjoying abundance, our man would not be grieved because they are not richer and cannot enjoy greater abundance. His benign attitude toward the poor and unfortunate, then, did not spring from love, but rather from grief and pain for the unfortunates and therefore he befriended them. The pity which he felt for their misfortune, and which stirred him, did not spring from love for men but because his capacity for cruelty had expired. Cruelty too has its limits. But the Torah demands love for man because man is God's creature, made in His image, because man's origin is God. This being so, you must love not only the unfortunate and tormented, but even the well-fed and the haughty. If they need help of some sort, you must be prepared to help them, too. For example: In the case of a wealthy man who becomes impoverished, it is not enough to provide him with sufficient food, but you ought to give him the kind of repasts he was accustomed to when he was rich, and even a horse and carriage, if that is what he was used to. For now that he is poor, he lacks those things just as the ordinary poor man lacks bread.

One can attain this level of doing good and loving others when one meditates, trying to penetrate the real purpose of man in the world. That is man's purpose in improving himself, as when he studies musar.

The Old Man used to say: "If I knew that I could be only what I am, I could not endure it; but if I did not strive to be like the Vilna Gaon, then I would not be even what I am."

He used to say: "In this world no one pays for good deeds. A small town has no facilities to change large bills. After all, what are the pleasures that man can enjoy in this world? How many earthly pleasures can man delight in? Eating well, sleeping well — how much can man savor? But if he can enjoy someone else's well-being by transferring the enjoyments of others to himself, then perhaps pleasure is worth thinking about."

From time to time the Old Man would disappear. People thought he was probably at home, for where else would he be? But those close to him knew he was not at home. They began to trail him. They caught up to him just as he was setting out with a band of gypsies. His friends appealed to him: "Teach us, rabbi, what is the meaning of this?"

"Gypsies are the most forlorn people in the world. They do not know of rest or home. They torture themselves and their families in their wretched travels. So they ought to be heartened by a cheerful mien, a friendly smile in their roaming and wandering."

Because he believed wanderers were the most forlorn people, he used often steal out to the nearby railroad stations. There he found much work for himself — helping travelers by carrying a bag, or giving advice or comforting them with a kind word, cheering them with a chat and sometimes with a loan. The Old Man used to say: " 'Love thy fellowman as thyself.'

Just as you do not love yourself because it is a commandment, do not love him because it is a commandment."

Winter, he would rise early, cross the bridge into town, setting out for all the prayer houses and places of study, to start and stoke the ovens. He said that if the prayer houses and study houses would be warm early in the morning a coachman, a porter, or just a poor man would come in to warm up and find himself in a sanctified place. His closest friends asked him: "Rabbi, is it your business to start the ovens and carry packages?" He answered: "Even if it were as hard as you think it is, that would not be the point. The maskilim demand 'light,' humanity must be given light. But we must not forget that a light sheds light for all, but itself is extinguished. Otherwise, it would not be a light."

Man is an angel, indeed above the angels. For when God created the world and exhibited all its creatures before the angels, they could not think of any names for them. But Adam did. The First Adam understood every creature's nature. He comprehended each one's spirit and their relations to one another. Their relations affected the whole community; the absence of one would mar the perfection of all creation.

The Old Man treated each yeshiva student individually and differently. He took the soundings of each in a different way to be able to perfect him. He saw through every student, yet he never spoke ill of anyone, for a human being is a creature of choice. When he did encounter rebels, he exhausted himself trying to bring them back on the right path. When all attempts failed, he would fast. Once he said of a rebel, "He cost me dearly." His close friends understood the meaning of his words.

Every day at twilight, between afternoon and evening services, and particularly on the Sabbaths, the yeshiva used to seem like a sinking ship. The Holy Sabbath was ending; everyone tried to retain the Sabbath tranquillity as long as one could. But the day passed, the darkness neared, the shadows grew longer and denser. The weekdays were coming. One could not light a fire or a lamp; it was too dark to read or study. Then all turned to meditation and musar. There were those who lamented their sins aloud in sobs and those who smote the lecterns so hard with their bare hands that sparks flew to scatter their evil thoughts, and those who soared silently on their thoughts, as if on wings, and punctured themselves as if with needles: "Envy, lust, and coveting honor put a man out of the world."

"A man must be one who walks forward."

"A man worries about the loss of his money, but the money can be replaced."

A black cloud crouched overhead. Men were sinking into an abyss and sought rescue. The Sabbath was departing. The weekdays were upon them. Suddenly, as after birth pangs, a rap and the evening service: "And God being merciful forgives transgression."

It is bearable. God is good, He will be merciful and forgive our sins. After the evening prayers, all in unison, weeping, all chant the psalm Maschil of David. Someone sings with a heartbreaking melody that moves stones to tears. Everyone sorrows and everything mourns. Suddenly the Old Man emerges from the crowd. He chants the *havdala* with such sweetness the tension eases and the atmosphere becomes more cheerful. He moves quickly from bench to bench greeting everyone purposively: "Good week."

A circle begins to form around the Old Man, spreading like circles in the water. The students surround him and wait. The Old Man leans on a lectern and begins to talk, just as one chats in company.

"We know that man's greatest obligation is that he submit to the yoke of God's rule. He expresses this obligation by blessing everything that gives him pleasure. It would seem, then, that submission to God's rule is a sort of subjugation, an enslavement. The blessings appear to be a sort of tax which man must pay for his pleasures. Yet the truth of the matter is quite different. Obedience to God's will is neither enslavement nor levy, but rather the source of all pleasure.

"Thus, it is man's nature to be impressed only by innovation. Things to which he is accustomed do not arouse his curiosity nor appeal to his feelings. But things which we see for the first time awaken feelings of pleasure. Hence, man cannot really enjoy the beauties of the world because he is accustomed to his surroundings. He can appreciate their pleasures only after he has missed them.

"For, in truth, all the world is a source of pleasure and beauty, every detail of Creation, every manifestation in matter, every movement in nature affords us immense pleasure. Man views the radiance of nature in a mass of colors. Should this not give him endless joy? Yet it does not delight him. His ears hear; his sense of hearing unites him with his surroundings. He hears every sound and echo in the creation of the world. This should, one thinks, give him boundless joy, but no. For man has been accustomed to hear and see. He finds nothing new in this that should awaken joy.

"God bestowed upon man all the senses and perfected him from the day of his birth. Therefore, man does not appreciate God's charity.

"To liberate man from the paralysis of habit, to awaken his frozen senses so he can feel the beauty of creation and the good which fills the world, our blessed sages prescribed the recitation of blessings. The blessings accustom man to be aware always that 'with goodness the Creator renews the history of creation every day.' This means all creation, as if everything were now created for the first time and as if man were first born. The blessings teach man to reflect: a moment ago he was not yet born into the world, or was a body without a soul, without feelings, like a blind man who does not see, a deaf man who does not hear, without understanding and intellect. Suddenly God shed light upon his eyes and brought him into a new world. He opened his arms and strengthened his bones, made his ears hear and his understanding grow. How great, then, was man's rejoicing!

"Such insights make man's life pleasant. They come from pondering on the blessings: He opens the eyes of the blind; He sets free those in bondage, He raises up those who are bowed down, He restores life to mortal creatures."

Everyone listens, absorbed, open-mouthed and open-eyed. Then, all of a sudden, almost unnoticed, the Old Man has vanished. He is wandering in lonely, forgotten, dark streets.

He was a poet, the Old Man, a gentle philosopher. Yet there were times the philosopher became a warrior. He taught: "Every man must be a King David — poet and warrior. One should compose psalms, but, if necessary, gird his loins and go bravely to war." When the Old Man perceived danger threatening God's abode, he became a merciless and fearless warrior.

In 1905, the students in the Slobodka yeshiva rebelled. Jewish revolutionaries on the outside had propagandized them, with some success. The revolt swept the yeshiva. The insurgents demanded greater freedom, secular studies, permission to read secular books and newspapers.

The Old Man did not falter. All day, in the yeshiva, he prepared for war — his pointed beard cropping out of its hiding place, his gentle limpid eyes gleaming like blazing spears. Who could resist them?

With a firm hand, he warded off the attack. He excommunicated some of the students. No one in town would rent them rooms or sell them food. He persuaded some students to his side. Others, impervious, were sent out of town with the help of some cooperative coachmen. The rest were crushed and subjugated. Who could resist him?

At such times he used to teach: "People say, when you cannot pass over, you pass under. But the musarists say, when you cannot pass over, you must rise above."

16 In the Service of
Isaac Elhanan Spektor
by Jacob Halevy Lipshitz

ISAAC ELHANAN SPEKTOR was born in Rosh, province of Grodno, in 1817 and died in Kovno in 1896. He was considered the leading rabbinical authority in Russia and maintained regular contact with rabbinic and Jewish communal leaders all over the world. He was the exemplar of the modern rabbi in Eastern Europe, combining religious authority and communal leadership. He was involved in all major rabbinic, educational, and social questions affecting the Jews of his time. His influence extended far beyond the borders of the Tsarist Empire.

Jacob Halevy Lipshitz, Rabbi Isaac Elhanan's biographer and personal secretary for twenty-six years, was born in Vilkomir, province of Kovno, in 1838 and died there in 1921. His memoirs, an extract of which follows, present the Orthodox point of view in the conflict with the haskala.

MY YOUTH

What follows is a record of many historical events which I witnessed and in which I took an active part as a writer and as an aide to our great Jewish leaders in their work on behalf of the Jewish community. May I, therefore, give a brief account of my own history?

I was born in Vilkomir, 5th of Tebet, 1838. My sainted father, Eliezer Lippman Halevy, was a rabbi, scholar and teacher. My mother, the pious Esther Ethel, was his second wife. She agreed to marry him even though he told her he would not accept a rabbinical post. The only position he was willing to accept was preacher, at a small salary, in Vilkomir. My mother, an energetic and experienced businesswoman, supported the family respectably. She had two sons and a daughter by her first husband and four sons with my father. My older brothers had the good fortune to be educated by our father. Two became rabbis and acquired some reputation as authors of rabbinic works. My third brother became a writer.

My father died in Vilna, where he had gone for treatment, during Sukkoth, 1843. My mother then had to provide for all four orphans. I was five years old then.

Boys of my age used to have tutors to teach them to read and write in Russian, but my mother's earnings kept declining and she could not afford a tutor for me. Several years later, I went to Keidany to study under the supervision of my brother Judah. For nearly two years, I studied in the Keidany yeshiva, in the company of learned and God-fearing men. Here, the foundation for my later education was laid.

A DELUSIVE SPIRIT

The spirit of freedom which swept across the land in the wake of the Crimean war was delusive. Many people, sensible ones at that, thought the days of darkness were over. The sun of knowledge would purge men of evil, no man would harm another because of his beliefs or views, hatred for different religions and nationalities would disappear without trace. Even among observant Jews, these ideas made some headway. The deceptive light of haskala deluded them, too, and some thought the days of the Messiah had come. Enlightened people of our generation had wandered so far afield they even thought Jewish national and messianic hopes would be fulfilled. It was then Moses Hess's *Rome and Jerusalem* was published. Hess was the first to express this new spirit of nationalism.

Yet no generation lacks men learned in the Torah who can predict the outcome of these transitory moods. We, too, had our scholars, of whom it could be said that "a wise man is better than a prophet." For instance, I recall a time around 1860, when the rabbi of Keidany, Abraham Simon Traub, was discussing with prominent townspeople the notion that the spirit of freedom spreading across Europe would be a deliverance for the Jews. The rabbi said: "Do not be deceived by this spirit. Do not believe it will bring us any good. Dear brothers, I believe firmly that the present mood is fleeting and will pass. Thirty years from now, Jews will be hated once more and persecuted even in free and progressive France."

"How can you say that, rabbi?" The people were astonished. "Have you not read the newspapers that promise brotherhood and freedom of thought, that foretell the time when religious hate and enmity among peoples will cease to exist and that men of goodwill will be ashamed to recall such prejudices?"

"Dear brothers," Rabbi Traub replied, "Seven times daily do I praise God for the respite from the persecutions which our people have suffered until now. But we must remember the respite is temporary, as our sages commented on the passage '. . . put a space betwixt drove and drove.' This is not our deliverance. Those who know Jewish history realize such periods occurred many times, when Jews rose to prominence in the lands they lived in, but the people turned on them and brought them suffering, followed by deportations and exile. If only we may be worthy of the coming of the Messiah. Only then will true deliverance be ours and an end to our suffering will come."

Though many pious Jews shared these views, some Jews were seduced by the haskala, captivated by the spirit of assimilation. Some even denied God. All this brought us grief.

Hitherto, the leaders and defenders of our people had been God-fearing Jews and distinguished rabbis. But during the haskala, new leaders, close to the government, came to the fore, weakening the influence of pious Jews. But many of these notables repudiated our people. Some even failed to employ Jews in their own business enterprises. They allowed Jewish affairs to drift, without trying to halt their downward course.

As early as 1840, even before the morning star of the new era had risen, our freethinking maskilim in Russia were stirred by the freedom gusting from France and Germany, where Jews were enjoying equal rights. Observing our low estate here, the maskilim concluded — strange logic — that the fault was in us, in our lack of good manners and in our fidelity to the Torah and to Talmudic injunctions. These shortcomings rendered us ineligible for citizenship. Hence, they argued, every step toward the haskala would help to liberate us from antisemitism and bring us closer to civic equality. Those who deviate from this path create a harmful image of the individual Jew and of the whole Jewish people, and ought to be condemned.

But the maskilim did not understand the ways of God or the course of human history. In 1861, when the beacon of freedom and brotherhood shed its light on the whole country, 23 million serfs were liberated not because they had improved themselves and were worthy of liberation, but because Alexander II in his charity liberated them, for they had been created human beings. Their liberation made them civilized beings. So, too, with the millions of American Negroes, who were freed not because they had better education or nicer manners, but out of the love of mankind, which always accompanies progress. Some persecuted groups or peoples were helped, not because of their own good traits but because the political changes in their own countries made it possible for all people to be considered equal. This should have held true also for Jews. Certainly any shortcoming in social manners ought never to have justified depriving us of civic rights.

Starting from 1840 when the haskala began to burgeon, freethinking maskilim tried, in vain, to reach the Jews with their freethinking ideas. No secular Jewish literature existed, neither Hebrew journals nor miscellanies. Not until 1844 did some Vilna maskilim publish a journal *Pirhe Tsafon* ("Blossoms of the North"). Even then, only two miserable little issues appeared. The blossoms did not flower. The masses looked upon the haskala book as atheistic and called them "forbidden." Anyone caught reading a forbidden book was considered an unbeliever. Thus, their literature made little headway. Then the maskilim applied the pressure of governmental authority. In olden days the European settlers in America — the bearers of culture — subdued the wild Indians and ruled them with brute force and cruelty. The maskilim conducted themselves in much the same way, trampling over God's holy people. Their intercession induced the government to issue an edict forbidding Jews to wear their traditional garb. The maskilim carried tales to the government about the "rebels against the light," who kept ignorance and darkness alive by adhering to the Talmud. Their talebearing found favor with the government, and the maskilim succeeded in influencing the government to pile up prohibitions and restraints on the rabbis and the yeshivot.

After the Crimean War, *Ha-Maggid* was founded in 1856. Then, in 1860, two more Hebrew periodicals appeared: *Ha-Karmel* in Vilna and *Ha-Melits* in Odessa. They were followed by *Razsviet*, a Russian journal. All had many readers. At that time the railroads and the telegraph contracted the world. (In 1860, tracks were laid between Petersburg and Warsaw.) Newspapers became an everyday commonplace. The power of the press opened new channels for the propaganda of the freethinking maskilim. Their influence grew and then, following the ways of the Berlin maskilim at the Brunswick Rabbinical Assembly in 1844 and the Kassel assembly in 1848, they began to introduce reforms in Judaism. This movement was led by J. L. Gordon, M. L. Lilienblum, Alexander Zederbaum (the publisher of *Ha-Melits*), and their circle, whose freethinking ideas seduced many of our young people to substitute secular education for Judaism.

But then came 1881. The pogroms started and the tattered mobs, slashing bedding and pillows, spared no Jews, not even the apostates who set icons in their windows. It was then the freethinkers repented, running to the synagogue to recite penitential prayers. When the maskilim admitted their bankruptcy, they cogitated and deliberated and came up with a new trade name. They now identified themselves as Lovers of Zion and repudiated their literature of the sixties. They wept for their twofold sins — because they had believed the haskala would bring equality and because the movement for religious reform had weakened Judaism.

After the pogroms of 1881, the Jewish communal leaders were stupefied into inaction. The government had justified the pogroms on the grounds that Jews were socialists. But it was clear to me that the Jewish misfortunes were caused by the reactionary forces seeking to destroy us. I approached Rabbi Isaac Elhanan with a plan to help our people. I had given the subject some thought and proposed that Rabbi Isaac Elhanan get in touch with Nathaniel Rothschild in London, through Dr. Asher Asher, to ask him to intervene on behalf of the unfortunate Jews of Russia. Since the Russian government was stirring up mobs to kill the Jews and pillage their belongings for no reason but that they were Jews, the progressive nations ought publicly to protest. We would ask Rothschild to activate expressions of protest from distinguished non-Jews.

At the summer's end of 1881, in the penitential days before Rosh ha-Shana, I went to Vilna to meet Rabbi Isaac Elhanan, who was just returning from a meeting of Jewish leaders in Petersburg. They had assembled at Baron Günzburg's in sorrow and anguish, to discuss a petition to the government for equal rights for Jews. Just then Ignatiev's circular was issued, creating commissions to protect the Russians from the Jews! There was even the trace of a suggestion that pogroms were a good thing. The Jewish leaders realized then that the government itself put Jews at the mercy of the mob. We stopped in Vilna to confer about these commissions and how to ward off future calamities.

I put my proposal about Dr. Asher before Rabbi Isaac Elhanan and his son Zvi Hirsh. They approved, but they wanted first to confer with Baron Günzburg and Poliakov and others. I disagreed. What I had proposed had to be done in strictest secrecy and presented later as accomplished fact. If, with God's help, we would succeed, we would be credited with wisdom. But if we failed, that would be our secret.

The month of Tishri passed in constant consultation. The fear of fresh pogroms grew daily. In Heshvan, Rabbi Isaac Elhanan and his son agreed to act. Since no one could go to London, the only thing to do was write, but because of the censorship, did we dare to tell the stark truth? I had an idea: the rabbi would write to Dr. Asher saying that the next day he would send him a long responsum signed "Nahal Isaac," about an abandoned wife, which would start with the words: "Be Thou with the mouths of those who have been sent by Thy people." * Dr. Asher was to occupy himself

* From the additional service for the first day of Rosh ha-Shana:
    Our God and God of our fathers, be Thou with the mouths of those who have

with this case and do everything necessary on behalf of the abandoned wife, to liberate her from her difficulties.

On the 5th day of Heshvan, 1881, the rabbi wrote this letter with his own hand and gave it to me to send off. The next day I made an appointment with my nephew (and my daughter's fiancé), an artist and calligrapher. We attended afternoon services together and then, after dinner, composed the text for "Be Thou with the mouths." We wrote it, page by page, reread it, edited it. Then my nephew copied it in his elegant penmanship. We sat at this until eleven at night, when I went to Rabbi Isaac Elhanan. Reading the text, he shed tears over it, kissed me, put it into an envelope, and hoped it would be successful. That was the beginning of a correspondence with Dr. Asher which culminated in the impressive protests which came from London against the persecutions of the Jews in Russia.

The benefit to the persecuted and oppressed Jews of Russia from the Mansion House meeting was that the Russian government learned the Russian Jews were the object of world concern and that the world knew they were being persecuted and murdered because of the policies of a brutal government.

One day in Tebet, 1882, while I was sitting with Rabbi Isaac Elhanan, Bernard Maneshewitz, one of Kovno's leading well-to-do Jews, came in. "Rabbi," he said, "today is not Purim, but I have brought you something to be read that deserves the same piety as the story of Esther. Besides, we ought to say a blessing for joyful tidings." He unfolded *Golos* (The Voice), the most distinguished newspaper in Russia. He began to read and translate for the rabbi the dispatches about the London meetings and the protests against the pogroms. He read with great emotion and tears of joy, often interrupting: "Is the rabbi not impressed by this? Why not? Doesn't he believe in these press reports? How can he fail to appreciate that distinguished Gentiles took the side of Jews and protested against the injustices of this regime."

The rabbi asked him to excuse us for a few moments. Outside, the rabbi asked me: "Reb Jacob, do you consent to our telling him? I think we ought to disclose this to a selected few, and it would be an act of piety to tell them." I consented.

Maneshewitz was astonished: "How did you do this?" To convince him, the rabbi showed him the full correspondence, and Maneshewitz read the letters in amazement. He gaped at us, "I would never have believed that a

---

been sent by Thy people, the house of Israel, to stand before Thee in prayer and supplication, to entreat Thee in their behalf.

diplomatic task of such magnitude could have been accomplished by an Orthodox rabbi, without fuss and bluster. I would never have believed it had I not seen it."

"And who is this Reb Jacob, who is your colleague?" asked Maneshewitz. "He," Rabbi Isaac Elhanon replied, "is the director of the local Talmud Torah, and he distinguishes himself by his ability and his sincerity. He is my confidant and my advisor and assists me without renumeration in communal matters. It was he who wrote these letters. We three — he, I, and my son — did all this."

Maneshewitz wanted to give me some golden coins, but I refused: "We all work on behalf of our people. When we ask your help, you give it. We, too, donate our resources to succor our people from their oppressors. I cannot accept money for my work on behalf of our people; that is a privilege given by God. For this I have striven and for this I was born."

17   Upholder of the Faith: The Rebbe of Belz

by Joseph Margoshes

JOSHUA ROKEACH was one of five sons of Sholem Rokeach, founder of the hasidic dynasty in Belz, Galicia. Joshua became head of the Belz court in 1855 after his father's death and ruled until 1894, when he died. He maintained his father's conservatism and engaged in an active campaign against the Galician maskilim. He innovated the use of the instruments of modernity — the press and politics — to propagate and perpetuate the traditionalist and conservative point of view in religion and politics. Thus, Joshua Rokeach may be regarded as a precursor of the Agudat Israel in the politicalization of Orthodoxy.

Joseph Margoshes, born in Lemberg in 1866, died in New York in 1955, was a Yiddish journalist who settled in New York in 1903. The following selection was taken from his memoirs.

In 1868, the society Shomer Israel ("Guardian of Israel") began to publish a fortnightly, *Der Israelit*, intended to exercise a "modern" influence on Galician Jews, particularly in Lemberg. For four years, the paper was written in a sort of Galician German with Hebrew letters; in its fifth year, it changed to pure German. During controversial issues or election campaigns, *Der Israelit* put out supplements in good, modern Hebrew. This paper, constantly agitating for "progress," naturally was a thorn in the side of the pious Jews. They, for their part, thought of founding a society, with its own publication, that would oppose Shomer Israel and defend Orthodox interests. My father, the animating spirit of this Orthodox oppositional movement, searched for an able man to help him. He found him in the person of Mordecai Pelz of Lemberg.

Pelz, whose real name was Enser, was an interesting man. His father, Moses Zvi Enser, who died in 1871, had been a leading maskil in Lemberg, a close friend of Solomon Rapoport and Nahman Krochmal, a frequent contributor to Hebrew publications, and the author of a Hebrew grammar. How the son of a maskil — and an important one at that — turned into a hasid, I do not know, but since Pelz first began to come to our house in 1877, I remember him always in his high fur hat, part of hasidic garb at that time. He was then private secretary to Joshua Rokeach, the rebbe of Belz, and also his political spokesman. Himself an educated man who knew Hebrew, German, Polish, and French, Pelz nevertheless did not give his children a secular education.

Under Pelz's influence, my father became closer with the Belzer rebbe and other hasidic rebbes. I came to know the Belzer rebbe quite well. He was a guest in our house several times. In his humility, he did not think himself worthy of the hasidic title "rebbe" and insisted on being called "rabbi." The son of Sholem Rokeach, founder of the Belz dynasty, Joshua inherited the Belz hasidic court at his father's death in 1855 and remained its head until he died in 1894. He had tens of thousands of followers in Galicia, Poland, and Hungary. The whole town lived off the rebbe's court. Every week several hundred hasidim assembled, and on holidays even more. During Rosh ha-Shana some five thousand hasidim used to throng to Belz.

The Belzer rebbe was tall and well built, with a heavily bearded face and thick brows. His massive frame housed an ardent and fearless spirit. Always certain he was right, he was convinced he was someone special in his relationship with the heavenly Household. He was constantly on guard wherever his influence extended, lest the old piety diminish and the slightest whisper of modernity be heard in his domain. In the first twenty-five years of his rule over the Belz court, he was satisfied to limit his influence to Belz and the surrounding towns. But later, with Mordecai Pelz as his secretary, and with the growing influence of the Shomer Israel in Lemberg, the rebbe of Belz realized the time was ripe for him to extend the area of his influence.

With Pelz and other leading Jews of Lemberg, my father had already worked out a plan for an association to be called Mahzike ha-Dat ("Upholders of the Faith"), whose center was to be in Lemberg, with branches in towns and villages. But this simple practical idea ran into obstacles, particularly the opposition from Shomer Israel. Its distinguished and influential membership of doctors, lawyers bankers maskilim had taken control of Jewish communal organizations and become spokesmen for the Jews. But these spokesmen did not observe *kashrut,* held themselves aloof from Judaism, and sometimes even mocked it. They introduced innovations in the community councils and wanted to imitate the pattern of German Reform Judaism. They aspired also to speak for the Jews in the Lemberg Landtag and in the Reichsrat in Vienna. For a long time, Galician Orthodoxy watched helplessly, unable to organize against Shomer Israel. Finally, they awoke from their sleep and began to fight the modernists.

In those days, a government permit was required for any new organization, even a society to study the Talmud. My father's plan for an organization with branches in many cities required a permit from the authorities in Vienna. When he and Mordecai Pelz submitted their application, the Shomer Israel went into action. They spread word that the founders of the new group were obscurantists whose fanatic purpose was to halt the spread of culture among the Jews. They used their influence to slow down the wheels of the bureaucracy, always a tiresome and complicated process in Galicia. In *Der Israelit,* they attacked the proposed Mahzike ha-Dat. The Orthodox, for their part, having no paper, could respond only by issuing leaflets, written mostly by my father. Even I was an active participant in the war against Shomer Israel: I was in constant motion, delivering copy to the printer and distributing the leaflets.

Though all doors were closed to them, the founders of Mahzike ha-Dat did not give up. They sought out Ignaz Deutsch of Vienna, who succeeded in eliciting a permit for the organization and for the newspaper. Deutsch, born in Pressburg around 1809, had studied in the yeshiva there under Rabbi Moses Sofer, the Hatam Sofer. Later he moved to Vienna, became a wealthy merchant and, finally, a banker. (He was bill broker at the court of Emperor Franz Joseph.) Orthodox Jews in the Habsburg Empire, especially the Hungarian Jews, found in him, a most pious Jew, their protector. (For example, he convinced the government that students who spent four years at the Pressburg yeshiva ought to be relieved of military service; the yeshiva then was publicly recognized as a theological institution.) About two months later, my father received the permits from the Austrian Ministry.

The next step was to select the president of the organization — an honorary office. The logical candidate was the rebbe of Belz. But since he had his own following, my father felt the other rebbes would be reluctant to join an organization which he headed, risking their own following. Besides, Orthodox Jews in Galicia were not all hasidim: there were mitnagdim, many observant maskilim, and educated people who held the rebbes in low esteem. It was decided, then, to invite Rabbi Simon Sofer, the rabbi of Cracow and son of the Hatam Sofer, to accept the presidency. A quiet man, he was reluctant at first, but I heard it said that he could not resist the prestige and my father's promise that, with the influence of the rebbe of Belz and of the other hasidic rebbes, he would be elected to the Austrian Reichrat. And, indeed, in 1879, he was elected from the heavily Jewish Galician districts of Kolomyja, Buczacz, and Sniatyn. He remained deputy until his death in 1883. (He supported the Polish Club and never spoke up in the Reichsrat, allowing the Poles to represent Jewish interests.)

When the newspaper *Mahzike ha-Dat* began to be published — its editorial office was in our house — I was ten or twelve years old. Its editors were Herz Goldenstern, my brother Joshua, and Joseph Joel Philip, who knew German well and was conversant with what was going on in the Lemberg kehilla, which our paper continuously assailed. In time, the circulation of the paper rose to 3,000.

18 The Golden Dynasty: Rebbe of Sadeger

by Isaac Ewen

ABRAHAM JACOB FRIEDMAN, born in 1820, was the second son of Israel of Rizhin (Ruzhin), founder of the hasidic dynasty of Sadeger (Sadagora), Galicia. Abraham Jacob assumed the leadership of the dynasty at his father's death in 1850, remaining head of the court until he died in 1883.

The court at Sadeger was an unusual combination of high mysticism and high living, Messianism and a splendid, regal way of life. The rebbe's immersion in the Kabbalistic mysteries, on the one hand, and the court's conspicuously lavish furnishings and costumes, on the other, seemed to embody the kingship qualities which the dynasty had inherited from its founder, Israel of Rizhin.

Men of the world were impressed by the Sadegerer rebbe not only because of his outward regal accoutrements but also because of his extraordinary spiritual qualities. This tension between the spiritual and the material seemed to be the hallmark of the Sadegerer court.

Isaac Ewen, who was born in Rozwadow, Galicia, in 1861 and died in Vienna in 1925, spent some time at the Sadegerer court and was later editor of the Belz *Mahzike ha-Dat*. He came to New York in 1908. He was a journalist, who wrote several books about hasidism. The following selection has been taken from his book about the dynasty of Sadeger.

THE rebbe of Sadeger, Abraham Jacob, was venerated not only among Jews, but also by prominent Christians. It was not unusual for princes, counts, and famous writers to journey to Sadeger to see the "wonder rabbi" and speak with him. Articles about him appeared in the press of Vienna, Berlin, Frankfort, Prague, and elsewhere. For such audiences, the rebbe relied on a translator, since he himself spoke no German. (Monish Weichselbaum, a boyhood friend of mine, was his translator.)

I was in Sadeger in 1880 when Sir Laurence Oliphant advised that he was coming to see the rebbe. Indescribable the preparations that were made for his reception — and extravagant. The whole court was redecorated and all the rooms refurbished. The commotion was stupendous. Sir Laurence, a wealthy and eminent Londoner, was said to have an enormous influence on the English government. For political reasons, he took an interest in the settlement of Palestine. At the time, there was talk of eventual partition of Turkey. Oliphant tried to convince his government that the Jews should, in that event, have Palestine, the land of their fathers, where they could once again make their home.

The news of Oliphant's imminent visit prompted all sorts of rumors among the hasidim. Many swore that Oliphant was bringing important political secrets that, affecting the Jews, could not be committed to writing.

That is why he came for a personal meeting with the rebbe, whom he considered the leader and spokesman of all Jews. Other hasidim believed that Oliphant wanted to become a Jew and that he wanted the rebbe to convince him of the moral superiority of the Torah of Moses and of Judaism. Sir Laurence would then bestow half of his fortune on the rebbe to do with as he chose; Sir Laurence would become a Jew — a Sadegerer hasid, at that. The hasidim even bickered about how the rebbe would spend the money. Some hasidim read strange and farfetched interpretations into the visit. The rebbe, of the seed of the House of David, was surely heir to the soul of Rabbi Judah ha-Nasi, of the House of David, and Sir Laurence, the Gentile noble, was surely the transmogrification of Antoninus, who, in his time, had gone to pay homage to Rabbi.

And indeed Oliphant came. The old rebbe and his sons gave him an unforgettable reception. He did not stay long in Sadeger, departing immediately after his visit. Weichselbaum, the translator and Nahum Ber, the rabbi's son-in-law, were the only ones present at the interview, but they never talked about it. Thirty years later, in hints and allusions, Weichselbaum told me something. Oliphant, he said, believing the Sadegerer rebbe was the leader of world Jewry, wanted his help to establish a national fund to buy Palestine from Turkey. The rebbe was supposed to have refused on the ground he was a Turkish subject, living on a Turkish passport. Moreover, he believed Jews must await redemption by a miracle, not by purchasing land.

After the rebbe's death in 1883, Oliphant described his visit in a Viennese journal.

When I was in Vienna, people I trusted told me so much about the Sadegerer rebbe I wanted very much to meet him, I thought, come what may. A man who by spirit alone rules thousands of people cannot be an ordinary commonplace creature. Since I was then situated near Sadeger, I advised the rebbe that my wife and I would like to meet him. Immediately, he sent us his splendid carriage. The whole Jewish community of Sadeger awaited our arrival, lining both sides of the street to see the Gentile coming to their rebbe. At the entrance of the rebbe's house, his sons and sons-in-law, in Polish dress, greeted us. Inside, the rebbe's daughters were hostesses to my wife. I was led into a room, much like a princely court, furnished with precious gold and silver antiques. There I met the rebbe, accompanied by two servants. Regal authority was in his face. He spoke intelligently about the situation of the Russian Jews. Though I did not quite understand his conduct, I was nevertheless con-

vinced that he could lead and command his people with just the barest
gesture.

The songs of Sadeger were so overwhelming that, once heard, they
could never be forgotten. Hasidim tell a story: A Sadegerer hasid had a son,
who, when he married and became independent, took to modern ways. He
ceased to make pilgrimages to the rebbe; he stopped observing the dietary
laws and publicly violated the Sabbath. Grief stricken, the father turned
his back on his son.

Once the Sadgerer rebbe asked him: "What has happened with your
son?"

"I no longer want to know of him," answered the hasid. "He has forsaken the Living God."

"A hasid who was once at my table cannot forsake the Living God," said
the rebbe. "If he has sinned, he will not die without repenting. Go home
and reconcile yourself with him."

Coming home, the hasid heard his son singing a moving Sadegerer melody, with the supplicating tones of deathbed prayers. Seeing his father, the
young man stopped singing, but in his surprise forgot to dry his tears.

"What business do you have now with a hasidic melody?" his father
asked. "You have so little connection with Judaism."

"In certain circumstances," the son replied earnestly, "one can cease to
be a Jew, but one can never cease to be a hasid. To some extent, Judaism
depends on reason, intellect. Intellect can, sometimes, reverse things and
interpret them contrariwise. But hasidism depends on the heart, on feeling.
Feelings and the heart cannot persuade or convince one by arguments and
delusions. A person feels a certain way and nothing can be done about
it."

And the young man repented his former ways and returned to the
rebbe.

Belz and Sadeger differed about how to safeguard hasidism against modernity. Belzer hasidim had a deep antagonism to Sadeger, for they could
not forgive the Sadegerer transgressions in dress — donning the styles of
modern Europe. Among hasidim of Belz, Jewish traditional dress was a
dogma, a fourteenth credo. Men had to wear a high fur hat (Polish style)
and flat shoes with white socks (German style). Belz was especially outraged by the high-fashion clothes of the women of the Sadegerer court.
But, in the long run, who was right?

In 1878, the Belzer rebbe, Joshua Rokeach, convened a rabbinical assembly in Lemberg to found the Mahzike ha-Dat. Its purpose was to publish a newspaper to strengthen hasidism and piety among Galician Jews, and to combate the Shomer Israel of Lemberg and the many periodicals of the haskala. The Mahzike ha-Dat was to be directed by Belz. The Sadegerer rebbe and his two brothers, the rebbes of Czortkow and of Husiatyn, were invited to the conference. Their delegates at the meeting supported the establishment of local societies to strengthen Judaism, but they utterly opposed the newspaper. In their opinion, that would bring about precisely what the Mahzike ha-Dat was intended to combat.

"An unheard-of thing," cried the Belzer indignantly to Mordecai Pelz in the presence of the Cracow rabbi, Simon Sofer, " 'the native below and the stranger on top!' I, who all my life waged war against every single innovation, understand that now is the time to serve God, that we need a paper to strengthen Judaism. But *they,* the 'enlightened,' have suddenly become worried that a paper can hurt our faith more than help it. What an upside-down world!"

But who was right?

I was editor of the *Kol Mahzike ha-Dat* ("Voice of Mahzike ha-Dat") for several years. I do not want to spit in the well from which I drank, but I must speak my mind. The historian writing about the Jews in Galicia will have to give much credit for the modern cultural development of today's Galician Jews to the Belzer rabbi and *Mahzike ha-Dat.* For the truth is, not Joseph Perl, nor Isaac Erter, nor Nahman Krochmal, nor Herschel Schorr succeeded in raising the intellectual level of Jewish youth in Galicia as much as did this hasidic Hebrew paper. Without intending it, not even aware of what it was accomplishing, this newspaper made fertile the soil on which Hebrew schools, the modern Hebrew language, and Zionism flourished. The Sadegerer rebbe was right. This fanatic hasidic paper, which dared not mention a word about the Zionist Congress, stirred hasidic youth from their lethargy and propelled them out of the prayer houses, first into the tents of the maskilim, and then into the arms of the Zionists.

That was the time Belz dominated Jewish Galicia. The young people were confined within the narrow limits of the prayer house. They were forbidden to study Hebrew as a modern language, to read the Hebrew press. Study even of the Prophets and Writings was a sin. Then all at once, a paper was issued in the sacred tongue, under the holy imprint of the highest authority, the Mahzike ha-Dat, its president the Cracow rabbi Simon Sofer, with the explicit approval of the Belzer rabbi. It became permissible to read a newspaper even in the prayer house — for this was a sanctified newspaper. It even became possible to look into Prophets and

Writings, not to study it, but to check on the meaning of a word in *Mahzike ha-Dat*. Every Thursday evening in the prayer houses, the young men used to read the paper and discuss it. Now their fathers approved. Sometimes *Mahzike ha-Dat* engaged in a controversy, for the sake of Heaven, with *Ha-Ivri* or *Ha-Maggid*. It naturally became a small matter of curiosity to have a look at these godless papers just to see what they were saying. In this way, these pious readers of *Mahzike ha-Dat* became fluent readers of the modern Hebrew press and belles lettres. Some even became maskilim and writers themselves. So, after all, the rebbe of Sadeger was right.

19   The Two Lights of My Life

by Isaac Jacob Reines

ISAAC JACOB REINES, a rabbi and Zionist, was born in Karlin, near Pinsk, province of Minsk, in 1839 and died in Lida, province of Vilna, in 1915. He received a Talmudic education from his father. He also studied mathematics and philosophy from Hebrew works and was said to have known both Russian and German, a most unusual accomplishment for an observant Jew of that time and place. In 1855, he studied for two years at the yeshiva at Volozhin. In 1859, he married the daughter of Joseph Reisen, rabbi of Horodok (Grodek), and studied with him for some years. In 1869, Reines became rabbi in Swieciany, province of Vilna, where he remained until 1885.

In 1880 he developed a new and modernized plan for Talmudic study in an enlarged program that included also secular subjects, an innovation severely condemned by the Orthodox. Only his own unblemished orthodoxy saved him from being attacked as a freethinker. In 1882, at a conference in St. Petersburg of rabbinic and communal leaders, he proposed that his educational plan be adopted instead of the one prevalent in the yeshivot, as a means of attracting greater numbers of young Jews and also of meeting the pressure of the Russian government for the introduction of Russian and other secular subjects into the yeshiva curriculum. But after his program was rejected, he undertook to institute it in a yeshiva he himself organized in Swieciany. This was a ten-year course combining a rabbinic course of study leading to ordination with a program of general studies. But opposition among the ultra-Orthodox was so great and so well organized that they prevailed upon the Russian government to close down Reines's yeshiva. For years, Reines hoped to be able to reopen such a modern yeshiva. In 1905 he had this opportunity in

Lida, where he had been rabbi since 1885. It appeared to be quite successful, attracting particularly the sons of well-to-do Jews who might otherwise have been sent to Russian schools, since general education had already become a basic necessity.

Reines's modernism was not limited to education. In the late 1880's he had already become interested in the Hibbat Zion movement and, after the first Zionist Congress, became an active member of the Zionist Organization and later a founder of Mizrachi. Also for his dedication to the Zionist movement, Reines suffered the abuse and harassment of the ultra-Orthodox. Excerpts follow from his memoir, recounting his experiences in the Zionist movement and in establishing the yeshiva at Lida.

Reines, a generation after Israel Salanter, tried in a more systematic and organized way than Salanter to combine Talmudic education with general education and reconcile Jewish rabbinic tradition with the modern world. Reines was a sort of unsuccessful Eastern European Israel Hildesheimer, without sufficient communal support among the Orthodox to help him achieve his great purpose. Had Reines found more understanding among Orthodox rabbis for his goal of conserving rabbinic learning in a modern world, raising its prestige by acknowledging the necessity for general secular education, he might indeed have become a great luminary instead of remaining a half-forgotten figure in Jewish memory.

THESE memoirs describe, first, my involvement in the Zionist movement and the founding of Mizrachi, and then how, with God's help, I founded the yeshiva at Lida. The idea of Jewish resettlement in Palestine has engrossed me for over forty years. On this subject I corresponded extensively with Rabbi Zvi Hirsh Kalischer and Rabbi Elijah Gutmacher of Grätz. Thirty years of my life I devoted to the yeshiva. In my later years my lifelong commitment to both these undertakings became even more intense, perhaps because they caused me so much suffering. I think some law of nature makes the object of one's love more precious because of the pain it causes: the greater one's love, the readier one is to suffer for it. Suffering, in turn, enhances the beloved object and becomes transformed into still greater devotion.

This may have some bearing on devotion also to a national or communal cause. Those who abandon a cause because of some unpleasantness may not have been sincerely committed to it in the first place. Otherwise, obstacles would not only not have made them withdraw, but would rather have increased their dedication. One reason prompting me to publish this memoir is, indeed, to describe publicly the difficulties I encountered while engaged on behalf of my beloved projects. But I have another, even more valid, reason for its publication.

In an essay elsewhere, I said two factors helped preserve Judaism and faith throughout the years of Jewish dispersal: influential leaders wholly devoted to their people, and a disciplined people prepared to obey and follow these leaders. Clearly, the presence of great leaders — a sign of Divine providence — in each generation was crucial in maintaining the nation's loyalty to its faith, but they needed also absolute obedience from the people.

Some people think that rabbinical authority today is bankrupt and ineffectual. But that is not so, though rabbinical leadership nowadays is not sufficiently outspoken. Had the influence of the rabbis waned, our people would not have remained true to Judaism. Though deterioration of moral values can be seen in individual instances, the people as a whole abides by Jewish tradition, and in many places true piety abides. Almost every community boasts a circle for the daily study of Talmud and the yeshivot enjoy a large enrollment. But in our times, more than ever, national discipline is indispensable, for the winds of free thought are blowing from all directions, the high-rising waters threaten to inundate the very foundations of our national structure, washing away the sacred precepts of Israel. Only obedience can save us, only national discipline. Obedience requires leaders and followers.

To be a source of strength and inspiration to his people, a leader must have an unblemished reputation, or his voice will be calling in the wilderness. No taint of gossip must be linked with his name, for obedience is based on respect, which vanishes before gossip or slander. A leader must not pursue profit, nor deviate from truth, as it is written, "men of truth, hating unjust gain." Both are in the same category, and anyone suspected of either untruth or unjust profit will lose the respect of the community.

There is a popular saying that if you are aware of a personal failing, you must reveal it before others do. This can be applied to the Jews. This saying influenced me to express publicly what was in my heart.

For some decades now, Jews have shown symptoms of a disease — perversion of the truth. This is a dangerous and contagious disease which we must seek to cure. A man dedicated to truth will fearlessly and honestly defend his views, even if he arouses opposition or displeasure, but some people, to please everybody, openly applaud one set of beliefs while in their hearts they believe otherwise. This is flagrant dishonesty. The symptoms of this disease were most apparent when the Zionist idea began to spread, for many supported it in their hearts but spoke against it. There were those who opposed Zionism because they feared that nonbelievers infiltrated the movement. But this argument was a deliberate distortion, concocted for mass consumption, and any sensible person knew it was untrue. Whether or not freethinkers take part in the movement, no one can deny that all activity on behalf of the Holy Land is sanctified and moral. Most opponents of Zionism know their fears in this regard are groundless, yet they exploit them. There is no greater perversion of the truth. While I can understand that some of these people fear the consequences of publicly supporting Zionism, it would have been much better had they defended their beliefs. The only way I knew how to prove they had nothing to fear from Zionism's opponents was to publish this memoir. It describes my experiences and how many reputable people tried all sorts of devices to humiliate me. Yet they failed. With God's help, I succeeded in my undertakings, my person and honor unimpaired. I hope that my words will allay the fears among Zionist supporters and they will no longer conceal their sympathies.

Among the antagonists of Zionism are many God-fearing men whose opposition comes from the depths of their heart. Zionism's supporters, too, include deeply reverent men. What, then, is the critical point which caused the conflict in views? The antagonism to Zionism is, I concluded, essentially psychological. One who had been reared from early childhood in the tradition of the Torah and whose constant support is in Judaism, which is bone of his bone and flesh of his flesh, is as deeply shocked when his religion is put to shame as if his own son were disgraced. His indignation will, in turn, set in motion thoughts of persecuting the offenders, without pausing to consider whether such persecution will be efficacious.

Each rumor of irreligion within the movement — not by Zionism itself but by individual Zionists — shocked the Orthodox. They immediately resorted to counteraction — withdrawing from the movement and urging others to withdraw. I confess that I, too, contemplated resigning at certain times, especially after the 1911 convention adopted a resolution favoring the inclusion of Jewish secular culture in the movement. For many years I fought this proposal. When it was adopted, I was shocked. Had it not been for my lifelong devotion to the ideal of resettling the Holy Land, I would have followed the natural course and resigned. But on second thought I realized nothing could be gained by condemnation or resignation, which would hurt rather than help the religious issue.

In 1897, the year of the first Zionist Congress, when the Zionist idea first received world attention, many rabbis participated in the movement. They even held a caucus convention in Warsaw. At that time I was not yet involved, since my practice has always been first to study all aspects of an idea, especially one of such vital importance to Jews and Judaism. I believe one cannot expect too much of those who join a movement on the spur of the moment, but those who give their support to the movement after seri-

ous consideration may become its standard-bearers. It took me two years to
accept Zionism; in those two years I studied its religious and intellectual
aspects and the personality of the man heading this movement. When I was
satisfied with the results of my investigation, I became an active member
and attended every Zionist convention and Congress. Leaders of the opposition tried to dissuade me, because they feared my presence would attract
new members. But they failed, for they had no understanding of Zionism
and their arguments were often ludicrous. A most eminent man from the
opposition appealed to me with the tired arguments about irreligion in the
Zionist movement. When I demonstrated how groundless his objections
were, he argued that I was harming my own prestige and reputation. Were
I not with the Zionists, I would be more sought after and consulted. But I
replied that I had no intention of resigning unless I had real evidence of the
alleged misconduct in the movement. Even more, I told him that a Jew
should not only not estrange himself from the Zionist organization, but it
was his duty to join it. Furthermore, I told him, to my knowledge many
rabbis were favorably inclined toward Zionism but hesitated to endorse it
publicly because the opposition was so skillful in character assassination.

I refuted all the arguments advanced by my eminent opponent. When
the opposition realized that the ideal of Zionism remained rooted in my
heart they unloosed a campaign of slander against me. But I ignored the
endless stream of calumnies they issued against me in the press, as I had in
the past.

As a matter of fact, I was distressed and heartsick by the absence of the
Orthodoxy in the Zionist movement. Since the sad lot of the Jews kept
deteriorating, any concrete plan to alleviate the troubled situation, however
uncertain or impractical it might seem, should have received a helping
hand. Yet many of our fellow Jews rejected it and urged others to do likewise. Since I knew the opposition based its arguments on unfounded rumors of irreligiosity in the movement, I undertook to remove this suspicion
and to silence the rumormongers. To safeguard the Zionist idea against
slander, it occurred to me to convene the truly Orthodox to discuss this. I
knew I would encounter many obstructions but the urgency of organizing a
special Orthodox Zionist section became apparent after the Fifth Congress
in 1902, when some young and radical Zionists broke away from the general organization, attacking also some matters of religion. Returning from
the Congress, I became ill in Frankfort and had to stay there a few days.
With some of my visitors I spoke of my plan to organize an Orthodox
Zionist section, and upon my return home I devoted myself exclusively to
this objective.

The hardships I encountered in the process defy description, but my efforts were crowned with success, and the Orthodox group, under the name of Mizrachi, came into being.

The yeshiva in Lida, I must admit, I cherished even more than the Zionist idea, for I count it as the recovery of a loss. For when one loses something valued and cherished and then recovers it, his joy is endless — as if he had discovered a new treasure. For over thirty years I tried to organize a yeshiva of this particular type, which supplemented the usual religious studies with secular subjects. I had once done something along these lines on a limited scale, but it did not last. Thereafter, the idea continued to engross me. God, seeing my sorrow, helped me found the yeshiva, which now has become a permanent institution. In existence for eight years, it keeps expanding every year and its renown has no limit. Thousands of students come here from all parts of the country. My joy and satisfaction are great because I founded this yeshiva.

The responsibility of the individual toward his people is felt in direct relation to his emotional sensitivty. The more sensitive he is, the stronger his bonds to his people. A man must also be sensitive to his people's faults and seek to correct them. This is his obligation. If he does not do what he knows ought to be done, he is like a debtor unable to repay a loan. For years, I thought that so long as we did not establish yeshivot which instructed also in secular studies we would never prevail over the haskala, which was becoming ever more influential. In war, before taking its own positions, each side must know the size of the enemy's forces, their morale, the number and strength of their defenses and, most important, their weapons. If the enemy's weapons are superior, then he avoids battle, for without hope of winning, why send thousands of people to be killed?

So we, too, must see that our weapons are not inferior to those of the maskilim. As long as we use only weapons of the spirit, when they use weapons of substance, we can never win. When we ponder on the tremendous upheaval among Jews, we must conclude that it came about not because we changed our attitude toward Judaism but because our way of life changed and economic conditions changed all over the world. In earlier times, Jews lived in a world of their own from which they drew their livelihood, without need of general education or special training. It was sufficient that a man be learned in Torah so that God would love him and his fellowmen respect him. Fathers could provide for their sons studying the Talmud, and the sons themselves did not strive for anything else. But the world is changed now. The economic barriers between peoples have fallen. Trade, industry, and handicraft differ radically from what they used to be. To be employed nowadays, a man needs general education and training. Now, when making a living is as hard as dividing the Red Sea, parents are glad if they can provide for their small children; the burden of supporting grown sons is too great for them to bear. Nor can the young people themselves be blind to their future. Nowadays, when a father selects a groom for his daughter, he demands, even of a rabbi, general education in addition to traditional Jewish learning. Little wonder, then, that fathers and sons see no future in the prayer house. We have done nothing to prevent this. Did we try to face these new conditions which loomed up like a barrier before our young people? No, we did nothing. Now the Jewish community is being swayed by an alien voice; the Jewish voice has been silenced. For where there is no Torah, there is no Judaism.

The obvious conclusion, then, is that young people, while being educated in Torah and its commandments, should also be given a general education and taught subjects which they need in life. If we will not act soon, our young people will forsake us for places where they can find this general education. That was why I was convinced that a yeshiva, concentrating as it does on the study of Judaism, must at the same time prepare the students in general subjects. Only this sort of yeshiva can rescue Judaism.

20   Mother of the Beth Jacob Schools
by Sarah Schenirer

SARAH SCHENIRER, founder of the Beth Jacob schools, was born in Cracow in 1883 and died in a Vienna hospital in 1935. The daughter of a well-to-do Belzer hasid, she received what was then the typical education for Jewish girls — a general elementary education in a Polish school, with a weekly hour of religious instruction. She grew up to become strictly observant and deeply pious; her autobiography is unfortunately reticent on how she came to be so different from her contemporaries. Aware of the powerful impact of secularism and modernity on Jewish girls and young women, she conceived a new system of Jewishly educating Jewish girls that eventually became known as the Beth Jacob movement ("house of Jacob": "O house of Jacob, come ye, and let us walk in the light of the Lord," Isaiah

2:5), described in the following extract from her memoirs. Her first school was founded in Cracow in 1917 with thirty pupils. Shortly before World War II, over 35,000 girls were enrolled in nearly three hundred Beth Jacob schools in Poland. Sponsorship of these schools had been taken over by the Agudat Israel.

The expansion of the Beth Jacob school system made the question of teacher training urgent. Sarah Schenirer spent the last years of her life as head of the Beth Jacob Teachers Seminary, training orthodox Jewish teachers for Beth Jacob schools. A Beth Jacob movement exists today in the United States and in Israel.

Herself a product of the modern world whose influence she sought to minimize in the face of the centrifugal forces that beset traditional Judaism, Sarah Schenirer originated for girls a revolutionary educational program whose purpose was to conserve and preserve. However traditional in her beliefs, she represented the modern woman and the important new role of women, outside the home, in shaping Jewish life.

I was born in Cracow in 1883. My father did his utmost to bring up his children in the ways of Torah and Judaism. When I was six, I was nicknamed Miss Hasida. In school, religion was my best subject, though I was good in all subjects and received some distinction each time I was promoted. I was also good at sewing.

It gave me great pleasure to spend the Sabbath reading the *Tsena-Urena*, reviewing the portion of the week and its *haftora*. My sister and her friends used to spend the Sabbath singing and dancing. I went off into a corner, immersed in the portion of the week. They used to say that I was so absorbed in my religious books, I would never have noticed if the house was being robbed. It hurt me even then to see my Jewish sisters transgress the spirit of the ancient Jewish people and disregard Judaism. Sometimes I scolded one of the girls, but they mocked me and called me Miss Hasida. I did not mind the ridicule or the nickname; I continued in my way.

As I grew older, the income at home was small and I had to find work. I became a seamstress. I worked all day; in the evening, however, I worked on myself. I bought a Bible with a Yiddish translation and studied every evening. My pleasure was boundless.

On one Friday evening a cousin invited me to attend a meeting of the organization called Ruth. I was shocked to see with my own eyes one of the officers lighting candles on the Sabbath. I had known this group set no records in piety, but I never imagined they would have publicly violated the Sabbath. The lecture of the evening, distorted and impious, was heard by girls whose hasidic fathers were that moment studying the Gemara and whose mothers were reading *Tsena-Urena*. There it first occurred to me: If only these girls would be in the right environment, things would be different.

After the great war broke out in 1914, we left Cracow for Vienna. That translocation was to influence the future Beth Jacob movement. Vienna was a seething cauldron of the masses of migrant Jews from Galicia who had fled the Russian advance. Our first weeks there, we practically roamed the streets looking in vain for a place to live in the Jewish quarter. Finally we settled in a non-Jewish section, about an hour's walk from the Great Synagogue. But my landlady told me of a nearby Orthodox synagogue. I went there on the Sabbath during Hanukka. The rabbi, Dr. Flesch, delivered an inspiring sermon about Judith, calling on the daughters of Israel in our time to follow in her footsteps. As I listened I thought: If only the Jewish women and girls of Cracow could hear him and learn who we were and how great is our heritage. But I realized that unfortunately our daughters knew little of our splendid past, a lack of knowledge that estranged them from their people and their tradition. Then I dreamed of great deeds, but Providence decreed a long time would pass before something practical would come of these thoughts.

Listening to Dr. Flesch's sermons, I kept thinking how to bring his message to the Jewish women of Poland. As time passed, my plan became concrete. How would Cracow respond to my plan to establish a school in which Jewish girls could be educated in an Orthodox environment? I knew they would ask: "Now, in the twentieth century? Do you want Jewish girls to return to the past?" But an inner voice kept calling me: "It is your responsibility to submit your plan to establish an Orthodox school. This is the only way to rescue for Judaism the new generation." I decided that when I returned to Cracow, I would convene a meeting of girls and women and submit my proposal.

I went back to Cracow in the summer of 1917 and invited a small group of observant women to listen to my plan. They approved. I was afraid that even if adults were excited about my idea, the younger generation would laugh at it. But I persisted. One Saturday afternoon I lectured to about forty girls on *Pirke Avot* ("The Sayings of the Fathers"). Dwelling on the passage "and make a hedge about the Torah," I spoke about the hedges and fences with which our sages surrounded the commandments. The girls, I could see, were amused, I could see their ironic smiles. My talk was received coldly, mockingly. I knew how hard was the road I had marked out for myself, but I did not give up.

The High Holy Days approached. On the eve of the Day of Atonement I was especially emotional and sentimental. Before my eyes floated visions of the past, the Temple, the High Priest at his service. That was the splendor of Israel. What of today? Who will continue the tradition in our times? Where are the Jewish hearts whose fervent prayers can substitute for the High Priest's holy service? The sons of Israel who attend the synagogue do so only out of habit; their hearts and souls are not in the service. How much truer for the girls who know neither the greatness of our people nor the meaning of the prayers. Until Kol Nidre, these thoughts obsessed me. What did obstacles and impediments matter? What did ridicule and mockery matter? Or my personal feelings? When the cantor concluded the Yom Kippur service, singing, "Hope to God and strengthen your heart," these words reawoke my hope.

The days turned into weeks; my plan began to take shape. The girls' organization I had founded began to grow; yet I feared it would not bring the results I hoped for. Was it possible to influence grown girls who had ideas of their own? I decided to move in another direction. One must begin with little children. A young shoot bends more easily. Orthodox schools should be organized, in which girls could be educated in the spirit of the ancient Jewish people. The idea preoccupied me. I wrote my brother, asking advice. At first he cautioned that I would become involved in disputes with the Jewish parties already operating their own school systems. But he suggested that I come to him in Marienbad, where we would visit the Belzer rebbe and ask his advice. Though I could ill afford the trip, my joy was so great I went. My brother took me to the rebbe, to whom he submitted a note explaining: "My sister would like to guide and teach Jewish girls in the ways of Judaism and Torah." Then the rebbe gave me his blessing and his wishes for my success. It was as though new energy poured into me.

In 1917 I finally had my own school. Who could understand how I felt with twenty-five beaming little faces before me? Once I had sewn clothing for many of them. Now I was giving them spiritual raiment. The school expanded from day to day. Soon I had forty pupils. The children were choice material; they had not yet tasted sin. They learned that man does not live by bread alone and that everything comes from God's mouth. They came to know that only by serving God sincerely could they live truly happy lives.

As for me, I am so absorbed in my work nothing else exists. I do not notice how the hours, the days, the weeks pass. But this is only the beginning.

21   When Hasidim of Ger Became Newsmen

by Moshe Prager

ABRAHAM MORDECAI ALTER was born in Poland in 1865 and died in Israel in 1948. He was the third generation of the hasidic dynasty of Ger (Gora Kalwarja), the great-grandson of Isaac Meir, the Hiddushe ha-Rim and follower of Menahem Mendel of Kotsk.

Under Abraham Mordecai, Ger became the most influential center of Orthodoxy in Poland, providing a common ground for hasidim and mitnag-dim. He may perhaps be designated as the political genius of hasidism, which found its expression during the German occupation of Poland in World War I. A founder of the Agudat Israel, he helped to bridge differences not only between hasidim and mitnag-dim, but also between East European and German Jews, who met on common ground in the Aguda.

Moshe Mark (pen name Prager), a Yiddish and Hebrew journalist, was born in Warsaw in 1908 and now makes his home in Israel. The following selection was taken from his memoir about the Orthodox Jewish press in Poland.

THE Orthodox Yiddish daily press had a long history of failure and disappointment. Its first nonsuccess goes back to 1907, the very high point of the Jewish press, and to the Hebrew daily *Ha-Kol* with its Yiddish section. But the history of disappointed hopes goes back even further — to the sixties, when *Ha-Maggid*, voice of the haskala, began to appear. Rabbi Isaac Meir Lewin, leader of the Polish Jewish Orthodoxy, wrote: "An old hasid once told me that when *Ha-Maggid* appeared, the Gerer rebbe, Isaac Meir Alter, said that we ought to counteract immediately and publish an Orthodox paper. But regrettably no one did."

The third Gerer rebbe, Abraham Mordecai Alter (1865–1948), tried to realize his great-grandfather's hope, after he took over the Gerer court. Isaac Meir Lewin recounts: "My father-in-law, the Gerer rebbe, knew the importance of an Orthodox newspaper, and he invested considerable energy in starting one. In 1907, he and his brother Menahem Mendel published a daily newspaper in Yiddish and Hebrew in Warsaw, and a weekly, too."

Another contemporary wrote: "The initiator of this venturous plan was Menahem Mendel Alter. He scoured among Orthodox circles for talented journalists who were deeply committed hasidim, but there were few. He found a teacher in Bedzin, a learned Jew and a skillful writer whose thankless task it became to edit *Ha-Kol,* the first Orthodox daily. Unable to find writers among the Orthodox, the editor recruited his staff from maskilim, Hebrew teachers, and anyone else who could write. But after a year, the paper failed, for the editor and his motley staff could not fulfil the expectations of the founders."

Another abortive attempt occurred in 1912, after the Kattowitz conference at which the worldwide Agudat Israel was founded. Once again, the Gerer rebbe conceievd an ambitious communal program for Orthodox Polish Jewry, of which a daily newspaper was an integral part. Some of his well-to-do followers in Warsaw and Lodz undertook to finance the proposed daily. To gain wider support, the rebbe wrote an open letter to all his followers: "Some distinguished men of Warsaw and Lodz have undertaken to sponsor a popular newspaper to be written and edited in a truly religious spirit. I ask all of you to join in the solemn task of obtaining subscriptions and readers. This is the most effective way to halting the freethinking that has spread among many Jews."

The Gerer rebbe's letter was considered an open attack on the Yiddish press of the time, which sought to attract readers with trashy and lurid serials. But by the time a permit for a Yiddish paper had been obtained from the Tsarist government, an editor found and hired, the war broke out.

Success came at the third try, in Warsaw during the war. Two rabbis of the German occupying army, Dr. Pinchas Kohn and Dr. Emanuel Carlebach, distinguished German Orthodox Jews, of the Frankfort school, advised the German occupying authorities with regard to the Jews and the Jewish community. The Union of the Orthodox was then established and *Dos yidishe vort,* the Orthodox Warsaw daily, came into being.

A staff member of the early days recalled the reception of the paper: "I will never forget the powerful impression the first issue of *Dos yidishe vort* made when it appeared in the summer of 1916. Observant Jews and old hasidim pronounced the benediction 'Who hath preserved us in life' over each issue. The literary material appealed to the young people, because it was suspenseful without being obscene."

Once again the Gerer rebbe wrote to his followers:

"Long have I wanted a newspaper true to the Jewish spirit, where freethinking and indecency would have no place. How many of you have come to me weeping, seeing your sons and daughters turn from us and flee elsewhere because they read wicked books and newspapers which poison the body and the soul? Now I appeal to you: Let this undertaking not appear trivial in your eyes, because with only a few pennies a day you can help this paper grow and benefit the community. I appeal particularly to my own followers."

In 1919, when Poland became independent, the Gerer rebbe helped establish a new Orthodox paper, *Der yid* ("The Jew"), which was conceived as an official organ of the Agudat Israel in Poland. Started as a weekly, it became a daily in December, 1920. *Der yid,* nicknamed by Zionists *yid ha-kodosh* ("the holy Jew"), was always in a sorry situation. Sometimes it appeared only once or three times a week; several times it stopped publication altogether. In 1929 it finally closed down.

From its ruins arose *Dos yidishe togblat,* the first Orthodox paper established on a solid financial basis and with a crystallized ideological position. The paper struck roots in the religious milieu and in the Jewish community at large, appearing regularly until September, 1939.

Probably the chief reason for the paper's success (how ironic!) was that it originated as a cooperative venture on the part of the Orthodox journalists' association and the Socialist Bundist printers' union. Since the government's anti-Jewish discriminatory policies had hit the Jews hard economically, all Yiddish newspapers were affected and the consequent decline in circulation threatened their very existence. The cooperative agreement, then, made economic sense. Still, because the Orthodox and Bundist papers were printed in the same plant, occasional typographical absurdities occurred. The slogan "Down with clericalism" might turn up under an announcement by the Agudat Israel, and the expression "God be praised" would appear in a report of a Bundist meeting.

No doubt another reason for the paper's success was the fact that the Agudat Israel was not its publisher and did not dictate its political line. Editorial management was in the hands of observant men, reared in the ranks of the Agudat Israel, competent to formulate the Orthodox view in political matters, though they sometimes disagreed with the particular political views of Aguda leadership.

Mendel Kaminer, the paper's cofounder and business manager, made it possible for the paper to stay institutionally independent. A man of royal stature, with a commanding presence and a wise smile, he had been brought up in a home of princely riches. He had both self-reliance and family prestige (he was a brother-in-law of the late Gerer rebbe and an uncle of the regnant rebbe). Hot-tempered and ambitious, girded with prestige in his own right, he had been one of the chief organizers of the Aguda in Poland, but he was not flexible enough to share power in its leadership. Though his name did not appear on the masthead, he was the support behind the scenes. It was he on whom the editors leaned.

It was feared when the *Togblat* first appeared in the fall of 1929 that it would be labelled as belonging to Ger and therefore would be spurned in Galicia, where Belz reigned supreme. But the course of events prevented that. In February, 1930, a conference of Jewish religious authorities convened in Warsaw under the chairmanship of the ninety-year-old Hofets Hayim, the outstanding rabbinical authority of the time.* Bringing together the religious leaders of Crown Poland, Galicia, and Lithuanian Poland (the Hofets Hayim flanked by the rebbes of Ger, Belz, and Alexander, all competing dynasties), the conference was reminiscent of the historic convocations of the Council of the Four Lands. The meeting itself was secret, but the later dramatic public procession of these four rabbinical eminences with a petition to the Polish Premier, the Interior Minister, and the Education Minister created a sensation.

All this was propitious for the *Togblat,* which having firsthand access to the news sources, brought the message of unity among Orthodoxy to Galicia, Lithuanian Poland, and the Eastern borders, where previously a publication associated with Ger would have been ill received.

22   From Freethinker to Believer
by Nathan Birnbaum

NATHAN BIRNBAUM, seminal Jewish thinker, was born in Vienna in 1864. His father had come of a Galician hasidic family and his mother was the daughter of a Carpathian mitnagid rabbi. Having moved to Vienna, however, his family was only moderately observant; his father was even something of a maskil. Birnbaum attended German schools, and German culture had a considerable influence on him.

As a student at the University of Vienna in 1883, he founded the first Jewish nationalist student society, Ka-

* Isaac Meir Lewin has described the purpose of this conference: "The new Polish government had appointed an assimilationist freethinking Jew to the Education Ministry to supervise Jewish religious and educational affairs. Backed by the authority of the government, he had begun to introduce religious reform and changes conforming to his own outlook. To counteract his activity, the Hofets Hayim came to Warsaw to organize a unified opposition."

dima, based on the idea of national renewal in Palestine. For some years he published a paper called *Selbst-Emanzipation*, named after Leon Pinsker's *Autoemanzipation*.

In 1885 he obtained his law degree but after four years gave up his position with a law firm to devote himself to writing and Jewish communal affairs. He eventually became deeply involved in the early Zionist movement. He read a paper at the first Zionist Congress in Basel in 1897 and was elected secretary-general of the first Zionist Actions Committee.

But he became dissatisfied with political Zionism and began to question the validity of its approach to Jewish existence. Leaving the Zionist movement, he turned toward East European Jewry, which he considered to be the real and living Jewish people, embodying a vital Jewish culture. From this perception he evolved a theory of galut-nationalism, which led him directly to Yiddish, a galut-language, and he entered into a lifelong battle to raise the prestige of Yiddish among those who spoke it and those who did not. In 1908, he went to the United States to lecture and plan the Yiddish Language Conference, held later that year in Czernowitz (Cernauti).

In 1911, Birnbaum went to Poland and Russia, where he lectured in every important Jewish center: Lodz, Warsaw, Vilna, Riga, Kiev, and St. Petersburg. While there, Birnbaum had a great mystical experience, which he described in an autobiographical essay:

I must first go back a few years. Even before my trip to America I had doubts about my materialist world outlook, which I had for so long accepted. But the first truly religious feelings, the first perceptions of God, first awoke in me when I was travelling on the sea. I myself did not know what was happening to me. Later, I looked upon it as a dream. But my doubts about materialism continued to harass me until I vanquished it totally. I began to understand the achievement of religion in the world. I recognized it as the axis on which human history revolved. I was already close to the recognition of the eternal and living substance of religion, but I still somehow resisted, until the blessed moment arrived and He showed himself to me in His whole creative splendor. Yet still I did not get the idea that from this recognition some greater accomplishment still awaited me. It was when in Russia, at a discussion in St. Petersburg, after a lecture given by someone else, that suddenly it became clear to me that I must rise and bear witness to the Lord God. And I rose and in a passionate speech poured out my whole heart. Then I first realized that a great new obligation awaited me.

After this public testimony of his conversion from secular materialism to Orthodox Judaism, Birnbaum devoted himself to writing about Messianic Judaism, teaching that Judaism and Jewishness had a single divine origin and that one could not exist without the other. In 1919 Birnbaum, who had arrived at professing Judaism by way of a mystical experience, joined the Agudat Israel, which had politicalized Judaism. For a short time, he was its general secretary. The following selection was translated from an autobiographical essay first published in 1919.

Birnbaum lived in Germany until 1933. After Hitler's advent to power, he settled in Scheveningen in Holland, where he died in 1937.

I_F I am to explain how from a freethinker I became a believer, I must first answer another question: how I became a freethinker to begin with. Born of East European Jewish parents in the West European metropolitan Jewish community in Vienna, I grew up with the concepts, and amidst the practice, of traditional Judaism — yet in an environment that no longer retained much of that strong and vital Judaism we still find among the Jews of Eastern Europe. Nevertheless, I was a believing child and youth, eager to practice Judaism as I had been taught. And so until the early years of high school. Only later was I to be influenced by the sort of education I received and the non-Jewish culture around me. I did not, however, experience that precipitousness, that painful inner conflict and pathos so characteristic of young East European Jews who abandoned the old Jewish life for "enlightened" ways. My way of life did not, after all, differ so greatly from the non-Jewish way, as did the East European Jew's, yet I felt real satisfaction that there was a difference between me and the world outside, and not a small one at that. But bad influences did not appear to have played a role in the change I underwent. At first it showed itself only in the fact that calmly and without fuss I stopped observing one or another commandment. I gave no thought to the important questions. In my basic principles, I remained a believer and, as I recall, I had no doctrinal objection to the observance of the commandments. The change in me became more violent when, at about sixteen or seventeen, I began reading a certain type of literature, especially Büchner's *Force and Matter,* then in fashion. Antiphilosophic natural philosophy succeeded in doing what the culture of my environment had not been able to accomplish — that is, to uproot me. I felt as if the scales had fallen from my eyes and suddenly I could see. The world was so simple to understand: it exists and that's that. Life evolves from dead matter and multiplies by sexual intercourse. Soul, spirit are simply functions of matter or, if you wish, their excrescences. Philosophy and, it goes without saying, religion — idle words. This materialistic, monistic turn in my opinions about the most important things in the world would probably have greatly reinforced the revolutionary anarchistic sympathies which I had already had, had not something else kept me from wandering far off. This was the insight which I, the young Western Jew of East European Jewish origin, had at the end of the seventies — that assimilation was a delusion, a fallacy we might well bewail, and that we must remind ourselves of the fact of our peoplehood. Realizing this, I had, still in my early years, begun to work with great impetus among the educated younger Jews then unquestioningly assimilationist. It happened that I did not make much of my brand-new freethinking and even tried not to flaunt it. I did not have enough time for that. My national outlook had led me to look upon religion and the commandments as a national mode, cherished by the people — a mode freethinking nationalists could use, and one to which they ought even adapt themselves, if that was necessary for their purposes. Perhaps some nationalist romanticism intruded and perhaps also — so it seems today, looking back — an instinctive satisfaction that I had once again come closer to the old domain of the faith of my childhood years. But my freethinking did not long permit me to put it aside. If my free thought had not been fitted into a general scheme of the world, it was simply because I still had not had such a view. Things became quite different when I outgrew boyish unaccountability and arrived at the responsibility of manhood, when in all my work I reached the stage of viewing everything under the sun from a single point of view. Freethinking did not then seem to me to be an isolated phenomenon, but something which a modern man's world outlook ought not to lack. To me, modernity meant the liberation of the individual from all his bonds. My old anarchistic sympathies became clearly defined socialist demands. I was concerned about the individual, about saving his individuality, which economic exploitation menaced. As for our people, my concern was to liberate Jewish group individuality and Jewish individuals from their especially pressing poverty. Likewise, my freethinking seemed to be the cure for the disease of religion which, in my view at that time, enslaved and crippled the human spirit and thereby shrivelled the happiness of the individual and of peoples. I had no choice, then, but to destroy all bridges leading to religion, and I did so. But I did not wage any particular war for my freethinking, as I had done for my national ideals and for some of my social ideals. I was reluctant to insult the most sacred feelings of others, and besides, I continued to make allowances for national needs because, even then, my greatest interest and my outlook were tied up with the question of peoplehood. Perhaps, also, a remnant of doubt persisted, though I would not have admitted it. During the period of my freethinking, there were moments when something out of keeping with my principles stirred in me, but, unwilling to submit to weakness, I always managed to throw it off with determination. In any case, the fact is that for over twenty years I served nationalist, socialist freethinking modernity in its most extreme mode. I was quite certain, and with cause, that I would never disbelieve in my disbelief.

And yet I did. I know many are angry with me for this — many more than those who were offended because, for twenty years, I have been critical of Zionism (though I doubt not at all the peoplehood of Jews and though the land of our ancestors is precious to me) and of modern Hebraism (though I love Hebrew, the sacred tongue). Many, though not all of them, resent my conversion and think the worse of me. First, there are those who believe I had dishonest motives. To them, I have nothing to say. Whoever is acquainted with the course of my life knows what to think of it. For those who interpret my becoming a believer in the usual manner, that is, as a sign of mental deterioration, I cannot of course act as my own defense and demonstrate that I am still of sane mind. I can only say that their interpretation substantiates my opinion, based on many other facts which I have observed and about which I have learned: that the slogan "free thought" appeals particularly to those who do not have the least comprehension of the deepest essence of thought and who are, besides, the most stubborn and conceited fanatics imaginable. To a third group, who say I force myself to believe because I have somehow been disappointed in Judaism, I would like to reply. But I feel it is beyond my ability, for how can I convince them to imagine what they cannot imagine — that the "sensible man," the "educated man," the "man of intellect" can be religious nowadays? I cannot give them the sense they lack, though they see how large and towering the religious beliefs of men have loomed in all periods and among all nations, especially those of the greatest historical figures. For example, one of my critics, mentioning my conversion, wrote that God has no heirs. How can I make him, however superior intellectually, understand that indeed I do not pray to his God, who, in his eyes, is dead, but to the God that lives forever, the Lord of the Universe?

I wrote elsewhere that when I discarded ideological nationalism, putting greater stress on peoplehood as a living reality, I came to realize that the innermost nature of the Jewish people ought to be expressed in its religion and that it therefore deserved serious attention and the utmost respect. But this was not yet the start of my conversion, because I still held that religion in general was obsolete, and therefore the Jewish religion also could not survive. I pondered: "Is it not conceivable that something new will succeed Judaism and undertake to express what it hitherto expressed? Why could not the essence of the Jewish people appear everywhere in life in all its breadth?"

My conversion apparently began when my materialistic outlook showed its first spiritual traits. I cannot say precisely when this happened, except that some twelve to fourteen years ago I began to feel somewhat uncomfortable with materialism. It was harder for me to deny that modernity, which had once entered the world with great promise and was welcomed with very great expectations, had reached a stage in which its bankruptcy became evermore apparent. Its individualistic programs could not resolve the confusion of life; everything it had given rise to became resolved in disharmonies; its high priests turned out to be comical little figures. I began more frequently to suspect that the natural sciences refused to listen and learn about anything which seeks to emerge from the other side of our senses and our reason, lest we recognize it or understand it better. Little by little, I realized that the limits which materialism set on thought, and even tried to set on feeling, were the limits of those people who had succumbed to it, that there was a higher stage of thinking than logic, of which the senses are aware, and a higher level of emotion than pure psychophysical sensitivity, and that, in essence, we cannot interpret the great and elevated revelations of spirit in history as the inevitable effects of senseless dead matter. More and more, I understood that even the fact of peoplehood, of each peoplehood, could not be explained by materialism, that economic materialism, based exclusively on economic data, could not explain the differences among peoples. Even racial materialism, supplementing economic materialism, could not, as I examined it closer, fulfill its promise. It was too obvious that from peoples of one race many cultural groups emerged, peoples with differing cultural ideals because of differing spiritual outlooks.

But the true and great revelation came to me when I had conquered my materialistic superstitious fear of the subject of religion and when I suddenly encountered the most grandiose and significant expressions of the spirit, the originators of the greatest cultural achievements of nations and the whole human race, the most magnificent cultural structures. What a boor I must have been to have passed them by unaware, busy instead with collecting all kinds of little facts and proofs. I felt the distaste rising in me for that cheap materialistic interpretation of religion which seeks to reduce the most elevated religious philosophies of the world to fetish, totem, taboo, and other such cute things. I even bowed before the pagan heaven of ancient Greece, however alien and remote from me. I bowed to it because I saw in it man's striving for the world of spirit and his inadequate understanding of the response of that spirit, because I saw the greatness this striving and this response wrought in human history. That was the great discovery, when before my very eyes the one and only true spiritual revolution took place, whose purpose is to divert man from the path that leads to the gods and set him upon the path that leads from and with God into the world, when before my very eyes unfolded the great innovations which Judaism introduced into human history. Though I was deeply aware how Christianity and Islam differed from Judaism, their mother, and though I could never forget how meanly they expressed their gratitude, nonetheless, seeing how these religions raised nations from a gray mass of heathens, teaching them the ABC's of Jewish thought, recreating them into work-shops of fine cultures in which at least the sacred seed of Judaism remained, I could look upon them only with profound respect as magnificent experi-ments in which Jewish thought was poured into non-Jewish forms. But for the mother itself, for Judaism, in its uniqueness and majesty, I was seized with awe. I felt that the hope of the world was preserved in my people, that it was seeding the world with the future; the meaning of the religious way of life of the Jewish people transcended all historical measures. The axis of all axes around which world history revolved for thousands of years was revealed to me.

In the light of the awe I felt and the insight I had, I abandoned materi-alism completely and even left far behind ordinary philosophic idealism, for this was merely the bare philosophic assent that spirit is the original and creative force in the world. I was already carried along, as I understand today, by the vigorous religious stream of humankind, and particularly in a stream that originated in the profoundest depths of the Jewish belief in God. This was the first outburst of my suppressed religious ecstasy, the day of crisis when the soul returned from abroad, forlorn in a long night illu-mined only by artificial light. But I was not yet aware of it, because I had neither the time nor the courage for self-understanding and because con-sciously I still served an alien power. My brand-new happiness then seemed only like painful restlessness, from which one question constantly cried out: What good is it that you have become absorbed in things that actually can have meaningfulness only on one premise which has no place in your phi-losophy? What are these huge cultural apparatuses, these great emitters of light rays, if He does not live, in whose name and with whose power they say they work? And what if this God, whose heralds they are, does not exist? Or, if machines create the spirit and function as the fiction of "God," then why the fiction, why the roundabout path? Is it only to prove that matter, brute force, must travel roundabout paths, *golem*-paths, if it is to express spirit?

For a long time I found no answer. The suppressed longing which sud-denly erupted in many of my thoughts, sometimes even in waves of feeling, and in a few spiritual experiences had long pointed to God. At the end, only a thread held me to disbelief, the last thin thread of the materialistic web, with its haskala woof, which still encased my soul. But the thin thread was unbelievably strong, and strong also my obstinacy. Not only did I feel I dare not yield, that I dare not repudiate the philosophy which recognizes

only a world that can be touched and computed, and which I served faithfully for twenty-five years, but I also feared, and with reason, I would sink
into a bottomless abyss. I continued to cite everything wrong in the world,
in the life of individuals and nations, as proofs against God. If there is a
God, why does He need these progressions with their remote periods, catastrophes, and extremes? I was just not yet convinced that God existed.

So the years passed until a day came — I no longer know when it was
— when the thin thread snapped by itself and I recognized God, recognized Him in His full obviousness, the Creator and King of the world.
Then I understood that all the arguments that I cited against Him and His
existence proved only that one could not approach Him, but did not remove
the assurance that He existed. Once more, everything seemed so simple that
I could not comprehend how I could have so long resisted this simple insight while assenting to a vulgar platitude. I remembered various things of
the time of my disbelief which I had then disregarded and which were
expressions of my imprisoned and suppressed volition. Then I also realized
that the sorrow of recent years was nothing more than one great heralding
of the Lord of the World, before He entered my consciousness. At the same
time, I felt, as I wrote in *Gottesvolk,* a "burning shame" that "I should have
been for so long among those who do not know Him, that the wisdom of
my ancestors — the most magnificent on earth — lay dormant in me for so
long, that the voice of my people was for so long silent within me."

After all I have said so far about my change, I was obviously not eager
to qualify my tardy recognition with all sorts of fashionable and unfashion-
able "ifs" and "buts." I could not be satisfied with a nonpersonal god that
does not exist, in whose name one could not proclaim moral law, shape
human history nor form culture. Not for this, I thought, were we the first
to be privileged to know God — to permit Him to be ground into a kind of
God-dust and blown out into nature, or to let our megalomania stamp a
formula by which He and our own humanness are identical. Nor could I
accept a barren deism for myself alone. Not for this did we undertake to
serve God as a people, that we should now renounce the power of communal service. Nor did I want to belittle our chosenness. For, if there was a
God — and now I was sure of this — and if it was true that the Jewish
people, obdurate against circumstances which affected other peoples and
against the arrogance of the senses, thus became different from other peoples and became the first to recognize God (and this is true), then doubtless
God decreed this differentness and chose the Jewish people to be the pioneer in recognizing Him, bestowing upon them special duties and responsibilities, and putting them on a special plane. Then it is also clear that all

the laws which were given this chosen people, according to which they were to live and work, must have been given deliberately as a means or way or goal of chosenness. The Torah, then, which is the foundation of this Law, and the great records of the tradition which were built on this foundation cannot be regarded merely as Israel's national literature, but as documents which Almighty God gave to the Jews, setting forth their chosenness and the rights and obligations derived from it. Then, Revelation and the tradition are authentic, so authentic that it does not matter to me whether or not the arrogant faultfinding of errant generations recognizes them. It follows, then, that every word of the written and oral tradition is binding — on me just as much as on anyone else. It is not enough that I condescend to recognize God's existence, but I must stand among my believing people and go in its ways with its means to its ends.

I admit I did not always succeed in accommodating my actions to my belief, nor could I have succeeded. I had to surmount strong inner opposition, besides outer obstacles. A man who for decades valued and served individualism in its subservience to matter cannot simply divest himself of the effects of his education, of all Western habits and traits which contravene the meaning and the rigorous will of Judaism, as he would take off clothes he had put on a few hours before. Perhaps some trace of an alien sin will always persist in the blood of the soul which was among strangers, a trace which one hopes God in His mercy will forgive and the community of Israel in its strength will absorb. Nor is it any more possible to comprehend instantly the full seriousness of the commandments; it is even less possible swiftly to adjust to performing them. This is the last thing to be convinced of. It takes a long time until one ceases to be discouraged by the superiority of the enlightened Jew toward the ritual ceremonies, understanding that his is nothing but the old arrogance of the half-educated vulgarian toward the cultured man of history, of the easygoing, lax man toward the God-fearing man, of the pseudoreligious charlatan toward the truly and consistently pious man. It takes a long time until one understands that the commandments really require strictness and that this strictness preserved us from becoming common and vulgarized; and until one comprehends that special mercy of the Almighty who gave us the commandments on our solitary journey among the peoples as a guarantee that they would not absorb us and that we would survive, with our Jewish way of life and our Jewish outlook, until the Messiah will come, for our sake and theirs.

True, the more I became part of traditional Judaism, the fewer my complaints against it and the greater my demands on observant Jews. I could not help feeling that they did not attain the height of their task, and I could not keep from saying it. I realized that observant Jews had become lax in that cardinal article of faith concerning the Messiah and that in all respects they were non-doers, nothing-doers. They still struggled with the idol of time, before which Westerners, rested or restless, kneeled in the dust, but they did not try to do something that would for always keep Judaism above time. Submitting certain proposals, I demanded of them deeds and a new beginning to their old, old heritage, or, more accurately, to their everlasting heritage.

If someone starts talking about "reaction" and "clericalism," I must state these words do not frighten me one bit. They displease me to the extent that they sound as uncomfortably European as, for instance, "revolution" and "liberalism." But I accept these designations with affection, if people mean to say of me that I dislike the everlasting European bustle around progress, which in the end adds up to nothing, and that I recognize the union of men with God and their organization based on this union to be of the highest importance. I am bored with Europe's progress and its "emancipated humanity," with the masquerade of little people who play god and keep sinking into the mire. If they choose to stay there, that is their pleasure.

If someone should charge me with having repudiated Jewish peoplehood by becoming a believer from a freethinker, I would respond to his stereotyped European nationalism with only a contemptuous laugh and continue to believe that a community of Jews, truly God-fearing, faithful to the tradition and observing, must perforce be the most national and most creative community, and that no other Jewish community, howsoever conceived, can compare with it with regard to creative power.

I can think of no better way to conclude this essay than by telling my friends and opponents that I have never felt stronger and happier. Since I rejoined the great Jewish congregation of the past, the present and the future, with its Jewish outlook and its Jewish way of life, since I have been working in it, a brother among brethren, I have realized the greatness of authentic Jewish life and its joyfulness. Because for so long I ate the bread of exile, I am now gaining new strength at home.

V

Scholars and Philosophers

23   On the Death of
Nahman Krochmal
by Solomon J. Rapoport

NAHMAN KROCHMAL was born in Brody, Galicia, in 1785 and died in Tarnopol in 1840. The facts of his life are recounted in the following eulogy written by his friend and follower, Solomon Judah Rapoport.

Krochmal stood on the border between East and West, seeking a reconciliation between faith and reason, eschewing the rationalist philosophy of the Berlin Haskala and scorning the ultra-Orthodox for their rigidities. He described his time thus: "At both extremes there is a lack of true faith in our time. Both extremes are alike in believing that religion is what they used to believe in childhood; and the difference between them is only this: that some rejoice when they can find opportunity to cast suspicion and doubt upon that faith, while the others — and they are the majority — endeavor to strengthen and sustain faith with fantasies and various exagger-

ations — futile measures in an age when knowledge is widespread." [*]

Krochmal used Jewish history to mediate between faith and reason. According to Julius Guttmann, Krochmal, in his great, unfinished *Guide to the Perplexed of Our Time*, "interpreted the outer history of the Jews as the outcome of the inner relation between the Jewish people and the absolute spirit. Because of this relationship, the existence of the Jewish people is not bounded by time, as is true of other nations, but after periods of decay and degeneration, the Jewish people again and again revive with the strength of youth."

Scholars today believe, as did Solomon Schechter, that Krochmal's greatest innovation was the historical method, his ground-breaking historical researches, and his introduction of the perspective of time in Jewish history.

Solomon Judah Rapoport was born in Lemberg in 1790 and died in Prague in 1867. Like his friend and mentor, Rapoport was one of the galaxy of the Galician haskala, forging their own unique accommodation of scientific knowledge and traditional Judaism.

[*] Sholom Spiegel, *Hebrew Reborn*, rev. ed. (New York, Meridian Press, 1957), pp. 109–110.

Once again it is my sad lot to place a wreath of bitters midst the flourishing leaves of this journal. Only recently I lamented the loss of one great scholar and leader of Israel [Joseph Perl]. Now another great scholar, philosopher, teacher, Rabbi Nahman Krochmal, has gone the way of all flesh. The former was close and familiar, a father to me since childhood; the latter, a true companion and intimate friend. Thus, one by one, my comrades are snatched away to that region which lies beyond the range of mortal eyes. Since their departure from this vale of sorrow, I too was led away to a new dwelling place. Which loss shall I now mourn: those dear lives faded and extinct, or my birthplace, Galicia, which I shall never again see?

Oh, brothers, and loved ones! My land and people! I recall you now as a dream that has flown away and is no more. These two valiant souls have gone to their rest and, you, land of my youth, are bereaved. Those who had both power and will to bring you glory have departed from your midst. Among those who strove on your behalf, I count myself. Yet you regarded us as naught and heeded not the word of loyal counselors, trusting the wisdom of merchants and rich men in every town. If some fault of yours was noticed, some error pointed out for the sake of correction, you saw in this sedition, mockery, antagonism — though, in truth, the criticism derived of a pure and loving source and was directed toward your interest. You do, indeed, possess many great and expert Talmudists, fine scholars in science and languages, merchants and men of means. But few fulfill their mission, and most stray from their rightful way. Those who pore over the writings of our rabbis do not note their lesson or observe their teachings. They observe only those texts which, at first sight (at first sight only!), express an attitude of vengeance and scorn of the intellect, ignoring the real meaning and logic provided by an understanding of time, place, author, context. These same scholars avoid those texts which convey love for every man, all knowledge, all work, moral teachings, insight — being dominated by so-called hasidim who rule through slander, intimidation, a glib tongue. Scientists and linguists, for the most part, abuse their knowledge, addressing shameful charges to the government, engaging in polemic, in Hebrew, before readers who know little of the actual issues, all this for the sake of profit or to be provoking and vindictive. Only the smallest minority seek truth and wisdom. Most of the rich idolize money. They do not know and do not want to know what is the lot of our people. Like demigods, they look down upon the community and take no part in its affairs, for good or ill. They think it beneath their dignity to associate with the less-fortuned, a situation which is most prominent in the larger towns, with the exception of Brody, whose rich preserve a measure of modesty. Elsewhere, wealth is coupled with arrogance. Few recall how often sons of the rich are reduced to poverty. All this may be traced to a decline in the social feeling essential to every community of Israel.

Gentlemen, take note and observe the cities of Germany: there one still sees the spirit of the people as it was in the days of yore. Peace reigns throughout, and there are none who seek to advance themselves by sowing dissension. Many are the men of property and means, dignitaries, individuals in close contact with the government. Yet their hearts remain bound to the people, the wise and poor, the houses of learning, hospitals, all community matters, large and small. These communities will be long-lived and their situation will improve steadily until the day when God redeems all of Israel together.

Make no mistake — as for piety, learning, scholarship, righteousness, the level is higher in their old communities than in your midst, though certain malicious persons have led you to think otherwise. The masses of your people are lifeless, their spirit dissipated. Who estranged them from you? Who destroyed your house? Those, who pretending virtue, usurped power because of their positions. Brothers of my land and of my city! It is time to cast off the yoke from your backs, to reject the magic-makers, to cast out the conjurers from your midst, for too many victims have already fallen prey to their craft.

Now news has come that in one of the big cities a number of distinguished citizens wish to set up a house of prayer to be conducted in an orderly manner, appointing a cantor capable of singing with a choir, of articulating clearly. This gladdened me, and I urge you to be strong in purpose and undismayed by those enemies of our people who gyrate at services like savages and who caper like goats. God does not demand that. God chooses deep feeling, pleasingly delivered, arranged with order and charm. Heed not the false prophets who urge you to serve the Lord with madness and confusion. Turn away from those vile, despicable creatures who bathe in defiled waters, who pass the day in the toilets, calling this clean and pure, sanctioning their practices with the text: "Prepare for thy God, oh Israel!" Take up your task and God will be with you. He will stir the hearts of the rulers to help you, and from the cities and towns of Germany you will also have assistance.

My brothers, those of you dwelling in Galicia! A great and wise man, your crown of glory, has been plucked from your midst, yet you take no notice. Do you not know that the crown has been taken from your head? Believe me, had this great man's life come to its untimely end in Germany, there would surely be grief and mourning in every Jewish settlement throughout the land. You, however, remain silent and some of you, perhaps, rejoice secretly. I shall speak words which would be uttered by thousands of you, were you not misled by those who disdain all wisdom and knowledge, all concern for the people's welfare.

Regarding the death of this high priest, Rabbi Nahman, let me paraphrase our rabbis: the town of Brody conceived and gave birth; the town of Zolkiew raised her beloved child; alas, cried Tarnopol, for she has lost a precious vessel.

The town of Brody conceived and gave birth: Born there in 1785 to parents of considerable means, he was raised in the ways of Torah and piety, studying with prominent teachers, who were generously rewarded. The lad, as he grew and developed, earned a reputation among his peers, for God had granted him a fine and clever heart. When it was time for him to marry (at sixteen or seventeen as was then the custom), he was given the daughter of a wealthy family from Zolkiew. He settled in that town and lived there many years, supported by his wife's father.

The town of Zolkiew raised its beloved child: He gave pleasure to all his acquaintances, to all who came to his home. He learned to read German and pored over volumes of poetry and philosophy, beginning with the words of the great scholar, Moses Mendelssohn, and advancing rapidly to the works of Kant, the wisest man of his time, whose position was unrivaled in the world of scholarship. Mark this and marvel, you who live in Germany. It is no great feat in your country for a man to master several disciplines, for there are many schools and teachers for every subject. In the lands of the north, however, to this day, more so thirty or forty years ago, there was no one to teach and no one to guide the Jew who desired to expand his knowledge beyond traditional areas. Anyone who wished to embark on a new course had to pave his own road, having no model to follow, having to overcome many obstacles, to cope with disparaging friends and relatives who would go so far as to urge that all books of science be removed from the house, even threaten to burn them lest they be discovered by would-be pietists who defame the names of scholars and destroy their property too, as reported, to our great shame and disgrace. Usually, even the lion-hearted were forced into submission. Thus, to this day there are few true scholars, for only the individual whose soul is guided by God could withstand this terror.

Such an individual was this marvelous man. His frail body, always susceptible toward the chest and lung ailment from which he died (as did a younger brother in his youth), was further strained by the rigors of scholar-

ship and related problems. It is some thirty years since I first met him and
saw the splendor of his presence, this when he was in my city to consult a
doctor. Yet in spirit he was always stalwart. When I spoke to him, I fell
under the spell of his knowledge and understanding, being almost transformed. A passion for learning emanated from his person to all those who
spoke with him.

As Joseph Solomon Delmedigo observed, though the invention of the
printing press brought untold benefit to the other peoples, the availability
of books on Jewish subjects had as many disadvantages as advantages.
Without dwelling on this subject, let me point out that, our people being
poor and without means in most countries, most intellectuals were unable
to afford the price of a book, or the space to keep it, or the time to keep up
with the flow of literature, in our language as well as other languages, concerning our religion and our position in the world. Formerly, in Israel, the
number of copies of a book testified to its value and appreciation by scholars. That which was not well received was soon abandoned and forgotten,
to the author's consternation. Not so now. Anyone — a boy, a wise man, or
a fool — may publish his thoughts, be they original or plagiarized, clever or
mad, delicate or crude, adding to the burden of those who seek truth, for
who can ignore a book before he knows what is in it, and whether it does,
perhaps, offer a single redeeming quality? After being exposed to a particular literary folly, one can only be consoled with the hope that it will disappear in darkness.

Let us consider the way of our ancient rabbis who sought to limit written literature to the Bible. All other material, law, legend, and so on, was to
be communicated from one scholar to the other and concealed from the
masses, lest each man regard himself a judge in high matters. The scholars
were cautioned against publicly divulging what was passed from mouth to
mouth, from ear to ear, in the academies of learning. Such was also the
custom of the ancient Greek philosophers, Pythagoras and those who followed him being notable examples. They wrote nothing down but communicated their teachings to their students, through whom their legacy was
preserved.

Such was the practice in Poland among those scholars worthy of their
title. They accomplished more with their oral tradition than others with
their books. So, too, our great scholar. This wise man exercised great influence through the charm and pleasing quality of his teachings. He feared no
form of slander or intimidation and continued to study and teach others. All
of his acquaintances, among them youths as well as mature men, were enriched by his company. He made them aware of the sublime power of poets

such as Goethe and Schiller, and of the extraordinary beauty of the Hebrew poetry of Luzzatto and Wessely. Through him, others discovered the
wonders of mathematics. So great was his impact on colleagues that a few
of them became fine poets themselves, some writing in Hebrew, some in
German; others gained erudition in mathematics, still others achieved distinction in the study of the human mind. He mastered Latin and Syriac,
also Arabic, though hampered by the scarcity of textbooks for the Oriental
languages. I recall various occasions when I visited him for a precious day or
two, or a week, or when he came to me — our walks through the countryside were among the chief pleasures of the world. My ears could not tire of
hearing his wisdom; his every word was a lesson.

When at home alone, he devoted himself mainly to philosophy, studying the works of Kant, Fichte, Schelling, Hegel, and became especially
involved with the last. Still, he never lost touch with our own Jewish heritage, keeping up with the old as well as the new. He was alert to new
trends in every field. He faithfully observed every letter of the Torah's
commandments as interpreted by our rabbis. All who knew him respected
and loved him, spreading his good name far and wide. You, enlightened
gentlemen, who have declared your intention to establish a place of prayer,
orderly, esthetic and in accord with the spirit of the time, are much indebted to the soul of this dear man. For his role was great in disseminating
these ideas. They did not fall down from Heaven upon you.

The weak body of this man could not always sustain him and thus it is
that much of his profound thinking is not preserved for future generations.
Ill health and indolence led to his financial decline, though the fortune he
inherited, along with that acquired through marriage, was considerable. But
God bestowed upon his offspring wisdom and knowledge. His eldest daughter was given in marriage to a fine and educated man of Brody, a doctor of
medicine, whose articles appear in professional journals, his reputation being so widely recognized that he was honored by a distinguished Viennese
society of scholars and elected to join it. His medical opinion is regarded as
the word of God by many in the highest circles of our population. Nor did
this man abandon his own heritage with which he had gained intimacy in
childhood. A perceptive and tasteful person, seeking the advancement and
welfare of his people in every way, he urged his father-in-law to set down
his ideas in writing, but did not succeed in this matter. The few things thus
far published, meager in quantity and great in quality as they are, hardly
begin to reflect the scope and greatness of the man we now commemorate.
I, too, on several occasions, addressed myself to him in this regard. Other
friends sought to influence him. It was, in fact, my son whose efforts bore

fruit. He secured a pledge which motivated the writing of *More Nevuke ha-Zeman* ("Guide to the Perplexed of Our Time"), to be prepared for publication by Yom-Tov Lipman Zunz, as requested by the author. I glanced, only briefly, at two of the pieces in it and remember seeing in them the author's characteristic insight and verbal skill. The work will, undoubtedly, teach much to many generations to come.

Alas, Tarnopol, because she has lost a precious vessel: In Zolkiew, after the death of his wife, his financial situation deteriorated further. His eldest daughter, who had kept house for him, went with her husband and sister to Tarnopol, leaving him alone with his youngest son, Abraham, a lad gifted in Talmudic studies. (Another son, learned in the wisdom of Israel as well as in the sciences, particularly medicine, was an outstanding physician in Odessa.) In the winter of 1838, he followed his two daughters to Tarnopol, carrying with him what remained of his possessions, looking forward to peace and tranquillity. Before long, the town's intellectuals recognized his singular qualities and began to gather about him to glean of his wisdom. A few months before his death, he was approached by a few gentlemen from Berlin and asked if he might be willing to become their rabbi and religious leader. He replied that he could not go, because of his health. The people of Tarnopol valued him all the more then, for he had chosen to remain in their midst. He was the glory of the community, especially after the death of Perl. Then he, too, was snatched away, suddenly, midst the lament of his children and the sighs of all good people. Alas, Tarnopol mourns the loss of a precious vessel, and the entire land echoes this dirge.

Great honor was accorded him in death. All the city was astir. An enormous crowd walked after the bier, despite a driving downpour. The city's leading citizens were his pallbearers. Two weeks later, a moving eulogy was delivered in the new synagogue by a leading rabbi and scholar.

Let me add this: We enjoyed twenty-eight years of close friendship, seldom allowing a month to pass without meeting to engage in scholarly banter, this though we were often situated far apart. These pleasantries were of more than slight value to me, and I address my gratitude to his spirit now resting in the shadow of the Lord, though in the year and a half preceding his death our intimacy had, in fact, dwindled.

I felt, and now feel, that it was not I who brought about this unfortunate breach. His friends and close associates have confirmed my feeling. If, in some way, I, nonetheless, was not innocent and contributed to the gap, I ask forgiveness of his pure soul, clasped in the clasp of eternal life.

Some months before I left his town, the breach was repaired and we were intimate and attuned to one another as always. I find it necessary to dwell on this in order to anticipate the devious tactics of those who may now seek to sully his name. Before long I shall join him and a clear verdict will be rendered in Heaven, each of us being judged according to his true qualities. I trust that there is nothing to fear, for we shall each be vindicated by this trial. Should any man find flaws in either of us, these flaws, I hope, will not become a blemish. The good Lord will, surely, forgive us. May man, created in His image, follow in His way! Amen.

24   Under the Sign of Historicism
by Simon Dubnow

SIMON DUBNOW, Jewish historian, was born in Mstislavl, province of Mohilev, in 1860 and died in Riga at the hands of the Nazis in 1941. Reared in a traditionalist home, he grew up in a world that rejected the foundations and fundamentals of the old society and sought to rebuild anew on the basis of individual emancipation and Western culture. Early in his intellectual life, Dubnow turned to history and in the study and writing of Jewish history he found the surrogate for Judaism, the modern means by which he could identify as a Jew, which would give him inner satisfaction and keep him part of the Jewish community.

After Graetz, he was the first great Jewish historian with universal scope, and he was the first to introduce Eastern European Jewry into the Jewish historical picture. He introduced sociological methods into the study of history. In all his work on the Jewish past, the living reality of the Jewish present was always there, demanding his involvement in the Jewish community. Thus, his researches on Jewish communal institutions led him to formulate a theory of Jewish communal existence based on national-cultural autonomy.

Dubnow remained all his life a man of reason whose rationalism penetrated even his emotional being. Even in his pioneering studies on hasidism, Dubnow's rationalism shines through. In this sense, he was a completely modern Jew who was willing to take the risks of a free society. In one of his last essays he wrote: "In our epoch of counteremancipation we dare not posit the ironic question: 'Well, what has emancipation brought us?' True, it brought assimilation, but also freedom and human dignity. It revived the free person in the Jew. The task of our great national movement in the past fifty years consisted of the struggle for emancipation *without* assimilation, for both civic and national rights."

Yet despite his rationalism, despite his modernity, Dubnow believed in a mystic force — the Jewish will to live, which he described in his essay "Jewish History: An Essay on the Philosophy of History:"

Above all, Jewish history possesses the student with the conviction that Jewry at all times, even in the period of political independence, was preeminently a spiritual nation, and a spiritual nation it continues to be in our own days, too. Furthermore, it inspires him with the belief that Jewry, being a spiritual entity, cannot suffer annihilation: the body, the mold, may be destroyed, the spirit is immortal. Bereft of country and dispersed as it is, the Jewish nation lives, and will go on living, because a creative principle permeates it, a principle that is the root of its being and an indigenous product of its history. This principle consists first in a sum of definite religious, moral, or philosophic ideals, whose exponent at all times was the Jewish people, either in its totality, or in the person of its most prominent representatives. Next, this principle consists in a sum of historical memories, recollections of what in the course of many centuries the Jewish people experienced, thought, and felt in the depths of its being. Finally, it consists in the consciousness that true Judaism, which has accomplished great things for humanity in the past, has not yet played out its part, and, therefore, may not perish. In short, the Jewish people lives because it contains a living soul which refuses to separate from its integument, and cannot be forced out of it by heavy trials and misfortunes such as would unfailingly inflict mortal injury upon less sturdy organisms.

The following selection has been translated from his memoirs.

AT the outset I want to explain the meaning of this title. By "historicism" I mean not the passion for the writing of history, which grew stronger as the scope of my works expanded, but my whole world outlook, which was then in transition from stormy antithesis and passive resignation. I could have boldly quoted Victor Hugo:

> L'historie m'apparut, et je compris la loi,
> Des génerations cherchant Dieu, portant l'arche,
> Et montant l'escalier immense marche à marche.

In historicism I found a counterweight to religious and philosophical dogmatism. (Later I extended it to the limits of philosophical relativism.) My thinking went along these lines: I am an agnostic in religion and in philosophy with regard to their attempts, each in its own way, to discover the meaning of the enigmas of the world, but I can find out how mankind lived in the course of millennia and in what ways mankind sought truth and justice. I myself have lost faith in personal immortality, yet history teaches me that there is collective immortality and that the Jewish people can be considered as relatively eternal, for its history coincides with the full span of world history. The study of the Jewish people's past, then, encompasses also me in something eternal. This historicism admitted me in the national collective, drawing me out of the circle of personal problems onto the broad highway of social problems, less profound but more timely. National sorrow became nearer to me than the sorrow of the world. Here the way opened to national synthesis, synthesizing the best elements of the old thesis and the new antithesis — Jewish and universal ideals, the national and the humanistic.

When I came to Odessa in the fall of 1890, I knew that this capital of New Russia, the least historical of Russian cities, had fewer research facilities for the historian than St. Petersburg. I knew, also, the atmosphere of this southern trading seaport was scarcely suited to its growth as a literary center. In addition to its southern landscape, Odessa attracted me only as a large Jewish community, with the luster of European culture and a large Jewish intelligentsia, albeit mostly assimilated. Yet it turned out that this intelligentsia just then stood at the crossroads and that the literary circle which expanded with my arrival was destined to play no small role in attracting the community to the national movement.

Heavy premonitions oppressed me on New Year's Eve of 1891, which proved fateful in the history of Russian Jews. The wave of anti-Jewish hatred on the part of the government kept rising and the semi-official press, such as *Novoye Vremya*, intensified its attacks on Jews. A new administrative pogrom was in the making.

I put aside my journalistic work then to absorb myself once again in history. I began to work out the plan of an organization for historical studies, which was why I had moved to a large cultural center. I was engaged in systematizing a large number of documents which were dispersed in hundreds of volumes published by Russian learned societies. I devised a procedure for extracting documents from community records and from public and private archives, and I drafted a program for a historical society. This developed into a small book, *On Studying the History of the Russian Jews and Establishing a Russian Jewish Historical Society*. My historicism was easily recognizable in the initial chapters. After quoting Cicero — "not to know what has been transacted in former times is to continue always a child" — I developed the idea in the first chapter that a conscious awareness of the past signifies man's higher intellectual level. Consciousness of the present inheres even to a child in its direct perception of impressions, and the conscious awareness of what is to come inheres to everyone, out of a sense of self-preservation and practical purposefulness; but the awareness of the past satisfies only the higher needs of the intellect, instituting the orderliness of phenomena as a chain of causes and effects. In the second chapter, I stated that historical consciousness was the basis of the Jewish national idea, for with the loss of the physical characteristics of nationhood, we are held together mainly by the community of historical fate (I based my remarks on Renan's definition of nationality). The introductory theoretical chapters were followed by a survey of the development of Jewish scholarship in the West and in Russia, the proposal about studying the history of the Jews in Poland and Russia and a very detailed classification of the sources, published and in manuscript, and, finally, the proposal for collecting materials and also the draft statute for the historical society.

I wrote the essay in a state of great excitement. Having finished the larger part, I had to stop in the middle because of overexhaustion. In between, on March 13, I noted in my diary: "While I am writing I become ever more infused with the greatness of the idea for which I am ready to devote my whole life. The work is complicated, demanding extraordinary efforts of the mind. But the physical exhaustion is nothing against the intellectual pleasure it provides. You forget all the troubles and prickly thorns of life, you rise to the heights of sublime ideas."

Nevertheless, exhaustion overcame me, and two days later I wrote to Adolph Yefimovich Landau, publisher of *Voskhod*, "I am sick," and asked for a half-year's leave from my journalistic work. I had not even finished the letter when the doorbell rang. That was March 15. The local agent of *Voskhod* came, holding a telegram from St. Petersburg: "Decree of the Ministry of the Interior to the monthly journal *Voskhod* and the weekly newspaper *Nedelnaya Khronika Voskhoda*: For persisting in their most harmful course, a third warning is issued with the simultaneous suspension of both publications for six months."

The blow was twofold: social and personal. The suspension of *Voskhod* and the subsequent suspension of the liberal Petersburg paper *Novosti* portended new repressions. And two weeks later, Alexander III issued a cruel decree expelling thousands of Jewish workingmen and merchants from Moscow, where his stiff-necked brother, Grand Duke Sergei, had been appointed General Governor. *Voskhod's* suspension meant losing my only source of income. The Minister of Interior gave me my half-year's leave, not only from journalistic work but from any sort of work.

I made the final effort to complete the essay on studying Jewish history; a sensitive reader could sense my depression in the last chapter. In my diary for April 2, I wrote: "I have finished my large work. In the last chapters, words flowed without pause, passionate and persuasive. At times it seemed I was writing my intellectual testament." I was ill from mental fatigue and from the cold which I had caught in the winter in the chill, damp apartment.

Voskhod reappeared at the beginning of October. A collection of articles was published as a substitute for the issues during the suspended half year. The lead article was my essay "On Studying the History of Russian Jews." The essay was published in St. Petersburg also as a pamphlet for propaganda purposes. In the tenth year of my literary work, my expectation to see an article of mine in book form was fulfilled. The pathos of historicism, which permeated the whole book, impressed various circles of the intelligentsia. The first response came from St. Petersburg, from a circle headed by Maxim Vinaver, Vasily Berman, and Samuel Gruzenberg, inquiring how they could help organize historical studies and along what lines they should be conducted. I replied that the Petersburg circle could most successfully undertake to collect all documents relating to Jews — documents scattered in hundreds of volumes of official records issued by various archival commissions. These materials should be compiled so that they might later be issued in a series of documentary collections or listed in a register. My advice was accepted, and shortly thereafter this group of young energetic people in St. Petersburg founded the Historical Ethnographic Committee of the Society for the Promotion of Culture among the Jews of Russia. In the course of several years, the committee completed the monumental volumes *Regesty i Nadpisi* ("Lists and Inscriptions"). Associated with the committee was a group of Moscow university students who had, even earlier, been engaged in compiling their *Systematic Guide to Russian Literature Concerning the Jews,* an exemplary bibliographical monument of a literary era. (This was published as a supplement to *Voskhod* in 1892.) The Moscow group was headed by Leon Bramson and Julius Brutzkus, who had corresponded with me back in 1890 about principles of classifying the bibliographical material. Early in the nineties, they moved to St. Petersburg and merged with the Vinaver-Berman group in the Historical Ethnographic Committee. From this nucleus of Jewish intelligentsia in St. Petersburg emerged the men who were to play a leading role in the communal and political life of Russian Jewry. Later, their paths diverged in various directions and parties, but it gratifies me to testify that the first love of this generation of intelligentsia was Jewish history and literature.

The Historical Committee of the Society for the Promotion of Culture thus became a sort of substitute for the independent Jewish historical society which I had envisaged in my book and which, under the conditions of police censorship at that time, could not be legalized. Besides, I was separated from this group by the enormous distance which lay between north and south Russia. By its composition, the Petersburg group could carry out only part of the preparatory work which I had outlined; I had to organize the rest myself. To gather these materials, it was necessary to involve the entire Jewish public, kehilla representatives, rabbis, and educated people in the Pale of Settlement. At the end of 1891, I appealed in *Voskhod* for voluntary cooperation in collecting historical materials, especially records of the oldest communities. Thereafter, I began to receive from various places documents or information about where to locate them; the number of my voluntary collaborators gradually increased.

I had barely begun to set up these preparatory projects when the news came that our historian Graetz had died (September, 1891). The death of the teacher whom I had emulated in the first period of my scholarly work aggrieved me, and I willingly accepted Landau's proposal to write a detailed article about Graetz. For two months I lived with the spirit of the dead man. Once again I read his splendid work, volume after volume, and before my eyes unfolded a grandiose picture of the historic path of the Jewish people. I decided, then, to recreate this picture in Graetz's biography and to add an evoluation of his scientific methods. A complete study came out of this, which I wrote at the beginning of 1892 and published in several issues of *Voskhod* of that year, under the title "The Historiographer of the Jewish People."

In the New Year's Day entry for 1892 I wrote: "My aim in life has become clarified: to spread historical knowledge about Jewry and particularly to work on the history of the Russian Jews. I have become a missionary of history." I was under Graetz's spell. The exalted mood in which the study was written can be seen in these emotional passages of the introduction:

Amid the noisy chorus of the battle slogans of our time — Baron de Hirsch, Argentina, total emigration of the Russian Jews, foreign committees, conventions — the grievous words suddenly intruded: "Graetz has died." The same day the bier with the remains of the deceased historian moved from Munich to Breslau, a line of wagons, not less sad, though not in a funeral cortege, proceeded over the whole length of the East Prussian border. Thus, by the tens of thousands, the sons of the homeless people were departing from their homeland, preparing to cross an ocean in search of bread and a small corner for a sorrowing heart. . . . The historian has died; history provides materials for future Jewish

martyrs. . . . Shall we not preserve for generations the memory of him
who preserved for generations the whole past of our people in one magnificent literary monument?

Sorrow of the present and pathos of the past permeated the series;
throughout, one could feel the union between myself and the soul of the
departed historian, my identification with the dead scholar's methodology.
Each volume of Graetz's work I described with lyrical and, sometimes, critical commentaries. I took under my wing, for example, against Graetz, the
freethinkers of all ages, from Aher to Uriel Acosta, Modena, and Spinoza,
the heroes of my youth. I even found extenuating circumstances for the
heroines of the Berlin salons; I explained their flight from the community of
Israel by the "spring torrents" of the revolutionary era. But simultaneously I
also recognized Graetz as the first to express the idea of a "spiritual people,"
though it was not yet clearly formulated, "a world people, a cosmopolitan
people." Some of my friends told me, others wrote, that they had read the
study about Graetz with great excitement.

I was exalted by the thought that I was destined to continue Graetz's
great accomplishments in the field of East European Jewish history. (I had
not yet considered that I would, on my own, write a universal Jewish history.) I eagerly continued my preparatory studies. For Ravnitsky's literary
miscellany, Pardes, I wrote an article dealing with the subject matter of my
essay "On Studying the History of the Russian Jews." It was adapted for
Hebrew readers, especially for rabbis and yeshiva students on whom I was
counting to help me gather community records and other Jewish communal
materials. In this article I deplored the fact that although the rabbis of the
past eras had left very many books on Jewish law, they had not been concerned about preparing a source book for our history. I appealed to the
descendants of those rabbis to remedy this fault by collecting historical materials according to the plan I had outlined.

In those September days of 1892, when most of the country houses
were vacated, we remained at our summer place outside Odessa. I began
writing my introduction to our Russian translation of Graetz's history. I
wanted to synthesize our historical experiences and from this derive a national ideology. The sketch was completely imbued with the extreme spirituality of Zunz and Graetz. Their thesis of spiritual history (Geistesge-
schichte) and the history of suffering (Leidensgeschichte) I expressed in the
poetic phrase "Thinking and suffering." As a motto I set down Pascal's
words that the duration of Jewish history equaled the duration of all man-

kind's history. I characterized the Jewish people as the "most historical people," as "Methuselah among the nations." I designated the content of Jewish history in strictly idealistic terms: its first half as "the account of the people as teacher of religion," and the second half as "the account of the people as thinker, stoic, and sufferer." The basis of the national idea is "historical consciousness," the spiritual territory of the Diaspora. Having paid tribute to the idealism of Western historiography, I bypassed the historical literary method in periodizing Jewish history, dividing the eras, instead, according to centers of hegemony, though with an admixture of the old divisions, according to spiritual and literary characteristics. My earlier views about the Talmud had changed; I now saw an objective justification for the Talmud: "A spiritual people must have spiritual weapons of defense. Such weapons were forged and deposited in the vast arsenal called the Talmud. The Talmud represents a complicated spiritual discipline, enjoining unconditional obedience to a higher invisible power. Let no one ask, then, to which purpose the innumerable religious and ritual regulations. Every regulation is necessary, if only it contributes to the desired end, namely, discipline. It is a uniform with insignia by which soldiers of some regiment recognize one another."

My introduction was completed in the second half of September. In my diary for September 25, I find this entry: "I worked two weeks; because of my great exertion I frequently tired and had to take breathing spells. I expended considerable spiritual energy on the study. But it seems to me that I partly achieved my purpose: I presented a philosophy of history and a historical credo, though on a small scale." I later added: "A philosophy — no; a credo — yes." This was a sign of the self-criticism which I applied toward my initial synthesis. As I immersed myself in the processes of Jewish history, I introduced many substantial emendations in this synthesis and realized it did not merit the title "A Philosophy of History," but rather "The Poetry of History," for this was essentially pathos, lyricism, and the passionate preachment of a missionary. When this lyric of historicism was published as an article in *Voskhod*, its poetry rather than its scholarship caused a great sensation. Particularly suited to the taste of Western Jews, it was twice published in German in Germany and also twice in English, in the United States and in England. The Russian original never appeared in book form. I did not have the opportunity to rework it in the spirit of the system in which I completed the final revision of my general history of Jewry, a work over which I was yet to labor for three decades. My a priori theses were amended by a posteriori conclusions.

Since I published my appeals for the collection of historical materials, I received information from many localities about historical documents. With an annual grant of three hundred rubles a year from the Odessa branch of the Society for the Promotion of Culture, the project took on more life. I obtained manuscripts or copies, early editions, and collections of documents. Every day letters arrived from various cities with information and news, proposals and inquiries. I answered all on substantive matters, gave advice, guided the work. This correspondence took much time, but I felt a deep moral satisfaction. This was the realization of my idea of a collective preparatory work for historical study.

I became ever more engrossed in systematizing the sources for the history of the Jews in Poland and Russia. I had started to lay the foundation: I began to keep a large book for "chronology," in which every year had a separate page. There I entered the historical facts, hypotheses, and comments from the sources; thus, the book would serve both as a handbook of information and as a chronological compilation of the material. How much love was invested in every page of this chronology, whose many comments were the result of untiring searches and scholarly ingenuity! How often were the distressing day-to-day worries lost in ardent dreams of the time when a magnificent structure would rise from this foundation, when these thousands of facts and hypotheses would be merged in one luminous portrait of the 800-year-old history of Jews in Eastern Europe! Meanwhile, I wanted to keep the public informed about my research, and I decided to issue periodic progress reports. Beginning July, 1893, my "Historical Notices" appeared in *Voskhod* for three years. At first they consisted of news and replies to questions from the collectors. In time, the new sources, together with earlier materials, provided the basis for studies, for example, on communal autonomy and the communal councils.

Engaged in the areas of special studies, I thought it necessary, in introducing the "Historical Notices," to dissociate myself from the "guild scholars," with their narrow intellectual horizons, who strove to transform that liveliest of sciences, the "instructress of life," into a museum-piece mummy. "History is a science about people and for people," I wrote, "and therefore cannot be a guild discipline. The priestly cult of castes is abominated in the writing of history; its place is not under the academic cap but in the open forum. We are striving for the people's self-recognition, not for our own intellectual diversion. Tedium, which is usually ascribed to academic studies, is not at their required attribute. Tedium more often hinges on the scholar's temperament than on the subject studied." I confess that in writing those lines I had in mind such embalmers of science as Harkavy and the undistinguished mass of researchers in the field for the sport of it. Even in my younger days, I resented the intellectual games of the Talmudists, and since then I have all my life opposed all types of sport in modern science, philosophy, and belles lettres. Later, I often told my pupils that the purpose of scholarship is to seek truth, and not to provide an arena for mental exercises.

In the spring of 1894, I received an invitation from a group of Jewish intelligentsia in Kharkov to lecture on Jewish history. There I talked for the first time about the basis of spiritual or cultural-historical nationalism, on which I later expanded in the "Letters on Old and New Judaism." I began by defining the concept of "nationality" as collective individuality, entitled to ask for the same freedom of development that every individual has. Here the circle of my thinking closed: in my youth I had advocated Mill's thesis of absolute freedom of the individual against the discipline of society. Now I limited this absolutism by advocating the principle of individual freedom or self-determination for a collective unit. I spoke about four stages of the Jewish national idea, from primitive racial unity, through state and religious unity down to modern cultural unity in a free national community. The capstone of my doctrine was the new genesis of the Jewish people, transcending the thesis of tradition and the antithesis of assimilation toward the synthesis of progressive cultural nationhood. My talk evoked lively dispute. My opponents disagreed with the very principle of Jewish nationality as opposed to the dogma of assimilation. Our discussion lasted late into the night.

The next evening I had a similar talk with the students at Kharkov University and the Technological Institute. In a modest apartment, several dozen Jewish students assembled, among them Palestinists and socialists. Both groups challenged my theses. The first thought that a national ideal without Palestine was too abstract; the other completely rejected the idea of national self-preservation, substituting instead the social struggle and participation in the Russian revolutionary movement. Here, for the first time, I observed how Marxism was beginning to influence our young people. I recognized the first signs of socialist assimilation, which I deplored, as the evening before I deplored assimilation of liberalism. I remember how hotly I argued with my youthful audience that taking part in the struggle to free the persecuted Jewish people in Russia, this proletarian among the family of nations, demanded a higher ethical standard than taking part in the struggle to free the Russian peasants and workers.

The path toward the synthesis of the old and new Judaism grew wider.

I had not yet reached the last stage, but the milestones on the road had been set in place. That same year, in "Interacting Ideological Trends" (*Voskhod*, 1894), I tried to clarify my attitude toward other ideologies of national identity. I concentrated on two trends in modern times: the "Western" or idealistic, and the "Eastern" or realistic. Western ideologies paired the achievements of Western emancipation with the ideal of the spiritual or cultural nation and the continuation of establishing Jewish centers in the Diaspora. The "Easterners" supported the "real" or, to be exact, the territorial center of our ancient Eastern fatherland. I demonstrated that we "Westerners" were in fact grounded in reality, continuing to spin the thread of Jewish history in the age-old Diaspora, whereas the "Easterners" created a Utopian ideal of a new Judah. I believed that the spiritual territory which our history had shaped was more real than the earthly nonexistent territory of the Palestinists. From this point of view, I analyzed other explorers of national ideology — Nahum Sokolow, in his role as editor of the yearbook *He-Asif* and Ahad Ha'am, who advanced his ideas in *Pardes*. I cited Sokolow's transition from an earlier opportunism to broad eclecticism embracing elements of both Western and Eastern systems, and contrasted Lilienblum's simplified philo-Palestinism with Ahad Ha'am's neo-Palestinism. Ahad Ha'am had then formulated his concept of transferring the Jewish spiritual center from the Diaspora to Palestine. I argued that if the spiritual hegemony of Palestine strengthened the national Diaspora, that would create the possibility of interacting influences between the Eastern and Western centers. Soon a clear-cut differentiation of these ideological viewpoints emerged: Sokolow eventually joined the ranks of Herzl's political Zionists; Ahad Ha'am stood in opposition to Herzlian Zionism, in the name of spiritual Zionism; I came to formulate my theory of autonomism.

25 When Lawyers Studied History
by Maxim M. Vinaver

MAXIM MOYSEYEVICH VINAVER, attorney and Jewish communal leader, was born in Warsaw in 1862 and died in Menthon-St.-Bernard, France, in 1926. He completed the University of War-

saw in 1886, then moved to St. Petersburg where he established himself as a lawyer. He was one of the leading members of a rising group of middle-class Jewish professionals who had found ways of accommodating their Jewishness to their enlightened, educated, and secularized way of life and also to their second-class status as Russians.

He was a moderately observant Jew. (Chagall sketched a Passover at Vinaver's in a few strokes: "The reflection of the blazing candles, their odor mingling with the dark ochre of Vinaver's complexion, glowed in the room. . . . The table shone in anticipation of the prophet Elijah.") His greater passion was reserved for the Jewish community, impoverished and persecuted, and all his life he combined his pervasive concerns for the Russian Jewish community with his profession of law and his love of "the other Russia." For Vinaver was a modern man also in this way, with his deep loyalty to Russia, its people and its culture, which even the oppressive reactionary Tsarist regime could not extirpate.

Vinaver's loyalty to Russia was served by his role as one of the founders and leaders of the Constitutional Democrat (Cadet) party, a centrist party founded in 1904. As a Cadet, he was elected to the first Duma. A liberal whose vision of justice, equality, and liberty was a constitutional democracy, Vinaver found that the intransigence of the Tsarist regime often turned him into a radical and revolutionary. Thus, in his reply to the address from the throne, in the Duma on May 13, 1906, responding to the government's omission of all references to the status of Jews, he said: "By your silence in response to the cry of despair

arising from the hearts of this people of six millions, you have indicated your intention to continue in your old ways. Be then advised that our voices will blend with all those others who say to you: Be gone! We shall support only that government which represents the will of the people."

Vinaver believed that not the Russian people, but the Tsarist government was responsible for the antisemitic outbursts throughout Russia. During the debate in the Duma on the pogrom in Bialystok in 1906, Vinaver said: "We are deeply convinced that not the Russian people is our enemy, but only that clique which for its own ends seeks to set the Russian people against us. . . . We see no other solution for ourselves but to rescue all of Russia from this handful that bosses it. . . . We Jews are small in number, but we have one imponderable strength — the strength of despair — and we have one ally — the whole Russian people, which is rich in human compassion."

During the Kerensky regime, Vinaver was a justice in the Supreme Court of Cassation. In 1919 he went to Paris, where he published a weekly in Russian and French to combat antisemitism and taught Russian civil law at the Russian University at the Sorbonne.

The following memoir, an address delivered at the opening of the Jewish Historical Ethnographic Society on September 16, 1908, describes how Vinaver found himself as a Jew in the study of historical documents.

Our historical society did not appear spontaneously in this, God's world. It has an ancestry. It is a time-honored custom that before embarking on a new venture, we recall its predecessors, those who worked in this field before us. This is a most suitable approach for a historical society, for in doing so it fulfills part of its task.

It happened just seventeen years ago, in a Petersburg autumn like to-day. The first meeting was convened by some young lawyers under the leadership of Alexander Yakovlevich Passover,* who proposed to compile a volume which would document, with living facts, the legal status of Jews in Russia. A committee headed by a few older lawyers was set up for this purpose. But these dropped away, except for Passover, who directed the work and attended the meetings regularly. The whole field of Russian legislation affecting the Jews was apportioned to the younger men, and each prepared his paper and read it at the meetings. I remember I was assigned the Ignatiev decrees of May 3, 1882, and I read my paper at that very autumn meeting where the idea for our historical society was born.

The plan for the documentary volume came to nothing. It seemed to have died by itself, without any reason. Originating in a vague desire to engage in Jewish communal work, it fell apart when we blocked out a plan for a vigorous and broadly inclusive organization concerned with Jewish affairs. It happened on a Sunday, during a recess we took in the meeting when the only senior advisor present had to leave. V. L. Berman took from his pocket a thin booklet which had just appeared under the title *On Studying the History of the Russian Jews and Establishing a Russian Jewish Historical Society*. It was written by the man sitting next to me today, S. M. Dubnow. Then, seventeen years ago, it proposed establishing a Russian Jewish historical society. It concluded with the words: "Let us begin to work. Our work will grow out of the soil of the past, but its harvest will belong entirely to the present and the future. I appeal to all right-thinking people, Jews and non-Jews, to cooperate in this consecrated work — the writing of Russian Jewish history. We will demonstrate that we Russian Jews are not just a branch of the most historical of peoples but that we ourselves have a rich past and we can appreciate it. We can benefit from our past. An ancient people, hoary with age, wise in the experience of centuries, with a truly incomparable past — can this people neglect its history?"

Berman proposed we accept Dubnow's challenge. We gladly committed ourselves, and in our youthful zeal widened our scope. We decided to form an organization which would embrace history, customs, and legislation — everything that, within the scope of the internal life of the Jewish community, ought to be systematized and studied. Later, we liked to define our purpose this way: In times of peace to study and cultivate scholarship, and in battle — if it would come — to resist in closed ranks. Meanwhile, study and research were most important. We elaborated a plan of study to attract

* Alexander Yakovlevich Passover, 1840–1910, outstanding Russian jurist.

a wider circle. That meeting took place in my home. I remember the bustling liveliness that filled my bachelor room when in our youthful enthusiasm we laid the foundation for our new structure. I am happy to see that
many of us, then young and today rather gray, are here. But many, alas,
have gone: Vasily Berman, that elegant, graceful blond young man whose
whole life was dedicated to bringing people together on behalf of the common good; Ludwig Ossipovich Seidenman, who came to us as a Polish
specialist and who lectured us on Polish Jewish history. Departed also is
Sergei Alexandrovich Bershadsky,* who helped us in our inexperienced
efforts and later excavated from the archival dust incomparable original materials of Russian Jewish antiquity. He was built like a giant, and he was
the first to swing a giant axe through the abandoned forest of Jewish history. He guided our first steps — the first register of source materials we
prepared could not have been done without him. He impatiently awaited
the time when we would at last be ready to publish in Russian the Hebrew
material of the sixteenth and seventeenth centuries: "Give me the record
books of the sixteenth and seventeenth centuries and I will write you a
Russian Jewish history." But he did not live to see our first product, the first
volume, *Regesty i Nadpisi* ("Lists and Inscriptions"), which we dedicated
to his memory. Gone, too, Vladimir Soloviev, who, in *Vestnik Evropy,* was
the first sympathetically to greet the publication of *Regesty.* He used to
deliver lectures at our meetings. It was significant that he, an evangelical
Christian, a prophet in appearance and in conscience, came to teach us,
descendants of the prophetic people, about the prophets.

We divided the domain of Jewish life in eleven sections, of which I
remember only seven: history, law, economics, literature, customs and education, health and medicine, emigration. Each section had its own head. I
was put in charge of the history section, only because I had once prepared a
legal historical study that had no bearing on Jews.

All the sections were under one dome and together they constituted the
Historical Ethnographic Commission. But very soon the whole complex
structure collapsed, except for the historical section and the dome — the
Historical Ethnographic Commission. And thus it remained, this strange
structure in defiance of all the laws of architecture.

First about the historical section, the only surviving part of the nonexistent whole. Under the influence of Dubnow's booklet and partly as Bershadsky advised, we decided, at the start, to engage in solid research, to

---

* Bershadsky, 1850–1896, Russian historian and jurist. He began his historical
studies of Jews in early Russia "as a confirmed Jew-hater," according to his autobiographical notes.

extract the Jewish material out of published collections, records, and documents. We soon learned this was no easy task and required knowledge and methodological experience. No one was available to guide us in the historical section, for we were just young men who loved our people and wanted to serve them. In the second year of our work, 75-year-old white-haired Emanuel Borisovich Levin joined us and collaborated for over ten years, attending meetings regularly (he had to climb up four flights). He compiled about one-third of the material for *Regesty*. Our group used to meet regularly every other Monday, continuing punctually for fifteen full years. People came and went, but the institution remained. The ebb and flow of people brought us freshness and youth. The young people met two evenings a month, stayed long past midnight, and left pleased and exhilarated.

What attracted them? What interested them? Anyone watching the crowded room where this performance took place would have been astonished. Some ten to twenty people assembled, each with his parcel of documents and pride on his face to show off his catch. Those unfortunates who did not net even a single "Jew" came sad and dejected, begging to be believed that they had searched some ponderous tome which had yielded nothing. Sometimes the catch was so abundant that the evening was too short for everything to be read.

Then the reading began. What did we read? Extracts from public records, with perhaps the barest reference to a Jew. That was how the evening was spent. The records were read in chronological order. Sometimes there were comments, emendations, additions, explications of doubtful matters. It took on the aspect of a collective study.

This long, persistent labor, warmed by the love for it, gradually filled the lacunae in the compilation of historical sources, for when the great volume *Regesty i Nadpisi* appeared, after eight years of work, the scholarly reviewers unanimously praised it. That volume contained only half of the material we collected, and we continued to collect. When the section stopped functioning we had more than double, perhaps triple, the published material. These documents were to be a second volume, down to 1800, and we had also a supplement to the first volume. The second volume went to press in 1905 but the political events brought our work to a halt. Our last meeting was held January 8, 1905, in an atmosphere of disquieting reports and fears for the coming days.

After his death, Bershadsky's rich archival materials passed to the Historical Commission. Analyzing this material, annotating and publishing it, was the second task of the Historical Commission, which handled it the same way as *Regesty*. In 1903 the material was published as the third volume of the Russian Jewish archives (Bershadsky himself had published the first two volumes).

We also worked on published and archival Hebrew sources. The published sources, which have been preserved until today but not used, we compiled in a register, in the style of the *Regesty*. The archival materials were mostly community records which we had read and discussed at our meetings. Of these, we decided to publish the most important — the record book of the Grodno community and of the Lithuanian Council — with an accompanying Russian translation, which was checked, analyzed, and discussed at a section meeting.

So the years passed, fifteen full years. Two generations burrowed year after year among the dried old parchments which were so far removed from their everyday interests, and yet a piety remains for those years which we spent in this eccentric reading. Every December, for some years, the old and young archivists met for an annual dinner, a happy friendly occasion, which grew ever more familiar and intimate. The dinner usually started off with a humorous account of current events in the style of public documents. We even published some, as a miniature *Regesty*. During dinner there were toasts and speeches about then and now. The speeches usually ended with unresoluable differences — about Zionism. So we debated until long past midnight and the next day, in a most amiable fashion, settled the legal dispute between Yankel Khatskelevich and Feivish Movsheyevich over three grams of honey.

Ah, these inconsequential casuistries of life — how closely, yet invisibly, they were bound with our existence, despite the distance separating us in time and historical circumstances, how they forged us in one! In all these explicit expressions of a way of life, so much was your own that you felt a blood relationship with them, as with a departed world, even before you realized consciously that this relationship was called "nationality." We did not debate the "national idea"; we felt its vigorous influence. Inspired by feelings more than by ideas, we spent fifteen years — despite the tedium — over these old documents, witnesses of the authentic life of our people.

"From all of these sources," we wrote in the foreword to *Regesty i Nadpisi*, "streamed facts, pictures, ideas. A rich new world of our own cherished past unfolded before our eyes. Then what? The very reading of these dry documents about ordinary happenings of no particular fascination affected us in the same way as Antaeus's contact with Mother Earth. The past was woven into the present, and in the old we saw the new, in the new the old; and life with all its glory, multiplicity, and immediacy captured us. We

waded in over our necks in details and minutiae, scowling and unenthusias-
tic, and emerged fortified and serene. We achieved that solidity and self-
satisfaction which give life inexhaustible worth and richness. Vernunft fing
wieder an zu sprechen und Hoffnung wieder an zu blühen. The most important thing for us was the life of our people."

26 My Father, Baron David
by Sophie Günzburg

BARON DAVID GÜNZBURG was born in
Kamenets-Podolski in 1857, and died
in St. Petersburg in 1910. He was the
third generation of a famous Jewish
baronial family of financiers, philanthropists, and communal leaders and
was himself a paragon of aristocracy,
an exemplar of *noblesse oblige*.

David Günzburg bridged the many
worlds of Russian Jews of his time. He
presided over rabbinical conferences
concerned with communal affairs with
sympathetic understanding and courtesy, and yet he was also an admirer
and friend of the apostate Daniel

Chwolson (see Part VIII). Conservative in politics, he nevertheless also befriended and helped Jewish socialist
and Zionist radicals. A true aristocrat
and a good Jew, he transcended class,
party, and sect, acting out in his life
an old Jewish tradition that all Israel
are responsible for one another.

In the following memoir written by
his daughter Sophie, he appears in all
his roles: son, husband, father; gentleman and scholar; linguist, philosopher,
and patron of the arts; educator and
communal leader.

M Y great-grandfather, Joseph Yozl Günzburg, known as Ossip Gavrilovich, lived in one of those towns of western Russia which swarmed with
Jews and produced some of Israel's great men. He took to wife Rosa Dinin,
the eldest daughter of one of the prominent families of the day. When he
rose to greatness, all his in-laws, those close and those remote, gloried in
their link to him. He used to say: "The Dinins are not a family but a tribe."
He was generous to all; to provide funds for dowries and exemptions from
military service, he bought 50,000 hectares of land in the Crimea, the income of which was set aside to aid indigent relatives.

One of his sons, Horace, settled in Kamenets-Podolski. There, in 1857,
my father was born. After fortune smiled on him, my great-grandfather

decided to go for the waters to Spa, in Belgium, stopping in Paris on the way. He took along his three married sons with their families; his fourth son, a bachelor; his only daughter; a nurse for the small children; his barber; a whole retinue of servants, and two or three older women to assist his wife.

That was in 1863. They travelled leisurely: to Berlin by carriage and from there to Paris by railroad. The city fascinated my great-grandfather, and he decided to settle there. After taking the cure in Spa, the whole family returned to Paris. He rented a house and established the family in it. On the upper floor of the building, a synagogue was set up which, before long, attracted many worshippers from those in the neighborhood for whom the Great Synagogue in Rue Victoire was too far to walk to on Sabbaths and holidays.

Ossip Gavrilovich adapted himself to Western ways, but his wife, a loyal daughter of Israel who wore a *sheytl* and dressed in the style of Russian provincial gentry, spoke only Yiddish and was far from the spirit of the time and its ways. She was critical of her husband's conduct, seeing it as a quest for wealth, honor, assimilation. She did, nonetheless, allow herself to be escorted to the table by the guest of honor, as was customary, though often the two would sit side by side unable to exchange a word. Her husband having gained considerable position in Paris, there were elegant dinners and splendid parties attended by ministers and ambassadors. Immediately after the meal, my great-grandmother would retire to her own quarters. How happy she would have been to forego the entire proceedings, but it was her husband's wish that she act as hostess.

Actually, the guests were attended to, menus planned, and preparations supervised by a daughter-in-law, Anna, who was also Ossip's niece. Anna, who was young, charming, clever and tasteful, was popular in Paris, but the rush of compliments and praise did not go to her head. She came from a small town in Russia and, though she had social status in Paris and had many admirers, she maintained her quiet, reticent manner. She had all a woman could desire: a loving husband, healthy children, great wealth, jewels, the affection of friends and family, a life free from personal shock. She had only one wish: that she be spared the death of any loved one, and this wish too was granted.

Anna died at thirty-six, after bearing her eleventh child. She was the first to be buried in the family sepulchre built by my great-grandfather in the Montparnasse cemetery, with a mausoleum which had seventy-two places. My father, nineteen at the time, recalled his mother with love.

Ossip died in 1877, only one year after his devoted daughter-in-law. His wife outlived him by many years and attained such a ripe old age that even my older sister and brother remembered her.

As for how we became barons, let us work backward. My great-grandfather visited Petersburg and, once granted the right to settle there, founded a bank bearing his name and bought a large building with ninety-two suites, some elegant, others more simple. It had only two stories but occupied a large area and had many interior courtyards.

Shortly after being widowed, Grandfather Horace settled in this house with his children. After my father's marriage in Paris, he too came to Petersburg and took an apartment in this large house.

In 1875, Grandfather Horace handled the affairs of the Grand Duke of Hesse-Darmstadt, a high officer in the Russian army, the father of Alexandra, future Tsarina of Russia. The Duke had been in great financial distress. Wishing to express his gratitude, yet unable to grant father an estate in Germany, he bestowed upon him the title of Baron. Approximately a year later, that same personal title was extended to the entire family so that my great-grandfather became a baron as did all the brothers and grandchildren. With the permission of Alexander II, we were also made Russian barons. Napoleon III, however, refused to extend the title.

Of the eleven children in his family, my father was the only one to display intellectual leanings. When he was eight, one could often find him in the great vestibule, where the statue of Moses stood. He would be rolling a hoop with his right hand, while holding in his left hand an open book from which he studied his lessons. Later my father studied in the famed German university of Göttingen.

When Father was twenty-one he served in the Russian army, in the Ulan regiment in Lomza. As a volunteer and an intellectual, his term was reduced to eleven months. An aide was assigned to him, as was the rule with officers — in this case a young Jewish soldier from Warsaw, Alexei (Aaron) Fliderbaum, who appears again in the course of these recollections. After serving in the army, my father resumed his studies in Paris, mastering new languages, passing many hours with the rare book dealers on the banks of the Seine and in his own stacks on Rue Napoleon. He was, by temperament, withdrawn, and did not enjoy parties or concerts.

In 1883 he became engaged. Father had decided, when he was twelve, that no girl could vie with Uncle Uri's daughter Matilda in beauty and charm, and, accordingly, informed his parents that when he grew up he would marry her. My mother, at that time, was five. From year to year this love grew stronger and there continued to be no woman to rival Matilda in his eyes. When my mother, at eighteen, entered society, she had almost no suitors since it was already generally assumed that she was betrothed.

The wedding was to take place in December, which allowed my father to take a six-month trip to the Caucasus for the purpose of learning Georgian and Armenian. In Caucasia, Father lived among people who were cruel and primitive, but utterly loyal. They welcomed him and gave him a handsome horse, a gift which pleased him very much. He had to leave the horse behind when he returned home, but he did bring his servant with him to Paris.

My parents were married on the 18th of December. The day was cold and dreary. My mother was the first of the Günzburg girls to marry. The beautiful ceremony took place in the synagogue on Rue Victoire. The young couple then left for a honeymoon which turned out to be a series of visits to relatives in various towns in Germany.

Returning home, my parents reached the Russian border on a Friday evening, and as my father refused to travel on the Sabbath, Mother spent the night on a hard bench in the waiting room. Saturday night they resumed their trip, arriving in the apartment which awaited them in Petersburg. The adjacent quarters were occupied by Horace, my mother's father-in-law as well as her uncle, and his unmarried children. The little ones soon grew fond of their cousin — sister-in-law — who entertained them with great skill so that she was soon their confidante.

My mother was well received in Petersburg, having youth, beauty, charm. My father worshipped her. He composed poems to her every day, thought only of her, spoke only of her. Returning home from his office in the Ministry he was overcome with joy at the mere sight of her. When he was out with her, displaying his prize to the world — this was a thrill to him. My mother's relation to my father was somewhat different. She respected his judgment, generosity, talents, and courage. She was grateful for his abundant love. But Father used to fly into quick rages. The outbursts would subside just as swiftly. Though they were never directed at her, still she was very disturbed. Besides, Horace's sons were brought up in a religious and traditional spirit, whereas my mother's family did not observe the commandments. In their kitchen, dietary laws were not followed. It was not their custom to attend the synagogue. The children were not taught Hebrew prayers; they travelled on the Sabbath. When she married my father, Mother was burdened by the dietary laws and by the requirement to dine with her father-in-law on Sabbath eve. Nevertheless, my parents had a peaceful life together. Their principles and ethic were identical: boundless kindness, an uncompromising sense of justice, pride in their Jewishness, good education, pleasant character, the capacity to understand others. In Petersburg they were considered a model couple. I was born to them in 1890, the fourth of five children.

My father inherited from his grandfather Ossip a library of 10,000 volumes. He was constantly supplementing this, purchasing entire collections, as well as individual volumes, through catalogues received from Paris.

Father had bookcases sent from Paris to Petersburg, four meters high, one meter deep. They were of oak, with glass doors. Every shelf had a side vent to allow for air circulation. The lower sections had no glass. There, about 2,400 rare manuscripts were kept. There were oversize folios with engravings by Gustave Doré (the Bible and La Fontaine's fables), the works of Molière in large format, many art works, sheathed in rollers, one of them, very large — decorated with illustrations and elaborate inscriptions, arabesques; copies of gravestone inscriptions and ornamentation, colorful engravings of Jewish interest. The description of this collection, entitled *L'Ornement Hébreu* (Berlin, 1903), was prepared by my father. He devoted years to it and was assisted by Vladimir Stassov, a famous Russian art expert. The project, involving the study of ancient art, consumed considerable time, devotion, research, and money. Happily, their efforts were crowned with great success.

Alexei Fliderbaum, who had been my father's aide in the army, had become his secretary. Twice a year he cleaned all the books, now numbering 52,000, this not counting the collection of French and Russian newspapers and magazines. Father would not discard anything. The library, which had grown at such a rapid rate, included the collection of Vladimir Soloviev, the philosopher and Father's close friend, and many volumes ordered from Paris. The King of England was said to have the largest private book collection in the world; my father's library, so I was told, was considered second or third to it.

Let me here mention that my father, even on a very short trip, always kept a small Hebrew Bible in his pocket, a French Bible in his suitcase, two volumes of Lermontov's poems, as well as two large dictionaries, Arabic-French and French-Arabic, which he needed for his work.

When we were little, my father used to teach us to love and take care of books. He used to show us old parchment volumes, bound in heavy leather, warm brown or white, often fastened with metal pins. He would call our attention to the colorful engravings. But we also loved the simpler volumes. Among the 2,400 manuscripts, there were three volumes salvaged from an auto-da-fé in Spain. The fringes of the pages were tattered and singed. These were my favorite books. It is difficult to describe my feelings when I fingered the parchment that had been brushed by the flames.

We were educated at home. We had a French governess and a Russian teacher. Chief Rabbi M. A. Eisenstadt gave us Hebrew lessons. Also, we studied piano, drawing, dance. Our parents were not present at our lessons, not wishing to burden the teachers, but both of them took an interest in our studies.

As the library expanded and the children grew, our quarters were no longer adequate. We moved to a new apartment on the second story of a handsome house. Two or three years later, we noticed the floors sagging under the weight of the books and were compelled to move to the ground floor.

Two or three rooms in a small suite were set aside to house Jews refused residence permits in the capital city. Here they lived in hiding until my father could obtain the proper documents for them. They did not leave the house; food was brought into their rooms by our servants.

My parents were intimate with the sculptor Antokolsky, born in Vilna. He was so talented that Nicholas II commissioned three busts from him: one of himself, one of his wife, one of his mother. This was a great honor for a Jewish artist. My father had great respect for Antokolsky but enjoyed irritating him, saying jokingly that he spoke poor Russian, French, and German, but would not, alas, speak Yiddish. Most of Antokolsky's works were acquired by the Museum of Alexander III. Father's friend, Vladimir Soloviev, used to come to our house often and sit with him in his study. My mother was always sending tea up to them. Soloviev, however, never came down to the drawing room.

We used to spend at least two months a year in our estate in Podolia. The estate was large, including our house, a huge garden, the caretaker's house and garden, the stable, barn, chicken yard, laundry, houses for the coachmen and their families, the laundress, and so forth — about fifty persons in all. A small distance away was the village of Mohilna, population 5,000, with a pretty church and peasant huts — whitewashed, straw-thatched surrounded by cherry trees and rose bushes. One kilometer from our house, in the valley, was our sugar factory, as well as the manager's home, overlooking a freshwater pond that provided us with water for drinking, cooking, laundry, washing, and gardening.

Our closest neighbor was fifty kilometers away. He was a Polish noble-man, hence we had no contact with him. Some ten kilometers distant was a second village; in another direction, toward the railroad station, about 25 kilometers from our house, though not on our land, was a third village. We were, thus, along with the factory, quite isolated from the world.

Father used to spend the entire vacation period with us at the estate. He liked the factory manager and his family and enjoyed our visitors and, in the peaceful countryside, devoted himself to his work. He loved nature, plants, animals. We used to go on excursions, sometimes by foot, other times by horse and carriage. We would go to the shores of the Bug River and collect shells.

About eighteen kilometers from our estate there was a Jewish town called Khashtchevata (Khashchevatoye). The authorities were not particularly hostile to this town but did not allow it to expand beyond set boundaries. Its inhabitants, being faithful observers of the commandment to be fruitful and multiply, soon found themselves in a grave situation.

Two or three times a year, our parents would visit this town, sometimes taking us along. The people, deeming it an untold privilege to be neighbors of Baron Günzburg, considered these visits a holiday and flocked to welcome him. The crowd would swarm about the carriage so that it could not move ahead. My parents would descend. Then the "attack" would begin. They kissed my mother's hands, her shoulders, the hem of her gown. She would go into a hardware store and buy a pan; in a dry-goods store she would buy a ribbon; at the inn she would take tea. About fifty people clothed in rags followed her everywhere. Those who could not find a corner within, pressed against the windows and peered. Others stroked the horses, the wheels of the wagon. It was utter madness!

Then the entire crowd besieged my parents, all at once, crying, sobbing, each with his problems: one had a sick daughter, another needed a dowry, another had a son who sought to enter a vocational school, a fourth had a paralyzed mother. My parents recorded each case, distributed candy to the children and money — a good deal of money — and even promised to attend to every request. They used to return home very tired and worn out from all the sorrow they had witnessed.

Since we, the children, were Günzburgs whose duty it was to assist the Jews of Russia, we were taken to this town at an early age to see how its unfortunate population lived. In Petersburg we were taught to listen to those whose hearts were encumbered and to help them, not merely with money.

My father was employed in the Ministry of Education. He was accepted unquestioningly by the staff and introduced many innovations and improvements. He also served in the Foreign Ministry, which was ordinarily closed to Jews. But my father was a noted linguist who learned a new language almost every year. (A short time before his death he mastered a thirty-fourth tongue — Mahratti.) He was the only man in Russia who could translate any European or Middle Eastern tongue to any other in these families. Since Russia maintained diplomatic relations with all countries, but because Russian was known only in a few, a group of prominent citizens demanded that my father be appointed official translator in the Foreign Ministry.

As a Jew, my father could not be a professor at the University of St. Petersburg, though he was the leading expert in Near Eastern history, Hebrew, Arabic, Turkish, Assyrian, Aramaic, and so on. Students gifted in these subjects were sent to my father by their professors. We had a special hall for his lectures, many of which I attended, becoming acquainted with all the students. Later, my father opened a school of his own, with the right to confer degrees. He taught most of the subjects, but other qualified scholars were there too.

When I arrived in Israel in 1953, I was welcomed by my father's former students, first in Jerusalem, then in Tel Aviv, a large number of them now scholars and professors themselves. Among them were Rachel Ben-Zvi, widow of the late president, and Zalman Shazar, now President and formerly Minister of Education. It would have pleased my father to know of his students' course in life. As a teacher, he had concerned himself not only with their studies, but with their spiritual and material problems as well. None of this was forgotten, and much gratitude was conveyed in the greeting offered me.

My father served in two ministries, taught in his school, was active in community affairs, wrote books and articles, even gave us Hebrew lessons at 7 every morning. He used to eat quickly, as it was his custom to receive the public between 8 and 9:30 A.M. When we left his study after our lesson, we would see people seated in the entrance, the drawing room, the dining room — sometimes as many as twenty — all petitioning for help. All comers were received graciously without regard to distinctions of education or dress. Father would shake everyone's hand and, one by one, hear each plea. My grandfather and my father took an interest in a number of young musicians, financing their studies at the Conservatory. Many of them, Misha Elman and Josef Ahron, for example, earned great renown.

In Petersburg, father's positon was, for a Jew, among the highest. Even when his father, the head of the Jewish community was still alive, he used to intercede with the authorities in crucial matters: thwarting plans (which somehow became known to him) for violence against Jews, freeing an innocent Jew from prison, obtaining residence permits, providing an accused Jew with a fair defense lawyer.

He never sought favors for himself. Being a shy, modest person he would not have known how to ask for a favor. When he appealed, the officials knew that he was pleading another's cause, seeking to right an injury rather than being capricious or partial. They listened to him with respect. His simple, honest manner was convincing and his pleas were seldom rejected.

Father had little time to spare for society. He often had to attend meetings in the evening, and this prevented him from going to the theater. He was eager to be with his brothers and their wives, to maintain contact with friends and with the families of his colleagues. He therefore tried to arrange his affairs so that he would be free to accept evening invitations and also be available for special festive dinners at home. We had large dinners, sometimes simple (with family and friends), and sometimes more official. Scholars, members of the Russian nobility, government officials and their families were frequent guests. On one occasion, the Minister of Education came to us; this was a great event.

In 1908, a dance was held at our house in honor of my parent's silver anniversary. The company refused to play cards, although a quiet room had been set aside for this purpose. It was known that cards were not played in our house and no one would dream of violating this, though in Petersburg society, playing cards was the practice at every big party.

In the fall of 1910, my father became ill. By November, his condition was grave, but he still took an interest in his family, his friends, and the life of the Jewish community. The day came, late in December, when he no longer opened his eyes or spoke; not long afterward came the end.

The cemetery, founded by my father, was thirteen kilometers from our house, on land granted by the government. Father had had a synagogue erected there, where it was his wish to be buried rather than in the family plot in Paris. He had, after all, lived in Russia, loved the land, devoted his life and work to its Jews. There was no equivalent past linking him with Paris.

The funeral was very large. The streets, covered with snow, were lined with carriages bearing family, friends, acquaintances, and with large numbers of paupers who had come to pay final tribute to their benefactor.

I recall only the sound of the coffin striking the earth, which was covered with water — so close was this spot to the river Neva. (Besides, the city was built on swampland.) It was shocking — the sound of the waters which would soon begin to wear away the coffin. Surely Ossip must have recited the Kaddish; surely there must have been eulogies, but I do not remember them.

27   How I Became a Yiddish Linguist

by Nokhum Shtif

NOKHUM SHTIF was born in Rovno, province of Volhynia, in 1879 and died in Kiev in 1933. Most of the facts of his life are told in following selections from his brief autobiography. He was one of the founders of the Yiddish Scientific Institute (Yidisher visnshaftlekher institut) — YIVO and was its ideologue.

In the study of Yiddish and in ad-vocating for it a central place in Jewish life and thought, Shtif found his identity as a Jew. Living in a milieu where Judaism and its traditions had largely been abandoned, and himself having rejected a religious way of life, he was nevertheless able to sink deep Jewish roots through his extensive researches into the origins and early history of Yiddish.

I was born in Rovno, province of Volhynia, on November 17 (Old Style), 1879. My father, Jonah, came from the small Volhynian town of Varkovich, of a poor, respectable Jewish family. As a boy he went to Odessa, to which young maskilim were attracted. There he picked up some general education and learned Russian. My mother, Pesa, came of a middle-class "enlightened" family in Rovno. Her father, for whom I was named, was one of the first teachers in the then new government schools for Jewish pupils (he taught religion and the code of Jewish law). He gave his sons a modern education. One studied in the Rovno *Real-Gymnasium* and later became a doctor.

At any rate, it was a foregone conclusion in our home that the children would be given a better education than that usually received by Jewish middle-class children. My brothers, sister, and, especially, I owe our education to our father, who had a long-range outlook and who sacrificed a great deal — much beyond his resources — to educate his children.

Like all children in a pious Jewish town, I began studying with private teachers, first with one for ABC's and then with another for more advanced lessons. In my eighth year, my father instituted the first revolution in our educational style. I was sent to a tutor for Bible and Hebrew. At that time, studying the Prophets and the Writings was equated with nonbelief — all the more, studying Hebrew grammar and the literature of the haskala. Thanks to this teacher and his successor, I had a thorough grounding in Hebrew. At twelve, I knew practically all the Bible by heart, had read all the Hebrew literature of the time, and wrote a flowery Hebrew. I also studied a good deal of Gemara.

My father undertook a second revolution in 1894, when I was fifteen. He enrolled me in the Rovno public *Realschule*. (I was admitted to the third-year grade). No one in our middle-class status then dared do such a thing. Nevertheless, I did not cut myself off from the Jewish milieu. I continued to read Hebrew and even continued to study Gemara until I was well along at the university. At sixteen, I even founded a Hebrew-speaking club, with which I busied myself for about a year.

In 1897, after the first Zionist Congress at Basel, I became an ardent Zionist (my first love), founded societies, made speeches, and in various transmogrifications remained true to Zionism until about 1904. Zionism was the only movement in our town; there was no trace of a socialist party until 1903–4.

In 1899 I completed the Realschule and, after highly competitive examinations, was admitted to the *Polytechnikum* at Kiev. There I studied — first in the engineering school, and then in the chemistry department. I owe much to the Realschule for the systematicness I gained from studying mathematics. The Polytechnikum reinforced this with higher mathematics, physics, and chemistry.

In Kiev I belonged, at first, to the general Zionist organization. Later, under the influence of socialist propaganda and the student revolutionary movement in which we were active, we seceded and founded a leftist radical group, without clearly knowing what we wanted.

In 1902 I wrote a long study in Russian, in response to an anti-Zionist article, in which I argued on behalf of the proletarian-Zionist point of view and seasoned it with "economics" and statistics. It was practically the first rationale of the ideology later associated with the socialists-Zionists — that the nonproletarization of the Jewish masses leads to emigration which, in turn, must lead to colonization.

My radicalization continued further. The Kishenev pogrom broke out during Passover, 1903. In Kiev we responded with a self-defense group and with revolutionary proclamations. I played a leading role in the self-defense. We expanded our work, providing the region with arms. I had practically stopped studying at the Polytechnikum. With some other students, I submitted a demonstrative announcement to the rector that at a time when such dreadful things were happening to our brothers, I was in no position to take examinations.

In May, 1903, I met friends in Kharkov who had gone through the same intellectual process. The result was that in the fall of that year we convened the first conference of the group that was known as *Vozrozhdenie*, later the Seymists (Jewish Socialist Labor Party), in which I was quite active until 1907–8.

In November, 1903, during mass arrests of students, I was arrested. Police had found, under my pillow, Lenin's *What Is To Be Done*. I was in jail until May, 1904, when I was released temporarily and expelled from the Polytechnikum. In October, 1904, I fled to Switzerland, where I stayed a year in Bern and some months in Geneva. In January, 1905, I returned to Kiev on a false passport and reentered the Polytechnikum. But I did not really study; I worked in the Seymist party, first in Kiev and later travelling as a party professional in Vilna, Vitebsk, and Simferopol. I married in the summer of 1907 and moved to Vilna. But after the political reaction had set in, party life was throttled; consequently in the fall of that year I moved again — to St. Petersburg, on a temporary residence permit as a merchant's clerk. I lived from writing, participated in the Jewish Literary Society, and began to be interested in the work of the Society for the Promotion of Culture among Jews; I became a purposeful Yiddishist and began to propagandize Yiddishism.

I was given a post in the emigration division of the Jewish Colonization Association in 1909 and the same year I was admitted to the Law Lyceum in Yaroslavl. In the fall of 1914 I submitted my dissertation on "Criminal Law in the Torah and the Talmud," and received the bachelor of law degree.

I came to literature rather late and to Yiddish literature even later. Yiddish literature was then something alien to me. In my circle in those years, the idea of Yiddish literature did not even exist. I first heard about Yiddish in a serious vein when Sholem Aleichem read his stories at Zionist gatherings in Kiev in 1900–2. Though brought up in a Jewish home where Yiddish was always spoken, where I lived until I was nineteen, I believed, like all my friends, that I did not know Yiddish, and even more certainly that I could not write it — so much so that when I had to write two pamphlets about the attempt on Krushevan's * life, I wrote in Russian and asked someone to translate into Yiddish. These two pamphlets were my first published writings, printed outside Russia in 1903, and without my name, of course. At Bern in 1905, Yiddish made a more enduring impression on me, thanks to Ansky and his poem "Asmodai," to the traces of Yiddish propaganda which Zhitlowsky had left behind (he was then in America), and to the Bund's underground literature. In August and November of 1905, two of my articles were published, under the Russian pseudonym "Mechtatel" ("Visionary"), in the Zionist monthly *Yevreyskaya Zhizn* ("Jewish Life"). They were an outpouring of the heart about nationalism, assimilation, Zi-

* Russian antisemite whom a young Jew, Pinhas Dashevsky, unsuccessfully attempted to assassinate for his responsibility in the Kishenev pogrom of 1903.

onism, Jews, Ahad Ha'amism, and the younger Jewish generation, with all
the rhetoric and fervor of youth and inexperience. But at that very time
something happened that determined my cultural and literary orientation.
Until today I cannot figure out how it happened. In the emigrant colony
one had to look with a light to find a Yiddish book or newspaper, and I did
not look particularly hard. There was not, I think, a single person who was
serious about Yiddish, and certainly not about propaganda for Yiddish.
Everyone was involved in political agitation — in Russian, of course. We
were cut off from Jewish life in Russia. Yet, suddenly I told myself: I must
begin to write in Yiddish. Something had touched me off. One after another, there had appeared in 1904–5 David Pinsky's *Familye Tsvi* in Yiddish, and, both in Russian, Yevgeni Nikolayevich Chirikov's *Jews* and
Semyon Solomonovich Yushkevich's *Jews*. These three works were somehow associated in my mind, psychologically rather than literarily; I told
myself that I must write about them and only in Yiddish. It was a vision, a
lyrical dream, rather than a clear idea. I was at fever heat. In the hot Bern
summer, in deserted surroundings — even the émigré colony was breaking
up — lonely as only a poor student all alone in a strange place could be, not
knowing how to live through the day, I sat in a sweltering attic and worked
eight to ten hours a day without seeing the daylight, struggling bitterly
over the diffuse, imprecise, and elusive idea and even more over language
that I had to extract from the memory of my mother's tongue and of my
undeveloped taste. I worked at fever pitch for about six weeks and finished
my work: a lyrical outburst, nearly fifty pages long, flowery rhetoric in
journalistic form, about man and universe, Jews and Gentiles, Zionism and
socialism, all in a pretentious style. But its contents were the purest idealism. I did not even think of publishing it; I did not know where. Someone
later told me the St. Petersburg *Fraynd* published also a monthly called
Dos lebn ("Life") and advised me to submit it there. With a pounding heart
I counted the days, waiting for a reply that never came. Four or five years
later, the editor told me that he had intended to print it, but the revolution
of October, 1905, intervened and cut off *Life*'s life.

This youthful literary effort had a twofold effect. I became infected
with writer's itch; I realized I knew Yiddish, I could know it better, and it
was mine.

In Kiev in the winter of 1906, I contributed a great deal to the Seymist
journal *Di folks-shtime* — my first published work in Yiddish, which included political articles and controversial pieces. I wrote a folksy Yiddish
that I later deliberately cultivated. This was new for our circles that were
used to the highfalutin, Germanized Yiddish of the political parties, and it

made a great impact. My stylistic reputation was made with my first-published Yiddish articles. Committed to the Seymist concept of autonomism, living in a resuscitated Jewish community, especially in the natural Yiddish milieu of a workers' party, and pursuing my literary work, I came to regard Yiddish as a culture. I knew definitely what I wanted. I began to speak in Yiddish, and it seemed strange to me that it could ever have been different. I had already seriously begun to study Yiddish literature.

I was more of a nationalist than a comrade. "Proletarian psychology," I must admit, always took a beating. From 1908 to 1912 I worked along two lines: (1) Jewish culture — the struggle for Yiddish in print, in schools, among the intellectuals; Yiddish as a culture, not merely as a tool to enlighten the masses; writing critical studies about Yiddish literature, and (2) the struggle against russification, against russified banality and its influences, to which I gave a national-mystical underpinning.

Particularly in my literary criticism, when I wrote in Yiddish, I tried to free myself from that communal attitude which dictated that our critics extend pity and silk-glove treatment toward every mediocrity, just because it was "ours," magnifying every triviality. I defended the artistic-esthetic point of view, the criteria of world literature, ideas, emotions, literary techniques, style, which affected us like everyone else. I was certain that in this way I could really serve Yiddish literature. With this outlook, I tried to revise the attitude toward Sholem Asch, for example, and even more toward Morris Rosenfeld and Abraham Reisen. For these articles I was subjected to much abuse. Nomberg called me a roughneck who talked about art. But I stuck to my attitude towards Yiddish belles lettres. In the literary cliques I was always like an outsider, a visitor, partly because I avoided the Warsaw literary hubbub. I broke the habit of polemics: I did not reply to attacks. One must say what one wants to say in an affirmative form.

In a collection of essays about Peretz, published in Minsk in 1922, I said Peretz was not our greatest literary talent — compared with Sholem Aleichem, for example, and not our most elegant writer, compared with our contemporary ones. But Peretz himself had a great literary culture and introduced that culture among us. He was the first to make a literature out of scattered authors and books, with faith and determination, in his own way, because he wanted and clearly strove toward it.

In an article on Sholem Asch, I showed that the chief defect in many Yiddish writers, except the three literary fathers, was their lack of culture and knowledge. They wrote from memory about their small towns, and stayed with that, quickly draining themselves, repeating themselves, without any critical sense for what was new, for what was happening in Jewish life. The shtetl was our culture of yesterday. Whoever records it with naïve infatuation, without understanding the revolution which took place within our Jewish society, is a man of the past. Yiddish writing had already passed that stage of literaryness and had arrived at the stage of literature.

From 1908 I gained a new interest: research in Yiddish. I began to visit the Asiatic Museum in St. Petersburg that is, the libraries of the Eastern peoples, which included also collections of Hebrew and Yiddish. Old Yiddish literature — the *Shmuel-bukh,* for example, made an enormous impact on me. I began zealously to study this literature and Yiddish linguistic works. By myself, without a guide, without any philological background at all, it was hard labor.

In Rovno, with only pennies, but with energy and discretion, I collected a large library — from Elijah Levita's *Tishbi,* published in Isny in 1541, to the rare editions of Aksenfeld and Linetsky. I had the most important old works of research on Yiddish, Wagenseil's *Die Belehrung der Jüdisch-Deutschen Red- und Schreibart* (Koenigsberg, 1699), a considerable literature about Middle High German, a large collection of Yiddish periodicals (from *Kol Mevasser* on), a collection of responsa with Yiddish glosses and texts — a rare library for the study of Yiddish and Yiddish literature.

My first publication on the study of Yiddish was an article in the *Pinkas* (1913), "Dr. Pines' History of Yiddish Literature." I exposed the book, showing that its author had never actually seen with his own eyes anything of Old Yiddish literature and had badly put together the history of modern Yiddish literature.

The years between 1915 and 1921 were the most unfortunate for my work; since I worked at the Jewish Colonization Association, I could not study at the Asiatic Museum, which was open only during my working hours. In 1920 in Kiev, I did have the rare opportunity of studying the Cremona edition of 1560 of the Pentateuch in Yiddish. In 1919 and 1920 I busied myself rather with Jewish history, especially studies in the rich provincial archives of Kiev.

After March, 1922, I resumed my linguistic studies in earnest in Berlin. Here I got to examine not only the rare holdings of the Berlin State Library, but also those of other libraries. I studied the most important sixteenth-century publications (Bible, morality books, prayer books, books on customs, secular writings), all the Berlin manuscripts, and some manuscripts in Munich, Hamburg, Karlsruhe, Oxford, and Parma — the entire linguistic literature about Yiddish which I had not seen before. I worked seriously on Middle High German, on German dialectology, partly on the history of the Jews in the German lands in the Middle Ages. With photographic copies of some published and manuscript works, I got some idea of the books and manuscripts which the Berlin library could not borrow.

I made a special study of Yiddish translations of the Bible. When I began to write, I thought it would be a lengthy article. But I soon realized that I had material for a book. I continued such studies: on the *Shmuel-bukh*, the *Mase-bukh*, sixteenth-century Yiddish works printed in Cracow, sixteenth-century literary and colloquial languages, especially in Poland. I amassed an enormous quantity of material for an anthology of Old Yiddish literature.

In the journal *Yidishe filologye* I published an article on "Dietrich of Bern: Secular Motives in Old Yiddish Literature." I then wrote a lengthy study on the connective *ven-den* in sixteenth-century Yiddish literature, which was "too long" for the journal and so has remained in my desk drawer. In the summer of 1918, during the great famine in Petersburg, I wrote a small book *Yidn un yidish* ("Jews and Yiddish"), in simple language to show the great value of Yiddish for our children's education and for our national-political equality, that is, national autonomy. The book was published in Kiev in 1919 and reprinted in Warsaw in 1920.

In the summer of 1920 in Kiev I wrote another small book, *Humanizm in der elterer yidisher literatur* ("Humanism in Early Yiddish Literature"). This was a survey of Yiddish haskala literature from Isaac Ber Levinsohn down to Mendele, showing the dominant ideas and the passion of this literature — humanism, the desire to fraternize with the world and its culture, matter versus spirit, humanity versus Judaism, a program of social and cultural reform, knowledge versus mind speculation, productive work versus idleness and Jewish trades. That was the reformation in Jewish life.

28 Balance Sheet of a Jewish Historian
by Jacob Shatzky

JACOB SHATZKY was born in Warsaw in 1894 and died in New York in 1956. He received a doctorate from the University of Warsaw in 1922, and five years later came to the United States.

His first encounter with the secular modern world was through Polish history and literature, and all his days he remained loyal and indeed enamored of Polish culture. In becoming a modern man of secular learning, in a milieu where religion seemed irrelevant, Shatzky found a meaningful and personally satisfying form of Jewish identity in his study of the Jewish past and in his search for a Jewish-Polish symbiosis.

A historian of Polish Jewry, his most outstanding work was a three-volume history of the Jews in Warsaw. The following selection has been translated from two autobiographical addresses.

I WAS born under the sign of Jewish history. If that predisposition toward recording the Jewish past was restricted in my childhood to those Warsavians whom Jews considered the "last of a passing generation," such was the effect of the milieu in which I was born and reared. My father had a weakness for the funerals of those he thought of as "great Jews." His notion of a great Jew was exaggeratedly maskilic. He believed one of the best Jewish educational methods was to make a child pay his last respects to great deceased Jews. I recall he took me to Hayim Selig Slonimski's funeral. That was in 1904, and I was ten years old. My father said to me: "Son, know that the last great Jew of our generation has died." We were standing on the corner, waiting for the funeral coach. It was a lovely spring day. The street was swarming with people, Jews, who congregated because others did. A man dressed in the traditional long coat of Orthodox Jews — my father's collective epithet for them was "Itche-Meir" — approached, asking, "Who died?"

"Hayim Selig Slonimski," my father replied with feeling.

"He must have been a big businessman, so many Jews have come to the funeral."

My father had a temper, but the funeral atmosphere cooled his hot-headedness. He did not respond with a single word. To me he said, "What a pity when a great Litvak is at the mercy of these Itche-Meirs."

We always found out at a funeral whoever was great or distinguished in Jewish Warsaw. I used to attach myself to every funeral procession that seemed to me important — according to the number of mourners. Often I did not even know who the deceased was, but hearing the eulogies at the cemetery, I felt that it was a privilege to be there in such lifeless proximity to a living past. Instinctively I inherited that impersonal attitude toward one whose life had graced Warsaw's Jewish life, a life which first revealed itself to me at the cemetery.

That was decidedly the approach of a Jewish historian.

I remembered 1908, when Mattias Berson, philanthropist and collector of Jewish antiquities, died. His collection formed the basis of the Warsaw Jewish community museum. The funeral was authentically Polish — Sarmatian faces, aristocratic women, the chill atmosphere and decorative flowers, without tears and without Kaddish — it was all a world I was seeing for the first time. I was standing very near the grave when an elderly man asked me, in Polish: "Son, what are you doing here? Are you a relative of the deceased?"

"No," I replied, "I came to pay my respects to the author of *Starożytne Bóżnice w Polsce.*"

The effect of my reply was tremendous. He introduced himself — Alexander Kraushar, Berson's son-in-law. Then I surprised him again, telling him I had been unable to get a copy of the second volume of his history of the Jews in Poland, published in 1866. (A few days later he sent me a copy as a gift — the first autographed book I ever owned.) The inscription was so allusive that my youthful mind did not grasp it then, but years later it became understandable:

> Młodzieńciowi, który, gdy dane mu będą warunki odpowiednie, stanie się tym, czym autor tej książki chciał być w jego będąc wieku, ale życie inaczej postanowiło.

> (To the boy who under auspicious circumstances will grow into the kind of man the author of this book wanted to be when he was his age. But life decreed otherwise.)

After every funeral I used to stay on at the cemetery and copy tombstone inscriptions. From my father I received my first lesson in how to calculate Hebrew dates and years and the most precious gift — Kalman Shulman's popular history *Milhamot ha-Yehudim* ("The Jewish Wars").

But when my father died I had to relinquish my dreams. I worked in a tea store on Leszno Street, but to recite Kaddish I went to the Tlomackie Synagogue, even though it was far away. Protected by an orphan's immunity, I did not have to return to the store, and I could stay a while in the synagogue library. There I found a guardian angel named Abraham Gavze. He was a fair librarian, a good journalist, but an even better human being. He showed much fatherly love to me and to other dreamers like me who used to crowd the tiny reading room in the cold winter evenings. There I used to study Latin and Greek from the polyglot Bible, repeating from memory whole sentences in a Gemara intonation: "In principio creavit Deus caelum et terram."

One cold December evening, after Kaddish, I sat down in the library to study my mentor, Steinschneider, and began copying titles, some of which

I did not even understand. Then Gavze beckoned to me. A woman wearing a professorial pince-nez wanted some information. The question was apparently too difficult for Gavze. It was the first time I had ever been asked anything. I poured out everything I knew on the subject in a mass of details. She seemed quite pleased and wanted to talk further with me. When the library closed, I escorted her home. She asked all sorts of questions about me. Then, suddenly, "Young man, would you like to study?" She listened while I, indecisive, played Hamlet, then asked for my address and said she would speak to someone about me.

About a week later I received an invitation from Bernard Lauer, a banker reputed to be a patron of Jewish artists. He lived on Święto-Krzyska, a street famous for its shops of antiquities, where I had spent my hoarded pennies. Save in my imagination, I had never seen anything like his home, with expensive bookcases filled with handsome books, with paintings by Wyspianski, Moritz Gottlieb, and others.

We began to talk about books and antiquities, as if he wanted to test me. Then he went into another room, returning after a while with two letters. "Here are two letters: one is addressed to Rabbi Dr. Poznanski and the other to Samuel Adalberg." I squealed in adolescent surprise: "Adalberg, the author of *Księga przysłów polskich*? I wish I owned that book! But it is so rare that even if a dealer on Święto-Krzyska Street gets a copy, it sells for twenty-five rubles. And I earn ten rubles a month."

Lauer laughed. "Don't worry. I'll give you the book if Adalberg says you deserve it."

I saw both men, and they conducted a sort of colloquy with me, a disguised test. Both interviews greatly flustered me. What would come of them? A few days later I received a summons to visit Lauer. He gave me a sealed envelope, saying: "Go to Cracow right away. Here is a letter to my brother, a bank director. For ten years you will receive a monthly grant so that you may complete gymnasium and also university. I cannot depend on God's unseen ways and I do not think he will let an unbeliever like me live ten years more. I must provide for you, for my dream, also, had been to be a historian of Jews, but money strangled that desire. Hunger, too, can do the same thing. I will provide for you, especially since Poznanski and Adalberg said you were worth the risk. You will get a set of tutors in Cracow who will prepare you to enter the sixth or seventh class in gymnasium, and my brother will pay them."

"You will go away to Cracow. There you will inhale the spirit of free Polish culture. There, in Cracow, you will understand not only the spirit of

Poland but also the spirit of historical Jewry in Poland. In Warsaw one cannot be as Polish as in Cracow. You will complete the gymnasium and then study in the ancient Jagiellonian University. Only then, when you return to Warsaw, will you be able to write a history of Jews in Warsaw."

So spoke to me Samuel Adalberg, whom most Jews knew only as Wawelberg's* realty agent and a bank clerk, and whom Poles valued for his monumental work on Polish proverbs. Later he was to become head of the Department for Jewish Affairs in the Polish Ministry of Education. From childhood on I had known and heard of Adalberg. That I was destined to know this extraordinary man and that he would play a decisive role in my life seemed beyond any of my dreams. It happened by accident, whatever the determinists may say. Not a Jewish historian, but a Polish cultural historian, Adalberg headed a fund for Jewish historians which Wawelberg had established at the University of Lemberg at the advice of the great historian Szymon Askenazy. Adalberg naturally consulted Askenazy about me and received his assent. Both had an *idée fixe* that a true Jewish Polish historian must be a Warsaw Jew. In this instance the geographic factor had enormous psychological significance. It meant more than being merely a historian of Jews in Poland. In Galicia there were such men as Meir Balaban, Isaac Schipper, Weissberg, and N. M. Gelber. In Prussian Poland, rabbis wrote regional communal histories, often better conceived than similar works by the Lithuanian rabbis or scholars, though politically biased and culturally Germanic. Askenazy used to argue that though the Galician historians wrote mostly in Polish, they had no emotional ties to the language and hence they could not be thought of as Polish historians of Jews. They were neutral, he would contend, about the partitions of Poland, without feeling for the tragic end of ancient Poland, for which he, Szymon Askenazy of Zawichost, still mourned. As for the German-speaking rabbis, they were explicitly anti-Polish, apologists for Prussian imperialism.

At that time, Russian Jewish scholars started to create a clearly defined Russian Jewish school of historical writing. Thematically this meant that the history of Jews was located in the kingdom of ancient Poland up to the time of the partitions. Some Russian Jewish historians formulated the idea that the Jews had been badly off in Poland because it was governed by nobility and that the situation of the Jews, particularly in those areas occupied by Russia, improved politically and economically with the fall of Poland. Levanda had written that the liquidation of Poland had been a pro-

---

* Hippolite Wawelberg, 1844–1901, who was born and educated in Warsaw, lived later in St. Petersburg and was a prominent banker, Jewish communal leader, and philanthropist.

gressive act of historic justice. The same tune was sung by the rabbis of
Posen, who dated the paradise for Jews in Poland from the days when
Prussian soldiers liberated the country from the Slavic nobility.

But in Congress Poland the Petersburg historians had no influence and
no collaborators. In all Poland there was a bare handful of supporters of the
Jewish Historical Society in St. Petersburg, mostly non-Polish Jews. Congress Poland had been Polish even in the most difficult years of brutal russification; its Jews had not been among the russifiers and took no part in
Russian Jewish cultural institutions. The few exceptions confirmed the
fact.

In his first interview with me, Askenazy developed the idea that Polish
Jews needed their own historians; acknowledging the Jewish Historical Society in Petersburg, he said, was like approving the Russian occupation of
Poland. In his eyes, Russian-writing Jewish historians were Litvaks, to
whom the spirit of Polish history was totally alien. They were not Polish
historians of the Jewish past in Poland, but Russian historians of that past.
The difference was great, for the function of a Polish historian of Jews in
Poland, he continued, was to prove that Jews were always well off in Poland and the situation grew worse when Russia helped topple Poland. Was
it chance that the Russian Pale of Settlement coincided with the whole
territory of former Poland, that Russia did not admit the Jews into Russia
proper even after these provinces had been incorporated in the Russian empire?

The russification of the Jewish intellectuals, Askenazy argued, was careerist assimilation, whereas in Poland assimilation was passionate Polonization, for it offered no practical benefits. Even the Jewish lower classes who
did not speak Polish felt themselves part of Poland. Askenazy believed that
the history of an oppressed people is above all their political weapon. Hence,
Petersburg could not set the standard for Warsaw even in matters of Jewish
historical writing.

In 1912, Askenazy began to publish a journal for the history of Jews in
Poland, of which only three meager issues appeared. St. Petersburg did not
like its tone; Dubnow did not like its Polishness. It did not occur to either
side that there could be a third party, a Jewish one, unassociated with either
Polishness or Russianness — Jewish not necessarily in language, but in the
internal rhythm of the Jewish historical process, played out, it is true,
against a background of political reality but not always closely intricated in
it.

Sometimes I wonder why hasidism rooted in Poland rather than in
neighboring countries where the Jews were just as pious. And at the same

moment I wonder why Treblinka happened to be in Poland and not elsewhere.

Why did the Posen Jew become German, the Vilna Jew Russian, and the Warsaw Jew Polish, emotionally at least, if not culturally, but certainly not Russian? What were the forces that caused Warsaw Jews to reject the rich culture of the Russians? Indeed, more Jews in Warsaw knew French better than Russian. Warsaw Jews joined with Poles in complete unity in their boycott of the Moscow Art Theatre. That was a *genius loci,* creating special conditions and hence deserving particular treatment, more than merely as the local history of another Jewish community.

It was no accident that my first published work was about Jews in old Warsaw. I spent my first leave from the then new Polish army in Warsaw, which had just been liberated from Russian occupation. Askenazy threw open the doors of the Warsaw archives to me. I became the first Jew in Warsaw to work on a Jewish theme in Polish government archives.

Thus, the circle of my life revolved around the past of the city where I had been born of a father from Bialystok and a mother from Berdichev. It was not just biological chance that made it my city, but emotional attachment. There my historical consciousness had been shaped by attending the funerals of Warsaw's great Jews.

VI

Literary Men

29 Notes for My Literary Biography
by Mendele Mokher Sforim

MENDELE MOKHER SFORIM (Sholem Jacob Abramovich) was born in Kopyl in 1836 and died in Odessa in 1917. Many of the facts of his life are told in the following autobiographical memoir. Known as the "grandfather of Yiddish literature," he guided Yiddish literature through its transition from being no more than an instrumentality of the haskala to becoming a full-blown expression of modern literary creativity. His enormous literary power enhanced his didactic purposes and transformed even his harsh and bitter depictions of traditionalist, unemancipated Jewish society into social criticism of a high order. He was the first, apart from the hasidic storytellers, to introduce the individual and his individual sensitivity into Yiddish literature, and thus to bring Yiddish literature into the mainstream of nineteenth-century European writing.

M Y birthplace, Kopyl, is a small town in the Slutsk district of the province of Minsk. God did not endow this town with resources and wealth or favor it with business and trade. Instead, He bestowed upon it a lovely landscape, beautiful forests, and a placid life, with valleys and lovely fields all about. The date of my birth was not recorded anywhere, for we Jews did not bother about such things then, especially in the small towns. But I have assumed I was born in 1836 and my family decided on December 20 as my birth date.

My father, Hayim Moshe, was a most respectable householder in town and was known in the district for his religious learning and his good manners, his generosity, and his familiarity with worldly matters. He allotted half of his time to God — for religious study by himself and teaching others without charge — and half for himself, for his own affairs and for communal matters, to which he was devoted. My father loved me very much and of all the children picked me to be educated in a way that had until then not occurred to anyone in our town. When I was six and could already read Hebrew, he hired one of the best tutors to teach me the Bible and study the Prophets and the Writings with Targum. My teacher studied with me twelve hours a day and after three years of study I knew all the books of the Bible by heart and God's Torah was in my belly.

Seeing how I savored the sweet words of the divine Prophets and walked with great divine visions from time immemorial, my teacher brought me into the domain of the Talmud, forever the giant, Og the King of Bashan, of world literature. There I was like one who comes for the first time to a great fair, gaping, his amazement unceasing at all sorts of goods and many strange things. He is openmouthed at the bustle and tumult and noise on all sides. Buyers and sellers, brokers and merchants hurry-scurry, seized with the desire and greed for business. They dash dazed and bedazzled, one with his pitcher and one with his barrel, jostling one another, asking, answering, nodding and winking, strutting, they deal and wheel, dicker and haggle, with a boom and bellow in the crowd! My fantasy gave form and face to everything that appeared to me in the Talmud. I understood everyone's language right away as soon as I was introduced to them, but still much of their talk remained obscure. But that was just at the start, when I had entered the gateway of the Talmud. In time I became accustomed to it and came to love it. I used to pass the night in the depths of the halakha, awed by towers flying in the skies and mountains hanging by a hair and other such wondrous matters in keen casuistry.

I used to love to stroll in the garden of the Agada. It was not like an orchard, fenced in, with gates and padlocks, its tall trees planted in rows, each kind set apart, and where nature is hemmed in with park palings. But it was like a wide area of forest and wheat fields without end or fence, without order, in a dense intertwining of plants. There were flowers without number, diverse strange plants growing as commonly as grass in the fields. The lily is the lily of the valley and the rose is the rose of Sharon. Thousands, millions of grasses rise before you in a riot of colors blended together. Imagination roams freely in this garden and does wonders. Sometimes it drops the heavens to the earth and lowers God's chariot, and sometimes it raises the earth up to heaven where mortals and angels embrace.

When I was twelve I left the heder. At that time the schedule of my studies was this: after morning prayers my father studied Mishna with me in the prayer house; during the day I continued studying there by myself; in the evening I returned home, where my father, having finished with his business affairs, helped me understand a page of Gemara with all its commentaries. If he had no time in the evening, he would wake me at dawn and we would both go to the prayer house to study Torah. True, for a young child to be awakened from a sound sleep, especially in winter days, is great grief, yet after I was up and out, I was pleased at heart, and my reward for rising at dawn to study was very great: a heavenly stillness in the town streets, still sunk deep in sleep. The moon and the stars in the sky wakened my imagination, and I saw and heard many things: I saw Gabriel, crowing like a rooster and announcing in the heaven that night was departing. The angels in heaven leaped up, danced, and sang Moses' song in sweet tones. After a while, the gates of Paradise opened with fanfare, and Almighty God entered. The angels, seeing how God had shown Himself in His Holiness, remained motionless in great awe — no wing fluttered and no breath was uttered. Suddenly God roared with thunder and then wept, weeping for His temple that was destroyed, for the city of Jerusalem His crown, which was desolate, and for His people, the dear children of Zion, who wander homeless among alien peoples, and for the Shekhina, dishonored, wandering homeless with them in exile, sorrowing for their sorrows. Tears flow from His eyes, dew that falls on earth, night drops on my locks. Hearing God's voice, the just men of the world tremble and with the good angels weep bitterly. And I, imagining these fantasies, begin to study with all my heart. I chant sweetly and hum while studying. My heart yearns for God's Torah, for all the secrets of the Talmud. And I yield myself completely to it.

This way of studying had a twofold effect on me. It sharpened my intelligence by its deep probing of subtle arguments, making me sharp witted, digging until I reached rock bottom, to get the simple truth. It also awakened my emotions and my imagination with large sublime conceptions and made me receptive to imagery and pure feeling. At that time I possessed nothing but the halakha and knew nothing but the Talmud. I had not seen or even heard about worldly books and still knew nothing about literature, theater, and such. For my birthplace was a lonely nook in a forgotten corner of the world where no foot trod. Being innocent, like the chick in the egg, I thought this was the whole world and beyond Kopyl a desolate desert with mountains of darkness and the Sambatyon River with strange weird creatures. The little houses in my town were in my eyes like rich palaces, the synagogue with its house of study unequaled in the world — here alone resided wisdom. The townspeople were the chosen of all creatures, all sages among sages, especially those with long beards and advanced years. For I then held to the theory that with age went also wisdom and learning. Those whom God had blessed with a cow or a goat seemed rich as Korah and goodly his portion in this world. The shofar, and the street organ which had somehow found its way into our town like a marvelous object, and the ordinary fiddlers who played at a wedding, all made the most exquisite music, and fortunate the ba'al-tokea, who could blow the shofar so that hearts would tremble hearing his quavers.

I had not yet tried my hand at writing. When some marvelous feeling awoke in me, I did not pour it out in rhetoric on paper, but I sat silent, while torrents of feelings raged within me and my heart wept, thinking this was the work of the devil, the evil spirit seducing me with sinful thoughts, leading me to disregard my Torah study. To save my soul from the devil, I had no other counsel than prayer and entreaty to God. In such prayers I expressed my feelings, tasting the sweetness of Paradise. I became happy. Then, if the Evil Spirit encountered me, I led him into the woods, on hills and knolls and fields. There I passed the time in a state of bliss, looking at nature in its splendor, and in time it charmed me with its radiance and beauty. I fell in love with nature and loved her like a groom his bride. Every day I went out in the fields to see my beloved. I sought my love in the dense forest and in the grove, on the green grass and at the river bank, and she revealed everything she had. I leaped after her on the hills, climbed the trees, and sat among the flowers to hear the lowing of the cattle. The nightingale sang for me and the voice of the turtle dove was heard in the chorus of birds. The love in my heart glowed like fire, a spiritual love, a pure love, without form or body, a secret love for the good, the beautiful and the exalted, a love which gladdens man, clothes him in humility, makes him good, a lover of his fellowman and elevates him above ordinary things.

Thus I sat peacefully in my nest until I was thirteen. I thought I would stay there forever. But things happened otherwise. Suddenly my father died at forty-one, leaving a widow and children in great poverty. Out of need, I wandered homeless from one yeshiva to another in Lithuanian towns, near and far, fulfilling all the obligations of studying the Torah and living in suffering like all learned men. After a few years I went back home. My mother had meanwhile remarried and gone away with the younger children to her husband in the village of Melniki. I remained alone and forlorn in Kopyl. I was very miserable then and life was unbearable for its pain and despondence, for I was still a boy, young in years and old in troubles. So I was dejected and melancholy, until my stepfather took me into his house, and to earn my keep I instructed his children a few hours a day.

My stepfather's house was surrounded by woods — great, ancient forests in which wild animals roamed. The wolves howled at their prey through the nights and the bears came from time to time. Birds in their nests twittered among the boughs, and wild geese and waterfowl screeched from the weeds in the swamps. A great river curved and cut its way through the trees of the forest, flowing to the mill and from there into a waterfall driving the wheels with a roar and a noise, and the noise of the mill and the whirling of the waters split the ears.

In this lonely isolated place, my muse appeared, the beloved of my
youth. The charm of her lips induced me to follow her into the woods
under a young tree and fragrant place, where we made a pact with the trees
and fields, the birds and the fruitful things of the earth, and she taught me
to understand their language and to observe their way of life. My heart
yearned for these comrades who told me their eternal riddles and the events
of their world and of the greatness of God who created them and was good
to them. Also, I told them my feelings. That was the first time I took a pen
in hand to express what was in my heart. On paper I sang a new kind of
Hallelujah. The river applauded and the echo of the hills resounded. Until
today I still have my first poetry but it will never see the light of day, for it
was unripe fruit with the taste of crab apples. And a wondrous thing: as
soon as I had written the first thing, the Devil came, the mocker who rules
over me now in the shape of Mendele Mokher Sforim and who talked me
into mocking people and tearing off their masks. Then I wrote a drama in
verse on the style of Rabbi Moses Hayim Luzzato's *La-Yesharim Tehilla*. I
had no notion what a drama was and had never read books of that sort.
Mine was only buffoonery, a mockery of the Satan of my youth who
mocked me.

This tranquillity did not last long. It seems heaven had decreed even
before I was born that I was to be a writer for my people, for my poor
unfortunate people, and God wanted me to learn their customs and observe their ways. Therefore He said: Wander, little bird, over the world,
unfortunate among the unfortunates, a Jew among Jews. A wind picked me
up, buffeted me about and carried me on the heights of life. An angel of
God lowered me to my suffering brothers on the lowest level, to live a life of
sorrow with them, to feel their pain, and of their sufferings I had a double
share. Sometimes he raised me to the very summit of life, making place for
me among our rich men, the leisurely and the smug, the leaders of the
Jews, to see their demeanor and their deeds, their actions and transactions
— but only to observe their advantages, never to enjoy them.

From that time on, after God set me wandering from my stepfather's
house, a new chapter in my life began, of wanderings, trials, and great
sufferings.

I will skip these chapters and now tell only about how I became a
Jewish writer, the purpose to which I dedicated my thoughts and pen, and
about the books and articles I wrote.

Hebrew literature was a rare thing in the days of my youth. There were
no Hebrew books, dailies, weeklies, monthlies, and annuals as there are
today to stir Jewish feelings and awaken love for our sacred tongue. There

was no stimulation and no competition and hence, few writers. When I lived in Kamenets with my father-in-law and also after I divorced my wife and became a teacher in a crown school, I devoted myself to seeking general education and with great effort obtained the knowledge I was lacking. If anyone would then have told me that I would become a writer among Jews, I would have thought he was mocking me. I thought naïvely that writers were divine creatures and who was I to aspire that high? But accident made me a writer, suddenly and unexpectedly.

One winter night, dark, cloudy, and overcast, with a whipping wind, I sat alone in my room, sad and dejected. To occupy myself and calm my spirit, I took up a pen to reply to a letter from a teacher. Without pause I wrote a lot about education, covering both sides of a large sheet. The next morning I copied some of it for the reply to the teacher, tossing the original sheet away.

One day the letter carrier brought me a sealed envelope from abroad. I was curious to know who wrote me from a strange country where I knew no one. There, before me, was *Ha-Maggid*, Vol. 1, No. 31, with some familiar text in the leading article, entitled "Letter on Education." How surprised I was to see my name signed to it and below it a note praising the article to the skies, with the request to scholars to translate it into other languages. I was quite bewildered. In a complimentary letter the publisher, Eliezer Lipman Silberman, asked me to make a friendly agreement with his journal. This amazed me even more. But soon the whole affair became clear. My friend and teacher Emanuel Borisovich Levin had been pleased by what I wrote about Jewish education; he had sent it to Abraham Ber Gottlober for his opinion, and thus it had come to the editor of *Ha-Maggid* and was published. Both men drove my article like a nail into Hebrew literature, and it was the start of my later work.

I became interested in our Hebrew literature, wanting to know what it was like and what was taking place in it. I hoped to find something of utility, knowledge, and wisdom, something cultivated and beautiful, but of these I found very little. Hebrew literature, then, was a desolate garden, forsaken in the autumn, without fruit, without fragrant flowers or lovely plants, the leaves withered and the trees bare. Here and there some outcroppings and weeds, but all neglected. As for its writers, the watchmen of this garden, like innocent children, amuse themselves in pranks, praising and admiring each other.

I found this literature like a garden without an owner — the calf feeds there, ruining the seeds, the pig digs up the plantings, and the little foxes destroy the planted beds. People think it is no calamity to enter this garden, breaking and smashing, and stashing something in your pocket, for the garden is ownerless, and we are among ourselves. No one sees, no one knows, there is no judgment and no judge besides God in heaven and no one will speak a word against you. I pondered these things and on this subject wrote *Mishpat Shalom* ("Peaceful Judgment," Vilna, 1860). This book exploded upon the smug writers, placid like wine before fermentation. I had disturbed their peace, insulted their honor and reputation, and from their ranks came a loud wail. A literary war broke out in *Ha-Melits* and *Ha-Karmel*, which had just begun to appear. I continued to provoke them and to attack them in my writing, and many joined me and encouraged me. Not for me to judge if I was right or if I always hit the target, but I know I brought new life into our literature. After me, from the younger people emerged literary critics, and many writers learned their lesson and changed their course. The literary polemics introduced a lively spirit into the literature and attracted many new readers.

Writers ought, it seemed to me, to aspire to a threefold purpose: to bring our people good taste and knowledge, to make literature depict the real life of the people — to bring it closer to them — and to educate and be utilitarian. With all my heart I wanted our writers not to fly in the sky with silly fantasies nor write of Lot's daughters and Potiphar's wife long gone from this world. They ought not to write about the dead for the living, but they ought to come down to earth, observe how our people live, at home and in society, and depict it for them. Writers ought to refine our people's taste for language, instruct them in science, and make them knowledgeable.

Therefore I divided my literary work into three parts. My first work was *Sefer Toledot ha-Teva* ("Natural History"), translated from H. O. Lenz's *Naturgeschichte*, which dealt with the animal, vegetable, and mineral world, arranged by genus and species, each with its characteristics and habits. The first part, on animal life, containing eight pages of illustrations, was published in Leipzig in 1862.

At the same time I also tried to compose a story in simple Hebrew, grounded in the spirit and life of our people of the time. At that time, then, my thinking went along these lines: Observing how my people live, I want to write stories for them in our sacred tongue, yet most do not understand the language. They speak Yiddish. What good does the writer's work and thought serve him, if they are of no use to his people? For whom was I working? The question gave me no peace but placed me in a dilemma. Yiddish, in my time, was an empty vessel, filled only with ridicule, nonsense, and the twaddle of fools who could not speak like human beings and who had no reputation at all. The women and the commonest people read this stuff, without understanding what it was they read. Other people, though they knew no other language, were ashamed to read Yiddish, not wanting to show their backwardness. If one was tempted to read something in Yiddish, he made excuses: "I just look at these women's books to see what these foolish females read. It is only to amuse myself."

The Hebrew writers, concerned only with the style of sacred language, uninterested in the people, despised Yiddish and mocked it. If someone ever wrote in the reviled language, he hid it beneath lock and key, lest the shame be discovered and his reputation harmed. This was my dilemma, for if I started writing in this "unworthy" language my honor would be besmirched. My admirers, lovers of Hebrew, warned me I would dishonor my name among Jews, if I dedicated myself to this outcast. But my concern for utility conquered my vanity and I decided, come what may, I would have pity for Yiddish, that rejected daughter, for it was time to do something for our people. A good friend and I convinced Alexander Zederbaum, the editor of *Ha-Melits,* to publish a journal in the people's language. We should recall his name gratefully, because the journal, *Kol Mevasser,* proved very successful. I was inspired and wrote my first story, *Dos kleyne mentchele* ("The Little Man"), under the pen name of Mendele Mokher Sforim (Mendele the Bookseller). It appeared in the paper about 1864 and later in book form.

This story created a sensation among Jews and was published in many editions. It became the cornerstone of modern Yiddish literature. I fell in love with Yiddish and wedded her forever. I gave her the spices and herbs she needed and she became an attractive helpmeet and bore me many sons: *Dos vintshfingerl* ("The Magic Ring," 1865), *Di takse* ("The Tax," 1869), *Fishke der krumer* ("Fishke the Lame," 1869), *Der luftbalon* ("The Balloon," 1869), *Di kliatche* ("The Nag," 1873), *Der ustav* ("The Statute," 1874), *Yudl* (1875), *Masoes binyomin hashlishi* ("Travels of Benjamin III," 1878), *Der priziv* ("Conscription," 1884).

30 I Become a Hebrew Writer

by Reuben Brainin

REUBEN BRAININ, Hebrew writer, was born in Lyady in 1862 and died in New York City in 1939. A young Hebrew journalist, he was in his day the exponent of modernism in Hebrew literature. As he describes in the following selection from his autobiography, he sought to modernize Hebrew as a language for contemporary discourse, simultaneously seeking to modernize also the intellectual milieu of that language. A prolific writer and translator, he first introduced modern European literature into Hebrew literature and was the first to champion esthetic standards in a literature that had hitherto been essentially didactic and regarded as merely a weapon in the hands of the enlightened against the obscurantists, rather than as a vehicle for creative experiment. Because of the influential position he attained as editor and contributor to many Hebrew journals, he became a figure of importance in directing the course of Hebrew literature, encouraging young people to strike out in new directions in their creative writing.

WHEN I begin analyzing and burrowing in the hidden recesses of my soul to discover the moods and impulses which made me become, and remain, a writer — it has been remarked that I am the only Hebrew writer who holds no office, has no occupation other than literature, no outside jobs and, no extra income — I seem to enter either an enchanted world or a dark labyrinth.

But even today, after forty-five years of writing, despite the hard times en route, despite the hardships attendant on being a professional writer among Jews, especially in a transitional era, I confess, if I had to be reborn and if the angel would ask what kind of creature to make me and what should be my fate, I would reply: I want only to be a writer and only among Jews.

Before I began writing for the public, I asked myself: Am I a born writer, God-gifted, or self-deluded, seduced by false instinct which has drawn me magnetically to literature? Examining myself, searching the hidden recesses of my inner life, and analyzing my abilities, impulses, and inclinations, I found that many contradictory spirits dwelled within me, that I lacked inner unity, consistency, balance.

The wide world with its innumerable wonderful potentialities and prospects pulled me in various directions. Mathematics, for one, was my passion. Even before I could write or read numbers, before I had heard the names of the four basic operations of elementary arithmetic, I could swiftly do the most complicated mental calculations of percentages and fractions. My only teacher was my father, who had taught me, two or three times, how to do mental arithmetic, and that was enough for me.

Before I had any notion that Hebrew had a literature of poetry and fiction, I had studied Hayim Selig Slonimski's *Yesode Hokhmat ha-Shiur,* from which I learned algebra; Gabriel Judah Lichtenfeld's books, from which I learned geometry, Zvi Hakohen Rabinowitz's *Ha-Menuha ve-ha-Tenua, Even ha-Shoevet,* and others, from which I learned physics and mechanics. I did not even know of Mapu's *Ahavat Zion,* a historical novel in Hebrew, or of Smolenskin's modern novel, *Ha-To'eh be-Darke ha-Hayim.* With great effort I had obtained the Vilna Gaon's *Ayil Meshulash,* a treatise on trigonometry, geometry, algebra, and astronomy. Besides the ten hours a day I spent studying the Gemara, I studied as much mathematics as was possible from Hebrew books with inadequate theories.

Still a boy, I corresponded with Hayim Selig Slonimski and Zvi Hirsch Jaffe about mathematics. Ignorant of the basic mathematical literature, I discovered long-discovered things in algebra and trigonometry. Later, when I began to read European languages and became acquainted with the mathematical literature in French, I thought I was a born mathematician and that would be my true calling. I thought in mathematical terms. I disliked casuistry, supercleverness, expositions making something of nothing. Everywhere I sought logical grounding, exactness, and precision. I believed that the natural sciences would someday solve problems of life and death, social problems as well as the ultimate metaphysical questions. I could not comprehend how grown people with good minds could read novels, stories, invented tales without sense or reason. For one great mathematician, chemist, or an engineer like Lesseps; for one inventor like Thomas Edison, I would have traded all the novelists, poets, and dramatists, with even Homer, Shakespeare and Goethe thrown in.

When I emerged from my narrow nest, my hasidic birthplace Lyady, and came in contact with the great outer world, with various cultural circles, I began feverishly reading world literature, fiction and non-fiction, and became a frequenter of museums. I avidly swallowed Tolstoy, Turgenev, particularly Dostoevsky, Emile Zola, Hippolyte Taine, Georg Brandes, Goethe and Victor Hugo, Friedrich Spielhagen and Berthold Auerbach, Heine and Börne, Dante and Carducci. A world of sound and song opened for me, a world of color and line, esthetic feeling, everlasting beauty, a world of grace, poetry, winged fantasy, love and human passion, a world of struggle and heroism, delicate plastic forms, a world of social ideals, men fighting for a good world, dreamers of a future mankind, free and fortunate.

These newly discovered worlds enchanted me and captured my imagination. After I left the *bet-hamidrash* and put aside my mathematical books, I became a dreamer, a visionary of beauty, harmony in nature and art. Beauty became my cult; everything beautiful was ethical and moral.

In this intoxication, in a surfeit of youthful pride, the desire to become a writer matured in me. It drove me to express myself, my new philosophy of life. Then, I thought, I was a born writer. Everything in me strove for expression, for beautiful artistic form. I thought I had something new, fresh, and vital to communicate to the Hebrew reader.

When I definitely decided to dedicate my life to Hebrew literature, I was most earnest about my purpose, though my friends thought it madness. So you want to become a Hebrew writer? Nonsense! For whom will you write? Who will read you? Who will understand you? Who will publish you? Is there any Hebrew publisher, any Hebrew press, any audience? And other such basic questions — is there any chance of earning a living from a Hebrew pen? Is it not a fact that Hebrew authors are forced to become shnorers and go begging for their works? Should an able and vital young man dedicate himself to such a thoroughly lifeless thing like Hebrew literature? What bearing does it have with the modern times and progress? Yet such questions and doubts could not shatter my firm resolve to dedicate myself totally to Hebrew literature. But I was disturbed by the questions bearing on my ambition to humanize, to simplify, and clarify Hebrew and to create a new form for new content. I was then avidly reading modern Hebrew literature, from Moses Hayim Luzzato to Judah Leib Gordon. Reading modern Hebrew literature and comparing it — if comparisons were at all possible — with modern European literatures was most sad. I had to admit, despite my nationalist outlook, that no Hebrew work made much of an impression on me, that no Hebrew writer influenced my thinking, that none affected my youthful soul and my hopes.

The contemporary Hebrew writers, even the most prestigious, were either pitifully disguised assimilationists or petty backward types, out of touch with the great intellectually influential trends of the times.

Hebrew literature, in its circumstances, could not, on the one hand, attract those untalented and unprincipled scribblers who push their way into the press just to make money. These could not expect to get anything in the Hebrew press. But neither could Hebrew attract those better minds, who, raised in a world of culture and general education, even if they knew Hebrew, even if they were idealists and did not look for material advantages out of writing. They thought the Mishna was modern Hebrew literature. They could not, if they wished, express themselves freely in Hebrew, which they counted among the dead languages of archeological value only.

Studying modern Hebrew writing, I became convinced I had to create my own instrument to express my thoughts and feelings. Reading the best Hebrew writers of the time, I thought their ideas appeared as through a fog, vague, without a clear outline. The Hebrew writers used usually to pay with gold where small change was required. The most ordinary day-to-day needs were expressed in rhetoric, in elevated language and bloated phrases. One prick of a critical pin could puncture the phrase and turn it into nothing more than a burst soap bubble. The sentence was a maximum of words with a minimum of content, lacking precision and correct shading. Seldom did anyone reveal any individual style. None could free himself of the domination, the constraining power of biblical verse. One writer was influenced by Isaiah, another by Ezekiel. The greatest art of style consisted of mosaic, piecing together bits of biblical verses, or tired, tasteless, and often senseless rhetoric of the Epigoni. Practically no Hebrew writer dared to speak in a human language of his own, in his own accent and his own rhythm.

The Hebrew poets and fiction writers saw only those colors in nature for which the Bible had names. They did not see colors and shades in nature and life unmentioned in the Bible. Their nature descriptions were, then, mere variations of Biblical rhetoric, as though the rulers of the republic of Hebrew letters had all been born color blind. The world of flowers, too, was poorly represented in Hebrew, by only those blossoms and flowers which happened to have been mentioned in the Bible. People, when they were not eating dry bread, ate "delicacies," but what these were the reader could not imagine. Clothing, too, had the same limitations, the same impoverishment. Hebrew vocabulary had to be enlarged and enriched. I always was a strong advocate of preserving in Hebrew the spirit of biblical language. But Hebrew words, even biblical ones, without the primordial spirit of the Hebrew style, as preserved in the Bible and in the oldest Hebrew documents, are what you will, but not Hebrew and not organic.

Besides, Hebrew had not stopped developing, even if in an abstract bookish form, but yet neither mummified nor ossified. The rich treasures of Hebrew literature, accumulated in the course of thousands of years, influenced by many cultures and intellectual movements, preserved words and expressions for all human thought and feeling and for everyday needs. The question was how and how much and in what context to use these scarcely tapped linguistic resources.

The fathers of the haskala, like Adam Hakohen, Joshua Steinberg, Kalman Shulman, Joshua Lewinsohn and others, did not tolerate mixing the language of later writers with biblical diction. In their eyes, that was language impurity, or a lack of style. Writers who ventured to adopt Talmudic or later Hebrew phrases could not combine the old and new linguistic elements proportionately.

My masters in Hebrew style were, in addition to the Prophets early and late, Maimonides and Rashi. The simplicity, clarity, and brevity of Rashi's style had an enormous influence on me in my youth. Later, Eliezer Hakohen Zweifel, who was the first to seek and, in some degree, also to find a synthesis of the biblical and rabbinic style, influenced me. Mordecai Aaron Gunzburg enchanted me with his successful attempt to simplify Hebrew style and introduce newer linguistic elements, though his grammar was a little lame.

In my youth I had spent much time and effort in studying Hebrew as a potential instrument for free expression, with exactness and clarity, without artifice, a language in which ideas would not be constricted in a straitjacket or a bed of Sodom. I brought no knowledge of Hebrew as a language from my early education.

When I began to study Hebrew, I turned to the first sources. I applied myself to the Bible, Mishna and Agada. Happily, but with no small effort, I obtained a copy of Moses Mendelssohn's German translation of the Bible with its commentaries, and Ben Zev's *Talmud lashon ivri*. The Bible, the book of books, now became my most wonderful discovery. With new eyes and fresh senses, I began to appreciate its incomparable beauties and profundities. In heder, Pentateuch had been a needless burden; now it was a source of enrichment, inspiration. I began to appreciate the greatest creation of our national genius, and that appreciation stayed with me all my life.

I was shocked that some widely acclaimed Hebrew writers knew little of the structure of biblical Hebrew or, if they did, disregarded it. The development of Hebrew had outgrown the dated Hebrew grammars. Even Zachariah Frankel's scientific grammar of the Mishna was theoretical, rather than practical. My friends deplored the time and energy I spent on dead subjects.

Studying the haskala literature, I found it dry, without a drop of life, remote from the reality of Jewish life, isolated from the living stream of European thought. I expressed this opinion to some fanatic admirers of this haskala literature and they could not forgive me for it. Maskilim now, they idolized the haskala writers, as once they had idolized their rebbes when they had been hasidim.

Though I was critical of haskala literature, it had nevertheless influenced my early youth. Renan once said that he who ridicules his spiritual bonds is not yet liberated from them, and even if he has freed himself from these bonds, he drags them behind him for a time, not even aware of them. I was convinced one could change the fundamental tenor of our life, that one could annul, recreate, transmute human character with words — beautiful, spiritual, vigorous, or prophetic — without changing or transforming the political, economic and social conditions. My faith in the power of the word was then limitless. The word was the beginning and the end. Preparing myself for my later career in Hebrew literature, I hungrily devoured the masterworks of European literature. Yet, despite their decisive influence, in my heart I believed that dynamic and vitalizing power resided in the Hebrew word, even in its very square letters.

31   Isaac Leibush Peretz As We Knew Him

ISAAC LEIBUSH PERETZ was born in Zamosc, province of Lublin, in 1852 and died in Warsaw in 1915. In the words of S. Charney Niger, "Peretz set his personal imprint on the nascent Jewish literature and the movement whose aim it was to instruct the average Jew and to raise his cultural level. He was not the leader of that movement, because leadership demands a more circumscribed and set credo than the one Peretz possessed. Not being the standard-bearer of the Jewish cultural movement, Peretz became its standard."

Peretz was the great innovator of Yiddish literature: he modernized and individualized it, urbanized, intellectualized and personalized it, and transmitted its folk heritage into high artistry.

Master of a Literary Generation
by Hersh D. Nomberg

Hersh David Nomberg was born in Mszczonow, near Warsaw, in 1874 and died in Warsaw in 1927. A novelist and short story writer of subtlety and distinction, he was also a Yiddishist and a

founder of the Jewish *folkspartey*, steering an independent course between the powerful left and
right Jewish political groups in Poland. The following autobiographical essay was written on the
fourth anniversary of Peretz's death.

I KNEW Peretz about eighteen years, the last years of his life and the most productive of his literary career. These years also mark an era in Yiddish literature, a whole literary generation. Peretz was the leader of this era — more correctly, its midpoint, a center of influences. Everything was reflected in him and refracted as by a prism. He was not a founder of a literary school, for until the last day of his life he was a seeker and a striver, always springing from style to style. The literary generation around him, his disciples, did not walk in his steps. Nearly everyone had his own trodden path, his domain, and his style. Peretz was a father of a literary family. His living interest for literature, his urge to create, his deep love for everything beautiful and sublime which ruled all the passions of his stormy nature — these acted magnetically upon all that was alive and creative in our world. These eighteen years also signified Peretz's growth, when he wrote his maturest works, his late summer, when singing he sowed what he had once frivolously seeded, as if without purpose or hope, the years of his growing renown. About these years I wish to write.

Elul is a month of worry, earnest thoughts, and heavy heart for a small-town young man still bodily and spiritually stalled in the world of religion. That Elul came just at the time of the great religious breach when the earth seemed to give way beneath my feet and the heavens toppled on my head. It happened that suddenly, with such definitiveness. In the morning the skies still hung over me. I struggled, fortified myself, and with my last strength clung to my religious outlook. By evening it was all over. I realized how futile was every effort to sustain the structure that barely stood on its rickety legs. I despaired, and the structure collapsed like a pile of rotted beams. My "I" remained buried under the ruins.

That was the catastrophe of people reared in deep and true religiousness, a catastrophe from which one rarely emerges intact, seldom without evident traces for his whole life. The cure is painful and slow, and the deeper the religiousness, the more shattering the catastrophe.

I pounced ravenously on worldly books, the Hebrew literature of the time. But instead of giving me some support, instead of filling the frightening void which inhabited me, these books only angered and repelled me.

Frivolous people, it seemed to me, had written them. A young man falls in love with a girl, the girl loves him, or not; a rabbi forbids a deserted wife to remarry because of a trifle — they wrote about everything, but not about what mattered, about the root question: How does one live in a world so empty and so desolate? What sense has life which is confined to seventy years and ends with death and destruction? I felt despondent, weighed down by morbid melancholy, psychically and physically crushed.

On the first night of Selihot, when coolness already touched the air, I lay in a hut in an orchard which a friend, a maskil, had rented. He showed me a new book which he had ordered from Warsaw, called *Ha-Ugav* ("The Flute"). The portrait of the author, I. L. Peretz, showed a young man, a clean-shaven face, with a thick mustache and extraordinarily wise eyes. The fur collar suggested a winter outfit. I began to leaf through the book with apathy, beforehand convinced I would not find anything in it, as I had not found anything in all the other books. But, a mystery to me, not aware of how it occurred, the book so captivated me that my friend could not understand what had happened to me. I read the verses, reread them, and unconsciously began to chant them aloud. When I came to "Tell me, Temurah," my eyes filled with tears.

When my friend asked me to explain what had so stirred me that my depressing apathy changed into a strange ecstasy, I was unable to do so. I myself had only the barest notion of the real meaning of "poetry" or "beauty." Something was roused in me that night, the first powerful impact of poetry. It came from the man in the fur coat, unknown and yet intimate. When I later lifted up my eyes to the starry dark sky, its desolate empty endlessness no longer frightened me. From then on, whenever melancholy oppressed me, my imagination sketched a wintry, snowy landscape, a one-story house with a narrow garden in front of its windows and trees with frozen dew, and a young man in a fur coat strolling about.

That was my dream.

I gave no thought to how this young man with wise eyes would answer my great question. But I was certain the answer had to come from him, that the singing little book must have a connection with the great enigma of the world.

That was my first impression of Peretz. The first impression, it is said, is decisive and most enduring. I think it is characteristic of the attachment of a whole literary generation to its literary rebbe. Outwardly, everyone expressed it differently and experienced it differently. Inwardly, it was the same attitude of faith and trust which is proffered to the progressive in spirit.

In his lifetime, Peretz came under many influences. He had little attachment to ideas — he was indeed free as a bird, a Don Juan in the world of ideas, living with the latest and loveliest idea that captivated his heart. The reason he treated ideas like pretty women came from the depths of his world outlook. He demanded of ideas what one wants of a woman — that she be seductive, radiant and amusing, yet not insist on a wedding canopy or a marriage certificate or union forever. In this sense, he was doubtless the most ardent advocate of free love with regard to all sorts of political, moral, and esthetic credos. But under one condition — that it not be only lust, but real love, which captures, enchants and dazzles, makes the eyes glow and the blood throb quicker in the veins.

I met Peretz when he was intoxicated with socialist ideas that were not yet crystallized. It was soon after the appearance of *Yomtov-bletlekh* ("Holiday Leaves"), at the start of the labor movement among Jews. Several young socialists had formed a coterie around Peretz, among them David Pinsky, whose socialist point of view was evident in the *Bletlekh*.

It was quite a step forward from the *Yidishe bibliotek* ("Jewish Library") to the *Yomtov-bletlekh*. In the former, Peretz had been close to a circle of Polish Jewish university-trained professionals. The introduction to the *Yidishe bibliotek,* though brilliant in style, could pass as original only in form — it can doubtless still serve as a model in Yiddish journalism — but in substance it belonged to the haskala school: its slogan was "education," the "jargon" was the instrument. True, willy-nilly, this instrument was fondled and shown affection, quite out of keeping with the official line. In the *Yidishe bibliotek,* Peretz did not stand apart from his contemporary circle of Warsaw maskilim. Some years earlier, he had been very actively involved in conducting the Jewish census planned by the apostate millionaire Bloch to show the government the extent of Jewish poverty: Peretz's *Rayze-bilder* ("Travel Pictures") was the literary heritage of that undertaking, its only positive result, worth more than all the statistics, which came to nothing, scientifically or practically.

In *Yomtov-bletlekh* the old maskilic tone disappeared altogether. This was not an external change, an adaptation to circumstances. Inwardly, Peretz broke with the ideas of the Warsaw maskilim. He became alienated from the generation of writers among whom he lived and stood in the most intense opposition to the entire contemporary Hebrew press and literature.

At the time I met him, there was no writer, no literary figure, whether Ahad Ha'am or J. L. Gordon, for whom Peretz had anything but a few curt words of utter contempt. My first impression of him was of a man who denies everything and everyone. That, of course, most suited my current mood, and it greatly impressed me. When I became curious to know also the positive side, beyond the "nothing," I was less fortunate.

I had come to Warsaw with the assistance of a circle of Warsaw socialist students. The early socialist academic circles at the Warsaw University engaged in educational propaganda, agitating able young people in the provinces and preparing them to enter the university. I had told the student who arranged my trip that I wrote poetry and I asked him to show my verses to one I. L. Peretz. He did so reluctantly, never having heard of Peretz. In a few days he brought me the news that Peretz was greatly pleased with my verses and had invited me to visit him. The student had only the faintest notion what this message meant to me — this prospect of meeting Peretz. To be able to speak with Peretz at length had been the purpose of my trip — the university and the socialist propaganda had been an excuse, perhaps a side issue.

My coat was cut long, but that did not embarrass me. Why should it? Would he be affected by such purely outward things? Indeed, he received me very cordially, warmly. We spoke Russian, a little of which I had managed to learn at home from a manual.

"Your verses are worthless. They are immature, yet there is much talent in them."

He began to point out various passages, praising and criticizing. In the course of the conversation, he finished off all the great men of the time. I found favor with him because he met no opposition from me to his merciless criticism and to his sharp disparaging words. At a very cutting remark about Ahad Ha'am, I reacted: it seemed too biting against this writer for whom I had much respect, who was someone special, not one of those frivolous writers who babble and twaddle.

Peretz needed no more to goad him, and he was off. He directed spears of sarcasm not only at Ahad Ha'am, but against everything and everyone, against the whole intellectual inventory of that time — Zionism, Hibbat Zion, and haskala. A heap of ashes remained.

I had no reason to bewail these ruins, because I had built neither home nor nest there after the great conflagration in my religious world.

Suddenly in the middle of the conversation, Peretz turned to me. "Discard the Hebrew verses. Write in Yiddish. You will do the world good."

"What of it, then?" I asked.

He gave me an altogether different look. The voluble colorful tone of this conversation changed:

"If you do good, you will be morally satisfied."

"If one is morally satisfied, then what? One can live and die and not be morally satisfied."

He no longer had a smile for me. He answered with cold words, "That you must feel."

I asked nothing more. The vanishing luster from his eyes and the smile gone instantly from his lips reminded me of the distance between me, a young man from the provinces in a coat cut long, and — I. L. Peretz.

I have said that Peretz was, above all, a center of influences, a prism for the intellectual rays of the era, and let us look at him in this aspect. Only after we are clear about all these influences, can we determine which were lasting and deep, which casual and transitory, which he internalized and which enriched his personality and his work, and which he merely reflected like a mirror.

Nietzsche was the protest against the earlier generation's materialism, against vulgar democratism, against the demand that the individual submit to community and society. Individualism had found its greatest prophet. This great wave of individualism broke up into various small waves, one of which was modernism. Its spokesmen were Stanislaus Przybyszewski and Strindberg; traces of it could be seen in Maupassant and even Chekhov. Edgar Allen Poe, that old spirit of young America, who had lived and written much earlier and had died, neglected, lonely, and unknown outside his country, had just been "discovered" in the period I am talking about, honored and read. This modernism was different from the elements out of which it had originated, yet it was its true child. Nietzsche preached belief in self, in power, and in glory. The modernism of these writers tore and fragmented the personality, was imbued with the deepest pessimism, with disgust for life. It is interesting to note a singularity on which I had commented. Schopenhauer, the pessimist, comforted the spirit; Nietzsche, the optimist, briefly intoxicated at first and then depressed. After Schopenhauer, one becomes wiser, more perceptive, calmer; after Nietzsche, more disquieted, thirstier, tense, and wretched. This was a kind of reaction of intellect, of which modernism was an expression.

Peretz, too, did not escape that modernist wave. He fell under its influence, like everyone else. But Peretz's quality, his inner being, was different in that he threw off this modernism at the first possible moment. I observed him then, and I remember how he struggled with the modernist influence as one who struggles with dark spirits and dreadful, hostile forces. In the depths of his soul he could not endure the breath of death and demolition which the movement exhaled. Inwardly it was foreign to him and remote, but it was then the last word, modern and most up to date, and how could he turn his back on it?

Because Peretz could talk and think about anything at all in the world, nothing human was alien to him — except death. Death he ignored completely, drove it out of his consciousness. For many years he had been an official in the Warsaw Jewish community council, whose duties were with the dead, yet I doubt he ever in his life saw a corpse. He practically never went to funerals, avoided sickbeds, and never talked of the dead. I know of instances when people nearest and dearest to him died in their most flourishing years and took into their graves his deepest love, yet he stubbornly resisted mentioning them. He hated death and he hated drooping age, with its scent of graveyard leaves. He hated, and kept his distance from, everything related to these sordid matters.

But the modernist wave was overpowering, ravaging on all sides. For a year or two it constricted Peretz in his creativity. The singing and radiant qualities in Peretz's depths needed another milieu. Like his rebbe in the *Goldene keyt,* he absolutely refused to let the workaday enter his soul. At the first chance he shook himself free.

A dark-haired young man from Lithuania, who spoke Russian like a true Russ, hung around Peretz then and could be found, with the others, every Saturday in his house on Ceglana Street. This young man had brought Maxim Gorky's first book of short stories. Never in my life have I seen a greater delight, greater spiritual enjoyment than that which Peretz had from this book. His eyes lit up as he talked about it. This delight and love he transferred even to the young man who otherwise was not in any way special. Maxim Gorky's short stories were then seized upon by the entire intelligentsia as a return to a healthy powerful optimism, a call to life. Peretz had often liked to thrust an angry sarcastic epithet at Russian literature, like "Russian barbarism." After all, he lived in a Polish-Jewish milieu. But this little book's coming was timely, as if releasing him from an oppressive nightmare.

Dr. Eliashev (Ba'al Machshoves) was then in Peretz's coterie. He had come from Berlin even more influenced by modernism. He himself, in mood and style, was quite modernist; besides, being naturally analytic, he was in Peretz's set the living embodiment of modernism, which both attracted Peretz and frightened him with its uncanny and alien elements.

Peretz teased and taunted us with Gorky's stories, like Prometheus liberated from his chains. I remember an incident involving Dr. Eliashev and, I think, myself, when Peretz let fly harsh words at us. Who could then understand their origin, the source of the poet's caprice? Now, in the perspective of two decades, it seems so clear and obvious. For about two years Peretz was under the spell of some heavy mood, an oppressive world view, which was utterly alien to him, which he could not absorb and assimilate. Yet he could neither brush it aside with the old sweeping contempt of the maskilic-skeptical style, nor tolerate it inwardly. Gorky was his triumph, his victory. Just as he had suddenly come to like the dark-haired young man and held him up as the model of culture and intelligence, so he transferred the hostility toward modernism toward individuals. Children act that way, women act that way, and poets act that way.

Peretz used to like to tell a story, I think, from Arabian Nights, but he used to adorn it and ornament with his own colors and pictures and when he told it, that always meant he was in high spirits.

"An enchanted prince lives in a castle filled with the treasures and splendor of all the world, but he is melancholy and pines for something different, without knowing what. A small fence separates the prince from an exquisite garden, where graceful palms and mighty cedars grow, beauteous roses and snow-white lilies. But the prince has been sharply warned not to step over the fence, lest he come to a bad end. The prince is guarded on all sides, watched over by day and protected by night, lest that misfortune occur. But his desire is great and the prince cannot resist it. Once, at dawn, when the guards are dozing, he steals out of the castle and into the garden.

"The wonders and beauties of the world are revealed to him. The loveliest blossoms, the most marvelous creatures — all are colorful, gentle, amiable, all affectionate, attractive, and appealing. Every flower wants to be picked by him; every creature dumbly pleads: hold me, stroke my velvety fleece. He picks his first flower, but opening his hand, he sees he holds only slimy mud and throws it away with disgust. He entices a creature near him, and as soon as he holds it in his hands, it turns ugly, a revolting crawling creature. He walks on. Again a flower motions to him, again an animal coddles up to him. He fears to pluck the flower, to caress the dumb creature, but his heart longs to. He plucks the flower, and again holds slime in his hands; he strokes the animal and, once again, touches a reptile. He walks away, his restraint greater, for he has already had many lessons, yet the longing in him grows stronger and his soul hovers between desire, fear and disgust. Suddenly heaviness seems to affect his youthful legs. A dwarf emerges from a cave, bringing him a mirror and in it he sees an old, decrepit graybeard — himself."

This struggle with desire, longing, and revulsion went on all of Peretz's life. He used to tell this story as the final answer to all possible questions, as the word of ultimate wisdom. And that was always when he was at fever pitch, when his eyes glowed and smiled. I heard this story many, many times from him and always I had the impression he was reciting his credo. What is plucked, attained, felt, is slime and disgust; only longing is beautiful and attractive.

With this story he tried to justify his own weakness of switching often from style to style, not having his own marked-out path like Mendele and like Sholem Aleichem who, after years of search, finally found their own style. His skepticism toward all variety of beliefs and programs was expressed in the story. Everything is illusory, valuable only as long as it is untouched, all the same if it is a loved one kissed only once, an idea which once inspired, or a style which was once exploited.

Peretz told this story only when he felt elated and vigorous, when he had had some success, particularly with something he had written, when he had won inner security. But hidden from all and from his own consciousness, in the depths of his soul, the urge to find himself, the dissatisfaction, still existed. Anyone who penetrated the secret of the gloomy mood often reflected in his eyes understood that. How, then, could it be otherwise? The same force that makes the apple tree "love" only apples and produce only apples drives the artist to find himself, his personality, his style. Though Peretz often ridiculed walking a beaten path, though he attacked it with the bitterest sarcasm as one-sidedness and niggardliness, still, without being aware of it, he sought his own one-sidedness, longed for it, strove toward it. But it was destined for others to find his ego, his artistic individuality, before he himself noticed it. The supreme expression of his unique style, his originality, was revealed in two short stories: one, written originally in Hebrew as "Mishnat Hasidim" and the other, "Mekubalim," originally in Yiddish in the *Yomtov-bletlekh*. Like true first-rate works of art, they were new, even strange, in form and content, the characters and their treatment. Like everything newly created, which stands out from the hackneyed and the commonplace, the stories were not particularly noticed, not even by their author. Which works of Peretz did we, his admirers, not talk about in his house? Everything from *Monish* to the latest article in the *Bletlekh* against the Hoveve Zion. But I do not remember that we talked at all in the early years about these two stories. Peretz himself never mentioned them. They became valued because of an outside influence. Once again, a breeze blew in from abroad, from a Jewish student circle in Berlin, infected with contemporary Nietzschean and modernist ideas, and led by Micah Joseph Berdichevski, a profound and original thinker. Individualists, they were quite different from the young socialist Jews. Berdichevski made the first try to transport these new ideas into the Jewish world or, more correctly, into the world of Jewish thought. He declared war on Ahad Ha'am for his dry rationalism, his spirituality, and his moralizing about what ought to be the essence of Jewish thought. Going in this direction, he became an advocate of the hasidim, with their individualism and absorption in self, as a contrast to dry Talmudism. At their own expense, these Berlin students published Berdichevski's Hebrew pamphlet *Shinui Arakhin* and others, which no one else wanted to publish.

What Berdichevski had come to by way of analytic reasoning, Peretz had long ago revealed as a prophecy. Berdichevski's battle cries and his heated apologia for hasidism reached Warsaw. In Peretz's literary circle, people became aware of Berdichevski and discovered as well the treasures which had long been lying open — true hasidic poetry, complete and ready for use.

This also affected Peretz, who, more consistently and in full consciousness — with premeditation, one might say — applied himself to the subject of hasidism. Whether these works, created in full consciousness, surpassed those first two stories which emerged like lightning from his still beclouded soul — that is another question. In any event, Peretz began to draw near his own path, his own style, and his own roots.

The first folksong collection was a scholarly compilation by Marek and Ginsburg in St. Petersburg. But even before the book was published, we used to sing folksongs at Peretz's every Saturday. In the group that used to assemble there was Judah Leib Cahan, by occupation a watchmaker, who was truly enamored of folksongs. He scooped them up firsthand, in the Warsaw barrooms and in all the places where fellows and their girls used to dance and sing. Cahan was the expert in Yiddish folksongs. He was always able to transmit the special charms of each song, the most subtle nuances of the heartfelt, simple melodies.

On Peretz and on his circle these songs acted like prophecy, revelation. We all felt that a fresh spring had been tapped, lively and bubbling. The songs appealed not only with their artless poetry, their inner truth, and their deep feeling, but they also evoked and beckoned to a world utterly unknown to Jewish intellectuals, the old-style ones — the traditional, religious scholars, and the new-style — the maskilim and worldly educated. Behold, a people lives and sings! Sings of love and longing, of joy and pain! A people that knows nothing of the zigzags and dilemmas and hairsplittings of our traditional and modern intellectuals. This revelation set off an easily imagined revolution in thought and outlook. One need only remember how widespread was (and perhaps still is?) the conviction that Jews were, on one hand, a Chosen People, elected, pure spirit, and on the other, crippled, without feeling for nature, for simplicity, for love, beauty and poetry.

That is a lie! An innermost protest challenged this common view. That is your deformity, your unnaturalness, which you, religious scholars and worldly intellectuals, transfer to our people. The people are natural, healthy human beings. You spoke on behalf of the people and that is why they looked like monstrosities. The people did not speak. But let them speak for themselves and you will hear, not the voice of the prince and not the voice of the dog, as in Heine's poem, but the voice of a human being!

For the time being, the folksongs had only an esthetic import. Half the time of Sabbath gatherings at Peretz's was spent in singing folksongs, in a strangely high-spirited mood, orgies of poetic delight, experiences in which the spirit is tempered like steel in a flame. These experiences also brought Peretz closer to his "I" and to his roots. Their product matured later in the *Folkstimlekhe geshikhtn,* where the over-clever, crafty Peretz, the seeker of new paths, the advocate of an allusive intricate style, returned to the simple and openhearted — and yet so individual, so characteristically Peretz.

The secret of a unique style, which Peretz achieved in the *Folkstimlekhe geshikhtn,* lies always in the process combining the different elements of the artist's nature, those with which he came into the world and those which were a product of his life and environment. This process organically transforms these elements into new matter, which is original, for the artist's soul is his laboratory, and which is individual, for he is unique in the world of appearances.

A good many years elapsed between the time the folksongs first made such a decisive impact on Peretz and the *Folkstimlekhe geshikhtn* appeared. The time passed with various experiments Peretz made in drama, under Wyspianski's influence, and other tries which succeeded in one degree or another. I skip this period partly because I was not present, being often far from Warsaw, and partly because I do not consider it played an important role in Peretz's inner development.

In *Folkstimlekhe geshikhtn* the two chief traits in Peretz's creativity were united: the hasidic fervor which was in his very nature, and the return to his people, the striving for openheartedness and artlessness, which he attained only after searching long and wandering about on his own and others' ways and paths.

When Asch appeared and then Weisenberg, the true depicters of the popular spirit, through whose mouths the people themselves spoke, everyone felt that the prophecy which the folksongs had foretold had come to pass. The people had become articulate and talkative. That was also the time when he, too, who had transmitted what was most beautiful and most radiant from generations of traditional religious spirituality, the quintessence of a generation of haskala, refreshed his spirit with the clear water of a newly discovered stream, found himself, and sang his loveliest song.

Peretz at Home
by Jehiel Isaiah Trunk

Jehiel Isaiah Trunk was born in Osmolsk, near Lowicz, in 1887 and died in New York City in 1961. Of a rabbinically prestigious and wealthy family intermarried with hasidic dynasties, he broke with tradition and, having literary aspirations, was drawn to Peretz as a filing to a magnet. This crucial period in his life is described in the following memoir, which epitomized Peretz's role as rebbe to his hasidim and father to his literary children.

Trunk was a versatile writer; his most enduring work is his seven-volume *Poyln* ("Poland"), which he described as "the portrait of my life in the framework and in relation to the portrait of Jewish life in Poland."

WHEN my Uncle Yosel left Kutno for Lublin, he wanted to have nothing to do with the hasidim there, but he did bring with him his enthusiasm for haskala and literature. In his free moments he even tried to write a Hebrew poem extolling the virtues of that heavenly daughter haskala and castigating the sinister forces that denied the light. The maskilim of Lublin at once recognized in my uncle a kindred being, theirs body and soul, even though he was a grandson of the greatest Polish rabbis and hasidic rebbes; it was, in fact, just because of his distinguished forebears that the renegade impressed them. He was welcomed into the circle of Lublin maskilim and became their darling. When a Hazomir was organized there, Uncle Yosel naturally became cock of the walk. All his spiritual ambitions blossomed like flowers in the sun.

One day, out of the blue, I received a letter from Uncle Yosel. The famous writer I. L. Peretz had come to Lublin from Warsaw for a lecture at the Hazomir, and Uncle Yosel had shown him my essays in *Ha-Kol*. Of course, my uncle was not pleased at my works being published in a "reactionary" hasidic paper, but still, it was something in print. I don't know what Peretz really said about my efforts in *Ha-Kol*, but Uncle Yosel wrote: "Your writing has found favor in the eyes of the great writer Mr. I. L. Peretz." I could hardly believe what I read. The letter was a terrific shock, especially since Uncle Yosel revealed that he had told Peretz I had many manuscripts, and Peretz had suggested that I visit him in Warsaw to show him my work. I thought the ceiling had opened over my head and all the angels of Heaven were beckoning to me. Peretz's name was something to conjure with. Imagine, that I should myself go to see him! It was too frightening. My awareness that Peretz's mind now contained a consciousness of my name awakened the wildest dreams, but I lacked the courage to take the daring step I so desired.

I answered Uncle Yosel immediately, saying that even though his news had put me in seventh heaven, I still could not face the idea of going by myself to Peretz, who probably had forgotten the whole business. I would come to him like a beggar at the door, and he wouldn't even take a second look at me.

Uncle Yosel told me not to take after my family. He said if I would just spend an hour with Leyzer Lam, his father-in-law, he would beat out of me the old unworldly delicacies of Kutno as the dust is beaten out of an old carpet. But, knowing the Trunk family, Uncle Yosel realized he could accomplish nothing by mail: I would remain the same trembling and delicate young gentleman who would always have to be kept in hot-water bottles. Uncle Yosel decided that as soon as he could leave some of his urgent business with the Lams, he would come to Warsaw and personally escort me to Peretz. He had to be in Warsaw anyway to purchase some books for his Hazomir library, and it would give him a chance to go to the opera. He longed desperately for good music. If I were not such a delicate mollycoddle, he said, I would spit on all the hasidim and their traditions and go along to the opera. Only then would I realize that we live in a wonderful world with opportunities for a free and beautiful life. But no — he knew beforehand that I would not have the nerve, and who knows if I were not a lost soul altogether — unless some *shikse* should come along to make a man of me. This is the essence of Uncle Yosel's letter, written in a maskilish, euphuistic Hebrew, cursing all bigots and reactionaries and telling me to prepare my best manuscripts to take to Peretz.

I counted the hours until Uncle Yosel's arrival. Brightest hope and darkest fear took hold of me by turns. I searched through my writings to find something suitable. At that time I was already writing in Yiddish, but it seemed better to take a long Hebrew story, a sort of autobiographical novel into which I had poured all my experience, past and present. It seemed the best window through which Peretz could peer into my being.

Late one afternoon several days later, Uncle Yosel turned up. He was dressed in European fashion and seemed quite self-satisfied. Nevertheless, he still looked like a yeshiva student masquerading on Purim: he could not so easily efface the signs of his rabbinic home in Kutno. He had let his fingernails grow long, probably to spite God by showing that he no longer cut them every Friday as he had done in Kutno. He had to show in every possible way that he belonged more to the Lams than to the Trunks.

Uncle Yosel told me he had already bought the books he needed for the Lublin Hazomir. Last night he had been to the opera and later to a cabaret where naked *shikses* danced and sang gay, spicy couplets. But would a Trunkian mollycoddle like me know about that? He had also learned that Peretz received visitors after four in the afternoon. I was to prepare to go with him and take along a manuscript. Uncle Yosel would stay two days more in Warsaw, and if only I were not such a milksop, he would take me to a movie and show me something of the beautiful world. He wouldn't even propose the theater: he knew I wouldn't have the nerve to take such a revolutionary step.

It was nearing four o'clock. Uncle Yosel said it was time to go.

I felt myself turning pale and my hands trembled. I wrapped my story in a newspaper and we went out.

It was just a few blocks from Grzybow to Ceglana 1, where Peretz lived, about a quarter of an hour's walk. Even today I cannot forget this most decisive walk in my life. Thirty-odd years later when I passed these streets, my heart still beat excitedly in remembrance of that earlier walk. I have never forgotten the cobblestones, a certain street lamp, a newspaper kiosk, and a dozen other details that caught my eye.

Passing the court of Twarda 10, the hasidic prayer house of the Aleksander (Aleksandrow) rebbe, I paused for a long look inside, as if taking a desperate farewell.

We crossed the street at Ciepla and Ceglana. A tall smokestack rose from the red factory building, and opposite stood a large spacious house resembling a barracks, with lots of windows. We approached the gate. Unlike other houses, this gate was always locked, and it seemed to me pregnant with the mystery of Peretz's being. We entered a small and tranquil court-yard, in the center of which grew some trees. These trees, too, growing in the quiet of a Warsaw yard, seemed to have something of poetry and of Peretz.

Entering a side door, we came to an ancient and spotless hall stairway. Its cleanliness was like something Gentile, unlike the Warsaw I knew. The staircase was shining, narrow, and curving. It was as quiet as if no one had ever climbed those steps or even lived in the house. Everything seemed subdued to the unseen presence of Peretz. I felt my heart beating like a hammer, and I wanted desperately to put off the great moment my feet were bringing me to.

We stopped before a small, wood-panelled vestibule on the second floor. A metal nameplate on the door said in Hebrew, in large characters: "I. L. Peretz receives from 3 to 4." At the door hung an old-fashioned bellpull.

Uncle Yosel rang the bell. The thought leaped into my mind to dash down the steps and leave my uncle at the door. We could hear the door being unlatched and then opened. On the threshold stood Isaac Leibush Peretz.

I had occasionally seen him at a distance. In his long black cape and soft felt hat, he had seemed quite tall. Now there stood before us a short, stout figure, with graying short-cropped hair. A long yellow mustache concealed his mouth; the ends of his mustache drooped over the corners of his lips and trembled upon his cheeks. He wore a silk smoking jacket. His shirt collar was open and revealed a short, rather heavy neck. He wore pince-nez, with half lenses. He raised his limpid eyes to us and asked in Polish what we wanted. But as soon as he recognized Uncle Yosel, he changed his tone and began to speak in Yiddish.

"Is this the young man you told me about in Lublin?" he asked, looking at me. I was dressed in a long *kapote* and the traditional black serge cap. I was already growing a small yellowish beard. Peretz saw the newspaper-wrapped package in my hand and his face broke into a smile. "Come in," he said.

Peretz's home overwhelmed me; everything seemed to me full of poetry and fame. His study was a large light room, though the old fashioned win-dows, set with small panes of glass, seemed somewhat countrified. In the center of the room stood large wooden bowls of full-grown oleander plants, which filled the room with flaming crimson, a crimson that seemed dewy in the light of the sun pouring in. The windows of the study showed a gen-erous portion of sky because there was no building opposite, only the tall factory chimney just opposite the window at which Peretz's desk stood. The desk itself was covered with large vases of flowers that overshadowed everything else, making it seem like a fragrant flowerbed. The walls were densely hung with drawings and photographs, including portraits of Peretz in various poses.

In the naïveté of my emotions, everything contributed to my fantastic imaginings. Here the Muses really soared; no one but Peretz could live like this.

Peretz sat down at his desk and asked us to be seated. The odor of the flowers intoxicated me. Peretz pointed to the package in my hand and said, "Well, young man, show what you have."

Timidly I gave him the thick notebook. Peretz opened it, let his eyes rest upon the densely written pages, and began to read.

Silence reigned. Uncle Yosel raised his head and studied the portraits on whose strong colors the sun played. I sat lifeless. I felt as if I had given up all initiative and all will, and was overcome by a profound inner emptiness. Peretz read a little, passed over some pages, and then read some more.

At last he raised his eyes and peered at me over his half lenses. He closed the notebook and put it aside.

"You have interesting ideas like . . . (he mentioned the name of a well-known Yiddish writer), but you don't know Hebrew. You think in Yiddish and translate yourself into Hebrew. No, this has no point. Why don't you write Yiddish? Doesn't it suit you, a son-in-law of the Priveses, to write in the language of the common herd?"

I answered that I did write Yiddish, but I had wanted to bring him a bigger piece.

"No, no, bring me some of your Yiddish pieces," he said and returned the thick manuscript.

He was silent a while and then said: "I'd just like to read you something of mine which I wrote today."

He took up a large sheet of paper overlaid with tiny characters. He moved closer to the desk. His gray short-cropped hair seemed to become stiffer, and his clear eyes took on a dewy youthful brilliance. He began to read.

It was a prose poem, "Cain and Abel." I would not today rank it among Peretz's best work. But at that moment I considered it the greatest spiritual experience of my life.

Peretz's voice was unlike any I had ever heard, at once crusty and tender, metallic as gold and sweet as the subtlest honey. In this voice Peretz could express with mastery his emotions and turbulence, his longings and his unquieted temperament. He could threaten like an enraged lion and be gentle as the most peaceful dove. With good reason, he had the reputation of being a great public speaker, capable of swaying the largest crowd.

When he had finished reading, he rose from his chair. We, too, stood up.

"Bring me some of your work in Yiddish," he said as we shook hands, "and we will see."

I was dizzy when we left the apartment. But the trees in the courtyard seemed to grow more familiar.

The next day Uncle Yosel took me some place along Ujazdowskie Aleje where there were no bearded Jews in long kapotes. With great furtiveness he led me into a movie.

I did not consider my Yiddish writings as containing the essence of my spirituality. In Hebrew I hoped to express my intellectual moods, my introspections, the subtlety of my observations. In Yiddish I wrote about my milieu and especially my feeling for nature, which was always strong — I had spent my childhood and many months of my later life in the country. Yiddish evoked for me the fragrant fields and orchards among which I had been born and brought up. Hebrew called forth the Gemara and the intellectuality of my father's family. Hebrew was the language of the Trunks; Yiddish was the language of my mother and my Grandfather Boruch.

It had seemed most proper to present my intellectual side to Peretz, and so I had brought only my Hebrew writings. As for Uncle Yosel, no matter how much he detested rabbis and the Gemara, no matter how impressed he was with the turbulent simplicity of the Lams, he was still, at bottom, an intellectual Trunk and a grandchild of Reb Yeshuele Kutner. He reckoned only with my Hebrew accomplishments. A maskil to the marrow of his bones, he considered Yiddish something for the ignorant masses. Why should I come to Peretz with Yiddish when I wrote excellent Hebrew and could express myself conceptually and intellectually? Why should I tell Peretz about fields and orchards when I could show him something more elevated?

I had to rely on my own courage to go to Peretz a second time and bring him, as he had bade me, my Yiddish writings. It was a struggle and I put it off from day to day. I did not dare write to Uncle Yosel to take me again. Ashamed of my own timidity, I was afraid to appear ridiculous before Peretz. The longer I postponed the visit, the surer it seemed that Peretz would long have forgotten me, that he would not recognize me, and would make short shrift of me at the door. But at length I overcame my cowardice and resolved, come what may, to take my fate in my hands.

Going to Peretz, I relived once more all the scenes of the first visit. The cobblestones and houses on the street imprinted themselves on my mind. At the corner of Ceglana, seeing the factory smokestack and the big house where Peretz lived, I almost lost my new-found courage. I stopped. But it was now or never. I marshalled my failing energy. And there I was standing again before Peretz's door and pulling the bell.

Again, I heard the door being unlocked, and again confronted Peretz with his silk jacket and clerical pince-nez.

My face must have been very white. And Peretz must surely have noticed my anxiety, for his smile was very friendly.

"Why haven't we seen you until now, Trunk?" he asked. "Come in and take off your coat. Have you brought something in Yiddish?"

When I saw that the great man remembered my name, the burden of fear fell from my heart.

Peretz waited until I had removed my coat. Then he led me into his study. This time, too, the desk was covered with flowers and plants. A dwarfish creature, gray-haired and gray-bearded, sat at the desk, absorbed in rolling cigarettes.

"This is Jacob Dineson," Peretz said. "Get acquainted."

Dineson turned around to inspect me. To him I was a new face, a young man in a kapote. As for me, it was with great awe that I looked at him. This gray, dwarfish man was the famous author of *Der Schvartser Yungermantchik* and of *Yosele*, a book over which I had wept a sea of tears. My mother had wailed aloud over it. And even hardhearted Grandfather Boruch, reading it, had broken into sobs and had groped for a cane to beat up Berl the cruel *melamed*. More than ever, Peretz's home seemed peopled with the figures of my secret dreams.

Peretz said to Dineson: "This is the young man I told you about, old man. Perhaps something will come of him."

Then he turned to me again: "Sit down at the desk and show us what you have."

I pulled a short story out of my pocket and handed it to him. It was a story about our village of Dlutow. The narrative itself was sprawling and ill constructed; the chief thing was the landscape motif. I had described the fields of Dlutow very sentimentally.

Peretz said that though the story had many defects, he liked it very much. He advised me to go on writing similar things. "You will develop into a pastoral poet," he said. I remember that is how Peretz expressed himself. Then he took a pen and began correcting a lot of sentences, changing many words and phrases. At that time, Peretz believed that Germanic words should replace the Slavic elements in Yiddish; for example, where I had written *lonke* (meadow), Peretz substituted *Wiese*.

Then he returned the manuscript, continuing to encourage me, and said to Dineson, who had not stopped rolling cigarettes, that he hoped something would come of me. (Dineson rolled the cigarettes for Peretz; he himself did not smoke.)

"Continue writing," Peretz said to me, "and bring it to show me."

My face beamed with joy. Thinking that my audience was over, I arose to take my leave. But Peretz asked me to stay and have coffee.

Peretz and Dineson rose and we went into the kitchen. On the way, Dineson began talking to me with intimacy as if I were one of the family, and encouraged me to keep on writing and show my pieces to Peretz.

As we sat at the table in the rather dark kitchen, Peretz talked familiarly and jokingly to the maid, an elderly, stout Polish woman who had worked for him untold years and considered herself part of the literary family. He told her, pointing to me, that this young man was a new visitor who would come frequently now, and she was to make especially good coffee for me.

I must confess that I suffered the torments of hell drinking the strong and aromatic coffee with Peretz. I knew the milk wasn't kosher.

Then I heard several shrill rings of the doorbell. Peretz went to answer it. From the corridor came the sounds of two new voices; one was high-pitched and singsong and talked to Peretz with familiarity; the other was low and harsh. Soon Peretz returned to the kitchen with the two men and introduced them to me. One was Menachem Boraisha and the other S. L. Kave. They sat down at the table, Menachem continuing to talk in his singsong voice, in a slight Lithuanian dialect. His sentences always seemed to end in midair.

The stout maid served more coffee. I felt I was in seventh heaven. For the first time in my life I was in a real literary milieu, with Jewish writers.

32 Between Two Worlds: S. Ansky

S. ANSKY, pen name for Solomon Zaynvl Rapoport, was born in Vitebsk in 1863 and died in Warsaw in 1920. A Yiddish short-story writer and dramatist known especially for his play *The Dybbuk*, he was an extraordinary personality only barely illuminated by the data of his life or an analysis of his literary output. The progression of his life was as cyclical as Nathan Birnbaum's and though the steps in the progression were somewhat different, its cyclical character was similar. Ansky was an early maskil, as he describes in the following story. Thereafter he became a leader among the Socialist-Revolutionaries; because of this activity he fled to Paris in 1894, where he was secretary to Peter Lavrov. But upon his return to Russia, he became ever more drawn back to Jews and Jewish life. He turned his attention to Jewish folklore, which he regarded as a struggle between spirit and matter.

In 1910, in an address on the occasion of his twenty-fifth literary anniversary, he said:

Twenty-five years ago when I first began writing, my striving was to work on behalf of the oppressed, the laboring masses, and it seemed to me then — and

that was my error — that I would not find them among Jews. I thought it was impossible to hold oneself aloof from politics and, again, I did not find any political currents among Jews. Bearing within me an eternal yearning toward Jewry, I nevertheless turned in all directions and went to labor on behalf of another people. My life was broken, severed, ruptured. Many years of my life passed on this frontier, on the border between both worlds. Therefore, I beg you, on this twenty-fifth year of summing up my literary work, to eliminate sixteen years.

In 1911 he headed one of the more extraordinary undertakings among Russian Jewry — an expedition, originally financed by Baron Horace Günzburg, to gather Jewish folklore, particularly in the Ukrainian settlements where hasidism had originated. When World War I broke out, he contrived to obtain permission to visit, as a medical aide, the Jewish communities in the war-torn areas, and his three-volume work *Der yidisher khurbn* ("The Jewish Catastrophe") reflected the intensity of his return to the Jewish world. The following narrative was taken from a collection of his autobiographical stories and essays.

I Enlighten a Shtetl

by S. Ansky

At the beginning of 1881 I left Vitebsk, my birthplace, to become a tutor in the town of Liozno. Seventeen years old, this was the first independent act in my life, but I abounded in dashing self-reliance and was greatly inspired by the high ideals which lit up my vision. About a year earlier, I had left the straight and narrow; I became engrossed in worldly books and turned into an ardent maskil. I was then most influenced by Lilienblum's *Hattot Ne'urim* ("The Sins of Youth").

I did not go to Liozno so much to teach as to spread haskala among the young people, to open their eyes. I took a bundle of haskala books along: I. B. Levinsohn's *Zerubavel*, Mapu's *Ahavat Zion*, Smolenskin's *Kevurat Hamor* and, of course, *Hattot Ne'urim*.

At that time, the Jewish towns of Lithuania were congealed in the old Orthodox ways and absolutely refused to face up to new trends and movements. Liozno, once the residence of the old Lubavicher rebbe, Schneur Zalman, was in this respect even more backward than the other villages. Until my arrival, the town had had only one teacher, a former yeshiva student, whom the rabbi and the *melamdim* persecuted at first and then persuaded to repent. They cut his hair, took him to the ritual bath, burned the hair with the short coat, dressed him in a long garment and a skullcap, and sat him down in the synagogue to study the holy books. But their joy was shortlived: a few months later the penitent ran away and became converted.

It was not easy for me to find jobs tutoring. To avoid provoking malicious acts against me from the start, I put on a mask of piety and showed that my only purpose was to earn my keep. I played my role well, I obtained lessons, and soon I was in touch with several boys. Despite its isolation from the great world, the town nevertheless had a few "infected" young people, who reached out for light and knowledge and thirsted for a word of haskala. They understood immediately I was not as pious as I made out, and wordlessly, but with expressive glances, they hinted they wanted to establish contact with me. They soon succeeded. Once, late at night, I heard a cautious quiet tap on my window. Opening it, I saw before me two boys who, quietly but joyously and spiritedly, told me they came to discuss an important, a most important matter. Not waiting for an invitation, they entered my room through the window.

A conversation began which lasted till dawn. It would be hard to define what we talked about. The conversation consisted almost entirely of passionate exclamations (whispered, of course, so the landlady would not overhear) extolling the radiant and sacred haskala. I do not remember what I told my new comrade-pupils, but the substance was not in my words but in the exalted mood of the listeners, who saw some sort of prophecy in my words. They left, joyous, as if newborn, with a firm decision to throw off their yoke, run away from home, and begin a new life, bright and promising.

The nightly visits repeated themselves. After the first two boys, others also so idealistically inclined came. Soon they formed a peculiar club of six or seven. They usually assembled at my place Fridays late at night when the town slept soundly: the visits were so furtive and conspiratorial, the discussions conducted so quietly that for the several months I was in the town, no one learned of these meetings. When I became better acquainted with my comrades and became convinced that they could be trusted, I began to lend them my secret books, even the most precious and most "dangerous," *Hattot Ne'urim.*

But over my head, clouds began to gather little by little. It began with a ludicrous incident. I had told one of my pupils to order from Vitebsk a chrestomathy. The melamed whose classroom I had used surmised this must be a book about Christ's mother and made a commotion in town. It took considerable effort to convince the parents that the reader had no connection with Christ or Christianity.

A few weeks later, an even funnier incident happened. I kept a diary in which I used to write down my impressions, describe all sorts of scenes and types, my pupils, their parents, and others. I wrote the diary in the form of letters to my childhood friend Chaim Zhitlowsky. Once, when I forgot to lock the box where I kept my manuscripts, the landlady's daughter, a grown girl and apparently a literary connoisseur, came in during my absence. She fished out the diary and began reading. Interested in its subject matter, she assembled a few of her friends for a literary soiree. The next day, the contents of my diary were known all over town.

Unaware of all this, I went as usual to give my lessons. When I arrived for the first lesson, the lady of the house, a well-to-do shopkeeper, greeted me at the door with this welcome:

"Listen here, you writer! I hired you to teach my children to read and write, but not for you to write down that my Abie's nose is dirty, and that my Frieda has big teeth and that I go about in a bedraggled dress. I can assure you that even if I wear a bedraggled dress, whatever I put in the garbage is worth more than you and your fine learning. And you can go back where you came from. Writers like you I don't need."

I got the same turning out at the next lesson. I was beside myself with despair, not knowing what had caused this misfortune. I expected that I would find the same reception at my other lessons, but apparently my dear first reader had no time to read the whole diary or forgot to tell everything. At the other homes, I was received not only without anger and abuse, but even with more friendliness than usual. These women, splitting with laughter, begged me to come read for them how I described their neighbors and acquaintances.

The episode concluded in my losing only the two lessons. But it also hurt my reputation with the solid householders. Besides, no matter how carefully I conducted myself, people began to suspect I was masquerading, and talk that I was a nonbeliever spread in town.

Just at that time, the pogroms took place in southern Russia, calling forth the deepest despair and bitterness among the Lithuanian Jews. At the same time, the religious mood became stronger. Reports about the pogroms reached our town not from the newspapers, which no one received, but from unclear rumors. One day the rabbi received a letter from, I think, the Vitebsk rabbi, describing the horrible events and proposing that a communal fast be decreed. The letter was read in the synagogue and had a powerful impact. A fast day was decided on. Then the rabbi chastised the people, calling them to repent and pointing out that there were those in town who had forgotten God and allowed their children to study forbidden subjects. Precisely then, the mishap with my clandestine maskilim had to occur.

A few days before the fast, one of the maskilim, a sixteen-year-old boy, came to me about midnight. From the nervous tapping on the window, I realized that something unusual had happened. When my nocturnal visitor entered through the window, he was white as chalk, depressed, and upset. In answer to my question about what happened, he shot out despairingly: "Oh, what a misfortune happened! We are lost!" With much effort on my part I managed to find out what had happened.

About a week earlier, I had lent the boy *Hattot Ne'urim*. He read it several times and memorized several passages. Since he had a fourteen-year-old brother whom he had already led astray, he let him enjoy the book too, warning him to be careful. The boy sat up all night in a tiny room and read. In the morning, after prayers, he went to the study house where, under the cover of a Gemara, he continued to read. But the sleepless night and the excitement had their effect, and he fell asleep, leaving the book on the lectern. A yeshiva student entered, approached the lectern, and immediately recognized one of those secular books. He began leafing through it, till he came upon the sentence: "Who can prove there is a God?" He became so terrified that he began screaming. The boy awoke and, seeing the book in a stranger's hand, leaped to retrieve it. He managed to tear the book out of the yeshiva student's hands and run away. The yeshiva student went immediately to the rabbi, telling him of the horrible occurrence. A couple of hours later, the father of both my maskilim was furiously beating the younger one, demanding he confess where he got the forbidden book. But the boy did not talk. Then the father locked him in a dark room, threatening to starve him until he would talk. The older boy got a beating, too. In short, the town was in a real uproar, and all as one claimed that only the "writer" could have lent the boy such a book; they were convinced that the "writer" had been sent from Vilna by those nonbelievers to demolish the town.

Relating this story, the boy shed bitter tears. He brought me the salvaged *Hattot Ne'urim*. But in what a condition — all tattered! He insisted that I must burn it immediately, because the townspeople would surely come to search me here.

Calming him, I proved to him that his and his brother's sufferings were a sort of self-sacrifice for the Sanctification of the Name — on behalf of the haskala. This reasoning encouraged him. He even exclaimed spiritedly: "Very good, this will bring things to an end sooner and we will both run away from home!"

Early the next morning, I found out that there had been a meeting the night before at the rabbi's house in which the affair was discussed. They spoke a great deal about me, and the rabbi even proposed excommunicating me.

I went to the synagogue for services. My arrival at this time agitated the congregation. The rabbi, a little old thin Jew, stood at the eastern wall, his head enveloped in a prayer shawl, and he prayed. I walked boldly toward him and called, "Rabbi!"

He looked up. Seeing me, he turned his frightened pleading glance to the people nearby; someone whispered to him: "The writer." Hearing who I was, the rabbi lowered his head, turned, and began to move further away from me.

I took several steps toward him and I spoke out, purposely loud and bold:

"Rabbi, I came to ask what you have against me that you consider ex-communicating me. I want you to tell me here, in the synagogue, in front of everyone!"

The rabbi began to wring his hands and without looking at me, backed still further away, stammering in fear, "Go, go, go. I don't know you, I don't know you."

I stepped right up to him. Then someone grabbed me by the hand and shouted in anger, "Unbeliever, where are you crawling? Can't you see the rabbi does not wish to look at you and does not wish you to remain in his presence?"

"Out of the synagogue, unbeliever," came the shouts.

I had no choice but to leave. But now I was relieved. What did I care if they excommunicated me? I had long excommunicated them. But I worried about the boy caught with the book. His father had beaten him with such violence that he had fainted.

I had an idea. I noticed that in speaking about the heretical book which the yeshiva student found on the lectern no one called it *Hattot Ne'urim*, but "Two Days and One Night," the title of a story by J. L. Gordon, bound with *Hattot Ne'urim*. The yeshiva student had apparently just glimpsed at the title page and remembered the name of Gordon's story. I tore the story out of the book, took it to a young, somewhat worldly, lumber merchant. I asked him to read it and testify before the rabbi that there was no disbelief in it and that it did not contain the incriminating sentence "Who can prove there is a God." The young man read the story and found only flowery rhetoric, not a word of heresy. He went to the rabbi, explained to him that I and the boy were less guilty than he had thought, and warned him not to think of excommunicating me because the government could punish him severely for this.

That worked. The father released the boy from his cell, extracting a holy vow from him never to read such books or associate with me. All talk about excommunicating me ceased. But on the fast day, the rabbi in his sermon showed that I, and such as I, were the only ones to blame for the pogroms. He demanded that I be discharged as tutor. Besides, he issued rulings which were posted that same day in all the prayer houses. Of these rulings, I remember only four:

1. All males, from thirteen years up, must wear skullcaps and not re-move them at night;

2. Girls and, especially, married women must not sing in the presence of a man, or even when alone;

3. At weddings, women and girls must not appear immodestly exposed;

4. A search should be made in all homes and in all attics; all books, except religious books, that might be found were to be brought the next day to the synagogue courtyard for burning so that evil should be purged from the town.

About six or seven Hebrew books, quite innocent ones, were turned up, including also Gordon's story, which the young man had not returned to me. To this, they added about a dozen Yiddish novels, mostly by Shomer. They made a pyre in the synagogue courtyard and set it afire. From the distance I could see only the smoke of the auto-da-fé. It reeked of the Middle Ages.

The next day, Saturday after *havdala,* a townsman came and in a calm businesslike tone ordered me to leave town — unless I wanted to be marched out by the police. Besides, why did I have to stay? I would not have any more lessons anyway. In answer to my question as to how someone as innocent as I could be sent out with a convoy of prisoners, he said quietly, with a smile, "Can't you understand? You're not a child. Two pounds of tea to the police commissioner, and tomorrow you march out with the prisoners."

I do not know if they would really have carried out the threat. But since there was no longer any point in my staying in Liozno, I left.

For a long time I kept the tattered *Hattot Ne'urim* as a memento.

A Half Year with Ansky

by Haykel Lunsky

Haykel Lunsky was born in Slonim in 1881 and died in Vilna, killed by the Nazis. He was a Hebrew and Yiddish writer, bibliographer, and librarian of the Strashun library in Vilna, a renowned Judaica collection. The following memoir was written shortly after Ansky's death.

I BECAME acquainted with Ansky before the first Russian revolution. Vilna was then a place of refuge for many Russian Jews, and Strashun's library was their cultural center. Ansky had lived in Vilna before; he had married there in March, 1908. Later, he left for St. Petersburg, where he organized the Historic-Ethnographic Society. He returned once again to Vilna in the fall of 1918, sick and wasted, in flight from the Bolsheviks. He was in the hospital several weeks, then took a room far from the center of town.

I met him one evening and accompanied him home. I was drawn to him like a magnet. His room was practically unfurnished, just a bed, a pair of chairs, and a small table piled up with cigarette boxes — he was a chain smoker — and with his manuscripts. On the walls hung many oil paintings which he liked to buy in the marketplace, where they could be had cheaply. There were several bookshelves which he had also gotten at a ridiculous price. Near the door lay a couple of dozen logs which he used to split to heat his stove. He likely suffered great poverty, for I noticed that bread and tea then were his entire meals.

This wretched little room soon became the center for all the communal leaders and writers in Vilna, because he was there, their father, the patriarch of the Jewish literary world, the man with the great heart toward whom everyone was drawn.

In that little room he talked to me about forming the Historic-Ethnographic Society, which had become the ambition of his life. A month earlier, he had delivered a brilliant address on this subject. His words flowed like water from a quiet stream. Then he straightened his tall figure, shook his large leonine head; his gray hair tousled over his radiant face and in his wonderful eyes burned a flame that kindled all hearts. Like a prophet, he spoke about justice and truth and he closed with these words: "Their folk-creations are mostly about women and bloodshed, whereas Jewish folk-creations are all about truth and justice. Truth stands so high that it calls even God to judgment; if the Almighty issues a harsh decree, the righteous man comes to nullify it."

On February 20, 1919, the Historic-Ethnographic Society was formed. We had compiled a list of names of people and written the invitations. Typically, we distributed the invitations ourselves. In three hours the society was established. A board was chosen and the work organized in five sections. Ansky sat all day with the people assigned to the sections, like a rebbe with his followers, showing them what was to be done. His knowledge was enormous, and while teaching he also enchanted everyone and they were inspired in their work.

In less than two years, in a time of destruction and convulsion, practically without funds, he assembled a treasure of tens of thousands of documents. Even while he was sick he kept working. A day before his death he sent, from Warsaw, gifts for the museum.

Ansky was cheerful and talkative. His cheerfulness did not forsake him even when he was in great pain. But he was not gay when he confessed that for a long time he had been sundered from his own people, the poorest among the poor, the most unfortunate among the unfortunate. His face clouded and his voice grew silent in sorrow.

When he was preparing his will, he asked me also to keep the anniversary of his father's death, which he had always observed. Later, in July, 1919, when he was sick in Otwock, he wrote for his prayer shawl, which he had left in Vilna.

Once I saw him as propagandist at a Zionist youth meeting. Someone there attacked the hadarim and yeshivot, besmirching them along with all Orthodoxy. Then Ansky spoke out in a fiery speech: "When the Russian schools gave us careerists, the yeshivot gave us idealists, fighters, and public leaders. I love all my people and all its classes and I have strong faith in its healthy senses."

33   Torments of Berdichevski's Last Days.
by Fischel Lachower

MICAH JOSEPH BERDICHEVSKI, Hebrew writer, was born at Bershad, Podolia, in 1865 and died in Berlin in 1921. Brought up in a hasidic home, and having studied at the yeshiva at Volozhin, he became a maskil, and then wandered about from city to city in search of education. He studied at the universities of Breslau, Berlin, and Bern, from which he received a Ph.D. in 1897. His contact with Western culture had a shattering effect on him and he became the first Jewish Nietzschean, a Jewish transvaluator of values. All his life he was tormented by the conflict between his Jewish heritage and European civilization.

Berdichevski described his inner conflict in one of his essays: "With my hands I destroy old values, but simultaneously I remove my shoes from my feet — in good biblical tradition — not to desecrate our holy soil. I strive for reconciliation and unity in my inner self as well as for the creation of a new people, but in vain. The soul remains divided and for generations we will continue thus."

A rebel and a heretic, he nevertheless returned to Jewish sources and to Jewish tradition, searching for Jewish unorthodoxies out of which he could create a modern Jewish tradition of rebellion. In so doing, he reaffirmed Judaism for the modern Jews of his day.

Fischel Lachower, Hebrew writer, literary critic
and editor, was born in Chorzele, Poland, in
1883. He lived in Warsaw until 1927 when he
settled in Palestine, where he died in 1947. He
was very close to Berdichevski, whose last days he
described in the following memoir.

Nᴏᴛ much is known about Berdichevski's early days. This man was always strange and mysterious. Whoever knew him did not really know him, and whoever knew him in one period of his life knew nothing about him in another. In that final period of his life, full of mysteries, I was close to him and for about a year, that last year of his life, I was near him. Had I a storyteller's talent, I could tell about that last year of his life, but since I cannot do that, I will content myself with less and tell about his last days.

We were then occupied with one thing — sorting out Berdichevski's manuscripts and preparing them for press. This was not complicated, for the material had mostly already been printed and part had even been gathered in various collections. But nothing was simple with Berdichevski. Everything had to be considered from all sides. Doubts always arose; when everything seemed clear, suddenly a "perhaps" loomed up. Sometimes things went so far that our whole endeavor was put in doubt: why publish these writings at all? How can one make of something fluid something solid? How can one set down for perpetuity things which originated in relation to a given period and are associated with that period?

Sometimes the great question arose from another side: Is it at all right to publish these works, to revive the problems and uncertainties about the very nature of our people and its existence? He raised this great question usually during a catastrophe or a crisis in the life of our people. Such a catastrophe occurred in the spring of 1921, the last year of his life — the pogroms in Palestine. Talking about this, Berdichevski told me what his father, the rabbi, had told him: "I read other writers and they are nonbelievers, but you are an utter disbeliever, even in the essence of being a Jew."

Berdichevski told me many stories about his sainted father, the rabbi of Dubovo. One bears on our subject. "Once," Berdichevski told me, "when I lived in the same town with my father, after I had returned from abroad, I heard a knock at the door very early in the morning. I then lived at the edge of town, at the far side of the Jewish section. Who could that be knocking at my door so early? I opened it and there stood my father. 'Hurry, get dressed, and come out, I have an important matter to take up with you,' he said to me.

"I dressed fast and went out. He began right away. 'All night I tossed on my bed and searched for the meaning of this: that this rabbinic chain of thirteen links, reaching back to Reb Shmuel Shmelke of Nikolsburg, the disciple of the Maggid of Mezritsh and the Ba'al Shem Tov — thirteen generations of rabbis, one generation after another — has ended with me. It was my great wish that God Almighty, Who estranged you from my ways and the ways of my fathers, would tell me the meaning of this enigma. Only when dawn came did I find the answer. It must be one of these two: Either God did this so that you would become famous among the non-Jews' " — Berdichevski was then writing in German and had been translated into Russian — " 'or this is what was destined in Heaven. Forty days before a child is born it is announced in Heaven that so-and-so's daughter will marry thus-and-so. How could the son of a small-town rabbi marry an educated woman who lives somewhere far away at that? That was how things unfolded, that you became a doubter, moved abroad, and became an educated man. Now, God having accomplished that, the time has come for you to repent.' "

This voice calling him to repentance from time to time found a response in Berdichevski's heart. His father's martyr death, in horrible torture, was the force that at times reunited the links of the chain. Berdichevski learned of the death of his father only after a long time, but even before that, the Ukrainian massacres had deeply affected him. I had come to Berlin in 1919, shortly before Rosh ha-Shana. On the eve of Rosh ha-Shana I was at Berdichevski's home. As I was leaving, he asked me what I planned to do that evening. I told him I had arranged to go to the theater with a friend. "I am disappointed in you," he said, "that after a year of such ghastly massacres in the Ukraine, you should go to the theater on Rosh ha-Shana."

Berdichevski sometimes had the feeling that some secret power obstructed his collecting and publishing his writings. To him, a recluse removed from the practical world, the impediments seemed insurmountable.

We were in Leipzig a few days in connection with the publication of his works. We stayed in a hotel near the railroad and ate in the restaurant at the station, a large airy structure bathed in light and always crowded with people coming and going. This put us in a good mood, and we had long talks. When Berdichevski got in the swing of talking, he would tell a story or some hasidic saying. He would begin, "My father used to say." Once, when he closed with a hasidic saying which pleased him, as if he had just penetrated its deep wisdom, he added, quite unlike his usual self, "My father was, nevertheless, a wonderful man." Suddenly his face clouded up and he became silent. Then he broke into a wail in front of everyone in the station. People watched us in astonishment, as if asking what had happened to this elderly man who was just conversing so cheerfully and all of a sudden was shaken by sobs.

The next day we returned to Berlin and resumed our work. It seemed to me he yearned to take up again the scholarly work he had neglected when we began to sort his writings. He wanted to finish, finish, and kept repeating the question: "Can I live several years more to be able to finish what I began?" In this scholarly work he saw the purpose of his life. "Without this purpose," he told me several times, "life has no meaning for me. If not for this work, after what happened to my father, I would have secluded myself off in a corner to end the remaining days left to me." He had, in fact, secluded himself since his father's death; he did not go to any places of amusement or even to public gatherings. Occasionally he visited a friend. He was absorbed in his work and there he sought refuge. He found it in the scholarly work in which he had been engaged for fifteen years, and which was still far from complete. He thought it was his obligation to finish it.

In his last year, he became animated only when he spoke about this work, but he seldom spoke of it. That was his secret. I had to use all sorts of stratagems to get him to tell me this secret. He led me into an inner room and showed me the cornerstone of his work, telling me about it in detail. I observed him as well as his work; one could see that while shedding light on our past and its essence in its profundity, he himself became radiant. His eyes, which had always had the glint of steel, now suddenly flashed with a wondrous light, the light of a distant vision.

A great scholarly work always has something of vision, but Berdichevski was then seized with a vision of life. The poet in him came to life again with great force in his last years. The more time drove him, the more he strained to bring forth what was within him. Much of his novel *Miriam* was written in this last year of his life — many chapters in his last days. This novel was part of a trilogy which he had conceived. Miriam, the heroine, was supposed to come from a provincial town to Odessa, and from Odessa to Switzerland, in the circle of revolutionary students. He intended to portray the great city of Odessa with its maskilim, then the life of the students abroad, the revolutionary types. Miriam was then to become entangled in a tragic love affair with her best friend's husband, and find death in a Swiss lake.

External distractions, many and frequent in his life, became inner ones. At that time, his father's widow and his brother's family (his brother had also been murdered in the Ukraine) came to Poland. They wrote him often, asking help. He gave willingly and beyond his means, but the letters brought to life the horrible picture of our life, and awoke a strange fear in him, fear for the life of Judaism and of Jews. He was drawn to them and yet at the same time he wanted to flee from them, to observe them from outside and also to judge them. He often thought he was losing his balance, he was losing his freedom, the freedom for which he had fought even with himself so heartlessly for thirty-five years. This freedom he cherished above all else: freedom of thought, without design, without ulterior motive of love for his ancestral heritage, for the burden of this heritage. But he bore the burden on his back, in his whole being and his whole life.

VII

The Arts

34 Visiting Goldfaden,
Father of the Yiddish Stage
by David I. Silberbusch

ABRAHAM GOLDFADEN, Yiddish playwright and poet, was born in Old
Constantine, province of Volhynia, in
1840 and died in New York in 1908.
His tombstone is inscribed with these
words: "Abraham Goldfaden, the
father of the Yiddish stage." A maskil,
a poet first in Hebrew and later in
Yiddish, he became renowned for his
plays and musical comedies. He may
be said to have been the first Yiddish
writer and maskil who addressed himself to the common man, the Yiddish-
speaking masses, seeking to entertain
and comfort. His great success was
made possible by the emergence of
these masses as consumers of literature
and drama. Thus, Goldfaden was probably one of the earliest producers of
mass culture.

> David Isaiah Silberbusch, who was born in Za-
> leszczyki, Galicia, in 1854 and died in Tel Aviv
> in 1936, was a Yiddish and Hebrew writer. He
> lived in Vienna most of his life, settling in Pales-
> tine in his last years. The following selection has
> been translated from his memoirs.

I T was a Sunday morning when I went to visit Goldfaden, as had been arranged by a mutual friend.

Goldfaden was then staying in one of the best rooms in the Black Eagle,
then Czernowitz' best hotel. He had a large sitting room, with an alcove for
bed and washbasin, the doorway was hung with blue velvet drapes. A thick
carpet covered the floor. There were a sofa, a polished dark-wood table,
with leather-upholstered chairs around it. In a corner, near a window, stood
a piano and a writing desk.

When I arrived about eleven o'clock, he had, I think, been sitting at the
desk. He was wearing a gray dressing gown with blue stripes at the collar,
and embroidered velvet slippers. On his nose, highly polished, gold-framed
glasses. None of this shocked me. I was innocent in the correct way to

receive visitors. What impressed me were the golden frames and the expansive style of living of a Jewish author.

The elegance cost me. In keeping with hasidic custom of paying the rebbe for his advice, I had prepared three Austrian guldens to pay in advance for a half-year's subscription to his paper *Izraelitishes folksblat,* which he was planning to publish in Czernowitz. I knew this was a way to soften the heart of an editor. But three guldens seemed too paltry for an editor with gold-framed spectacles, who treads on a thick carpet in embroidered velvet slippers. I dug into my pants pocket and extracted a crisp five-gulden note and put it down on the table, saying that besides the paper I would like also his two books, *Tsitsim u-Ferahim* and *Dos Yidele.* To win more favor in his eyes, I said I had already read these books.

Then, with a deep sigh, I poured out the words I had rehearsed: "Jews still shuffle around in the dark and do not see the splendor of the haskala . . . Jews still do not know how to appreciate the great value of their own great poets. . . ."

Goldfaden smiled and with great conceit said, "Against my Jews I have no complaints. I have only to concoct a concoction for them and they pay the rent."

I sat stunned like a dummy. His language was so common, so irrelevant. He walked over to the piano and strummed the keys as though searching for a melody. Then he came back to me and said, "However little the Jews appreciate us, their poets, we appreciate them even less. A Jew, even if he is hard as flint, does not have to be beaten to strike water. Heaven forbid. The Jew is beaten enough. One need only bend close to his ear, sing a song of his thousand-year-old accumulated sorrow, put a dressing on his sore, sing him a cheerful song about hope for deliverance. He repeats your song with feeling. He becomes soft as dough and, singing, lets you reshape him. Or tell him a charming story. Hold up to him the true mirror of his own life. He will seat himself on your lap and listen with open ears — and you can get whatever you want from him. Of course, he must trust you; he must believe you mean well. It is hard, very hard, to deceive him. He can tell you by the tip of your nose. My Jews love me, because they recognize my love for them in my poems . . . I concoct them a concoction and they pay the rent."

Again the "concoction" and the "rent," but now I understood him better and gazed at him with great respect. Yet I asked him, somewhat modestly, "Why do you put such stress on the words 'my Jews'?"

"My Jews," he replied, "are the common people, who do not worship the Golden Calf, whose tablets are not yet broken, whose ears and whose hearts are not closed. These are not necessarily the poorest of the poor. Quite a few of them have good incomes, yet their Jewish spirit has remained fresh and their Jewish heart still throbs. The number keeps increasing of those who refuse to give for the Golden Calf, but who give for the Tabernacle and will continue to give. You need only to know how to sing into their ear."

I endeavored to engage him in a more prosaic conversation. "I heard that your friendship with Isaac Joel Linetsky, your collaborator in *Yisrolik*, dates back to when you attended the Rabbinical Seminary at Zhitomir. Why has he now parted company with you?"

My sudden question did not please Goldfaden very much. But he replied with a smile. "Don't expect me to tell you all the reasons. You must be satisfied with one. Linetsky and I were friends at the Rabbinical Seminary, but remember, he had family status, a child of a rabbinic line, the son of the rebbe of Vinnitsa. I was just common flesh and blood, the child of a workingman, the son of Hayim Lipa the watchmaker, in Old Constantine. As a boy I studied my father's trade."

I understood the mordacity in his reply, yet I did a foolish thing. I wanted to show off my rabbinical learning; I quoted our sages who said "Greater is he who enjoys the fruit of his labor than the fearer of Heaven," and "whoever does not teach his son a trade teaches him to become a robber." Then I gave him the whole list of Tannaim and Ammoraim who were artisans: Rabbi Isaac the blacksmith, Rabbi Johanan the sandal-maker, Rabbi Hillel the woodcutter, Rabbi Shammai, the mason, and many more. "Besides," I added, "I know from the poem which you published on the first page of *Tsitsim u-Ferahim*, which you dedicated to your father, that you are as proud of him as the son of a great rabbi is of his father."

Goldfaden laughed aloud. "Young man, one can see that you are a scholar and very well versed. Yet you forget something. You forget the words that our sages selected when they wanted to say that thus-and-so would not be interpreted in any other way. They did not say 'a rabbi and the son of a rabbi,' but 'there is no artisan and no son of artisan that can solve that.' "

Now I laughed. Then becoming serious, Goldfaden told me, "You see, my dear young man, that is also the difference between me and most of my friends at the Rabbinical Seminary. A snob, a rabbi's son, deceived his parents and family, secretly studied forbidden books, at night stole money from his mother's pocket for expenses, and then ran away from home in the middle of the night and fled to Zhitomir. He arrived there, an embittered hero, at least half-enemy to his parents and even more so to his milieu, and thought himself a big hero. He broke his fetters and became a free man! Brought a sacrifice before the altar of that heavenly daughter, the haskala. All his life this young man's bitterness against others remained and also his exaggerated notions of his own courage. But as for me, little Abraham Goldenthread, the son of Hayim Lipa the watchmaker, I was never embittered and not much of a hero. My father was himself a maskil of the older generation, who wanted his eldest son to be a Jewish human being with all the virtues. He sent me to the best teachers in Old Constantine, later to school, and then to the Zhitomir seminary. The one who understood this best of all was the best teacher in the seminary, Jacob Eichenbaum, the author of the famous little book about chess, *Ha-Kerab*. Himself a Hebrew poet, he was always ready to listen to every poem, not merely to the sound of its words, but also to the subtlest stirrings in the poet's soul. Two pupils at the seminary were reputed the best writers of Hebrew verse — Solomon Mandelkern and I. Each of us wrote a poem about Bathsheba and submitted it to a teachers' jury. The teachers could not decide which was better. I must admit I myself liked my friend's poem very much. I felt very discouraged. But Eichenbaum proved that mine was better. 'In reading a poem, whatever its language,' he said, 'one must see how much purity of feeling and poetic simplicity it has and how much refinement and ingenious speculation. The greatest virtue of Goldfaden's poems is their simplicity, their quiet flow from a pure mountain source.'"

"When did you begin to write Yiddish poems?" I asked him.

"Someone else wrote my first Yiddish poems, not I."

"How is that?"

"I will tell you the story as it was. I cannot remember when I first had the itch to write rhymes, that is, to rattle off a short-lined crambo. I remember, when I was six or seven and already studying Gemara and knew the first two books of the Pentateuch by heart, my mother took me to a wedding at a neighbor's. There was a big-bellied man with a trimmed beard. He pushed the visor of his cap to a side, struck a happy-go-lucky pose, his right foot forward, to celebrate the bride before the ceremony. Afterward, he struck the same posture, calling all the relatives by name for the bridal dance, and everything he recited and sang rhymed artfully. I listened in complete absorption. Then we went home. I turned my cap aside, put my right foot forward, and whatever I had to say to my mother I said in rhyme. She held her sides with laughter. Hearing this, my father came in, smiling under his mustache, addressed me as 'Little Abie, the badkhn.' But then seriously, he scolded me: 'It's not nice for a boy studying Gemara to be so foolish.'

"At a later time, rhymes were always dancing in my head. Sometimes they seemed to compose themselves into a pleasant little poem. Then I would fit some cantorial melody which I had heard to the poem. I would sing it to myself with great pleasure. But it never occurred to me to write it down. Now a Hebrew poem was something different. I could take pride in it and my father would admire me.

"I was fourteen years old. A new journeyman came to work in my father's watchmaking shop, a boy from Brody called Nahman, about seventeen. He was a good worker, but an even better singer. In Galicia he had been a chorister for many cantors. Here, too, in Old Constantine, he worked all week in the shop and on Saturdays assisted the cantor. Singing came naturally to him, whatever he was doing. He took watches apart to the melody of the Rosh ha-Shana hymn 'As a shepherd counts his flock' and he put them together to the tune of the Yom Kippur hymn 'Today strengthen us.' He sang all sorts of cantorial compositions and also Berl Broder's and Velvel Zbarzher's songs. So I hung around him. My father did not like this; he said I was neglecting my study of Gemara because of Nahman. But I think he meant something else. At fourteen, I was taller and more broad-shouldered than Nahman at seventeen. His black forelock, his pale face, the black hairs already showing on his upper lip, and above all, his lovely way of singing Yiddish songs, won the girls and young women of Old Constantine. My father was afraid I would become corrupted.

"But Nahman attracted me like a magnet. He knew all my secrets. I sang him all my songs. He rendered them with exceptional sweetness. That gave me the urge to write more poems and compose more melodies.

"Then I heard my songs sung also by a friend of Nahman's. Later I heard them sung by the girls and women sitting in front of their houses on a summer Saturday afternoon. That gave me particular pleasure. It was the secretiveness that was intriguing. I used to imagine how it would be when they knew whose songs they were singing.

"Then something happened. Nahman was not in the shop. I needed his knife. I looked into an open drawer and found a notebook. On its title page I read the printed letters:

Songs and Verses
Composed with original melodies
by Nahman Broder

I kept reading. I became quite upset. These were my songs, word for word, letter for letter, just as I had passed them on to him.

"The time had come for me to reveal myself. Nahman had to admit in public that the pretty songs were not his but those of his master's son."

"Did your teachers in the Rabbinical Seminary know that you wrote, besides Hebrew, also Yiddish poems?"

"Certainly. And how they knew! As soon as I came to the seminary, things began to get lively. Between classes the students used to sing my songs. Soon the teachers found out. Some of them, like Eliezer Hakohen Zweifel and Hayim Selig Slonimski, played at not hearing and not knowing. Some of them, like Eichenbaum and other ardent Hebraists, forgave me this because of my contrived verses.

"At that time, quite a few of the most adamant Hebraists, who had sworn eternal fealty to the Hebrew tongue, flirted in gay and frivolous moments with the 'jargon,' the 'servant girl.' Abraham Ber Gottlober, for instance, my former schoolteacher in Old Constantine and later at the Rabbinical Seminary, wrote a Yiddish parody of Schiller's 'The Song of the Bell.' He called it 'The Song of the Pudding.' At first it was all in jest, but serious things often come from such jests.

"Besides, at the Rabbinical Seminary I had a strong partisan in the inside management. Principal Hayim Selig Slonimski's wife, who liked to busy herself in communal affairs, was very fond of me. It was her idea, and she carried it out, that the seminary students produce *Serkele,* Dr. Solomon Ettinger's Yiddish comedy. I was her right hand. In making the sets and rehearsing the students I was the big wheel. And I also helped myself to the leading role."

Goldfaden looked at his watch. It was after twelve. Smiling, he said, "Enough, young man. You have cross-examined me enough. Now it is your turn. Your friend wrote me you crow like a Hebrew rooster. Show me something you've knocked off. I will read it after dinner. If I will like it, I will cross-examine you, about what happened to you on the way from the prayer house until today's visit to Abraham Goldfaden."

35 Joel Engel, Champion of Jewish Music
by Jacob Weinberg

JOEL (Julius) ENGEL was born in Berdyansk in 1868 and died in Tel Aviv in 1927. He was the first of a generation of Russian Jewish musicians who, on the advice of a Gentile Russian, turned to Jewish folk music to find their own identity as musicians and as human beings, as described in the following essay by one of his friends. The Jewish composers who sought out the Jewish folk and religious musical sources, taking a lead from Engel, included Josef Ahron and Ernst Bloch.

Jacob Weinberg, who was born in Odessa in 1879 and died in New York in 1956, was a composer and music teacher who, after living in Palestine a few years, settled in the United States in 1926.

THE name of Joel Engel is still unknown among many people interested in Jewish music; others know only his name; a few have heard some of his songs. But his significance as father of Jewish art-music and as a symbol of our musical renaissance by far exceeds all other aspects of his heritage.

He attended the gymnasium at Berdyansk and was graduated at seventeen. The nearest place of higher education was Kharkov University, in which he enrolled together with his brother Gregory (Hirsh). While a law student, Joel showed musical propensity and enrolled in the local music school. He completed his musical education at the Moscow Imperial Conservatory, under Sergey Taneyev, director of the conservatory and teacher of an impressive array of composers such as Scriabin, Miaskovsky, Medtner, Sabaneyev, Glière, and Alexandrov. Upon graduation in 1895, Engel became music critic of *Russkia Vedomosti*. Despite his youth and inexperience, he soon succeeded in winning broad recognition in the artistic and academic circles of St. Petersburg, Moscow, and other centers. Authorities like Rimsky-Korsakov, Taneyev, and Cui acclaimed "the outstanding articles of the young critic Engel."

I mention all this only to show that Engel was assimilated into Russian life. There seemed hardly any specific Jewish culture or Jewish national self-expression in his life. Yet, all of a sudden, as by a magic stroke, Engel's chief concern became Jewish music. For many years Engel's transfiguration remained an enigma to me, for I had lived in Moscow and knew that environment. Years later I met Engel in Tel Aviv, and once I finally asked him the crucial question: "How did it come about that you, a typically Russian intellectual, suddenly turned about and became an ardent exponent of Jewish music?"

Engel smiled. "You see," he said, "strange as it may seem, I owe this to the Russians, or rather to one Russian." And he told me of the remarkable episode which caused that decisive turn of his life. It happened on the eve of the Russian Easter in 1897, in Moscow, when the young Russian music critic Engel met his friend the sculptor Antokolsky, who was to introduce him to Vladimir Stassov, the champion of Russian national art. Stassov lived in St. Petersburg and usually visited Moscow on his Easter vacation. When Engel and Antokolsky arrived, they found Stassov in the company of the painter Repin, both absorbed in Stassov's beloved topic — nationalism in the arts. Stassov, a genuine Slav, was a great admirer and student of the Bible. He felt the inner profound relationship between the Bible and Western culture. Thereupon Yuli Dmitrevich Engel was introduced by Mark Matveyevich Antokolsky. Stassov immediately started a vigorous attack on both, as Jews who used Russian names instead of their own Hebrew ones. "Look here," he shouted at Antokolsky, "what is the idea of calling yourself Mark, a genuine Roman, Latin name? What have you in common with Mark? Certainly nothing. Are you ashamed of your own Mordecai? I simply cannot understand it. Where is your national pride in being a Jew? Can you not see the magnificent biblical splendor, the nobility of that 'Mor-de-cai'? Yes, yes, you should forget Mark and become proud of your ancient aristocratic forefather Mordecai. The great Mordecai!" So Stassov as if in a delirium of ecstasy.

Young Engel was overwhelmed, bewildered. The tall man with his long gray beard looked like a biblical prophet. His thundering voice sounded like that of an Isaiah, Elijah, or Jeremiah. His words struck Engel's imagination like lightening, and the Jew awoke in him. That was indeed the greatest moment in Engel's life. For that was the night when Jewish art-music was born.

Two months after meeting Stassov, Engel spent his whole summer in the western provinces of the Pale of Jewish Settlement, listening, and noting down, Jewish musical folklore. Upon his return to Moscow, he assorted the material, harmonized the choicest tunes, and prepared them for publication. Two more summers of similar activity followed. In 1900, he published at his own expense the first *Album of Ten Jewish Songs*. One of the first copies went to Stassov with a personal acknowledgment. Later that year, Engel organized a public lecture with illustrations on Jewish music, the first ever delivered on the subject. It took place at the Moscow Polytechnical Museum and was sponsored by the music section of the Imperial Society for Natural Science, Anthropology, and Ethnography. Its president, Professor Anuchin, was then chief editor of *Russkia Vedomosti;* the chairman of the society's music division, Yanchuk, was Engel's friend.

The lecture coldly recorded facts. They hardly meant much to assimilated Moscow Jewry. But to the nationally minded few, mostly young music students, the lecture was a revelation, indeed, a revolution. *Voskhod,* the Russian-Jewish periodical read by the whole Jewish intelligentsia, published a detailed report on Engel's lecture and awakened a response from Jews all over Russia. Jewish musical activities started simultaneously in several cities and culminated in the eventual founding of the Society for Jewish Folk Music in St. Petersburg. When the request to form "a society for Jewish music" was presented to Major General Drachevsky, governor of St. Petersburg, he refused to issue a license: "What? A society for Jewish music? What kind of business is this?" He was told about Engel's activities in collecting and publishing Jewish folksongs. To which the General replied: "You mean a society for the development of folksinging, do you? That is an altogether different proposition. Then it must be called Society for Jewish Folk Music." Thus the society attained official sanction for its existence. The first Jewish musical organization received its license November 30, 1908.

Despite his heavy schedule, Engel organized several tours of Jewish music lecture-concerts through Russia. In addition, his summer visits to the hasidic centers to collect Jewish music continued. He began also to compose music to Jewish-Russian poems. The first author he used was S. G. Frug. Thanks to Engel's educational activities and with the support of Rabbi Jacob Maseh, Jewish concerts became more frequent and their standards improved. As a student of the Conservatory and University, I often participated in these concerts and thus I met Joel Engel.

Five years after the Society for Jewish Folk Music was founded in St. Petersburg, its Moscow branch began to function, with Engel as its permanent president. Engel's prestige in Russian circles kept rising. Even during the Communist regime, after *Russkia Vedomosti* was suspended, Engel was appointed principal of a school in Malachovka, a Moscow suburb. There he wrote his famous children's songs in Yiddish and later in Hebrew. During this time he composed the music for the Habima's production of Ansky's *Dybbuk.*

As time went on, it became evident that Engel's national aspirations were throttled under the Bolshevik regime. In January, 1922 he left Russia and came to Berlin. After two years in postwar Germany, with its billion-mark inflation, he finally managed to come to Palestine on December 4, 1925, as instructor of music theory at a conservatory in Tel Aviv.

Though he was exhausted by ten years of privation and frustration, Engel plunged into work of composing, teaching, conducting, lecturing, writing articles in newspapers and magazines. His leadership of the "Ohel" chorus attracted crowds of young men and women. His concerts were very successful. The climax of his achievements, however, was creation of new music. Recognition came quickly. After a few months Engel's name was on the lips of every music-loving Palestinian. Song after song appeared and through the "Ohel" chorus penetrated into *kvutsot, moshavot,* and towns, being acclaimed as genuine music of the country.

Despite his love of Jewish music, Engel never overestimated Jewish composers. A man of highest musical standard and supreme taste, he knew that the Jews did not yet have their Bach or Mozart. He used to say: "Jewish art-music was born only yesterday. Let us give it a chance to grow. Let us nurse the baby." Once, at a writers' convention in Tel Aviv, Menachem Ussishkin said, "I see no need to give special attention to Jewish folksongs. Let us listen rather to the great composers of the world." Thereupon Engel jumped up from his seat and retorted: "True, there is not yet a Jewish Beethoven; however, *our* songs are still dear to us, just because they are our own. Take as illustration yourself, Ussishkin; you are not yet a Gladstone or Bismarck. But to us Jews, you are more precious than all of them, just because you are our own Ussishkin! So, let us love our own songs. They will prepare the ground for a future Jewish musical genius like Beethoven or Bach."

In spite of his ill health, his overwhelming productivity did not cease. In December, 1926, just two years after his arrival, he caught cold at a concert; the illness turned worse. In February, 1927, I visited him. He seemed to feel better, saying that the cold was just a trifle, soon his new "Peretz Suite" would be played. But his heart failed, and on February 11, 1927, he passed away.

36 What Is a Jewish Artist?
by Marc Chagall

MARC CHAGALL was born in Liozno, province of Vitebsk, in 1887 and was brought up in the city of Vitebsk. He now makes his home in France. He is perhaps unique among artists in his openhearted acceptance of his Jewish roots and of the Jewish milieu of his childhood and youth.

The following autobiographical essay appeared in a book commemorating Vitebsk.

AND still you insist that I write and speak about Jewish art. I will, for the last time.

What sort of thing is it? Only yesterday Jewish artistic circles fought for this so-called Jewish art. Out of the tumult and the heat emerged a group of Jewish artists and among them also Marc Chagall. This misfortune occurred when I was still in Vitebsk. Just returned from Paris, I smiled in my heart.

Then I was busy with something else. On one hand, the new world, Jews, my hometown's narrow streets, hunchbacked herring residents, green Jews, uncles, aunts with their questions, "You have, thank God, grown up."

And I kept painting them. . . .

On the other hand, I was a hundred years younger then and I loved them, just loved them. . . .

This engrossed me more, this captivated me more than the idea that I was anointed a Jewish artist.

Once, still in Paris, in my room on La Ruche, where I worked, across the partition I heard Jewish emigrant voices quarreling: "What do you think, was Antokolsky not a Jewish artist, after all, nor Israels, nor Liebermann?"

When the lamp burned so dark and lit up my painting, standing upside down (that's how I work — laugh!), and finally when at dawn the Parisian sky began to grow light, I gayly scoffed at the idle thoughts of my neighbors about the fate of Jewish art: "So be it, you talk — and I will work."

Representatives from all countries and peoples — to you my appeal. Confess: when Lenin sits in the Kremlin, there is not a stick of wood, the stove smokes, your wife is not well, do you have national art now?

You, wise B., and you others who preach international art, the best Frenchmen, and (if they are still living) you will answer me: "Chagall, you are right."

Jews, if they have a feeling for it (I happen to), may weep at the passing of the decorators of the wooden shtetl synagogues (why am I not in the grave with you?) and of the carvers of the wooden synagogue clackers (saw them in Ansky's collection, was amazed). But what really is the difference between my crippled great-grandfather Segal, who decorated the Mohilev synagogue, and me, who painted murals in the Jewish theater (a good theater) in Moscow?

Besides, I am sure that if I let my beard grow, you would see his exact likeness. . . .

By the way, my father.

Believe me, I put in no small effort. And we both expended no less love (and what love). The difference was only that he took orders also for signs and I studied in Paris, about which he also knew something.

And yet, both I and he and others as well (there are such), taken together, are still not Jewish art.

And why not tell the truth? Where should I get it from? God forbid, if it should have to come from an order! Because Efros writes an article or M. will give me an academic ration!

There is Japanese art, Egyptian, Persian, Greek, but from the Renaissance on, national arts began to decline. The distinctive traits disappear. Artists — individuals arise, subjects of one or another country, born here or there (may you be blessed, my Vitebsk) and a good identity card or even a Jewish passport expert is needed so that all artists can be precisely and fully nationalized.

Were I not a Jew (with the content that I put in the word), I would not be an artist at all, or I would be someone else altogether.

There is nothing new in that.

As for myself, I know quite well what this small people can accomplish.

Unfortunately, I am modest and cannot tell what it can accomplish.

Something to conjure with, what this small people has done!

When it wished, it brought forth Christ and Christianity. When it wanted, it produced Marx and socialism.

Can it be then that it would not show the world some sort of art?

Kill me, if not.

VIII

Marginals

37   Daniel Chwolson: A Christian Jew
by David Günzburg

DANIEL CHWOLSON, Orientalist, was born in Vilna in 1819 and died in St. Petersburg in 1910. He is the Jewish careerist par excellence: he became an apostate for a university professorship in Tsarist Russia. Everyone who knows his name knows the Chwolson folklore: When asked if he had converted to Christianity out of conviction, he was supposed to have said, "Yes, I was convinced it was better to be a professor in St. Petersburg than a melamed in Eyshishok [Eiszyszki]." In other stories that coursed the Pale of Settlement it was said he had become a Christian only so he could render effective aid to his Jewish coreligionists.

Chwolson had received a traditional rabbinical education. At eighteen, he learned the Latin alphabet from Polish store signs. Then, from dictionaries, he learned German, Russian, French. In search of secular education, he went on foot to Riga, where Max Lilienthal gave him a letter of introduction to Abraham Geiger in Breslau. Geiger helped him in his studies during the four years it took him to qualify for the university. In the introduction to his first published work, originally his dissertation, *Die Ssabier und der Ssabismus* (1856), Chwolson wrote:

"Finally my heart compels me to express my gratitude to a man who actually has no relation to this book, yet he has other claims on my grati-

tude — the widely known Dr. Geiger of Breslau. Poor in all respects, I arrived many years ago in Germany, in a land whose language I scarcely understood, where I knew no one and no one knew me. I might have died there physically and mentally. This fine man received me as a father would, worried about my spiritual and material state. To him I am especially thankful that I have reached that level of scholarship at which I now stand."

In 1851 Chwolson returned to St. Petersburg. In 1854 A. S. Norov, having become Minister of Public Education, had obtained Imperial permission to establish a department of Oriental studies at the University of St. Petersburg. It is said that Chwolson helped Norov draft the plan for the departmental divisions and that Norov offered Chwolson the chair for Hebrew and Syriac, if he would convert. In 1855, Chwolson accepted the Greek Orthodox faith and the University professorship.

Nevertheless, he served the Jews all his life, as recounted in the following memoir by Baron David Günzburg, a student and lifelong friend. His children, however, no longer had contact with Jews, living nearly always in the company of sons of converts, in a shadowy land on the margins of both Gentile and Jewish society. Their children disappeared completely from Jewish view.

David Günzburg, whose daughter's recollections
of him appear on pp. 248–256, edited a *Fest-
schrift* in honor of Chwolson on his eightieth
birthday, *Recueil des travaux rédigés en mémoire
du Jubilé scientifique de M. Daniel Chwolson*
(Berlin, 1899). The following selection was
translated from an appreciation written on the
same occasion.

WHOEVER knows Professor Daniel Abramovich Chwolson loves him;
whoever has heard of him respects him. His name is associated with scholarship. From the cradle on, that was his purpose. Scholarship filled his life,
gave it meaning, and raised him to the level of a most distinguished teacher
and a discoverer of new literary paths. Scholarship did still more for him,
its admirer: it made him the champion of light and truth. In the name of
scholarship, he fought against prejudice and superstition and emerged the
victor. With his learning, he liberated the whole people from the chains
with which their oppressors wanted to bind them forever until they per-
ished. Himself free and fortunate, he did not, while free, forget, like Pha-
roah's cupbearer, those whom he left behind in prison cells. He remembered always that a blood covenant existed between him and the downtrod-
den people from whom he came. He was always proud that he came from
the tribe of Judah, which gave the world David the royal poet and Solomon
the sage. All his life he was engaged in studying the foundations of Jewish
love for man and reverence for God. He investigated and illuminated the
development and ramification of these profound ideas. He acquired mastery
of many languages to learn the truths preached throughout the globe.
Through his linguistic attainments, he gained knowledge about the human
soul. From his study of books, he evolved a world outlook of boundless
religious tolerance, a passion for the philosophy of history, and an impartial-
ity in the history of philosophy.

Scholarship taught him sympathy for people, to be satisfied with little,
to respect the individuality and opinions of others. He enjoyed the good
things of life, but did not pursue them. He was full of kindness and consid-
erateness, but he never humbled himself.

At eighty he is hale, strong, and energetic. He keeps abreast of the
scholarship of others and undertakes his own.

It is instructive to consider the fate of this excellent man, to search out
his beginnings, to learn how he achieved his tranquillity and his fame, what
he gave his contemporaries, and what he has prepared for posterity, though

he has not yet spoken his last word and the world will still enjoy the fruit of his thought and scholarship.

Because of his position, Professor Chwolson was able to disseminate through Russia a true conception of Jewish learning and of Jewish ideals.

He returned to Russia at the time of the famous Saratov trial. Shaken to the depths of his soul by the despicable lying accusation that Jews used Christian blood, he spoke out against that dark superstition with all the force of his intelligence. He came forward as an expert and mercilessly fought the false blood accusation. With memorandum upon memorandum, refutation upon refutation, he let nothing remain undisclosed that could merit the attention of the Imperial Investigation Commission. Yet by a strange course of events, when the commission was to issue its opinion, it submitted the fabricated evidence, but Chwolson's brilliant presentations were not attached. Now, before me lies his hitherto unpublished summary in which with scientific and logical proofs he demolished the hypothesis that a sect among Jews permitted the use of blood.

He solemnly declared: "With my hand on the heads of all who are dear to me in this world, I swear before the Almighty Creator of heaven and earth that this is a lie, a lie, a lie! Jews never used Christian blood for religious or any other purposes, so may God help me, my dear wife, and my only child. Amen, amen, amen." In 1861 his famous book appeared, in which he demolished the antisemitic constructions of the Eisenmengers, Prikulskys, and all the rest of them.

Seeing how this superstition had penetrated the flesh and blood of the Polish population, he took advantage of the fact that he taught Hebrew from 1858 to 1884 in the Roman Catholic Theological Seminary. Each year he delivered a lecture showing the fraud of this accusation which the heathens had first directed against the early Christians and which, after these heathens themselves became Christians, they then applied to the Jews. Every time someone raised a hostile voice against the hounded people — whether his name was Kostomarov, Liutostansky, or Count Gagarin — the answer was ready and the arrow found its target.

Following the blood-ritual case in Kutais, his richly documented study on the blood libel was issued in an edition of ten thousand copies. Later, that excellent work "Several Medieval Accusations Against Jews" (1880) was published in a revised and doubly enlarged form. Not content only with the work of his pen, Chwolson in a lengthy audience in the Caucasus with the Tsar's brother and deputy, Grand Duke Mikhail Niko-layevich, undertook to demolish the Grand Duke's suspicions about ritual murder.

Rabbis blessed Daniel Abramovich's name. In 1881, after attending an archeologists' conference in Tiflis, he passed Kutais. He learned from the judges that their belief in the innocence of the accused derived from his ardent defense of the Jewish people. He was conducted into the synagogue by the head of the congregation, attended by a Jewish escort all the way. The synagogue was brightly lit up. The Holy Ark was opened and the congregation blessed him. The venerable rabbi, a magnificent figure with biblical bearing, delivered an emotional sermon in Hebrew. Another rabbi spoke in Georgian, and the congregation's president translated and then gave Chwolson an address of thanks.*

Now we celebrate his entering upon the ninth decade of his life with fresh strength in body and spirit. It was touching today to hear from the mouth of this graybearded scholar a talk on the importance of issuing without delay a German edition of his attack against the obscurantist medieval accusations against the Jews, which he himself is prepared to revise in the interests of the Austrian Jews.

The Society for the Promotion of Culture among Jews, which has been so close to his heart, which so often exploited his pen and his counsel, is proud to have him among its honorary members and with affection its members commemorate each step in the brilliant path of his life.

38   I Confess to Dostoevsky
by Abraham Uri Kovner

ABRAHAM URI KOVNER was born in Vilna in 1842 and died in Lomza in 1909. Much of his early life he recounted in the following letter to Dostoevsky. He began his literary career as a maskil and Hebraist who attacked both the haskala and Hebrew rhetoric for their pretensions and impracticality. A positivist, he was known in Jewish literary circles in the late 1860's as the "Jewish nihilist."

He then turned to Russian journalism, becoming fairly well known. After the bank defalcation which he describes to Dostoevsky, he was sentenced to four years of hard labor and then banished to Tomsk, Siberia, where he lived many years, employed as a minor government official. In 1893, at fifty-one, he married a twenty-three-year-old Gentile Russian girl who had fallen deeply in love with him.

* Chwolson's concern was stirred not only by the medieval accusations. When the pogroms plunged the Jews into misfortune, he wrote moving letters on their behalf to Count Tolstoy, newly appointed Minister of the Interior.

Two weeks before their marriage he was baptized. The conversion had no religious meaning or careerist purpose; it was only to enable him to marry the girl, who was his only comfort the rest of his life. After a while he returned to European Russia and began writing again, under a pseudonym. Once more, in public and private correspondence, he undertook to defend the Jews against antisemitism, particularly in a long-lasting correspondence with V. Rozanov, correspondent for *Novoe Vremya,* the most explicitly antisemitic newspaper, representing official Tsarist policy.

Kovner's tragic life history, which encompassed the great culture con-flicts of the emancipated Jew of his time, including conversion, suggests that his loyalties to the Jews as a community could not easily be destroyed or denied, though he denied Judaism and, in fact, all religion.

In the issue of March 1877 of his *Diary of a Writer,* Dostoevsky replied to Kovner's letter: "I shall quote certain passages from a long, and in many respects, beautiful letter, addressed to me by a highly educated Jew, which aroused in me great interest." But apart from the personal compliment, Dostoevsky's reply was nothing more than an elaboration of his anti-Jewish views.

January 26, 1877

Most honored Fyodor Mikhailovich:

A strange idea occurred to me: to write you this letter. Though you get letters from all corners of Russia, many doubtless quite stupid and strange, yet you could never have expected to receive a letter from me.

Who, then, am I?

I am first of all a Jew and you are not very well disposed toward Jews (about this I will speak later). Secondly, I am that sort of journalist you despise: I have insulted you (that is, your literary works) vehemently, in great fury and malice. If I make no mistake, at the time you were editing *Grazhdanin* ("Citizen"), you commented very shrewdly about me, without mentioning my pen name, that I tried in every way to involve you in a personal argument, challenging you to respond. But you passed over my attacks in silence, wounding my self-pride. Thirdly, and finally, I am a criminal and I am writing these lines from prison.

Actually, this last-mentioned circumstance must rather appear in your eyes an excuse for my turning to you, whom everyone — that is, the trifling number of intellectuals — in Russia knows as the author of *Memoirs from the House of the Dead.* But no! I am not one of those criminals with whom you can sympathize, for I was sued in court and convicted of fraud and swindle. Since you attentively follow more or less striking events in public life and, especially, legal proceedings, you must have guessed by now, I am sure, that I am that Kovner who wrote the articles on "literary and social curiosities" in *Golos,* later worked in the St. Petersburg Loan and Discount Bank, and who on April 28, 1875, by forging a check, robbed the Commercial Bank of Moscow of 168,000 rubles, hid out in Kiev with all the money, then was delivered to Moscow for investigation and sentenced to a heavy four-year jail sentence.

What, then, is the real purpose of my writing?

A deep psychologist, you will believe me that my purpose is not to give an accounting of myself and that it is quite likely I have no purpose at all. What animated me to write you was your *Diary of a Writer,* which I have been reading with the greatest absorption and whose every installment impels me simultaneously to praise and criticize, to reject what appears paradoxical and yet to admire your brilliant analysis.

Yet before I turn to what seems to me your strange and incomprehensible social and philosophic conceptions, I think it necessary to sketch for you in brief my moral physiognomy, my *profession de foi,* and some details of my life.

No one, I think, knows better than you that a man can be honest his whole life long and under the pressure of circumstances commit a great crime, but thereafter again remain forever a perfectly honest human being. Can you take my word for it that I am indeed such a person?

I am a man without manners (this was the title of a novel I wrote which a Ministerial Committee banned, under the law of June 7, 1872, in that very same year). I arrived in the world into a sizable poor Jewish family in Vilna, whose members cursed each other over a piece of bread. I received a thorough Talmudic education and, according to Jewish custom, was supported, until I was seventeen, at the expense of strangers. At seventeen, I was married off to a girl much older than I. At eighteen, I fled from my wife to Kiev, where I started to study Russian grammar, foreign languages, and general subjects, everything starting from *A.* I had the firmest intention to enroll in the university. That was at the beginning of the sixties, when Russian literature and youth were celebrating the honeymoon of progress. With my abilities, I soon learned Russian and, like so many others, let myself to be ensnared by Dobroliubov, Chernyshevsky, *Sovremennik* ("Contemporary"), by Buckle, Mill, Moleschott, and others of the then reigning authorities. I took a strong dislike to classicism and therefore did not go to the university. Because I knew Hebrew and Talmudic literature thoroughly, I conceived the notion to become the reformer of my unfortunate people. I wrote several books, in which I demonstrated, with European scholarship, the absurdity of Jewish superstitions, but the Jews burned my books and cursed me. Thereafter, I flung myself into the arms of

Russian literature. I went to Odessa and lived only from writing for the local press and as correspondent for the St. Petersburg papers. In 1871 I moved to St. Petersburg. There I became a contributor to *Delo, Yevreyskaya Biblyoteka, Vsemirny Trud, Peterburgskia Vedomotsi;* later I became a member of the staff of *Golos.* After a falling out with the editor, I decided to give up writing, to allow my brains to rest and to take on some mechanical work. I got a job at the Loan and Discount Bank. This new milieu, which ran counter to my upbringing, my habits, my convictions, corrupted me. After two years of experience in bank operations, I was convinced that all banks were based on deceit and swindle. I saw how people made millions; temptation came upon me and I decided to steal a sum that was three percent of the annual net profit of the stockholders in the richest bank of Russia. That three percent amounted to 168,000 rubles.

That was the first and last blemish on my conscience, and it destroyed me. Love for an honest girl of a decent family played the main role in this crime which I committed. By nature blessed with spirit, quite healthy, but ugly, I had never known the love of a woman. In Petersburg I won the affection of a pure and splendid girl. It was a love freely given, deep and ardent. She loved me, naturally, not for my appearance, but for some spiritual qualities, for some little understanding and kindness of heart, for my readiness to do good. She was very poor, had only a mother (her father had long since died) and three sisters. I wanted to marry her, but I had no sure livelihood, for I was employed in the bank without a contract and the director could let me go at any moment. Besides, I had debts, not large, but they gave me no peace (in the matter of paying off debts, I am the most unimaginable stickler).

Was it not natural, with all that, that I laid hands on the three percent? With that three percent I could take care of my infirm parents, my large beggar-poor family, my small children by my first wife, my beloved and loving girl, her family, and many more "insulted and injured," without inflicting any significant damage on anyone. These are the true motives of my crime.

I do not want to justify myself, but I tell you that after I had committed the crime I did not feel the least pangs of conscience, nor do I now. Doubtless my conduct is contrary to social and literary morality, but I do not see it at all as the shocking crime about which almost all the Russian press foamed, besmirching me as some deformity of humankind.

But you know by now that I did not enjoy the fruits of my crime. I was caught right away and arrested with my wife (we were married in prison a second time), then brought before the court; I was convicted, but she was acquitted. But the poor girl (you understand that being married under such circumstances my wife still remained a girl) could not endure my arrest, my ignominy, the separation from me for many years, and died soon after her acquittal. This last blow was the most terrible of all for me and I nearly lost my mind over it. I remained alone, abandoned in prison, spat upon, covered with disgrace, without any livelihood. I do not know if any other person in the world has endured such soul's torture — that is why I have set everything down in detail in my diary, which may perhaps sometimes see the light of day. But that is not the point. I am convinced that you can understand my moral character from this senseless incoherent sketch.

As for my *profession de foi*, I share all the ideas you expressed in your *Diary* about suicide and the conclusions that flow therefrom. I will therefore not expand further on them here. But naturally I cannot share your opinions on patriotism, nationality in general, the Russian national spirit in particular, the Slavs, and even on Christianity, about which I will not debate with you either. But there is one subject I would like to touch on, that I can in no wise explain to myself. That is your hatred of the "kike," which shows itself in practically every installment of your *Diary*.

I would like to know why you are against the Jews and not against exploiters in general. I hate the deficiencies of my people no less than you and I have suffered enough under them, yet I would never concede that unscrupulous exploitation is in their blood.

Can you really not rise to accept the fundamental law of any social life, according to which all citizens without exception must enjoy all the rights and privileges so long as they accept the required responsibilities for the existence of a state, and that for violators of the law, harmful members of society, one and the same measure of punishment must be applied equally to all? Why should all the Jews be restricted in their rights and why should special legislation be enacted against them? How is exploitation by foreigners (Jews are, after all, Russian subjects), by Germans, Englishmen, Greeks, with whom Russia is overfilled, better than exploitation by Jews? How are the Russian Orthodox kulaks, bloodsuckers and vampires, how are these people, with whom all Russia swarms, better than the Jews, who operate only in a limited area? Why is one better than the other? In what respect is Gubonin better than Poliakov? Why is Ovsyanikov better than Malkiel? Why is Szamanski better than Günzburg? I can ask you a thousand such questions.

Yet when you speak of the Jews, you include in this term the whole terribly wretched race of three million Jews in Russia, of whom at least 2,900,000 lead a desperate struggle for an unfortunate existence, and who are more moral than other nationalities, and also than the Russian people, whom you idolize. You include in this term also that considerable number of Jews who enjoyed the benefits of higher education and who have contributed in all areas of civic life: I mention here only Portugalov, Kaufman,* Schapiro,** Orshansky, Goldstein (who died a hero's death in Serbia for the Slavic idea), Wywodzev, and hundreds of others, who worked for the good of society and of mankind. Your hatred for the Jews extends even to Disraeli, who probably does not know that his ancestors were Spanish Jews and who does not, of course, conduct Conservative Party politics in England from the Jewish point of view. (By the way, you mention in one installment of your *Diary* that Disraeli "begged" the title from the Queen, though it is generally known that the Queen offered him the title in 1869, but he refused it because he wanted to remain in the House of Commons.)

No, unfortunately you know neither the Jewish people nor its way of life, neither its spirit nor, finally, its forty centuries of history. I say unfortunately, because you, an honest, absolutely sincere man, remain unaware of the enormous harm you are inflicting upon this unfortunate people. But the influential Jews who receive government ministers and members of the city council in their salons naturally fear neither the press nor the powerless wrath of the exploited. But enough of this.

Perhaps you may wish to discuss some of the subjects touched on in this letter in your *Diary*. You may do so, naturally, without mentioning my name.

With the greatest respect;

U. KOVNER

---

* Probably refers to Illarion Ignatevich Kaufman (1848–1916), Russian political economist, in government service.
** Probably Heinrich Schapiro (1853–1901), Russian physician, military surgeon during the Russo-Turkish War.

39 Jan Bloch: The Loyal Convert
by Nahum Sokolow

JAN BLOCH was born in Radom in 1836 and died in Warsaw in 1901. One of the most extraordinary men of his time, financier, railway contractor, economist, scholar, pacifist, and visionary, he was baptized as a young man. Yet in his testament he wrote: "I was my whole life a Jew and I die as a Jew." His adult life he lived as a Christian, but he was motivated and largely directed by Jewish interests and concerns for the Jewish community. One of his great research investigations was an incompleted five-volume Russian study of the economic and social situation in the Western, Great Russian, and By-Vistula provinces, in which he compared conditions in the provinces where Jews lived with those from which they were barred. In these volumes he produced a tremendous mass of statistical data to prove the baselessness of the Tsarist government's antisemitic arguments against the Jews. (The completed volumes were printed and ready for publication in 1891, 1894, or 1896, according to various sources, when a fire in the printing plant destroyed all but twenty-five copies at a bindery.) Bloch had had access to data collected by an official Tsarist commission, but aware of the lack of objectivity in these sources and the methods used, he set up the equivalent of a private statistical bureau to compile and analyze data about the social and economic life of the Jews in the Polish provinces. His staff included Samuel Adalberg, the Polish folklorist, Nahum Sokolow, and Isaac Leib Peretz. Most of the original materials were subsequently lost: Bloch, who had, in the meantime, become a friend of Theodor Herzl, was said to have given the accumulated mass of raw data to Herzl, who was to have them analyzed and published in summary form, but no more was heard of it. Apparently, the only tangible product of this fantastic private census of the Polish Jews was Peretz's *Rayze-bilder* ("Travel Pictures").

Bloch's six-volume work, *Budushchaya Voyna* ("The Future War"), appeared in 1898 and is said to have led to the convening of the First International Peace Conference at The Hague in 1899.

All his life he supported Jewish institutions, and in a letter he once critized wealthy Warsaw Jews for contributing to Jewish philanthropies only as little as "their weak Jewish hearts permit them." His Jewish heart was great, yet his son and four daughters were completely estranged from Jews and the Jewish community.

Nahum Sokolow, writer and communal leader, was born in Wyszogrod, province of Plock, in 1859 and died in London in 1936. He had a traditional Jewish education. His father was reluctant to send him to the gymnasium, but because of the boy's exceptional talents he allowed him to study privately several hours a day with several gymnasium instructors. That concluded Sokolow's formal education, yet he was one of the most learned and cultivated men of his time, with superb facility in many languages.

His literary talents blossomed early. He came to Warsaw in 1880 and shortly thereafter became a contributor to Hayim Selig Slonimski's *Ha-Tsefira*. In 1884 he became its assistant editor, a year later associate editor, and then, because of Slonimski's advanced age, its managing editor when the paper became a daily in 1886. He was a most prolific writer, editor, and anthologist. Besides his work in Hebrew, he was contributor, and later editor also, of the Polish weekly *Izraelita*. As a Hebrew author and editor, especially in *Ha-Tsefira*, he advocated modernism, Hebraism, and Jewish nationalism to his readers. In *Izraelita*, which was read by assimilated and assimilationist Polish Jews, Sokolow concentrated more on Judaism and less on nationalism. Chaim Weizmann wrote of him: "This duality in his attitude was not repellent, for it was part of his nature to seek to harmonize extremes."

He became a Herzlian Zionist after the first Zionist Congress and soon thereafter became general secretary of the Zionist Organization, making his residence in Cologne. When World War I broke out, he moved to London, working with Weizmann on Zionist political affairs.

But Sokolow as man and literary analyst of men was more fascinating and enduring than as Zionist or even communal leader. Himself a radiant and radiating personality — the only man to compete with Peretz in all Warsaw — he was interested in other men and their origins, and particularly in men of marginality or duality, cosmopolites, whose Jewish roots or Jewish loyalties were tenuous, fragile, or even broken, but which Sokolow detected and which he tried to heal and restore, as in the following eulogy written on Bloch's death.

The apostle of peace, whom the rude hand of death had just led over the threshold of this earthly existence, Johann Gottlieb de Bloch, was something more than a great financier and capitalist. A phase of Jewish history sinks with him into the grave, a personality vanishes that was no less epoch-making than all those mighty figures that open the new sluice gates of development and force the stream of history into a new direction. One could read, as on a weather glass, from the phases of the varying fortune that Jan Bloch experienced in half a century, the changes which the upper classes of assimilated Jews have undergone in this memorable century. An ambitious Jew in the fifties, an international pioneer of peace at the end of his career, this testifies not only to the changes which this genial personality passed through in the long period from youth to old age, but, apart from personal circumstances, to the diversion of Jewish talents, of Jewish ability and capacity, through conversion to another faith, into strange channels of intellectual life. The transformation from a Jewish self-taught and self-made man to one of cosmopolitan capacity, as in the case of the practical, highly talented, and extraordinarily businesslike Bloch, does not occur to every individual who has emerged from the ghetto.

Adaptability, which plays an important part in the whole process of assimilation, was the chief characteristic of the departed, who, despite the profundity of a hard-won and self-acquired culture, was eminently a practical man. His first deeds and thoughts belonged to the practical commercial world and not to the theoretical or the ideal. As a railway contractor, he built railways; as a capitalist and merchant, he founded and conducted a large and flourishing business; and as a member of the Consulting Committee of the Russian Ministry of Finance, he introduced many reforms that have become epoch-making for the industry of the country. As a citizen of Poland, he interested himself in the practical questions of economic life rather than in the war of theories and shibboleths which the contending parties waged. Nay, in genuine Jewish fashion, loving learning and striving after knowledge, just as the *gevirim* of the old stock who, having become rich, took upon themselves the furtherance of study, and in noble dilettantism tried their hand at literary work, Bloch founded at the corner of Krolewska and Marszalkowska Streets, Warsaw, his statistical-scientific bureau, where he kept himself apart from the eddies and counter-eddies of Polish party politics and confined himself to the undisturbed labors of his study. He gathered eminent Polish writers and publicists around him, and the influence that he exercised on economic conditions was none the less important on that account.

In the banks and exchanges of Warsaw and St. Petersburg, Bloch may be regarded as having been one of the leading spirits. His skillful hand always knew how to diminish the clashing of interests of the capitalists and landowners. He remained "the clever Jew," and the more he was known the more he was appreciated.

A genuine Jewish type — an intellectual, mild, thoroughly good face, a high *lamdn* forehead, clever piercing eyes, in his youth somewhat chic, but in his "old days" the features marked, and the inner natural characteristics once more brought out; speech, style, thought, taste, Jewish — humanly Jewish — intellectual, quiet, deliberate, tactful, but — always Jewish. An old, clever, good Jew. One was almost tempted to call him "Uncle."

And his biography? The old story "that is ever new." A Jewish boy born sixty-seven years ago in Radom. His father was a Jew of Lomza, a dyer by trade. He leaned slightly towards reform, wrote Hebrew well, wore the *kaftn* somewhat shorter than his contemporaries; in short, he was intellectually inclined. He eked out an existence for himself and his family by his work, dyeing prayer shawls, and worked for the Jewish Aged Home when he moved to Warsaw fifty years ago. The young Jan — of course, in those days he was not called Jan — visited, in his earliest childhood days, the heder. He is said even then to have astonished the rabbi by his capabilities. Under the eyes of his father, he was instructed outside the heder in the vernacular, arithmetic, geography, etc. That Bloch passed through a gymnasium, as stated in the obituary notices in the Polish papers, is not correct. At a very young age he entered the office of a Jewish solicitor, Rosenblum, as assistant clerk, where he worked for some years. Later, he obtained a situation in the Teplitz banking house, and then went to St. Petersburg, where under the patronage of General Tysenhaus (probably in the meantime, owing to his sojourn in the capital, having gone over to Calvinism), he developed a capacity for commerce and finance which in the course of years brought him fortune and influence. Having returned to Warsaw and entered the ranks of railway contractors with Kronenberg — whose sister he married — and having swung his way up to the highest rung of the ladder of financial success and political honor, Bloch remained with the remarkable characteristics of a Jewish autodidact and was left a Jewish "poet and merchant," half financial genius, half dreamer, Polish citizen, Russian statesman, European scholar, perhaps more than a scholar; on the whole, a marvelous product of the Diaspora.

But Bloch was frustrated in the desire to emerge from his own nation, or, in spite of the formal separation, in accomplishing something great for it. And this is the tragic side of this highly sympathetic and remarkable figure. The former son of a dyer, the *ilui* hailing from Lomza, Radom, and Warsaw had to arduously fit himself for the surroundings to which he desired to attain. For some time he was forced to estrange himself from the people that lived in his blood and in his mind. Others, even those formally baptized, without individuality, without personality and characteristics, vanished in the chaos. He could not be lost. It was an open secret that J. G. Bloch was bound up, if not in faith, at any rate in sympathy, with the Jewish people. The upheavals in the eighties brought him to the forefront of the vindicators of the Jews.

At that stage he completed his great and incomparable statistical work, the economical statistical apologia of the Russian Jews. The sphere of his activity centered then in St. Petersburg, where he mixed intimately with the leaders of the Jewish community. Bloch not only accomplished a great literary work, but as a pliant and intellectual statesman he brought the whole weight of his mighty influence to bear in order to produce a change in current opinion. Many of us have seen him at work with the ever-to-be-remembered Hebraist and popular scientific writer, Hirsh Rabinowitz.

He had come to the conviction that the solution of the Jewish question was to be sought elsewhere. In the next phase of his efforts, he displayed a lively interest in the undertakings of Baron de Hirsch. He was desirous of accomplishing something in this direction, too; we remember that he was thinking of sending his agent to the Argentine. But, on the one hand, he was prevented by his surroundings from working openly, and on the other, the necessary ideal was lacking. Then, after the death of Baron de Hirsch, we see him anxious to further the work of the Jewish Colonization Association in the earliest stages of its existence. He was then in Paris; that was in 1897. He took part in a private meeting. His Jewish sympathies impressed those Jews present. He afterward came to a meeting here in Warsaw. There was something tragic in his eagerness that was never productive of any great result.

Then began his peace work. He did more for this cause than his contemporaries imagine. Who knows whether he did not really seek the solution of the Jewish question and did not strive for international peace as a condition of the realization of Jewish ideals? At all events, this shows a great and untiring spirit. New studies, conducted with the ardor of a Benedictine friar, an heroic desire to open up a sphere of knowledge that for a layman was *terra incognita,* an enthusiasm, an energy, a disinterestedness that had never been seen in anyone before, combine to convey the impression as if an old Jewish national idea, a prophetical inspiration had been once more revived in the heart of a son of our race.

In his very last years, J. G. Bloch's interest was enlisted on behalf of the Zionist idea. From being skeptical and hypercritical, his sympathies were at last given a powerful impetus. Unhappily too late! Death surprised him in the middle of the work he had begun. The weaknesses of assimilation will not be attributed to the son of the Lomza dyer in his grave. Thus are we bereft of strength. So, without leaving a trace behind, vanishes what the potential energy of the Jewish race accumulated through a thousand years, what Jewish industry has built up, so does it all vanish through want of a national foundation. In spite of his assimilation, he was the best of half Jews: a penetrating Jewish mind, a warm Jewish heart, a practical genius, and a poet. Thus does a generation die, thus our strength departs, and thus do the blossoms fade! And so they will continue to fade as long as we have not a foot of earth we can call our own beneath our feet, nor a stretch of heaven above our heads. These blossoms are still beautiful and poetical: the poetry of the redemption.

40 Henri Bergson's Old-Warsaw Lineage
by Nahum Sokolow

It has been generally known that Henri Bergson, who was born in Paris in 1859 and died there in 1941, was "of Jewish origin." In the following memoir, Nahum Sokolow traces that origin in a brilliant portrait of the family's lineage. But if Sokolow knew the origins of that great Jewish family, he did not know its tragic terminus. The newspaper rumors Sokolow referred to in 1918 had, even then, some truth to them. Jacques Chevalier, Bergson's biographer, quotes French Catholic philosopher Joseph Lotte: "Under the twofold influence of Bergson's psychology and Péguy's ethical critique, the framework of Taine's *scientisme*, Renan's intellectualism, Kant's moral-

ism was shattered to bits as far as we were concerned. It provided an escape from determinism, a soaring upwards toward the rediscovery of God."

Not a Catholic when he died, but a Christian *in voto*, in a last will and testament dated February 8, 1937, Bergson wrote:

My reflections have led me closer and closer to Catholicism, in which I see the complete fulfillment of Judaism. I should have become a convert, had I not seen in preparation for years . . . the formidable wave of antisemitism which is to sweep over the world. I wanted to remain among those who tomorrow will be persecuted. But I hope that a Catholic priest will be good enough to come — if the Cardinal Archbishop of Paris authorizes it — to pray at my funeral. Should this authorization not be granted, it will be necessary to approach a rabbi, but without conceal-ing from him, nor from anyone, my moral adherence to Catholicism, as well as my express and first desire to have the prayers of a Catholic priest.

Nahum Sokolow's enormous reputation among Jews as a diplomat for Zionism, a grand gentleman of high culture and noble grace, made him something of a legendary figure. In a tribute to Sokolow in 1923, Sholem Asch wrote:

This man Sokolow was like a legend among the denizens of the prayer houses in the Polish towns. Between afternoon and evening services, when they sat around talking about Napoleon and about the English queen, the conversation shifted to Sokolow, then in Warsaw, a caller at the homes of kings, who engaged them in debates about Judaism. Sokolow was the cynosure of every young man in the prayer house, sitting over the Gemara, beneath which he surreptitiously read *Ha-Tsefira*, daydreaming of the time he would leave his town, his father-in-law's board, and his young wife, and go on foot to Warsaw. There he would sit on the doorstep of Sokolow's house, waiting for him to emerge, and approaching him say, "Mr. Sokolow, my heart is yearning for the heavenly haskala and I want to taste its fruits."

In the ancient prayer houses of the land of Poland, in the twilights between the afternoon and evening prayers, the young men used to sit near the stove and tell stories about Sokolow, about his journeys to the royal courts, about his encounters with emperors and princes, and with the Pope, all of whom loved to converse with him and hear him express in seventy tongues his wisdom and his learning, and consulted with him how to govern their peoples. And Sokolow, in his sagacity, pointed them toward the right path, told them against whom to conduct war and with whom to make peace, never omitting an opportunity to be an advocate on behalf of his fellow Jews.

This legend which coursed among the young men of the prayer houses was in the last years something of a reality.

Trembling figures, insubstantial, very like shadows but white, flying, fluttering, soaring like clouds of snowdrops, blossoming with the purity of the morning star in the crystal sea of air, yet less corporeal — like the immateriality of a melody, a chord, a child's smile, a rose's fragrance — unseen, intangible, yet more potent than giant forces.

Generations, types, personalities, whole companies — a long procession! All beckon like old friends; you think they are calling you. You did not know all of them, but you have relived their lives down to the most sensitive fibril of your nervous system. You do not have to brush off the archival dust, you do not have to burrow in old manuscripts nor decipher riddles on gray tombstones. They are part of you, they live in you. And indeed you knew many of them.

If you are a Polish Jew, and especially a Warsaw Jew, then you recall our ancient men of wealth, our community leaders, our scholars and philanthropists: serious faces, wise eyes, long beards, moiré coats, high sable hats, heavy silver collars on voluminous prayer shawls covering their heads — my grandfather, your grandfather!

Reb Shmuel Zbitkower! Do you know who he was? Look him up in the encyclopedia! No — let the pedants learn from the encyclopedias who and what a man of wealth was and who and what a philanthropist, what and when Zbitkow was. That is their business. A lot they will understand. But you know. Do you remember Reb Isaiah or Reb Yosl Krel? Perhaps you knew my grandfather, Reb Akiba from Plock? I am thinking of their pride in their worldly goods, their extensive businesses, the esteem in which they were held by government and aristocracy, yet they were not servile. On the contrary! Others danced attendance on them — these ancestral fathers, with famous sons and select sons-in-law, with learned men for in-laws, philanthropists who gave without stint and in the strictest secrecy and who carried the responsibility for the community on their broad shoulders. The community — aristocrats and the common people alike — but respect was due only the learned. (Impudent fellows, boors, vulgarians with or without money, had no say.) A Jewish democratic aristocracy? Not a bit of it! That was the typification of the real types of real life, our own virtues and our own faults, our own strengths and our own misfortunes. It was not a Purim play of make-believe copying. Did you know them? Then you surely knew also Reb Shmuel on the other side of the Vistula, in Praga!

Praga, the threshold of Warsaw — the aroma of the country, with its broad fields, so many times desolated by wars and fires and rebuilt, remnants of trenches, a battlefield and a cattle market, too large to be a suburb and too small to be a separate organism, a gateway to Warsaw. But for us, Jews, an older community, squeezed together — where the old synagogue was secluded and the old cemetery hidden, with large stores and the tiniest shops, and where Jews had the right of residence when they did not yet have it in Warsaw proper — except with privileges, or during fairs or only on certain streets, like Deutz near Cologne, for example, and many other suburbs of large cities. As it is said, "Prepare thyself in the vestibule, that thou mayest enter into the chamber." The Jews waited in the corridor and meanwhile were beaten up.

If you traveled from Warsaw to Serock, Nasielsk, Pultusk, as I used to in a coach over the old bridge, through Praga paved with cobblestones, and all your insides jolted, and if the coach stopped a while at a station with warehouses, with a spacious tavern, with old stone-built huts, semi-rural, semi-urban in which lived semi-peasants in derbies (which they picked up in Warsaw), and where my old friend Leib, the blacksmith, used to sit outside the smithy, shoeing horses while the sparks scattered in the enduring mud, and about him stood the little flaxen-haired Janeks and Marusias — then you were in Szmulewizna.

If you are anything of a Warsavian, then you surely know what Szmulewizna means. It belonged to Shmuel Zbitkower, a son of Reb Jacob (that is why he was called Jakubowicz), who had come from Zbitkow to Praga, having traded in thread, ribbons, and yard goods. Then he became a dealer in wheat, loaded barges on the Vistula to Danzig, and enriched himself and all his neighbors. Then he bought woodlands, built sawmills, transported lumber on rafts, built houses, bought estates, employed a multitude of people — a sort of Meyer Anschel in Praga (but a little earlier). He, too, had his equivalent William IX, Landgrave of Hesse-Cassel — Frederick, King of Prussia, who gave him "a privilege to live in Warsaw, South Prussia, Silesia, and other places," probably because of his businesses, from which Prussia also raked in something. In other countries, a man of such distinction was called a court Jew or a court banker, but in Poland, especially in that generation, it was just simply a privilege. Reb Shmuel, a Jew with beard and sideburns, in a long silk coat with a *gartl*, engrossed in business and community affairs in Praga, provided a livelihood for many Jews. He was a man of parts to the government which was then changing, a bit implicated in the web of those historical dramas, and contented that the Jews loved him. "Community leaders used to serve at his parties," I heard one of my grandfather's pupils tell.

Yet we would know as much about Shmuel Zbitkower as we know about thousands of other wealthy Jews who had privileges, which is to say we would not even know his name, were it not for the legend which every Jewish child in Warsaw knew — about the two barrels of gold which Reb Shmuel put in front of his house in Praga in 1794 when Suvorov captured the city: a ducat for a live Jew, a ruble for a corpse. And the Cossacks began to bring the merchandise and soon both barrels were empty.

Was it a legend?

What is the redemption of prisoners? What is the commandment to bury the corpse of an unknown Jew? Not barrels of gold, but the last drop of blood that Jews wrung from themselves to save a brother Jew from ill-treatment, to give a Jewish corpse a Jewish burial. An ordinary matter! The Russ had captured Praga (from ancient days a place marked for misfortune) — a hurricane of brutality. The Cossack whips (who does not remember them?) were unleashed; Jewish blood flowed like water. The crazed beast could be restrained only one way — so Shmuel Zbitkower sacrificed his gold and saved a good many Jewish lives. Why else then are Jews Jews? Otherwise, we would not deserve to live on this earth.

Thus the authentic Jewish heritage. Reb Ber, Reb Shmuel's son, known as Berek, was more Warsaw than Praga. Born in 1764 — he was thirty at the time of the Praga massacre — he enlarged his father's inheritance. A very wealthy man with many enterprises, he also was engrossed in Jewish studies. In 1810 he received a privilege from Governor General Zajączek to live anywhere, to wear traditional Jewish garb and not to be required to shave his beard. Zajączek, an old general from Kościuśko's time and later in Napoleon's army, a little spoiled by foreign heresies of freedom, a friend of the Berek family, was prepared to grant everything, but he had to present the matter to the Tsar himself — no small matter this privilege — and Alexander I restricted the privilege specifically only to Berek, and, after him, only to his eldest son.

An important Jew, devoted heart and soul, he donated Torah scrolls to all the synagogues. All his days he was a bridegroom of the Torah and had much to say in the community. Yet no one would have made much stir over him. We never lacked for distinguished Jews, wealthy men steeped in Torah. Berek would have been forgotten, were it not for his wife Temerel.

The loveliness of a flower, the modesty of a dove, a soul with wings of gold, and fruitful as an olive tree. Four sons: Jacob, Michal, Leib (Leopold) and, I think, a fourth whose name I cannot remember, and an only daughter — Perel-Mirel. Temerel was a sort of mother Rachel in Warsaw Jewish legend. One hears less of Berek: he was her prince consort. That in itself was enough. He left five million gulden, most for charity and philanthropic funds.

I see it all before me, as if it were today, but even more clearly do I see the continuation. From here on I am completely at home. Comrades, old Warsavians, who of you did not know Perel-Mirel, Temerel's daughter? Who did not meet her in the neighborhood of Nowolipki, Dzielna, Pawia and Dzika Streets, when she used to visit Maria Blumberg or Madam Sarah Slonimski, to come to us at *Ha-Tsefira*, when it was still a weekly on Dzika Street? Poor — all those millions and philanthropic funds had run out — but like a widowed queen in her bonnet with its dark-blue ribbons, in her Turkish shawl like an antique Gobelin. Her gait — as in a ceremonial procession, yet quite natural. A century strolled from Nowolipki to Dzika Street, a century of old charm, boudoir beauty, and wisdom. You should have heard her speak Yiddish. You would have held your breath, not to miss a syllable. Only two people spoke Yiddish like that — Perel-Mirel and my grandmother Yutta, rest her soul, from Plock. How she could tell stories! About the first uprising, about Constantine, about Paskiewicz, about 1864 and Rabbi Berish Meisels and Mathias Rosen, about Kraszewski as editor of *Gazeta Polska* and an associate of Kronenberg. These were people of destiny with fabulous traditions, like heirs of those heroes about whom they told stories. Listening to her, I had to lower my eyes, compelled by an inner feeling of reverence. This was truly Jewish, she was truly a heroic Jewish matriarch, not on stage, but in real life.

The name Bergson — actually Berekson — came into being after Berek, Shmuel's son. I have mentioned Berek's sons before — Jacob, Leopold, and Michal. I heard many stories about Jacob and Leopold — the best from Perel-Mirel. Jacob was a great philanthropist, a man of learning, a quiet, withdrawn man. I myself knew Michal when he was eighty. He was a whole chapter in himself. He was born in Warsaw in 1818. In 1825, all the brothers received a privilege "to reside where they choose and to dress according to Jewish custom." Michal, then, in his early youth, wore his coat cut long, but he grew up a musician! He escaped, as Perel-Mirel used to tell, from his privilege, his long coat and his wealth, to the musicians, and fell in love with that genius musician called Chopin, with that sweet, entranced music in which the soul of Poland sang the harmonies of its pains and hopes. Temerel's son became a pioneer for that gifted son of a French father and a Polish mother, in whom the mother's side conquered. But Warsaw was not yet ready for that, and so Michal, son of Ber, went abroad. This Warsaw young man, grandson of Reb Shmuel of the two barrels of gold and son of the wealthy, pious Temerel, a full brother of Perel-Mirel, was the first to popularize Chopin in Europe. A pianist and composer with the dew of youth still on his brow, he set out for France, Italy, Belgium,

England with Chopin's other-worldly music, deep and soft, psalms from Polish harps, green corn from Poland's fields, poetry of imprisoned heroes, longing of Polish emigrants, blossoming hymns, music of flowers and human souls, secrets and moods. His grandfather had poured out gold coins to ransom the Jews of Praga; his mother was the crown and adornment of Warsaw synagogues; his sister had married a great Lithuanian Jewish scholar; and he introduced Zbitkow and Chopin into world music. Travelling about, he played himself into the directorship of the Brussels conservatory, where he worked many years; from there, to France, Italy, England, distinguished himself as a virtuoso much more than as a composer, wrote two long operas, many études, songs, hymns, marches, became friends with the geniuses of the musical world of his generation, and in his old age settled in London (his wife was an English Jewish girl, Dr. I. L. Levinsohn's second daughter), where he had a house. There I became acquainted with him in 1896.

He longed for Warsaw and inquired about the old city square and other parts of the city. He spoke Polish in high-flown style, with grammatical mistakes and a French accent, a little Yiddish with a rolled Warsaw *r*, an artist-aristocrat down to his fingertips. When he spoke of Chopin, he became a boy: his cheeks glowed and his excited Jewish, Polish Jewish, eyes burned like fiery coals. I told him about Warsaw and he was especially interested to know about the old-age home over which his nephew — also Michal, our communal leader — presided and about the vocational shops of which his other nephew, Samuel, was chairman, and about the trade-employees association where I was active several years.

In 1898 he died quietly, as if he had fallen asleep, in his little house in London. A day before, acquaintances told me, he had played some Chopin nocturnes. His wife, Kate, survived him.

In 1900 I was in London again, for the Zionist Congress. There I met Michal Bergson, the nephew, my old Warsaw friend. He had come to visit his Aunt Kate. He was no Shmuel Zbitkower, and no Berek, but decent, a thoroughly decent man, diligent in community affairs, without compare. Honesty, precision, dignity, conscientiousness in business and communal matters. He used to attend services in the synagogue and all his life had the honor, as he stood fasting, to open the Ark at Ne'ilah, a strong character, assimilated, but God-fearing at heart. . . . Here the thread of these reminiscences snaps. Why repeat what you all know? Rather tell what you do not know or not well enough. Back to our Chopin-Michal.

He had two sons: One, less known, occupied himself with English literature in London under a pen name, did not accomplish much, then disappeared like thousands of others into anonymity, an honest, quiet man. The other, the important one, Professor Henri Bergson! He was born when his parents lived in France, and so a Frenchman. His mother, Dr. Levinsohn's daughter, was a fine Jewish woman in England; he himself married a Miss Cahan of a good Jewish family in England. That is why his English is as good as his French. Needless to describe what Henri Bergson has been in our generation. He wields the scepter of philosophy; he casts his luster on the Sorbonne, the French Academy, he nourishes the world; he is the guide — in the kingdom of intellectual scholarship, Temerel's grandson reigns.

The essence of Bergson's philosophy is that intellect is not at all the highest degree of human perfection and that with intellect alone man cannot comprehend the truth. Intelligence, in Bergson's system, meant man's ability to distinguish and classify all things around him according to their similarities and their differences, to identify them by different names and formulae, and to discover the laws which determine their form and cause their events. Thus, man had the ability to invent language and science; on these two foundations he rests his control over all things and the power he possesses to bend and exploit them for his needs. But neither language nor science nor intelligence can penetrate the true significance of these things. Only philosophy can do so. That is something quite different from science. Science is external and utilitarian. Philosophy is knowledge for the sake of knowledge (Torah for its own sake) and is practically without utility. The power through which this nonutilitarian purpose can be attained is not ordinary intelligence which concerns itself with the outward appearance of objects, dividing them here and there; *that* power is quite different; it is called intuition. Through intuition a man can come to grasp the profound pulse of life's domain. Through necessity and the needs of everyday life, human intelligence became the chief factor, strengthening itself and developing at the expense of the precious and sensitive force of intuition. Only at certain moments in human life does the true meaning of its existence show itself, make us recognize our personality and cast a weak fluttering light on our liberty, on the place we occupy in the whole of nature, on our origin and perhaps also on our destiny. The light is feeble, the lamp is practically extinguished, it flickers at intervals and for an instant, but it shatters the darkness of night in which the intellect has left us.

"There is no durable system," Bergson wrote in one of his early works,* "that is not, at least in some of its parts, vivified by intuition. Dialectic is necessary to put intuition to the proof, necessary also in order that intuition

* Henri Bergson, *Creative Evolution*, trans. Arthur Mitchell (New York, Modern Library, 1944), pp. 260–61.

should break itself up into concepts and so be propagated to other men; but all it does, often enough, is to develop the result of that intuition which transcends it. The truth is, the two procedures are of opposite direction: the same effort, by which ideas are connected with ideas, causes the intuition which the ideas were storing up to vanish. . . . Intuition, if it could be prolonged beyond a few instants, would not only make the philosopher agree with his own thought, but also all philosophers with each other. Such as it is, fugitive and incomplete, it is, in each system, what is worth more than the system and survives it."

No wonder that, apart from its scholarly value, Bergson's theory of intuition had a magnetic effect with its inward, unintended poetry. All Paris awoke — the salons, the women, the intellectuals. Even the Catholic Church was resuscitated. Actually, in Bergson's philosophy there is as little Jewish religion as Christian, but it cannot be denied that religion and a suggestion of mysticism are there. Intuition is the divine spirit, intellect is secular — "Trust in the Lord with all thy heart and lean not upon thine own understanding," "the fulfillment of the commandments requires intention," "the merciful God asks for heart," and thousands of other sayings, come to mind to anyone versed in Jewish tradition. Bergson had never dreamed of this. A nonbeliever, without religion, a scholar, a mathematician, a logician, he had never heard of these citations, did not think of pleasing anyone, but drew on his own resources and created, and by chance came to a conclusion that shattered rationalism. Perhaps something in his blood? According to Taine's theory, every great man is a product of his race, his environment, his time, or all three combined. Two generations of literary historians have been riding this theory. If so, then originality does not exist at all, for if it is true that the great man is only a repetition of his ancestors, who then was the innovator, the originator? "Our tongs are made with the help of tongs: who made the first tongs?" We must begin some time! I suppose Taine's theory was not given at Sinai; it has some truth, but only a part and that is nothing new, especially with regard to race. But one must not exaggerate, for each exaggeration results in caricature.

I remember in 1908 I was in Paris, and I visited our old master Max Nordau. Besides Zionism, we had an interesting talk about literature. Bergson was then in vogue. His career was that of a successful French professor. Born in 1859, he entered the École Normale Supérieure. At twenty-two he became a professor in the same École Normale in which he had studied. In 1900 he became professor in the Collège de France and a member of the Institute de France. In 1908, his works were first translated into English.

That year the third international philosophical congress was held in Heidelberg, and there Emile Boutroux read a paper on French philosophy since 1867 and for the first time mentioned the great influence of Bergson's ideas. Bergson himself was not there, but in Paris he was already quite well known. Our Nordau, the rationalist, the ironbound mitnagid, was blisteringly opposed to the Bergson mode. The old master then told me, in his hammer-splitting-rock style, that Bergson inherited these fantasies from his ancestors, who were fanatic and fantastic "wonder-rabbis" in Poland. I explained then to Nordau this was a mistake but where he took it from I did not know. I know of no documentation about hasidic rebbes as Bergson's ancestors or about Shmuel Zbitkower's being a devout hasid. Reb Shmuel was a simple pious Jew. In his time, hasidism was not widespread. Perhaps he prayed in the Sephardic rite or provided for a rebbe — one cannot build a case on that. One thing I do know from Perel-Mirel's stories: her parents, Ber and Temerel, deeply revered Reb Isaac, the famous rebbe of Vurke (Warka). Reb Isaac was one of those on the board of the charitable funds that Ber and Temerel bequeathed. One can suppose that in their lifetime they admired him a great deal, but this would not mean that Berek was a dedicated follower of the Vurker rebbe. He was a man of charity and an admirer of learned men. As in all large Jewish families of that time, its members were sharply divided between the pious and the worldly, so much so that one group had no relation with the other. I knew, in my time, many Orthodox Jews in Warsaw related to the Bergsons. I remember one, a maskil who wore a long coat, contributed to *Ha-Tsofe*, the supplement to *Ha-Maggid*, and who also wrote a history of the "Berekson" family. In any case, even Ber's hasidism is very dubious. His son, Michal, Henri's father, was altogether so freethinking that Perel-Mirel, his sister, used to sigh, "He has gone completely!" Here, and not in imagined rebbes or in exaggerated hasidic devoutness, is the key to understanding Bergson's national psychology.

Michal was not a disciple of the Vurker rebbe; he was a disciple of Chopin, Chopin's first disciple in Europe. Chopin was by nature a wonderful racial combination; Michal, by his family's history, his revolutionary youth in the ghetto, his wanderings and multifarious artistic conflicts, by his libertinage and his overripe artistic nature, was a unique combination. And Henri, to whom his mother's Anglo-Jewish element was added and then the powerful influence of French culture and education, life and environment — he was a combination of combinations. One needs strong intuition to orient oneself in all these subtle nuances, but there is no choice. Otherwise one cannot approach this problem. But nevertheless, a fundamental temper underlies these subtleties. As the Marrano with Spinoza, so with Bergson; beneath his consciousness lay a specific sort of Warsaw Jewish wealthy aristocracy, an old artistic tapestry of patrician ancestry with its own specific quality. The barrels of ducats which Reb Shmuel had put out in public, real ducats, became, in his great-grandson, ducats of ideas, put forth with the same modesty, the same patrician simplicity that no parvenu — financial, intellectual or political — can imitate.

Several years ago I had a long, a very long and very cordial conversation with Bergson. It took place on a Sunday in February, 1918, in his Paris home. The newspapers had then published a false, sensational report about him. Newspapers! They pick up a word, make a headline, and that's that. With all due respect! But the only truth is that Professor Bergson remains what he was born. He is a Jew, with a Jewish wife, and has great, profound human ideals. He almost transcends time and place, seeking the meaning of meaning. He is as subtle as his father; he penetrates into the soul's secrets with musical subtlety. A wealth of poetry is in his philosophy. He has a modest, aristocratic nature. He is no stuff for propaganda, that is too profane.

Whenever an encyclopedia article, a biographer, or a newspaper hints or suggests — it is said or it is supposed — that Professor Bergson is "of Jewish origin," or when someone asks if it is true that "Professor Bergson has some connection with Jews," I am consumed with a raging anger. "Jewish origin," "suppose"? Of course he is a Jew and of Polish-Jewish stock, a grandson of Reb Ber and Temerel, the exact image of the portrait of Reb Ber, with the modesty of his grandmother, the large deep-set eyes of Perel-Mirel, the famous brow of the family. What is he? What he must be, whether he wishes it or not. Has he any choice?

Warsaw Jews — migrated like a flock of birds, dispersed in the atmosphere of the world, from the ancient privileges down to the French Academy, our eggs laid in strange nests, gold given to the Cossacks, pioneers to music, philosophy to the world. Warsaw, old Warsaw!

41   Neither Pole Nor Jew
by Leopold Infeld

LEOPOLD INFELD, scientist and writer, was born in Cracow in 1898. In 1921 he received his doctorate in physics at the University of Cracow. As a boy, he had felt oppressed by his Jewish background, by what he refers to as "the ghetto" and sought to escape, through education, from what he perceived as burdensome and constricting. But Polish society, and especially the Polish academic world, rejected him. Though he received the first doctorate in theoretical physics in independent Poland, he was denied a university research or teaching position because he was a Jew. For years he earned a livelihood by teaching in Jewish gymnasia and by writing popular science. Nevertheless, as the following extract from his autobiography *Quest* shows, he retained deep affection for that Polish world which rebuffed him and contempt for the tradition that shaped him.

In 1936, with Albert Einstein's help, Infeld received a fellowship to the Institute for Advanced Study in Princeton, N. J. In 1940, he became professor of applied mathematics at the University of Toronto. In 1949, he returned to Poland, where he now lives.

D URING my childhood, and later in my youth, my thoughts and desires centered about a peaceful life, around teaching and research, around an occupation which promised uneventful, quiet days, in which emotions were drawn from studying, reading and contemplation.

But this life remained a mirage, a picture which faded the moment I felt that I might grasp it and keep it. I fought for a peace and rest which did not come, and I experienced a strange change, a substitution of means for ends. I thought that peace and security were my aims, but ambition and tension grew from my desires to achieve these ends. I thought that I was approaching my goal by a difficult and bitter road. Obstacles, defeat, victory, and again defeat, all taught me to enjoy the fight with its strategy and its continual ups and downs. Through such a life, the longing for peace may change into an aversion toward the boredom of harbors and havens, into a desire for new adventures.

Is this perhaps not the reason for the nervous restlessness characterizing Jews? Is this not an inevitable reaction against the obstacles and frustration which are so often their lot, so that they welcome contention and struggle?

To achieve peace of mind for scientific work, I had to leave the country in which I was rooted. Perhaps I welcomed the defeat because I had developed a taste for a restless life. I burned my days hoping to accelerate the rhythm of time, to bring me nearer future events. I wanted each day to pass quickly in my impatience for tomorrow.

This was not my reaction alone. I developed the characteristics which grow in every member of a suppressed nation or race. Though, curiously enough, I do not believe that the same applies to a suppressed class.

An exploited worker who knows that he is exploited joins a union, fights for better conditions and a better social order. In his fight he finds an emotional outlet and hope for tomorrow. He identifies himself and his interests with those of his own class; he feels the support of the working class and knows that he is not alone. He may try the way up by leaving his factory, by educating himself, and he may succeed. If he does, he will not suffer for his worker's past. He always has in his background the class on which he can lean, and before him the goal which he wants to achieve. If he despises the class from which he grew, he deserves contempt.

It is different for one who tries to escape from the ghetto. His driving force to escape is rooted in contempt for the environment from which he comes. I hated the Jewish school. I disliked the Jewish language. I was not attracted by the Jewish religion. These were the driving forces. I never had — as the worker has — the struggling background of the class from which he comes. The ghetto is full of misery, dirt, sadness, but there is not even so much as a spark of fight. Religion and obedience to the Almighty make the misery bearable and throw over life the weak luster of poetry.

From early childhood, I nursed the same emotions toward my environment, and from those feelings I drew the strength which carried me toward the outside world. The realization of this desire to escape formed the first serious problem from which I learned to think and act, and it was this struggle for achievement which formed my character.

To escape, I was forced to fight against my environment. I tried hard, and often cynically, to burn out of me the traces left by my upbringing. Every successful step outside was bound to increase my contempt for the small, sad world from which I came and my desire to erase its visible signs. I did as a prisoner does after escape. His first deed is to change his prisoner's garb and rid himself of the chains still hanging about his ankles. As brutal and ugly as this sounds, it is still better to acknowledge the existence of this attitude than to be entangled in self-deceit. Jews who succeed in leaving the ghetto must go through a period in which they despise and detest their old world, because these emotions form the driving force for escape. This contempt and the force directed outside are strongly connected: they nourish and, by mutual induction, intensify each other.

Just before I left for America, I went to Cracow. I wandered through the ghetto of my town. On a summer morning the voices of Jewish boys singing in chorus the words of the Torah reached me through the open window of the school. "There may be among them someone who hates this place as I hated it and who dreams of going to a gymnasium." I went nearer. The school windows were open, the first-floor windows of a dreary house. I smelt the foul air of the room. It was the same air, the same smell of onions and potatoes, which I had smelled over thirty years before. I saw the tired, thin, badly nourished faces with burning dark eyes, and for the first time in my life I was conscious of a touch of poetry in this sad ghetto scene.

"What did I do to help them? I did nothing in the past and can do little in the future. No one here will listen to my voice. We no longer speak the same language. Most of them would spit in my face and throw stones at me. But there may be one among them whose eyes burn with desires, who will try the hard and lonely path which seems to lead outside. If I meet him in life I shall try to help him, because I know the hardships and sufferings of this long journey."

No! It is not true that I had only scorn and contempt for my environment. There is a curious mixture of hate and love. I could say to myself; "What do I care about Jews? I am above racial, religious problems and prejudices." But all my continued attempts to tear off the bonds only prove that these bonds exist, and they will exist to the last day of my life. Hate and scorn carry subtle overtones of love and attraction.

It is not easy to gain freedom and to escape. It is a bitter fight repeated over and over again, until one's system absorbs the necessity of fighting and the restlessness created by it destroys the peace so ardently desired but never to be attained. There is no harbor, no haven anywhere.

The struggle to leave the Jewish environment and to mix freely with non-Jews creates and must create the characteristic features for which Jews are despised. The bitter struggle deforms character. Antisemitism nourishes itself. It is a monster which increases and grows by the laws governing hate. Barriers created by antisemitism shape the characteristic features for which Jews are hated and by which antisemitism attempts to justify itself.

There are only two ways to solve the Jewish problem. One is the simple, brutal way — to destroy the suppressed. The other way is to destroy the suppression. The growing monster of antisemitism can be forced to kill itself; it can be nourished by reaction or annihilated by progress.

I know that my destiny is the destiny of thousands and that my feelings are reproduced in thousands of others. I felt that the roots of my life had been taken away with the earth of the country in which they grew. It is not true that I and others treated far more brutally are without a country. Poland is, and will remain, my country. I shall always long for the Polish fields and meadows, for the air smelling of flowers and hay, for vistas and sounds which can never be found elsewhere. I shall long for the countryside with its bad roads and peasants' huts, for Polish food and the smiles of Polish girls. And, above all, I shall long for the sound of the Polish language, the language in which I expressed my earliest joys and sorrows and incoherent silly thoughts — the only language in which I can make stupid puns, tell ribald stories and curse roundly. I will never forget my country. It is the coordinate system to which I refer the most important events of my life. There I spent the childhood which determined my future. There I met Halina and there I endured the day of her tragic death. There I was taught and there I wanted to teach. I shall try desperately to put out new roots in a new earth. My intentions may be strengthened by the friendliness and opportunities which will be offered me. But the mirage of my country, idealized by thought and vividly painted by the force of imagination, will always be before my eyes.

IX

In the Zionist Movement

42   One of the People: Ahad Ha'am

AHAD HA'AM, pen name of Asher Ginzberg, was born in Skvira, province of Kiev, in 1856 and died in Tel Aviv in 1927. Probably the most interesting and intellectually influential of all Zionist leaders and thinkers, Ahad Ha'am conceived of a national cultural revival, the Jewish state in Palestine serving as the spiritual center of world Jewry and the stimulant for a new appreciation of Jewish moral and cultural values.

With Dubnow, Ahad Ha'am shared the hard-to-define, nearly mystical concept of a national Jewish will to live,

though the two men differed in how this national spirit could best express itself. Like Dubnow, too, and many others of his time, a positivist and agnostic, he was nevertheless unable and unwilling to jettison his heritage of Judaism and Jewish tradition. As Leon Simon, his biographer, has pointed out, Ahad Ha'am nationalized supernatural sanctions and transcendental values, elevating a collective Jewish moral sense into a substitution for Godhood. The following selection has been translated from Ahad Ha'am's reminiscences.

A Few Facts of My Life

by Ahad Ha'am

UP TO NOW, July 6, 1926, my life has been divided in five periods: (1) The period in my native town, where I lived until I was twelve. There I was mostly occupied in studying Talmud and its commentaries, with a teacher my father hired. I have written about this period in various places and perhaps I will still have an opportunity to return to it. (2) The period in the country, when I left my native town (1868) and came to my parents in the village which my father had leased from a landowner. In this village I acquired most of my educational baggage — Bible, Hebrew, and general knowledge. This period lasted nearly sixteen years, until Nisan 1884, when I went to Odessa. (3) The Odessa, or literary, period which lasted until 1907. In this period, my place in our national work and our literature was

367

determined. (4) The London period. I left Odessa for various reasons in 1907 and settled in London. There I lived until 1921. In London my life did not change much, for the life of the Jews in London did not attract me very much and I spent my time mostly in the society of Russian maskilim and Zionists, just as I had been accustomed in Russia. The main point is that these were war years and because of the events it was not possible to do anything but our national work. This period lasted fourteen years. (5) The Palestine period. I finally settled in Palestine, fulfilling a hope for which I had striven for decades. I arrived January 9, 1922, with my wife, my son, and daughter-in-law, to settle here forever.

Much has been written about the B'nai Moshe and a book by S. Tchernowitz on its history has already appeared, but I believe one essential thing has not been mentioned anywhere. Everyone attributes the founding of this organization to me, that I conceived the idea and I carried it out myself. This is really not so. The idea to form a secret society originated in Palestine. A group of youngish people were engrossed with the idea of opposing obstructionism with silence. Among them was Barzilai (J. Eisenstadt). When he came to Odessa he became acquainted with M. A. Lubarsky, and both decided (I do not know who was the initiator) that I should head this organization. I knew nothing about what transpired between them, but one day Lubarsky invited me to an important meeting to take place that evening in his brother's house. I promised to come. When the meeting opened, I was amazed when everyone turned to me, as if they expected me to explain the purpose of this meeting. It appeared everyone thought, or had been told, that I had called the meeting and that I would explain its purpose. But as a matter of fact, I knew nothing more than the others; the real conveners were Barzilai and Lubarsky. From the discussion it became clear that the purpose of the meeting was to form a secret society, the B'nai Moshe, and they had picked me to found it and head it. They thought I was competent, for at that time I had published my article "The Wrong Way," in which they found things similar to this idea. The proposal appealed to me and I agreed to undertake it. And so, after a series of discussions at several meetings the organization was founded and I was its head and leader. Gradually I became more absorbed in this undertaking and devoted much time and work to it. Barzilai was a sort of apostle, traveling around in various places to get members and extend our influence. Since it quickly became known in the circles close to us that I was the founder of the organization, I could not reveal the truth lest I harm the society. But eventually the truth must be known, that the idea to form the B'nai Moshe was brought to Odessa by Barzilai, and I was not its initiator.

The Society existed for about eight years, and almost all the best of the Hoveve Zion were members of it. In its early years it was very vigorous. It had a marked moral influence on its members, and through them on the whole Hibbat Zion movement; but gradually it lost its drive. It was also the victim of misrepresentation and baseless slander on the part of malicious persons, and in the end it went to pieces. So long as it existed, I was regarded by the public as its head; but in fact I held that position only for a short time — till I went to Palestine in 5651 (1891) — after which the leadership was in other hands, first in Warsaw and afterwards in Jaffa. Looked on as its founder, however, I was regarded by the members as head of the Society in the purely moral sense. Someday I may publish its full history. To this day the most absurd stories are invented about it, and most people do not know the truth about this interesting development of what may be called the "twilight" period, a development which might have been of great service to the national revival had it not been ruined by unfavorable circumstances which combined with fanaticism and jealousy to spoil it.

The Most Important Person in My Life
by Chaim Nahman Bialik

Chaim Nahman Bialik, Hebrew poet, was born in Radi, province of Volhynia, in 1873. In 1924 he settled in Palestine. He died in a Viennese hospital in 1934 and was buried in Tel Aviv, next to Ahad Ha'am.

Moving to Odessa in 1899, he became close to Ahad Ha'am, whose disciple he was to remain all his life, as he describes in the following eulogy written upon Ahad Ha'am's death.

Bialik has been called the poet of the modern national renaissance, but his roots have been in the Jewish tradition. The last years of his life he wrote little poetry, devoting himself to a cultural educational project of incomparable grandeur. He sought to make available to twentieth-century Jews — children and young people especially — the centuries-old accumulated treasures of Jewish literature: Bible, Mishna, Agada, Midrash, and the Hebrew poetry of the Middle Ages.

I FIND it difficult at this moment to speak on Ahad Ha'am, because it is a kind of undressing the soul in public. For me, Ahad Ha'am was much more than a writer: he was the most important person in my life. He himself always avoided putting on the mantle of author for all to see. Somewhere in his work he tells us that the idea of becoming an author made him tremble all over. It may sound paradoxical that he always influenced us more by his personality than by his writings; even his books and articles work upon us primarily because of the personality which in spite of himself percolates from them, though, I repeat, he tries mightily to hide it. I wonder whether we can find even one instance of "I" in his work; he is forever suppressing it. But his efforts notwithstanding, it is precisely the "I" of this great man — this magnificent personality — which comes through to us.

I distinctly remember Ahad Ha'am's influence on the yeshiva students. His first articles reached me while I was a student at the yeshiva of Volozhin. We were impressed not only by the new style, the brilliance, the powerful thinking; it was the personality in the words which struck us most, revealing as it did a leader of extraordinary stature. At that time we were not able to explain it, but in our hearts we knew that this man was charting a new road. Many of us were then dreaming about literature, and here we found loftiness of spirit. Here was a man to lead us, not merely an author in the accepted sense, but a teacher, a pathfinder, a trailblazer. And because study is the craft of the yeshiva students — it is their only way of taking root — we tirelessly expounded every "verse" of Ahad Ha'am with every method of exegesis known to us. We spent many an evening on his words in the same kind of thorough, minute analysis we used to give, day and night, to Torah texts. Ever since those days he has held me captive: it was clear to me that I would have to wander about until I reached the place in which the great teacher lived.

That was the twilight of the haskala period. In our circumscribed world we still had a man who symbolized this period: J. L. Gordon, lion of the group of writers who ruled our souls. But Gordon was already on the way out. Grown weak and disillusioned, he was indeed "the last of the poets" as he called himself. True, we already had the "Love of Zion" movement, which was really a direct outgrowth of the pogroms; but it failed to take into account the individual and the unfolding of his life; that is, it did not spell out the individual's role in the drama of national rebirth. The movement was an indefinite call Zionward which smelled of the haskala.

Suddenly a man appeared who put redemption in the center of the nation's thought, not because of external persecutions, divine visitations, or

evil decrees but simply because he could not conceive of an honorable existence for the image of God in exile. Here at last was a thinker who could
fashion a national *Weltanschauung* as the tendon of the rest of our ideas.
You might call it the transmigration of the idea of "the Shekhina in exile,"
the realization that there is no power of resistance without the revival of the
Shekhina, the spirit, the soul — call it what you will — and that there is
nothing more important than building this power of resistance in ourselves.
When a limb hurts, the whole body seems to contract into that limb. Similarly, the very being of the nation and all its thoughts ought to contract into
this central idea; and instead of looking for a multiplicity of highways and
byways — education, religion, literature, the rabbinate, and the like — we
ought to perfect one road which will fulfill all our needs.

This is exactly what Ahad Ha'am brought us — a new "way of life." A
Jew ought to adjust his personal affairs to the improvement of the nation
and its ways; his main concern ought to be the nation, and he should subject his will to its will. True, he did not provide a detailed Shulhan Arukh,
but he did lay down clear guidelines, including the objective to which every
Jew ought to direct his thoughts: namely, how he can adapt his life to the
upbuilding of the community. Our whole national heritage which outwardly seemed poor and dried up passed from the narrow limits of religion
to the broad domain of the nation and thence, in its national guise, to the
domain of humanity. Our national riches became human riches. The men
of the haskala regarded our past as a stream of vapors; some of them maintained that Judaism consisted of rubbish heaps scattered in many places
and that Maimonides collected them into one large dunghill. It was Ahad
Ha'am who made Judaism a foundation stone; who brought us to the realization that those sources which have absorbed the life of all our generations
ought to be tapped for the revival of Israel.

His work, which became the backbone of a whole period, was a ceaseless effort to direct the mind of the people to one central point: the sin or
the punishment of galuth is characterized by a disease of the spirit: namely,
the weakening of the will which leads to ever diminishing confidence in
our own strength.

He raised the prestige of literature in the eyes of the writer himself. He
made us feel honored to be Hebrew authors and to do literary work. We
had come to such a pass that even we who had been reared on Hebrew literature no longer respected it. Ahad Ha'am put a backbone in our backs. He
came to us at the age of thirty-three, highly cultured, a member of a rich
family (also no small matter), but our real respect for him developed after
we had been privileged to work with him and to grasp his attitude of the

sacredness of literature. He would labor religiously over a passage to extract its quintessence. As was his way, he chose the shortest and most direct mode of expression. According to him, every expression has one pure form, and it is the duty of the writer to find it. He always had a strict attitude toward his ideas: in conveying them to others he neither added to, nor subtracted from, them. When we saw his uncompromising attitude toward literature, our self-respect increased because we began to have more respect for literature. This man with his clarity of mind taught us not to pour out our feelings as one pours out dirty water.

I do not remember exactly when my attention was first called to the name Ahad Ha'am. I think that it took place when I was still quite young, perhaps about fifteen, with the appearance of his article, "The Wrong Way," which caused a considerable stir in the circles of the Hoveve Zion. There was even greater interest in Ahad Ha'am at the yeshiva of Volozhin. By that time his other articles had reached us, especially those debating with Lilienblum. In the first place it was Ahad Ha'am's audacity which drew us like a magnet. For many of us, Lilienblum was our first literary love and seemed to us the brightest and most important of personalities. Here an anonymous writer came out and spoke with Lilienblum as if he were his equal; at times he even appeared superior to him. Though there was some murmuring over such presumption people could not withstand the magic of the newcomer, and they soon began to feel that his courage was well founded. Two adversaries of equal powers were squaring off. But for every good point we found in Lilienblum we were able to discover more of it in Ahad Ha'am. He had a special charm and fascination for us; and, as you know, if there is charm, the rest will follow. Magic is not given to measurement. How did he come by that charm? This was a question we could not answer. Many writers reeked of pedagogics and their tone was that of the Talmud student in the bet ha-midrash. But Ahad Ha'am's work had substance; in his style we sensed the discipline, as it were, of business and industry. This was something new to us.

We heard that the man was in his middle years. Up to this time he had written nothing; suddenly he revealed himself and his powers. With us a writer makes his debut forty days before his conception; in his infancy, poems and stories cascade from him. But here was a man who held back about thirty-five years, which meant that he had grown so strong as to attain to his full powers in one sweep.

And there were stories of his origin. He came of a rich family possessed of estates and factories. He was the son of a great merchant who did business with Ignatiev himself — the man who fathered the May Laws against the Jews of Russia. Because of our innocence, this item enhanced the literature for us and perhaps even increased the self-respect of the writers themselves. This showed that not all who were engaged in Hebrew literature were idlers and piddlers. In addition there were mysterious rumors. He was the head of a secret society, B'nai Moshe, a mysterious group working on missions and tasks whose nature we did not know.

I came to know Ahad Ha'am in connection with my first poem. I had two friends, one of whom was a fellow student in the yeshiva. While in Odessa I stayed at their home. Their father was a rabbi. Now I had a strong desire to see Ahad Ha'am. But how? I was a youngster with no business of any kind that might take me to him. I did not dare just go to see him, for what would I say to him? So I asked my friends to help me. Ahad Ha'am used to go to a certain tobacco factory; so we made up that when he came, they would call me. One day, both of them rushed to tell me: "There he goes in that cab!" I hurried with all my might, but to no avail; the cab had already darted by. I saw him from the rear wearing his round "Catholic" hat. I had to be satisfied with that: "the saintly Rav saw the back of Rabbi Meir."

I would have left the city without seeing him. But it happened that I was trying to publish a poem of my own. My friends' father, the rabbi, was Lilienblum's friend. So he took me to Lilienblum, who, after reading the poem, gave me a note to Ahad Ha'am. It was a recommendation, and I remember only one sentence of it, "and he deserves not to be spoiled."

With buckling knees I entered the great man's home on a murky, Odessa winter day. The door of his study was opened, and I saw him standing at the table with a little girl, apparently his eldest daughter, cutting the pages of a foreign journal. I handed him my poem ("To the Bird") together with Lilienblum's note. He said: "Come around in a few days." I somehow managed to get through the next few days; then I went back. He received me standing and told me that my poem pleased him, but it all depended on Ravnitsky, editor of *Pardes*. If he liked it and there was space, it would be published. I then took it to Ravnitsky; you all know the result. That meeting with Ahad Ha'am was not at all satisfactory; it took place while standing on one foot, and the foot itself was trembling.

Nine years later I returned to Odessa to stay. Ahad Ha'am was already the editor of *Ha-Shiloah*. I went to visit him one evening. At that time I found a curious person named Frankfeld with him; Frankfeld had some connection with literature and was Ahad Ha'am's friend. (I used to find him in leisurely conversation with Ahad Ha'am about the Russian writer Uspensky.) I sat there waiting for Ahad Ha'am to emerge from his study.

It was a miracle that my soul did not leave my body out of fear — I was twenty-seven then. When he entered the room, I arose; I thought I would fall to the ground. But he was wonderful: he put me at my ease, giving me counsel and asking me to come again.

For a long time I did not dare to visit him on Saturday nights when his friends used to gather. From time to time I would make up my mind to go, only to be seized with fright when on the point of starting out. I finally conquered my fear but God alone knows how much it cost me. Even when I did make my appearance, I sat like one deaf and dumb with my mouth tightly shut.

Maybe it was my timidity, but I have a feeling it was something nobler. We were afraid to approach him because of our reverence. Wittingly or unwittingly, we were keeping our distance. I do not know whether he himself was particular about this, but the fact is that for many years that distance was dear to me. And it was precious for me to conquer it step by step. I gave myself a long time in which to gain the privilege of getting closer to him. I remember my fear when I brought him my poem "The Dead of the Wilderness" one morning, because the morning hours were sacred to him for serious work. His daughter Leah opened the door. I handed her the manuscript and fled. I did not return to his home. Afterward my friends told me that he had read the poem to them and expressed his opinion of it. For a long time I was simply afraid to come and hear his opinion; and when I eventually gathered enough courage, I would stand on the threshold, hear his verdict and take to my heels.

Many thought that Ahad Ha'am was dry but this was not so. He once said: "I know how to feel, though I do not usually become excited." I recall the twilight when we parted in Odessa. There was a small group at the station. He was excited and in a bad mood. He kissed and embraced us with great emotion. Standing by the window in the train, he drummed nervously on the glass.

I met him afterward at one of the congresses. Something extraordinary took place at this meeting: I suddenly had the feeling that the distance between us had gone. The horns of glory had been cut off. It was as if his stature had been lowered, as if that special brightness of forehead and face which had been his, especially during moments of elation and excitement, had departed for all time. We sat together like two friends who had chanced to meet, as he spoke disconsolately of his disappointments. He was uprooted from that vital soil in which his spirit had been firmly planted. In London he was bereft of the Divine Presence. He was changed: it was a different Ahad Ha'am. I had already sensed it in The Hague, but London had really changed my Ahad Ha'am. There he lacked the fellowship, the necessary environment that at one time had nourished him.

We had our last meeting in Eretz Yisrael. On one occasion I poured out my heart to him with respect to the Jewish situation in the *yishuv* and in the Diaspora. I remember saying to him: "At times I want to put on prayer shawl and phylacteries, go to the synagogue, and become part of all those Jews who still bear the yoke of the Commandments." He replied: "Oh, my friend, if you have such a desire, heed it; do what your heart dictates. If I were young now, I would do many things altogether differently."

For us the image of Ahad Ha'am has remained not that of the broken man but of the leader who captured our imagination with the splendor of his power; it was then that he gave us his ideas, the glowing quintessence of his thought. No later image can replace this one. As just such a teacher, he exerted his influence on the younger writers. Would that we had in our generation such a figure from whom rays of glory emanate and from whom we would keep our distance in the sense of "they were afraid to approach him." There is no such personage in our literature today. It may be the fault of our generation; or has the democratic spirit done away with the idea of distance?

43 My Early Days
by Chaim Weizmann

CHAIM WEIZMANN, first President of Israel, was born in Motol, near Pinsk, in 1874 and died in Israel in 1952. Most of his life his Jewishness and his Zionism competed with his scientific interests in chemistry, each aspect vying with the other for the whole man. (In explaining his flight from Switzerland to Manchester in 1904, he later said he had been "in danger of being eaten up by Zionism.") The following selection from this autobiography describes the formative period in his life.

Weizmann's role in Jewish history needs no recounting here. He was the modern man of Western culture, a scientist, a man of vision and yet a practical man, but, above all, as David Ben-Gurion has characterized him, "he was first and foremost a *Jewish* Jew."

THE TOWNLET of my birth, Motol, stood — and perhaps still stands — on the banks of a little river in the great marsh area which occupies much of the province of Minsk and adjacent provinces in White Russia; flat, open country, mournful and monotonous but, with its rivers, forests and lakes, not wholly unpicturesque. Between the rivers the soil was sandy, covered with pine and furze; closer to the banks the soil was black, the trees were leaf bearing. In the spring and autumn, the area was a sea of mud, in the winter a world of snow and ice; in the summer, it was covered with a haze of dust. All about, in hundreds of towns and villages, Jews lived, as they had lived for many generations, scattered islands in a Gentile ocean; and among them my own people, on my father's and mother's side, made up a not inconsiderable proportion.

Just outside Motol the river flowed into a large lake and emerged again at the other end on its way to join the Pina; that in turn was a tributary of the Pripet, itself a tributary of the Dnieper, which fell into the Black Sea many hundreds of miles away. On the further banks of the lake were some villages, mysterious to my childhood by virtue of their general name — "the Beyond-the-River." For them, Motol (or Motelle, as we affectionately Yiddishized the name) was a sort of metropolis.

A very tiny and isolated metropolis it was, with some four or five hundred families of White Russians and less than two hundred Jewish families. Communication with the outside world was precarious and intermittent. No railway, no metaled road, passed within twenty miles of us. There was no post office. Mail was brought in by anyone from the townlet who happened to pass by the nearest railway station on his own business. Sometimes these chance messengers would hold on to the mail for days, or for weeks, distributing it when the spirit moved them. But letters played no very important part in our lives; there were few in the outside world who had reason to communicate with us.

Motol was situated in one of the darkest and most forlorn corners of the Pale of Settlement, that prison house created by Tsarist Russia for the largest part of its Jewish population. Throughout the centuries, alternations of bitter oppression and comparative freedom — how comparative a free people would hardly understand — had deepened the consciousness of exile in these scattered communities, which were held together by a common destiny and common dreams. Motol was typical Pale, typical countryside. Here, in this half-townlet, half-village, I lived from the time of my birth, in 1874, till the age of eleven; and here I wove my first pictures of the Jewish and Gentile worlds.

The first fundamental change in my life took place when, at the age of eleven, I left the townlet of my birth and went out "into the world" — that is, to Pinsk — to enter a Russian school: which was something not done until that time by any Motolite. From Motol to Pinsk was a matter of six Russian miles, or twenty-five English miles; but in terms of intellectual displacement the distance was astronomical. For Pinsk was a real provincial metropolis, with thirty thousand inhabitants, of whom the great majority were Jews. Pinsk had a name and a tradition as "a city and mother in Israel." It could not pretend to the cultural standing of great centers like Warsaw, Vilna, Odessa, and Moscow; but neither was it a nameless village. The new Hibbat Zion movement, the forerunner of modern Zionism, had taken deep root in Pinsk. There were Jewish scholars and Jewish public leaders in Pinsk. There was a high school — the one I was going to attend — there were libraries, hospitals, factories, and paved streets.

The years of my childhood in Motol and of my schooling in Pinsk coincided with the onset of the "dark years" for Russian Jewry; or perhaps I should say with their return. The reign of Alexander II had been a false dawn. For a generation, the ancient Russian policy of repression of the Jews had been mitigated by the liberalism of the monarch who had set the serfs free; and therefore many Jews believed that the walls of the ghetto were about to fall. Jews were beginning to attend Russian schools and universities, and to enter into the life of the country. Then, in 1881, came the assassination of Alexander, and on its heels the tide of reaction, which was not to ebb again until the overthrow of the Romanovs thirty-six years later.

Parallel with these repressions, and with the general setback to Russian liberalism, there was a deep stirring of the masses, Russian and Jewish. Among the Jews, this first folk awakening had two facets, the revolutionary, mingling with the general Russian revolt, and the Zionist nationalist. The latter, however, was also revolutionary and democratic. The Jewish masses were rising against the paternalism of their "notables," their *shtadlanim*, the men of wealth and influence who had always taken it on themselves to represent the needs of the Jews vis-à-vis governmental authority. Theirs was, even in the best cases, a class view, characterized by a natural fear of disturbing the status quo or imperiling such privileges as they enjoyed by virtue of their economic standing. In the depths of the masses an impulse awoke, vague, groping, unformulated, for Jewish self-liberation. It was genuinely of the folk; it was saturated with Jewish tradition; and it was connected with the most ancient memories of the land where Jewish life had first expressed itself in freedom. It was, in short, the birth of modern Zionism.

By 1886, when I entered high school in Pinsk, the atmosphere of Jewish life was heavy with disaster. There had been the ghastly pogroms of 1881. These had not reached us in Motol, but they had shaken the whole Jewish world to its foundations. I was a child, and I had lived in the separateness of the Jewish life of our townlet. Non-Jews were for me something peripheral. But even I did not escape a consciousness of the general gloom. Almost as far as my memory goes back, I can remember the stampede — the frantic rush from the Russian prison house, the tremendous tide of migration which carried hundreds of thousands of Jews from their ancient homes to far-off lands across the seas. I was a witness in boyhood and early manhood of the emptying of whole villages and towns. My own family was once caught up in the fever — this was about the time of the Kishenev pogrom of 1903 — and though we finally decided against flight, there were cousins and uncles and more distant relatives by the score who took the westward path.

The school regime in Pinsk, and for that matter, I suppose, in all other Russian cities at that time, was very different from that of the Western world. There was no contact between teachers and pupils, and little inter-course among the pupils themselves. As far as the Jewish boys were con-cerned, the teachers were looked upon as the representatives of an alien and hostile power; they were more *tchinovniks* ("officials") than pedagogues, and in them human emotions and relationships were replaced by formalism and by the instinct for climbing inherent in the Russian official. With few exceptions — and there were some — the teacher had his eye not so much on the pupils as on the head of the school; the road to the good opinion of his chief, and therefore of promotion, was not the road of pedagogics, but of strict adherence to the decrees and ukases issued by the higher authorities.

There was one outstanding exception among my teachers, a man by the name of Kornienko, to whom, very possibly, I owe whatever I have been able to achieve in the way of science. He was a chemist, with a genuine love of his subject and a considerable reputation in the world at large. He was, in fact, the glory of our school, and this perhaps explains why he was able to do as much as he did without falling foul of the authorities. He had managed to assemble a little laboratory, a luxury which was then almost unknown in Russian high schools. His attitude toward his pupils was in wholesome contrast with that of the other members of the staff. He was a decent, liberal-minded fellow, and treated us like human beings. He en-tered into conversation with us, and did his best to interest us in the wider aspects of natural science. I need hardly say that most of us responded warmly, and there grew up a kind of friendship between pupils and teacher — a state of affairs unimaginably rare in the Russian schools of that day.

Jewish Pinsk was divided into two communities, Pinsk proper and Karlin, each with its own set of synagogues, rabbis, hospitals, and schools. Karlin, where I lived, was considered, as they say in America, the right side of the tracks. It was here that I grew from boyhood into early manhood, here that I had my social and intellectual contacts, and here that I was inducted into the Zionist movement. Pinsk, then, set the double pattern of my life; it gave me my first bent toward science, and it provided me with my first experiences in Zionism.

We must not think of Zionism in Pinsk fifty-odd years ago, long before the coming of Theodor Herzl, in terms of the modern movement. Organized activity in the present-day sense simply did not exist. A youth organization was undreamed of. There were casual meetings of the older people, at which the youngsters sneaked in, to sit in a corner. On rare occasions when a circular was sent out, we were permitted to address the envelopes. Our financial resources were comically primitive; we dealt in rubles and kopecks. One of the main sources of income was the collection made on the Feast of Purim. Youngsters were enlisted to distribute leaflets and circulars from house to house, and modest contributions would be made by most of the householders. Not all, by any means. Not the very rich ones, for instance, like the Lurias, the great clan of industrialists with branches in Warsaw, Libau, and Danzig, who owned the match factory in Pinsk. For already, in those early days, the classic divisions in Zionism, which have endured till very recent days, manifested themselves. The Jewish magnates were, with very few exceptions, bitterly anti-Zionist. Our supporters were the middle class and the poor. An opposition — in the shape of a labor movement — did not exist yet, for the Bund, the Jewish revolutionary labor organization, was not founded until 1897 — the year of the first Zionist Congress.

During my student years in Berlin and Freiburg, as well as later on, when I was teaching at the University of Geneva, I invariably went back to Russia for my holidays. Nine months of the year I spent in the free Western world; but every June I returned to the East, and until the autumn I was the militant Zionist in the land where Zionism was illegal. In the East our opponents were the *Okhrana*, the Russian secret police. In the West it was an open fight, in the East a conspiracy. The West preached liberty, the East practiced repression; but East and West alike were the enemies of the Zionist ideology.

It was in the fen and the forest area about Pinsk that I did my first missionary work, confining myself to the villages and townlets. In these forlorn Jewish communities it was not a question of preaching Zionism as much as of awakening them to action. I went about urging the Jews of places like Motol to enroll in the Hoveve Zion; to send delegates to the first Zionist Congress, when that was called in 1897; to buy shares in the first Zionist bank, the Jewish Colonial Trust, when that was founded in 1898. Most of the meetings were held in the synagogues, where, in case of a police raid I would be "attending services" or "preaching." My dreams were opulent, my demands modest. It was a gala day for me when I managed to raise twenty or thirty rubles for the cause.

With the years, the areas assigned to me by the local committee widened out. Mozyr was the first fair-sized town to which I was sent as an apostle. Mozyr had a large synagogue; it also boasted an intelligentsia. So, from the tiny communities of the marshlands I graduated to Vilna in the north, to Kiev and even Kharkov, with their large student bodies, in the south.

Here the missionary work was of a very different order. I no longer had just the folk to deal with. Among the Russian-Jewish assimilating intelligentsia, and among many of the students, there was an ideological opposition to Zionism which had to be countered on another level. These were not the rich, orthodox Jewish families of Pinsk, obscurantist, reactionary. They were not, either, the *shtadlanim*, the notables, with their vested interests, their lickspittle attitude toward the Russian Government, their vanity, and their ancient prestige. Nor were they like the German assimilating Jews, bourgeois, or Philistine. For these last strove, in their assimilationist philosophy, to approximate to the type of the German *Spiessbürger*, the comfortable merchant, the *Geheimrat*, the professor, the sated, respectable classes. Most of the Russian-Jewish intelligentsia, and above all the students, assimilated toward the spirit of a Tolstoy or Korolenko, toward the creative and revolutionary classes. It was, I think, a tragically erroneous assimilation even so, but it was not base or repulsive. In Germany we were losing, through assimilation, the least attractive Jewish groups. The opposite was the case in Russia.

For me, then, it was a time of threefold growth. I was pursuing my scientific studies systematically, and to that extent resisting the pressure of bohemianism in my surroundings. At the same time, within the Russian Jewish Society, I was working out, in discussion and debate, my political philosophy, and beginning to shed the vague and sentimental Zionism of my boyhood. Third, I was learning, one might say from the ground up, the technique of propaganda and the approach to the masses. I was also weaving the web of my life's personal relationships.

If Russian Jewry was the cradle of my Zionism, the Western universities were my finishing schools. The first of these schools was Berlin, wth its Russian-Jewish Society; the second was Berne, the third Geneva, both in Switzerland. The second and third may be lumped together; and they differed radically from the first.

I finished my third year in Berlin; for the fourth — in 1898 — I went to Freiburg to take my doctorate. My favorite professor, Bistrzycki, a distinguished German chemist, of Polish origin, had moved from Berlin to Freiburg, and I followed him. There were very few Jewish students at Freiburg; but in the neighboring university town of Berne — three-quarters of an hour away — there was a very large Russian-Jewish student colony, and here conditions were not at all like those which I had left behind me. Switzerland — and this meant chiefly Berne and Geneva — was, at the turn of the century, the crossroads of Europe's revolutionary forces. Lenin and Plekhanov made it their center. Trotsky, who was some years younger than I, was often there. The Jewish students were swayed — it might be better to say overawed — by the intellectual and moral authority of the older revolutionaries, with whose names was already associated the glamor of Siberian records. Against them the tiny handful of Zionist students could make no headway, having no authority of comparable standing to oppose them.

Actually the fight was not of our choosing; it was thrust upon us. Our sympathies were with the revolutionaries; they, however, would not tolerate in the Jewish youth any expression of separate attachment to the Jewish people, or even special awareness of the Jewish problem. Yet the Jewish youth was not essentially assimilationist; its bonds with its people were genuine and strong; it was only by doing violence to their inclinations and upbringing that these young men and women had turned their backs, at the bidding of the revolutionary leaders, on the peculiar bitterness of the Jewish lot. My resentment of Lenin and Plekhanov and the arrogant Trotsky was provoked by the contempt with which they treated any Jew who was moved by the fate of his people and animated by a love of its history and its tradition. *They* could not understand why a Russian Jew should want to be anything but a Russian. *They* stamped as unworthy, as intellectually backward, as chauvinistic and immoral, the desire of any Jew to occupy himself with the sufferings and destiny of Jewry. A man like Chaim Zhitlowsky, who was both a revolutionary and a Jewish nationalist, was looked upon with extreme suspicion. And when the Bund was created — the Jewish branch of the revolutionary movement, national as well as revolutionary in character — Plekhanov sneered that a Bundist was a Zionist who was afraid of seasickness. Thus the mass of Russian-Jewish students in Switzerland had been bullied into an artificial denial of their own personality; and they did not recover a sense of balance until the authority of the "old men" was boldly challenged and in part overthrown by the dissidents — that is, by us.

We held our first organizational meeting in the back room of the Russian colony library; and we held it standing, for "the others" had got wind of our projected meeting and had removed the furniture. But we founded, on our feet, a Zionist society, the first in Switzerland, under the name of Ha-Shahar, the Dawn; and we resolved to carry the fight into the open.

The mere proclamation of our existence created a scandal. The "reactionary bourgeoisie" was on the march! The colony was in a turmoil, and attempts were made to browbeat us into submission. We refused to be browbeaten. Instead, we called a mass meeting of the Jewish student body for the purpose of increasing our membership, and the notices proclaimed that I was to read a paper and submit a resolution in favor of the Zionist program.

I cannot help saying that this step called for a certain degree of moral courage. Lenin was not the world figure which he became later; but he already had a name. Plekhanov, an older man, was widely known. We, on the other hand, were nobodies. So if the founding of Ha-Shahar was a scandal, this step was revolution. The other side mobilized all its forces; we, for our part, invited down from Berlin two gifted young Zionist speakers, Berthold Feivel and Martin Buber. The meeting, which was held in a *Bierhalle*, expanded into a sort of congress, and lasted three nights and two days! It was before the dawn of the third day, at four o'clock, that the resolution was put to a vote, and we scored a tremendous triumph. A hundred and eighty students enrolled in the Zionist Society — a striking revelation of the true inclinations and convictions of a large part of the Jewish student body.

This was the first real breach in the ranks of the assimilatory revolutionists in Switzerland. I recall that Plekhanov was particularly outraged by our success. He came up to me after the close of the meeting and asked me furiously: "What do you mean by bringing discord into our ranks?" I answered: "But Monsieur Plekhanov, you are not the Tsar!" There was already, in those days, something significant in the autocratic spiritual attitude of the revolutionaries.

Seen from this distance, and across a turbulent period of human history, that incident in a Swiss university may seem to be rather unimportant. It had, however, serious repercussions in our young world. The shock of the

Berne rebellion was felt throughout the student body of the West, and Zionism was strengthened at a dozen different points. The struggle was on for the possession of the soul of that generation of young Russian Jews in the West. It must not be forgotten that of the thousands who were then preparing for a career in the West, a large proportion returned to Russia. The students who had been won for Zionism became influential cells in their hometowns. I found them there later, carriers of the movement in the Jewish communities.

44 Defenders of the City
by Schneur Zalman Shazar

SCHNEUR ZALMAN SHAZAR (Schneur Zalman Rubashov) was born in Mir, province of Minsk, in 1889 and settled in Palestine in 1924. Since 1963 he has been President of Israel. He was one of the early Labor Zionists, as he describes in the following memoir about the organization of self-defense groups in 1903. In his later quest for education, he came to St. Petersburg and was one of the students at Baron David Günzburg's Institute of Oriental Studies and thereafter worked in the emigration offices of the Jewish Colonization Association. All his life active in the Labor Zionist movement, he nevertheless remained deeply committed to his historical scholarly interests and continued, whenever the pressures of party work permitted, to make his contribution to Jewish historical and literary research. The following selection has been translated from his memoirs.

STOLPCE, city of my childhood! Pride of my youth! I still do not believe that you were led like sheep to slaughter. For did I not know your young heroes, reared on the banks of the Niemen and skilled in border fights? I remember your brave butchers and coachmen, ships' caulkers and river raftsmen, the tough peddlers who used to take on drunken peasants, and the Jews from the nearby villages nurtured on hard labor, and the young men at the markets experienced in handling weapons.

Aye, that handful of partisans who came to Palestine through the seven divisions of hell from the forests of Polesia across the border of Rumania and Italy are witness that also in that calamity, your heroism did not fail you. But I was a witness at the start, when first the spirit of resistance and

defense was kindled in you. I remember well when first that powerful ignit-
ing word "self-defense" fell among your young people, when the self-
defense movement had barely begun to be organized.

Self-defense itself was older than its formal organization. The town,
surrounded by villages, lived by trade and handiwork. Sunday was market
day and a day of misfortunes. On market days a crowd used to collect
around the town inn and in front of the homes of Jonah and Mordecai
Isaac, the vintners, scaring everyone. Jonah and Mordecai, devout and
learned Jews, used to make raisin wine for kiddush and havdala for the
townsfolk on Fridays, and on Sundays they sold vodka to the village peasants. Ever since liquor had become a government monopoly, the peasants
used to line up every Sunday afternoon in the marketplace in front of the
liquor store. There they left all the profit from the produce which they had
brought to town. With extraordinary virtuosity, they used to pop the corks
out of the bottles and swill one flask of vodka after another. That always
boded danger. When Easter approached or Christmas Eve, when the town
priest had duly inflamed the peasants' fantasy, after the long procession
wound around town and passed the gates of the liquor store, the stirred-up
peasants released their piety and their hostility in government liquor. Panic
seized the Jewish households. Schoolboys used to tell stories that in such
days Reuvele the coachman used to keep an iron rod in the leg of his boots
— for any trouble that might come.

Reuvele the coachman was the eldest son of Moyshke the coachman.
Moyshke in his younger days used to drive his coach as far as Smolensk and
Nizhny-Novgorod, carrying the town's merchants to the trade fairs. I knew
him only when he was getting on in years. Once a year he drove us, my
mother and the children, to see the doctor in a village five hours' drive from
Stolpce. En route he kept reciting Psalms, in a sweet voice and a marvelous
intonation, until in the course of the trip, while sitting on his coachbox, he
recited from memory all the Psalms, and between one book of Psalms and
the next he instructed me in how to write a most flowery Hebrew letter.
Reuvele, his eldest son, was the first of the town's defenders. He would
never take orders from an organization, mocking the help he could get from
friends, certain that by himself he could drive off all the enemies of the
whole town. At first sight, one could see nothing at all valorous in him. He
was thin, not tall, but he was fearless, and all the villages spread the fame of
his heroism. Once, it was told, seven peasants attacked him, one alone. He
clobbered them all, laid them out cold, and came running back to town
with a knife in his belly. Without organizations and without a special election, the town knew Reuvele was its protector.

The other strong man was Shmuel Tunik. In appearance he was just the opposite of Reuvele. Head and shoulders, he towered over Jews and Gentiles in town. He was a giant and a handsome man too. The ends of his thick blond mustache were pointed like spears. When he strode at the head of a unit of firefighters, whose commandant he was, with his copper helmet and the brass trumpet at his lips, the ground beneath him trembled. I do not recall that he really ever fought with a Gentile, but every drunken peasant feared even his glance. He had only to stroll around the market grounds to assure the townsfolk no harm would come to them.

Both these defenders had sufficed so long as times were normal. But then came the days of the first revolution, and the Black Hundreds were organized. Came the massacre at Kishenev, and the pogroms in Homel, and the dark clouds lowered also over the area of Stolpce. Since January 9, 1905, the wave of agitation against the Jews had not subsided. The newspapers were filled with news about pogroms. Suspicious characters turned up in town, neither buying nor selling, but loitering among the peasants and stirring them up. The peasants came out of church all keyed up. Decent, friendly peasants told us that agitators came to the villages and that the day and even the hour had been set. . . .

In town, a clandestine labor movement had already come into being. The Bund had been in existence for some years. In 1905, a Labor Zionist group was organized, attached to the Minsk region. At one Zionist meeting, a speaker described the events of Troyanov. A group of young people had set out from Chudnov to bring help to the endangered Jews of Zhitomir. They passed the town of Troyanov, but its Jewish inhabitants were afraid to shelter the young people. As a result, seven were murdered on the road. A writ of excommunication was issued against the Jews of Troyanov. We, in our youthful rage, recited the age-old verse:

> "Curse ye Meroz," said the angel of the Lord,
> "Curse ye bitterly the inhabitants thereof,
> Because they came not to the help of the Lord,
> To the help of the Lord against the mighty."

The thought ripened among the Labor Zionists that we too ought to form a self-defense unit at Stolpce. To buy arms we needed money, and we had to approach the townspeople. We decided to hold a meeting in the synagogue. Organization of the meeting was put in the hands of Pinye Kushnir, a baker's son and a nephew of the Cherikover rabbi, one of the first supporters of the Mizrachi whom I had heard speak out in town on behalf of Zionism. I was assigned to make the speech in the synagogue. The panic that seized me before speaking could not be stilled — I was only a boy, a month in the party; it was my first political speech at a public meeting. The meeting was held in the old prayer house after evening services. Pinye ascended the pulpit, rapped the lectern, and announced that no one had better try to leave. Besides bolting the door, two of our comrades guarded the exit.

Surrounded by my "bodyguards," I went up to the pulpit and began to speak. I started out with some Talmudic quotations, proceeded to call on the young people to enroll in the self-defense group, and urged the well-to-do townspeople to provide us with funds. Then Pinye began to announce the donations.

A week later we received instructions from the regional party committee in Minsk that our branch was to organize the self-defense in the nearby villages. On this assignment Pinye and I visited Swierzna, Horodziej, Baranowicze, Musz, Lachowicze. It was our first propaganda tour. We initially approached the local Labor Zionists, but the assembly was always public, held in the synagogue. As for the self-defense organization, that was always nonpartisan; whenever possible we saw to it that a local leader, Zionist or Bundist, also addressed the meeting. Soon the police found out about our trips and the solid citizens became afraid to go to the synagogue. Even Pinye's threats and bolting the door did not always help. There were even such heroic types who, out of fear for the illegal meeting, leaped out of the window and fled. Yet when we came later to their homes, they received us well. I remember especially the assistance of a Zionist in Lachowicze, a son-in-law of one of the town's rich men. Though he refused to join us on the pulpit, he accompanied us to the homes of the rich, spoke sharply to the well-to-do, and got decent contributions from them. We used to assemble the young people separately, in the women's gallery of the synagogue. Pinye used to divide the volunteers into units of tens and appoint their commandants.

When we returned to Stolpce, we found it engulfed in fear. We decided to call a meeting in the old synagogue on the Great Sabbath, following the rabbi's sermon. Speaking with me was the leader of the Bund in Stolpce, once my fellow pupil in heder. Then we had a surprise: After we had both finished speaking, my uncle, Joel Ginzberg, warden of the burial society, ascended the pulpit. I was afraid he would castigate us for having dared to have invaded the synagogue, especially on the Great Sabbath. But his words astonished us:

"I am no preacher, neither am I a preacher's son. I have nothing to do with any of these parties. But this time the boys are right. It is God's commandment to help with money and with muscle, for the situation is bitter indeed."

After the Sabbath, the most distinguished townspeople brought my uncle their contributions. The next morning Pinye went to Minsk to get spitters, as we called revolvers. At our next meeting, held late at night in the hasidic prayer house, our organization counted about a hundred registered and armed members.

Twice during that period we used our organized strength. The first time, we were alerted to come to the aid of the nearby town Swierzna, across the Niemen. A town smaller than ours, it was renowned for its Jews who leased the orchards from the landowners. They used to guard the fruit trees all week until the fruit ripened; then they sold the apples and pears at the nearby markets. No prayer-house types, these Jews had been brought up in the outdoors, always had business with tough peasants, and knew the craft of self-defense. But at that time, the pogrom panic had seized everyone and fear confused even the bravest. Early in the morning we heard the news that "it" had begun in Swierzna. Friendly peasants came to Stolpce to tell us that their young people had set out to loot and terrorize Swierzna.

We assembled our self-defense unit and set out to aid Swierzna. It just happened to be the thaw, when the Niemen was rising. Normally, the trip from Stolpce to Swierzna took twenty minutes, but with the Niemen overflowing its banks we had to go roundabout and cross swampy streams. The wagon in which we had our weapons — iron rods with round lead ends and iron prongs — could not traverse the marshes. We had to haul the weapons ourselves, crawling over the mud. That procession took us, defenders of Stolpce, six hours. When we arrived at Swierzna toward evening, fatigued and battered, but ready to fight, we found a ghost town. All the shops were barricaded, the streets silent and empty; one could not see a living soul in the houses. We learned that the Jews, frightened at the oncoming peasants, had locked homes and stores and hid in the cellars. We went from cellar to cellar, with our commandant Pinye leading, informing the Jews in hiding that the danger was over, their defenders had arrived. After having spent a whole day in terror in dark cellars, they regarded us as saviors from heaven. I remember how the young rabbi of the town, out of deep gratitude, kissed Pinye on the forehead. The women brought jugs of sour milk out of the cellars and briny pickles to refresh us. Then we learned that the thaw and the perilous roads that had not deterred the Stolpce defenders had dissolved the determination of the peasant pogromists. They changed their minds en route and returned home empty handed.

Some days later we heard that "it" was coming to Stolpce itself the following Sunday. This time we were ready. We knew that agitators had come from afar. We saw peasant women coming into town with empty wagons, and we knew they were coming to loot and wanted to be able to take the stolen goods home. In the morning, our comrades were on the street ready with iron rods, lead bars, and whips with rounded pieces of lead at their tips. The commandants of the units of ten, armed with revolvers, stationed themselves at many points in the marketplace. At noon, when the peasants poured out of the white church, rabid and worked up, ready to assault the Jews, one of the outside agitators gave the signal and started to lead the peasants to break into the shops. Then all at once our unit commanders fired their revolvers — in the air, not hurting anyone. The shots came from all sides of the marketplace, creating panic and confusion among the crowd of attackers. The horses broke wild, the peasant women began screaming as though they were being slaughtered. One wagon collided with another. With what seemed their last gasp, the peasants ran in fear from the Jews firing all over the marketplace. It took only a few minutes before the marketplace was emptied of the aroused pogromists.

No, Stolpce, pride of my youth, I cannot believe that you were led like sheep to slaughter.

45 A Mind of My Own
by Puah Rakowski

PUAH RAKOWSKI, Zionist leader, was born in Bialystok in 1865 and died in Haifa in 1955. A precocious Hebrew student, she was reading modern Hebrew literature at fifteen and even studying Gemara. She translated from Russian into Hebrew and also wrote for Ha-Tsefira. At seventeen she was married, but after five years she left her husband, taking her two small children with her. She then completed her education and became a teacher-principal of a girls' Hebrew school in Lomza.

The following extract from her memoirs takes up her story.

Puah Rakowski was a revolutionary figure, one of the earliest of modern women who sought and won her independence as a woman, both by making a career for herself and by choosing a husband on the basis of love and compatibility, rather than by traditional family arrangements. As teacher, school administrator, writer, and Zionist leader, she was an innovator, making a place for the modern woman in Jewish communal life.

I LIVED in the hope of tearing myself away from the provincial town of Lomza and becoming a teacher in Warsaw.

My uncle's friend Tykocinski went to Warsaw on business, where he stayed with a good friend of his, Eliezer Kaplan. Kaplan was a Zionist, belonged to the B'nai Moshe and was a member of the newly formed Hebrew publishing house Ahiasaf. I used often to correspond with Tykocinsky about my personal affairs, and I wrote only in Hebrew. Tykocinsky used to show my letters to Kaplan to prove how well a woman could write Hebrew. Kaplan began to inquire about me. He found out about my background and family and, learning that I ran a school in Lomza, he inquired if I was interested in becoming a teacher in a Hebrew girls' school which the B'nai Moshe had established in Warsaw. They needed a licensed Hebrew teacher and had been unable to find one in all of Russian Poland. The founders of this school included Saul Pinhas Rabinowitz, Nahum Sokolow, Abraham Shalom Friedberg, and Eliezer Kaplan.

During the Passover holidays I closed my Lomza school and went to Warsaw for an interview. The committee members agreed to everything: Yes, they said, I was a good teacher in all subjects, including foreign languages, because I had the license. But how could they be sure that I could teach Hebrew? They were justified, and I suggested that I give some model lessons in Hebrew. On one of the intermediate days during Passover they assembled some pupils and in the presence of Rabinowitz, Friedberg, and Nahum Sokolow, I took my Hebrew-teaching test. Of course, I pleased them and they hired me at thirty roubles a month for six hours of daily instruction. I was to settle my affairs and start work soon after Passover.

But things did not go smoothly. Bad luck ran ahead of me. A committee member had gone to school with my husband and he knew my story. He advised the committee not to hire me, because he knew for sure that my husband would soon come to take me away, who knows, perhaps even with police. He convinced them, and they called me to a meeting to inform me that they would not hire me until I had a divorce from my husband.

Obviously, this upset me. Not enough that my parents as well as his kept me fettered, would not permit a divorce, but they did not even let me move freely, nor let me arrange my life as I chose, on my own. Suffice to say, it was a terrible experience. Finally I hit on a daring scheme. A month before Rosh ha-Shana I wrote three letters, in Hebrew at that: one to my grandfather, the rabbi of Mariampole, another to my father in Bialystok, and a third to my husband in Odessa: "If you do not release me and send a divorce as soon as possible, I will convert to Christianity and baptize the children, too." These letters had the right effect.

Neither my parents nor my husband's parents knew how contrary to my nature such a step was; not even my husband understood. They knew only that I was not observant, and they assumed therefore that one could believe such a thing of me. The first to respond to my letter was my grandfather. He wrote my father that a divorce should be issued to me. His letter was severe, actually a command. Then the in-laws got together with my husband and sent the divorce to the Lomza rabbi. He found some rabbinic deficiency in the divorce and wanted to return it, but I prevented him from doing so, arguing that if the divorce were returned, I would never get another, my husband being very pious would consider this the hand of God. I got the divorce and immediately wrote to the school committee in Warsaw that I would arrive after the holidays to begin teaching.

In September, 1891, at twenty-six, I began to teach Hebrew and Russian in the girls' Hebrew school which the B'nai Moshe had founded. It was called the Yehudiya. I had my eight-year-old son and six-year-old daughter with me.

At about the same time I began teaching here, I became strongly attracted to the Hibbat Zion movement. The groundwork had been laid in Bialystok, where the Zionist idea had appealed to many circles and had produced leaders like Rabbi Samuel Mohilever and A. S. Hershberg. It is hard to say when and how I became a Zionist. Sometimes it seemed that I had been a Zionist from my earliest childhood. I suppose the foundation had been laid in my education, the heder, the Bible, and later, perhaps, also the pogroms.

When I came to Warsaw in 1891, I heard that a young woman, Leah Levin Epstein, had recently returned from Palestine where she had spent a year with her brother, the founder and manager of Rehovoth. I learned her address and went to see her, saying directly: "I heard you were in Palestine. I would like to have a look at you and get to know you." We became friends from that time on.

Soon afterward Leah became interested in Yehudiya and its financial situation, which was shaky. Many Zionist-minded parents did not appreciate the importance of Hebrew for their daughters. The more observant parents held to the rule that "he who teaches his daughter Torah is like teaching her obscenity." As for the more progressive, they were eager to teach their daughters foreign languages, but certainly not Hebrew. Jewish fathers argued that the sacred tongue was for boys. So Yehudiya, as a girls' Hebrew school, had a hard time financially. Leah organized a women's committee which was to broaden the school's membership base and thus provide monthly contributions. The women's committee did so well that I was able to propose we organize evening Hebrew courses for poor children.

Yet I was not quite satisfied with the school or the evening courses. The pupils did not stay long; after a year or two they went to larger schools. Not everyone thought Hebrew was good enough for them, not even Zionists, for they took a more practical view of their children's schooling. The situation was so bad that I thought of turning my girls' Hebrew school into a regular elementary school. I got the permit from the education department without difficulty because I introduced Russian as the language of instruction. The change helped. The enlarged curriculum in a three-year course brought better educational results, also for Hebrew, and the school's financial situation improved. But that still did not satisfy me. Hebrew is a difficult language, but a necessary one. It is not used at home or on the street, yet do not our fathers and brothers have to study it for years in hedarim and yeshivot to master it properly? What does one girls' Hebrew school in this great Jewish Warsaw amount to? We ought to establish a chain of Hebrew schools so Hebrew might penetrate all hearts.

Thinking along these lines finally led to deeds. I proposed to the school committee that since Yehudiya was now quite popular, they could run it. Let me apply to the Ministry of Education for a permit to open a seven-grade girls' school, with Russian as the language of instruction and Hebrew as a subject to be taught more than three hours a week. I wanted to run such a school on my own responsibility. My proposal evoked differences among the school board, but eventually I won. I remained principal of Yehudiya until I received the permit for the seven-grade school, which I opened in the heart of Jewish Warsaw. Yehudiya was transferred to a more well-to-do part of town and eventually became a Hebrew gymnasium.

Things did not go badly, though my life, like the life of all Jewish teachers, was not easy financially. The school, known as "Puah Rakowski's First Hebrew School," had a large enrollment, particularly of middle-class girls. But the ideological battle for the revival of our old national language had to be conducted patiently and stubbornly. If we are to teach our children Hebrew, how can we fail to associate it with our past and with Palestine? I taught my pupils about Palestine and the girls used to know when to tell one another: "Now teacher will cry." (Yes, I admit I could not speak about Palestine without tears in my eyes.) I devoted myself fully to the school. Despite the hardships, I loved it.

When the Jewish National Fund was organized, I thought that was the most suitable time to form a Zionist women's organization. The Jewish National Fund had opened a broad field of activity for Jewish women. The practical work on behalf of Zionism would be sure to give a woman spiritual satisfaction, and in time she would be infused with the ideology of our movement. "By all means let a man engage in the study of the Law and in good deeds, even if not for their own sake, for through the work for a selfish purpose he will arrive at the stage of doing good for its own sake." When I expressed my thought to one of the leading Zionists, he said with the male's customary contempt: "Comrade Rakowski, you will not establish any Zionist women's organization."

"Perhaps I will," I said, cutting off the conversation.

This brief exchange annoyed, but did not discourage, me. Without procrastinating, I convened a group of rather active women and proposed that we create a separate women's committee of the Jewish National Fund. It was high time, I told them, for us to stop being errand girls for our male comrades. Our participation in practical work was actually much greater than theirs, but they took the credit. We, for our part, do not ask for appreciation, because this is our duty. But as long as we have the same duties, we demand equal rights and we can win these only when we succeed in forming our own Zionist women's organization. The founding of a women's division of the Jewish National Fund was the first step on this road. My proposal was well received and unanimously adopted.

How did the men in the B'nai Zion regard this revolutionary step? The older men simply looked upon it as an assault on the biblical precept "and he shall rule over you." The younger ones thought it contravened democratic principles, which did not recognize a women's organization. But our opponents took no action against us. The women's committee carried on its work with no less success than the men and eventually became the basis of the Zionist women's federation in Poland, B'not Zion, the Daughters of Zion.

Eleven women took part in the first Zionist Congress, mostly wives of leading Zionists and a few students at Swiss universities who were for a time interested in the Zionist movement. Though they had been given equal speaking rights and voting privileges, without having to demand them, they sat silent, just observing and listening. Only at later congresses did women begin to show signs of activity and that kept growing. Beginning in 1921, a year after the founding of the Women's Zionist Organization (WIZO), the women's conferences were held simultaneously with the congresses.

However extraordinary it may sound, some forty years ago Jewish women, and young women, too, who had been brought up on the old-fashioned notion that "All glorious is the king's daughter within the palace," never felt as comfortable at general meetings as they did in the women's federations. Rarely did a woman have the courage to speak publicly. Most had not liberated themselves of the absurd notion that any man was allegedly wiser than a woman. Nor did the contemptuous attitude on the men's part encourage them.

Yet despite the difficulties, the Daughters of Zion grew and in a few years had thousands of members in seventy branches in Russian Poland.

In 1918 a new radical *halutzot* ("women pioneers") movement emerged that symptomized the changes in the woman's role in Jewish Poland. The halutza had originally been the simple girl, of the typical middle-class Jewish home, sometimes of the great hasidic dynasties, whose one and only purpose in life had been to wait for her promised one. This girl made the first revolution in the Jewish world. With her hitherto-suppressed youthful ardor, in stubborn combat with her milieu, she broke out of her enslaved condition, shattered the Chinese Wall of old, moldy traditions, and prepared for a new life on economically healthy and normal foundations, a life where her religion would be a religion of labor, of creativity. Yet the initiators of the movement were not women. The cradle of the Hehalutz movement had been in Russia. After the Bolshevik revolution, the movement was transferred to other European countries, but concentrated particularly in Poland, where large-scale intensive agricultural preparation and propaganda work were conducted and from which a mass emigration of pioneers streamed to Palestine.

Our propaganda work, oral and printed, brought results. The halutzic ranks kept increasing: not only the leftist young people, but also middle-class youth became imbued with the revolutionary halutz ideal. The hopelessness of any economic future in Poland was the chief drive in motivating these so-called middle-class idlers to become the avant-garde of a movement of youthful workers on their way to Palestine.

46 Memoirs by My Typewriter
by Vladimir Jabotinsky

VLADIMIR JABOTINSKY was born in Odessa in 1880 and died at Camp Betar, Hunter, New York, in 1940. The product of assimilated and easy-going Odessa, which he describes in the following selection of his unfinished memoirs, Jabotinsky became the intensely nationalist and militant Zionist leader, the founder of the Jewish Legion during World War I and later of the Zionist-Revisionist movement. Though the movement he fathered has often been accused of militarism and fascism, he himself has been less critically regarded because of his own gifts and great personal appeal. His ideas and his movement were a strange hybrid of his Jewish loyalties and his Westernized, romanticized notions of modern nationalism. Yet he made it possible for even the most un-Jewish Jews, for whom force had a mystique of its own, to find their place within the Jewish community.

SOMETIME in a man's life comes a turning point when he must pause to give himself an accounting, however brief, of the sins he has committed, and when he must see if he can promise God, man, and himself to try to shun these sins in the future. The undersigned is at such a turning point.

A furious tempest in our Jewish teacup, a small teacup full of the bitterest water in the world, and a bitter tempest. Young Jews beat each other with fists, sticks, and stones in Jerusalem, Warsaw, Lemberg, Paris, and who knows where else. In the course of demonstrating our national unity in this charming way, the undersigned's name is often mentioned, usually as a word of abuse. Standing before an audience that brings with it this dowry of enmity, an accounting is really called for. It even seems that all these assembled regard you with this question in their eyes: You must really have sinned heavily; what then were your sins and will you perhaps shun them in the future?

In the old days when a writer paused to ponder, he used to bite his pen. That was both a comfort and a source of ideas and reminiscences, but not nowadays — try to bite a typewriter! Yet the typewriter is a friend and a colleague, firm in its loyalty. A pen cannot imitate that — a pen cannot serve ten years. Ten years! This means, then, that my typewriter has lived through a good number of my sins. As for the others, the earlier ones, committed before it came into my life, it probably heard of them not just once or twice. True, one cannot bite a typewriter, yet in the end such a machine is not less like a living creature than a pen made of the same steel. If a writer can sometimes allow his pen to take over and write what it wishes, why should the same experiment not be made with an old friend like the typewriter?

Melancholy and pessimistic rings its iron confession. It tells the undersigned that it is not new for his name to be mentioned only for ill. Thus it was long ago, so it always was. Have you forgotten? I will remind you, dear friend.

You remember — the typewriter says — some twenty-five years ago (before I was born) an election campaign to the Russian Duma, somewhere in Volhynia, a meeting of voters in Rovno, a list of candidates, with your name on it, too, and a hall full of people who do not like that name. Just look at these people: all classes, all political wings, both the solid citizens of town — the doctors, the lawyers, the businessmen — and also the honest poor carpenters of the purlieus. All rant and rage against you and reject you. What was your sin at that time? Simple: you were a Zionist. Not, heaven forbid, a member of some Zionist faction, but just a plain Zionist, nominated by the central committee of the General Zionist Organization in Russia. Why were the people shouting? They shouted that you would bring misfortune upon the Jewish people by injecting Zionism into the Duma, that you would bring harm to the struggle for equal rights. Whom did they want to elect instead of you? Was it a Social Democrat or even a Jewish Labor Bundist who could represent the interests of those carpenters? Not at all. They supported a middle-class Cadet [Constitutional Democratic Party] even less left than you (you had already been in Russian prisons a few times), just as long as he was not a Zionist. Even the carpenters preferred the Cadet to you and kept shouting at you: "Down!" And you, still a boy and deeply affected by the whole atmosphere and the opinion of a mass of people, felt as if throttled by communal hatred and you asked yourself: Is it then a sin to be a Zionist?

Several years later, in Odessa, again an election, but now in a Jewish institution, in the Society for the Promotion of Culture, then a stronghold of russifying assimilation. The "nationalists" proposed a rather mild and moderate program of reforms. It was called "Two-Fifths," because it proposed that at least two-fifths of the school days in the Jewish schools should be devoted to Hebrew and Jewish history. The list of candidates was quite distinguished, headed by Ussishkin, Bialik, and Druyanov. But because you could shout better in Russian, you became the chief shouter, all the hostility concentrated on you. A most selected assemblage — the best-known upper crust of the Odessa community and, about midnight, after the theater or a concert, their overdressed wives turned up. They were not interested in the discussion and did not care to listen, for they came only to vote against the nationalists. They looked at you with hostility and applauded each speaker that proved you were a foe of education, a religious fanatic, an advocate of hate against the Russian people and against European culture. Shortly before dawn you leave that meeting, spat upon, and standing alone at the shore of the sea, you ask yourself: Am I an enemy of the Russian people? Am I one of the Black Hundreds? I, who just lately helped establish the self-defense organization? Am I the opponent of culture and an advocate of religious intolerance?

Still later: in 1913, in Vienna, at the Russian Zionist caucus before the Eleventh Zionist Congress. You are on the platform, proposing that Hebrew become the language of instruction in all Jewish schools in Russia. In Russia, just as in Palestine. Here members of the audience are not assimilationists, and the question is not whether or not one is a Cadet. This is a conference of Zionists like you. But do you remember the reception your proposal received? "Nonsense," shouted the delegates. "Childish talk — journalist, why are you butting into educational matters?" Once again, you feel it is not just that they disagree with you (how could they fail to agree on such a matter?), but that you disrupt, you arouse resentment, they rather dislike you — only a little, of course, not quite so heartily as those carpenters and those overdressed women, but coming from your own comrades it is a thousand times bitterer.

Why are you surprised, asks the typewriter? Is this anything new? Every person at birth receives his portion and all his life must bear it and cannot unburden himself of it. This is probably your portion. It is futile to resist, you cannot change it. You will always be in the wrong, weighed down with black sins. You were a sinner yesterday, you are a sinner today and tomorrow, a sinner who is hated and whose name sounds like a scare-word. Take my advice, the only advice for such a creature. You recall only the beginning, but you must not forget also the outcome. Remember what those voters in Volhynia did a year and a half later at the next elections to the Duma? They sent a collective plea to you to be their candidate. And the schools of the Society for the Promotion of Culture in Odessa finally became "nationalist," and Hebrew as the language of instruction became the basis of the educational policy of the Russian Zionists. Remember the outcome and try to forget the beginning. A good conclusion is worth much, even accepting with love the pain and even a portion of dislike. As for the dislike, I have advice: Try to convince yourself that dislike is but the first stage of friendship and gratitude. I cannot swear this is true — perhaps it is only a lie. But talk yourself into believing it is true. When you stand before an audience, particularly at a moment when you are heavily weighted down by your bitter portion, bow politely and respectfully to your audience, though there are probably some among them who dislike you, and say, "Sholem aleichem, brothers."

Nowadays everybody writes memoirs and it begins to look odd if one does not. It almost gives the impression of coquetry, of trying to convince people one is still young. Second, the process of writing and reading personal memoirs must be a sort of relief for both writer and reader, who are probably tired of struggling. I want to try too, not (Heaven forbid) regularly, but from time to time, when the spirit wants respite, without struggle. Just one comment: True memoirs mean communicating "the truth, the whole truth, and nothing but the truth." This I cannot promise. Truth is perhaps not such an everyday thing and not so cheap as to be wasted even on personal memoirs. Memoirs, I think, are not journalism, where truth is obligatory. Memoirs are a branch of belles lettres (my memoir-writing colleagues must pardon me; I am referring only to myself), and here it is perhaps best to mix truth and poetry, as Goethe said. In other words: It must not absolutely be your own biography, how you actually are. First of all, no one asked you to tell your biography. It ought to be a narrative about a certain period and about a milieu. This idea was best put by the Russian writer Korolenko, when he titled his memoirs: "Memoirs of My Contemporary." This dear, good-hearted man is long since dead, but I think even if he were alive, he would forgive me this plagiarism.

The custom is to start with a description of one's own family. But since the writer of these lines is just a beginner in this field of literature, he does not have the daring to start off with purely personal matters. May he be permitted to put this off for later? Here we will talk only about his hometown. I think a hometown is a very important factor in a person's education, especially such a town as mine.

Odessa was one of those few cities which create their own type of people. In all Russia before the war there were only three such cities: Moscow, St. Petersburg, and Odessa. About St. Petersburg there is a question whether the Petersburger was really a native type or only a farrago of other concepts: bureaucracy, capital, careerism. But about Moscow and Odessa there is no doubt — two clear types, as if hewn from marble.

The Jewish characterization of my fellow residents was an insult: "A thieving city." But this must be understood philosophically. No one probably meant that we were all thieves in the sense of pickpockets (though this profession flourished among us). The word "thief" in Yiddish ("*ganev*") has a much deeper meaning. It characterized a person who would fool you before you could fool him — in short, experienced, shrewd, a trickster, a manipulator, a maneuverer, a man of ingenuity, a screamer, an exaggerator, a speculator — but I said "in short." Many readers will think all these are not compliments, but I think they are, and in this sense I support the Jewish characterization of my hometown.

Even if it was a city in Russia and in my time very russified in language, Odessa was not really a Russian city. Nor was it a Jewish city, though Jews were probably the largest ethnic community, particularly when one takes into account that half of the so-called Russians were actually Ukrainians, a people just as different from the Russians as Americans from Britons, or Englishmen from Irishmen. At least four great peoples — three ancient ones and the fourth a young one — united to build the city: first the Greeks and Italians, a little later came the Jews, and only in the 1840's did the actual Russian influence begin to grow. The city was also full of Poles, Armenians, Caucasians, Tatars, Moldavians, and a half dozen other peoples. Yet it did not look like Constantinople, where the Levantines were foreigners and lived apart from any Turkish influence, nor like New York where people are divided into natives and immigrants. In Odessa, everybody was an Odessan and everyone who was literate read the same newspapers and thought about the same Russian problems. And thus the Greek, the Pole, the Jew, and the Russian all developed that same uniform and unique psychology to which I referred "in short" before.

Was this assimilation? Yes and no. The best illustration was perhaps my gymnasium class. We were thirty classmates, representing eleven nationalities, and ten of us were Jews. One would have searched fruitlessly among those Jews for even a glimmer of what today we call national consciousness. I do not recall that one of us was then interested in the Hibbat Zion movement for example, or even Jewish civil disabilities, though we all personally suffered from them. Everyone of us had had a hard time being admitted into the gymnasium and knew that it would be still harder to enter the university; we knew but did not realize it, for that knowledge played no role in our consciousness, in our thoughts, and dreams. At home some of us studied Hebrew (because father said so), but I never even knew who did and who did not, for the whole thing seemed so unimportant, like taking private piano lessons. Once, when the gymnasium offered us a one-hour-weekly course in Jewish religion (prayers and Jewish history), only three of the ten responded, and those only because their parents wanted them to. Of the books we read, I do not recall one of Jewish content. The whole subject of Jews and Judaism just did not exist for us. The same was true for the Greeks, the Armenians, and the handful of Italians. But not for the Poles — they forced even me to read Mickiewicz.

Yet, at the same time, we all lived in rigidly separated national groups, especially we Jews. Without any propaganda, without any ideology, we ten Jews used to sit on one row of benches in class, next to one another. As far as I remember, this was true in all our classes. For a long time we had a reading circle to study philosophy, and it simply never occurred to us to invite any non-Jews. At home, after school, one rarely encountered a non-Jewish student as a guest. We used to go about only with Jewish boys and flirt in the park only with Jewish girls. Why, I do not know. At that dead time in the early nineties (in Russian it was called "untime"), even anti-semitism drowsed — not, Heaven forbid, in the government, but in society. We were quite friendly with our Christian classmates, even intimate with some, but we lived apart and considered it a natural thing that could not be otherwise, or did not consider it at all. How does one explain this condition? Was it assimilation or was it instinctive nationalism? I do not know. Perhaps both. I believe the same situation held true, more or less, for the other nationalities. The five Poles, I recall, used to sit always in their "Polish corner," like the three Greeks, the three Armenians, and the two Moldavians in theirs.

Life in Odessa was easy and gay. The city had a sort of oral tradition: "As long as you have your next meal, you can whistle at the whole world." Under the impact of such a philosophy, our parents did not intrude too much in how we were getting on in school and where we passed our time. So we did not study very much and most of us never picked up a textbook at home. There were many ways to fool the teachers, who knew all about it and did not want to upset the system. As for our parents, it was not even necessary to deceive them.

Odessa reared healthier types than more traditionally Jewish cities. Odessa did not have any tradition, but it was therefore not afraid of new forms of living and activity. It developed in us more temperament and less passion, more cynicism, but less bitterness. On balance, is it better or worse? I do not know. But I would add the truth: Were I asked, I would not choose to be born in any other city.

Odessa is a great city; Kiev, too; Nikolayev, Kherson, Taganrog — all important cities; the whole Ukraine — an important land, a blessed country, forty million people at the opening of this century, which supplied wheat for probably another hundred million, if not more, in Russia and abroad. Who built all this? Who was the true creator of these enormously beautiful cities, harbors, railroads, highways, the grain elevators and ships, the theaters and the hospitals and the universities? The merchant. Not just the Jewish merchant alone, ten other peoples participated, and I mentioned them before. Without the merchant — no harbors and no ships, and no cities (villages would have sufficed), not even the wagoners. Why the piles of wheat? Those grain merchants, on a small steamer or even on a common wagon, travelling from place to place, discovering a wheat field here and a market there, a producer here and purchaser there — they united the earth with thousands of threads and wove a net of arteries for the blood traffic of the economy, laid the foundations for everything which is called culture.

This is perhaps the greatest positive influence which I inherited from my father, whom I practically do not remember — the pride of a calling. If you are a doctor or a tailor's apprentice or a rabbi, trade is not your calling, but it was my father's calling and my grandfather's and probably yours too; in the historical sense, the collective chief calling of our people in the course of seventy generations. They began when the world was a wilderness with wild beasts, and through their connective labor they transformed the wilderness into a chessboard of cities and roads.

Once an Odessa contemporary said, "Such and such happened just in that year when you were expelled from gymnasium." I was much amused there was such a myth; one is quite pleased with a bit of a myth about one-self even if it is only among a half dozen colleagues who join you for coffee in the same café. I did not deny it then, but a word in print, as everyone knows, must be the truth, the whole truth, and nothing but the truth. The myth is an undeserved honor. There was no reason for me to be expelled from the gymnasium. I was not engaged in any revolutions. The extent of my liberalism was that I forgot to get a haircut. Though I hated school like poison, I was not expelled. It was much worse. I ran away on my own — two months before the end of the term, of the seventh, the next-to-last class. Running away from a Russian gymnasium, which had been so diffi-cult to get into, was a great foolishness, especially a year and two months before completing it. And until today I thank the Lord that I did so, not listening to the advice of friends and uncles and aunts. Because I believe that life is logical. If one completes a Russian gymnasium in the normal way, then one must go to a Russian university; and then one becomes a lawyer. Then, when a war comes, one already has a wealthy practice and one cannot leave for England and become a soldier. So one remains in Russia until a Bolshevik upheaval erupts and then, considering my deeply reactionary world outlook, one would lie six feet underground without a gravestone. But I am continuing another career, one which started with a foolishness. I am thinking of writing a scientific tractate on the importance of not being afraid to commit foolishnesses. It is one of the most successful ways of living like a human being.

X

In the
Revolutionary Movements

47   Socialist Jews Confront the Pogroms

by Pavel Borisovich Axelrod

PAVEL BORISOVICH AXELROD, early socialist, was born in a village in the district of Meglinsk, province of Chernigov, in 1850 and died in Berlin in 1928. His family was very poor, his father the lessor of a small village tavern. Around 1858 the family moved to Shklov, where Axelrod, as an object of charity, had an opportunity to start his education. He then set out on his own to Mohilev, where he entered the gymnasium and continued to live in the direst poverty.

As a gymnasium student, he encountered Russian literature. Turgenev and Belinsky molded his new outlook. Axelrod has written of this period in his life. "When I was still in the fourth class I consciously strove to disseminate culture among Jewish youth. I wanted these young Jews to liberate themselves from their religious and national superstitions and I thought to accomplish this quite simply: I intended to disseminate among them the ideas, the concepts, and the aspirations which evolved in my head under the influence of these Russian writers and also under the influence of Börne and Dobroliubov." Somewhat later he came across Lassalle's *Arbeiter-Program* and Karl Ferdinand Gutzkow's *Die Ritter vom Geiste,* a novel about the revolution of 1848 in Germany. These two books literally and figuratively revolutionized his outlook and his future.

Thereafter, the "Jewish question" seemed trivial as compared to the idea of the "Fourth Estate," which he believed would solve all questions arising out of the injustices and misfortunes of the masses.

In 1872, Axelrod began his revolutionary activity, and his first successes came in Kiev, while he was working among Jewish students. In 1874, during a period of severe Tsarist repression and a wave of arrests, he managed to escape abroad, living for a while in Berlin. There he studied and observed intensely the German socialist movement, whose West European influence left a permanent mark on his thinking and in part accounted for his subsequent split from the populist movement.

After a few months, Axelrod settled in Geneva, where he lived until 1906. In 1883, George Plekhanov, Vera Zasulich (who in 1878 had attempted to assassinate General Trepov, chief of police in St. Petersburg), Pavel Axelrod, and Lev Deutsch (one of Axelrod's Kiev recruits of 1872) — all of whom had belonged to Chorny Peredel — formed a group called Osvobozhdenie Truda ("Liberation of Labor"), the first Russian Social Democratic organization. Axelrod became one of the editors of *Iskra* and in 1903, when the Russian Social Democratic movement split, he joined the Mensheviks.

He retired from politics after the Bolshevik revolution and lived his last years in Berlin.

The pogroms of 1881 and the indifferent, or even approving, attitude of the Russian revolutionaries toward them shocked the Jewish radicals. On August 30, 1881, the executive committee of *Narodnaya Volya* issued to the Ukrainian people a proclamation which justified and praised the pogroms.

Good people, honest Ukrainian people! Life has become hard in the Ukraine, and it keeps getting harder. The damned police beat you, the landowners devour you, the kikes, the dirty Judases, rob you. People in the Ukraine suffer most of all from the kikes. Who has seized the land, the woodlands, the taverns? The kikes. Whom does the peasant beg with tears in his eyes to let him near his own land? The kikes. Wherever you look, whatever you touch, everywhere the kikes. The kike curses the peasant, cheats him, drinks his blood. The kikes make life unbearable.

Some populists, it must be said, were highly dissatisfied with that leaflet and some even refused to distribute it. But according to *Narodnaya Volya*, October, 1881, that proclamation represented the official position of the party's executive committee: "We have no right to respond hostilely or even indifferently to a truly popular movement." That "truly popular movement" was pogroms.

Pavel Axelrod then began to write a pamphlet, describing the disillusionment of young Jewish radicals in the revolutionary movement. He tried to reformulate the goals of the Jewish socialist intelligentsia, specifically with regard to the pogroms, their causes, and effects. The following memoir is an extract from that pamphlet. But his idea of expatiating on the Jewish question from a socialist point of view found little response among the emigrant revolutionaries. Even Axelrod's own circle of former members of Chorny Peredel, Jews and non-Jews, objected to his writing on the subject, fearing to alienate the Russian masses.

Though Chorny Peredel agreed to permit its press to print, for a fee, Axelrod's pamphlet, he finally withdrew it and left it unfinished. Apparently the opposition he met was too strong. Axelrod's own explanation was that since he could not raise the money to publish, he did not finish writing it. Nonetheless, Axelrod's loyalties to the revolutionary movement persisted, and thereafter he was and remained not so much a Jew as a Russian revolutionary.

BEFORE I come to the main subject of my pamphlet, I would like briefly to consider why the Jewish socialists deserted the Jewish masses and what is the current state of mind of a substantial segment of Jewish socialist youth.

Before they became active revolutionaries, many Russian Jewish socialists may likely have thought of devoting themselves to the social and spiritual renewal of the Jewish people. But most, paricularly those nurtured on Russian literature, lost interest in the Jewish masses as soon as they learned even a little socialism. I still remember, when I first read Lassalle, how ashamed I became because I was interested in Jewish affairs. What significance can the interests of a handful of Jews have, I thought, compared with the interests and the "idea of a working class," with which socialism was imbued? For there is actually no Jewish problem, but only the general question of liberating the working masses of all nations, including also the Jewish masses. With the victory of socialism, this so-called Jewish question will be solved. How senseless then and indeed how criminal to devote oneself to the Jews who are only a small part of the vast Russian empire!

Thus the young Jewish intelligentsia sundered themselves from the Jewish masses and dedicated themselves wholly to the Russian revolution, to those organizations and circles that had no understanding of the Jewish situation. Yet the persecution of the outstanding spokesmen of these revolutionary groups and the long list of their martyred heroes reinforced the moral and spiritual attachment of Jewish socialists to non-Jewish socialists in Russia. It even eradicated our last bit of interest in the fate of our people, which needed the help of its own intellectuals as much as the other poor classes in Russia. We forgot, too, that a substantial part of Russian Jews was proletarian in the literal meaning of the word and that even the petit bourgeois elements among Jews, though parasitic exploiters of the peasants, were, in their huge majority, nonetheless dreadfully poor; they themselves were monstrously exploited by the military, the great bourgeoisie, and the government.

Now, having a more realistic attitude toward real life, we realized that the cosmopolitan aspect of socialism did not demand that we be indifferent to the conditions of life among the Jewish masses. We should have approached the Jewish masses not with liberal ideas and ideals in national coloring, but with propaganda about class conflict and the solidarity of the oppressed working masses regardless of nationality or religion. Jewish socialists might surely have been closely associated with Russian revolutionary groups, even as active members, while forming revolutionary groups in the larger Jewish centers like Odessa, Kharkov, and Kiev. This would have brought them closer to Christian workers' groups. Such Jewish groups would doubtlessly be a great help in the social revolutionary struggle in Russia. (Many revolutionaries, for example, found that observant Jews helped them wholeheartedly when they had to flee Russia as political criminals.)

Conceivably, after ten years of systematic socialist propaganda among Jews and a close association of Jewish socialist circles with true Russians, the one-sided unworthy nationalist aspect of the "anti-Jewish disorders" would have been considerably weakened. Such a Russian-Jewish association might have prepared some leadership elements to divert the mobs from attacking the poor and direct them toward the rich Jews, if they could not be directed against all exploiters in general.

Be that as it may, the Jewish socialist intelligentsia abandoned the Jewish masses, leaving them "to the natural course of events." The natural course of events led to pogroms which ruined the poor among Jews most. The horrifying scenes of havoc and the atrocities committed against tens of thousands of Jewish families and, hard upon that, the cynical anti-Jewish agitation by much of the Russian press — in a word, these repulsive excesses of a thoroughly medieval character towards the Russian Jews — opened the eyes of the Jewish socialist intelligentsia, revealing the mistakes they had made and the injuries they had inflicted on the Jewish masses, and finally aroused their concern and compassion.

I should like to quote from letters lent to me for this purpose. They reflect the state of mind among Jewish socialist youth at that time.

"Out of the blue in Yelisavetgrad, first came the whooping and howling of the city mob, 'Down with the kikes.' They began to loot, not making distinctions, not excepting the poor, nor the women. They flung children about. Groans and screams were heard everywhere. We, of the Populist circle, were joyful. We thought these were the signs of the Russian revolution, expressing itself first on the Jews, but then it would develop in depth and breadth."

Then the Kiev disorders began. One is horrified by their description, writes a student. Yet, he says, "We were convinced that all Jews were swindlers and that we ought to stand on the sidelines and not interfere. We belong to the Russian people. We were nurtured on its labor, our minds sharpened on its literature. We, the intelligentsia, are the brothers of the Russian people. Russian society, the Russian intelligentsia is united with us."

"How comical we were, how childishly naïve," comments the letter-writer.

At that time, a movement "to go to the Jewish people" had already been initiated among the Jewish students in St. Petersburg. But both that appeal and proposed program were at first angrily rejected in the provinces, and also by the writer of this letter:

"There is no Jewish question, but only a Russian question. If we will solve the general Russian question, then all other questions will be solved as a matter of course. Russian society is with us. The general Russian question will be solved by political changes, economic reforms, and the spread of education. This will unite the Russian Jews, the Pole, the Tatar, and the gypsy.

"But then the Christian students began to submit petitions and memoranda to the effect that the Jews were defilers, that they had seized the university chairs, the laboratories, education. The professors began to fail Jewish students in their examinations. Yet we comforted ourselves with the notion that only the outcasts of Russian society were doing this, that the better Russians were with us. And each of us continued calmly to go about his business."

Here is another letter. "The blood runs cold in the veins when we look at the insulted and humiliated. They seem only ghosts with deathly pale faces, expecting they know not what. At all levels of society, from the university intelligentsia to the ignorant peasant, a savage attitude toward Jews can be observed. This has stimulated both the Jewish masses and the Jewish students. The masses are leaving in groups for America; the student youth are forming groups to work out an emigration program. Relief committees for poor emigrants are being set up. Many students who could not stand being treated like dogs, even worse, like worthless animals, have quit their studies and are leaving. I have read letters from V., and B., and others in St. Petersburg. B. plans to leave the Institute. Meyer, too, plans to leave the Institute, to enter the Petrovska-Razumover Academy, become a good farmer, then leave for wherever everyone else is going. Many people plan to do the same."

Another student wrote from Kiev, February 18, 1882:

"Though the May Laws are directed mainly against Jewish economic interests, they have nevertheless so humiliated the Jews, so trampled their human pride, that the common Jew feels wronged and insulted. And, therefore, the Jewish masses are looking hard for a corner somewhere without restrictions and humiliation. Jews are ready to emigrate anywhere, let it be America, Palestine, even beyond the mountains of darkness, as long as it is as far away as possible from Russia. But the fat bourgeoises show little energy in the matter of emigration and unfortunately they have the last word because they have the big money.

"As for the young people, the first to respond were the Petersburg students. When a general fast was decreed, they all went to the synagogue. It was their first step toward their own people. Afterward, they threw themselves into Jewish life with all its pains and woes and have been trying to solve the Jewish question theoretically and practically. Then the Kiev students were heard from. After two nights of stormy debate, they also decided to go all together to the synagogue, not merely as silent witnesses during the services, but to encourage the despairing, to declare that they are ready to help, body and soul, that all Jews should be united. They prepared speeches in Russian and in jargon [Yiddish]. One student composed a poem for the

occasion and printed it. The presence of the students in the synagogue,
their warm and fiery speeches, and the poem brought tens of thousands of
Jews to the synagogue. Since there was not enough room inside, they just
stood outside. That was something quite extraordinary and of course the
police could not help but observe it. It was quite a successful demonstration.

"Now the students here are organizing an emigrants' society. Many students want to leave together with the common people and settle with them.
Others, who are not leaving, want to help them here. They are already
collecting money for emigration purposes. . . ."

Such reports came from various places in southern Russia. In all of
them the oppressive state of mind of the whole Jewish intelligentsia is evident, and most particularly among those who believed they had already
been fully assimilated into Russian society. Most shocked of all were the
Jewish socialists. The pogroms and public opinion, especially among the
Russian intelligentsia, after the pogroms were a revelation. Little by little,
after a bitter struggle, they acknowledged the full meaning of these events.
Long accustomed to the idea that there was really no such thing as a Jewish
people, that Jews were merely a group of Russian subjects who would later
become a group of Russian citizens, that Jews could not be segregated socially or culturally from the "native" population, the Jewish socialist intelligentsia suddenly realized that the majority of this Russian society did, as a
matter of fact, regard the Jews as a separate nation and that they considered
all Jews — a pious Jewish worker, a petit bourgeois, a moneylender, an
assimilated lawyer, a socialist prepared for prison or deportation — as kikes,
harmful to Russia, whom Russia should get rid of by any and all means.

The Jewish student youth suffered their greatest disappointment when
they realized that the socialist-minded Russian students sympathized with
the crusade against the Jewish masses and, worse yet, exhibited their antisemitic feelings toward their Jewish fellow-revolutionaries.

Thus, the pogroms made the Jewish socialist intelligentsia realize first,
that the Jews as a people are in a unique situation in Russia, hated by the
most diverse segments of the Christian population; second, that they, the
Jewish socialists, had committed an error in overlooking the actual condition of the Jews as a people different from the rest of the population. Nor
should they, Jewish social revolutionaries, in the name of cosmopolitanism
have forsaken the Jewish masses. As for the "native" masses, they lacked not
only cosmopolitan feelings and ideas, but were wanting even in the idea of
class solidarity among the poorer classes of Russia's nationalities. These
were the conclusions to which a sizable part — perhaps even most — of
Jewish youth had come.

48   The Jewish Factor in My Socialism
by Chaim Zhitlowsky

CHAIM ZHITLOWSKY, Socialist-Revolutionary and Yiddishist, was born in Ushach, province of Vitebsk, in 1865 and died in 1943 while visiting in Calgary, Canada, as a lecturer. He had lived in the United States since 1908. Zhitlowsky is the example par excellence of the modern radical Jew drawn to non-Jewish intellectual and revolutionary society, yet reluctant, despite his ambivalence toward the Jewish group, to divorce himself from it.

The following excerpts from the early part of his memoirs shed light on the tensions between him and his father, and on his hatred for the middle-class Jewish society whose embodiment his father seemed to him to be. His intellectual, literary, and scientific pursuits led him in a rational progression toward the populist movement — he was later to become active in the early Socialist-Revolutionary Party, but his feelings and, indeed, something akin to a mystical experience kept him within the community of Jewish interests. An eclectic thinker, he evolved theories of Jewish existence and solutions to Jewish problems that had in their time considerable influence. Yet for all his concern for a future Jewish existence in a future egalitarian society, his conceptions of Jewish nationalism — or Jewish nationality — were by and large hostile to and destructive of Jewish tradition. His first major

work on the Jewish situation was "Thoughts on the Historical Fate of the Jewish People," published in 1887 in a Russian journal, which the Jewish press reviewed as the work of a "negator of Israel" and a "Jewish anti-semite." Dubnow, Zhitlowsky's contemporary, wrote that this work was beneath any historical standard.

In the course of later years Zhitlowsky evolved the theory of Yiddishism which advocated the Yiddish language as the basis for a renewal of Jewish culture, to parallel a renewal of the Jewish people along economic lines — Jews were to became "productive" and "nonparasitic" elements in a socialist economy. Zhitlowsky advocated Yiddish as a national language, the vehicle of a national cultural entity. His was not the approach of the maskil and early radical whose attitude toward Yiddish was that it was useful merely as an instrument of instruction. Zhitlowsky constructed a theory of Jewish national existence that grew out of his recognition that Yiddish was a language used by the common people and belittled by middle- and upper-class Jews. Hence, Yiddish was a class-war weapon. Yet, however iconoclastic Zhitlowsky was toward all Jewish tradition, his theory of Jewish nationality served to keep many antitraditionalists within a Jewish framework.

THERE was a time I called myself a "cosmopolitan," an "internationalist," for to me both names signified the same thing: the antithesis of a "national-ist," a "patriot," a "chauvinist," which I thought were synonyms. Yet my cosmopolitanism, even my early radicalism, was not so much cosmopolitan as internationalist. It accentuated not the disappearance of nations, but rather their fraternal union. That certainly deviated from current thinking.

Did I assimilate this concept of internationalism from our Jewish prophets? True, the best of them first promulgated the pure internationalist ideal of a fraternizing society, with nations living like brothers within it. But I knew almost nothing of the prophets. We had learned about them in heder, but only incidentally and according to the interpretation of a later Jewry uninterested in such "trivialities." Did it perhaps come from the first founders of true socialism, who antedated me in the socialist movement — from Moses Hess, Karl Marx, Friedrich Engels, and Ferdinand Lassalle? But I did not come upon Hess's name until 1889. I had heard of the other three, yet had had no interest in their position on the national problem and in the ideological revolution which they had made in socialism on this sub-ject. Without exaggeration, none of us knew their views.

Did my internationalism originate in a Jewish religious world view which reigned in our world of Jewish ideas? That would seem likely. The enduring diversity among nations first appeared in the idea of Jewish chosenness. But also this conjecture I reject. First, Jewish religion was of no interest to me. I could not care less. The idea of chosenness was con-spicuous for its glaring chauvinism. Second, national diversity in the Jewish world view was distorted to mean that Jews differed from Gentiles, but all Gentiles were alike. Third, even nationalism, a basic element of interna-tionalism, was not quite a pure element because it was pervaded with religion.

No choice, then, but for me to search for the seeds of my thinking in my childhood years, especially in my father's direct or indirect influence on the early shaping of my personality. Now I realize that my father and, to a lesser extent, also all of us showed clearly decided and differentiated atti-tudes toward three non-Jewish nationalities: the Germans, the Poles, and the Russians.

Toward Germans my father felt deep respect. The German type enor-mously impressed him and he valued the German highly for his absolute honesty, for valuing highly his own human dignity, for having a stiff back-bone, and for demanding respect for himself as a human being. My father had quite a different feeling for Poles. Here it was not so much respect for the Polish type as tender friendship. Like most Jews in our environment, my father would, if he had thought about it, have considered himself a Polonophile. This period I am writing of came about ten years after the Polish uprising of 1863, which had repercussions even in Vitebsk, and was still spoken of. The heroism of the Poles and their contempt for death at their executions evoked our deepest admiration. We all suffered Poland's martyrdom. We had not the slightest doubt that Russia had committed the most brutal sin against Poland.

Besides, there was the specific circumstance that our family had many business associations with Polish landowners, from whom they bought woodlands or leased estates and breweries. These Poles used to visit us, laden with a wagonload of gifts from the country, their arrivals and departures punctuated by kisses and embraces.

Thus from the earliest childhood years, I absorbed from our environment at home and my father's influence something I designate a "heart-idea," something impressed deep in the heart, of which one is not always conscious, which is not often clearly articulated, but which underlies conscious thought. Such a heart-idea was my boyhood concept that nations are diverse in their nature and that non-Jewish people have many virtues deserving our respect and admiration: Germans for preserving their own inner human dignity, Poles for their heroism and tenderness, for their sufferings and their passionate love for an ideal — their people, country, and language. I am articulating this now; in those days, these were heart-ideas, vague sympathies and antipathies.

But our attitude toward Germans and Poles is less relevant here than our attitude towards Jews and Russians. My own attitude changed tremendously, tragically, and dramatically toward Jews, radically and joyfully toward Russians. From home I acquired Jewish patriotism and a rather strong anti-Russianism. Jews? Aha! No joke that Jewish Gemara-head! The Jewish heart! Moses Montefiore! Moses Mendelssohn! Beaconsfield! Russians? Our whole environment was completely permeated with hate for Russian landowners and officialdom that milked us dry, conscripted our children for the army, persecuted us in every way possible, and treated us like dogs. As for the Russian masses, we regarded them as brute animals. My father, particularly, was anti-Russian. We had only fiery hate for the power wielders, ridicule and contempt for the whole people. There was no other name for a Russian than the derogatory epithet "Fonye" — "Fonye thief," "Fonye murderer," "Fonye drunk," "Fonye louse." Writing my memoirs, I suddenly recalled the conversations and jokes around our dining table about the ignorance and stupidity of the Russian peasants. I wondered what bearing that had on my subject — explaining how I became a socialist. But my subconscious stream of thought did not betray me.

I will never forget those evenings when our handyman, a Russian peasant, sat in a corner of our dining room, his plate on his knees, while my family regaled itself at table with jokes about Jews outwitting the stupid Russian peasants. Who would have thought then that I would regard our Russian servant as the symbol of the whole Russian people? That I would feel we all lived and enjoyed ourselves at his expense and thought ourselves toweringly superior to him, whereas in truth we owed him so much — this indebtedness of ours rested most heavily on me.

From our own way of life, I first understood the true meaning of exploitation, that it was a way of living at the expense of someone else's labor. All the merchants, storekeepers, bankers, manufacturers, landowners, both Jew and Gentile, were exploiters, living like parasites on the body of the laboring people, sucking their lifeblood, and condemning them to eternal poverty and enslavement.

The antisemitic press made charges against Jews and these anti-Jewish accusations were at least partly true, though the antisemitic press had no right to make them. Yet it was true that, with very few exceptions, Jews engaged in exploitation and led a parasitical existence. But the blame lay not on our lack of civil rights, but rather on the whole social order. Both antisemites and philosemites would have to disappear, because they belonged to the old world.

From my friends I learned about socialism, which in their proud conviction was the last word in scientific knowledge. New horizons opened up for me with new methods of measuring and evaluating phenomena, foremost among them socialist science, the last arbiter in all matters of human concern. I learned much of this, not systematically but from my socialist friends. These ideas deeply affected me. Their conclusion that Jews were, in the main, parasites filled me with sorrow and shame. It was not easy to submit to the judgment issued by socialist science. But still, think of it: science, socialism!

This new socialist ideology did not vindicate antisemitism, but if I would then have asked "Are you for us or against us," the answer definitely could not have been "for you." Socialism was a stream of ideas containing elements inimical to Jewish existence in the Diaspora. (I could not even conceive of another kind of Jewish life. It was still before the pogroms and before the Palestinian movement.) Years later Bebel referred to the relation between socialism and antisemitism — in his famous saying that "antisemitism is the socialism of fools." That would not have applied to Russian antisemitism, which was pure evil on the part of evil men, without the barest trace of a socialist idea. But between my Judeophilia and this social-ism which regarded the whole Jewish people as a multitude of parasites yawned a chasm which I had to vault. It was not pleasant to think that Moses Montefiore was a louse, that your father and mother, your relatives and friends whom you loved and respected were these same repulsive crea-tures.

For me personally, the idea of cosmopolitanism was for a time like heal-ing balm for the pain I had felt ever since it had been explained to me that we Jews lived a parasitic existence. Jews were parasites, but not Jews alone. Even Heine did not treat the stock-exchange Jews of his day with kid gloves. No one had any *special* responsibility to maintain a *special* Jewish existence. The messiah would soon come, and then differences among nationalities would vanish. So we became cosmopolitans — intellectually. But feeling is not so rational. Having lost our national Jewish orientation, our feelings nevertheless demanded a people to belong to, to unite with, to serve. And so we became Russians.

Many of that generation, having shed their tears over Nekrasov's poetry, made a binding covenant of tears with the Russian people. Why not with the Jewish people? Pondering the assimilatory effect that Russian literature with its Turgenevs and Nekrasovs had on us, I find it was because we had no such Jewish literature. That was before Sholem Aleichem and Peretz; there were only individual works in Yiddish that had not yet converged in one stream of literary development. These individual works presented de-scriptions of Jewish life that could not evoke love or even feeble sympathy for their Jewish characters and situations. They described a world decrepit and moldy, rotting away and fouling the air with its stench of corpses. Those literary works were the product of the haskala, with a totally nega-tive attitude toward prevailing Judaism and to all the institutions it had shaped. It was enough to compare descriptions of childhood in Yiddish liter-ature with those in Russian literature, and you could understand the differ-ences between our life and "theirs."

Later, when I had again become Jewishly conscious, I realized that had we had a progressive cultural Jewish environment in Yiddish and a Yiddish literature which would have depicted Jewish life as the Russian or Polish literatures depicted theirs — then our radical youth would not have made such an assimilationist break. But the fact remains that both the Russian language and Russian literature made us Russians. From untold sources, Russian life, Russian ideas, Russian hopes and aspirations streamed into our inner consciousness.

It was to take some time until I was truly an adult and able to follow an independent course in my life. Yet one thing was then sure: I knew definitely *that I was not a Jew.* From this I concluded that I must change my Jewish name to a Russian name. I still remember how I chose a name. When I had first enrolled in gymnasium, as an ardent Jewish patriot, I had not been ashamed of my name Chaim; on the contrary, I bore it with pride. Now it was different. Since "Chaim" meant life, the logical name would have been "Vitali," which sounded quite elegant. But I thought it was too elegant, suggesting an upstart. Yefim, the usual Russian equivalent for Chaim, was more natural. Besides, I remembered I knew a coachman called Yefim, which meant it was truly a democratic name. That was how an aspiring Russian revolutionary came to be called Yefim Osipovich.

I finally decided that the best thing for me was to prepare myself earnestly and systematically as a socialist propagandist, to go to the people, either village peasants or factory workers. It occurred to my friend Ansky that I should go to Tula, where he had an uncle. In that way it would be easier for me to leave home and extricate myself from the bourgeois atmosphere which caused conflicts between my parents and me.

Though our family life had its spiritual side — rabbinic learning, hasidic fervor, and a smattering of newfangled haskala, there was also another side, much less spiritual. Among almost all the wealthier members of our extensive family, a true cult of materialist pleasure prevailed. My father, who was very learned in Talmud and qualified as a rabbi, tended to be a lenient interpreter of Jewish law, permitting some things toward which other authorities might be stricter, like the length of time required to soak herring to make it permissible for use during Passover. At table they often spoke of culinary delights, like mushrooms marinated with little cucumbers. Corpulence was considered God's gift, a sign of grace.

These respectable and pious people were not ashamed to tell unseemly stories and jokes, even with the children at the table. What could children understand? They did not notice how the children blushed and that their minds were captured by these sweet, enigmatic secrets which they could not yet understand intellectually, but which stirred their blood. Once there was some talk about my parents' early married life, when they lived with my mother's family and I was a year-old infant. My mother was saying I had made it a habit to beg myself into her bed at night, screaming at the top of my lungs. "Then," she related, "Papa took a thin strap and lightly whipped his fingers. Little Chaim really wailed then." My mother had told this story so melodramatically that the tears welled up in my eyes — I was then six or seven and felt terribly sorry for that baby.

"What else?" My father defended himself, with an ironic grimace. "I needed him in our bed like a hole in the head."

At that time our family lived well and had a good income. Each year the desire for worldly pleasures grew. When we moved from the wooden house at the end of town to a large brick house in the very center of town, quite a new life began — in which more liberal ideas lightened the former strict piety. My mother uncovered her hair and my father began to wear his coat shorter. In place of the old spiritual ideals came the thirst for luscious living and luscious earnings. Material wealth became their idol. The old values of religious learning, piety, and family were replaced by the cult of money.

From this bourgeois atmosphere I had to escape. I was then only about sixteen, bound with innumerable ties to my home and my mother, whom I loved dearly and who loved me, and to my father for whom I had the greatest respect from earliest childhood. There were, however, no tragedies and no conflicts at my leaving. At first, my mother tried to dissuade me, but then both parents gave their consent and, of course, their financial support.

I had gone to Tula as a Russian to work for the Russian people, among whom I counted the Jews who would become just as Russian as I. But I had accomplished nothing. In the summer of 1883 I returned to my birthplace, the little Jewish village of Ushach, where all my youthful fantasies of living as a Russian among Russians faded. In the foreground emerged the Jewish question, confronting me like a Sphinx: Solve my riddle or I will devour you.

The philosemitic solution of the Russian-Jewish press, demanding equal rights and justifying Jewish merchantry and its achievements for Russia, could not impress me. In fact, it revolted me. I sensed it as an absolute contradiction to my socialist ideas and ideals, which had a pronounced Russian populist, agrarian-socialist character.

Samuel Solomonovich Poliakov built railroads for Russia. Those railroads were, according to Nekrasov's famous poem, built on the skeletons of the Russian peasantry. My uncle Michal in Ushach distilled vodka for the Russian people and made a fortune on the liquor tax. My cousin sold the vodka to the peasants. The whole town lived off the Russian peasants. My father hired them to cut down Russian woods which he bought from the greatest exploiter of the Russian peasant, the Russian landowner. The lumber was shipped abroad, while the Russian villages were full of rotting, dilapidated huts, covered with rotting straw-thatched roofs. They could have used my father's merchandise. Wherever I turned my eyes to ordinary, day-to-day Jewish life, I saw only one thing, that which the antisemites were

agitating about: the injurious effect of Jewish merchantry on Russian peasantry. No matter how I felt, from a socialist point of view, I had to pass a
death sentence not only on individual Jews but on the entire *Jewish* existence of individual Jews.

Assimilation, the complete disappearance of the Jews and their merging
with the Russian people so that the Jewish abscess would not be distinguished from the Russian one, was the most logical and consistent solution
to the Jewish question. The most logical, yet for me psychologically impossible. For why fool myself? I felt myself a Jew. I was happy and comfortable in my Jewish world. Jews were closer to me, more my own kind, than
many Russians with whom I was good friends and closely associated because of our common views. Why fool myself? After all, I was a Jew.

What then? Must we Jews disappear? What an insult to me and those I
love and cherish! Were the Jewish nationalists right with their Palestinism,
which had its logic and consistency? So, the balance rose and fell, with
assimilation on one scale and Palestinism on the other, until an experience
in February, 1884, when assimilation was hurled off the balance.

All my doubts were removed by a purely literary experience. One of
Shchedrin's fables, "The Old Wolf," hit me like hammer blows. I interpreted the old wolf as the personification of Jews in Russia. The wolf attacks the bear. At the end, the bear says to him: "You are a most unfortunate beast. I cannot judge you, but I will tell you: I, in your place, would
consider death as your good fortune. Ponder on these words."

As I read this story, I thought — so, we are wolves, are we? Must we
die? Must we assimilate? Cease to exist as a people? I trembled with rage
and fury. I cannot say that my ideas flowed in any logical order. These were
rather aroused feelings of national pride. I felt deeply insulted. The idea of
assimilation disappeared like smoke.

The collapse of assimilation as an ideal and the upsurge of my Jewish
nationalism was not a result of a theoretically based and logically thought-
through mental process. Now I know it was intuition, like a waking from a
light sleep in which fantastic elements are mingled with real ones. Upon
waking, the fantastic disappears and one sees clearly what is real.

It became clear to me that the subject of nationalism, Jewish nationalism, particularly in relation to both progress and reaction, was a trouble-
some matter which had first to be researched and theoretically clarified. I
began to gulp every serious book and discussion that offered a theoretical
analysis of our progressive outlook. The intellectual world of the sixties,
with its Chernyshevskys, Pisarevs, Zaitsevs, Dobroliubovs gradually faded.
Other names, other intellectual worlds — more profound and more fundamental — replaced them.

I read Ferdinand Lassalle in German. Then Karl Marx — the first vol ume of *Das Kapital* in Russian and *Poverty of Philosophy*, his polemic against Proudhon, in German. How many hours of strained concentration it cost me till I mastered "value" and "surplus value."

As the old radical authorities faded away, two new intellectual leaders grew in stature: N. K. Mikhailovsky and Peter Lavrov. Mikhailovsky made the greater impression on me, though I did not yet understand the original-ity and significance of his new approach to theoretical problems. Mikhailov-sky's ideas massaged the rigid muscles of my dogmatic and self-satisfied logic, making them more flexible, so they could move freely in different ideational worlds. Both Lavrov and Mikhailovsky, though they represented different philosophies, sounded the same basic theme that neither logic nor common sense was the source of true knowledge, but only scientific investi-gation, which is inimical to every form of metaphysics. Positivism, whose foundations were laid by August Comte, replaced materialism. This com-pletely new approach to philosophical problems opened up for me a new intellectual horizon with stars of the first magnitude, each revolving around the central sun — August Comte. Thereafter, the order of reading was Spencer, Mill, Buckle (in Arnold Ruge's German translation), Lewes. All this had only an indirect effect on the development of my Jewish program. It gave me a wider perspective, richer knowledge and, most important, total liberation from those intellectual chains with which the radical outlook of the sixties had fettered our thoughts.

In those days there were not yet any socialist Jews, but only Jewish socialists, who did not care to be identified as Jews. I never heard of any socialist theories that harmoniously united socialist ideals with the problems of Jewish life. That formulation was one of the most important goals which engaged me a great part of my life. I think I am justified in saying that my theories about national socialism played a role, one way or another, in the development of Jewish socialist movements. These theories, too, it can be proven, had a great effect on the formulation of the nationalities program of the Socialists-Revolutionaries, a movement which emerged in the nineties, and one of whose first flag-bearers I was.

My position on the nationalities problem was also given serious consid-eration by the Austrian Social Democrats, even before Otto Bauer's and Karl Renner's splendid theoretical studies appeared. But all this came later. The prehistory of how I came to view these matters is what I am now describing.

All during this period when I was thinking of my Jewishness, my emo-tional state was poor. I was suffering from acute neurasthenia which at times reached a stage near hysteria. It was impossible for me to remain at home in the kind of atmosphere which I described before. I told my mother I was going to live by myself. She was very upset and, as a compromise, I agreed to come home every day for dinner.

I had a few hours of tutoring to cover my small expenses, and I rented a small room from a Polish widow. There I moved my library of semilegal publications which young people, Jewish and non-Jewish, used to borrow. The library kept expanding, thanks to my older brother's purchases of classical radical literature. He worked in my father's lumber business and always had some ready money.

I did not conduct any propaganda. I merely advised the young people what and how to read so they could become "intellectually developed." I used to show them where they could find explanations for one or another problem that interested them. Such tiny intellectual centers like my library were then coming into existence all over Russia. The more reactionary the government became, the tighter the censorship of the printed word, the more backward the trends in official educational institutions, the more the young people needed sources from which they could draw free ideas. But this work among the youth did not satisfy me very much. I was busy reading and writing poetry.

Without any conscious Yiddishist forethought, my poetic muse expressed itself in Yiddish. One poem I wrote was so descriptive of my mood at that time, I will set it down in prose, for it may not even have deserved poetic form:

"I myself know not why my heart grieves; why I am bathed in tears; why I have no peace and nothing can subdue my wild ideas. I know not what drives me hence and uproots me; what attracts me elsewhere? A feeling grows within me I cannot understand and wild thoughts sans words."

"Bathed in tears" was not pure rhetoric. I often used to weep, sometimes hysterically. Several such attacks occurred in the summer of 1884. That was when I first read Goethe's *Faust* in Russian translation. It had an extraordinary effect on me. Its ending stirred my soul to its depths. I had to exert my utmost control to restrain the hysterical lament that arose in me, for it was obvious that the final scene had a deeply symbolic significance for me.

For me then, Gretchen was our Jewish people. Our people is sitting in a dark prison, its mind unhinged, clutching to its breast a bundle of rags instead of a living child. Faust the liberator arrives, but the people do not understand his words. But when they comprehend what the liberating intelligentsia demands of them, they choose instead the dark prison, the doll and certain death, instead of freedom and life. The intelligentsia is then forced to abandon the people to their fate.

Need I explain the symbol of the doll which the people embraced? I was then still hostile to every religion, and especially Judaism. I then still had not the faintest idea that for us religion was the only source of life which gave us the spirit to exist as a people.

On a hot, quiet afternoon that summer, I rowed downstream on the Dvina. I pulled up near the hilly, overgrown shore, resting in the shade. Everything about me was frozen in silence. Suddenly, from above, as from the heavens, I heard a lamenting singsong feminine voice: "To whom have you abandoned me?" Above, on the hill, a young woman was weeping at a grave in the Jewish cemetery.

That single lament tore through the air, and then again the motionless silence. I felt hysteria coming over me and hastily I began to row upstream, back home.

The long-drawn-out despairing lament reechoed within me like a symbolic reproof. It evoked from me the pledge I had given to myself — always to remain faithful to the Jewish people, never to abandon them, to solidarize myself with their historic fate, whatever befell them.

Thereafter I never had any doubts or hesitations in thought or feeling about my moral responsibility. That was the central axis around which all my efforts revolved, in communal work, and in large part in my theoretical studies.

At this point the practical question emerged: What should I do?

Among the various plans I had in mind was one to which my thoughts kept returning. That was an idea to publish a legal monthly journal in Yiddish, an organ of enlightenment and struggle for those universal foundations of human progress which could be advocated even under Russian censorship. The decision to issue the journal in Yiddish did not originate from any conscious Yiddishism. The theoretical works on nationality, with which I was familiar, gave no particular importance to language, which was merely one of the characteristics of national existence. My later studies were to introduce considerable revision in this outlook, but at that time I shared the view that language was no more than a means of expressing and communicating ideas. My reasoning then went something like this: One must talk to a people in its own language. But our people use two languages: Hebrew and Yiddish. In the world in which I grew up, both languages had the same prestige. None of my pious relatives looked down upon Yiddish. After all, Torah was studied and interpreted in Yiddish. Hebrew, the sacred tongue, was valued more, but only religiously. As a secular language, in which one read the paper or a haskala book, it may have outranked Yiddish slightly, not for any inherent reason, but because of its association with education.

The question facing me was to decide in which language to appeal to Jews, not just the ignorant masses, but the whole people, to train an avant-garde to fight for the ideals of universal progress and for their realization in Jewish life. I decided on Yiddish. This was my calculation: We, the carriers of ideas of universal human progress, had to appeal to the people with our message about quite a new world, the world of modern, progressive West European culture. Vis-à-vis this world the whole Jewish people were like the ignorant masses. My father, greatly learned in rabbinic literature, a sharp mind and a thorough one, was just as ignorant as the shoemaker or tailor of Western culture. One could make no distinctions between classes and levels of education. One had to use the language that everyone understood. That was Yiddish, the vernacular of every Jew. I did not go into this matter any further, but it was easy to see what this first step meant and in what direction it would take me.

49   When Yiddish Literature Became Socialist
by Abraham Liessin

ABRAHAM LIESSIN, pen name of Abraham Walt, socialist and poet, was born in Minsk in 1872 and died in New York in 1938. He came of a prestigious rabbinic family and in his early youth was renowned for his Jewish learning. At thirteen, he entered the Volozhin yeshiva but was expelled at fourteen for smoking on the Sabbath and writing poetry. He came to Vilna where, befriended by socialists, he began to study secular subjects. But his fiercely independent character prevented his joining any group. After a few years he returned to Minsk, where he conducted socialist propaganda among Jewish workers. He was perhaps the only Jewishly Jewish populist who, it was said, had thought of returning to his rabbinic studies so that, being ordained, he could then use rabbinic authority and Talmudic teaching to propagate socialism among Jews. The following autobiographical essay reveals his uniquely Jewish approach to socialism at a time when only few socialists among Jews thought in Jewish categories. His warmhearted Jewishness, his lectures combining socialist propaganda with Jewish history, and his Yiddish poetry made him famous and beloved among Jewish workers' groups in Lithuania.

Early in 1897 he had to flee the Tsarist police and left Russia for America, the very year the Jewish Labor Bund came into existence. In America, he continued to work in the socialist movement, concentrating on journalism and poetry. From 1913 until his death he edited *Di tsukunft*, Yiddish monthly of politics and literature.

I FIRST heard David Pinsky's name in 1894, at my cousin's home in Vilna. I had come from Minsk for a few days to discuss the "national question." For about seven years I had been out of touch with Hebrew (I had not looked at a Yiddish book in even longer) and I was estranged from Jewish matters. Pushkin and Nekrasov, Uspensky and Zlatovratsky had practically made me a Russian populist. The only stumbling block in my mind was whether Russia could bypass the capitalist stage. While I studied this problem, Marxism became my ardent faith. Besides reading the legally published Populist literature, I devoured also the illegal literature which Liberation of Labor published — Marx, Engels, Plekhanov. I also studied in deadly seriousness the works of Lassalle and Marx which could be obtained in Russian. I do not know what and how the connections were made, but it just so happened that when I learned I was a convinced Marxist, I also discovered I was what I was: not a Russian, not just a human being (which is merely an abstraction), but a Jew. Marxism intensified my sense of reality and the reality surrounding me was Jewish. This Jewish reality found no expression in Marxist literature or in the practical movement which this literature had fostered in Jewish communities. I realized that Geneva, whence this literature emanated, was as far from us as the Russian village and that the German worker could as little serve as our model as the Russian peasant. In vain did our young minds struggle to adapt the accepted abstractions to the unfortunate Jewish reality, to our past and our future, but without success. At first I tried to fight off these sinful thoughts and gropings, just as ten years earlier I had tried to struggle with the religious doubts which tormented me. But I saw that the struggle was lost: I had become a nationalist, just as ten years earlier I had become an unbeliever. Though I had never been a disciplined member of the socialist movement, I felt lost nonetheless, like a tired migratory bird parted from the flock.

I decided to put my doubts before the leader of our movement. Alexander Kremer, known as Arkady, whom I had loved and respected from my earlier days in Vilna. Kremer, a man with a sensitive soul and vulgar speech, with a soft voice and rockbound opinions, was too de-Judaized to grasp the meaning of my confession. Since my inner world of Jewish experience was totally alien to him, I tried to argue with him in terms of the movement's practical aspects. I remarked that it was un-Marxist to adapt life to a pamphlet, especially if the pamphlet came from as far away as Geneva, where, as a matter of fact, it had been reworked from pamphlets in Berlin. Kremer gave me a withering look and began to scold me. I, in turn, shouted even louder that the Jewish worker was a fiction, that in our towns the worker became a petit bourgeois as soon as he married. That was why the movement had to emerge from its narrow economic outlook and become broader, more political, more national. We must formulate a Jewish national program. That way our socialism could appeal to larger masses — to the whole gamut of Jewish poverty. But my arguments ricocheted off him like balls off a stone wall. Against him I was a boy, and uncultivated at that, who did not support the organization and refused to go on trodden ways.

That evening I went to visit my cousin. Her parents' home was one of the most prestigious in Vilna, where one could encounter a rabbi together with a university student, where one man would recite evening prayers while another discussed Pisarev. Some seven years earlier, when I had first come to Vilna, not quite fifteen and already expelled from the Volozhin yeshiva, I had wanted to convert my cousin to Zionism and Hebraism. But she just kept on reading Russian novels and went to the Vilna opera. Later, when I became a socialist, I used to bring her illegal literature and try to make a revolutionary of her. But socialism did not stick any more than Zionism. She remained the wise daughter of a very wise mother. In time I became estranged from my relatives. Now, I was surprised to see that my cousin was active in the Jewish community; she knew Hebrew, interspersing her Russian with biblical phrases, the way the old-fashioned Russian aristocrats used French. She was a leader of the Vilna Daughters of Zion. The atmosphere of Vilna had become so saturated with social movements that even such a girl could not resist them.

This very cousin told me about Pinsky. She said she had met him at a small meeting of young intelligentsia where he advocated that they become "jargonists."

"Jargonists?" I repeated.

"Yes, join the party of the jargonists," she burst out laughing.

"What sort of person is he?" I was curious.

"A drugstore clerk," a friend of my cousin's replied and smirked.

I was angry: "A drugstore clerk may not rate high for a girl with a dowry, but Pinsky is a writer whose value you do not at all understand. Leave it to a marriage broker who knows better than you how to grade rank."

"Pinsky is, as a matter of fact, a military man," said my cousin, and laughed again. "At that gathering he stated belligerently that he had come to wage war on God and capitalism."

That was the attitude in those circles to "jargonist" writers. I said good night.

I walked the Vilna streets until late at night. I felt alienated, forlorn. I had nothing in common with the bourgeois Zionists and now also I had left the assimilationist-minded socialists. I had nowhere to turn. Then I thought of Pinsky and his "jargonism," and my heart grew lighter and happier. I perceived that perhaps here I would find what I sought, a synthesis of nationalism and socialism.

I myself had for some years been writing Yiddish verses. I had begun to write Yiddish because I wanted to stop writing Hebrew, but that sterile fanaticism did not last long. The Yiddish verses I wrote were mostly satiric, to ridicule something or someone, but occasionally I wrote a poem suitable for recitation at workers' meetings. Later on I became a real Yiddishist, not in the anti-Hebraist sense, but in the anti-Russian one. When the Russian *intelligent* went to the people, he first learned to speak the language of the Russian peasant, but the Jewish *intelligent* expected his people to speak not their own language, but his — Russian. I believed that the language of the masses had to be the language of socialist propaganda, and for me, revolutionary poetry became an important part of socialist propaganda. In "jargonism," whose purpose was to fight also capitalism, I saw something new, an overturn in Jewish society, an intimation that the common man would come to demand his share in intellectual life.

The next day I returned home to Minsk. A little later I was pleased to hear that Pinsky had come to Minsk and wanted to see me. Pinsky did not strike me as a fighter, not against capital and certainly not against God. He was completely a writer, living only in literature and for literature. Someone like me, reared in the radical movement, could understand him but not sympathize with him. Besides, Pinsky was well dressed, looked prosperous, was high spirited and self-confident. Everything about him was so precise and neat that he rather shocked a vagabond like me. Yet he exuded such honest enthusiasm for our young popular literature, so much active energy and youthful zestfulness, that I forgave him everything.

Yet we quarreled. Pinsky, I recall, kept praising the Yiddish writers and extolling them at the expense of writers in other languages. As long as the belittled writers were Gogol, Turgenev, and Saltykov I did not mind, but when Pinsky began to derogate Judah Leib Gordon, that was too much. Gordon and M. J. Lebensohn, two great Hebrew poets, had an enormous influence on me in my youth. (Later my inspirations were Pushkin and Lermontov.) When Pinsky praised a small, recently published book of Hebrew poems by Peretz, *Ha-Ugav*, more highly than Gordon's poems, I became outraged. But we parted amicably after I read him some of my revolutionary and didactic-satiric Yiddish poems. Curiously, I did not read him the purely lyrical or nationalist poems which I had already begun to write in Yiddish. I knew then the significance of a poem or story as a thing of beauty, but it had seemed to me a quaint luxury for our poor Yiddish, something like having a roof before the foundation was laid. After my meeting with Pinsky, my views changed.

Soon thereafter I became wholly absorbed in the practical labor movement. The leaders who came from Vilna attacked me for my heretical nationalist views; the police were always on the lookout for me. Where I passed the day I could not spend the night. Yet, always on the jump, in controversy and anxiety, I was always aware that in Warsaw, where Peretz and Pinsky were, the mansion of Yiddish literature was being built from foundation to roof. The more the Jewish masses awakened, all the more would builders of our literature emerge.

50   The Youth of a Bundist
by Vladimir Medem

VLADIMIR MEDEM, born of assimilated Russian-Jewish parents in Minsk in 1879 and baptized at birth in the Greek Orthodox church, devoted his life wholly to the cause of the Jewish labor movement as a leader of the Jewish Labor Bund. He died in New York in 1923. His tombstone bears, in Yiddish, the inscription: "Vladimir Medem, legend of the Jewish labor movement."

Medem developed as a political personality during the period of conspiratorial revolutionary activity in Tsarist Russia. He was arrested several times and was frequently forced to seek refuge abroad, usually in Switzerland, where he came into contact with various leaders of the Russian revolutionary movements: Plekhanov, Lenin, Trotsky, and many others. Shortly before the outbreak of World War I,

Medem was arrested by the Tsarist authorities. In 1915, he was released from a Warsaw dungeon when the Russians fled before the Imperial German Army. Medem remained in Warsaw until 1920 as a member of the Central Committee of the Bund; during these five years he became one of the most popular labor leaders among Eastern European Jews. His poor health, combined with internal party differences, caused him to leave Poland in 1921 and to come to the United States, where he retired from public life and devoted much of his time to writing his memoirs, a selection of which follows.

By constant study of, and immersion in, things Jewish, Medem came to know a great deal about Jewish history and customs, Jewish thought and politics. He learned Yiddish so well that established Yiddish writers declared his style impeccable. During his work with the Bund in Warsaw, he turned his attention increasingly to the educational and cultural aspects of the Bund's program, especially in the area of the Yiddish secular school. Steeped in Jewish history and politics, Medem was, even in the consistently anti-Zionist Bund, one of the most outspoken critics of political Zionism, and in his journalistic work he frequently attacked Zionist parties for drawing the attention of Polish Jewry away from the immediate, local struggle to improve their civic and economic conditions.

Because of his unique personal history in returning to the Jewish people and because of his selfless devotion to the Bund, the austerity of his personal life, his gentleness, modesty, and integrity, Medem even during his lifetime attained a stature considerably greater than that of most contemporary political leaders. His death grieved Jewish workers the world over; tens of thousands of Jewish laborers braved a raging snowstorm to join his funeral procession. Memorial meetings were held in many cities throughout the world. But most of all, the Jewish workers of Poland grieved and, in every Jewish community of that country, left their factories and workshops in the middle of the day to assemble in the greatest tribute of sorrow ever offered a Jewish political figure.

MY MOTHER sits in the dining room. Before her stands a little old woman. I remember her name was Leyeh or, as she was called in our house, Leyke. My mother sits, Leyke stands, and they don't stop talking for a moment. I don't remember what they talked about, but I do remember that they spoke Yiddish.

I, a child of six or seven, hover near my mother. I hear Leyke calling her "dear Madame," I hear my mother replying in "jargon" [Yiddish], and I am beside myself with anger. Who ever heard of such a thing: an intelligent, educated woman, the wife of a Russian general, speaking "jargon"? I can hardly wait for my father to come home. Such goings-on aren't allowed in his presence. And indeed, when my father is heard coming, Leyke disappears hastily into the kitchen. I breathe more freely. Our home is once again truly Russian.

Leyke used to come to our house every Friday to make Jewish-style fish. True, it wasn't for Friday night suppers as in Jewish homes, but for Friday dinner. Nevertheless, it was a relic of old Jewish times, a trace of vanished Jewishness. Such traces became less and less frequent from year to year. Our house was increasingly becoming really Russian, not only in language, but in the full content of our lives.

Both my parents were Jews by birth, real honest-to-goodness Jews. I think that my father was even a kohen. He came from Shavli (Kovno region) and had settled in Minsk; my mother came from Vilna. I never met

my paternal grandparents, but I know that my father's generation was
stricken by conversion, as was my mother's family. Practically all my uncles
and aunts were Christians, and some of their children did not even know of
their Jewish origin.

To understand this, we must remember that this epidemic of conversion
began much earlier. My father, for example, was born in 1836. As a boy he
studied in a Russian gymnasium and later attended the St. Petersburg
military medical academy. When he was graduated, he became an army
doctor and established himself in a Russian environment. He had left traditional Jewishness very early, if he had ever known it. Insofar as he had any
contact with Jewish life, it was permeated with assimilationist leanings. In
the sixties, the springtide of Alexander II's regime, the attitude toward Jews
was liberal, and the Jewish community responded ardently in its desire to
fuse with the Russian people.

Then came a shift in events. The political honeymoon ended and was
replaced by years of reaction, pogroms, and antisemitism, especially when
Alexander III ascended the throne. With political persecution also went
social rejection of the Jews. The situation had changed. No matter how
hard one had tried to forget one's former Jewishness, the outside world
refused to allow it. "You are a Jew" became an insult, a detraction. And the
Jew then began to feel ashamed of his Jewishness.

This shame about Jewishness and the desire to conceal one's Jewish
origin were typical for our milieu. I remember how, in my childhood, my
family was speaking about someone: Is it known or not known that he is a
Jew? I remember that some of our relatives strictly prohibited the use of the
word "Jew," lest the servants hear. A sort of code was developed which only
the family could understand. Instead of using the word "Jew," they said
"Italian" or "our kind." In our house, the shame of Jewishness never
reached this absurdity, but the same atmosphere prevailed. I myself, as a
young child, was completely acclimated to it. My Jewish origin was a burden. It was a shame, a degradation, a sort of secret disease about which no
one should know. And if people did know, then, if they were kind and
friendly, they took no notice of it, just as one ignores the deformity of a
hunchback so as not to hurt him.

This is why I used to become upset when my mother spoke Yiddish to
old Leyke. Every word reminded me of the ugly disease: You are a Jew, a
cripple. I did not want to be a Jew, I did not consider myself a Jew, and I
used to prattle in imitation of the grown-ups: We are Russians.

This was the atmosphere of our circle and it led to conversion as the
final and drastic cure for the secret disease. Actually, conversion was no

more than a formality, the last rung of the ladder. My parents did not take this step until quite late. My father became converted at the age of fifty-six, a few months before his death. He was one of the most distinguished citizens of our city, a division doctor, a *statsky sovetnik*, a rank between colonel and general. He could not become a full general because he was a Jew. But that was not why he became converted. As I understood it (I was about thirteen years old then), new restrictions against Jewish officials had been introduced, and my father's position was endangered. Since he had no private practice, was old and sick, and could not possibly dream of beginning his career anew, he decided to join the Lutheran Church.

My mother became a Christian a short while later, soon after my father's death. She was very sick, and we children convinced her that her conversion had been our father's desire. She gave in unwillingly and with considerable distress.

At that time, all the children were Christians. My sister had become converted together with my father in order to marry a Russian. My oldest brother had long been an army officer and, necessarily, a Christian. Two other brothers had been converted, but it was spoken of so little that I don't even remember when. Oddly enough, all became Lutherans, as did most Jews who joined the Christian church. I believe it was because conversion to Protestantism involved less ceremonial and fewer technical difficulties than Orthodoxy. Thus, our whole family gradually became Lutherans. Only I was an exception — I belonged to the Greek Orthodox church.

I was the first Christian in our family, even though I was the youngest. When I was born (July, 1879), my parents decided: We have suffered enough because of our Jewishness; let our youngest not know such sufferings. And I was baptized in a Greek Orthodox church just as if I had been born into an Orthodox family, while they themselves remained Jews for a long time.

Thus, I was a Greek Orthodox child, reared in a Jewish, later a half-Lutheran, and finally a wholly Lutheran family. I never felt any inconsistency between my Orthodoxy and the Jewishness around me. Actually, I was for a long time convinced that my father had become converted much earlier than he had in fact. In our home all the Russian church holidays were observed. On official festivals my father even used to go to church, so that I never felt any barrier to the full and free development of my religious feeling.

I was about five when I first went to church. It made a great impression on me: the dark gold, holy pictures, the glowing lights and candles, the somber mien of the priests in their extraordinarily beautiful vestments, the mysterious ceremonies, the vibrant bass of the proto-deacon, the singing of the choir. It is indeed hard to describe the full beauty of Russian church music with its earnest and sublime harmony.

But as I grew older, my religious emotions, based on externals rather than conscious religious awareness, began to dissipate, and when I reached my second year in gymnasium, I began to develop critical attitudes. During my last years in gymnasium, my circle gradually and imperceptibly turned Jewish. The adults who visited us were still mostly Russian, but the friends with whom I associated were almost exclusively Jews. One was Alexander Eliasberg, the son of well-to-do Jews, who himself had already traveled, read much, and who influenced my taste in art and literature. Another was Yasha Kaplan. I used to visit him quite often, and there I found an unmistakably lower-middle-class Jewish house. Eliasberg's home was Jewish too; his family observed Jewish customs, so much so that he was afraid even to ride on the Sabbath lest they find out. But I hardly ever saw his family. With Kaplan's family, it was different: the home was more sociable, more familiar. A portrait of Baron de Hirsch adorned a wall; Yiddish was heard frequently. Once, I remember, some people came and sang Yiddish songs, some by Goldfaden, I think. By that time the sound of Yiddish no longer pained my ears.

There were other Jewish boys with whom I was friendly and who visited me. At home, my Jewish acquaintanceships did not pass without comment. My older brother used to joke good-naturedly about it. He would say, "Go on, one of your Ginsbergs has come; I don't know whether Kaplan or Eliasberg." But it was no more than a joke; no one disturbed my friendships.

At that time, I had two other Jewish friends of a different sort, not fellow students. They were sons of a Jewish storekeeper who had his shop in the yard of our house. All day the boys played in the yard until their mother drove them inside. When I outgrew the games, I turned to "education." I decided to teach them Russian, hygiene, and gentility.

Yet even though I made friends with more and more Jews, I cannot definitely say that I began to consider myself a Jew. The question of my own Jewishness was not yet posed.

In 1897, I enrolled in the University of Kiev. During this year, I learned about Karl Marx and his *Capital* from Yasha Kaplan. I used to consider socialists a group of dreamers who with fantastic plans and bombs and riots sought to change the order of the world. Now I learned there was another kind of socialism, not a fantasy nor a dream, but a logical and necessary product of human development. The next year I began to study political economy, and a little later I met real live Marxists and learned the name of the Bund.

Besides studying Marx, I decided to learn Hebrew. But my interest in Hebrew was literary rather than Jewish. I wanted to read the Bible in the original. I did not consider the Bible a Jewish book, for, after all, it had been part of the Christian religious teaching I had had as a child. At home during the summer vacation, I did not have to search far for a teacher. Mitche, the older of the two boys who lived in our yard, agreed to teach me in exchange for Russian lessons. We began with Genesis. He taught me the alphabet and pronunciation. He did not have to translate because the Bible we used, one that my father had cherished, had a French translation. We used to sit in the yard and read aloud. But I wanted to study with system and I asked Mitche to teach me grammar. He began to tell me about dikduk, but I suspect that Mitche himself didn't understand very well what it was. His reputation as a Hebraist fell in my eyes. I never did learn Hebrew, but I did accomplish something: I learned the alphabet, gaining the key to the Yiddish language. I read very poorly at that time, but the first step had been made.

When I returned to the university, I became active in the student movement. My political work increased my homesickness for Jewishness. Even though no distinction as to Jew or Christian was made among the students, there was one specifically Jewish institution among them — the Jewish student kitchen. Actually, I don't recall that I had ever been there. It was not merely an eating place; it was an intellectual gathering place, a kind of club for the Jewish students. At first I had paid no attention to it, but getting back from a visit home, I felt something akin to envy. I saw that my Jewish friends had their own group from which I was excluded. It was as though I stood before a closed door that shut me out from warmth and hominess. I felt homeless, and longed for a home. This home was Jewish life. This feeling of envy was a sign that I was still on the wrong side of the door, that I still did not consider myself Jewish. But also it was an expression of an awakening desire to become one of those to whom I was drawn.

In various ways and for various reasons, I began to turn to Jewishness. Here I should mention my friendship with Isaac Tumin, a man considerably older than I, who had read and seen much, been to America, Switzerland, seen the world, been imprisoned, and was associated with the Jewish labor movement. Tumin was a person with strong Jewish feeling. He came from a traditional Jewish family, knew Jewish life intimately, and loved it. This love communicated itself to me.

I was in Minsk during the summer and early fall of 1899. On Yom

Kippur, Tumin took me to the synagogue. I remember that evening well. Earlier, I had wandered through the streets. Minsk is a Jewish city and the stores were closed, the streets empty and desolate. I recall the figure of a Russian hussar, in a light green coat and raspberry trousers with silver band, and a long sword. His strange figure in the empty streets enhanced the extraordinarily solemn appearance of the city. A gray dusk hung over a gray quiet. You could feel that the day was different from other days.

Later, Tumin and I went to the synagogue. I had been to a synagogue before, but that had been the large, new-style synagogue in Kiev, with its Western architectural style, its choir, and its rich Jews in top hats. Now for the first time I entered an old-fashioned synagogue.

First we went to the large synagogue and immediately I felt the presence of a new, hitherto-unknown atmosphere in all its uniqueness and magic. It was different from the Russian church. There, the large mass of people stood quiet, grave, and silent, and only the priest and the choir spoke and sang on behalf of the congregation, spoke and sang in lovely, carefully harmonic and measured tones. But here, it was as though I had fallen among torrential waves. Hundreds upon hundreds of worshippers — each one taking his own case to God, each in a loud voice with passionate eagerness. Hundreds of voices ascended to the heavens, each for himself, without concord, without harmony, yet all joining together in one tremendous clamorous sound. No matter how strange to the Western ear, it makes a deep impression and has a great beauty derived from the passion of mass feeling.

Afterward, we went to a small synagogue; it may have been a hasidic prayer room. There too, I was carried away by the passionate stream of hundreds of voices. Above the vast mass rumbling there rose a sharp and high-pitched voice, the voice of the old graybearded *ba'al-tefila*. This was no singing or preaching. It was a lament, a true lament in which you could feel the scorching tears of an anguished heart. There was none of the solemnity or measured harmony of a Christian prayer. It was the true Oriental passion of a suffering soul, a voice from the gray past which wept and beseeched its old age-gray God. In it lay a great beauty.

In the fall of 1899, Yasha Kaplan and I were expelled from the University of Kiev for our political activity among the student body and ordered by the police to return to Minsk. It was a foregone conclusion that we would sooner or later join the "movement," the Bund. We had enjoyed the taste of political work and it was clear that our place was in the local movement in Minsk. Even though I had some doubts as to whether the Russian workers

were at a stage of readiness to accept socialist doctrines, I was well enough
acquainted with the Jewish labor movement to know that its existence was
an accomplished fact, and that there could be no doubt about its survival.
In the winter of 1899-1900, I became a member of the Bund.

At that time, I don't believe I understood the concept of the Bund as a
Jewish organization, and its proper role in Jewish life. But, looking back, I
realize that Bundist thought on this subject had not yet been clarified;
Bundism as an ideology with its own concept of Jewish life and of the
Jewish labor movement was still in the process of crystallization. The first
formulation of the Bund's Jewish national program was made at the Bund
convention of April, 1901, when I was in prison. At the time I began working for the party in Minsk, we were still in a period of searching, groping in
the dark. The national question was hardly ever discussed in Bundist literature, and what there was of such discussion was inaccessible to me, for I
still could not read Yiddish.

I remember once Yasha's coming to ask: "What do you think — are the
Jews a nation?" I didn't know what to answer; I had never thought about it.
But so far as the Jewish labor movement was concerned, we all recognized it
then as a unique and independent movement. I remember a conversation
concerning the uniqueness of the Jewish labor movement some time later,
in 1901. We were in prison, together in one cell, and behind bars we held a
discussion about the quality of our movement. I tried to summarize. Our
movement, I said, has two major characteristics. Most of our people are
employed in small or very tiny workshops belonging to artisans who themselves work. The second characteristic of our movement is that it consists of
Jews, children of the Jewish people. Thus, there are two forces impelling
the Jewish worker into our movement: his class feeling, the consciousness
that he is a worker who is being exploited, that he wants to fight together
with his brothers for a better life; and his Jewish feeling, the consciousness
that he is a Jew.

What was my personal Jewishness at that time? My new friends, Jewish
workers, used to call me the *goy*, and in externals I was really quite *goyish*.
I still had lots of trouble with Yiddish. I could understand it (I had heard it
around so much), and my knowledge of German came to my aid. But the
Hebrew elements used in Yiddish were strange and presented many difficulties. Nevertheless, I was able to follow the general content of a Yiddish
speech. In fact, I even remember that when I heard someone read Peretz's
Dos kranke yingl, I understood it very well. But I still could not speak
Yiddish. Once I went to visit a worker who happened to be out. I asked his

wife in Yiddish when he would come. They were just four simple words, but immediately she had the feeling that a *goy* was speaking and answered me in Russian.

The articles I then wrote in the *Minsker arbayter* were written in Russian and then translated into Yiddish. I had already developed some feeling for the Yiddish language, and though I wrote in Russian, I used such expressions as readily lent themselves to Yiddish translation. I could not read Yiddish either at the time, but I was learning.

Certainly the Jewish labor milieu influenced me greatly. I cannot say exactly how this influence expressed itself, but the constant association with Jews and Jewish life Judaized me. An especially strong influence was my friendship with Tumin.

I remember one evening when we went walking together through the Jewish quarter, in the outlying poor little streets with their poor little houses. It was Friday night; the streets were quiet and empty; the Sabbath candles burned in the little houses. We were talking about Jewish things. I don't remember the subject, but I do recall that I was strongly impressed by that unique charm of the peaceful Friday nights and felt a romantic association with the Jewish past, a warm, intimate closeness that one has with one's own past. And this feeling for the past has always remained associated with the small houses and quiet streets of a Lithuanian Jewish town. My sentiment for Jewry was always, as a Zionist might express it, a galut feeling. The palm trees and the vineyards of Palestine were alien to me. I think this is an indication that my Jewishness was really an ingrained living Jewishness, not a literary fancy.

As I have said, I cannot exactly determine how this "nationalizing" influence of the Jewish labor circles expressed itself. It was the quiet effect of day-to-day living. This life became dear and important to me. It was Jewish and it drew me into its environs. When did I clearly and definitely feel myself to be a Jew? I cannot say, but at the beginning of 1901, when I was arrested for clandestine political activity, the police gave me a form to fill in. In the column "Nationality," I wrote "Jew."

51   From Pole to Jew
by Bronislaw Grosser

BRONISLAW GROSSER, socialist, was born in Miechow, Poland, in 1883 and died in a St. Petersburg hospital in 1912. Much of his tragically short life is related in the following extract of a memoir he wrote in 1911, shortly after he was freed from a Warsaw prison when, ailing, he had gone abroad to try to regain his health. He wrote it for his then four-year-old daughter.

From childhood a Polish patriot and Polonist, Grosser found his Jewish identity as a consequence of the deep divisions between Poles and Jews and the nearly endemic antisemitism among Poles. Because antisemitism persisted even in revolutionary radical Polish circles, it was impossible for so sincere a human being as Grosser to propagate cosmopolitanism as a solution to the "Jewish question." The Polish socialists, by demanding the total assimilation (disappearance?) of the Jews as a precondition for political equality, forced Grosser into defense and advocacy of Jewish culture and the goal of a fraternity of national cultures.

AT A certain time in my life I said to myself: You will work in the Jewish movement.

How did that happen? Why did it happen? What influenced me in that direction and for what reason did I do it? Of course, the explanation that I set down here is one made much later, after many years passed. Perhaps I no longer remember exactly the external circumstances or my inner feelings. Perhaps some views and feelings which have long been mine came to me later than it now seems: in short, the usual difficulties of every historical undertaking.

I was born in Miechow, a small town in Kielce province, on the road to Cracow. My parents had lived there for many years and moved when I was, I think, five years old. Their home was thoroughly Polonized. Part of the worldly, educated circles, they were quite detached from religious matters. In my early childhood, I never saw anything about me that was at all Jewish.

My father was the most sought-after lawyer in that area, used to make a good living, was respected in town, and associated only with Gentiles. At home, my parents used to entertain the local gentry and also the clergy. I remember while playing in the town park near the church, I used to greet the priests like old friends; I used to go to church with the maid (that was probably her own idea), never realizing that I had any relation to Jews. I remember one fact distinctly. When about eight, I rode with my mother and sister in a Warsaw streetcar. A Jew sat down on the bench near us. Without a word, I arose and moved to another seat. I did it somewhat as if out of disgust, on purpose. Why has this remained in my memory? Perhaps my mother's dismay persisted in my mind, for it surprised me then and forced me to remember it. As I now understand, my mother was upset just because of her democratic instinct. Perhaps my mind was affected by the infinitely sorrowful gaze in this Jew's eyes. Now I wonder whether he really had that look or whether I just think so now. The incident was typical of my state of mind then. I do not reckon it was the man's Jewishness; more likely I was revolted by the filth. Yet peasants did not repel me; I would not have moved away from them. The awareness of something totally alien played some role in this. It never occurred to me that there was or could be any relation between me and this being. I think I became aware of being Jewish only just before taking entrance examinations for gymnasium. For the first time I heard that there were some special conditions for me, because I was a Jew. I remember only my indescribable shock when I learned of this, but nothing more of that time.

Attending the gymnasium opened an altogether new era in my life, a critical period for these feelings of identity. From the very start I knew and I felt I was a Jew. I did not attend the class in Catholic religion; I attended the class in Judaism. There were other Jews besides me in my class. In our school there were no Russians, just Poles and Jews. I soon realized these were two different categories: the handful of Jews clung to each other and were somewhat segregated from the others. Otherwise, there was nothing uniform about us. My friend Julian Natanson and I kept aloof from the Jewish group and associated only with the Poles. The segregation of the Jewish group seemed apparent only in their clinging to each other, but it was quite evident when the boys had a dispute, a row or a fight. In the fracas, in anger and excitement, the children's deeply rooted attitude toward Jews as different, worse, inferior rose to the surface. The word "Jew" — sometimes "goy" — rang out like an insult in the classroom. This may have been my introduction to the idea that I belonged to a special group of people, not only by the standards of our lonely little crowd, but also in the eyes of the outsiders.

That was my first encounter with the formula I was later to hear so often: You really are not a Jew; you are different. This formula, spoken with the best intentions, was so degrading, highlighting so distinctly the tragedy of one's Jewish origin, yet perhaps it gave me some satisfaction then. I think I was already aware how bitter it was to belong to a group from whom it was considered good to stay away and I was pleased that I was, after all, different, special, exceptional. I remember once talking with Julian about what our Jewishness meant and we had no answer. "Our home is like other homes," we used to tell each other. "I recite the Lord's Prayer," Julian bragged. "I don't pray," I replied, "but I know that prayer." We were then in first-year gymnasium.

In my second year something happened which created quite a stir. Speaking Polish was prohibited in school and severely punished. Naturally, then, we spoke only Polish; it could not have been otherwise. Everyone spoke Polish, even the Russian Jews. We all did so surreptitiously but nevertheless, we were caught. The penalties used to arouse feelings of obligation, solidarity, determination, and a desire for revenge. One day my mathematics teacher caught me in the very act of the crime, during his class. He began to lecture me. What he said was that in the final analysis one could forgive Poles for speaking Polish, but not a Jew, who could not extenuate his offense on the grounds of patriotic feelings or national habit. Deeply insulted, I explained that I was a Pole and, like the others, had the same rights and obligations. After an hour's arguing with the teacher, I was brought before the principal, and that exchange also lasted an hour. I remember only the beginning. He asked me: "Who am I?" In astonishment, I told him his name. "No," he replied, "I am asking what nationality I am."

"A Russian."

"No; I am a Russian Indian."

"That is impossible."

"Neither can one be a Polish Jew."

"Is it possible to be a Greek-Orthodox Indian?" I asked him.

"Certainly."

"Likewise, one can be a Jewish Pole."

This dialogue showed the ambiguity of Jews as a religion or nationality. The conversation, typical of the atmosphere in which I grew up, had been conducted before the whole class. My classmates aligned themselves with me. Upperclassmen used to come to look me over. Behind the backs of the school officials, our teacher of Polish, with tears in his eyes, made a speech to the whole class. Thereafter, I began to be recognized as leader in my class.

Boys are greatly impressed by outspoken convictions, fearlessly expressed to officialdom. The Polish boys began to regard me wholly as theirs. The Jewish boys were glad to accept me as a bridge that could link them with the non-Jewish world. But perhaps the most important consequence was that my logical mind was not satisfied with a temporary triumph. The Jewish question demanded my attention. I began to think about it persistently. Since then I have never ceased being interested in it.

When I was thirteen I began to study Hebrew with my uncle, Leon Grossglück, who, until twenty, wore his coat long. He had a bump on his forehead, the result of a stone thrown at him during a pogrom in the eighties. When I was going to school, he had already become Europeanized from top to toe. An autodidact, he had amassed a great deal of learning. Secretary of the Jewish community council, he was its real administrator. He differed from other assimilated Jews principally in that he did not cut his ties with Jews. My wish to study Hebrew was one more proof that being Jewish meant something to me.

When I was in the fifth grade, Grossglück celebrated his twenty-fifth anniversary with the Warsaw Jewish community council. On that day I presented him with a history of the Jews in Poland, in four handwritten notebooks, in which I had invested about a half year's work. I had read everything I could get hold of on the subject. Its closing pages were a defense of socialism, which would solve all questions, including the "Jewish question" — by assimilation, of course. I was obviously already a thoroughly convinced socialist, and I had a feeling, if not sufficient knowledge, for the relation between social questions and the Jewish question.

Thereafter, I made much progress as a socialist, active in the secret socialist self-study groups of older gymnasium students. We studied things we did not learn in school, but primarily we learned how to stick together and how to keep secrets. At the start there was not much diversity in views, but by the time I was to complete the gymnasium, we had two organizations — one National-Democratic and one progressive — that were the outcome of an internal struggle and a split. I played a great part in this. A gifted speaker, energetic, unyielding, in a short time I occupied an important position in the youth movement, of course, on the extreme left. During this struggle my socialist views crystallized and I also began better to understand the Jewish question. Suddenly and quite unexpectedly, I even made a statement on this subject. This is how it happened.

At a very stormy meeting of the youth organization, when the progressives had only a slight majority over National-Democrats, the basic program of the study groups was being discussed. The National-Democrats insisted that Polish subjects be given priority and we demanded equal consideration for social studies. A National-Democratic spokesman argued: "The members of the study groups are Poles; therefore, Polish subjects deserve major consideration." One of us answered: "Besides Poles, there are Lithuanians,

Russians, Ukrainians, Jews." To which the National-Democrats replied: "Non-Poles ought to be excluded."

Then it was my turn. I knew they stood in awe of me. I was the editor of the headquarters paper *Ruch* ("Movement"), the leader among the radicals. I decided to make my own person a test case. "Why then don't you bar me because I am not a Pole, but a Jew?" They were all shocked, confused. The progressives, who had been wavering on this issue, saw the point. If this National-Democratic theory would, in practice, exclude me, then obviously the theory was wrong. The National-Democrats, for their part, knew their position was untenable. One by one, they took the floor to announce that, whatever I said, they considered me a Pole and nothing they said referred to me. Here was a curious situation. The National-Democrats insisted on my Polishness and I emphatically denied it. Finally the question was put to a vote as "Grosser's affair." The study group with which I was associated declared that the question of excluding their entire governing body must be raised — they would not exclude only me. The majority supported the progressives' position, but feelings ran high. After the votes were counted, came the announcement that collaboration between the two factions was no longer possible. The organization split.

Those were the circumstances in which I had first stated publicly that I was a Jew. It was not a statement on the Jewish question, not a matter of rights for Jews. General principles are simpler to deal with than personal feelings. I had to fit my feelings artificially into a simple form that would illuminate general principles. But my own emotions were unaffected. A dissonance remained between the inner feelings and the external expression, between the real content and its form. Yet this Jewish question became intertwined in my personal life. Years have passed since those student days when my personality influenced Jewish-Polish relations. But the situation became just the reverse. I became the living embodiment of Jewish-Polish relations. Whatever was anti-Jewish and was directed against Jews was targeted first at my ego. Is it any wonder that this problem affected my deepest, most intimate, and personal feelings?

My view of the Jewish question was nebulous. I thought Jews were different, and I counted myself one of this different group. My sense of justice and self-respect forced me to demand complete equal rights for Jews as a group, but to tell the truth I had no clear notion what these rights ought to be. It was all rather metaphysical.

In the seventh class of the gymnasium, I met and became close with F. We shared the same feelings and ideas about the Jewish question. We decided to undertake to organize a socialist group for Jewish young people. In this connection we went to Plock where I met A. and I. G. I remember holding forth for them on my unformed views of the Jewish question. My main idea was that though Jews constituted a separate group, this separateness could express itself only when Jews, serving the idea of socialism, took on the role of the conscience of the other nationalities. A particularly Jewish kind of patriotism, a sort of belief in Jewish chosenness, was joined with a notion that it was impossible to treat Jews as a real people living in reality among other peoples. Generally speaking, my skeptical and sober intellect was not used to feeding on mystical experiences and being beclouded by them. The Jewish question was the only occasion when this happened to me, because, I suppose, of its personal application. After I. G. heard me out, he said, "When I listen to you, it seems you really take the same line as the Bund, but you are all mixed up. You add a bit of poetry, mysticism, some such sort of thing." I pondered on this, but said nothing.

I had heard about the Bund, but its organizations in Poland were then quite insignificant and weak, and uninfluential. I had had no direct contact with the Bund and only a very vague notion of its aims. (For that matter, the Bund itself at that time had no clear ideas on the Jewish question.) My next socialist venture was helping to form the Union of Independent Socialist Youth, which accepted all young people, regardless of nationality.

In time, the young people in this organization began to differentiate themselves politically. They were no longer satisfied with merely a progressive organization, with the educational goals which kept appealing to ever broader groups. Young people wanted to go among the workers and to join political parties. Cadres were organized to prepare for these activities. It was a dangerous game, its organization conspiratorial. One of these groups was a youth section of the prerevolutionary Polish Socialist Party. I was not asked to join, because this group united the "Polish" youth; for the first time in my life, my comrades did not count me among "Polish" youth. I formed a parallel organization which did not exclude any nationality and was also nonpartisan, independent of any party.

This organization became a training ground which directed many able young people into the parties. As its most influential member, I was sought after by the parties, but I declined to join any. Ostensibly, my reason was that I was not yet ready to join a party. But privately I kept asking: Is it not my duty to work among Jews? In any event I tried to serve also them, to the extent it was possible without belonging to a party. I wavered, I could not make up my mind. Leading Bundists were interested in me. I was able to give them a platform and contact with young people. I could be a link between the Bund and the Polish and Polish-Jewish community.

Once I had to be in Lodz on organizational business. There I went with some Bundists to an illegal meeting of workers that was held just outside town in the woods. For the first time in my life I saw a crowd of Jewish workers and heard them sing the Bundist anthem, the *sh'vue* ("The Oath"). I thought: I must work among Jews. If not I, the embodiment of Jewishness among the Warsaw youth; who then will work among Jews? If the Russian Jewish intellectual will come between the Jewish worker and the Polish worker, he will make it harder for them to understand each other. I will work among Jews, because I am a Polish Jew and I will not yield my role to anyone.

I was not sure I agreed with the idea of cultural autonomy, which the Bund had already formulated, though without much conviction. Nevertheless, at the student union I arranged some discussion meetings on this subject between a Bundist and a Zionist. When I arose to respond to a remark made by the Zionist, for the first time in my life I began, "We, Jewish Social Democrats. . . ." When the meeting ended, I went up to the Bundist and told him, "I am one of yours."

That is how I joined the Bund — the long way around — from complete alienation, into the ranks of a Jewish party; from extreme assimilationism, to principles of Jewish nationalism. By joining the Bund I thought I was fulfilling my duty to the Jewish masses as a socialist and a Jew. At the same time, I thought I was serving my country, because I hoped to link Jews with Poland, not by assimilation, but in full civic equality. My purpose was to defend the interests of the Jewish workers in Poland and to defend the interests of Poland in the hearts of the Jewish workers.

52 A Social Democrat Only
by Leon Trotsky

LEON TROTSKY was born Lev Davidovich Bronstein in Yanovka, province of Kherson, in 1879 and was assassinated near Mexico City in 1940.

The following excerpts from his autobiography exemplify the Jewish revolutionary as cosmopolitan, in flight from what he conceived as a parochially confining Jewish milieu. A story which Medem told of him is just as revealing. During a debate in 1903, Medem asked Trotsky whether he admitted the fact of belonging to a nationality. "You consider yourself, I suppose, either a Russian or a Jew," Medem said. "No," Trotsky responded, "you are wrong. I am a Social Democrat and only that."

In the country as well as in the town, I lived in a petit bourgeois environment where the principal effort was directed toward acquisition. In this respect, I cut myself off both from the country of my early childhood and from the town of my youth. The instinct of acquisition, the petit bourgeois outlook and habits of life — from these I sailed away with a mighty push, and I did so never to return.

In the spheres of religion and nationality, there was no opposition between the country and the town; on the contrary, they complemented one another in various respects. In my father's family there was no strict observance of religion. At first, appearances were kept up through sheer inertia: on holy days my parents journeyed to the synagogue in the colony; Mother abstained from sewing on Saturdays, at least within the sight of others. But all this ceremonial observance of religion lessened as years went on — as the children grew up and the prosperity of the family increased. Father did not believe in God from his youth, and in later years spoke openly about it in front of Mother and the children. Mother preferred to avoid the subject, but when occasion required would raise her eyes in prayer.

In my mother's family, the Schpentzers, religion was not observed at all, not counting the old aunt, who did not matter. My father, however, wanted me to know the Bible in the original, this being one of the marks of his parental vanity, and therefore I took private lessons in the Bible from a very learned old man in Odessa. My studies lasted only a few months and did little to confirm me in the ancestral faith. A suggestion of a double meaning in the words of my teacher, concerning some text in the Bible which we were studying, prompted me to ask a question which I worded very cautiously and diplomatically: "If we accept, as some do, that God does not exist, how did the world come to be?"

"Hm," muttered the teacher, "but you can turn this question against him as well." In this ingenious way did the old man express himself. I realized that the instructor in religion did not believe in God, and this set my mind completely at rest.

The racial and religious composition of my *Realschule* was very heterogeneous. Religion was taught respectively by a Russian Orthodox priest, a Protestant parson, a Catholic priest, and a Jewish instructor. The Russian priest, a nephew of the archbishop, with the reputation of being a favorite with ladies, was a young and strikingly good-looking man, resembling the portraits of Christ — only of the drawing-room type; he had gold spectacles and abundant golden hair, and was, in brief, impossibly handsome. Before the lesson in religion was to begin, boys of different persuasions would divide into separate groups, and those not of the Russian Orthodox faith would leave the classroom, sometimes under the very nose of the Russian priest. On such occasions he put on a special expression, in which contempt was only slightly softened by true Christian forbearance, as he watched the boys walk out.

"Where are you going?" he would ask some boy.

"We are Catholics," came the answer.

"Oh, Catholics!" he repeated, nodding his head, "I see, I see. . . . And you?"

"We are Jews."

"Oh, Jews, I see, Jews! Just so, just so!"

The Catholic priest came like a black shadow, always appearing right against the wall and disappearing so inconspicuously that throughout all my years there I could never get a look at his shaven face. A good-natured man by the name of Ziegelman instructed the Jewish boys in the Bible and the history of the Jewish people. These lessons, conducted in Russian, were never taken seriously by the boys.

In my mental equipment, nationality never occupied an independent place, as it was felt but little in everyday life. It is true that after the laws of 1881, which restricted the rights of Jews in Russia, my father was unable to buy more land, as he was so anxious to do, but could only lease it under cover. This, however, scarcely affected my own position. As son of a prosperous landowner, I belonged to the privileged class rather than to the oppressed. The language in my family and household was Russian-Ukrainian. True enough, the number of Jewish boys allowed to join the schools was limited to a fixed percentage, on account of which I lost one year. But in the school I was always at the top of the grade and was not personally affected by the restrictions.

In my school there was no open baiting of nationalities. To some extent the variety of national elements, not only among the boys but among the masters as well, acted as an important check on such policies. One could sense, however, the existence of a suppressed chauvinism which now and again broke through to the surface. The teacher of history, Liubimov, showed marked partisanship when questioning a Polish boy about the Catholic persecution of Orthodox Russians in White Russia and Lithuania. Mickiewicz, a lanky, dark-skinned boy, turned green and stood with his teeth set, without uttering a word. "Well, why don't you speak?" Liubimov encouraged him, with an expression of sadistic pleasure. One of the boys burst out: "Mickiewicz is a Pole and a Catholic." Feigning surprise, Liubimov drawled: "Is that so? We don't differentiate between nationalities here."

It hurt me quite as much to see the concealed cad in Liubimov's attitude toward Poles, as to see the Russian priest's nodding of his head at the sight of Jews. This national inequality probably was one of the underlying causes of my dissatisfaction with the existing order, but it was lost among all the other phases of social injustice. It never played a leading part — not even a recognized one — in the lists of my grievances.

The feeling of the supremacy of general over particular, of law over fact, of theory over personal experience, took root in my mind at an early age and gained increasing strength as the years advanced. It was the town that played the major rôle in shaping this feeling, a feeling which later became the basis for a philosophic outlook on life. When I heard boys who were studying physics and natural history repeat the superstitious notions about "unlucky" Monday, or about meeting a priest crossing the road, I was utterly indignant. I felt that my intelligence had been insulted, and I was on the verge of doing any mad thing to make them abandon their shameless superstititons.

Did the Schpentzer family have any political views? Those of Moissey Filippovich, my mother's nephew, were moderately liberal in a humanitarian way. They were lightly touched by vague socialist sympathies, tinged with Populist and Tolstoyan ideas. Political subjects were never openly discussed, especially in my presence; probably that was because they were afraid that I might say something censurable at school, and get myself in trouble. And when casual reference to what was going on or had taken place within the revolutionary movement was made in the grown-ups' conversation, such as, for example, "This was in the year of the assassination of Tsar Alexander II," it had the ring of a past as far removed as if they had said, "This was in the year Columbus discovered America." The people who surrounded me were outside of politics.

During my school years I held no political views, nor for that matter had I any desire to acquire them. At the same time my subconscious strivings were tinged by a spirit of opposition. I had an intense hatred of the existing order, of injustice, of tyranny. Whence did it come? It came from the conditions existing during the reign of Alexander III; the highhandedness of the police; the exploitation practiced by landlords; the grafting by officials; the nationalistic restrictions; the cases of injustice at school and in the street; the close contact with children, servants and laborers in the country; the conversations in the workshop; the humane spirit in the Schpentzer family; the reading of Nekrasov's poems and of all kinds of other books, and, in general, the entire social atmosphere of the time. This oppositional mood was revealed to me cuttingly in my contact with two classmates, Rodzevich and Kologrivov.

Vladimir Rodzevich was the son of a colonel, and was, for a time, the second highest in our grade. He persuaded his parents to allow him to invite me to their house on a Sunday. I was received with a certain dryness, but courteously. The colonel and his wife spoke to me very little, as if they were scrutinizing me. During the three or four hours which I spent with the family, I stumbled several times upon something that was strange and disconcerting to me, and even inimical; it happened when the conversation casually touched on the subject of religion and the authorities. There was a tone of conservative piety about that house that I felt like a blow on the chest. Vladimir's parents did not let him visit me in my home, and the link between us was broken. After the first revolution in Odessa, the name of Rodzevich, a member of the Black Hundred, probably one of the members of this family, was fairly well known.

The case of Kologrivov was even more poignant. He entered the school in the second grade, after Christmas, and was conspicuous among the boys as a tall and awkward stranger. He was gifted with incredible industry; he learned things by heart, anything and everything, whenever he could. By the end of the first month, his mind was completely groggy from incessant memorizing. When he was called on by the geography teacher to recite the map lesson, without even waiting for the question he started right in: "Jesus Christ left his command to the world. . . ." It is necessary only to mention that the following hour was to be a lesson in religion.

In conversation with this Kologrivov, who treated me, as the first in the grade, not without respect, I made some critical remarks about the principal and somebody else. "How can you speak of the principal in this way?" asked Kologrivov, sincerely indignant. "And why not?" I answered, with a surprise that was even more sincere. "But he is our chief. If the chief orders you to walk on your head, it is your duty to do as you are told, and not criticize him." He said it in just that way. I was astonished by this expression of a formula. It did not occur to me then that the boy was obviously repeating what he must have heard in his feudal home. And although I had no views of my own, I felt that it would be as impossible for me to accept certain views as to eat wormy food.

Along with the suppressed hostility to the political order in Russia, I began to create, in my imagination, an idealized picture of the foreign world — of Western Europe and America. From scattered remarks and descriptions, I began to visualize a culture which was high in itself and included everybody without exception. Later, this became part and parcel of my conception of ideal democracy. Rationalism implied that if anything was accepted as theory, it was of course carried out in practice. For this reason, it seemed incredible that people in Europe could have superstitions, that the church could exercise a great influence there, that in America the whites could persecute the Negroes. This idealized picture of the Western world, imperceptibly absorbed from my environment of liberal smug citizenship, persisted later on when I was already formulating revolutionary views.

After the seizure of power, I tried to stay out of the government, and offered to undertake the direction of the press. It is quite possible that the nervous reaction after the victory had something to do with that; the months that had preceded it had been too closely tied up with the preparatory work for the revolution. Every fiber of my entire being was strained to its limit. Lunacharsky wrote somewhere in the papers that Trotsky walked about like an electric battery and that each contact with him brought forth a discharge. The twenty-fifth of October brought the letdown. I felt like a surgeon who has finished a difficult and dangerous operation — I must wash my hands, take off my apron, and rest.

Lenin was in a different position. He had just arrived from his refuge, after spending three and a half months cut off from real, practical direction. One thing coincided with the other, and this only added to my desire to retire behind the scenes for a while. Lenin would not hear of it, however. He insisted that I take over the commissariat of the interior, saying that the most important task at the moment was to fight off a counterrevolution. I objected, and brought up, among other arguments, the question of nationality. Was it worthwhile to put into our enemies' hands such an additional weapon as my Jewish origin?

Lenin almost lost his temper. "We are having a great international revolution. Of what importance are such trifles?"

A good-humored bickering began. "No doubt the revolution is great," I answered, "but there are still a good many fools left."

"But surely we don't keep step with the fools?"

"Probably we don't, but sometimes one has to make some allowance for stupidity. Why create additional complications at the outset?"

I have already had occasion to observe that the national question, so important in the life of Russia, had practically no personal significance for me. Even in my early youth, the national bias and national prejudices had only bewildered my sense of reason, in some cases stirring in me nothing but disdain and even a moral nausea. My Marxist education deepened this feeling, and changed my attitude to that of an active internationalism. My life in so many countries, my acquaintance with so many different languages, political systems, and cultures only helped me to absorb that inter-

nationalism into my very flesh and blood. If, in 1917 and later, I occasionally pointed to my Jewish origin as an argument against some appointment,
it was simply because of political considerations.

Svierdlov and other members of the Central Committee were won over
to my side. Lenin was in the minority. He shrugged his shoulders, sighed,
shook his head reproachfully, and consoled himself with the thought that
we should all have to fight the counterrevolution anyway, no matter what
departments of the government we were in. But my going over to the press
was also firmly opposed by Svierdlov; Bukharin, he said, was the man for
that. "Lev Davidovich should be set up against the rest of Europe. Let him
take charge of foreign affairs."

"What foreign affairs will we have now?" retorted Lenin. But reluctantly he finally agreed, and I, likewise with reluctance, consented. And
thus, at the instigation of Svierdlov, I came to head the Soviet diplomacy
for a quarter of a year.

When I was declining the commissariat of home affairs on the second
day after the revolution, I brought up, among other things, the question of
race. It would seem that in war business this consideration should have
involved even greater complications than in civil administration. But Lenin
proved to be right. In the years of the revolutionary *ascendancy,* this question never had the slightest importance. Of course, the Whites tried to
develop antisemitic motifs in their propaganda in the Red army, but they
failed signally. There are many testimonials to this, even in the White
press. In "Archives of the Russian Revolution," published in Berlin, a
White Guard writer relates the following striking episode: "A Cossack who
came to see us was hurt by some one's taunt that he not only served under,
but fought under the command of a Jew — Trotsky — and retorted with
warm conviction: 'Nothing of the sort. Trotsky is not a Jew. Trotsky is a
fighter. He's ours . . . Russian! . . . It is Lenin who is a communist, a
Jew, but Trotsky is ours . . . a fighter . . . Russian . . . our own!' "

The same motif will be found in "The Horse Army," by Babel, the most
talented of our younger writers. The question of my Jewish origin acquired
importance only after I had become a subject for political baiting. Antisemitism raised its head with that of anti-Trotskyism. They both derived from
the same source — the petit bourgeois reaction against October.

53   Memoirs of an Assassin

by Sholem Schwartzbard

SHOLEM SCHWARTZBARD was born in Ismail, Bessarabia, in 1886 and died while in South Africa on Jewish communal business in 1938. Schwartzbard was catapulted into Jewish history when in 1926 in Paris he assassinated Semyon Petlura, Ukrainian nationalist and military leader. (During Petlura's short-lived political and military leadership when the Ukraine was briefly an independent republic, 1918–1920, and with his knowledge and reportedly at his instigation, the Ukrainian army and Ukrainian civilians barbarously massacred and pogromized Jews.)

Sholem Schwartzbard was a product of modern times. In 1905, at nineteen, he took part in a Jewish self-defense group during the pogrom in Balta and was thereafter active in the radical movement. A watchmaker by occupation, he was apparently too undisciplined to adhere formally to any organization, but he expressed publicly his sympathy for the anarchists. Assas-

sination as a political instrument of revolution had been glorified and popularized by the early populists — Vera Zasulich to begin with. Among Jews, Hirsh Lekert, a Bundist shoemaker, was the first to attempt assassination; in 1902 he shot at Vilna governor General Victor Von Wahl, who had flogged Jewish and Polish workers for participating in a May Day demonstration. Schwartzbard was, however, the first Jew successfully to use that most un-Jewish revolutionary-anarchist tactic of assassination for a Jewish purpose.* He murdered Petlura to avenge the pogroms and to let the world learn what Petlura and his Ukrainian hordes had done to Jews. The following extract from Schwartzbard's memoirs describes his feelings and motives in assassinating Petlura. The trial in Paris lasted a little over three weeks, and Schwartzbard was acquitted, the case having indeed sensationalized the tragic events of a decade earlier.

P ARIS, Tuesday, May 25, 1926, half past three in the afternoon. The car in which I had suddenly found myself honked and barely managed to drive through the dense throng, with people screaming on all sides: "Kill him, kill him!"

"Murderer!"

"Lynch him!"

"He's not a Frenchman, but a foreigner!"

"He should be torn limb from limb!"

Out of the tumult comes the weak voice of my escort, the policeman,

---

* Pinhas Dashevsky tried, and failed, in 1903 to kill P. Krushevan, editor of the antisemitic paper *Bessarabets,* for inciting to the Kishenev pogrom.

trying with all his might to ward off the crowd: "Let him alone. We have laws to take care of this. Let him go." The car moves very slowly, the mob surges forward with sticks and fists.

"Drag him out!"

"Let's lynch him. Kill! Kill!" Finally the car breaks through, as out of a fire. Rescued! Just barely saved! The chauffeur drives at full speed; the screaming grows fainter until it dies away altogether.

"The devil," says the policeman, as if to himself, "that was a wild mob. They would not have given me kid-glove treatment either." He wipes the sweat from his face and brow and straightens up his torn uniform.

"Out of danger at last," he says, again as if to himself. "That was some wild mob. That was some job." Then, turning to me, "Well, you got beaten up, eh?"

"Nonsense."

"Some nonsense," he says ironically. "That mob could have torn you apart right there. You really got off well."

"I've been through worse."

The car came to a halt. We were at the Odeon police station. We went into a room where two clerks sat, their heads buried in books. My escort greeted them and reported, "Murder."

No one answered, no one stirred, the clerks continued doing what they were doing, as if nothing had happened. They were not astonished; for them that was no news. My escort pondered a while, then took me into another room, where a man sat at a table, his back to me. Probably a stenographer, I thought. The policeman greeted him and reported, "Murder." The man did not even turn his head; the same indifference as in the other room.

The policeman did not know how to begin; in a little while he told me to sit in a corner. He himself wiped the sweat from his brow, talking, as to himself. "Oh, that was some job." And then grew silent.

The silence lasted a few minutes. All at once he said to me, "Empty your pockets — everything. The suspenders, the shoe laces, the garters, the belt, everything."

A door opened and a man entered — in his forties, medium height, with a large shiny forehead and a bald pate, a friendly face, and two black searching eyes surveying the room. My escort jumped to attention, taut as a string, greeted him, and reported: "Inspector, murder at the corner of Racine and Boulevard Saint-Michel."

But the inspector was not interested and went out. Several policemen came in, changing duty. My escort told them what a tough job he had just had.

"What about?" one of them asked, pointing at me.

"Murder," my escort replied indifferently, belittlingly.

"Whom?"

"I don't know, and I didn't ask. Some old bean pole. It just happened right in the street. Imagine, I'm standing at my station, all of a sudden I hear shots. I run in the direction of the shooting and I see this body stretched out on the sidewalk and this fellow standing over him with a revolver. The revolver was all discharged except for the last bullet, which jammed."

"Great!" the others beamed. One turned to me.

"Would you not have spared him even that last bullet?"

"Lucky for you the revolver didn't jam at the first bullet," commented another.

"Ah," remarked my escort, "he would have come off worse. The shot fellow had a cane. He surely wouldn't have spared him any blows."

"When you arrested him, did he resist?" someone asked.

"No. He stood there quite calmly and gave me the revolver."

"And the crowd attacked him?"

"And how. As soon as they saw I had taken his revolver, they attacked him like hornets and would have torn him to pieces. I got some of it too, but he got the better part. Lucky someone from the department came in a car. Even then, the crowd began to fight with sticks."

"Oh, people are like wild animals," someone commented. "If they see danger, they scatter like flies. Don't we know the mob?"

"That's just what it was like," assented my escort. "When they heard the shooting, they dispersed in all directions. Afterward, they wanted to lynch him. Oh, that mob!"

All at once they stopped the conversation and began to inspect me from head to foot. All the time they had been talking, I sat in a corner, resting from the blows to which the mob had treated me. My head ached badly and my face was inflamed. My eyes were burning and swollen. But my heart did not fail me. It beat calmly and quietly as usual. I felt as if I had been liberated from an enormous oppressive burden; instantly I felt good and relaxed. I followed their conversation without particular interest, as if it were not about me, and became aware of them only when they began to inspect me.

"Who is that someone you killed?" one of the police asked me.

"He was a Ukrainian general. Petlura was his name," I replied.

"What kind of bird is he?"

"A general, the leader of a barbarous army."

"That's good," a policeman responded.

"Once in a while they ought also to know the taste of death," another policeman commented, "instead of only sending others to break their heads. So it was a political act. That's not so terrible."

"He probably was a real bastard," said a second.

"Not worse than most of that rank," philosophized a third.

"Are you sure that he was the right one? You didn't accidentally shoot someone else by mistake?" one of the police asked me.

"I think not."

The last question, so innocently put, upset me. I felt disturbed. Perhaps? Who knows? I had to pull myself together. I tried to remember various details, but my head was not working. Had I made a mistake? Was it possible I had been wrong all along? What a calamity! What a crime! Suppose I had killed an innocent person? My breath grew short. My heart, which a few moments before had been relaxed, began pounding violently. Fear and despair seized me. I wiped off the sweat and tried to calm myself and banish the frightful thoughts. The harder I tried, the more impossible it became. How terrible! Now I would die like a common criminal undeserving of any sympathy.

The inspector came in, scrutinized me a while, and then told me to follow him into his office. He sat at his desk, and showing me a chair facing him, said, "Now we have time to talk."

"I am ready." I felt feverish, as if intoxicated, my eyes blurry, but I tried to control myself.

"Now, tell me, why did you do this deed?"

For a while I was silent. I felt everything I had to say was concentrated in one word and I blurted it out: "I am a Jew!"

"An Israelite," the inspector corrected me. "Proceed."

Slowly, with a beating heart I began to tell about the Jewish calamity, the horrible tragedy that had befallen us in the Ukraine, the massacres and pogroms, beginning with the bloody days of Chmielnitsky down to Petlura.

The inspector sat with his head bowed and kept writing, recording.

"All right," he said, "But I want to know who this Petlura is. All that stuff about the seventeenth and eighteenth centuries is pretty old. We are now living in the twentieth century. Tell me about the murdered man. Who was he?"

"In short, he was the second Haman. The first wanted to destroy the Jewish people and this one most brutally destroyed a great part."

The inspector smiled.

"Yes, yes. Put it in your report, do it at my request," I urge him, but inside, the painful question comes up again: Did I make a fatal mistake? Just then my arresting policeman entered.

"Inspector, I have come from the hospital. The wounded man died. His identity papers were found. He is called Semyon Petlura."

Then I was right! I had shot not an innocent man, but the murderer Petlura. To tell the truth, my original certainty that the man I had shot was Petlura was not very soundly based. After all, I had never seen the beast; I had no idea what he looked like. Despite all my investigations, it was impossible to find out anything about him. My numerous acquaintances in Jewish and non-Jewish circles could not satisfy my curiosity. When I first learned in a Russian newspaper that Petlura was in Paris, I could not rest. I began chasing around, searching, investigating. Many people thought my inquiries about Petlura peculiar, and some even mocked me, inquiring whether perhaps I planned to kill him. The futile searches and the ironic comments often brought me to tears. Sometimes I just became sick at the petty comments of friends who suspected something, who tried to dissuade me, saying that I should leave his punishment to other hands, not ruin the livelihood that I had. But the knowledge that this murderer was alive and well, and so near, would not let me rest. Ceaselessly I looked for his traces; at the end of each unsuccessful day I gnashed my teeth in sorrow. Often I wanted to express my anger against those whose irony exacerbated my hurt. Most of all, I suffered in the quiet night hours, lying on my bed and thinking about the further pursuit. It was impossible to conceal my sufferings from my wife, who began to notice my nervousness and even my tears.

"Why are you crying?" she used to ask.

I would pull myself together and put on an innocent mien. "What gives you such a notion? My eyes are tearing from my work." But my excuses were not always convincing. My wife kept noticing ever more that change that was coming over me.

Several months passed in dreadful suffering. In this time all I could find out was that Petlura went about incognito, had a younger brother, and was a frequent visitor in certain Jewish homes. But thereafter, all threads of information snapped.

My only photograph of Petlura I had cut out of my Larousse. But it could hardly do. It was absurd to hope to meet Petlura on a Paris street and expect to recognize him from this small, bad picture.

Then the lucky chance came. A Ukrainian paper which had just begun to appear in Paris came to my rescue by printing a photograph of Petlura with Pilsudski. If not for this chance, who knows how long my suffering would have lasted. For a time I was not yet quite certain that the person whom I had seen several times and heard speaking Ukrainian was Petlura. When finally I decided it was he, I found him several times in the company of a woman and a little girl. The fear of hurting an innocent victim restrained me. When chance once again brought me together with him when he was all alone, I was so struck with my luck that I abandoned any opportunity to check my information, and I raised my arm to punish. . . .

On hearing that he was in truth Petlura I felt a heavy burden had rolled off my heart. At that moment everything seemed to me radiant and beautiful. I felt happy, jubilant, satisfied, and like one born anew — like a young man in love who loves the whole world. Even though I had never felt any liking for the police, I wanted to embrace the policeman who brought me the news, to kiss him and press him to my heart.

THE SPEECH I DID NOT MAKE

My judges:

Whenever I read the chronicles of world history, my heart bleeds each time I encounter human injustice. As long as there have been people on this earth, the most pitiless enemy of any human being is another human being.

The classical world knew tyrants like Herod, Caligula, Nero, Diocletian, who drowned whole generations in blood. Those fine spirits Tacitus, Pliny the Younger, Marcus Aurelius in their writings mocked the unfortunate Jews and the martyred Christians. The Middle Ages witnessed Attila, the Crusaders, the religious wars, the Mongol Tamerlane, St. Bartholomew's Night, Torquemada, and Ivan the Terrible. Accusations about the use of blood were directed first against Christians, then by Christians against Jews, from the Middle Ages until today.

If we put the past on trial, is not history one long bill of accusation against humanity? Yet the old stories of brutal deeds and persecutions appear as child's play when compared to the horrible massacres which were enacted before our eyes. Our learned generation, with its diverse sciences, our fine philosophers, and gentle moralists have not succeeded in extirpating the bestial instinct in man.

I cannot contain my tears when I recall the great sufferings which our people endured the last centuries in the Ukraine, that vale of tears. For three hundred years Jewish blood flowed without halt on Ukrainian soil. In 1648, Hetman Bogdan Chmielnitsky and his Cossacks drenched the

Ukraine with our blood. They slaughtered old people, tore little children limb from limb, raped women and strangled them afterward. This massacre lasted until 1654, and 500,000 Jews met their death in the severest agonies.

The Jewish people was destroyed with fire and sword in the Ukraine. A Polish memoirist describes this epoch:

> When Kievan Ataman Charchevsky entered Kanev, the Cossacks massacred all its Jews. It was their custom thus to entertain themselves. In Nemirov an Ataman and his Cossacks lashed hundreds of Jews together and drowned them. Little children were ingeniously severed in half. Six thousand Jews were murdered in Nemirov.
> That was how the advance units operated. Then came the great Cossack hordes, headed by Bogdan Chmielnitsky and his aide Krivonos.
> In Tulchin all the Jews were assembled and ordered to be baptized. With one voice they cried out: "Hear, O Israel: the Lord our God, the Lord is One."

The same Polish memoirist tell us, the Cossacks assaulted the Jews, cut off their hands and feet, raped women in the sight of their husbands, smashed children against walls to crush their skull, carved open the bellies of pregnant women and forced cats in. . . .

They desecrated synagogues, ripped apart Torah scrolls, and sent entire towns up in flame and smoke. The Jewish communities of Pereyaslav, Borisovka, Piryatin, Boryslaw, Dubno, Lachowicze, and many others were destroyed. Streams of blood flowed over the Ukrainian roads.

That was the first time these wild Ukrainian creatures emerged in the arena of world history.

In 1768, one hundred twenty years after the first grim massacre by the Zaporogian Cossacks, Chmielnitsky's descendants, Ivan Gonta and Maxim Zheleznyak duplicated the atrocities committed by their ancestors. The heartless and soulless Haidamaks began their orgies and demons' dances in Lisyanka. Archimandrite Melchizedek Yavorsky gave them the blessing of the sword and promised them complete absolution if they would slaughter the unfortunate Jews. The hordes charged out and destroyed the Jewish communities in Uman, Zabotin, Chihirin, Smela, Kanev and Cherkassy.

In his poem "Haidamacks," Shevchenko described the following episode: A new Bartholomew's massacre was brutally enacted in 1768 by the Haidamacks and Cossacks in Uman. The chief actors were Gonta and Zheleznyak. Cooling their hatred of Jews and Catholics in streams of blood, the Haidamacks found, in a Jesuit monastery that they plundered, two children their chief Gonta had had by a Polish Catholic woman. They brought the children to their father, saying:

"You have sworn to destroy all Jews and Catholics, regardless of age or sex. Before you stand your own two children reared by the Jesuits!"

Gonta did not waver; with his own hand he stabbed his children.

Under the light of the conflagration which they had set, the Haidamacks feasted and celebrated their victory. Amid the ruins and heaped-up corpses they abandoned themselves to fiendish orgies. The horrifying spectacle lacked none of the usual ingredients: vats of wine, wild dancing, and virtuous Jewish daughters abducted to be violated. Gonta and Zheleznyak puffed their pipes, as the river ran red with blood.

Our tragedy is intensified when poets and historians glorify these grisly deeds. The barbarous epic of savage sadism committed by animals in the guise of men evokes no pity for our martyrs, no sympathy, no regret. For these poets and historians, too, the Jews are creatures without legal protection, scapegoats, animals to be driven and slaughtered with gratification. Historian Kostomarov, novelist Nikolai Gogol, and poet Shevchenko depicted these scenes of horror in tranquil tones and lauded the heroes who did these deeds. The victims appear to them as comical creatures. The Haidamacks boasted that they were heroes because they were cruel. They were thought vigorous because they were not deterred from butchering infants in their cradles.

The gruesome massacres, the ghastly acts committed by the Haidamacks of Ataman Petlura in 1918, 1919, and 1920, in their cruelty and evil surpassed the earlier deeds of the Ukrainian heroes.

I need only recall that dreadful time for a shudder to pass over my body. The hideous visions pursue me always, though I strive to ward them off. Though I seek to expunge them from my memory, they remain always fresh and fearful. Pogrom scenes I witnessed float before my eyes and at night keep me awake. I jump up from sleep and cannot shake off the bloody nightmares.

All the remembrances of my life are gruesome, as is our whole history of martyrdom. My anguish grows greater when I cannot aid my suffering brothers and sisters. There are times when private sorrows disappear in public woe, like a drop of water in the sea. But as for him who suffers for humanity, his sorrows continue and are vast as the world. These sensitive souls suffer every injustice done on earth, on their bodies they feel the whiplash, they cannot endure the oppressor's arrogance and the slow pace of justice. They must act.

The blood of the innocent and of the martyrs demands justice and vengeance.

My life was the theater of all misfortunes and afflictions. Sometimes actor, always witness and spectator, I was ever engaged in the struggle against tyranny and could never escape from it.

At the end of July, 1919 I arrived in Zhidowska-Grebla, two days after the Haidamack pogrom. The first Jewish home I entered looked as if it had suffered an earthquake. Two old women sat on the ground and lying next to them an old man, his face bloodied, his eyes bloodshot, blood still running from his bandaged head, and from him issued one lament, "My God, my God, why hast Thou forsaken me?"

In that town, eight of fifteen families were completely annihilated. A widow with six children, whose husband had fallen at the front, was violated and then strangled.

In Cherkassy on the Dnieper, the first Jew I encountered told me: "We have just buried a thousand victims of the last pogrom. All lie in one mass grave. One gets accustomed to calamity. It is Providence."

At the end of August, when I was in Kiev, Petlura's advance guard entered. They murdered all the Jews they met on their way. In the center of Bolshaya Vasilkovskaya Street, I saw the corpse of a young man stretched out on the pavement, and, her head on his dead body, a woman lamenting for her one and only son. Hoodlums shouted obscenities, mocking her despair. One sermonized: "This is good. We'll show you, damned Jews, we'll slaughter you all."

Kozyr-Zyrko, Petlura's aide, the hero of the massacre in Ovruch, selected thirty old Jewish men for his amusement. Haidamacks encircled them and ordered them to sing and dance. The Haidamacks were free with their whips and revolvers, mocking, deriding, goading the dancers. When one Jew or another broke out in a lament, the torturers beat them, ordering them to continue dancing and singing, and they shouted "Long live our Father Kozyr-Zyrko." Then they shot all the old men and piled the bodies in a heap.

Palenko, another of Petlura's aides, told a Jewish delegation in Kiev: "I will not listen to you. Do you think that for a few damned Jews I would disrupt my boys' amusements?"

And the great Petlura himself stated: "Do not make a quarrel between me and my army."

In all the cities they posted placards with insults, hatred, and threats against the Jewish population: "You, cursed people, whom all nations despise. . . ."

They forced unfortunates to eat their excrement. They shoveled earth over them and buried them alive. Nor did they spare the dead. They desecrated the cemeteries and refused permission to bury the martyrs.

In Tripole on the Dnieper, Petlura's birthplace, after the fifth pogrom, forty-seven corpses of the old, the sick, and the children were left lying in the street, and no living soul remained after them. Dogs began to pick at the bodies and pigs to nibble. Finally, a Gentile who used to work for Jews, out of pity dug a grave and buried them. The Haidamacks learned of it and for that they murdered him.

In Ladyzhin only two Jewish girls remained alive. They were raped, their noses bitten by sadists, and infected with venereal disease. They came for help to a hospital in Kiev.

Intoxicated with blood and uncontrolled hatred, the twentieth–century descendants of Bogdan Chmielnitsky, Gonta, and Zheleznyak completed the mission of their ancestors. Are these the flag-bearers of the New Testament, of civilization and of hope for a nobler mankind?

Judge me, my judges.

XI

In Political Life

54 Jewish Rights Between Red and Black
by Simon Dubnow

SIMON DUBNOW was not only a Jewish historian (see pp. 232–242) but a man of action in Jewish political and communal life. In the following selection from his memoirs, we see the scholar who researched the Jewish struggle for equal rights as totally compatible with the warrior for those rights in his own time and place. Dubnow was one of the founders of the Federation for Equal Rights for the Jewish People in Russia and, later, a founder of the *Folkspartey* (Jewish People's Party), short-lived in Russia, and subsequently renewed in Poland. All his life Dubnow saw the Jewish people as one community, undivided by class politics, despite the claims of the Jewish revolutionary movements. The purpose of "Jewish" politics was, according to his views, "national" political action for the emancipation of Jewish individuals and for the sociocultural development of the Jewish community.

B Y FEBRUARY 1905 both the liberal opposition and the revolutionary movement had taken hold of the entire Jewish community. The revolutionary terror (the assassination of Grand Duke Sergius, Governor General of Moscow, and others) had forced Nicholas II into compromises. A consultative council was appointed to draft a constitution, and all groups in the population were permitted to submit their recommendations. Also the revolutionaries started a flurry of petitions and resolutions. The Jewish community, too, prepared to take part. In St. Petersburg and Moscow, as in the provincial cities, Jews hotly debated drafts of resolutions moderately or sharply protesting Jewish disabilities. Petersburg led off. The "baronial" circles (Baron Günzburg) drafted a moderate proposal and distributed it to the largest Jewish communal bodies for their signature. I was in Vilna when a large assembly of Jewish communal leaders discussed that proposal. Its tone displeased me, for instead of demanding rights and justice, it pleaded that Jews were useful to the state and their persecution was harmful. I expounded at length to the assemblage that now we must come to the government as accusers, not as accused. But the majority favored signing the petition, while I, with the minority, refused. A few days later another meeting

461

took up a more radical proposal for civic and political rights, which had been brought from Petersburg by a young lawyer, J. G. Frumkin. I agreed with the basic text, but I insisted that it also include a demand for national group rights. After lengthy debates, my amendment was accepted. The entry in my diary noted how "interesting were the debates by the spokesmen of various movements: nationalists, Zionists, assimilationists, Bundists."

With such sociopolitical differentiation, it was natural for an idea to come up about forming a Jewish democratic party. Again, the initiative came from Petersburg, from L. M. Bramson and his friends, who had sent me the program of the new organization, suggesting we organize a Vilna branch and send a delegate to their first convention at St. Petersburg. We discussed this proposal in heated debate, as usual. I agreed with its general platform, but the extreme meagerness of its Jewish national plank aroused my apprehension that assimilationists would take over the party. The Vilna group wanted to send me to the Petersburg convention to defend my views, but my research commitments prevented my going. In the end, a small "Jewish Democratic Group," located in Petersburg, was formed. It was not the broad supraparty organization I had had in mind.

In the third week of March, some members of the Jewish intelligentsia came to Vilna from Petersburg and other large cities to form a Jewish people's federation to take part in the liberation movement. Its initiators were the Petersburg Jewish lawyers, members of the legal defense association which had been organized somewhat earlier to defend Jewish interests in the trials following the Kishenev and Homel pogroms. A large legal staff had been assembled to prove at these trials that the government was responsible for the pogroms. These lawyers, who turned into prosecutors at the trials, were particularly vigorous in the case at Homel where they represented Jews charged with armed self-defense. After lengthy wrangling with the chief judge over his high-handed conduct in obstructing their disclosures of evidence, they all demonstratively left the courtroom with an explanatory statement that rang like an indictment of the government. This demonstration, which had taken place at the end of December, 1904, on the eve of the revolution, popularized the names of the legal defense staff: Vinaver, Sliosberg, Bramson, Ratner. Now they proposed to form a nonparty Jewish federation to fight for equal rights.

That was the first time I met in person Maxim Moyseyevich Vinaver, with whom I had long corresponded about the Historic-Ethnographic Commission. A man, not tall, with a high forehead over deep-set penetrating eyes, with clear and masterful articulation and a rare gift not just to speak but also to listen, to fathom another's ideas, Vinaver immediately impressed

me as an accomplished political leader. It became clear to me why he occupied a distinguished position next to Miliukov in the new Russian Constitutional Democratic Party, the chief moving force in the opposition of
1905. His political skill and tact were evident in the way he conducted our
conference in which sixty-seven delegates of the most diverse movements
took part. Vinaver conducted this variegated assembly, calmed tempers, and
eased friction; his summaries of the debates created the basis for a com-
promising, synthesizing decision. His speeches charmed not with empty
rhetoric but with the clarity of his ideas and the forceful logic of his arguments. Henrik Borisovich Sliosberg, for his part, appeared an ardent advocate of Jewry, an excellent jurist who knew all the intricacies of Russian
legislation about Jews, and who was accustomed to challenging that legislation in government chancelleries and senate sessions. Compared to Vinaver
the *political* leader, Sliosberg was more of a *communal* leader. He was a
petitioner to the very government against which Vinaver had organized an
opposition. Sliosberg belonged to the right wing of the Cadet party,
whereas Vinaver belonged to the center. At the left, at this meeting, was
Leon Moyseyevich Bramson, later a member of the Labor Party in the Imperial Duma. Even more left was Mark Borisovich Ratner, a young lawyer
from Kiev who had joined the Socialists-Revolutionaries and the Jewish
group Vozrozhdenie ("Renascence"), which advocated autonomy. The Zionists formed a solid unit of their own at the convention. The assimilationists of the Society for the Promotion of Culture were there, and on the
extreme right was the official rabbi of Kovno, Hirsh Rabinovich. Only the
Bundists, at the far left, did not participate, refusing to enter any interparty
unions.

At that time freedom of assembly was not legally guaranteed in Russia
and, as we used to say in those days, we seized it by revolutionary right. We
did not let the government know about the convention, but to forestall a police raid, we held closed meetings in private homes and in the course of the
conference's three days and nights from March 25 to 27 prudently changed
the locus of the meetings several times. We were all in a festive mood: for
the first time representatives of Russian Jewry (self-appointed, to be sure)
assembled to discuss how to win civic equality in the constitutional state that
was promised. Tongues were loosened in open political debate for the first
time. People talked at length and with deep feeling. The first day we talked
about ensuring Jewish representation in the prospective Russian Duma, in
a torrent of speeches on various voting systems, parliamentary fractions, and
a special Jewish fraction. The second day I read a paper on the future goals
of this federation, advocating that it demand not only civic and political

rights for the Jews in Russia, but also national rights — communal autonomy, official recognition of Yiddish and a Jewish educational system.

The hottest debates centered on the issue of national rights in the federation's program. The Odessa assimilationists and some "practical" people feared this formula was dangerous, that it had no precedent in the Western European struggle for Jewish emancipation. Others believed that we first must demand only civic rights and leave national rights for the future. A Zionist opposed the idea of cultural autonomy in the galut on principle. Ratner defended my proposal hotly and volubly, trying to shame the timorous assimilationists and the Zionist negators of the galut. Vinaver and his group were neutral, but when the question was called, they, like most Zionists, supported my formulation. Thus, a substantive majority adopted the first plank of our program: "The goal of the federation: to attain, to the greatest degree possible, the civic, political and national rights of the Jewish people in Russia." This formulation was adopted only because of Vinaver's support, and I was particularly grateful to him because he himself did not agree completely with me on Jewish national rights. He believed Jews were a part of the Russian body politic, constituting only an ethnic group. He acceded to my formula (which he interpreted as cultural self-determination) apparently for tactical reasons, since he did not wish to lose the support of the nationalists and the Zionists.

A compromise name for the organization was adopted: Federation for Equal Rights for the Jewish People in Russia. The convention closed by electing a twenty-two-member executive board, half to be located in Petersburg. Vinaver and Sliosberg headed the Petersburg group. Shmarya Levin and I were elected from Vilna. I readily accepted. It was the first time my ideas were embodied in the program of a political organization. I hoped that with the success of the movement for freedom sweeping all Russia, they, too, would prevail.

In an unfestive mood we ushered in Passover, the festival of freedom, in 1905. Though the revolutionary movement had dealt heavy blows to despotism, it had received blows no less severe. "At such a time," I noted on April 10, "living between two terrors, from above and below, one needs superhuman strength to write the history of the sixteenth century. The illiberal reactionary government in Petersburg, the society's discontent boding no good, the patience of the people exhausted — something will soon give. There will be more bloody street demonstrations; labor unrest will grow; there will be Passover pogroms." Two weeks later my fears were fulfilled. During Russian Easter some pogroms of usual proportions took place in several towns, but in Zhitomir — it was a massacre, planned by the Black Hundreds, with the assistance of the police. That was a second Kishenev, in the very heat of the freedom movement. "My head aches. It is filled with ideas about a protest," I noted on May 7, "a declaration about our defenselessness, in addition to our civil disabilities. We dare not keep silent." I drafted such a protest in the form of memorandum to Prime Minister Witte, to be presented either on behalf of the Federation for Equal Rights or as a mass petition.

The government had issued a statement depicting the Zhitomir pogrom as the vengeance of the patriotic population upon the Jews for their revolutionary activity. My memorandum pointed to the inconsistency between this statement and one made recently by Witte at a Cabinet meeting that the revolutionary movement among the Jews was nurtured by their civic disabilities and would be only intensified by pogroms. Shmarya Levin took the memorandum to a Federation meeting in St. Petersburg, but it went no further.

Then a new concern worried me. A rumor spread that at a consultation between the Tsar and his advisors about a constituent assembly, they decided to deprive Jews of the right to vote. The Federation issued a directive for protests to be sent from all over Russia. I drafted such a sharp protest in the name of the Jewish community of Vilna that many people were afraid to sign it, but we collected enough signatures and it was published in the press with other protests. The protests succeeded. The Tsar's council of notables retracted.

On August 6, 1905, the Tsarist manifesto was issued, proclaiming the convocation of a consultative assembly composed largely of landed proprietors. The next day I noted: "Yesterday's manifesto will scarcely conciliate anyone. What sort of constitution is this without prior guarantees of freedom of assembly and press, with the complete lack of even elementary rights, under conditions of war and terror. Shall we rejoice that Jews are allowed into such a Duma? That may be the result of our protests, but after all how many deputies can we have and what composition can a Duma in a police regime have? Yet we must act, propagandize."

And indeed, in Vilna we began to work. There were tense disputes whether to participate in the elections or boycott them because the Duma with its propertied deputies and consultative functions did not meet the demands of democratic government. The board of our Federation decided to issue a call for participation in the elections so that "a bad Duma could be transformed into an instrument for a better one." At the board's request, I drafted a proclamation along these lines. We advocated support of Jewish candidates whenever they ran and, in their absence, of non-Jews who pledged themselves to support equal rights for Jews. We warned against partisan party-splintering at the polls and against altogether boycotting the election.

At that very time when Russian Jews were striving for emancipation, I was attracted to the history of the emancipation of Western Jews. I was convinced that I had learned the art of "standing on the volcano of the present and penetrating into the past and describing it." It was my hope soon to come to those chapters in which I could show my contemporaries how their forefathers fought for freedom in revolutionary eras. But the volcano on which I stood suddenly began spewing fire. The outbreak of the general strike brought about the ostensible surrender of the government on October 17. Until then, we were cut off from the world by the railroad strike — without newspapers, without correspondence, ignorant of developments elsewhere. For days there was violence and disorder. Then, abruptly, it halted. The police disappeared. The authority of the government vanished.

Early on October 18, while in my study, I heard a ring, then voices in the vestibule. Shmarya Levin and some other people came in with the joyous announcement: "A constitution!" They brought the first news of the Manifesto of October 17. The Tsar had granted all civic rights and a legislative Duma to be elected on the basis of universal suffrage. When I went out, it was a clear morning, not at all like autumn. Crowds had gathered on the corners and buzzed; friends greeted each other with jubilant faces and expressions. I met Dr. Kantor and we embraced, remembering 1881's start when we were in Petersburg; when expecting a constitution, we got pogroms. We did not yet know that now, too, a signal to instigate pogroms was being given all over Russia. We stifled doubts. That day I wrote in my diary: "Is not this near the realization of a dream which had each day for a quarter of a century been murdered? Are we not standing at the threshold of a real constitutional order? I await with impatience news about the Manifesto and newspapers."

The railroad strike had isolated us from the world. We had no knowledge of the terrors following the Manifesto, when the Black Hundreds started their work. Vilna was still in the hands of the revolutionaries. After attending a meeting of the Vilna city council on October 20, in which all the radical parties and nationality groups took part, I noted: "Is this perhaps not a brief episode, after which will come the reaction?" I had barely written these unfortunately prophetic words when news of fighting in the streets between police and demonstrators showed that the government had regained its authority. Then the news of the pogroms began to pour in — about pogroms in Kiev, Odessa, and other cities. That was the first we heard of the terrible October pogroms which began right after the promulgation of the Manifesto and submerged the entire Pale of Settlement under waves of blood.

With the arrival of the newspapers, a period of ceaseless mourning began for me. There were reports of hundreds of pogroms during that terrible week of October 18. On November 17 in Vilna, I spoke at a memorial meeting to mark the thirty-day mourning period for the victims of the first pogrom. I closed with these words: "Do not put your trust in Amalek, neither the Amalek of the government nor the Amalek of the people, for the old Russia may yet revert in the new!"

Three days later I went to Petersburg to attend the second convention of the Federation for Equal Rights. Petersburg was a seething cauldron, boiling with hundreds of assemblies and conferences, with thousands of delegates from all ends of Russia, the tumult of the earlier revolutionary underground now having risen to the surface of public life.

Our convention, in which about one hundred delegates from many cities took part, held its meetings in the salons of the wealthy St. Petersburg Jews. The proceedings during the first two days were devoted to what action we should take on the pogroms which the reactionaries had stimulated as a demonstration against the Manifesto of October 17: a public protest, a protest to the government, a deputation to Premier Witte, or organization of Jewish self-defense. Most delegates opposed sending a deputation to Witte to demand equal rights on the basis of the Manifesto. I remember the passionate outcry of a young lawyer: "We will not accept equal rights from the bloody hands of the autocracy. We will accept them from a free Russian Parliament!" A resolution was adopted condemning the government for not having tried the governors and other high officials who were guilty of not halting the excesses and even of abetting them. A committee was elected to investigate the pogroms and another one — to organize Jewish self-defense everywhere.

After January, 1906, I freed myself from scholarly work, devoting myself entirely to politics. The election campaign for the first Imperial Duma had begun. The Federation for Equal Rights and the Jewish members of the Cadet party in Vilna had formed a joint election committee in preparation for the Federation's third convention to be held in Petersburg in February to plan election strategy for all Russian Jews. The atmosphere in

Petersburg was red hot. That third convention, at that fateful moment, showed our differences more than our consensus. The question whether Jews should take part in the elections at all evoked the most heated debates. Terrified by the recent pogroms, perturbed by the counterrevolution of a government supported by the Black Hundreds, some people had lost faith in the possibility of free elections and of electing a progressive parliament. This state of mind led them astray along an irrational path. Instead of responding to government terror by taking an active part in the elections to produce an oppositional Duma, they conceived of a passive protest of boycotting the election, which, naturally, could please only the reactionaries. After heated debates our group, including Vinaver and Levin, won. An overwhelming majority adopted a resolution to take active part in the elections.

Then there was the question of strategy: a coalition or a bloc with non-Jewish parties. Our majority was for a bloc with Russian progressive parties, none further right than the Cadets; others thought it possible to reach agreement even with more rightist elements, the Decembrists, for instance, so long as they accepted the principle of equal rights. Ahad Ha'am advocated this position. A number of other proposals were debated which we introduced jointly with the Zionists: (1) voting only for candidates who supported the Federation's platform; (2) Jewish deputies may belong to various political parties which support equal rights for Jews, but not to any other nationality fraction (I pointed out the shameful role of the Jewish deputies in the Austrian Parliament and in the Galician Sejm who belonged to the Polish Club); (3) Jewish deputies ought to constitute a fraction of their own in the Duma with binding discipline regarding Jewish matters: (4) they must demand priority for the question of equal rights for Jews as part of the basic legislation about all civic liberties. In the end we decided not to create a Jewish fraction, but to ask Jewish deputies to pledge "to unite in common endeavors for the purpose of winning Jewish civic equality." The other proposals were adopted with a few changes.

March and April in Vilna passed in the fever of the election campaign which I had to conduct as chairman of the Vilna Federation for Equal Rights. We had chosen Vinaver as candidate from Vilna, considering him a first-rank political leader. When it was learned that Vinaver could run as a Cadet candidate in Petersburg, I was offered his place but I declined because of my commitment to my life's purpose — history. I urged Shmarya Levin to run as the Jewish candidate for Vilna, and he won the nomination against some opposition. On April 17 he was elected.

That evening we had a banquet to which Vinaver, already elected deputy, came. We made the usual toasts. I compared the Cadets to the Girondists, hoping nonetheless they would escape the fate of the Girondists in the Convention. Vinaver gave me a quick look. Did we both forefeel the tragedy of the Russian Gironde? For it was crushed between the pincers of the black and red terror.

In August, after the Duma had been dissolved and Stolypin had introduced field courts-martial, I was in Petersburg, where Baron David Günzburg had arranged to obtain a residence permit for me. I attended a meeting of the Federation for Equal Rights, which was nearing its death. We assembled in Sliosberg's apartment. Discouragement prevailed where not long before had been fight.

Having moved to St. Petersburg, I halted my historical work because of my political activity. The almost daily meetings on political affairs gave me no rest. The central committee of the Federation for Equal Rights was constantly in session, preparing for the elections to the second Duma. That the Federation's disintegration was inevitable was already quite clear. The Zionists dealt the first blow to our interparty union. At their Helsingfors convention, November, 1906, they appropriated all the Federation's principles as part of their program, even the plank regarding national rights in the galut. But they decided to support these policies only under their own party auspices. This induced the anti-Zionists, headed by Vinaver, to create their own organization, the Jewish People's Group, which adopted only a minimal section of the Federation's national position (self-determination), issuing a proclamation against the "principled emigrants." Bramson's Jewish Democratic Group also split off from the Federation. In these circumstances, we began to organize a national group in the spirit of my philosophy, called the *Folkspartey*, the Jewish People's Party. In Petersburg I found like-minded people. We worked out a twofold program; political and Jewishly national. Our political program was based on the principles of the Russian Constitutional Democratic Party (its left wing) whereas the Jewish national program was an extension of the Federation's, dwelling specifically on the institutionalization of autonomy through self-governing local and federated community councils. Our new party set down the principle of a national, rather than a religious, community council. In December, 1906, I wrote an introduction to this program, and both parts were published in Russian in *Razsvet* and in Yiddish in *Fraynd* and later in my "Letters on Old and New Judaism."

In February, 1907, the second Duma, with two extremist wings, black and red, and a weak center, was convened. It included only three Jewish deputies, and those politically without weight. The Federation for Equal Rights used to have consultations with these three deputies on the question of Jewish rights and with the leaders of the Cadet and Socialist opposition in the Duma. But the Federation was at its end. The emergence of differentiated political groups had destroyed it from the inside. There were only two alternatives: to liquidate it or transform it into a federation of these various political groups. I strongly supported the latter proposal. At a meeting in March we decided to preserve the Federation as a federative body of four groups — the Zionists, the People's Group, the Folkspartey, the Democratic Group, along with a fifth group of nonpartisans. But the Zionists had decided to act only under their own auspices, and nothing came of our planned reorganization. That was how the Federation expired after existing two years: a year of ascent and a year of decline.

55   A Good Russian — A Good Jew
by Henrik Sliosberg

HENRIK SLIOSBERG was born in Mir, province of Minsk, in 1863 and died in Paris in 1937. He was known as the legal advisor of Russian Jews, having been selected for that role first by Baron Horace Günzburg and then remaining in it by his own free choice, as he recounts in the following excerpt from his memoirs. The law was everything to him and its order was part of his nature. Hence, he was no revolutionary, and all his political energy was expended as an active member of the Constitutional Democrats (Cadets).

For years he engaged in what appeared a tragically futile attempt to annul and void the harsh and unjust legislation which the Tsarist regime imposed on the Jews. Yet he never became embittered, remaining what he had always been — an ardent Russian patriot, even in Parisian exile after the Bolshevik Revolution. As "attorney for Jews" against Tsarist antisemitic persecution, he managed to reconcile his identity with the Jewish community and his love for Russia — the "other Russia," which he believed to be the authentic face of Russian liberalism.

Shortly before his death he was preparing a book on Jewish values and ideals. He wrote to Saul Ginzberg, the Russian Jewish historian: "I would like our youth to know what Jewry gave to mankind!"

THESE memoirs are not just a depiction of Jewish life in Russia. The history of Russian Jewry was not created in a vacuum but in the environment and on the soil of life in the Russian empire. The Jewish question in Russia was not isolated from other problems under this regime, and the picture of Jewish life was not a unique fleck against the general background. Jews were not the only ones denied civic rights; actually 90 percent of native Russian peasants were without rights. There was high-handedness not just toward Jews alone, but toward other nationals as well; the Jews, however, received the hardest blows from Russian reaction, and the persecution of Jews became the barometer of the political outlook at any given time.

Since my childhood I have been accustomed to think of myself first of all as a Jew. But from the very start of my conscious life, I felt myself also to be a son of Russia. Now, at the end of my days, considering my whole life and work, I must admit that while loving my people and esteeming it above all, not just because of the accident of birth, but because of its noble spirit, its splendid ideals which have for me been the ideals of Judaism, I have also always loved Russia.

In a speech I made once, in which I spoke about national self-awareness, I compared Jewish attitudes toward Russia with the attitude of an ocean voyager in a private cabin toward the rest of the ship. He wanted his cabin always to be shipshape, yet he knew that the lot of his cabin depended on that of the whole ship.

To be a good Jew did not mean one could not be a good Russian citizen and vice versa. To be a good Russian citizen was no obstacle to being a good Jew, believing in national Jewish culture and being loyal to one's people and helping them as best one could. The affinity for Russian culture, which in the course of my conscious life, grew in giant strides, was in consonance with my loyalty to national Jewish culture. For that Jewish culture constituted a vast reservoir from which every other national culture could draw a great surge of energy and thus bring it closer rapport with the cultures of other peoples and help the cause of the union of all mankind — the ideal of Judaistic messianism.

It was my lot, together with others, to take part in activities to achieve better living conditions in Russia, to be concerned especially about the evils of the times. I could not omit these from my memoirs, for they are quite necessary for a better understanding of the condition of Russian Jewry. On the other hand, these memoirs are not completely without interest for those who see the history of the Jews in Russia as one of the lesser chapters in Russian history.

In 1891, a Tsarist decree deprived Jewish artisans and army veterans of the right of residence in both the city and environs of Moscow. They were banished from the city on the shortest possible notice. But these expulsions from Moscow were only the beginning. In 1899, Jewish merchants of the first guild were prohibited from being registered with the non-Jewish merchant firms in Moscow. This affected also Jewish merchants in Moscow who were registered with merchant organizations in other cities.

At the very height of these expulsions of Moscow Jews by the police, two Americans, Weber and Kempster,* came to St. Petersburg on behalf of an American committee investigating emigration. Since the Minister of the Interior put off seeing them, they decided to visit some smaller cities from which Jews were emigrating to America. They asked Baron Günzburg to recommend someone who could inform them about the civic-legal situation of the Jews in Russia and who could accompany them on their journey. I agreed to do so, together with another lawyer. The more we tried to explain to these Americans the anti-Jewish legislation, the less they, citizens of a free country, could understand it. Then we arrived in Moscow. We visited the Jewish sections of Moscow from which large numbers of Jews were being expelled. The Americans saw the abandoned houses with their barricaded doors and windows, stores closed down, their signs still hanging. Here and there desolate figures could be seen on the streets, grown-ups and children, eyes swollen with tears. Weber and Kempster were shocked by what they had seen in Moscow. From Moscow we went to Minsk. None of us had had any notion of the degree and extent of poverty which prevailed there. From Minsk we went to Vilna, where the poverty and want in the Jewish quarter exceeded any concept we had of how people could live in such conditions. Then we went on to visit Bialystok, Grodno, Warsaw.

Both Americans returned home, tremendously affected by the situation of Jews in Russia. They published a pamphlet which reported most accurately everything they had seen. They expressed their conviction that the situation of the Jews would not soon improve and that the American government ought to make it easier for Russian Jews to migrate to the United States.

Weber and Kempster both insisted that I ought to emigrate to America.

* John B. Weber, New York State Congressman, 1885–1889, Commissioner of Immigration, 1890–1893, and chairman of a commission to investigate in Europe causes of immigration; Dr. Walter Kempster, a physician specializing in the pathology of insanity.

They tried to convince me that I could be most valuable to American Jews. Later, in difficult moments of my life, when the atmosphere was oppressive, the struggle difficult and without hope of victory, I thought more than once of their proposal. But even in those difficult times, my love for Russia finally conquered, and despite all my troubles and the possibility of more troubles, I never regretted remaining in Russia. I would have felt like a deserter my whole life, like one who abandoned his suffering brethren.

Zionists considered as assimilationists those of the Jewish intelligentsia who did not support Zionism and who thought of themselves as Russians. The Zionists compared us, the non-Zionists, to the Polish assimilationists who thought of themselves as Poles of Mosaic faith. Nothing could have been more untrue. For there was an enormous difference between the Poles of Mosaic faith and the Russian non-Zionists. We non-Zionists considered Jews a nationality. We did not think of ourselves as Russians of Mosaic faith, but as Russian Jews. In our work we did not encounter the same difficulties that Polish Jews had with Poles. We were not a foreign element, for Russia had many nationalities, all of whom were part of the Russian nation, and no one dominant nationality tried to absorb them. The russifying pressures and antisemitism were matters of officialdom. The liberals never attacked the national culture of other nationalities. It was not difficult for us to reconcile Jewish nationality with Russian citizenship and to make Russian culture our own as much as our own Jewish culture. One culture complemented the other. We used freely to express our conviction that Jewish culture could contribute to the culture of mankind and surely also to Russian culture.

56 In the First Russian Duma
by Shmarya Levin

SHMARYA LEVIN was born in Svisloch, White Russia, in 1867 and died in Haifa in 1935. A Zionist from his youth on, he was an exemplar of the modern Jew, combining a traditional Jewish education with doctorate from German universities. As a government rabbi and preacher extraordinary in Grodno, Yekaterinoslav, and Vilna, he was in a position to bring more Hebrew and Judaism into the government schools, and into traditional Jewish society he brought modernism, particularly in the form of Zionism. His greatest talent resided in his personality and in his flow of speech. He was witty, sharp, passionate, graceful, one of the great talkers and raconteurs of his time. He talked in the Duma, too, to which he had been elected from Vilna. The following brilliant description of that first Duma, from Levin's autobiography, shows indeed that his verbal prowess found better expression at that Duma than his political stance, for indeed all were swindled, as Levin put it, Jews and Russians alike. In the long run, the caustic wit of a sophisticated Westernized Zionist in the Russian Duma was no more effective than the subservient intercessions of traditional Jews of an earlier time.

I was elected almost unanimously as the representative of Vilna to the first Russian Duma. There were twelve of us in all, the representatives of between six and seven million Jews, and I wonder whether any twelve men have ever carried upon their shoulders the responsibility of so many hopes and longings. Russia was — so it seemed — about to rise out of the abyss of oppression; the Jewish people was about to rise out of an abyss below the abyss. And these twelve men were to haul it out. To make their task the harder, these men had to bear in mind that they had been elected by non-Jewish as well as by Jewish voters, and frequently there was no correspondence between the work they had to do for their own people and the party needs dictated by their other constituencies. Even if there was no actual contradiction of interests, tactics might sometimes bring interests into a seeming conflict; when a thousand things had to be attended to by this first parliament, and every group was clamoring for first attention, the very order of affairs became an important matter.

The Federation for Equal Rights assembled in St. Petersburg after the Duma was opened. The Zionists, who formed half the Jewish group in the Duma, proposed that the entire group organize into a parliamentary faction, with the obligation to vote as a unit. The other six members demurred. They argued, with some show of reason, that to be consistent the Jews would have to step out of the various parties. A compromise was struck. It was decided that on all Jewish questions, the Jewish members should come together and try to act as a unit, though without party discipline. As a matter of fact, as will be seen, the discussion was almost purely theoretical.

Three groups were to be found in the Duma. First came the Constitutional Democrats, or Cadets. In this party were to be found the most advanced elements of the old Zemstvo, and the finest forces of the non-Socialist Russian intelligentsia.

To the right of the Cadets stood the Union of October Seventeenth, which had been organized after the issuance of the Manifesto; it included the mildly liberal elements and the less conservative representatives of the large landlords. The third group, under the name of the Trudoviki, consisted of the radical elements, Socialists and half-Socialists, who had been elected in spite of the official ban of the party in the elections. This group had no party program, and the only point on which they were united was the question of agrarian reform.

Of the twelve Jewish deputies, eight joined the Cadets, and three the Trudoviki. One remained without any attachments: or, as we said, he ran wild.

Among the Jewish deputies I occupied, in a certain sense, a special position, not for my virtues or abilities, but because of one of those fantastic anomalies which were so frequent in Russian Jewish life. I was the only one among them who had no right to stay in St. Petersburg. The others belonged, one way or another, to the class of the "privileged" Jews, either by academic association, or through their standing in the business guilds. But my degree had been taken at a foreign university, and I was no businessman. I was therefore one of the six million who could not leave the Pale. And so I walked around in St. Petersburg as the living symbol of the absurd system, as if to say: "I have no right to be living in St. Petersburg at all, and I am only here for the purpose of helping to make the country's laws." I did not neglect to point this out in my addresses, both in the Duma and at a meeting in Moscow.

However, there were absurdities enough in connection with that first Duma. One little circumstance, which had to do only with the Jewish delegation, I remember with amusement. Every delegate to the Duma had to register his name, together with his religion and his nationality. We were twelve Jews in the Duma; it was therefore expected that the twelve names would be repeated under the list of the religions, and under that of the nationalities. But among us there was the well-known journalist and economist Gregory Yollos, for many years the Berlin correspondent and then the editor of the foremost Russian daily, the *Russkia Vedomosti* of Moscow. Yollos insisted on enrolling himself as a Jew by religion and a Russian by nationality. But it appeared that the ancient dispensation could not tolerate the disappearance of one of the tribes, so there appeared on the scene the friend of Yollos, the former Jew Gerzenstein. *He* registered as Russian Orthodox by religion, and Jew by nationality. So the accounts were squared, though, as often happens in accounts, by means of a little cooking. There were twelve Jewish deputies, twelve on the list of the religions, and twelve on the list of the nationalities. Yollos too, it may be noted, was one of the members of the Duma to be assassinated by the Black Hundreds. These two men lived only as half-Jews, one with his nationality, the other with his religion. They died as full Jews.

The first official reception to the Jewish delegates was arranged by the Jewish community of St. Petersburg, under the leadership of the man who had, for many, many years, been the chief *shtadlan* of Russian Jewry — Baron Horace Günzburg. He received us in his palatial home, and spent a couple of hours with us. More active in the reception was his son David Günzburg, a famous Orientalist, and the possessor of one of the finest collections of Hebrew books and manuscripts in the world. The Günzburg family easily occupied the first place in Russian Jewry. In the days when *shtadtlanut* was still the only means by which anything could be done for the Jews, the Günzburgs set the example — not too often followed — of quiet, modest, and selfless service to their people. The old man invited us to his house as a sign of respect for the *elected* representatives of the Jewish people. But in this house the ancient system of shtadtlanut had for many years found its headquarters, and our appearance there was symbolic of the revolution that had taken place in Jewish not less than in Russian life. Baron Günzburg accepted us, too, in a spirit of symbolism. He accepted the new order.

Quite different in character was the reception given to the entire body of the Duma in the imperial palace, where the ruler by the grace of God was to come face to face with the men who would, from now on, make the laws for his empire. In one of his moments of weakness, when he felt the sword suspended above him trembling in the wind, the Tsar issued his own invitation to the deputies. But it needed much persuasion, almost compulsion, before he was convinced of this necessity. He regretted the step as soon as he had taken it. But it was too late. The comedy had to be played until the moment when the supporters of the throne had gathered enough strength to ring down the curtain, and proclaim it at an end. And then another play would begin, the play of revenge against those who had forced this humiliation upon the elect of God.

The day of reckoning was, in fact, close at hand. The ranks of the faithful were being increased and closed. In the interim the farce continued. Some six hundred of us, therefore, assembled in the palace and there, *standing*, we listened to him. Some two hundred of the country representatives came in their peasant clothes, and brought with them, into the perfumed air of the palace, the strong smell of the Russian earth, or, less figuratively, the still stronger smell of newly polished leather. Officials and lackeys of every rank crowded into the doors and corners of the hall. The

Imperial Guard was drawn up before us in two ranks. The Court Marshal entered, and struck three blows with his baton, to say: "The Tsar is coming!" And there he comes, an unimposing little figure, accompanied by a great suite. They advance in measured step, and the Tsar ascends the throne. Some of the lackeys try to raise a cheer. It dies in the hall without an echo. And standing by his throne, Nicholas reads forth his speech. He speaks of mutual trust and confidence between Emperor and people. He mentions the Duma and expresses the hope that the great heritage which he has received from his fathers he will be able to transmit in its entirety to his young heir. Once again the Marshal taps three times with his baton. The Tsar marches out. Once more a weak cheer. The ceremony is over.

In the speech from the throne, as in the October Manifesto, the Jews were not mentioned once. The government believed in adding contemptuous insult to injury — Jews could not be mentioned in important documents like these. The answer to the speech from the throne was composed largely by Maxim Vinaver, and in it appears the categorical statement that there can be no talk of a regular constitution for the country without civic equality for all its inhabitants. Once more, in its reply, the government ignored the point. And Vinaver, in the Duma, made perhaps the strongest speech of his career, declaring openly: "Let the government know, once for all, without civic equality there can be no tranquillity in this country."

The Cadets and the Trudoviki were united on this point. The point on which some of them were divided was the order of procedure. Was the question of civic equality — which meant, of course, the Jews — to take precedence over the agrarian question, which was the burning question of the day for all Russia? From this question had proceeded most of the unrest of the time. The Russian muzhik — more than three-quarters of the population—was crying out for land. The division of land had created injustices which it was difficult to look upon without feelings of revolt and disgust. While gigantic estates had accumulated in the hands of the aristocracy, the peasants were compelled to work tiny plots of earth which could not provide the barest necessities for themselves and their families. Not only the Trudoviki, but many of the left Cadets, were inclined to place the agrarian question first. But all of the Jewish deputies, and most of the Cadets, were afraid of the attitude of the muzhik delegates in the matter of equality of rights. In their opinion, it was the wiser course to take up the latter question first. I took part in the debate in the sessions of the Cadet caucus. Instead of using arguments, I asked the permission of the assembly to tell a Jewish story and, weary with the dry, monotonous debates, the delegates signified their consent.

It was a rather difficult story to tell, for I had first to explain certain Jewish laws and customs. One of these laws is that on the Sabbath the Jew may not kindle a light, even through the agency of a non-Jew. Having explained this, I went on to describe the dreariness of the long Friday nights in the winter. At five o'clock on Friday afternoon the prayers are over, and the Sabbath has begun. At six o'clock the family meal is over, and then follows sleep. At twelve they are through with sleeping—and there remain seven or eight hours of darkness. The poor cannot afford to leave a light burning through the night. This is the privilege of the "rich." One such "wealthy" Jew rose one Friday at midnight and saw to his horror that the light had gone out. He had a Gentile servant in the house, but it is forbidden to direct the servant to light the lamp. The Jew casts about in his mind and suddenly calls loudly to the servant. "Ivan, how would you like a drink of whisky?" Ivan did not mind being roused out of the deepest slumber for the sake of a drop. "Thank you," says Ivan. "I'd love it." "But it's dark," his master answers. "I can't find a thing." "That's perfectly all right," answers Ivan. "I'll make a light." The Jew is delighted. He had not told Ivan to kindle the lamp. The lamp is lit, the drink is poured out. Ivan swallows the drink gratefully, hands back the glass—and extinguishes the light. "Be careful with Ivan," I warned the Cadets. "He may get what he wants and then put out the light again." I was told that my story had its effect. The problem was taken up more seriously.

In court circles Count Witte was regarded as the chief criminal in exploiting the defeat of the Russian armies for the purpose of wringing concessions from the Tsar — in particular the Manifesto of October 17. Shortly after the calling of the first Duma, Witte was deposed as Prime Minister, and his place was taken by Goremikin, a black reactionary of the old school. This incident alone makes clear what was in Nicholas's mind even when he issued the Manifesto. One look at Goremikin was enough. His eyes were cold and glassy, he wore the old, ultra-orthodox side-whiskers of the typical Russian beaureaucrat. In all, he was the personified antithesis of a constitutional government. Goremikin was not the only sign of the real intention of the Tsar, but he was the most revealing.

And still the Duma believed that Nicholas meant well — or, at least, that with the Manifesto he had gone so far that retreat was now impossible. And who knows? If the democratic forces of Russia had been united at that moment, they might have emerged victorious from the struggle. But there was no such union. The interparty struggle, a bitter and obstinate struggle, was not suspended even for a moment, and the energies of the delegates were exhausted before they approached the question as a whole. The leaders of the fight against the government were the Cadets, and they were the most optimistic party.

In the Jewish group, Maxim Vinaver was the best informed on Russian political questions. He was a man of the Disraeli type, both in his brilliant intelligence and in his inexhaustible industriousness. He had not the opportunities of a Disraeli: but even a Trotsky could not have organized an army under the Tsarist regime. We followed Vinaver, some of us because we recognized his greatness, some of us because we had no alternative. I was among the former.

The catastrophe came closer, and once more it sent its shadow in advance in the form of a pogrom. The question of the Jewish pogroms had been brought sharply into the open in the sessions of the Duma, by interpellation of the government. The interpellation was formulated to indicate clearly that the government was held to be the party directly guilty. The Minister for Home Affairs, Stolypin, a graceful speaker with elegant manners, promised to give an answer within a month. But the pogrom leaders were impatient, and provided their own answer before the month was over — a pogrom in Bialystok. This was an orgy of beastliness after the fashion of Kishenev: bellies ripped open, heads with nails driven into them, children with their brains dashed out, and the rest. Eighty Jews were killed, and hundreds wounded. A tremor went through the Duma. It was not only the pogrom as such, but the hint that it contained. This, then, was the reply of the government to the interpellation. The Duma resolved at once to send a commission of investigation to the actual scene. One of the members of the commission was the Jewish deputy Benjamin Jacubson, who belonged to the party of the Trudoviki.

I had occasion to speak in the Duma on the subject of the pogroms, but I can no longer remember whether it was on the general question, or in connection with the pogrom of Bialystok. I said at that time, addressing myself to the Russian people: "It is well for you to know that we Jews are bound up with you, the Russians, like Siamese twins." I meant to say that the destruction of the Jewish people could be accomplished only at the price of the destruction of Russia. I was attacked from two sides. The *Novoye Vremya* accused me of having offered mortal insult to Russia. The Zionists attacked me for having insulted the Jewish people. Neither side understood my simile. I do not know whether it was particulary skillful or not, but in the sense in which I used it, I hold it true even today. There has been no case in history where a government has done violence to Jews without doing equal violence to itself.

Between the Bialystok pogrom and the dissolution of the Duma, I had occasion to visit the most Russian of the cities, Moscow. I had received an invitation from the general Cadet party to deliver an address on the Jewish question. The Bialystok pogrom had acted like a cold shower on Jews and liberal Russians alike, and many had begun to feel that the Duma would not live much longer. Among the Jews, the depression was of course at its worst. In Moscow I had the first occasion to declare the tragedy of the Jewish situation to a huge pure-Russian audience in the very heart of traditional Russia. My two friends, Yechiel Tschlenow, who was very popular among the Moscow Cadets, and Isaac Naiditsch, a rising public figure in the Jewish community of the city, participated in the meeting. I cannot forget the extraordinary reception that was given me, a Jewish deputy who had no right to be in Moscow at all.

On the second day of my stay I addressed a purely Zionist meeting. I took as my theme the question of what would happen after the Jews had obtained their "full rights." My text was the life of Herzl, and I indicated how the impulse toward the building of a Jewish homeland had come not only from Jews who lived in lands of oppression, but from those who had achieved civic equality. That impulse was not born of oppression, and did not die with liberation.

The commission returned from Bialystok. Fiery speeches were delivered in the Duma by Vinaver, Jacubson, and Rodichev. By an overwhelming majority the Duma accepted a resolution calling upon the Tsar to dismiss his Cabinet, in order that the rulers of the country might disassociate themselves from the disgrace of the pogrom. The atmosphere, during the debate, was heavily charged. The deputies knew that they now stood at the parting of the ways. Two days later, when they turned up at the chamber, they found the doors locked and guarded. Outside was posted the manifesto of the Tsar dissolving the Duma.

I went with a group of deputies to the Nevsky Prospekt, the main artery of St. Petersburg. We wanted to see for ourselves the effect which this action produced on the general public. There was nothing to be observed. There was not a sign of excitement. The crowded street looked as it had always looked — countless people hurrying around, intent on their own business. If two persons stopped to hold conversation, a third was sure to stroll by as if by accident, sidle up absent-mindedly, and overhear what was being said. There were agents enough in the capital to provide a third for every two that stopped to talk. Life was "normal" once more. The citizen had reverted to the subject.

We were called together in the club of the Cadet party. The deputies wandered around like lost souls. It was known that somewhere, in some secret place, the leaders were in conference, and there was nothing to do but wait. The hours passed slowly. The mood in the club was like that in a house of mourning before the corpse has been removed. The dead man can never be disturbed again, yet every visitor walks on tiptoe, as if afraid of waking him. It was toward evening when some of the leaders finally appeared. It had been decided that the whole party should transfer itself to Vyborg, the nearest town across the Finnish border.

The Trudoviki had taken the same resolve. There, in Vyborg, the two parties assembled, separately, and hour by hour there came relays of messengers from St. Petersburg, the emissaries of the revolutionary organizations. Stories were circulated of the excitement that reigned in the ranks of the workers of St. Petersburg. Others added that the unrest had spread to the barracks. And we ourselves could not quite make up our minds. Was *this* then the signal for the liberation? Was the dissolution of the Duma the necessary interlude before the curtain was raised on the last act?

The hall in which we assemble is small and overheated. The faces of the deputies are drawn and haggard, the voices weak. There are still some who preach moderation. This is not the moment for a revolution — peaceful victory is in sight. But the moderates are a small minority. The majority wants action, something to restore the dignity of the outraged Duma. The best speakers of the party follow one another, and the deputies listen intently, nervously. Vinaver takes the floor. The time has come, he declares, to ignore party programs. The government has practiced a deliberate swindle on the first representative assembly of the Russian people. The reply of the Duma will have to be fearless and dignified.

It is after midnight when the meeting is called to order. Sergei Muromtsev enters the hall. Every one rises. All eyes are fixed on the man who, as the first President of the Duma, has become the symbol of Russian freedom. We stand as if at prayer. The Vyborg manifesto of the dissolved Duma is read out. The Russian people is called upon to boycott the Russian government with all the means at its command, to arrest the entire machinery of administration, and to continue to a successful issue the struggle for freedom. Muromtsev is the first to append his signature. After him come the leaders and the other deputies.

The next morning we returned to St. Petersburg. On the train we received the "confidential and reliable" message that round the station in St. Petersburg hundreds of thousands of workers had assembled to greet us, and that there the first open conflict with the government would take place.

And sure enough at the station there waited for us a guard of honor —
two rows of gendarmes between which we walked as down an alley. No
one else to greet us. When the droshky driver asked us, with the famous St.
Petersburg courtesy: "Excellency, what address?" we did not know what to
answer.

Swindled again. It was the old game once more. It has been described
once for all in the book of books. Nine times Pharaoh swindled Moses. He
was waiting for the tenth plague. And even after the tenth plague he
changed his mind and pursued the liberated people. At the Red Sea he got
his final answer.

Many, many ages must pass before history changes into legend. But
after a long time — I do not know how long a time — the legend will arise
of the great swindler who was the last to sit on the throne of Russia. He
swindled, and swindled again, and kept on swindling until the Red Sea
swallowed him up.

57   Osias Thon: Statesman of Polish Jews
by Isaac Grynbaum

Osias Thon was born in Lemberg,
Galicia, in 1870 and died in Cracow,
Poland, in 1936. Thon was the unusual product of an unusual constella-
tion of influences. Having distinguished himself at the yeshiva as an
ilui, he was ordained at sixteen. Two
years later he began to study secular
subjects, finally receiving a doctorate
from the University of Berlin in philosophy. He had become a Zionist,
organizing the first Orthodox Zionist
youth group in Lemberg. Then, having become a rabbi, he studied at the
Hochschule für die Wissenschaft des
Judentums. Thus he combined East
and West, Jewish nationalism and rabbinic Judaism, and as such was the
spokesman of Polish Jewry in the
Habsburg Empire and then in independent Poland. Yet, being an individ-
ualist, a gentleman and a scholar, a
nineteenth-century man, he was unable as a Jewish politician to cope with
rabid Polish nationalism and its arrogant antisemitism, as Isaac Grynbaum
describes in the following autobiographical selection.

Isaac Grynbaum was born in Warsaw in 1879.
As a Zionist political leader in Poland, his fame
rested largely on the creation of the national-
minorities bloc. A leading Zionist, he settled in
Palestine in 1933, where he has been active in
politics and journalism.

D<small>R. O</small>SIAS T<small>HON</small> was not a fighting man. He had not intended to wage
war when he became a member of the Polish Sejm and when he headed a
creative and influential segment of Polish Jewry. It was his thought that
building and creating had nothing in common with destroying and more
than once he hoped he would succeed in removing himself from every destructive combat. He strove toward positive accomplishment. But he deceived
himself, almost deliberately. For in truth he stood on the battlefront and
commanded a fighting company. This was the tragedy of his life and work.

I remember my first meeting with Dr. Thon and our quarrel. It was at a
Zionist Congress in Vienna before World War I. We, who had come from
Warsaw from the battlefront of the boycott which the Polish parties conducted against us after the elections to the Fourth Russian Duma, wanted
to use the Congress rostrum to talk about the economic war being waged
against us. We wanted to tell all the Jews and all the world. Even if the
Congress would not adopt a resolution on the subject, we knew it would
hear us out. Thon opposed our proposal and persuaded his Galician supporters to vote against the boycott's being brought before the Congress in
any form. He thought that a speech about the anti-Jewish boycott in Russian Poland at the Zionist Congress, even if no resolution were adopted,
would set off a boycott also in Western Galicia, which had not yet been
affected by the antisemitic wave. He did not want to be counted among
those who started the war, though he was well aware that it was on its way,
that antisemitism from Congress Poland would inundate also Galicia. He
won at the Congress, and I did not get the floor.

I recall the episode because it illuminates that quality of Dr. Thon as a
politician that made him a tragic figure in Jewish life during the period of
Poland's independence. That characteristic of his was evident then though
he had not yet formulated it as he was to do later: "We do not wage war;
we merely defend ourselves."

He never attacked. He wanted to prove, to convince, to penetrate his
listeners' hearts, to speak to them in their language and their style, lest they
perceived in him the alien and the enemy. That was how he addressed the

Polish Sejm, and the deputies calmly heard him out. He spoke often in the
Sejm, demanding civic rights, even national rights, for Polish Jews, and
never did he arouse anger or wrath from the rightist deputies.

From a Western European political training ground, especially in Austria, he entered the Polish Sejm in Warsaw, in whose atmosphere the Russian spirit still lingered, the Russian ways of dispute, the political style to
which one was accustomed in Russia — clear and unambiguous words,
stinging and caustic expressions and slogans, no subtleties. All of this was
alien to Thon's spirit and style. He wanted to be a statesman, to negotiate,
to discuss, to win influence, but he was forced into a policy of radical opposition which had sometime to explode out of the framework of defense and
defensiveness. Sometimes it happens that your opponent does not appear to
attack you, but ignores you, overlooks you completely, doing so gracefully
under a hypocritical mask. He must then be unmasked and his true coun-
tenance revealed. Mere defense will not do in that case, for defense must
sometimes also be attack. That was Thon's tragedy: he began with peace
and never ceased to wage war; he wanted to build and had also to destroy.
That tragic predicament brought him sorrow and suffering which only few
understood or were aware of.

Thon belonged to the first Zionist generation in Galicia. His approach
to Zionism had much in common with Ahad Ha'am's outlook, but his scope
was broader, more modern, more European. He was the only one of this
group who took an active part in the organized Zionist movement, not
merely in its literature, but also in its life.

In a preface to a collection of his articles, Dr. Thon wrote:

There were times when I wanted to undertake to write a paper which would
scientifically validate Zionism. I studied the laws of history and economics; I became well versed in social psychology; I learned about universal
human phenomena and did research on the life and development of ethnic and national groups. On the basis of all that, I wanted to build a
system of scientific Zionism and establish a philosophic basis for Zionism, but merely fragments emerged from all of this: instead of a book,
only articles. I was carried away on the stormy waves of life, of daily
worries, in a sea of propaganda and organizational activity among the
masses of my people and I lacked time to concentrate my ideas. The
twinkling of the moment consumed me, disturbed my thoughts, and
transformed my valuable coins into small change.

But that, he admitted, did not cause him too much regret. He found satisfaction in the work to which he had completely dedicated himself. Its results gratified him. He saw how his people awakened, demanding their place in society and their share of freedom. And yet, I think, in the depths of his heart Thon always longed for quiet scholarly work on Zionism and for Zionism. He never let the pen slip from his hand. He wrote much in times of toil and turmoil, more than in tranquil times when he thought he could create scientific Zionism. Yet I think he always belittled his journalistic work, because, after all, they were only newspaper articles. Thon wanted to write and study, striving to interpret the works of others, but it was his fate, as often happens with people of great vigor and talent, to form and fashion life itself. From a teacher he became a leader, from a scholar and interpreter, a man of action and a fighter.

Thon was elected to the Constituent Sejm from Cracow on an independent ticket. Received in Warsaw with great honor and co-opted to the pro tem National Jewish Council, he was invited to contribute to *Ha-Tsefira*, *Dos yidishe folk*, and *Haynt*, after their merger.

In the Sejm we had established a loose association of the Jewish deputies, whose central focus was the Jewish Club, to which Thon also belonged. No votes were taken and the decisions were adopted with unanimous approval. Thon was designated senior member of the Jewish Club and participated in the senior assembly of the Sejm deputies.

According to Sejm rules, a fraction had to have at least twelve deputies in order to participate in various Sejm commissions. Since we had only eleven, we had no seat on the committees. Signatures of fifteen deputies were needed to present interpellations to the government, and thirty to introduce a resolution. For additional signatures we had to turn to the socialist fraction, the only fraction we could turn to, and even they did not always help us.

Dr. Thon's political line was apparent right from the start. It so happened that the Sejm was nearly equally divided at the election of its chairman, and our votes were decisive. The leftist candidate, whom Pilsudski supported, was Wincenty Witos, head of the Galician Peasant Party. Against him, the right put up the former head of the Polish Party in the Prussian parliament, Trampcinski, a member of the National Democrats (ND; Endecja), which had not ceased its fight against the Jews which it had initiated while yet under Russian rule.

It was clear to us, the deputies of former Russian Poland, that we could not support Trampcinski and it would be better to go along with the Sejm's left wing and with Pilsudski, the chief of state. But Thon opposed this move. He accused Witos of pogroms that his party had carried out in western Galician Jewish towns when the Habsburg monarchy was collapsing. We did not share this view. But Thon got in touch with the Sejmist right wing and brought back an offer: in exchange for our support, Trampcinski would give me a seat on the Constitutional Commission.

We did not know Witos and we believed Thon. We could not abstain, for that would have increased our isolation and the disesteem in which we were held. Had we supported Witos, we might have enabled the left wing to enter a closer union with the Peasant Party and could have formed a leftist government based on labor and the two peasant parties. But how could we support a man responsible for pogroms? Especially if our support of Trampcinski would open the door for us to one of the most important Sejm commissions, something which even the left wing could not guarantee us without right-wing approval.

So we accepted Thon's proposal and voted for Trampcinski. That vote aroused a storm of protest against us from the Jewish community and in leftist Polish circles. Thon entered the lists against his opponents and undertook to give the Jewish community of Russian Poland a lesson in practical politics, taking into consideration only concrete, practical accomplishments. He advocated political negotiations that were intended to fulfill our demands in exchange for political concessions on our part. For us, that was an alien course. We were prepared to conduct an open fight for our political rights.

But Thon's victory was incomplete. Who was to read our declaration in the first Sejm debate and what was it to say? Thon, naturally, proposed that he read it. He was the senior deputy, who had had political experience in a country that had had a constitutional government. We disagreed. In competing with the other Jewish parties, we insisted that the Zionist spokesman from former Russian Poland speak on behalf of all Jews in the Polish state. Thon yielded, and I was chosen to read the declaration, which we both composed. But it was my presence on the Sejm platform, not the statement itself, that displeased the right wing. I was the third Jewish speaker to get the floor, following the Aguda and the Folkists, though our fraction was the largest in the Jewish Club. The commotion and the catcalls at my appearance on the rostrum had been well rehearsed and intended to express dissatisfaction that I rather than Thon had been chosen. He, for his part, was shocked and depressed by the outburst. He saw that not the left wing whose candidate we had rejected started this uproar, but the right wing with whom we had reached an agreement.

Then Thon realized that only the left wing would treat us like equal partners and help us from time to time with the needed signatures for interpellations and proposals. Subsequently, the leftist deputy in the senior assembly succeeded in having our deputies accepted in the most important Sejm commissions.

Thon was the deputy of the Warsaw Jewish National Council to the meeting of the Jewish Delegations in Paris. I remained in my position in the Sejm's Constitutional Commission. That commission was trying to sidestep approving the Minorities Treaty which provided national rights for minorities. Under the conditions of the Versailles Treaty and the pressure of the Western powers, the Poles were indeed compelled to sign the Minorities Treaty guaranteeing minorities, including Jews, complete civic and national cultural rights. But simultaneously the Poles did whatever they could, under barely disguised antisemitic legislation and by administrative chicanery, to restrict Jewish civic and cultural rights. The Constitutional Sejm concluded its term of office by passing an electoral law which so gerrymandered the districts that Jews could elect Jewish deputies only in a few districts and then only if most of the Jewish parties formed a coalition.

I then proposed to create a national minorities bloc and, within its framework, a bloc of Jewish parties which would agree to join the minorities bloc. I proposed this during the debate on the electoral law but none of the Sejm leadership believed one could put together a bloc of Jews and Slavic minorities, along with Posener and Silesian Germans.

Thon doubted the effectiveness of such a bloc and feared it would arouse widespread opposition from the Polish parties. He strove for an all-Jewish bloc and pinned all his hopes on it. We debated the question many times at meetings of the Jewish Club. At times it seemed Thon had been convinced by our arguments, but each time he returned from Cracow his doubts increased. Yet he did not oppose my position in public, nor did he refuse to be on the minorities-bloc list. But when I had to submit to the demands of the Jewish religious parties and put them on the list ahead of Thon, I realized I had gone too far, that he would not forget that. Yet even then he did not relinquish his place on our ticket. Besides, he was simultaneously a candidate on the Jewish list in Cracow which remained independent of the minorities bloc.

The success of the National Minorities bloc exceeded all our expectations. We became one of the great fractions in the Sejm. Had we continued our ties with the other deputies of the National Minorities, we might have formed a coalition that might have played a decisive role. The bloc did, in fact, decide the presidential election, its votes electing Narutowicz, who was supported by Pilsudski and by the left.

The Endecja and the other right-wing parties responded with a massive demonstration. They even tried — unsuccessfully — to prevent the meeting at which the president was to take the oath of allegiance to Poland. The right-wing press did not cease to agitate against Narutowicz for having acceded to the presidency with the votes of a Polish minority that needed the help of other national minorities, thus violating the principle that Poland ought to be ruled by a Polish majority. A Polish painter decided to sanctify this principle. Stalking the president when he visited a Polish art exhibition, the painter murdered him and then committed suicide. Thereafter, the candidate of the rightist Peasant Party was elected with a Polish majority. Pilsudski did not oppose him.

The government which then came to power, headed by General Sikorski, tried to restore calm. To this end, Sikorski tried to disrupt a coalition of the national minorities. He succeeded in winning the Ukrainians and the White Russians by conceding to their demands regarding the use of their own language and culture.

The Polish press had laid down a new policy, whereby only those minorities that were territorially concentrated could enjoy national rights. Nonterritorial minorities, like Jews, Germans, and Russians, were not entitled to such rights. The Endecja renewed its antisemitic agitation and proposed to restrict the number of Jews admitted to the universities and other institutions of higher education.

To oppose this proposal, Thon was designated to represent the Jewish fraction in the Commission for Education and Religions, where the issue of introducing a *numerus clausus* was being argued. In the commission, Thon fought heroically against the majority favoring the restriction of Jewish rights; he continued his fight later when the proposed legislation was brought before the full house. The socialist wing and the deputies of the minorities parties came to Thon's aid, but it was clear that the legislation would pass. Before the third reading the debate was interrupted to introduce some amendments to the law. The National Jewish Council, in constant touch with the Committee of Delegations in Paris under Motzkin's leadership, demanded energetic action to prevent passage of the law. Motzkin succeeded in arousing public opinion in France and called the attention of the French government to this law restricting the rights of Jews. A letter which French President Poincaré wrote to the Polish president was published. It was a courteous warning against adopting a law that contravened Jewish civic equality. That letter struck like a clap of thunder. There was no third reading of the draft law and it was withdrawn. Instead of legislation, administrative regulations had the same effect of restricting Jewish admissions to academic institutions.

At that time Wladyslaw Grabski, the National Democrat premier, was engaged in a program of financial reform to stabilize Polish currency on the international market. Obviously that could not be accomplished unless Poland received a loan from the United States. It then became necessary to clear Poland's reputation as a country that restricted the rights of Jews and other minorities. The premier's brother, Professor Stanislaw Grabski, then Minister of Education, and Count Skrzynski, the Foreign Minister, were assigned to explore the attitudes of the Jewish fraction and, if they were interested, to start negotiation with them.

Thon and Dr. Leon Reich, who was then the president of the Jewish Club, began the negotiations. I was out of Poland at the time; when I returned I was not interested in whether the negotiations had been undertaken with the explicit consent of the fraction or if it had merely consented after the fact. In any event, the negotiations were conducted privately. There were announcements from time to time that Jewish deputies were invited to dinner or supper by the Foreign Minister or the Education Minister. That indicated the negotiations were being conducted in an amicable manner and that one could hope for a successful outcome. When the negotiations were concluded, a communiqué was published about a formal reception at which the Jewish deputies made a declaration of Jewish loyalty toward Poland and the premier responded by expressing his gratification for this statement and said he would see to Jewish needs and requirements.

Only twelve paragraphs affecting religious affairs and communal matters were made known of this agreement. The Jewish deputies involved said solutions to questions concerning Sunday closings and various economic and national questions had been formulated in other paragraphs which were not released and which the government withheld. We could not find out their content. The ND press, which responded gracelessly to the news of the agreement, stated that the twelve publicized points were quite enough and additions were unnecessary.

Jewish opposition to this agreement grew, even in the Aguda. For a long time the other items of the agreement remained undisclosed; the government postponed releasing them until it was convinced Jews would really meet its demands of loyalty in affairs of state. The government did not consider the declaration of loyalty which the Jewish deputies made at the reception a sufficient guarantee, having doubts that these Jewish leaders could influence their followers to take the desired course.

The severe criticism from all sides was hard for Thon and Reich to take. Reich released to some journalists the undisclosed points of the agreement, Stanislaw Grabski denied that the government was obligated to abide by

them. The agreement exploded and dissipated. The Jewish community realized that the government needed only the declaration of Jewish loyalty.
Its leaders had allowed themselves to be deceived by attractive promises.

The Pilsudski coup of 1926 and the formation of Professor Bartel's government, which discouraged the Endecja, basically changed the situation.
The premier declared that he would not take the line of making agreements
with groups of citizens of the republic, but would treat the minorities as
citizens with equal rights and would not deal worse with them than with
any other citizens. Thon was not feeling well and had stepped aside. Reich
resigned. At my suggestion, Hartglas was elected president of the Jewish
Club. I did not want to create bad feeling, for relations between the Jewish
Club and Bartel's government were quite good. Some of our national demands with regard to education were met. The attitude toward Jews in
government agencies in the capital and throughout the country became better. The Sejm session was nearing its end and new elections were ordered.
It then became apparent that the Pilsudski coup would not bring about any
fundamental social or political changes. Only those constitutional clauses
limiting the president's power were changed. The government's power was
strengthened and enlarged. Yet, despite its broadened competence, the new
government did not hasten to carry out the reforms which the nationalities
expected. Many proposed reforms were postponed. The Jewish demands
were at the bottom of the list.

With this situation, the Zionist Central Committee and the National
Jewish Council decided to revive the National Minorities bloc. The
Ukrainians and White Russians had, meanwhile, become more disillusioned with the Pilsudski government. Pro-communist leanings spread
among their supporters and a revolutionary underground took shape. They
were not suitable partners in a voting bloc. In their place we took the
Ukrainians of eastern Galicia who this time decided not to boycott but to
participate in the elections, and they joined the nationalities bloc.

The government and the Pilsudski party put on a bad face on the revival of the nationalities bloc. They established a kind of "nonpartisan"
bloc, whose purpose was to support the government. The Aguda and the
Jewish businessmen said they would support that bloc. It became obvious
that local authorities would interfere in the electoral districts and use all
means to harass the parties in the coalition of the nationalities bloc.

Thon and Reich thought a possibility existed of rapprochement with
the Pilsudski regime. By dissociating themselves from a bloc with the East
Galician Ukrainians, they thought they could prove they were neutral in the
Galician struggle between Ukrainians and Poles. Thon did not even have

to make an explicit statement of neutrality, for there were no Ukrainians in Cracow. His Jewish list in Cracow was independent and pro-government — which had already counted on a Jew's being elected from Cracow. In eastern Galicia the government disregarded loyalty statements by local Jewish leaders and took whatever seats they could. The number of Jews elected from the Galician provinces dropped sharply. The number of Jewish deputies elected by the minorities bloc also declined about half. The Ukrainian list in Galicia won. The only Jew on that ticket, Dr. Abraham Inzler, was elected.

But this Sejm did not have a long life. It was dissolved after a short and dramatic existence. In the 1930 elections we could not form a nationalities bloc. The Galician Ukrainians thought they could do without the Jews, the Galician Jewish leadership supported the government. We wanted to run a Zionist list, but at the last moment the Galician Zionists proposed their own list. We, then, had to submit also our own list. Both lists suffered defeat, ours was a decisive defeat. We were left with only two seats — one from Warsaw and one from Lodz. The Jewish masses had not withstood the pressure and had ceased to believe in an aggressive political policy.

Thon became the chief spokesman of Jewish national policy. The new Sejm had a majority which supported the government. Its function was restricted to endorsing the government budget at a special session. The government party tried to split the opposition parties and adopted repressive means against their leaders. Many former members of the Endecja joined the government party. The National Democrats in the government party and in the opposition used the "Jewish argument" to force the government on the well-trod path of anti-Jewish harassments.

The first assault was on higher education. The students began to torment the Jews, forcing them to sit on separate benches, and demanding that their admission be restricted. Even some professors supported the student antisemitic terror. Going out of the universities, students used to attack Jewish passersby and even ventured into Jewish neighborhoods, hoping to stimulate pogroms among the mob which followed them. But the mob was reluctant, seeing police did not support them, and meeting active Jewish resistance, especially among the strong-armed workers, coachmen, truck drivers, slaughterhouse workers.

Thon struggled, demanded protection for the harassed Jewish students, insisted the government curb the violence of the inflamed academic pogromists. It was hard for him to give up his cherished principle of the autonomy of universities, a principle sacred to him from his own university days. Yet his duty on behalf of the persecuted Jews prevailed, and he supported draft legislation to limit the autonomy of the higher educational institutions and to extend the government's authority over them.

In the midst of this conflict came the news that Hitler had seized power in Germany and had begun a campaign of terror against the Jews, also against Polish Jews for many years resident in Germany. These Polish Jews were expelled from Germany and assembled at the border town Zbaszyn, until they were permitted to reenter Poland. The government then declared that Jews who were Polish citizens would be taken under its protection. Speaking from the Sejm rostrum, Thon thanked the Polish government for protecting its Jewish citizens and courageously opposing the Nazi regime. Perhaps he had heard the rumor of Pilsudski's proposal to declare war on Germany and quash the Nazi movement at its very start. Perhaps he wanted to encourage such an undertaking and suggest how Jews would respond to an energetic anti-Nazi stand. But Pilsudski, seeing Poland between hammer and sword, between its two historic enemies, Germany and Russia, changed his policy. That change was heralded when Polish merchants rejected a Jewish proposal to boycott German goods.

Jews began to feel that bonds of understanding and alliance were secretly being forged between Warsaw and Berlin. Suddenly public opinion in Poland was shocked by Marshal Goering's friendly visit to Poland to join the hunting party in the Bialowieza forest near Bialystok. Antisemites of all sorts began to emerge in public. Then Thon spoke out strongly, in a style reminiscent of his early Sejm days. He thundered out against the rapprochement between Poland and Nazi Germany.

The cabinet ministers and their party members among the deputies could not understand what had happened to this moderate and cool Dr. Thon and why he was so agitated. After all, he had always believed that the political interests of the state transcended all else. But Thon no longer adhered to this principle. In the depths of his soul he felt the danger approaching, the sea of blood and tears with which Hitler and the German Nazis would inundate Poland and the Polish Jews. It was his last historic address in the Sejm.

Sources and Acknowledgments

AHAD HA'AM: "Pirke zikhronot," *Reshumot*, Tel Aviv, Dvir, 1927, 1930, pp. 128–30; 138–39; translated from the Hebrew by S. Dawidowicz and the editor.

ANSKY, S. (Rapoport, S. Z.): "Hattot Ne'urim," in *Zikhroynes*, Part 1, Warsaw, 1925, 5–16; translated from the Yiddish by the editor.

AXELROD, PÁVEL B.: "Pogromen un di revolutsyonere bavegung mit 43 yor tsurik: Vi di yidishe sotsyalistn hobn dan farshtanen zeyere oyfgabn," *Di Tsukunft*, XXIX (1924), 550–55; translated from the Yiddish by the editor.

BADER, GERSHOM: *Mayne zikhroynes: fun kroke biz kroke*, Buenos Aires, 1953, pp. 387–93; translated from the Yiddish by the editor.

BIALIK, CH. N.: "On Ahad Ha'am," trans. Maurice M. Shudofsky, abridged and reprinted with permission from *Jewish Frontier*, XXXI (1964), 15–23.

BIRNBAUM, NATHAN: *Fun an apikoyres gevorn a maymin*, Warsaw, 1927, 32 pp.; translated from the Yiddish by the editor.

BRAININ, REUBEN: *Fun mayn lebnsbukh*, New York, YKUF, 1946, pp. 165–86; abridged and translated from the Yiddish by the editor, with the permission of the publisher.

CHAGALL, MARC: "Eygns" in *Vitebsk amol*, ed. Gregory Aronson et al., New York, 1956, pp. 441–44; translated from the Yiddish by the editor, with the permission of H. A. Abramson.

CITRON, SAMUEL LEIB: *Dray literarishe doyres: zikhroynes vegn yidishe shriftshteler*, 3 vols., Warsaw, 1920–22; III, 130–51; abridged and translated from the Yiddish by the editor.

DUBNOW, SIMON: *Dos bukh fun mayn lebn*, 3 vols., New York-Buenos Aires, 1962–63; I, 231–77 ("Under the Sign of Historicism"), II, 28–73 ("The Movement for Civic Equality"); abridged and translated from the Yiddish by the editor, with the permission of the Congress for Jewish Culture, New York City.

EWEN, ISAAC: *Fun dem rebns hoyf: zikhroynes un mayses, gezen, gehert un nokhdertseylt*, New York, 1922, pp. 122–26, 164–65, 266–70; translated from the Yiddish by the editor.

FRISCHMAN, DAVID: *Geshtaltn*, Mexico, 1948, pp. 46–50; translated from the Yiddish by the editor.

GERZ, M.: *Musernikes: tipn un geshtaltn*, Riga, 1936, pp. 5–20; translated from the Yiddish by the editor.

GLIKSMAN, PINHAS ZELIG: *Der kotsker rebe admor reb Menakhem Mendl zal Morgenshtern: zayn opshtam, zayn lebn, zayne rebayim, zayne khaveyrim, zayn shite in toyre un khsides, zayne kinder un kindskinder*, two parts, Pietrikow, 1938–1939, pp. 17–21 (Simha Bunam); 25–35 (Menahem Mendl of Kotsk); translated from the Yiddish by the editor.

GORDON, JUDAH LEIB: *Kitve Y. L. Gordon*, I, Tel Aviv, Dvir, 1928, pp. 133–36; translated from the Hebrew by Gittel Allentuck.

GOTTLOBER, ABRAHAM BER: "Memuarn," in: A. Fridkin, *A. B. Gotlober un zayn epokhe*, Vilna, Kletzkin, 1925, pp. 164–77, 193–94, 207–217, 246–47, 340–43; translated from the Yiddish by the editor.

GROSSER, BRONISLAW: "Oytobiografye," *Royter pinkes*, I, Warsaw, 1921, 80–91; translated from the Yiddish by the editor.

GRYNBAUM, ISAAC: *Fun mayn dor*, Tel Aviv, Farlag Mokor, 1959, pp. 332–52; translated from the Yiddish by the editor.

GÜNZBURG, DAVID: "D. A. Chwolson," *Voskhod*, 1899–1900; abridged and translated from the Russian by S. Dawidowicz and the editor.

GÜNZBURG, SOPHIE: "David avi," *He-Over*, VI (1958), 152–65; translated from the Hebrew by Zeva Shapiro.

HELLMAN, CHAIM MEIR: *Bet Rabi*, Vilna, 1905, pp. 45–49; translated from the Yiddish by the editor.

INFELD, LEOPOLD: *Quest: The Evolution of a Scientist*, New York, Doubleday, 1941, pp. 231–36; reprinted with the publisher's permission.

JABOTINSKY, VLADIMIR: "Zikhroynes fun mayn ben-dor," *Jewish Morning Journal* (New York), December 4, 1932; January 15, 1933; February 5, 1933; March 19, 1933; translated from the Yiddish by the editor.

KOVNER, URI: Leonid Grossman, *Die Beichte eines Juden in Briefen an Dostojewski*, Munich, 1927, pp. 93–108; abridged and translated from the German by the editor.

LACHOWER, F.: "Yeme Berdichevski ha-Ahronim," *Moznayim*, I (1930), 1–3; translated from the Hebrew by S. Dawidowicz and the editor.

LEVIN, SHMARYA: *The Arena*, trans. Maurice Samuel, New York, 1932, pp. 291–305, reprinted with the permission of Harcourt, Brace & World, Inc.

LIESSIN, ABRAM: *Zikhroynes un bilder*, New York, 1954, pp. 112–20; translated from the Yiddish by the editor.

LILIENBLUM, MOSES LEIB: *Hattot Ne'urim*, 2 parts, Vienna, 1876; Part I, 20–43, 61–81; Part II, 20–33, 70–75, 132–39; *Derekh Teshuva*, Warsaw, 1899, 22–35, 45–49; abridged and translated from the Hebrew by S. Dawidowicz and the editor.

LILIENTHAL, MAX: "My Travels in Russia," in David Philipson, *Max Lilienthal, American Rabbi: Life and Writings*, New York, 1915; pp. 258–269, 282–99; 330–33.

LIPSCHITZ, JACOB: *Zikhron Ya'akov*, 3 vols., Kovno, 1924–1930, II, 19–26, 37–39; III, 20–48, 54–55; abridged and translated from the Hebrew by S. Dawidowicz and the editor.

LUNSKY, HAYKEL: "A halb yor zikhroynes vegn Sh. Anski (detsember 1918–yuni 1919)," *Lebn*, ed. Moshe Shalit, Vilna, December 1920, pp. 20–24; translated from the Yiddish by the editor.

MAIMON, SOLOMON: *Autobiography*, London, East and West Library, 1954, pp. 126–28.

MANDELSTAMM, LEV OSSIPOVICH: "Avtobiografiya," *Perezhitoe*, I (1908), 13–20, 44–50; translated from the Russian by Lynn Solotaroff.

MARGOSHES, JOSEPH: *Erinerungen fun mayn lebn*, New York, 1936, pp. 15–43; abridged and translated from the Yiddish by the editor.

MARK, JACOB: *Gdoylim fun undzer tsayt*, New York, 1927, pp. 67–104; abridged and translated from the Yiddish by the editor.

MEDEM, VLADIMIR: *Fun mayn lebn*, New York, 1923; translated from the Yiddish by the editor and reprinted with the permission of *Commentary*, in which it originally appeared.

MENAHEM MENDEL OF KOTSK: *Kotsker mayses: 50 vunderlekhe mayses*, ed. Luzer Bergman, Warsaw, 1924, pp. 126–33; translated from the Yiddish by the editor.

MENAHEM MENDEL OF RYMANOW: *Sefer tiferet Menahem*, Warsaw, 1926, pp. 18–20; translated from the Yiddish by the editor.

MENDELE MOKHER SFORIM: *Mayn lebn*, Warsaw, n.d., XIX of *Ale verk*, 135–59; translated from the Yiddish by the editor.

NOMBERG, H. D.: *Y. L. Perets*, Buenos Aires, 1946, pp. 57–72; translated from the Yiddish by the editor.

PRAGER, MOSHE: "Dos yidishe togblat: organ fun der yidisher ortodoksye in poyln tsvishn beyde velt-milkhomes," pp. 443–534, in *Fun noentn over*, II: *Di yidishe prese in varshe*, New York, 1956; abridged and translated from the Yiddish by the editor, with the permission of the Congress for Jewish Culture, New York City.

RAKOWSKI, PUAH: *Zikhroynes fun a yidisher revolutsyonerin*, Buenos Aires, 1954; pp. 59–71, 92–94, 108–20;

abridged and translated from the Yiddish by the editor.

RAPOPORT, SOLOMON JUDAH: "Al mot harav . . . Nahman Krochmal," *Kerem Hemed*, VI (1841), 41–47; translated from the Hebrew by Zeva Shapiro.

REINES, ISAAC JACOB: *Sefer Shne ha-Me'orot*, 2 parts, Pietrikow, 1913; Part II: 5–32; abridged and translated from the Hebrew by Gittel Allentuck.

SCHENIRER, SARAH: *Em be-Yisrael: Kol Kitve Sara Shenirer*, Tel Aviv, Nezah, 1956, pp. 21–42; abridged and translated from the Hebrew by S. Dawidowicz and the editor.

SCHWARTZBARD, SHOLEM: *Inem loyf fun yorn*, Chicago, 1933, pp. 183–197, 308–16; translated from the Yiddish by the editor.

SHATZKY, JACOB: *Shatski-bukh*, ed. E. Lifschutz, New York-Buenos Aires, Yivo, 1958, pp, 119–27, 129–35; abridged and translated from the Yiddish by the editor.

SHAZAR, ZALMAN: *Shtern fartog: zikhroynes, dertseylungen*, Buenos Aires, 1952, pp. 152–62; translated from the Yiddish by the editor, with the permission of the author.

SHTIF, NOKHUM: "Oytobiografye," *Yivo-bleter*, V (1933), 195–225; translated from the Yiddish by the editor.

SILBERBUSCH, DAVID ISAIAH: *Mentchn un gesheyenishn*, Vienna, 1922, pp. 66–77; abridged and translated from the Yiddish by the editor.

SIMHA BUNAM OF PSHISKHA: Martin Buber, *Tales of the Hasidim: Later Masters*, New York, Schocken Books, 1961, pp. 241, 266–67; reprinted with permission of the publisher.

SLIOSBERG, HENRY: *Dela minuvshikh dnei*, 3 vols., Paris, 1933; I, 1–5; II, 42–67, 306–07; abridged and translated from the Russian by S. Dawidowicz and the editor.

SOKOLOW, NAHUM: "Alt-varshe," in: *Haynt yoyvl-bukh 1908–1928*, Warsaw, 1928, pp. 121–24; translated from the Yiddish by the editor; "The Late M. Jean de Bloch: A Character Sketch," *The Jewish Chronicle*, January 24, 1902.

TROTSKY, LEON: *My Life*, New York, Charles Scribner's Sons, 1930, pp. 84–92, 340–41, 360–61.

TRUNK, J. I.: *Poyln*, IV and V, New York, 1949, translated from the Yiddish by the editor and reprinted with the permission of *Commentary*, in which it originally appeared.

VINAVER, MAXIM: "Kak my zanimalis istoriey," *Yevreyskaya Starina*, I (1908), 41–54; translated from the Russian by S. Dawidowicz and the editor.

WEINBERG, JACOB: "Joel Engel, A Pioneer in Jewish Musical Renaissance," *Bulletin of the Jewish Music Forum*, VII–VIII (1946–47), 33–38; shortened and revised by the editor.

WEIZMANN, CHAIM: *Trial and Error: The Autobiography of Chaim Weizmann*, New York, Harper and Row, 1949, pp. 3, 16–51; reprinted with permission.

WENGEROFF, PAULINE: *Memoiren einer Grossmutter: Bilder aus der Kulturgeschichte der Juden Russlands im 19. Jahrhundert*, 2 vols., Berlin, 1908–1910; I, 2–3, 9; II, 77–85, 96–100, 114–16, 129–40, 168–94; abridged and translated from the German by the editor.

ZHITLOWSKY, CHAIM: *Zikhroynes fun mayn lebn*, 3 vols., New York, 1935; I, 158–68, 184–86, 196–220, 236–37, 252–73; II, 37–57, 65–72, 80–87; abridged and translated from the Yiddish by the editor.

ZUSYA OF ANNOPOL: *Sefer tiferet ha-Ahim*, Warsaw, 1924, pp. 43–44; translated from the Yiddish by the editor.

Index